D1175777

Nicolas Point

S.J.

Nicolas Point
S.J.

His Life & Northwest Indian Chronicles

Cornelius M. Buckley
S.J.

LOYOLA UNIVERSITY PRESS
Chicago

Printed in the United States of America

Loyola University Press
3441 North Ashland Avenue
Chicago, Illinois 60657

Library of Congress Cataloging-in-Publication Data
Buckley, Cornelius M.
Nicolas Point, S.J.: his life & Northwest Indian chronicles

Bibliography: p. 499
Includes index.
1. Point, Nicolas, 1799–1868. 2. Siksika Indians—Missions. 3. Indians of North America—Northwest, Pacific—Missions. 4. Indians of North America—Great Plains Missions. 5. Jesuits—Missions—Northwest, Pacific. 6. Jesuits—Missions—Great Plains. 7. Missionaries—Northwest, Pacific—Biography. 8. Missionaries—Great Plains—Biography. 9. Missionaries—France—Biography. I. Title.
E99.S54P653 1988 266′.2′0924[B] 88-27341
ISBN 0-8294-0598-4

For the Jesuits of the Oregon Province who carry on the work begun by Nicolas Point.

“O Dieu, par quelles routes inconnues aux mortels
Ta Sagesse conduit tes desseins eternels!”

Jean Racine

Contents

Preface

This study grew out of the acquisition, over twenty-five years ago, of a manuscript containing a series of letters, accounts of excursions among the Blackfeet, and various anecdotes written by Nicolas Point (1799–1868), well-known missionary and amateur painter of Northwest Indians during the mid-1840s. This sixty-five page holograph written in a minute script and containing many corrections, emendations, and deletions, was never catalogued; therefore, it was unknown to Point students and compilers of bibliographical data. In 1962 it was housed in the archives of the Paris Province of the Society of Jesus, Chantilly, France. Now, privately owned, it is presently on permanent loan to the Gleeson Library, University of San Francisco, San Francisco, California.

A letter in the Jesuit Archives of the French Canadian Province, Saint-Jérôme, Québec, explains the reason for the appearance of this manuscript in France. On September 15, 1877, Nicolas's brother, Pierre Point, S.J. (1802–1896), a missionary in Canada, wrote to Father Elesban de

Guilhermy, S.J. (1818–1884), in Paris, advising him that he was sending him some of Nicolas's papers. Father de Guilhermy, the well-known menologist of the Society of Jesus, was the logical recipient of this material for the reason that he collected biographical data on noteworthy Jesuits. Moreover, since most of these items were written in letter form, they could easily have been directed to the sources responsible for publishing them for the general public in any number of French Catholic periodicals, or privately in the *Litterae Annuae* of the French Province, which were, according to St. Ignatius's admonition, marked for distribution, *"ad mutuam consolationem et aedificationem in Domino,"* among Jesuit houses through the province. By the time Elesban de Guilhermy received the Canadian packet, however, the Society of Jesus was fighting for its very existence in France; consequently, the Point manuscript, which would take some patient editing, was filed away for some halcyon day in the future that was never to arrive. Instead, in March 1880, the government ordered the dissolution of the society in France, and the Point manuscript was hurriedly collected with a number of other reports and papers and packed into boxes destined for England. After World War II, the various French Jesuit archival deposits were repatriated and reorganized, and it was at this time that Nicolas Point's holograph was discovered.

Before he died, Nicolas Point polished up, expanded, and reorganized much of the material contained in this manuscript into his "Journal," or "Souvenirs et mémoires illustrés," which is one of the treasures of the Saint-Jérôme archives. The "Journal" is made up of a number of separate essays which begin with Point's life as Jesuit in France in 1828 and end in Canada in 1862. The San Francisco manuscript may have been a draft of those essays of his "Journal" pertaining to some of the Rocky Mountain memoirs he later developed in greater detail. The theme of the manuscript is the Blackfeet. Some of Point's essays contained in the "Journal," pertaining to his life in the United States and in the Oregon country, were translated and published in *Woodstock Letters* (1889–1890). These essays and additional chapters from the "Journal" were published along with a fine selection of Point paintings by Joseph P. Donnelly, S.J. in a most impressive book, entitled *Wilderness Kingdom* (1967).

Nicolas Point is primarily known as a missionary who painted Indians. But first and foremost he was a Jesuit educator. When he founded St. Charles College, Grand Coteau, Louisiana, in 1837, there were three Jesuit *"collèges"* in existence in the United States: Georgetown, St. Louis, and St. Mary's, Kentucky. But all three were institutions founded by others and then taken over by the Jesuits. Grand Coteau was the first Jesuit boarding college in the United States begun "from the ground up," and its founder, Nicolas Point, modifying the "Fribourg Plan" he knew so well, attempted to endow it with a certain stamp that had distinguished Jesuit *collèges* operated by his fellow countrymen in Europe.

To understand Jesuit missionary and educational philosophy as it manifested itself in the United States during the nineteenth century, it is essential first to understand what the Jesuit Black Robe and classroom teacher was and how he was trained. Nicolas Point and his companions knew nothing about identification problems. They defined themselves by internal and external criteria. They wore a distinctive garb (black robe); they adhered to a structured schedule and a prescribed code of behavior; they had clearly articulated expectations of themselves and confidence in the integrity of their formation; they did not have to merit the esteem of friends or the deprecation of enemies. Those who trained them were not known for a tolerance of ambiguity in attempting to resolve psychosexual, interpersonal, emotional, and motivational issues. In fact, if they suspected such issues existed, the common good would demand a kind of immediate discharge from the service. The Black Robes of the 1840s and the Indians they dealt with have passed. The brief description of the milieu which created these historical entities is not intended to make a judgment on whether their passing is good or bad.

Acknowledgments

I am most indebted to Carla (Mrs. Philip) Hudner for her patient reading of the transcription of Point's manuscript and for her valuable suggestions for, and corrections in, the translation. A number of archivists have also been most helpful: Mrs. Nancy Merz, Associate Archivist of the Jesuit Missouri Province Archives, St. Louis, Missouri; the Reverend Joseph Cassette, S.J., archivist, Jesuit archives, Saint-Jérôme, Québec, Canada; the Reverend Francis Edwards, S.J., archivist, the Roman archives of the Society of Jesus; the Reverend Neill Meany, S.J., archivist, Oregon Province archives, Spokane, Washington; Brother Thomas A. Marshall, S.J., archivist, California Province archives, Los Gatos, California. The Reverend Robert Brunet, S.J., librarian at Les Fontaines, Chantilly, France, and the Reverend Wilson A. Aldrige, S.J., of the University of San Francisco, have also extended to me valuable help in preparing this book. Finally, I would like to acknowledge the professional and invaluable service of Jeanette Rubsam-Ertel at the Loyola University Press whose patience, encouragement, and friendship are most sincerely appreciated.

Biographical Introduction To Nicolas Point

BEGINNINGS
1799–1818

In France, May 1796 coincided with parts of the months Floréal and Prairial, Year V, on the Revolutionary calendar. It marked the turning point in French history, although it is doubtful if many contemporaries were aware of this fact. In Paris, François-Noël Babeuf, leader of the Communist movement for equality and editor of the obscene, scurrilous and vitriolic newspaper *Père Duchesne,* was arrested, thereby bringing the logical dynamic of the Revolution to a halt. The regicides who had turned against their chief, Robespierre, now had said "enough," set up their own government and pointed the Revolution in a more moderate direction. Meanwhile, General Lazare Hoche (1768–1797) had succeeded in pacifying the Vendée and the rebellious west, thereby strengthening both the Directory, which had taken over the reins of government the previous October, and the young Corsican general, who had taken command of the demoralized army in Italy. Napoleon Bonaparte had led his troops over the Alps, surprised and crushed the Austrians at Lodi, and was now entering Milan.

He promised the Paris Directors that the future belonged to their Revolution.

As for the Church, things were looking better only because they could not possibly have been worse than before. The Civil Constitution of the Clergy, passed on July 12, 1790, had split the country ideologically and geographically. The west, north, and northeast rejected the 'constitutional' church, but the center, the Paris area, and the southeast tended more to accept it. Throughout the country there were *constitutional* and *nonjuring* priests and *refractory* and *patriotic* areas. Priests who had refused to take the oath to support the Civil Constitution had been given fifteen days to flee the country or be sent to the "dry guillotine" of Guiana. Still in May 1796 *fanaticism* was a crime that rendered nonjuring priests liable even to death, so those who had not emigrated went underground where they managed to survive only because they kept two steps ahead of the police. A priest might appear briefly at a prearranged spot, offer a clandestine mass, solemnize marriages, baptize babies, encourage the faithful, and then just as suddenly disappear through the wall of silence erected by the people. One such priest paid a visit that May to the tiny Ardennes village of Cul des Sartes, near the town of Rocroi, where he joined François Point and Nicole Bourçois in marriage.[1]

Rocroi, some fifty miles northeast of Reims and less than five miles from the Belgian boarder, was tucked away in a corner of France that had never really accepted Revolution, much less the Civil Constitution of the Clergy. (In this sense it differed little from the majority of provincial towns.) Napoleon was realistic enough to see that the Church problem was not advantageous to the Revolution and—shortly after François and Nicole were married—he had his adjutant general, Henri-Jacques Clark (later the Duke of Feltre), write from Italy to the Directors: "Our Revolution, so far as religion is concerned, has proved a complete failure. France has become once more Roman Catholic, and we may be on the point of needing the Pope himself in order to enlist clerical support for the Revolution, and thereby the support of those districts which the clergy again controls."[2]

The growth of the Point family coincided with Napoleon's rise to power and the consequent triumph of the Revolution. The couple's first child, a girl, was born on April 5, 1797. She was given the name Marie-Jeanne. That same month Babeuf climbed the scaffold in Paris, and in far-off Leoben, Napoleon was negotiating a preliminary peace treaty with Austria. The second child, the author of the letters contained in this book, was born on April 10, 1799, the very day the helpless and humiliated prisoner Angelo Braschi, formerly Pope Pius VI, began a long, excruciatingly painful journey to his exile in France and where at Valence he died on August 29. April 10, 1799, therefore, represents the nadir of papal power and prestige in modern times. During this same period, Napoleon was seeking glory in the Near East where he had just routed a Turkish army in Palestine and Syria, although his earlier successes in northern Italy were being undone by the Austrians and Russians. The third child, Pierre Point, made his entrance into the world on March 7, 1802, twenty days after the remains of Pius VI were transferred to St. Peter's, Rome, and twenty days before Napoleon signed a peace treaty with the British at Amiens. In that year, August 15, the Concordat which Napoleon and the new pope, Pius VII, had signed on July 17, 1801, was solemnly promulgated throughout the territories controlled by France. Four days later another event occurred that was significant to Nicolas Point's development: René de Chateaubriand (1768–1848) published *Le Génie du Christianisme*. Finally, sometime in late 1803 or early 1804, Madame Point delivered her fourth child, Auguste, who lived but a short time and who was followed to the grave by his grieving father. Not long after, on December 2, 1804, Bonaparte, the conqueror of Europe, was crowned Emperor Napoleon I in the presence of Pope Pius VII at Notre Dame, Paris.

The untimely death of her husband forced the widow Point to assume a role she proved capable of sustaining, and if life was not easy, not even for this woman of rock strength, she had the advantage of caring relatives in Rocroi and about the countryside who could be relied upon to give her support when her own resourcefulness did not provide. Family cohesion among numerous aunts, uncles, cousins, and an uncommon bond between themselves became the distinguishing characteristic of Nicole Point and her children. Such fusion was seen as indispensable to a virtuous life. There was also the presence of Monsieur Richer. Shortly after Napoleon had made peace with the Church in July 1801, this former priest-in-hiding was given the parish of Rocroi and almost immediately he directed his energy into opening schools.[3] He persuaded one parishioner, his wife, and three elderly religious (one of whom was a cousin to the Points), whose congregation had been disbanded by the Revolution, to open a catechism school—for children between the ages of four and nine—beside the rectory. Meanwhile, *Monsieur le curé* himself conducted Latin classes in his presbytery for a selected number of boys who had already made their first communion. The opening of those schools was enthusiastically welcomed by Mme Point, who besides giving domestic management the highest priority, was also intent her children receive a proper education, learn good manners, and live in accord with precepts of justice, charity, and sexual purity. Years later, Pierre Point reflected that during this period, Nicolas "could be seen each day with a book under his arm and leading his little brother by his hand along the most direct path to school or to church: this was what their mother wanted."[4]

When he was in his seventies, Nicolas Point commented on the influence these first teachers had on shaping his character. As a matter of fact, many of the traits that would identify him as a missionary in the New World were already visible in the young boy. Highly imaginative and sensitive to the point of being touchy, he demonstrated a seriousness of purpose and a dedication to work that were nurtured in poverty and fostered by skimping during hard times. There was nothing casual about Nicolas Point, and if he dreamt the long dreams of youth, they were disciplined dreams. Pierre reported that from an early age Nicolas had espoused such virtues as orderliness, industry, and thrift; that his talent for drawing was already in evidence, for he loved to trace and sketch pictures of people and landscapes; and that his mother had taught him the importance of sharing bread with people who were less well off than they were. She frequently sent him off to run errands and care for the sick in their parish.[5] In 1810 he made his first communion, but no sooner had he enrolled in Monsieur Richer's Latin class than the old priest died, thereby forcing the serious-minded pre-teenager to reevaluate his academic career. He at last came to the conclusion that he had to put his books aside and concentrate his efforts on making money to support the family.

A local lawyer, a certain Monsieur Renier, needed a boy who could write legibly and had a tolerance for long working hours during which he would copy out letters, ledgers, and documents. Accordingly, Nicolas took a position with this solicitor and from here he soon moved on to a better job as a clerk in the establishment of Monsieur Briois, a wealthy man in town who was employed by the army as the local officer in charge of finances. Both men had the reputation for being upright and respectable; however, Pierre stated that while Nicolas was working for Monsieur Briois, he underwent the most serious temptation, "not in moral matters, which thanks to his steadfastness remained always religious and pure," but because of "a certain worldly atmosphere" that surrounded his new employment. Such an environment certainly seems benign by today's standards. It was made up of the splendor of glittering uniforms and the glamor of polished boots that came and went each day to and from Monsieur Briois's *bureau.* Sometimes these heroes of the *Grande Armée* would lean over and speak to the young clerk and then, in his hearing, congratulate Monsieur Briois for having such a fine boy working in the Emperor's service for him. No doubt he would feel two inches taller. Then at night he would return home where he drew strength from the family circle, "an antidote" for so pernicious a poison. On one occasion one of Napoleon's greatest marshals, Michel Ney (1769–1815), paid a visit to Monsieur Briois. He noticed Nicolas's fine, clear writing and showed glowing admiration for his sketches. He would become the boy's Maecenas, would send him away to become an engineer, and would adopt his family. Nicolas was overwhelmed, but his iron-willed mother bore the provincial's prejudices toward Paris and the scepticism of its schools, and so the military hero of legendary courage had to capitulate in the face of Madame Point's resistance.[6] The disdain for Parisians was the legacy Madame Point bequeathed to her son, a testament he would recall while working among the Coeur d'Alène Indians in years to come.

Other events during this period of his youth were to influence his life as a missionary among the Indians and some of them were referred to in the letters published in this volume. Once during the dead of winter, accompanied by his family and some friends, Nicolas spent a few days vacationing on the frozen banks of the Meuse, some twenty miles southeast of Rocroi. Imprudently the young boy attempted to walk on the ice which suddenly gave way under his weight. His companions pulled him out just in time from the black surging waters. In 1836 in Kentucky he would undergo a similar experience, and in the winter of 1847, as he watched Indian children skating on a river in the Blackfoot country, he would recall the bittersweet memory of the Meuse cutting through his native land, and he would immortalize the skaters and the winter scene in his sketchbook. There were also memories of 1813 that occur in these letters. He was fourteen then, and the war was going badly for the harried Emperor who was still reeling from his disastrous Russian campaign. To make matters worse, on August 12 Austria joined the coalition and declared war once again on France. Just two nights later the citizens of Rocroi celebrated the vigil of Napoleon's birthday, which coincided with the feast of the Assumption of the Virgin Mary, by firing off a series of volleys into the silent black sky. Surprisingly, these salvos were answered at four o'clock the next morning by sentinels in advance of a Prussian detachment. Awakened, Nicolas got up and ran to collect what he could from his employer's house when suddenly a shell landed a few feet from him. Its explosion covered him with dust and gravel, but miraculously he escaped without any injuries. He attributed this good fortune to the Blessed Virgin and, as these published letters testify, he alway had a special place in his heart for Our Lady of the Assumption.[7]

On April 4, the following year, six days before Nicolas Point's fifteenth birthday, Napoleon abdicated the throne in favor of his young son, but it was to the Bourbon's that the French turned for leadership. A month later the erstwhile conqueror of Europe was in his island prison of Elba. At Rocroi soldiers began returning to their families, but the peacetime regime did not last long because Napoleon made his escape and was back in France mustering a new army in March 1815. Ney was sent by the Restoration government to capture him and bring him back to Paris in an iron cage, but instead he joined forces with him, allowing the Emperor to make his triumphant entrance into Paris. Soon Rocroi was ablaze with renewed patriotism, for surely the ramparts rebuilt by Louis XIV's military engineer, Field Marshall Sébastien Le Prestre Marquis de Vauban (1633–1707), were about to see a repetition of the glorious events of May 19, 1643, which had made the name Rocroi immortal. On that day 32,000 men under Louis II de Bourbon-Condé (1621–1686), the Duc d'Enghien, henceforth known as the Great Condé, slaughtered the invincible Spanish army and thereby changed the course of subsequent world history. This time, on June 18, 1815, the decisive battle was fought at Waterloo, some sixty miles due north from Rocroi. The main part of Napoleon's army had marched through the small town and some soldiers were billeted in the homes of the townsmen, descendants of those who had been proud to billet Enghien's troops. Pierre Point recorded that hopes were high, but a few days after marching through the streets of Rocroi, "this army, beautiful as it was, was destroyed. The remnant, driven on by the enemy and by a terrible panic, came rushing pell-mell down the same road in great disarray: men and horses covered with blood and dust; shattered weapons and military vehicles in disrepair. Makeshift hospitals were set up and filled, and those wounded who could not be accommodated were laid out beyond the town, awaiting transportation further south where they would fall victims to fever and plague. After the vanquished army disappeared, the victors—Prussians, English, Russians, and finally famine—spread out over the land."[8] This small fortress town pitched on a high, out-of-the-way plateau in one of the most unattractive parts of France would witness more scenes in years to come like the one described by Pierre Point. Its withdrawn, brooding ramparts would be shelled by the Prussians in 1871, and afterwards victorious German soldiers would make their weary way down its rain-drenched streets. In August 1914, the French army which fought on the Meuse would be billeted under the seemingly perpetual gray skies of Rocroi, a fitting prelude Providence had arranged for this army's ill-fated destiny. Then, on May 14, 1940 what was left of French 61 Infantry Division tried to hold but soon abandoned the town to the Germans who made it their own until more battles during the first days of September 1944 brought back the successors of the Grande Armée to this battlefield of Europe, which had cradled, fostered, and formed Nicolas Point. It was fitting he should have come from Rocroi; it was his fate to know battles and to taste the fruits of defeat.

During the months that followed the rout from Waterloo, Nicolas worked tirelessly for his employer who had in the meanwhile become the town's mayor. In December, Marshal Ney faced the firing squad and in the spring Madame Point fell victim to the plague. For months she lay at death's door, but by late summer her health had improved. The past year had been most distressing for the family and particularly for Nicolas, who was now seventeen. He had come to the decision that if their mother should die, Pierre should begin his studies for the priesthood and at the same time look after the welfare of Marie-Jeanne. He himself had come to the conclusion that he was too old to take up again the studies he had set aside three years previously, and therefore he would join the army. Quick to point out that Nicolas had not given in to the temptation of his youth, Pierre wrote that his brother had not come to this decision "because of a love for glory, nor because he liked to see bloodshed, but only to find some place to spend his energy. Actually though he was right. He would become a soldier, a soldier for Christ."[9]

Besides his mother there were two other powerful personalities that left their marks deep in Nicolas Point's character. Not surprisingly one of them was a woman. The Revolution had produced an exceptional number of extraordinarily powerful women whose influence on the course of events from 1789 onwards has not been fully studied. In one of the most significant monographs on this subject, Olwen Hufton showed that women who until 1796 had "actually participated in the disintegration of the Roman Church" now "ended up on their knees and from then on worked wholeheartedly for the restoration of formal religion within France, the Roman Catholic religion of the *ancien régime,* but endowed with a new vigor from below. When Citoyenne Defarge, ex-*tricoteuse,* put down her needles and reached for a pair of rosary beads, an image to linger on if ever one was, she had to search out her priest and even force the opening of a church. From 1795 onwards, even in cities like Paris, which had demonstrated the most intense anti-clericalism, this is exactly what women did. They brought back the formal worship of God. . . . No government could hope to eradicate a church drawing on emotions which ran as deep as this: there was nothing so fundamental in circulation in the last fifty years of the *ancien régime*."[10] Of course, not all of the women in France had been like Citoyenne Defarge, who before 1796 had found her inspiration in the pages of *Père Duchesne*. "Religion remained powerful in rural France," observed one historian, "especially among the women; this was one reason for the antifeminism of the popular movement. Attacks on priests and *fanatisme* did much to alienate people from the Revolution."[11] It also paved the way for the return to the Church of Rome. Cults presided over by former priests and errant theologians made less and less of an appeal as the new century began. "Outside one or two *salons,*" wrote one of the foremost students of this movement, "the Ideologues had little influence [after 1800] and their predecessors the *philosophes* were universally decried."[12]

Gabrielle-Françoise Laroche (b. Chambley, Moselle, June 10, 1777; d. Metz, December 11, 1847) was a teenager when the Revolution declared war against Christianity. During the years when Citoyenne Defarge had scoffed at religion, Gabrielle-Françoise had developed an ardent desire to serve the Church and to bring the Gospel message beyond the frontiers of France. She found a kindred spirit in Madame de Méjanès, whose maiden name was Anne-Victoire Tailleur (b. Distroff, Moselle, May 11, 1763; d. Metz, October 2, 1837). With the encouragement of the Bishop of Metz, Monseigneur André Jauffert (1759–1823), the widowed Madame de Méjanès gathered about her a few lay women like Gabrielle-Françoise before the Concordat was promulgated. The group lived together in community, dedicating themselves to poverty, chastity, and to the service of teaching children and attending to the poor in Metz. In 1807 the group was recognized as the diocesean congregation of the Sisters of the Holy Childhood of Jesus and Mary of Sainte-Chrétienne—one more in the cluster of families of religious women that sprang up, like so many mushrooms after a rain, from the soil of post-Revolutionary France.[13] Gabrielle-Françoise, now known as Sister St. Gabriel, made her profession with the original group and was immediately sent to Rocroi where she arrived in January 1808 and where she remained for the next thirty-one years. Her assignment was to teach in the school reestablished by Monsieur l'abbé Richer.[14]

The inhabitants of Rocroi in no time recognized her as an exceptional woman. For her part, she bemoaned the fact that she had not been born a man. As a man, she said, she could have been ordained a priest and have been an apostle, one who could have baptized many, preached to more, and finally, she could have died a martyr's death in some far distant land for the faith.[15] Romantic ideas? Of course. We have noted that Chateaubriand had published his *Génie du Christianisme* the year Pierre was born, and that Romanticism had reached its zenith during the first part of the nineteenth century, not only in art, literature, and philosophy but in religious sentiment as well. Sister St. Gabriel was a product of her age; however, she was anything but a wooly-headed dreamer. On the contrary, she was a woman of eminent practicality, a realist, and a shrewd judge of character. The reality was she was not a man, not a priest in some far-off land; she was a religious woman sent off to a dull corner of northeastern France, but she certainly did not feel herself doomed on that account to play a minor role in the missionary activity of the Church. She spent long hours watching and praying before the Blessed Sacrament, for which she had a special devotion, and when she received Communion, which she did frequently, it was "always with transport and with abundant tears." In 1811, when there was no priest in residence at Rocroi, Sister St. Gabriel gave the First Communion retreat during which memorable occasion "she spoke to us of sin and of Our Lord with such a superhuman unction and vigor that she made us sigh and weep with her." It was her custom to fix attention on a student whom she deemed had or ought to have a religious or priestly vocation and then pray for this young person day and night. Once she received confirmation of her judgment in prayer she would approach the boy or girl and with terrible simplicity say: "God wants you!" Then she would call in the parents of the future priest or nun and advise them of God's plan for their child. Pierre Point reported that many young people in Rocroi traced the awakening of their vocation to Sister St. Gabriel. The good sister called all three of the widow Point's children aside and informed them God wanted each of them for a special mission. Their mother, who had easily resisted the proposals of General Ney, surrendered willingly to those of Sister St. Gabriel.[16]

During this same period a number of young men from the seminary would occasionally come to Rocroi where they used the Point home to practice singing. The unabashed piety and enthusiastic joy of these elder boys, whose harmonious voices were so appealing, provided Nicolas and Pierre with an added attraction to Sister St. Gabriel's confident assurances. But the man who was to have the most profound influence on the fourteen-year-old Nicolas Point arrived in Rocroi in 1813. His name was Pierre Charlier (b. Hannapes des Ardennes, March 19, 1767, d. Rocroi, March 14, 1840).[17] He had begun his preliminary classical studies late in life and had just completed his theological studies when the Revolution closed the seminaries. When he returned home, the civil authorities took for granted he had given up all ideas of becoming a priest, and so when he applied for authorization to run a small store out of his home, he was granted the requested permission along with a salesman's license to pass back and forth across the border. Taking advantage of the government's liberality, he tarried on one occasion long enough in Belgium to get himself ordained, and then he returned to France "bearing a load of eels on his back, the priestly seal on his soul, and in his heart apostolic zeal." From 1791 to 1801 he traveled throughout the country ostensibly peddling all types of wares, but actually offering clandestine masses and attending to the spiritual needs of the faithful. After Napoleon made his peace with the Church, he was appointed the *curé* in Neuville-en-Tourne-à-Fuy, a small Ardennes town near Rethel, and here he set up an informal seminary, similar to the one begun by Monsieur Richer in Rocroi.

Pierre Point wrote that some thirty to thirty-five priests "none of whom were unworthy of their master" and some of whom attained fame during the Orleanist Monarchy and the Second Empire, were directed to the priesthood by Monsieur Charlier. The priest was so successful in dealing with young men that he was appointed headmaster of the *collège* at Chimay, a town some ten miles from Rocroi, as the crow flies, on the Belgian side of the border. So, the former peddler returned to Belgium, this time bearing a burning desire to sell what he considered his most precious ware, the sacramental seal of the priest, to young men in the provinces of Namur, the Ardennes, and Champagne. From Chimay he came to Rocroi in 1813 to fill the post that had remained vacant since the death of Monsieur Richer. Hardly established in the rectory, Pierre Charlier made plans to reactivate the Latin school, the prime purpose of which was to prepare boys to enroll in the established diocesean seminary and the secondary purpose was to teach future laymen in the parish the wisdom of the Greeks under the scandal of the Cross. But the unsettled times prevented him from implementing his project until March 1815. At that date some forty young men and boys, a number of whom he set up in surrounding lodgings as boarders, were following his courses. Except for the Waterloo week, classes progressed without interruption for the next several years.[18]

The *collège* was separated from the Point house only by a small garden, but because of his mother's illness and other problems, Nicolas Point was not free to enroll in Père Charlier's school until the feast of St. Francis Xavier, December 3, 1816. From that day on it became clear that in this *collège* that provided an educational plan for boys who were anywhere from six to twenty years old, the seventeen-year-old Nicolas felt awkward around the younger boys.[19] He tried to compensate for the five years he had been away from any formal schooling; at the same time he strove to imitate the physical exploits of his athletic mentor for whom he had developed such admiration and awe. Typically he put all moderation aside. During the winter months he often rose at three or four in the morning to walk around the deserted streets before joining his companions at their five o'clock morning meditation, an exercise obligatory for all the boys. After classes he would again meet with his companions and Père Charlier for evening prayers and spiritual reading. At these sessions he became familiar with the life of St. Francis Xavier, whom he chose as his special patron, and with the *Lettres édifiantes et curieuses,* describing the exploits of seventeenth-and eighteenth-century Jesuit missionaries. It was during this period of his life that he also adopted a pious custom he was to retain as a missionary in the American Northwest, a practice he referred to in these published letters. Every year on the feast of St. Francis Xavier, December third, he would gather an assortment of flowers, each of which symbolized some special offering to his patron, and he would place the bouquet before a statue or picture of the saint. The period abounded in such devotions and Nicholas Point was a man of his age. On December 3, 1841, he baptized his first large group of Indians causing Pierre to comment that Nicolas "not only offered St. Francis Xavier a bouquet of flowers, but a spiritual bouquet made up of the first fruits of his mission."[20] But it was the accounts of the Jesuits in the Paraguay reductions that made the greatest impression on the receptive young romantic with the vivid imagination and the intense desire to give his life for a noble cause. The heroism and the successes of these Jesuits were the stuff out of which his vocation began to take shape. Soon he "burned with the desire to accomplish one day in the forests of North America what they had achieved in the forests of South America, along the banks of the Paraguay."[21] Père Charlier, who led a Spartan existence, encouraged him and often invited this supersensitive, overzealous disciple of his to accompany him as he made the rounds of his extensive parish on foot. Once his hero took young Nicolas on a walking pilgrimage of over one hundred miles, during which he pointed out to him all of the places where he had said mass and dispensed the sacraments during his nine-year stint as a traveling salesman. The young man returned exhausted but in a state of great spiritual elation. The priest then made him teach catechism to the youngest children in the parish in order to ground his idealism in the reality of the everyday world. It was precisely what he needed and, to a great extent, Charlier's pedagogical method was successful. Point, for all of his enthusiasm, sensitivity, and idealism, for all of his imaginings and flights into fancy, remained basically a realist all of his life.[22]

In 1818 Pierre and many of Nicolas's friends at the *collège* left to do further studies at the seminary, fully expecting him to join them. But he hesitated. He was now nineteen, and more than ever undecided, restless. Besides his studies in rhetoric, he pursued his interest in painting, and waited. On the feast of St. Francis Xavier that year, he reported he was drawn in some mysterious way to thinking about the vast wilderness of America. The thought persisted and, confused, he spoke about it to Sister St. Gabriel. She assured him this preoccupation came from God and he should bring it to prayer. But the turmoil did not abate. However sweet the attraction of America's wilderness, it meant leaving his mother, saying good-bye to his brother and sister. He redoubled his prayers and Communions and searched the meaning of all his confusion. As he reread Chateaubriand's *Le Génie du Christianisme*—a book he confessed had a profound influence on him—he discovered himself repeating over and over again: "If only the Jesuits still existed!"[23]

JESUITS 1819–1826

The fact of the matter was the Jesuits did indeed exist, even though legally they were still proscribed in France. On May 7, 1814, Father Tadeusz Brzozowski (1749–1820), whom the Holy See had already recognized as the general of the Society of Jesus in Russia, appointed Father Pierre-Joseph Picot de Clorivière (1735–1820) superior general of the society in France and authorized him to reconstitute the order in that country. As long as Clorivière and his companions did not dress in the traditional Jesuit *soutane* or call themselves Jesuits, Louis XVIII's government was prepared to cast a blind eye on their growing presence.[1] There were a number of liberals on the Left and Gallicans on the Right who called foul, but neither their number nor the number of Jesuits was large enough to make an issue of the affair.

By August 7, 1814, when Pius VII's bull *Sollicitudo Omnium Ecclesiarum* was published, officially reestablishing the society throughout the world, the Jesuits were already firmly rooted in France.[2] By the end of the year, three *petits séminaires,* or minor seminaries, sprung up: one at Saint-Acheul, near Amiens; one in Bordeaux; and one in Montmorillon.[3] The local bishops had taken advantage of the right granted to them by the Restoration government to open up such minor seminaries exempt from state supervision. They then turned them over to the shadowy Jesuits. The following year minor seminaries were opened up in Soissons and at Saint-Anne d'Aurray, in Brittany; in 1816 two more appeared on the scene, at Avignon and at Forcalquier.[4] Understandably, these "seminaries" were not in theory, much less in fact, institutions reserved exclusively for boys intent on becoming priests, even though this was the primary *raison d'être* of their existence. Many, and very soon most, of the students came from homes where a priority was placed on Jesuit education. The reputation of the earlier schools of the society conditioned parents to believe that academically, religiously, and morally, Jesuit education was a cut above the best schools in France. The parents who enrolled their sons in these Jesuit schools were royalist by inclination, and many were poorly instructed in matters of the faith. Their own parents had been unashamedly Gallican, and when the time came to choose between the Jesuits and the king, they chose the latter.[5] Each minor seminary showed a percentage of financially poor students supported by various bishops on its rolls, and there were also some students who worked for their board and lodging.

When Nicolas Point confided his yearnings for the society to Père Charlier, he undoubtedly learned about Father Clorivière, Saint-Acheul, and the other *petits séminaires.* Pierre Point recorded that the priest told him about a number of his own friends and former acquaintances at the seminary who had recently become Jesuits.[6] There was, for example, Father Nicolas Jennesseaux (b. Reims, April 9, 1769; d. Paris, October 9, 1842), a former Father of the Faith and presently the rector at Forcalquier, who had opened Saint-Acheul.

Another friend of Charlier, and like Jennesseaux, both a *champenois* and a former Father of the Faith, was the present rector at Saint-Acheul, Jean-Nicolas Loriquet (b.

Eparnay, August 5, 1767; d. Paris, April 9, 1845). Loriquet had not been as fortunate as Charlier, for when as a deacon he felt obliged to flee from Saint-Sulpice in June 1790, he was soon arrested in Paris. He was held prisoner in various jails during the height of the Revolution, but he finally managed to escape to England and eventually to be ordained. Certainly, he became one of the most influential of the Founding Fathers of the new society in France obtaining from Talleyrand his retraction and submission to the Church. A professional historian and author of the controversial *Histoire de France,* Loriquet promulgated the famous *Plan d'études,* or the basic curriculum for the *petits séminaires,* which he developed during his years as rector at Saint-Acheul. "Experience certainly shows us," Loriquet observed, "that even if it is sometimes useful, it is more harmful to innovate, and that in education, as in all other subjects, nothing is more dangerous than to let oneself be dazzled by appearances of imaginary perfection. For this reason, there is nothing new and extraordinary in the *Plan d'études.*" Rather, he explained, it was based on the educational principles expounded by French Jesuit educators before the suppression, and founded particularly on the writings and practice of Joseph de Jouvancy (1643–1719), "who was our principal guide, and in many places our *Plan* is simply the development of that which is mapped out in that precious work entitled *Ratio discendi et docendi.*"[7]

Loriquet, whose influences on Point were profound, was too modest in describing his innovative work. He did, indeed, expand and bring up to date what was implicit in the philosophy of the old society, but he was also an imaginative innovator in his own right. For one thing, his *Plan* had to provide an integrated core curriculum for boys and young men who were anywhere from six to twenty years old. This curriculum had to be constructed upon the ancient and rich tradition of Christian humanism, which was rooted in the soil of Rome and nurtured by the Jesuit schools of the old society. Since Latin was the vehicle of this culture, the *Plan* was built on the study of Latin grammar and literature.[8] However, Loriquet profited from the lesson Pascal taught his Jesuit predecessors. Factual information formulated with impeccable logic and phrased in a pleasing, precious Latin style was not enough. To a great extent the popularity of Pascal's *Lettres Provinciales* lay in their precise, beautiful, vigorous French. Because they were so stylistically pleasing, they were even read by many who disagreed with their content. Meanwhile, the Latin refutations by scholarly Jesuits were ignored. Because the value of communicating facts eloquently in French to Frenchmen was thus not lost on Loriquet, he placed the study of French grammar and literature high on the priority list of subjects to be mastered. He further argued that because theology and philosophy alone could not adequately explain the world Napoleon had made modern, it was of vital importance for the students at Saint-Acheul to be grounded in the study of history, which together with vernacular literature, had played a nugatory role in the old *Ratio*. For example, Loriquet argued that the causes of the Revolution could demonstrate the effects of accepting erroneous philosophical principles in politics and culture; they would also demonstrate to the students that the prevailing political dogma of the necessity of joining throne with altar was not necessarily good religion or good politics.[9] It would be difficult to exaggerate the influence of this Jesuit on the course of nineteenth-century education. As far as curriculum was concerned, Loriquet's *Plan* was not only implemented in the colleges established by French Jesuits in the United States and other missionary countries throughout the world, but it was also adopted and modified by the anti-Jesuit *Université*. It thereby became the official educational plan for all schools in the French-speaking world that prepared students for the pursuit of higher education.[10]

Another of Charlier's friends who had lately entered the society was Robert Debrosse (b. Chatel-et-Chehery, Ardennes, March 3, 1768; d. Laval, February 2, 1848), who became instrumental in making the devotion to St. Joseph popular in the new society and who, in 1818, while Nicolas Point was weeping over those burning pages of *Le Génie du Christianisme,* became the rector of the *petit séminaire* at

Bordeaux, the establishment destined to be the cradle of French Jesuit institutions in the United States and Canada. Debrosse, at a later date, would reestablish the society at Paray-le-Monial, the visible center of devotion to the Sacred Heart that so defined *l'ésprit* of nineteenth-century Jesuits. Point would one day dedicate the first mission he founded among the North American Indians to the Sacred Heart and his brother would become known as the propagator of this devotion in Canada.[11]

Two more seminary friends of Charlier, both natives of Reims, were Nicolas Godinot (b. February 6, 1761; d. Fribourg, Switzerland, May 26, 1841) and Jean-Pierre Varlet (b. March 3, 1796; d. Poitiers, March 26, 1854). As provincial, the former received Nicolas Point into the society and would play a pivotal role in determining his future; the latter founded the *collège* at Le Passage, in Spain, an institution where high adventure awaited him and whose customs he would introduce to the Indians of the Northwest.[12]

Père Charlier volunteered gladly to write to one or more of these good Jesuits on behalf of his spiritual son, who, like them, was also a native of the Ardennes and Champagne country. The returned correspondence from Père Loriquet encouraged the young man to come to the *petit séminaire* at Saint-Acheul, and so at last, on June 24, 1819, after bidding a tearful farewell to his mother and sister, Nicolas, his brother Pierre, and Père Charlier set off on foot from Rocroi to Amiens, some hundred miles or more to the northwest. The fact that a number of Nicolas's companions joined the trio as far as Chimay is a testimony to the warm friendships he had formed with so many of his peers. At Chimay, in Belgium, there were more farewells, another crossing of the serpentine border, and the long road to Saint-Acheul, where the three pilgrims arrived on the twenty-eighth.[13]

The imposing abbey dedicated to this obscure Picard saint had been built on a high hill, less than a mile from Amiens, in the seventeenth century by the Canons Regular of Sainte-Geneviève. During the intervening centuries the complex—abbatial church and palace, houses, garden, cemetery and farm—had changed hands and appearances a number of times and, what is more amazing, although scarred and battered, it did manage to survive the Revolution. In July 1814, when Father de Clorivière instructed Father Nicolas Jennesseaux to sign the lease on the property with the option of purchase, the buildings were in a deplorable condition; nevertheless, on the following November 3, the Jesuits welcomed 140 boys to the first class in this *petit séminaire*. "They called it a *minor* seminary," recalled Father Loriquet, part-time teacher and part-time master of novices, "but I have never seen a bigger operation."

In 1815 the Jesuits purchased another house, Maison Blamont, a hundred yards or so down the Amiens road, to accommodate the expanding student body, which, in 1816, already numbered 490. On September 14, 1819, three months after Nicolas Point arrived, the bill of sale for the Saint-Acheul property was officially transferred to Father Jennesseaux and his companions. That same year a fire almost destroyed the main buildings but the foundations for a new building were laid before the ashes were cooled. This structure, erected in a very different style from the original abbatial complex, was completed in the beginning of 1820. The following year the fathers purchased a cabaret of notorious reputation that was separated from the abbatial church by a wall and the Amiens-Noyon road, baptized it Saint-Firmin, and had it turned into a residence hall to accommodate 90 students. Six years later 225 were housed there.[14]

Nicolas was caught up in all of this activity and growth as a charter staff member of the French Jesuits' most famous *collège* from 1820 to 1830. Years later in Louisiana he would have the opportunity to emulate the daring of Jennesseaux and Loriquet and would try to create the kind of enthusiasm that he had known so well at Saint-Acheul. Some of that enthusiasm originated in the classroom where Nicolas studied philosophy under Father Jean-Paul Martin (b. Châteauneuf-Randon, Lozère, February 10, 1792; d. Lyon, December 5, 1859). Martin, a dynamic, personable, twenty-seven-year-old prodigy, was one of the founding fathers of the Province whom Father Clorivière had received into the society five years earlier, in 1814. All his lectures were delivered in sparkling Latin; French was never used in the classrooms of the older students. Martin had a remarkable influence on his students, many of whom, like Point, became missionaries and teachers throughout the world. For these young men Martin seemed to epitomize the ideal Jesuit, the scholar who had successfully integrated his intellectual life with spiritual principles, the teacher who seemed to have all the answers and whose door was always opened for counseling his students. After teaching philosophy and theology in various *collèges,* Martin was appointed dean and professor of dogmatic theology at Vals in 1836, the year after Point had arrived in the United States. Vals was a newly opened house at that date but already enjoyed the reputation of being one of the outstanding theologates in the society, Martin's photographic memory and voracious appetite for reading made him a living library of theological and philosophical knowledge. He was held in awe by his colleagues and he thrilled many young scholastics by his spellbinding lectures. It was during these years that he developed what his colleagues dubbed "Martinism" or the "Vals System" of theological speculation. Someone, however, became uneasy about where such speculation was leading and wrote about his concerns to the Jesuit general in Rome, Jan Roothaan (1785–1853). Martin taught, it was asserted, that in order to come to the necessary and eternal character of first principles, one had to see them in the first, eternal and necessary Truth, that is in God Himself. Was "Martinism" French Jesuit spirituality gone wrong, a form of ontologism? Would the "Vals System" eventually lead to a kind of pantheism? Rome responded quickly. Martin was asked to submit his lecture notes for investigation and Roothaan gave this material to three trusted theologians.

No judgment was forthcoming; however, in 1839 Martin was given a different assignment. Then in 1846, while Point was instructing his neophytes in wigwams, Martin was reassigned to Vals. When the 1848 revolutions scattered the Italian Jesuits, two former professors of theology took refuge in the French theologate. They were not favorably impressed by what they found was being taught there and so they sent a joint report to Rome on the "Vals System." Again the response was quick. This time Roothaan published the opinions of the three theologians who had studied Martin's notes along with the famous directives entitled *"Ordonnance pour les Etudes supérieures"* which forbade Jesuits to teach seventeen specified philosophical and theological theses. Martin was dispatched to the residence at Lyon and there, during the evening meal in the community refectory, he listened to the reading of the documents, which condemned his life's work, and he heard himself singled out for censure. His submission was immediate and sincere. At Vals, on January 6, 1850, the rector and the twelve remaining theology professors signed a statement protesting that "We adhere purely and simply with complete submission and without restriction to the Ordinance concerning Higher Studies." For Jesuit theologians in the "Age of Spiritual Awakening" submission to Rome was neither a luxury nor a formula of empty rhetoric. Martin's experience shows that there were times when those whose lives were consecrated to the assimilation and exploration of the Word of God had to remain silent for the greater good. They believed the alternative was to attenuate seriously that Word. Submission was a moral imperative. It was "expected of a religious"—one of Roothaan's favorite expressions. Indeed, the general in later years singled out Martin for always "giving great proof of a solid virtue." Martin's pupil, Nicolas Point, would be asked to make a similar submission in the very year when the work of the great theologian was being scrutinized. The fact that he did so, although it would seem with less peace and indifference, and the reasons for his submission can be appreciated in the light of the spirituality and ecclesiology that Jesuits like Martin held and taught.[15]

During 1819–1820, Nicolas was in his characteristic way excelling in Father Martin's class and for the most part he was rewarded for his efforts. Point was certainly intelligent, but his Muse did not have a speculative bent. In his second year of philosophy he was sent, as an aspirant to the society, to Maison Blamont where he was assigned teacher and prefect to the younger boys and served under the supervision of one of the Jesuit priests. This practice had already become a custom in the Province of France; its advantage was that the Jesuits in the community could judge the aptitude and prudence of young men who were thinking of joining the novitiate, and at the same time the candidate would learn by experience what was expected of him before he made a lifetime commitment to the society by applying to the novitiate. In December 1820, his brother Pierre also enrolled at Saint-Acheul. The following academic year, already a third-year philosopher, Nicolas was put in charge of Maison Saint-Firmin where he was responsible for forty older boys. Meanwhile, he continued teaching two classes of the younger boys and was expected to keep up with his own studies. At the end of the year he was so spent out that his superiors became concerned about his health and encouraged him to take a fifteen-day vacation so that he and Pierre could walk the more than a hundred miles back to Rocroi. By this date Pierre had decided to study at the newly opened seminary for the Archdiocese of Reims which had just been put under the direction of the Sulpicians, and therefore he did not intend to accompany his brother back to Saint-Acheul. In fact, it is not clear if Nicolas himself returned to the *collège* or if, after his brief vacation at Rocroi, he went directly to Paris where, completely exhausted, he entered the novitiate on September 23, 1822.[16]

As early as 1816 Father de Clorivière began looking for a country house for the fathers who worked out of the Paris residence on the Rue des Postes. He finally settled on a house with two and one-half acres of land in the suburb of Montrouge, some six miles south of the Paris residence, which he purchased at the beginning of 1818. The house was immediately expanded and other accommodations built for the arrival of fifteen novices (6 priests, 8 scholastics, and 1 coadjutor brother) who came from Paris on April 15 with their master of novices, Jean-

Baptiste Gury (b. Mailleroncourt, Haute-Saône, September 20, 1773; d. Dôle, May 6, 1854). Gury, the man primarily responsible from 1818–1830 for training aspirants to join the society had been described as "energetic and sanguine even though a bit brusque." He brought impeccable credentials with him to his new assignment. From experience he knew what life was like in the army barracks. Then, in 1795, he entered the Society of the Sacred Heart, which later fused with the Fathers of the Faith. He became the master of novices in Rome of this new canonical entity—a veritable refuge for former and future Jesuits—until his reception into the society by Clorivière in 1814.[17] Ultramontane both by instinct and training, he made sure his novices understood why the soldier Ignatius had placed his society under a special vow to the services of the pope and why "Laying aside all private judgment, we ought to keep our minds prepared and ready to obey in all things the true Spouse of Christ our Lord, which is our holy Mother, the hierarchical Church."[18]

Between April and December the number of novices had grown to forty and even a man as austere as Gury had to admit that the living conditions at Montrouge were deplorable. The food was scarce and poor; there was scant heat and that in only two rooms of the draughty building to fend off the freezing winter. He noted in his Journal that "the novices were often made to suffer the effects of a poverty which went beyond the bounds of what one would desire."[19] In 1820 the Twentieth General Congregation mandated that the decrees, rules, and ordinances of the old society be normative for the new, and to this end houses of formation be set up wherein applicants to the society could be trained in the authentic spirit of St. Ignatius. This meant that by 1822, the year Point arrived to begin his novitiate, the Polish and the English provinces and the Irish mission, which had no novitiates of their own, began sending novices to Montrouge. In this same year, moreover, a separate community was set up in the house as a tertianship for the benefit of seven of the original priests Clorivière had received into the society without the benefit of ever having made a novitiate. In 1822 a small chapel was at last constructed for the seventeen second-year novices, the forty-three first-year novices, and the fourteen coadjutor novices, cramped into the rabbit warren quarters.[20]

Among Point's fellow novices a few merit special attention both because they demonstrate the vitality of the society in Point's lifetime and because their careers enable today's reader of Point's writings to appreciate better his outlook on life, his expectations, and his priorities. The biographical data of these men also provide a necessary dimension to gauge the background from which he came.

Claude Guyon (b. Regny, Lyon, July 18, 1785; d. Lavaur, Tarn, November 25, 1845) was one of the best known preachers during the Restoration, a period when the art of rhetoric was regarded as the highest form of civilized achievement. He had been ordained in 1810 as a Missionary of Lyon and then immediately was chosen by Joseph Cardinal Fesch, Napoleon's uncle, to be his personal secretary. In this capacity Guyon was one of those selected to witness the marriage of the emperor to Marie-Louise in 1810. Dubbed "John the Baptist," he electrified those who crowded into the churches specifically to hear him during the second quarter of the century.[21] Another novice who would gain notoriety as a great preacher was Louis Marquet (b. Port-Louis, Morbihan, March 9, 1803; d. Nantes, April 21, 1880), the founder of a number of sodalities for men, called *congrégations,* and for women, *les enfants de Marie,* throughout Normandy and Brittany.[22] The great missionary of Brittany during the greater part of the nineteenth century, however, was Joseph Lestrohan (b. Plouhinec, Morbihan, December 14, 1800; d. Vannes, February 4, 1882), the acknowledged authority on preaching parish missions in French and Breton. During this period Brittany, the "Ireland of France," produced an impressive number of religious vocations, the great percentage of which went to the foreign missions. Lestrohan, through his parish missions, *pardons,* and pious confraternities, played no minor role in the Breton miracle during the "Age of Religious Awakening." He also had the distinction of having lived, when he was not out on the circuit, in the same community for more than fifty years, a fact which may have contributed to the judgment of one of his confreres who, curiously, described him as "a man sometimes caustic, always charitable." He outlived his fellow novice Nicolas Point by fourteen years and died in the home of a kindly family who gave him lodging after the promulgation of the decree of 1880, which outlawed the society in France and appropriated Jesuit properties.[23] Another one of Point's classmates shared the same fate as Lestrohan and, in fact, died one week after the "Apostle of Brittany" in the home of a family that had rescued him from the streets and had nursed him during the last year of his life. His name was Côme Lartigue (b. Rubempre, Somme, February 13, 1801; d. Amiens, February 25, 1882). In addition to being the "Lacordaire of Strausbourg," this Jesuit also became the prefect of studies, or principal, at the famous *collège* of Brugelette, from which so many missionaries were sent to the United States and other French missions.[24]

But unquestionably the best known of Point's fellow novices was Gustave-François-Xavier de la Croix de Ravignan (b. Bayonne, December 1, 1795; d. Paris, February 26, 1858). Armand de Ponlevoy, S.J. gives a stirring description of the character, life, and times of this man who, perhaps more than anyone else, is responsible for the reputation Jesuits enjoyed, among friends and enemies during Point's lifetime, as men of learning, industry, and dedication. Like so many of his contemporaries, Ravignan had spent time in the military, before joining the Jesuits. He had been a first lieutenant in the Royal Army that fought Napoleon on his return from Elba. After the defeat of the former emperor, Ravignan was named attorney general of the Royal Court, a remarkable appointment for so young a man, but it was expected that from this enviable post he would launch a brilliant career in the government. In 1837 he replaced Jean-Baptiste-Henri Lacordaire, O.P. as the *conferencier* at Notre Dame in Paris, a position he kept until 1848 when he organized the more famous lecturers for the men of the city. In the age of such giants as Bishop Felix-Antoine-Philibert

Dupanloup, (1802–1878) Charles-Forbes-René Montalambert (1810–1870), and Pierre-Antoine Berryer (1790–1868), it was Ravignan who was one of the most brilliant, diversified, and influential persons of the restored society, the acclaimed "spiritual father of his generation," and even though his fellow Jesuits secretly gave him the sobriquet "Old Iron Bar" because of his rigidity, Pope Gregory XVI decreed him the "Apostle of Paris." Before Nicolas Point was to leave for the American missions, Xavier de Ravignan had exerted considerable influence on him and, to a great extent, had molded his way of thinking.[25] Like Ravignan, but on a more modest plane, Pierre Cotel (b. Hangest-en-Sangterre, Somme, May 16, 1800; d. Nancy, August 4, 1884), another novice at Montrouge, also became a well-known retreat giver and interpreter of the *Spiritual Exercises.* He was also to become the beloved master of novices for the exiled French at Issenheim, Switzerland, at the same time that Point would be instructing the Flatheads in the Northwest.[26] Henri Delfour (b. Aurillac, Cantal, April 22, 1803; d. Toulouse, March 1, 1878) was another member of this famous novitiate class. He early gained the reputation as a gifted preacher but his asserted powers for healing the sick soon overshadowed his acclaimed oratorical abilities, and during the age of the apparitions at Lourdes, he gained the appellation "The Healer of Toulouse."[27] Finally some mention should be made of a man who entered Montrouge with Point but who subsequently left the novitiate. In September 1800, Father Louis-Barthélemy Enfantin (b. Brocards, Drôme, August 24, 1776; d. Lyon, November 7, 1855) was ordained secretly one night in a barn. Immediately afterwards he associated himself with the Fathers of the Faith who came out of hiding at the time of the Concordat. But when this society was suppressed by Napoleon in 1804, Enfantin became the director of the Missions of Valence, a group of priests dedicated to reevangelizing the poor parishes in that diocese. In 1820 he had gained the reputation of being a charismatic orator and one of the forces of the Church in France, and so it was not surprising that he was chosen to preach the funeral oration at the obsequies of the assassinated Duke of Berry, an event that carried great political implications. He entered Montrouge with Point in 1822, at the height of his career, but being "too ardent" he left after a nine-month stint to become the vicar general in the diocese of Valence and the author of many religious tracts. With Jeanne de Franssu (1751–1824) he founded the Sisters of the Nativity and wrote a Constitution for them that was modeled after that of the society's.[28]

Not all of Point's fellow novices remained in France, nor in Europe for that matter. A mathematician of promise Philippe de Villefort (b. Cornus, Aveyron, July 2, 1799; d. Rome, November 26, 1866) began his career trying to form the consciences of young scholars, but in 1836 he was sent to the generalate in Rome where he remained all the rest of his life. There he exercised a profound influence on the French community in the Eternal City. For example, he was Lacordaire's confessor and received into the Church such prominent people as Louis Veuillot (1813–1888) and the Ratisbonne brothers, Marie-Théodore (1802–1884) and Marie-Alphonse (1814–1884).[29] There were two novices at Montrouge with whom Point would have close dealings in the future: Pierre Chazelle (b. Saint-Just-en-Bas, Loire, January 12, 1789; d. Green Bay, Wisconsin, September 4, 1845) and Thomas Legoüais (b. Nantes, April 26, 1793; d. New York, May 15, 1876). The former, already a priest before coming to Montrouge, is rightly considered the Father of what became the two Canadian provinces and the New York and New England provinces. Even though he entered the novitiate directly from a military unit, he had been a professor at the same seminary out of which St. John Vianney (1786–1859) had flunked because of his inability to comprehend Latin lecturers. In fact, it is probable but difficult to prove conclusively that he had been a classmate with St. John Vianney.[30] Legoüais, "a pigmy in stature (his height was a trifle under five feet), was a giant in the vineyard of the Lord," He became the first chairman of the theology department and the first director of the campus ministry in what is today Fordham University. Some may see it as significant that he gave up these two ministries for what he considered a far more important work—hearing confessions at St. Francis Xavier parish, New York, where he was assigned in 1869, the year after Point's death.[31]

There were also co-novices with Point at Montrouge who became pioneers in diverse Jesuit missions. For example, Romain Dénieau (b. Guitre, Gironde, February 14, 1800; d. Nossy-Tally, Madagascar, July 21, 1861) was one of the first Jesuits to be sent to what became a famous mission of the restored society—Madagascar—where he collaborated in writing the first Malagasy-French dictionary and grammar.[32] Then there was Claude Gotteland (b. Bassens, Savoy, Kingdom of Sardinia, June 22, 1803; d. Zi-ka-wei, China, July 17, 1856). The French Jesuits had played no minor role in maintaining the China Mission during the seventeenth and eighteenth centuries, and in 1842, while Point was attempting to establish Paraguay-like reductions in Montana, Gotteland, who had been commissioned by Roothaan to rebuild the renown China mission was laying the foundations of what later became Aurora University and the Jesuit church in Shanghai, and also the remarkable Kiang-Nang Mission. The diversified Gotteland wrote on a number of topics—physics, chemistry, astronomy, Chinese grammar, moral theology—showing the wide variation of his interests as well as his competence in the world of academe. But, unfortunately, like so many French Jesuits missioned to China during this period, the dreaded typhoid fever brought him to a premature grave.[33]

Each of these men, and the many others, all fellow novices of Nicolas Point, went through a training at Montrouge which in some respects was like a Marine boot camp. "How will the sons of Ignatius, so *spiritually* weak become tough?" Roothaan asked Godinot, and he answered: "By being *soldiers, soldiers, soldiers of Christ!!!*" Then advising the provincial how he should govern his subjects, he added: "Let us not however lose hope. *Let them humble themselves in all things and they shall find favor with God.*" Roothaan was borrowing a metaphor from Ignatius, who in 1546, had written: "The other religious orders of the Church's army are like frontline troops drawn up in massive battalions. We are like light-armed soldiers ready for sudden battles, going from one side to the other, now here, now there."[34] And one of the Saint's early companions commented that Ignatius "supposed that the novices would leave [the novitiate] so mortified that they would need bridles not spurs."[35] It was at Montrouge they were fitted with spurs, and these men, trained in the Napoleonic era, appreciated well the connotations of the metaphor. The blueprint for their formation was St. Ignatius's book in which he described his own difficult path in finding the "glory of the Lord," which he called the *Spiritual Exercises.* These Exercises were designed "to conquer oneself and regulate one's life, and avoid coming to a determination through any inordinate affection."[36] They were designed to make athletes, frontline soldiers for Christ at the disposition of the sovereign pontiff. They indicated that the most difficult course was the speediest and surest way to reach perfection. Expressions like *ama nesciri* ("love to be unknown") and *agere contra* ("go against yourself") were sure ways to achieve self-effacement, to reduce the body to servitude in order to set the spirit free. Without judging whether they were right or wrong, the Jesuits that came out of Montrouge believed that Ignatius had made obedience the distinguishing virtue of his company of light-armed soldiers. Memoires written in later years by the men who did their training under Father Master Gury were in accord in stressing this fact, pointing to St. Ignatius's admonition:

> More easily may we suffer ourselves to be suppressed by other religious orders in fasting, watching and other severities in diet and apparel . . . but in true and perfect obedience and the abnegation of our will and judgment, I greatly desire, most dear brothers, that those who serve God in the Society should be conspicuous, and that the true and genuine progeny of the same should, as it were, be distinguished by this mark.[37]

By being strictly obedient to their superior these novices at Montrouge were expected even to mortify their own desire for mortification, that is their desire to excel in excessive generosity, to press themselves even further in realizing the "scandal of the Cross." Strict obedience and the desire to "do more" created a tension, a strain between counterpoised forces that is the source of the group dynamism and the highly personalized individualism so characteristic of the Jesuits of Point's generation. It was a delicate stress between the centrifugal and centripetal; however, the balance was not always easy to maintain. "The bow is broken if it is stretched too tight, and the soul is lost if it is [too] relaxed . . ."[38]

Understandably not everyone was suited for such a training just as not everyone is equipped today to go through a Marine boot camp. Father Master Jean-Baptiste Gury drew up a *compte-rendu* the year Montrouge closed, in which he cited the statistics during the ten years of the novitiate's existence. He revealed that during this period there were 316 scholastic novices accepted, of which number, thirty-four were already ordained priests. Thirty-four of the total left the novitiate on their own accord and eighty-two were dismissed.

Of the 138 coadjutor novices that were accepted fifty-four were sent home. "Amost all who left," he wrote commenting on the grand total, "were of the highest moral integrity. Some did not have the physical strength; others lacked the necessary talent; some were called home by relatives, and others did not give the indication of having a true vocation."[39] One of the casualties was Nicolas Point who was sent home at the beginning of May 1823.[40] He had been a novice about seven months.

Dismayed, the soldier retreated halfway across France. When he entered the novitiate he had resolved to conquer himself, to order his life without regard for the disorderly affections of his nature. And he had failed. He was so sure that he was called to be a Jesuit and to dedicate his life to converting the American Indians. Pierre reported that after his last year at Saint-Acheul he had never regained his strength; mentally and emotionally he was not ready to enter the novitiate. But now "his vivid imagination accused him of something, however hidden and unknown, as being the reason for his failure." This mysterious 'something' had caused Providence, "which had once been so favorable and was now so severe" to change toward him. We are not told, but he probably made the one hundred and fifty mile journey back to Rocroi on foot. We do know that he stopped off, exhausted, at the seminary in Reims to confide in Pierre and to make a difficult pilgrimage to the tomb of St. Remy. Then, confused, disgruntled, he left for home. Despite the fact that spring was in the freshness of the Champagne air, Pierre reported Nicolas moped about with feelings of guilt. He arrived in Rocroi with an overplus of gloom and profound sadness. His failure at Montrouge had put a full-stop to any hope of becoming a Jesuit missionary. "So, console yourself," Sister St. Gabriel told him with characteristic compelling conviction, "you are going to be a Jesuit after all." But there was no consolation; he was crushed.[41]

After awhile he made some effort to pull himself out of the slump. In Paris he saw how successful the Sodality of the Blessed Virgin had been in forming Catholic students; therefore, he persuaded Father Charlier to allow him to form a sodality, or *congrégation,* among the young men of Rocroi. But the enterprise failed to get off the ground. Suddenly, it seemed so unattractive and he just could not conjure up the energy to make it work. Licking his wounds, he consoled himself that "one cannot be a prophet in his own country." Then, little by little, as his melancholy of several months passed, the fires of his first love began to rekindle. The army had always attracted him, and now he found himself spending more and more spare time talking with soldiers in their nearby barracks. These conversations revealed to him that there were many men his own age who had not made their First Communion. Didn't St. Francis Xavier in his day prepare soldiers to receive this sacrament? All of a sudden, he found a project he could give himself to, one that eventually pulled him out of his funk. With this newfound fervor he began teaching catechism to the soldiers, and when they were sufficiently instructed, he enlisted some of the townspeople to decorate the parish church for a First Communion celebration that proved to be a tribute to his endeavors. Both a crowd of soldiers from the barracks and the townspeople renewed their baptismal promises on the day Nicolas's neophytes received their First Communion. The experience confirmed his desire to spend his life in the American wilderness; yet breathing "his native air" did not have the beneficial effects Father Gury promised it would. At last he wrote a letter to Prince Alexander Hohenlohe (1794–1849), a Bavarian priest of international fame, reputed to have remarkable powers of healing. The two men corresponded for awhile, and Hohenlohe invited Nicolas to join him each day at a specific hour for special prayers. Shortly thereafter the younger man regained some strength, which improvement he attributed to Hohenlohe's charism. He made contact with the authorities at Saint-Acheul and received an invitation from Father Nicolas Loriquet, who had recently been named rector, to return to the college. So once again, he set out on the long road to Amiens, and in August 1824, after an absence of almost two years, he arrived.[42]

Fear of future difficulties and the possibility that his plans would fail inclined Nicolas to be frequently despondent, and even though he protested that he eschewed honor and recognition, he was, "in fact," very much afraid of disgrace and humiliation. These characteristics of his complex temperament would become exaggerated in times of stress as the years wore on. Zealous and generous by nature, there was an excess in his zeal and an imprudence in his generosity. Pierre recounted how he was tempted to believe he was separated from God, a conviction that caused him to fall into the most terrible distress of mind, one that robbed him of confidence in himself and in God. At this point in his life he was plagued with scruples, and when he was not indulging in sentimental moods, imagining himself back in the society or converting Indians, he brooded over the malice and consequences of past sins.[43] What guarantee was there that this talented, sensitive, prayerful man would not fall into great despondency, inactivity, and even despair? Fortunately the new rector was more than a professional historian and a renowned educator. He was also a man who had the reputation of being a shrewd judge of character, singularly endowed with prudence, wisdom, and common sense, and he determined to keep a close eye on the twenty-five-year-old dropout whose desire was to re-enter the novitiate.[44] He decided that Nicolas was not to teach. Rather, Loriquet appointed him the *premier serveillant,* a kind of vice principal. This was the period when the rector was still drafting his *Plan* which placed training or moral formation *(éducation)* on an equal footing with classroom teaching *(instruction);* the former pertained to the will, the latter to the intellect.[45] As *premier serveillant,* Nicolas was to create an atmosphere in which community could be formed. The spiritual and moral development of the six hundred students assigned to him was his responsibility. Besides a few *serveillants,* who were his assistants, he was also assigned a number of *censors,* older students of trusted loyalty. These boys helped him carry out his day-to-day duties; for example, they assisted him in getting up his charges at five o'clock each morning. Afterwards, they led the students in prayers, introduced them to the sodalities and other religious confraternities that carried on particular religious activities, supervised outdoor exercises, sat in strategic places in the huge hall where the students met to do their homework and where no student was allowed to speak, and finally, after night prayers, made sure the students were in bed by nine o'clock. The discipline was strict and even rigid, but Loriquet, with whom Point met several times each day, made sure that Point had no time to think of himself and that he fell asleep exhausted each night.

The rector assured his newly appointed assistant that superior talent in a candidate to the Society was an advantage, but it was not essential. Prudence, on the other hand, *was* essential. Indeed, Ignatius placed it above charity in the hierarchy of virtues to be looked for in a prospective candidate.[46] By the end of the year the rector concluded that his *premier serveillant* was indeed a prudent, trustworthy candidate.[47] He was also obedient, docile, and not afraid of hard work—virtues looked for and highly extolled by Father

Master Gury. But if Point was eager to give the novitiate another try, Loriquet felt the society was in no rush. Time would confirm his judgment about this highly strung, competent associate who by that date had stilled the torments in his own soul.[48] Besides, breaking in a new *premier serveillant* at such a critical period of Saint-Acheul's history would not be easy; therefore, Nicolas's request to enter Montrouge was put off for another year. The society did not exist for Nicolas Point; Nicolas Point existed for the society. Finally, on October 16, 1826, after being away for almost three-and-a-half years Nicolas Point returned to the novitiate to begin again his two years of testing. He was twenty-seven years old.[49]

FORMATION

Part One: 1826–1833

In France: 1826–1830

The novitiate to which Point returned in 1826 was essentially no different from that which he had left in 1823. Montrouge was a place of prayer, work, and study; and the strict, Spartan regime was designated to protect, and at the same time, to try the vocations of the novices. The daily order was designed to maximize the time given to the stated purpose of the novitiate and therefore every minute of the day was carefully apportioned for the novices—indeed, such was the case for all Jesuits, even those in the colleges—by the 'bell-ringer', one of the most important officials in the community's hierarchy. But, in addition to prayer, work, and study, Ignatius had also prescribed that the novices in the society be given additional tests or experiments to exercise them in what he called abnegation, a virtue on which he placed the highest priority. At first these exercises were confined to teach catechism to children in the parish church of Montrouge and in the nearby parishes of Sceaux, Vanves, and Bagneus. Then in 1822, the year Point first entered the novitiate, the Paris Province took on a new apostolic project—caring for the spiritual and physical needs of the inmates of the hospital at nearby Bicêtre. This institution, the Bedlam of France, was a huge fortress that housed the indigent, the insane, and the abandoned. One section, where the mentally and emotionally disturbed children were locked up, was notorious throughout Europe. Jean-Baptiste Gury believed this massive hospital offered an ideal setting for novices and tertian fathers to learn the type of abnegation Ignatius looked for in his companions. Then, between 1825 and 1826, the Montrouge novices were sent to teach catechism and to instruct the prisoners in Bicêtre's equally notorious prison, and it was to this foreboding part of the fortress that Brother Point was assigned. Here, youngsters who had fallen foul of the law were consigned with the most hardened criminals, and it was to them particularly that he was missioned.[1] Each day, for several months during 1826 and 1827, he and a companion dressed like himself in cassock and hat, would walk either in silence or reciting the rosary together, the several miles that separated Montrouge from Bicêtre, and then each evening they would return to the novitiate. Years later Point confessed that his experience at Bicêtre had brought him the greatest consolation and peace. He learned that he had to possess himself in solitude and in silence before he could be any use to Indians in America. Moreover, during this Thirty Day Retreat his scrupulousness had left him and his doubts and fears had been put to rest.[2]

The inner peace and tranquility that permeated Brother Point's soul between 1826 and 1828 scarcely reflected the climate of turmoil that surrounded Montrouge, a turmoil which eventually made it impossible for the novices to continue the experiments at Bicêtre and in the neighboring villages. Each year the campaign against the Jesuits became more threatening, but by the end of Point's second year novitiate, that is, during the first part of 1828, vituperations bordered on the hysterical. It is not easy today to understand how the media alone could have aroused Dame Rumor to the point of what eventually became impassioned frenzy. However, it would be difficult to find a better example to support the theme of Charles Péguy's polemic about the transformation of the *mystic* into the *politique* than the anti-Jesuit mania of this period. During the late 1820s the liberals on the Left and what was left of the Gallicans on the Right saw in the growth of the ultramontane society an ominous sign for the future, and statistics supported their fears because the number of Jesuits in France had increased from 198 in 1820 to 456 in 1828.[3] Then there was the personality of the king to whom the Jesuits were, despite themselves, inexorably linked: Charles X did not have Louis XVIII's ability to neutralize and mollify political opponents, a tragic flaw when the Left found it profitable to use the presence of the illegal Society of Jesus as a red herring to defy the hateful Villèle, presently head of the king's government. For these reasons, among others less easy to define, the reign of Charles X witnessed a deluge of anti-Jesuit pamphlets, the most famous of which was the famous *Monita Secreta* containing purported instructions from Claudio Aquaviva (1543–1615), the fifth general of the society, to various superiors on the Machiavellian methods ordinary Jesuits should adopt to acquire wealth and power for the order. This clumsy forgery, written by a Polish ex-Jesuit named Heronym Zahorowski, made its first appearance in 1612, enjoyed considerable popularity just prior to the Suppression, and now in the 1820s was resurrected.[4] Then in 1825, while the anti-government faction was attempting to attack the king in both houses of the legislative bodies, the anti-Jesuit party found an even better advocate for their cause than the discredited author of the *Monita*.

Martial Marçai, a seventeen-year provincial of humble origins from Puy, entered the Montrouge novitiate in 1818 (he had changed the spelling of his name by that date to the more acceptably French Marcet) and in March 1823, while beginning his regency at the *collège* of Forcalquier, he was dismissed from the order. Embittered and reduced to poverty, he placed his unquestioned literary ability and vivid imagination at the disposal of those who were eager to sponsor him. It seems he had always admired the aristocracy, particularly those who identified with the old Gallican Right, and so, at twenty-two, he chose to write under the alias, L'Abbé Martial Marcet de La Roche-Arnaud, a name that hinted of lineage, crusaders for ancestors, and châteaux in the provinces. All his tracts and books, immediate best-sellers, had the same purpose—to alert the nation to the threat of the Jesuits in general and of Montrouge in particular. He turned the spotlight on the supposed machinations that took place daily in the novitiate; consequently, overnight Montrouge became the focus of the Jesuit menace.[5] He may have singled out this house because of its proximity to Paris or because of the novice master, Jean-Baptiste Gury, for whom he reserved special ill-will. But most likely the best explanation is that the novitiate was constructed at the center of a vast network of abandoned underground stone quarries, some of which were three stories deep. Long catacomblike tunnels which extended from these quarries gave a honeycombed effect beneath the countryside in and around the village of Montrouge. Critics of the society could not have asked for a better physical setting to support their accusations against the Jesuits.[6] Gury well-described the image Montrouge conjured up in the minds of many when he wrote that it was regarded as:

> a fortress in the midst of extensive grounds, surrounded by ramparts, fortified by bastions, bristling with canons, equipped with an arsenal that was filled with a variety of weapons and munitions. The Jesuits had daily drills with these weapons. Some said there were three hundred, others three thousand Jesuits stationed there along with the General, living like a mighty lord, surrounded by his court. There was an underground tunnel that connected Montrouge with the Tuileries, and the superior at Montrouge used it often to communicate with the king's ministers. The riches of Montrouge were vast. There were chests filled with gold and silver; there were mines that spread out far from the main building, and it was generally thought that the Jesuits could repel any attack with ease. This was the headquarters, the nerve center from where they directed all of their crimes, hatched all of their plots against public institutions and the commonwealth. There was not a single public or even private misfortune that was not blamed on Montrouge.[7]

Montrouge had reached the very height of its notoriety when, on March 9, 1828, Brother Nicolas Point pronounced his first vows in the Society of Jesus. The new scholastic was then sent back to Saint-Acheul where he was to be a counselor to the students. At the same time his own studies would not be neglected for he was to pursue the study of physics at the *collège*'s newly equipped laboratory. Physics was at that time regarded as an integral part of the education of a Jesuit, and Saint-Acheul was justifiably proud of its physics program.[8]

On the following June 16, Charles X, fearful his new government might meet the same fate as the last, grudgingly made a concession to the anti-Jesuit faction of various political hues when he signed legislation, called Ordinances, designed to end the practice of accepting into minor seminaries students who had no intention of going on to the priesthood and to place all ecclesiastical schools under the supervision of the *Université*. The not-so-thinly disguised purpose of these Ordinances was to close down the eight Jesuit *colléges* in France, because they forbade anyone to teach in any educational institution who had not signed an affidavit swearing that he did not belong to "a religious order not legally established in France."[9] In effect, these Ordinances of 1828 phased out Saint-Acheul, for the nine hundred boys were forced to leave; however, they did not close down the institution altogether because some twenty scholastics, like Point, who had already finished their philosophical studies, could stay on and begin their theological courses without being in contempt of the Law.[10] Nicolas Point recorded the many sad events and gave a vivid account of the final days of Saint-Acheul as a *collège* in the extended essay, "Dernière sémaine de Saint-Acheul," which he later incorporated into "Souvenirs et mémoires illustrés." The work is not a very successful combination of pietistic and romantic anecdotes, some of which are repeated in Pierre Point's "Vie," describing various educational practices at Saint-Acheul. But it has little direct historic interest in this presentation.[11] After the lay students made their tearful departures, two of his former novices of 1826, Father Thomas Legoüais and Xavier de Ravignan, joined the faculty of ten and began giving theology courses when the classes convened on September 27, 1828.[12]

The king's concessions to the Left, expressed in the Ordinances of 1828, only served to whet the appetite of the liberals intent on securing more freedom for themselves and more restrictions for the Jesuits. These Ordinances also had the effect of discouraging the ultramontane faction on the Right from cooperating with any constitutional program, much to the dissatisfaction of the Government. So, during the intervening months, as the Polignac ministry bungled from one crisis to another, it was the liberals that gained ground. The showdown was inevitable when the election results of June 29, 1830 were tallied. Emboldened, the liberal press stirred up a fierce fermentation against the government. On July 25, Charles X published four more Ordinances, the first of which called for muzzling the press, the liberals' most effective weapon. The resulting agitation on the part of students and republican societies grew to street riots and concern on the part of the bourgeoisie, and by July 31 Charles X was no longer king.[13] This July Revolution that brought the "Bourgeois Monarch," Louis Philippe of Orleans, to the throne had repercussions in Amiens. Here the "Three Glorious Days" began on the evening of the twenty-ninth. A band of miscreants wandered menacingly around the Hôtel de Ville not knowing exactly what they should do when a former student of the *collège* called out "À Saint-Acheul! À Saint-Acheul!" The crowd suddenly became rioters set on invading the school, which could offer no resistence. An improvised battering-ram opened up the halls to some four hundred yelling hooligans who, for two hours, smashed and burned everything in sight. Fortunately, the famous physics laboratory equipment was spared and the terrified Jesuits were saved when someone broke into the wine cellar and began passing its contents out to the excited, thirsty mob. It was at this juncture that the cavalry arrived and routed the invaders. Rumors that the mob was returning the next morning to take care of unfinished business convinced the rector, Achille Guidée (b. Amiens, August 18, 1792; d. Amiens, January 13, 1866) to order the community to scatter.[14] Point hid in a nearby wheat field where alone he watched the sun rise over the stifling Picardy plain on the feast of St. Ignatius Loyola, July 31. For the next two weeks he laid low, avoiding meetings with his confreres who, like himself, passed the time hiding in homes, barns, châteaux, convents and open fields, avoiding all contact with one another. By August 18 enough of the danger had passed to enable his old friend, the former rector and present provincial, Father Julien Druilhet, to make a quick and furtive appearance at the ravished Saint-Acheul. From here he summoned his subjects, one by one, and gave each his new assignment and a special blessing. The same scenario was repeated throughout that sweltering summer: Côme Lartigue was sent to Belgium; Jean-Pierre Varlet to Spain, and Pierre Chazelle, Thomas Legoüais and their companions were told to shake the dust of France from their feet to preach the Gospel in America. As for Point, he was ordered to keep his disguise and stealthily make his way to Paris where he was to request a passport for Switzerland.[15]

In Switzerland: 1830–1833

Apparently Nicolas's disguise was not convincing enough, for he reported that even before he arrived in Paris his identity was suspected and as a consequence he suffered considerable harassment before he was finally given the papers that entitled him to cross the frontier. The passport, however, did not exempt him from further tormenting. He does not report how he finally got out of Paris, a city he never loved, nor how he made it to the Swiss border, more than 350 miles from Amiens, where at last he could "breathe free air," but the assumption is that it was done by a circuitous, surreptitious route and for the most part by foot—his usual manner of travel. His ultimate destination was Brig, in Valais, a small town of one thousand inhabitants, where he finally arrived "under the protection of his Guardian Angel," at an unrecorded date in the fall of 1828.[16] Here he began his third year of theology under the direction of his old mentor Jean-Paul Martin and his former co-novice, Xavier de Ravignan. During the "siege of Saint-Acheul" a stone had cracked open the skull of Père de Ravignan and he had lost a great deal of blood but by this date he was apparently well enough to return to the classroom.[17]There was also a new addition to the faculty, a priest with whom Point would have dealings in the United States, Guy Gilles (b. Mende, Lozère, December 25, 1797; d. Baton Rouge, Louisiana, August 28, 1855).

Besides Point there were forty-two scholastics who followed the four-year course of theology at Brig and their subsequent careers illustrate the vitality and the diversity of the society in which Point was formed.[18] At the same time they show us how radically different were the times in which these nineteenth-century Jesuits lived. The principles by which they ordered their universe are sometimes the same, frequently different, and occasionally contrary to our own. Their beliefs and behavior appear alien, and yet these Jesuits are fascinating precisely because they dealt with many problems familiar to our contemporary world in ways that—from our enlightened vantage point—seem curious, contrary to the American spirit, and at variance with modern theological and psychological positions; that seem to us superstitious and even neurotic. But a cursory examination of the accomplishments of these men shows that the rigid bonds of their formation in no way trammeled their subsequent achievements nor manacled their personalities. The product of this formation, which placed so high a price on self-abnegation, was, paradoxically, a harvest of colorful personalities, self-assured, disciplined, highly individualistic, even to the point, in some cases, of eccentricity. Moreover, they were well adjusted to the world in which they functioned, despite their loud protestations of hating that world and desiring to turn their backs on it. Throughout his biography Pierre Point reminds the reader with what contempt his brother, always referred to as The Reverend Father Nicolas Point, regarded the world. "But this disgust with the world, so profitable to those who know how to use it," observed Nicolas's instructor, Xavier de Ravignan, with a nice touch of irony, "finds but few souls faithful to its counsels."[19] But even if few lived up completely to this lofty ideal, it did remain the standard of perfection that enabled many to excel in various fields where, under strict obedience, they fixed their interest; consequently, to these were given, sometimes grudgingly (but no less really) praise and respect by their "worldly" adversaries. The formation of Point and the men of his generation by no means ended with Montrouge. A Jesuit continued to be molded within the framework set forth in St. Ignatius's *Spiritual Exercises* and in his "Common Rules," which were read monthly in the refectory, in all *collèges* and houses of study. It was a mold whose object was seen as the way to foster interior recollection, love of prayer and silence, and self-abnegation. Study, discipline, a structured schedule, and hard work were peerless virtues since, again as Ravignan had impressed upon Point and those of his generation, "one could no more conceive of a laborer without work than a religious without observance of a Rule."[20] Unquestionably these Jesuits were firm and exacting, but their rigidity did not exclude generosity and friendship; however, it was a generosity geared to "the sanctification of both ourselves and of the souls entrusted to our care," and a friendship "*in visceribus Christi,* for unity of faith and charity is the strongest of bonds."[21] Adversaries of the Jesuits could be mean and violent; they castigated with withering, abusive, bitter language; they denounced with acrimonious vindictive; however, they recognized the Jesuits to be worthy, formidable opponents, and there is no evidence of any critic who accused them of being unfaithful in the matter of their vow of chastity. Whatever else their defects, they were honest in this matter, for any irregularities here meant instant dismissal. The result was respect both from friends and from foes.

Among Point's fellow scholastics at Brig, who like himself became missionaries, were Alexis Canoz (b. Sellières, Jura, September 11, 1805; d. Trichinopoly, Madras, India, December 2, 1888) and Félix Martin (b. Auray, Morbihan, October 4, 1804; d. Paris, November 25, 1886). The former left France in 1839 for the Madura Mission where eighteenth-century French Jesuits had so distinguished themselves and where, in 1837, the decision to reconstitute Jesuit presence in India had such a profound effect on the life and future of Nicolas Point. In 1844, while Point was working among the Blackfeet, Alexis Canoz was appointed superior of the Madura Mission, and in 1847, a particularly vexing year for his companions in France, this onetime prefect of discipline at the Fribourg school was ordained the first bishop of the restored society. Canoz's letters describing the work of the French Jesuits in India were subsequently published, offering a wealth of information about life on the subcontinent during the second half of the nineteenth century.[22]

Félix Martin is sometimes credited as being the founder of the *pétit seminaire* and *collège* at Vannes, but these institutions owed more for their existence to his generous father and his family.[23] After gaining the reputation for being both an outstanding preacher and mathematics and physics professor at the *collège-en-exile* at Brugelette, he was sent to the new French mission in Canada, where he arrived in May 1842. Here, as the first superior of the Montreal Mission, after the death of Pierre Chazelle, he was to found the famous Collège Sainte-Marie de Montréal. During this same period (1848–1857), he distinguished himself in caring and providing for the thousands of disease-ridden Irish refugees fleeing from the 1846–1851 potato famine.

It was in 1844 that the superior of the Sisters at the Hôtel Dieu, Quebec, presented Martin with a bundle of manuscripts, which had been entrusted to them by the last remaining Jesuit of pre-suppression days—Jean-Joseph Casot (1728–1800). To Martin's surprise and delight these handwritten originals covered the Mission Superior's annual reports between 1673 and 1679, including Jacques Marquette's account of his 1673 trip with Louis Jolliet, which resulted in the discovery of the Mississippi, and other invaluable documents relating to the history of Canada. This windfall enabled him to prepare, with the cooperation of the Canadian government, the famous *Rélations des Jésuites* in 1850, which in turn inspired the Jesuit scholastic, John Gilmary Shea (1824–1892), who left the society in 1852, to devote much of his life to translating and editing the various *Relations*. Then between 1896 and 1901 Reuben G. Thwaites (1853–1923) reprinted in seventy-three volumes the monumental *Jesuit Relations and Allied Documents*. So Martin, who was sent to Europe for research by the Canadian government in 1857, was responsible to a great extent for the reassessment of colonial history on both sides of the Canadian-United States border.

Besides translating, correcting, and augmenting numerous accounts written in Italian and English about the French Jesuit missionaries in seventeenth-century America, Martin also wrote biographies on historical personalities, such as the Marquis de Montcalm and Pierre Corneille. He was the author of more than two dozen books and during his lifetime he became a recognized specialist of Canadian history. John Gilmary Shea translated his popular biography of Kateri Tekakwitha, the seventeenth century "Lily of the Mohawks," and his biography of Isaac Jogues into English; and later, his novena pamphlet in honor of St. Francis Xavier, Point's special patron, was translated, introducing this popular devotion for Catholics south of the Canadian border. As if these accomplishments were not enough, Félix Martin, longtime superior of the Jesuit residence in Quebec, also gained fame for his architectural designs for St. Patrick's Church, Montreal, and for a number of churches in Ottawa.[24]

A third classmate of Point's at Brig who was later sent to the missions was the versatile Jean-Baptiste Hus (b. Les Loges-sur-Brécey, Manche, January 26, 1803; d. Paris, April 27, 1881). He first came to the United States while Point was laboring in the Northwest, as the companion to Father Clément Boulanger (b. Saint-Clement, Meurthe, October 30, 1790; d. Issenheim, Haut-Rhin, June 12, 1868), the especially dispatched Visitor from the Paris Provincial to the French Mission of Kentucky. When he returned to France he was appointed superior to the community at Metz. During the February Days of 1848, the local government attempted to close this Jesuit residence, but Hus informed the officials that during his brief stay in the United States he had learned that freedom was not the right of a select group; it was not something the liberals and republicans alone enjoyed, but that true democracy implied respecting the will of all of the people. He then made a dramatic appeal to the citizens of Metz, with whom the Jesuits had always been popular, and the authorities were forced to back off in the enthusiastic support of *"liberté à l'américaine."*[25] Then, in 1852, Hus was selected to lead four Jesuits back to French Guiana, the prosperous mission field of French Jesuits between 1651 and 1763. Even before they left France he and his companions dedicated themselves to caring for the four hundred convicts traveling with them to the Guiana penal settlement, known better throughout the world as Devil's Island. Transportation of convicts to this notorious colony ceased in 1935 and all of the penetentiaries there were finally closed in 1946, but not before the Jesuits of France had distinguished themselves in this thankless apostolate. The history of Devil's Island is intertwined with the history of the French Jesuit Mission of Guiana, for as early as 1855 there were already twenty Jesuits working on the mission begun by Hus.[26] But by this date Jean-Baptiste Hus, broken in health, was given a post where his superiors thought he would have time and leisure to recuperate, and here he remained—superior of the North American or New York Mission—until 1859.[27]

When Hus's tenure came to an end, he returned to France where again he became a source of annoyance to the government by getting embroiled in well-publicized confrontations with the anti-clericals and republicans. In the 1860s the besieged government of Napoleon III accused him of making provocative, pro-papal statements from the pulpit which offended those attempting to resurrect the age-old idea that the French Church was somehow different from that of Rome, and that the Roman ecclesiastical authorities did not understand the temperament and customs of the French people. Such accusations became a challenge to Hus who lashed back in an exaggerated way at those who were enemies of the temporal power of Pius IX, a tough subject for the government that had to maintain French troops in Rome.[28] At last, in June 1880, old, bedridden, and still suffering from the privations of Guiana, Hus took on the police and government officials who had come to the Jesuit residence in Paris in an effort to implement the Decrees of March 29, calling for the suppression of the thirty-seven Jesuit houses in France. Hus barracaded the door to his room, forcing the embarrassed authorities to crash through. He refused to leave quietly and so was pulled out by force. In the hall he encountered the superior who told him to comply. Hus, confident he was now acting out of obedience, knelt and received the superior's blessing. He then stood up and invited the police, government officials and the bystanders to kneel. They did. He then blessed the group and forced himself to walk out of the house unaided, a fitting symbol of the Jesuit trained at Brig.[29]

Life was no easier for Jesuits living in France during the second half of the nineteenth century than it had been during the first, but it could have been even worse had it not been for two Breton administrators who were fellow scholastics with Point at Brig in 1831. Ambroise Rubillon (b. La Chapelle-sur-Filix-Méens, Ille-et-Vilaine, September 10, 1825; d. Paris, December 10, 1888) was provincial of the Province of France between 1845 and 1851, at the time when the *collèges* were again forced to close and teachers compelled to scatter once more beyond the frontiers. Then as assistant for France, Rubillon took up residence in Rome from 1851 to 1883; that is, during the period of the second Empire and the first few years of the Third Republic. In 1850 the National Assembly of the Second Republic passed the Falloux Law guaranteeing liberty of education and thereby granting amnesty to the Jesuit teachers and legality to their schools. This enabled Rubillon to supervise from Rome the remarkable growth of the schools and houses of the society throughout France, which he did for the next nine years. During this time he saw to it that a steady flow of missionaries was channeled to the Americas, Asia, Madagascar, and Africa. But with the Imperial Decrees of 1859, which prohibited opening new religious schools, the tide began to turn and the spring of religious freedom had passed. After this date the situation went from bad to worse. In 1871 Jesuits were massacred in the Paris Commune uprising and finally when the Decrees of March 29, 1880 were passed, the whole Jesuit apostolate caved in before the onslaught of anti-clerical sentiment. During this crisis Rubillon saw to it that the Jesuit houses of formation were relocated, first in Wales, at Aberdovey, and later in England, at Slough, a few short miles north of Windsor Castle in Buckinghamshire. In March 1884, when the tertian director at Slough suddenly died, Rubillon took his place and, until his own death four years later, trained a new generation according to the precepts he had learned at Brig.[30] Both Hus and Rubillon came to Point's defense in later years and each was villified during his life: Rubillon was the object of Adolphe Thiers's diatribes in 1845 and 1846, and François Guizot singled him out in the *Mémoirs* as a crafty evil adversary.[31]

Another Brig confrere was Breton Frédéric Studer (b. Carhaix, Finistère, March 4, 1801; d. Laval, June 4, 1875). He began his career by teaching grammar and humanities at the *collège* in Dôle where he found time to publish a textbook on rhetoric. After his ordination he was assigned to teach philosophy at the *collège-en-exile* at Brugelette, Belgium, and then he was made principal and rector at the *collège* in Angers. His tenure here coincided with the publication of Eugene Sue's *The Wandering Jew,* which so inflamed popular sentiment against the Jesuits, and with the tirades of Edgar Quinet and Jules Michelet, so effective in forming the policies of the Bourgeois Monarchy. The energies of the unpopular government were directed in stifling the freedom of Catholic schools, and one of its last achievements was closing the Angers *collège* where Studer was rector, and running the Jesuits out of the country. During these trying times, from 1843 to 1851, Studer gained the reputation for being a cool, determined adversary under pressure. In 1851, when Rubillon was made assistant, Studer took his place as provincial, reorganized the *collèges,* built houses of formation and residences, and founded three more schools, one of which was the famous Sainte-Geneviève, Rue des Postes, in Paris. After his term of office as provincial of France, or of Paris, as it came more commonly to be called, Studer became provincial of the Toulouse Province; then rector of the houses of formation at Vals and at Laval. He expanded both of these facilities before being assigned to Quimper among his own Breton people. Dubbed "the Great Builder," he was responsible for sending many Jesuits following his and Point's generation to the foreign missions.[32]

Since the main thrust of the society in France between 1814 and 1880 was directed to the educational apostolate, it is not surprising that the majority of Point's fellow scholastics at Brig eventually found themselves assigned first to the several *collèges-en-exile* and then, after Jesuit schools were legalized in France, to the many *collèges* in the country itself. Some, like Studer, Point, and Canoz, were in the educational apostolate before passing on to different work; others spent many years, even all of their lives behind the desk, while still others juggled teaching with other ministries. All, however, owed much in their formation to the years spent with students in the *collèges*. For example, even though Eloi Solente (b. Mametz, Somme, October 7, 1796; d. Strasbourg, March 18, 1868), served as master of novices, director of tertians and rector of a number of houses and *collèges*, he was, nevertheless, singled out as "the model Jesuit teacher, devout, patient, exact, and religious."[33] On the other hand, one of Point's best friends, Ferdinand Brumauld de Beauregard (b. Poursac, Charente, July 28, 1798; d. Mende, August 10, 1863), a "fearless soul, a loyal heart, active, enterprising, bold," was associated with the *collèges* only at the beginning and the end of his exciting career. A physically powerful man, he was sent to the *collège-en-éxile* at Brugelette after he finished his tertianship in the spring of 1835. Here, a few miles over the Belgian frontier, he literally dug the foundations and helped construct the new edifice which opened the following October 29 with fifty students, a modest beginning for the *collège-en-éxile* that was considered, until it returned to France after the promulgation of the Falloux Law in 1850, as "Saint-Acheul Resurrected." But being a brick-and-mortar Jesuit did not excuse Brumauld from pastoral work. He was told to divide his time between teaching and preaching the *Exercises* to several congregations of religious women, and as a chaplain he was so successful and impressive that one convent tried desperately to keep him on as a permanent chaplain. However, he was about to march to a different drummer. In 1841 he was sent to Algeria where he became chaplain to the French troops, accompanying them on their desert maneuvers and giving them the *Exercises* in their barracks. Roothaan considered him the military chaplain without peers; indeed, he was probably the first military chaplain in the new society. But his principal work was with the Algerian orphans, for whom he got the French soldiers and sailors to help him build an orphanage at Ben-Akoun and another at Bouffarik, which won him the title "Father of the Orphans." It was through circulars, documents, and petitions that he forced the Imperial government in Paris to study the problem of the abandoned, abused, and battered Algerian children, and managed to have legislation initiated that remedied the problem—no small victory in that age of *laissez-faire* economics and anti-Jesuit sentiment. An intrepid supporter of French colonialism and the army, he envisioned setting up a Paraguay-reduction type system, supported by the government and protected by the army, that would provide education and, eventually, land for Algerian and French orphans. Point would devise a similar plan for the Indians. Brumauld became so successful, so well-known and so well-liked in Algeria and in France that he was given the thankless and frustrating job of fund-raising for the desperate Jesuit Missions of Syria, where also the Jesuits were involved in rescuing orphans and under more hostile conditions than in Algeria. Finally, however, he returned to the work of the *collèges* in the last few years of his life: he was made rector at the school in Mende. There, during a particularly heated confrontation with a government representative intent on closing the school, he suffered a fatal stroke.[34]

Another scholastic at Brig with Point, who later distinguished himself, was Pierre Faton (b. Dompière, Jura, April 17, 1805; d. Mongré, Rhône, December 17, 1869), who became a well-known mathematician and scientist. A student and close friend of the great mathematician, Augustin-Louis Cauchy (1789–1857), he was subsequently elected a member of the prestigious Academy of Sciences at Turin, despite the fact that he was a Jesuit. A brilliant monograph on the variations of atmospheric pressures, however, broke down all resistance on the part of the scientific community to his Jesuit affiliations. The year after he published this study (1843), he edited a highly praised textbook that reflected "the new ways of teaching mathematics" and containing "logarithmic tables and an explanation of the theory of arithmetic." Following each arithmetic principle was a series of problems designed to demonstrate how the particular theory worked in practice. This textbook, which attempted to apply the scholastic method to mathematics and which went through nine editions, became the standard text for advanced mathematics students in Jesuit and non-Jesuit schools in French-speaking countries in Europe during the middle years of the nineteenth century. Because Faton was the teacher of a number of Jesuit mathematicians and scientists who later went to the New York, New Orleans, California and Rocky Mountain Missions of the United States, this man, who had the reputation of being excessively modest and shy, exerted an influence on American educational theory and practice which has never been fully investigated, much less appreciated. The year of his death he published a study guide to his text and the following year a new text on the elements of basic arithmetic was published posthumously. In addition to these texts, Faton also published a Latin tract on the theory and practice of physics for Jesuit scholastics. The manuscript he was working on, when he suddenly died at the *collège* near Villefranche-sur-Saône, was a text in French on algebra. Unfinished, it is still in manuscript form awaiting a dissertation study.[35]

Like Faton and Gotteland, François-Napoléon Moigno (b. Guémené, Morbihan, April 15, 1804; d. Saint-Denis, Seine, July 14, 1884) was also a colleague of Augustin-Louis Cauchy, as well as other important figures in the Silver Age of French science and mathematics, such as the astronomer Dominique-François Arage (1786–1853), the chemist Jean-Baptiste Dumas (1800–1884), and the physicist mathematician André-Marie Ampère (1775–1836). After Moigno left Brig he returned to the classroom from where he published, in pamphlet form, readings for a type of Great Books Program in *collèges* and *petits séminaires*. He also published a two-volume syllabus for chemists and physicists and two shorter works about calculus and statistics. All of these efforts were autographic publications. Then, in 1840, while teaching at Sainte-Geneviève in Paris, an impressive printing company in Paris published his first volume of *Leçons de calcul différentiel et de calcul intégral, rédigées d'après de M. A. L. Cauchy*. This impressive work had just begun to be reviewed when the Provincial, Father Boulanger, ordered Moigno to drop his scientific investigations and turn his many talents to teaching Hebrew and ancient history to the Jesuit seminarians at Leval. Moigno, who was a fine linguist as well as a physician, and who had demonstrated that he could indeed teach Hebrew, protested, and for the next three years he and the provincial 'dialogued' about the matter. In 1843, while Point was undergoing a certain crisis of his own, his friend Moigno was dismissed from the society and immediately published the second and long-awaited volume of his calculus investigations.

Meanwhile, he had become incardinated into the Archdiocese of Paris and named chaplain to the former school Lycée Louis-le-Grand, a most esteemed assignment. From this post he contributed in an exceptional way to the Church's apostolate as a diocesean priest and later as a canon at Saint-Denis by preaching and writing. More of an exponent of science than an original thinker, he became the publisher and editor of two important scientific journals, *Le Cosmos* (1815–1863) and *Les Mondes* (1863–1865) and the science editor of a large Paris daily. He also wrote articles and books on such diverse subjects as optics, telegraphy, saccharimeters, the splendors of the Catholic faith, Church and State relations, stethoscopes, freedom for Catholic schools, and the lives of saints faced with the reality of science. In Point's time the society recruited and fostered men like Moigno, whose potential was greatness in various fields, and then encouraged them to realize their potential through discipline and industry, but obedience was always regarded as having priority over any natural talent or any particular work.[36]

If the vocation crisis of this gifted Breton noble was precipitated by the prospect of teaching history, there were scholastics at Brig during Point's time who later found Clio's charms attractive. For instance, there was Albin Leroux (b. Amiens, November 1, 1798; d. Paris, September 28, 1869), who became deaf shortly after ordination and had to leave the classroom. This handicap gave him the freedom to edit the *Litterae annuae Provinciae Franciae* between 1836 and 1852, and then again from 1856 to 1864. These detailed relations remain a gold mine of primary sources for the history of the society in France and in the missions conducted by the Province of Paris during these years of such dramatic happenings.[37] As a young scholar at Saint-Acheul, Leroux published his attempts at Latin poetry in the magazine *Hermes Romanus,* edited by Joseph-Nicolas Barbier-Vérmars (1775– c.1892), and his efforts won him a warm letter of congratulations from one of its most faithful and avid readers, another Latinist of repute, Louis XVIII.[38] Leroux's Latin style in the important *Litterae annuae* is calculated to delight a pure Latinist, but it is so refined and so precious that even Burnichon, no mean scholar himself, complained that what Leroux wrote about the history of the French Jesuits during this period is sometimes too difficult to understand.[39] Another Brig scholastic who eventually gave himself to the study of history was Fortuné Lhardy de Montézon (b. Paris, February 2, 1800; d. Paris, August 1, 1862). Like Moigno, he had been sent to Sainte-Geneviève at the time when this Paris *collège* on the Rue des Postes was gaining the reputation of being the leading educational institution in France, and it was here that he spent most of his life. Montézon was, however, more of a collaborator than an author who exclusively published monographs. It was he who did the spade work for Jacques Cretineau-Joly (1803–

1875), and therefore deserves much of the credit for the appearance of the controversial *Histoire religieuse, politique et littéraire de la Compagnie de Jésus* that was published in six volumes between 1844 and 1846. He also published *Clement XIV et les Jésuites* (1847), Cretineau-Joly's equally controversial and polemic study. When Félix Martin came to France in search of materials pertaining to the history of North America, it was to his former confrere of Brig days that he turned. Montézon was the gopher who dug up the material for the important *Rélations inédités de la Nouvelle-France (1672–1799) pour faire suite aux anciennes rélations (1615–1672) avec deux cartes géographiques* which appeared in 1861 under joint authorship.[40] This gifted research scholar was likewise the right-hand man to Xavier de Ravignan who published an apologetic autograph in 1854 entitled *Clément XIII et Clément XIV*. Incredibly, Montézon found time to write a few books of his own, including a history of the Guiana Mission (1857) and of the Indochina Mission (1858); unfortunately he has been accused of sometimes being careless with details.[41] He was pushed into the spotlight during a well-publicized controversy with Charles-Augustin Sainte-Beuve (1804–1869). The celebrated literary critic and lionized *littérateur* had printed false accusations against the society in the first volume of his much acclaimed work *Port-Royal* and he took pleasure in Jesuit-baiting, a popular sport of the day, in a number of his studies on the Jesuit-Jansenist controversies during the eighteenth century. Montézon published a mémoire on the matter in 1858.[42] Despite his historical and polemical publications Montézon's principal interests seem to have been pastoral and religious. He wrote a *Catéchisme à l'usage des Collèges*, which ran through four editions between 1844 and 1865, and a *Manuel de l'adoration perpetuelle . . . ou recueil de pieux exércises devant le Saint-Sacrament exposé* (1851), a meditation book for lay people (1856) and a book for instructing the young in religious and moral matters (1856). Finally, he took a great interest in analyzing the spirituality of bishop Jacques Bossuet (1627–1704), Louis XIV's tutor and one of France's great literary figures, an interest which resulted in the publication of two monographs on the subject in 1855. The number of books and articles published by Montézon becomes even more impressive when one considers that most of his time and much of his energy were spent in the classroom.[43]

These were a few of the sixty-two Jesuits in formation with Point at Brig (some others will be introduced later in this work), a tucked-away town in the Alps which "in the winter may challenge comparison with Siberia itself." Ravignan recalled there was heat only in the common room where the scholastics gathered to study and the fathers joined them to prepare their classes. "The Swiss shared everything with the French like brothers; but to tell the truth they had nothing but poverty to share." The hospitality and piety of these local mountain people caused Father Druilhet to weep when he visited his exiled subjects during the summer of 1831 when he encouraged the French to offer some sign of their appreciation. The following spring "the young French Jesuits who were come together in Switzerland determined to offer a proof of their gratitude to that Providence which had protected them, and to the land which nurtured them as her own children." They built a chapel "on a tolerably high hill called Rohrberg, and dedicated it to Mary, under the title Help of Christians." Point would relish planting crosses and dedicating shrines on "tolerably high hills" in the Rockies long after he left Switzerland. But if he had been part of the crew that planned the chapel, he was not involved in building it, for he had already left Brig.[44]

Some forty miles down the valley from Brig is the town of Sion, the capital of Valais, noted for its mild climate, its vine-covered hills and its picturesque site on the Rhône. The Swiss Jesuits had a *collège* there that the French sometimes used as a convenient meeting place between Brig and Fribourg. It also served as a refuge for those who needed rest or respite from the rigors of the winter in the Haut-Valais. The famous Doctor Joseph Recamier (1774–1852) of the Faculty of Medicine in Paris had a country home at Belfaux, near Fribourg, which he allowed the French Jesuits to use as a place of rest and recuperation. In the early days of 1831 there were four theologians and one coadjutor brother from Brig who were living in the Recamier chalet, but sometime before March these moved to the *collège* at Sion.[45] Very probably one of these students was Nicolas Point because he finished part of his third year of theology on the sick list, away from Brig, attached to the *collège* of Sion. On March 13 he was ordained subdeacon; deacon on the nineteenth, and finally on the twentieth he was ordained a priest by Bishop Fabien-Maurice Roten. He offered his first mass on Easter Sunday, April 3, 1831 at the altar of St. Francis Xavier, and in late June or early July he left Sion. Where he spent the summer has not been recorded, but in September he began teaching classes at the near-by *collège* of Fribourg.[46]

Joseph Burnichon, S. J. wrote in *Histoire d'un siècle* that "Fribourg and Saint-Acheul are the two names that sum up best the educational work of the French Jesuits during the first part of the nineteenth century. Even more than Saint-Acheul, Fribourg enjoyed the reputation of being really cosmopolitan."[47] This *collège* owed its reputation, although not its existence, to the Ordinances signed by Charles X on June 16, 1828. Jesuits, however, had been associated with Fribourg since the days of St. Peter Canisius (1521–1597) who founded St. Michael's College there in 1582. From its earliest days, St. Michael's thrived, and after the restoration of the society, the Swiss officials invited the Jesuits to reopen its doors. This they did in 1818, and the famous *Pensionnat,* or residence hall, operated by the Jesuits, was opened for students in 1822. The invasion of French students into Fribourg occurred in the fall of 1828 when some four hundred young men and boys came to enroll at St. Michael's. Many of the newcomers were refugees from the suppressed Jesuit *collèges* in France and almost all were scions of the finest aristocratic and richest bourgeois families in the kingdom, but this fact did not mean they were ready for resident life in what had been primarily a German-speaking *collège,* nor did it prevent them from trying to destroy the established order of the *Pensionnat*. The Jesuit superiors acted quickly and severely: the number of boarders was cut back to 220 the next year and the discipline was enforced with greater vigor. From that date until 1847, when the Sonderbund War closed the *collège* again, Fribourg had attracted students from almost every European country as well as from the United States, Canada, and a number of South American republics.[48] Between 1831–1833, that is, during Point's tenure at the *collège*, the Jesuit community consisted of about twenty-five priests, six brothers, and five scholastics. Two of the latter were studying physics and the other three were studying philosophy.[49] By 1847, the year Point left the Blackfeet Mission, there were some 180 priests and scholastics at Fribourg, and even though only eighty-seven of these were French, the *collège* managed to retain the Gallic character it had received from the refugees of Saint-Acheul in 1828. At the same time, even though fundamentally French, St. Michael's was an international center. This fact explains to some extent why and how the "Fribourg system" of Jesuit education became a worldwide system in Jesuit institutions.[50]

Point was invited to play an important role in the implementation of the "Fribourg system" when he arrived at the *collège* in September 1831. He was made responsible for the physical, moral, and intellectual development of a certain number of students, and he was also appointed one of the house consultors instructed to advise the rector, Jean-Népomucène Galicz (b. Polock, Witebsk, Belorussia, Russia, October 16, 1794; d. Ternopol, Galicia, Austria-Hungary, January 4, 1876), in the administration of the *collège* and the governance of the community. This White Russian, whom the French insisted on calling Galicet, was referred to long after his tenure of office at Fribourg as *"le grand recteur."* He and Father Joseph Barrelle (b. La Ciotat, Bouche-du-Rhône, August 26, 1794; d. Clemont-Ferrand, October 17, 1863) are regarded as the architects of the "Fribourg system." Barrelle who arrived at the *collège* the year Point departed, and in a sense replaced Point, was for eight years not only the famous prefect of studies in charge of the instruction of the students but also the director of the Sodality of the Blessed Virgin and therefore in charge of education. Barrelle perfected what Galicz had begun, but both men were indebted to Loriquet. In fact, it might be stated that Loriquet was the architect of what became the Jesuit method of education during the nineteenth century, and Galicz and Barrelle were the engineers who built the structure which preceded and so much influenced the *Ratio* of 1832.[51] Significantly, just as Point had been a key man in the implementation of Loriquet's *Plan* at Saint-Acheul from 1824 to 1826, so now, as one of the *grand recteur*'s four consultors, his role in the development of the "Fribourg system" at the critical time of its implementation was not insignificant.[52] Two other of Galicz's consultors were eventually sent to the foreign missions. These were Fathers Jacques Wilmet (b. Rulles, Luxembourg, Belgium, January 21, 1793; d. Negapatam, Tanjore, India, November 17, 1862) and Pierre Cotain (b. Bordeaux, April 15, 1796; d. Ile de Bourbon, June 2, 1871). In 1842, the year Point was missioned to the Coeur d'Alène Indians, Wilmet went from being the fund-raiser at the *collège* at Brugelette to Madura, where he immediately became known as *le Père de la joie,* the joyful priest, probably for reasons best known to retired Jesuit high school fund-raisers.[53] Cotain was one of the companions of Romain Dénieau and therefore one of the pioneer party of Jesuits who went to Madagascar in September 1844. Like Point, this future superior of the Madagascar Mission contributed to the magazine *Annales de la Propagation de la foi*.[54] Another member of Galicz's advisory board, the sub-minister of the Jesuit community and *collège* was Joseph Soller (b. Sausheim, Haut-Rhin, October 12, 1798; d. New Orleans, Louisiana, February 14, 1851), who had been a novice with Point and Cotain at Montrouge in 1822, and who was destined to be closely associated with Father Nicolas in the years to come.[55]

One of the members of the Fribourg community had had dealings with Point in the past. Just about the time Nicolas had left Saint-Acheul for Montrouge in the fall of

1822 for his transient life as a novice, he met a twenty-six year old Belgian organist who had arrived to take charge of the *collège* choir and music program. He was from Hamaide, near Charleroi Hainaut, Belgium, where he was born on March 27, 1797. His name was Louis Lambillotte and, like Point, he had come to Saint-Acheul because he was attracted to the society, which he entered in August 1825. By the time Nicolas returned to Montrouge in 1826, Louis was a second year novice and his brother François, also from Hamaide, where he was born March 22, 1802, was in Point's class.[56] A third brother, Joseph (b. July 3, 1805), entered the novitiate after it had moved to Avignon in 1842. The Lambillotte brothers did a great deal to make Jesuit education distinctive; Louis more so than the other two because their untimely deaths—François at Fribourg, June 2, 1835 and Joseph at Saint-Acheul, August 14, 1842—prevented the younger brothers from achieving the fame their talents promised.[57] Louis was only twelve years old when he began composing pieces for the organ and by the time he died, in Paris, February 22, 1855, he was recognized as the pioneer in restoring the Gregorian chant in the Church. In a sense, however, he was even more influential for his "simple, gracious, and totally singable" melodies, which continue to have an impact on the Catholic world. Some of his creations, such as "On this Day O Holy Mother" and "Come Holy Ghost" are still standard hymns in American churches.[58] But even in his own time his music had an important place in the *éducation* program of French Jesuit *collèges* and his melodies were soon exported beyond the walls of Saint-Acheul, Fribourg, and Brugelette.[59]

Jean-Baptiste Hus taught the condemned prisoners on the ships bound for Devil's Island how to sing Lambillotte's litanies of the Blessed Virgin, and Jesuit missionaries who had pronounced their vows with the strains of Lambillotte's "*Suscipe*" in their ears, taught people of various cultures his many "*O Salutaris*" and "*Tantum ergos.*"[60] Then these new converts from China, America, Guiana, India, Madagascar, Algeria, and Syria, gathered on their knees before the Infinite Presence, sweet-smelling censers, and unflinching candleflames to join the old formalities of Benediction and thereby insert themselves into a Catholic culture, so consciously emphasized in the 'Fribourg system,' until the latter half of the twentieth century.

Louis Lambillotte's career illustrates the importance of music and drama in the *éducation* part of the curriculum in the *collèges* between 1832 and 1880, and it also illustrates the tension it caused. Father General Roothaan confessed he frankly wondered if the stress on concert orchestras and choral groups Lambillotte organized did not go beyond moderation, and perhaps even create a climate inimical to that atmosphere of silence and recollection so necessary in cultivating *instruction,* the habit of mind necessary for learning the traditional Jesuit literary and scientific studies.[61] Frederic Studer, after he became provincial, forbade the practice of singing Lambillotte's arrangements at mass on those days which were not approved feast days, and at the same time he did away with the practice of having solemn or sung masses on Sundays, arguing that such liturgical pomp was not in the Jesuit tradition.[62] In this matter Studer was twenty years behind the prevailing traditions in those American *collèges* visited by Father Peter Kenney (1779–1841). At the time of his visitation to the St. Louis Mission in 1831, when Point, Lambillotte, and Studer were scholastics together at Fribourg, Kenney ordered that high masses were not to be sung oftener than twelve Sundays a year at Florissant and at St. Charles. Kenney argued: "We are repeatedly admonished in the Institute that High Masses and similar functions which occupy the time and distress the chests of our priests and scholastics are no duty of our vocation."[63] Since Kenney's regulations did not apply to the Kentucky and Louisiana Missions we may presume that Lambillotte's many masses, oratorios, cantiques, Benediction hymns, military songs, and hymns to the Blessed Virgin and saints fared better and longer in some parts of the United States than in others. Controversial in their own day, Nicolas Point's friends the Lambillotte brothers are composers who wait to be "discovered" by scholars interested in one particular aspect of nineteenth-century musicology or in the impact of *éducation* in forming popular Catholic culture during this era on both sides of the Atlantic.[64]

The two scholastics studying physics at the *collège* during Point's tenure at Fribourg gained fame in the years to come. Frédéric-Marie Guérin (b. Montélimart, Drôme, December 8, 1805; d. Avignon, March 3, 1869) became the author of a Greek grammar and a two volume work on the principles of persuasive speech, standard texts in French and overseas *collèges* during the latter part of the century.[65] Xavier Gautrelet (b. Sampigny, Saône-et-Loire, February 15, 1807; d. Montluçon, July 4, 1886) was, like Ravignan, a Renaissance man who became one of the outstanding Jesuits of the period chiefly because he was the founder of a movement called the Apostleship of Prayer. It would be impossible to overemphasize the importance of this Lyon-based association, founded in 1844 at Vals when Point was with the Indians of the Northwest, on the subsequent history of the Catholic Church and on the Jesuit missions in the United States during the second half of the nineteenth century. But Xavier Gautrelet's reputation and influence were not confined by his association with the Apostleship of Prayer. Like his brother, Francis de Sales (1814–1894), the founder of the Jesuit *collège* at Spring Hill, Alabama (1847), Xavier also became a missionary, serving in the French Jesuit Mission in Syria after he had gained the reputation for being an authority on Jesuit education. Like Point, he was an educator who met with no little success in implementing the Fribourg system in a mission land.[66]

When Point and Gautrelet were serving under Galicz, one of the essentials of this "Fribourg system," was integrating the German Swiss students with the French. Such a policy did not always meet with instant or happy results because, as Pierre Point wrote, "the spirit of young Swiss was not the same as that of young Frenchmen." By the end of the academic year, Nicolas realized that "prudence was needed to blend these very different spirits that were now physically and emotionally exhausted" and looking forward to vacation time. This scenario, he would learn, would be repeated with Louisiana boys in years to come. But in 1831 the term could not end quickly enough for the German speakers to quit the *collège* and head for home. The French boys were too far away to return to their families during the summer holidays and so Point got permission to take some of those in his division on a hiking tour of Switzerland. They climbed up the Simplon Alps and then descended onto the shores of Lake Geneva and from there, traveling westward, they climbed a bluff from where they could see France spread out, extending to the horizon. The view caused "the hearts of all to beat with force as they looked with fondness on this beautiful and unhappy land; memories flooded their imaginations as they cried out with one voice: '*Vive la France*.' They were intoxicated with joy." That night they camped beneath the stars that looked down on them and on their beloved homeland, and the next day Point went off and got a hold of "a bottle of champagne, popped the cork, filled their little glasses with bubbly stuff, and then with more enthusiasm than ever, they toasted '*à la santé de la France*' and cheers to their families and friends." It was a glorious moment, one that Nicolas could never forget, and one that gives good insight into at least one aspect of his personality: no matter where he was exiled, he remained a Frenchman with a passionate love for the country and the people of his birth.[67]

FORMATION

Part Two: 1833–1835

In Spain: 1833–1834

By the spring of 1833 the animosity generated by the July Revolution against the society had died down enough to enable the sixty-five Jesuits in formation at Brig to return to France. The novices were sent back to Avignon while the philosophers and theologians went to the newly founded scholasticate near Le Puy, at Vals.[1] A few months after this move Father Nicolas Point received a new assignment: he was to quit Fribourg to join the faculty at the *collège-en-exile* at Le Passage, Spain. He was asked to leave "the country he was beginning to love to make a new sacrifice," commented Pierre hinting at his disappointment in leaving Fribourg. But, in the characteristic rhetoric of the time, Pierre reflected that "a Jesuit's life is a long pilgrimage, mixed with sacrifices; nevertheless, let no one think that the frequency of such sacrifices makes it easier for the apostle to accept." So, as the summer of 1833 gave way to fall, and snow made occasional, short visits on the lower slopes, he said good-bye to his students and moved on to Geneva. Here he followed the Rhône down past Lyon to Avignon, and then turned southwest to Toulouse. Here he halted briefly, then continued on through Lourdes, an insignificant village then, but one he would remember in later years, and Pau, until he reached Bayonne. Here he lodged for awhile, resting and taking advantage of the hospitality offered him and his companion by a family friendly to the society. From this point he most probably boarded a ship for the short voyage to his new assignment.[2]

Le Passage, or, to give this historic town its correct Spanish name, Pasajes de Francia, faces a small harbor to the north on the Bay of Bisquay and is guarded on the east and west by twin mountain masses, Jaisquibel and Ulía. Isolated by nature, it lies midway between San Sebastián and the French border, a sleepy Basque town, once prosperous during Spain's Golden Age. After Charles X signed the Ordinances of 1828, the French Jesuits, with the support of the unpopular Spanish King, Ferdinand VII, were able to send twenty novices there from Avignon and open up a *collège-en-exile* at the same time when similar institutions were being established at Fribourg and at Chambéry in Savoy. But unlike these two *collèges-en-exile,* Le Passage never knew prosperity or success. In the first place it was inaccessible to all but those who lived in the southwest corner of France; moreover, unlike the peace that reigned in Sardinia and Switzerland, political instability punctuated by a series of uprisings characterized Spain during the last years of Ferdinand's reign. Finally, a cholera epidemic broke out on both sides of the frontier during the course of 1832 and, although no one at the *collège* was stricken, parents of a number of French students called their sons back home to enroll them either in exiled Jesuit schools that enjoyed the reputation for being flourishing establishments or in the *petit séminaires* under the control of the Université.[3]

On September 29, 1833, Ferdinand VII died; his wife María Cristina became regent in the name of the couple's young daughter, Isabella, who was proclaimed queen. This occasioned the First Carlist War (1833–1839), a savage conflict between urban liberals, the *cristianos* who supported the Regent, and rural traditionalists, the *carlistas* who gave allegiance to the late king's brother, Don Carlos, known to his partisans as Charles V. In general, the Basque states were for the traditional liberty of the Church and their *fueros* and against the centralism of Madrid; therefore, Don Carlos found his greatest support in the homelands of Ignatius of Loyola and Francis Xavier. The mountains of Guipúscoa became a hideout for guerilla insurgents while the central government held fast to the cities and large towns. Such was the political situation when Point arrived at Le Passage toward the end of 1833. Fifty Jesuits—sixteen priests, fifteen coadjutor brothers and nineteen scholastics, some of whom were students—served less than one hundred boarding students, all French, and forty day students, all Spanish. Unlike the policy adopted at Fribourg, at Le Passage the boys were separated according to language, and after June 1834 the number of Spanish students diminished dramatically because it was no longer safe for them to make the trip back and forth from their homes to school. As far as the French boarders were concerned, in June of 1834 there were fifty-six boys between the ages of ten and fourteen who studied grammar, and forty older boys who were either students of rhetoric and the humanities or of philosophy, which they studied with the Jesuit scholastics. These older students were housed in a residence hall named Saint-Joseph; the younger were lodged in a building called Saint-Roch, and it was at Saint-Roch that Nicolas Point was superior.[4]

He found a number of old friends and acquaintances at his new post. To restrict the list to three, there was Father Ferdinand Jeantier (b. Besançon, Doubs, February 20, 1799; d. Vannas, May 8, 1878), who had been a novice with him at Montrouge in 1822, lived with him at Fribourg, and very probably was his companion on the journey from Switzerland to Spain. Later in the century Jeantier won the epitaph "Father to the Angels" because of his work with children and because of his interest in the spiritual development of the young, many of whom attributed their subsequent vocations to the religious and priestly life to his care and concern.[5] Father Augustin Poissemeux (b. Molac, Morbihan, March 21, 1804; d. Shanghai, China, June 9, 1854), one of the young priests who had also been sent to Le

Passage that year, was a novice with Point the second time he entered Montrouge and he was stationed with him at Brig and Fribourg. In 1848 Poissemeux succeeded Claude Gotteland as the second superior of the China Mission and died, along with Gotteland and one-third of the French Jesuits in that fateful mission, from the ravages of typhoid fever in the great epidemic of 1854.[6] Point discovered another old friend at Le Passage with whom he would have later dealings: Father Paul Luiset (b. Lille, June 6, 1788; d. Sault-au-Récollet, Québec, Canada, May 1, 1855), the first *lillois* to enter the restored society. His family's house in the Pas de Calais was an oasis for Jesuits in need of rest and recreation and at least on one occasion Jan Roothaan, before he became general, had taken advantage of the Luisets' fabled hospitality. Paul had done his studies at Saint-Sulpice like Pierre Charlier and so many of the Jesuits who profoundly influenced Nicolas Point in the years he struggled with his vocation. After ordination Luiset entered the society, in 1821, and came to Canada in 1842 where he was appointed the first master of novices at Montreal and afterwards was assigned to the Jesuit *collège* at Fordham, New York. Toward the end of his life he lost his sight, but this handicap only enhanced his reputation as a spiritual director of remarkable perception and prudence for priests, religious, and laity on both sides of the Canadian-American border.[7]

In his essay "Dernier sémaine de Saint-Acheul" (1828), Point describes in detail the devotions the *collège* had adopted during *le mois de mai,* the month of Mary. In 1833, he developed this theme in an extended letter addressed to his friend, Father Ferdinand Brumauld, the future "Father of the Orphans" of Algeria. Subsequently he incorporated this letter along with his 1828 essay as parts of his "Souvenirs et mémoires illustrés."[8] May devotions were regularly fostered by a number of provinces in the society during the first half of the nineteenth century, and the custom of dedicating the fifth month, the most beautiful time of the year to the blessed Virgin, began with pre-Suppression Jesuits in those areas. Appalled by the lack of morals and solid piety among the students, a Sicilian Jesuit,

Francesco La Loma (1727–1789), introduced May devotions at the College of Palermo in the mid-1750s and in 1758 he published a small book entitled *Il mese di Maggio consecrato alla glorie della gran Madre di Dio, coll'esercizio di vari fiori di virtu.* This work gave structure to a devotion which had been practiced in various forms among Italian Jesuits since 1726. Then in 1767, the year the society was suppressed in the Duchy of Lorraine, Father Pierre Doré (1733–1816), a native of a town near Rocroi, was assigned to the College of Palermo where he was so impressed by what one might call today the Campus Ministry program that in 1778, seven years after the Jesuits had to leave Palermo and five years after the general suppression, he translated La Loma's book into French. It met with limited success chiefly in the northeastern part of the country and was reprinted in 1786 and again in 1807. Meanwhile, the dispersed Italian Jesuits were making the devotion popular in places on the peninsula where it had not been known. Finally, in 1812, one of these men, Alphonso Muzzarelli (1733–1813), accompanied Pius VII, as his personal theologian, to his place of imprisonment at the Chateau of Fontainebleau. Although Muzzarelli's life span was running out, it seems he did a great deal to make May devotions known throughout France, and by the time the society was restored in 1814, La Loma's translated prayers were becoming popular with the people and the devotion was taken on as a special project by the newly constituted French Jesuits. Doré's book was republished twice between 1816 and 1819, and four times between 1822 and 1826.[9] Although May devotions were slow to catch on in England, they had spread with rapid enthusiasm throughout Ireland after 1818. Essentially these devotions consisted in families setting up a house shrine to the Blessed Virgin before the first day of May, and then saying prayers, singing hymns, and bringing flowers to the shrine during the rest of the month. It was a popular, tender devotion, which fostered family prayer, self-conversion, and perseverence in sanctity, and although it had little relationship to the liturgy, Scriptures, and a healthy intellectual Christian life, it was one of the most powerful instruments in sustaining the Catholic revival in Europe during the greater part of the century.[10] May devotions played the central role in the academic year at Saint-Acheul, Fribourg, Le Passage, and other Jesuit *collèges*, and there seemed to be a type of rivalry in seeing which institution set up the most beautiful shrine where the students could sing the litanies, pray the rosary, recite homemade verse, and edify one another with specially composed memorized exhortations on titles and acclamations found in the Litany of Loretto. Perhaps no other activity, except the reception of the sacraments, contributed more in creating the animating spirit of the *collèges* than these May devotions. For this reason they played a central role in the *éducation,* the training, of the students in what was conceived to be the Jesuit spirit. Not only were these devotions designed to strengthen the faith of the students and to instruct them in a catechetical, apologetic way, but they also made strong appeals to the memory, imagination, and artistic creativity of the students as individuals and as members of a tightly-knit group.[11] Nicolas Point dedicated all of his artistic talents to making the 1834 month of May ceremonies memorable for the students and faculty of Le Passage. In this endeavour he was assisted by Ferdinand Jeantier, the chaplain of the young boys' sodality, and by the scholastic François Lambillotte, Louis's younger brother, some of whose cantiques and Benediction hymns, composed for the occasion in this, the penultimate year of his life, were posthumously published.[12] And, of course, each student had a particular role to play right up to the final day when they all made the solemn consecration to the Immaculate Heart of Mary.

Five weeks after the unforgettable pageantry that culminated the month of May at Le Passage, that is, on July 6, 1834, Queen Regent Maria Christina signed a decree ordering the *collège* closed and banishing all French students and teachers from Spain.[13] About four o'clock on the afternoon of July 12 the threatening clouds broke and the long awaited rain poured down on the sultry streets of Pasajes de Francia. At this moment, a detachment, wet and frustrated because a *carlistas* raiding party had slipped through their grasp, pounded on the doors of the Saint-Roch residence demanding shelter from the elements and all the wine in the house. Point obliged them. It was Saturday and therefore the students were in the chapel attending a sodality meeting. The wine gave the soldiers courage, and they roundly cursed Don Carlos and the partisans they were unable to capture.

Meanwhile, another group of soldiers had invaded Saint-Joseph and the adjutant-general of the local garrison accompanied by an officer went to the Jesuit residence and called for the rector, ordering him to hand over a list of the names of all the students, teachers, staff, and domestics at the *collège* and warning him that if this list was not received within fifteen minutes sanctions would be meted out. The list was readily provided. The officer then presented the rector with an order signed by the appropriate authorities and in a sententious voice announced: "As of now this *collège* is closed. You are given twenty-four hours to clear out." Further consultation allowed an exemption: four Jesuits and some domestics were given a continuance so that they could dispose of the furniture. About six o'clock the next morning, Nicolas Point ordered a convocation of all the students at Saint-Roch. The meeting took place in the chapel, where the boys had gathered for morning prayer. After a long peroration, he finally uttered the phrase, "we must leave," and could proceed no further because of the reaction of his auditors who broke out in loud weeping. "At that moment," Point recalled, "I too felt a rending of my insides that I have never felt before." Later in the morning Ferdinand Jeantier offered mass but broke down in sympathy with the continuous sobbing from the congregation. The boys did their packing and then assembled once more in the conference room where they were prematurely given their academic prizes: holy pictures for some, medals for others, and for the top two, crucifixes. They then marched to the pier and boarded the ships bound for Bayonne. Suddenly Jeantier remembered the Blessed Sacrament was still in the

Saint-Roche chapel. He grabbed one of the students, Henri de Carmejage, later an officer in the French army, and rushed back with him to the empty hall. There the priest had the boy consume the sacred species because his "own heart was too base." The two then rushed back to the small ship where young Henri knelt to make his thanksgiving surrounded by the others kneeling with him; in this way their ship joined the flotilla back to France.

On Monday morning, July 14, 1834, the exiles disembarked at Bayonne greeted by crowds along the quai cheering, *"Vive les Jésuites!"* The bishop had joined their ranks (Bastille Day was scarcely celebrated then) and gave them a hearty welcome. Jesuits and students remained together until the following Tuesday while arrangements were made to have the students delivered to their parents. On Tuesday, the fifteenth, agitated crowds in Madrid and in other Spanish cities began sacking religious houses, convents, and monasteries, killing a number of occupants. Among the fifty-nine dead were nine Jesuits: four priests, three scholastics and two brothers. With Gallic irony Burnichon commented that "the mobs showed their love for freedom and a constitutional regime by pillaging the monasteries and in killing the monks." Meanwhile, in the vacated *collège-en-exile* at Pasajes de Francia, all of the furniture and goods left by the French Jesuits was confiscated and sold by the government, although as a result of later negotiations some of the books from the library, equipment from the physics laboratory, and certain items from the chapel were redeemed. The buildings were "left empty with no other occupants than rats and spiders,"[14] Meanwhile, up in Belgium, a new country recently independent from the yoke of Protestant Holland and enthusiastic for Jesuit presence, plans were already in operation to replace Le Passage. In the following spring, the athletic Ferdinand Brumauld was sent to Brugelette in Belgium with orders to get the classrooms and living quarters ready in record time for the opening day of this new *collège,* the successor to Le Passage. Then, on October 29, 1835, Father Côme Lartigue, the newly appointed Prefect of Studies and professor of rhetoric welcomed fifty students, some of whom were alumni of the recently defunct *collège* in Spain, and he entrusted them to men like Fortuné de Montézon, Joseph Soller, Louis Lambillotte, and other founding fathers of the institution which would share with Fribourg the title of archtype for Jesuit schools throughout the world. Later that same year one of the statues salvaged from the Le Passage chapel was installed in the recently completed chapel of Brugelette. It was the statue of the Virgin Mary which was the object of the elaborate ceremonies Nicolas Point had orchestrated during the Month of Mary and now, under the title of "The Spanish Virgin" it would be given special recognition each May as long as the *collège* existed.[15]

During the last part of July 1835, there was no indication among the refugees at Bayonne that a new beginning was about to take place. Point was given the responsibility for seeing that his former boarders of Saint-Roch were delivered safe and sound to their families, and so he began the long trek northward in a caravan of stagecoaches with the man who would later be known in France as the "Apostle to Little Children" or the "Father to the Angels," his former fellow novice, Ferdinand Jeantier. On their long journey they crisscrossed France, going from Bayonne to Pau, and again through Lourdes to Toulouse, and then to Nîmes, Mende, Saint-Flour, Clermont, and Nevers, "leaving in safe hands along the way various pieces of their treasure," and gradually reducing the number of coaches. At Nevers they made a beeline straight north to Paris and then again north to Amiens and Saint-Acheul. In order to leave more coach space for the boys, Point planted himself alongside the driver, and during the almost eight-hundred-mile journey, he got to know him well. The good man was a rationalist, a scoffer who teased the priest and played little games with him, using blasphemy and coarse speech. Nicolas, who knew barracks life well, responded with patience and humor. Finally, "with only the stars as witnesses," he gave the rough and tumbled driver an abridged version of the Spiritual Exercises, and before they reached Amiens he heard his confession. This anecdote gives a good insight into the future missionary's personality.[16] Even though he could be rigid in judging moral conduct, and narrow in evaluating the beliefs of others (and in this sense he was a man of his time), he was nevertheless a man who dealt easily on a personal basis with common people and with those whose beliefs were radically different from his own. Whatever else he was, he was no prude, no bigot, and he demonstrated a genuine love and respect for soldiers, prisoners, coach drivers, German emigrants, French *chasseurs de bois*, Indian horse thieves, and Protestant Yankee bosses. Compared with many of his peers, he got along well with all of these and many others besides, in a surprisingly easy way.

In France: 1834–1835

In 1832, while Point was in Fribourg, a cholera epidemic broke out in Amiens (the same one that traveled south the next year, bringing such ill-fortune to Le Passage), and soon the hospitals were filled with the sick and dying. Father Guidée, the only Jesuit left at Saint-Acheul as a kind of caretaker, turned over the buildings to the municipality to accommodate the hospital crisis. In no time stricken soldiers from the local garrison filled the rooms and halls of the old abbey and these military men were nursed by Guidée and a few other Jesuits who had been allowed to function as secular priests in the surrounding countryside. By the beginning of 1833, as houses of formation were being reestablished in other parts of France, Jesuits were again openly living in the former *petit séminaire* at Saint-Acheul where their work with the fever victims had immunized them from harassment by the government authorities or by unfriendly mobs.[17] The next year the tertianship for the Province of France at Estavayer, Switzerland, was closed, and notices were sent out that it would reopen at Saint-Acheul under the direction of Father Sébastien Fouillot (b. Vesoul, Haute-Saône, November 5, 1798; d. Aix-en-Province, February 20, 1877), distinguished for his "original and powerful physiognomy," and for the fact that "no French Jesuit exercised a more profound influence over his religious family" for more than a half century.[18] François

Xavier de Ravignan, who had just completed his own tertianship at Estavayer, was assigned his assistant. He arrived at Saint-Acheul on November 2, 1834.[19]

This was the time where there was considerable discussion about the meaning and purpose of tertianship. Roothaan's objective in reorganizing the society inspired him to take a particular interest in both the novitiate and tertianship because it was in these houses of formation that the Institute of the society was to be studied and thoroughly learned. The Institute refers to the way Jesuits live and work within the guidelines of the society's constitutions, rules, and ordinances and in accord with decrees of general congregations that have been approved by the Holy See. Up until now tertianship had been more unstructured, but from now on the study of the Institute was regulated, and it is for this reason that Point's year of tertianship in 1834 at Saint-Acheul under Fouillot and Ravignan is considered the first formal tertianship undertaken by the Province of France.[20] This emphasis on the study of the Institute during tertianship was not missed by the new provincial, François Renault (b. Poubalay, Côtes-du-Nord, April 3, 1788; d. Paris, December 8, 1860), who wrote to Point's old mentor, Julien Druilhet, on December 3, 1834: "The tertianship augurs well. Our men are Father Fouillot and Father de Ravignan; unfortunately, there are few such men around because few study the Institute."[21] But besides offering an opportunity to study the Institute, tertianship, known also as the "third year of probation," was considered to be the "school of the heart," a time when future apostolic workers steeped themselves in the life of solitude, prayer, penance, and poverty with the purpose of obtaining from these practices the realization of the graces of the priesthood which they had recently received. Such was Ravignan's conception of what the year was to be for Nicolas Point and the fifteen other priests who experienced this *desert idyll* with him.[22]

Precisely when Point came to Saint-Acheul is not clear. Most probably he did not travel far from this house, which held so many memories for him, once he arrived there from Le Passage in late July 1834. Many of his co-tertians were known to him but there was one whose life was to be closely intermingled with his own. This was Guillaume or Líam or William—depending on whether one was French, Irish or English—Murphy (b. Cork, Ireland, April 29, 1803; d. New Orleans, October 23, 1875), a scion of a prominent Irish family. His brother Francis Stack Murphy (1807–1870), a graduate of the Irish Jesuit school at Clongowes Wood and of Trinity College, Dublin, was the representative of Cork in the Westminster Parliament from 1837 to 1853, and therefore a member of "the pope's brass band," an infamous group of affluent Catholic lawmakers more interested in advancing their own interests than those of their constituents, the many poor preoccupied with the struggle for existence. Called to the English Bar, he eventually became the Sergeant-at-Law in London where his wit became legendary and where there are yet many anecdotes told about him. He collaborated with his friend and former teacher Francis Sylvester Mahony (1804–1866), another sarcastic and cynical wit, in publishing many delightful *tours de force* in the famous "Father Prout" stories.[23]

Mahony, the son of a wealthy manufacturer of Blarney, was a student at Saint-Acheul when Point first arrived there in 1819, and then in October 1821, he joined the French Province and began his novitiate at Montrouge, where he welcomed Brother Nicolas Point when he arrived there to begin his novitiate the following September.[24] Superiors recognized Mahony's exceptional talents and predicted he, who at that date called himself O'Mahony, would become another Nicolas de Mac-Carthy (b. Dublin, May 21, 1769; d. Annecy, Savoy, Kingdom of Sardinia, May 3, 1833), one of the first Irishmen to enter the French Province and who vied with Ravignan as the society's greatest orator in France.[25] Mahony was back at Saint-Acheul as a scholastic with vows when Point returned in 1824 and during the July Days he was sent to Ireland where he became a professor of rhetoric and prefect of studies at Clongowes Wood. But his tenure there was short-lived. On one cold day the following November, he took Francis Murphy and a few other students, who later distinguished themselves in various professions, on a coursing expedition over the Irish countryside. When the happy group returned quite late that night it was more than obvious that the unsteady Prefect of Studies, who was not much older than his charges and certainly less experienced, had allowed the coursing exercise to become a carousing experience, and that the group had spent more hours in the warm homes of the Catholic gentry quaffing at the punch bowl's brink than gamboling over the green fields of rural Ireland. Retribution was quick. Mahony was ordered to pack his bags and head for Fribourg. From there he was sent on to Rome, but by the time he had reached Florence he found his dismissal papers from the society awaiting him. He was crushed. Today, in an age that supports the rights of the individual against those of the institution, such peremptory action seems unfair, self-defeating. But in the mid-nineteenth century, the society, ever conscious of its corporate image, had to remain strong, and tough discipline contributed materially to its strength.

Mahony continued on to Rome, where he finished his studies. Before he left Italy he was ordained for the diocese of Cork, returned to Ireland in time to give himself unsparingly to the victims of the 1833 cholera epidemic, and then clashed with the headstrong bishop of Cork over the design of the church he was building. This event caused him for all practical purposes to give up the priesthood, to move to London, where he joined Francis Murphy, and to take up the bohemian mode of life that characterized London's literary society. He soon became the lynchpin of the "Fraserians," a convivial group that contributed first to *Frasier's Magazine* and later to *Bentley's Miscellany,* which he had helped to found and which was edited by his fellow "Fraserian," Charles Dickens (1812–1870). Classicists may be a dying breed but there are still some today who can appreciate the wealth of Greek and Latin parodies composed in Pindaric and Horatian verse that flowed from the pen of "Father Prout," for that was the name Mahoney was universally called, and which appeared in *Frasier's Magazine*. A brilliant conversationalist, he claimed to be "an Irish potato seasoned with Attic salt."[26] Humorist and humanist, he had learned well the disciplined prosody of Loriquet and used it even in his outrageous theatrical sallies. And those who can yet relish Mahony can likewise appreciate Francis Murphy's talent for rendering "Hohenlinden" by Thomas Campbell (1733–1795) into Latin sapphics and for translating into mock Homeric Greek "Wreathe the Bowl" by Thomas Moore (1779–1852) and "The Groves of Blarney" by Richard Milliken (1767–1815).[27] In 1848 Charles Dickens sent Mahony to Rome as a correspondent for his new paper the *Daily News*, and from there he mailed back commentaries under the byline "Don Jeremy Savonarola." Mahony's commentaries from Rome seemed to have lost critical acumen, imaginative verve, and most of all *mesure*, that sense of proportion which was so essential in Loriquet's *plan*, and for Mahony that balance between hilarity and nonsense. After this assignment, ever restless and uncertain, he returned as if by instinct to Paris, the burying ground for so many Irish literary figures. Here, seemingly dead to the life of the senses and the mind, he lived the life of a hermit, eschewing all former friends and acquaintances, and here, almost blind and abandoned, he was reconciled to the Church. The Abbé Martial Marcet de la Roche-Arnaud considered Mahony the quintessential Jesuit, and it is significant that this man who mocked everything and everyone never showed animosity toward the society, but rather defended it in his Father Prout stories.[28]

Mahony's nemesis, the Bishop of Cork, was the uncle of Francis and William Stack Murphy. His name was Doctor William Murphy (1772–1847), a Lisbon-educated cosmopolitan who spoke a number of European languages including Irish, and who was the owner of the largest private library in Ireland (40,000 volumes).[29] When His Lordship refused to give his favorite nephew, who bore his own name, the necessary ecclesiastical permission to enter the society, the formidable Archbishop of Paris, Hyacinthe-Louis de Quelen (1778–1839), came to the rescue of "*pauvre Guillaume*." "Let him be accepted into my diocese," he advised the master of novices Father Gury, "and then I shall release him to you." He could not refrain from adding a

Gallic jibe at the man who considered himself the greatest patron of the arts in Ireland: "A bishop's charity ought to be catholic." Guillaume accordingly entered the French Province in 1823. He was perfectly bilingual, for his family roots were planted deep in French soil. He himself claimed to be French by training and sentiment; Irish in disposition and temperament; and since he had spent the past four years in Rome before returning to Saint-Acheul for tertianship, he had mastered Italian in a remarkable way.[30]

Ravignan gave the first conference of the Long Retreat on January 1, 1835.[31] What the great preacher's expectations were for the tertians and what Point gained from this unforgettable experience are outside the scope of this work except insofar as the tertianship might throw light on Point's personality and on his American apostolate. His meticulous notes reveal a sensitive, intelligent, prayerful man who was very serious, indeed, about the ends and means of tertianship. After his annual manifestation of conscience with the provincial, François Renault, he wrote down his reflections on their conversation:

> Everything the Provincial told me yesterday caused me to reflect and even fear. I know and have myself experienced all he said about adventurous and romantic fancies, but I go back and forth when I try to figure out how all this pertains to me; it is only after I think I have heard God's voice interiorly that I speak about it to those I should. I would be far from wanting to put such thoughts into execution now if they were contrary to the mind of those who for me stand in the place of God. But today I feel, as I have always felt, that my heart (if I can use such a comparison) is like a needle on a compass: it can be stopped by a strong, outside force, but when left to itself it points only to one direction—the conversion of the Indians in America or in America's islands . . .
>
> Yesterday, after speaking with the Provincial I was moved by the truth of these words: *Nihil sum, nihil possum, nihil valeo; omnia possum in eo qui me confortat.* (I am

> nothing, I can do nothing, I am worth nothing; everything I am able to do in Him who strengthens me). This feeling has nothing to do with either emotions or imagination; it seems to me a sentiment peaceful and deep, and rooted in my *faith in God*. The Provincial was gracious enough to read these lines and he too recognized that this inclination was one that came from grace.[32]

Father Provincial Renault seemed to have raised two objections to Point's request to be sent to America to work among the Indians. First, did Nicolas have the temperament to live alone? Second, seeing that the Province of France had no missions among the American Indians, where would he be sent? As for the first question, Point asked: "To live alone? My God, am I not alone in any situation!" And he continued:

> Isn't God my strength! My eyes are drawn to the crucifix in my room. Will not the cross be with me everywhere? If I am deprived of the sacraments at death, will not that death, providing I have the fortune of being with God through grace, be a sacrifice capable of meriting the mercy of God! To encounter death by being drowned, burned, massacred! Was this not the type of death the apostles met? What was Christ's life like? My crucifix answers all. God calls me to work for the conversions of the Indians . . . all my efforts must be directed there. How and when? When my superiors will it. How my superiors will it.[33]

François Renault at last decided that Nicolas Point and William Murphy were to be sent into the Bardstown, Kentucky area to St. Mary's College, founded by William Byrne and taken over in the name of the French Province by Pierre Chazelle in 1830. Two Breton coadjutor brothers were to accompany them: Michel Jary (b. Pontivy, Morbihan, March 4, 1793; d. New York, May 1, 1848) and Philippe Ledoré (b. Quiberon, Morbihan, February 13, 1800; d. New York, April 4, 1881). Point was to serve at the Kentucky *collège* until the French Province opened up a mission among the Indians. In the case that plans to inaugurate such a mission did not work out, Point would be assigned to the Belgian Jesuits, who had reestablished St. Louis College in 1829, eight years after Missouri became a state, and who were talking about sending men westward to the Indians. Meanwhile, just as Père Charlier had given young Nicolas Point the task to teach catechism to the young, eighteen years previously, so now Père Ravignan sent him out to teach the fundamentals of the faith to children and prepare pre-teenagers for their First Communion. However, this assignment was soon superseded by an order from Renault who had finally given in to the pleadings of Madame Point to allow her to see her son for the last time. This is the reason why Nicolas was sent to Reims in mid-September to preach the Spiritual Exercises to the Carmelite nuns in that city where his ailing mother and his brother and sister were living.

During this retreat he and the Prioress, appropriately named Mother St. Francis Xavier, became fast friends and carried on a lifelong correspondence which, unfortunately, is no longer extant. Born Marie-Jeanne Henry (Bouillon, Luxembourg, Belgium, February 4, 1793; d. Reims, November 14, 1869), this woman was a contemplative who enjoyed a reputation for gifted mystical prayer and had a special attachment to the foreign missions, a pre-figuration of the Carmelite Thérèse of Lisieux (1873–1897), whom the Church named co-patron with St. Francis Xavier of the foreign missions. By the time Point was on the high seas heading toward America, Mother Xavier left Reims to re-establish the famous Carmel Convent at Compiègne. On July 17, 1794, the sixteen nuns from this convent were executed in Paris. In 1957 Francis Poulenc (1899–1963) composed the opera *Dialogues des Carmélites* to immortalize this event. Poulenc based his drama on the 1949 screenplay of the same name by Georges Bernanos (1888–1948) which in turn was inspired by the novel *Die Letzte am Schafott* (1931) by Gertrud von Le Fort (1876–1971).[34] Point always had a special place in his heart for the Carmelites but because of his associations with Mother Xavier and the nuns at Reims, one of his tertianship resolutions was to wear the Carmelite scapular at all times. Toward the end of his life he even wrote a period-type monograph on the power and beauty of the scapular.[35]

The retreat at the Carmel Convent at Reims was not finished when Point received a startling communication from Ravignan, dated Saint-Acheul, September 29, 1835:

> Reverend and dear Father, P.C.
> As soon as you receive this letter return home. You could be leaving for your next assignment at any moment. I urgently enjoin you to make the greatest haste.[36]

Point quit Reims as ordered, but he did not consider it against obedience to stop over at the small town of Liesse, near Laon, to visit for the last time the famous shrine of the Black Virgin. After three knights brought this image back with them from the Crusades and built a church to house it in 1134, a devotion to the Virgin Mary under the title of Cause of our Joy spread about the Picardy countryside. Ironically this was the home of John Calvin, who was not known for an excess of joy. In the seventeenth century, as a result of books written by two Reims Jesuits, René de Cerisiers (1603–1622) and Germain Ripault (1605–1663), the devotion became more widespread, earnestly sponsored as it was by the society in France.[37] Père Jacques Marquette (1637–1675), a native of Laon, brought the devotion with him to North America. Finally, because of the centralized place this devotion had for Pierre de Clorivière, Our Lady of Liesse was regarded as a link between the old and restored society in France, the assurance of victory in spite of setbacks.[38] Father Sébastien Fouillot sent his tertians on pilgrimages to Liesse during 1834-1835, and after Point left France, the society built a residence there to care for the pilgrims and to indicate how important the devotion was to French Jesuits.[39] So, in late September or early October Nicolas Point spent a vigil in prayer before the Cause of our Joy and carried back with him relics from this shrine where wonders were reported to have taken place.

Ponlevoy gives the reason for the haste in his orders. The prefect at Amiens refused to issue passports to Murphy and Point. This administrative harassment brought the lawyer Ravignan to his feet. During the previous Lent he had preached the conferences in Amiens' cathedral with extraordinary success, and as a result he won the admiration and respect of this same prefect as well as other local authorities. So now, in September, when he came forward in favor of these future missionaries he was given a reception not accorded to an ordinary clergyman, much less a Jesuit. So, all the obstacles for granting the requested passports melted away before the force of his rhetoric and the suavity of his charm.[40] But experience showed how prudent it was to strike while the iron was hot; consequently on October 14, armed with the required documents, Point and Murphy along with Brothers Ledoré and Jary headed for Le Havre, their port of embarkation.

Of the sixteen priests in Point's tertianship there were others who also eventually went to the missions, and each one testifies to the diversity characteristic of these Jesuits of Point's vintage. Louis Tassis (b. Carpentras, Vaucluse, November 11, 1801; d. Trichinopoly, Madras, India, May 14, 1888) had been with Point at Fribourg and later on, like Point, wrote vivid accounts of the people to whom he had been sent.[41] Tassis, Antoine Sales (b. Saint-Laurent-d'Olt, Aveyron, September 3, 1802; d. Trichinopoly, Madras, India, July 11, 1875)[42] and Alexandre Martin (b. Nîmes, December 14, 1799; d. Jedeicatour, Madras, India, May 30, 1840) were pioneers to the Madras Mission.[43] Moreover, Martin and Sales were two of four veterans of the first mission, Portugal, established by the restored Province of France in 1829. When the society in Portugal was once again suppressed in July 1833, Martin, Sales, and their two companions were consigned to the infamous Dungeons of São Juliano where, in 1761, Sebastião José de Cavalho e Mello, Marquês de Pombal had imprisoned 220 Jesuits for eighteen years. Thirty-seven others had died there or were driven mad on that occasion. In 1833, however, thanks to pressure on the part of the French government, the Jesuits were released after a few months of confinement.[44] Finally, there was also a future veteran of the Madagascar Mission represented in this tertian class: Ambroise Neyraguet (b. Espalion, Aveyron, December 7, 1800; d. Toulouse, January 28, 1861) who had been with Point at Brig.[45]

AMERICA
1835–1836

The four Jesuits, Fathers Murphy and Point and Brothers Ledoré and Jary sped off to Le Havre and placed themselves in the hands of a certain Monsieur Legros, a benefactor who regularly assisted missionaries with the complexities of embarkation. Legros in turn consigned them to the care of Madame d'Ingouville, an elderly lady, "even more respectable for her virtue than for her age," who lodged them in her spacious château and for five days doted upon them until their ship, the *John Arrow*, was ready to weigh anchor on October 18, 1835.[1] As he saw the lighthouses at Le Havre fade in the distance, Point recounted, "It was then that the missionary realized he was French, realized he was making a sacrifice in leaving his country; we felt the need to raise up our hearts to God and remind ourselves why we were leaving: for the glory of God and the salvation of souls."[2] Among the passengers there was one young American and forty-eight German emigrants, twenty-eight of whom were Catholics. There was also a young stowaway named Pierre of undisclosed nationality, but probably French, who had stashed himself in a rowboat until the third day at sea when he jumped up and "ran gaily about crying, *'me voici.'*"[3] Point reported that none of the crewmen of the *John Arrow,* an American ship out of New York, was Catholic, but he had the highest regard for them; moreover, "all of the Germans seemed to be very honest people and we soon realized it was going to be very easy to live with them on the best of terms, despite national and religious differences."[4]

The passage over was terribly rough. Point had developed a bad case of housemaid's knee, a probable relic of the excesses of tertianship, and Murphy and Jary became seasick on the first day out and did not recover until the *John Arrow* docked in New York fifty-seven days later.[5] Brother Ledoré, who had spent eight years as a seaman, later confessed that in all of his experience he had never seen rougher seas nor more continuous storms.[6] On November 11, the ship's rudder broke and during the next forty-eight hours the *John Arrow* was totally out of control as it spun about aimlessly in circles. Murphy and Point vowed a novena of masses in honor of St. Francis Xavier if ever they made it to shore.[7] The four missionaries redoubled their prayers, and on the thirteenth, the feast day of St. Stanislaus Kostka, patron of Jesuit novices, the captain ingeniously (Point maintained miraculously) made the necessary adjustments and the *John Arrow* pointed again toward her home port. On the eighteenth, they were off the Newfoundland banks where they began to fish in order to replenish the dwindling stores. In a matter of minutes, they caught twenty-five gigantic cod all of which weighed more than forty-two pounds a piece, but as the captain was attempting to pull the net ashore, he fell into the turbulent sea. Just in time, Brother Ledoré threw him the line that saved his life. On the twenty-first, they hit a storm that in comparison minimized those that had already struck the ship. This time Brother Ledoré set up a tiny statue to "Good St. Anne," patroness of Breton fishermen, while Point threw relics from the shrine of Our Lady of Liesse, the Cause of our Joy, into the foaming waves. On the twenty-third, the sea suddenly became calm; they had met the Gulf Stream and for the next fifteen days there was scarcely any wind to drive them on.[8] Point noted in his journal: "On the 27th, the sun rose in all his splendor: What beauty! What riches! What variety! The eastern part of the sky, framed irregularly by fluffy clouds, was all blue and rose, which the Christian interprets as promises of blessings to come. France lies beyond all of that. It is about her that I am thinking. I am a priest. All of my life I have felt my heart throb at the very sound of the word, 'America'. So, I do not understand what secret seduction now draws my heart back toward the east. When I am not consciously thinking of that other country, all my affections converge on France."[9]

He admitted being enthralled by sunsets on the calm sea, declaring at one time that the glowing sky "recalled Chateaubriand's most beautiful descriptions,"[10] It is striking how profound an influence France's greatest romantic, who wrote exotic accounts of American Indians and poetic appeals of Catholicism's glory, had on Nicolas Point. One is also struck by the number of sunrises and sunsets over the American landscape he painted and in the last of the "Assorted Anecdotes," which end his sketches in this book, he attempted to paint in words, in imitation of Chateaubriand, scenes he so frequently depicted on canvass. As the *John Arrow* brought him closer to the American shore, he also witnessed for the first time an atmospheric optical phenomenon appearing as luminous spots beside the rising sun. Sometimes these parhelia are called sun dogs or mock suns. Point commented that French sailors called these rainbow colored balls *"oeils-de-boeuf,"* or "bull's eyes."[11] In his writings about the Rocky Mountains he again spoke of such parhelia, declaring that the Indian medicine men referred to them as *"oeils-de-buc,"* "buck eyes." These, too, became the subject of his paintings.

On December 2, vigil of the feast of St. Francis Xavier, he administered the sacrament of baptism for the first time in his life. One of the German women had given birth the previous day to a daughter, Marie-Philomène, her eleventh child. Point had become particularly close to this family because one of the older boys had almost died on two occasions and each time was nursed back to health by Point. "The ceremony was performed with decency and reverence," he recorded, "but not without discomfort; at the moment of pouring the water we were so tossed about by a storm, that the font, the priest, and all of the assistants were on the verge of being thrown upside down."[12] The storm continued all night, and on the following morning the passengers and crew witnessed a waterspout. Point saw in the phenomenon a spectacle of sheer beauty, a symbol of what had taken place on that same day in 1552 when Xavier's soul arose in a like manner to the Lord. Later in the afternoon two shore birds were spotted: a snipe and a robin, harbingers to the weary travelers that land was not far off.[13] After the third, ennui settled in on the *John Arrow.* For a long time provisions had been rationed, but just before December 8, the captain announced he was no longer able to feed the German emigrants. The Jesuits protested and vowed that they too would fast. On the ninth the captain did relent and issued everyone a small amount of bread, which kept the children, who received their share, from crying.[14] On the twelfth, a brig, which had been at sea for eighty-two days, was sighted and within moments so also was land. The crew and passengers on the brig, another American ship from New York, were starving and begged for food. The captain spontaneously shared the little that was left in the stores of the *John Arrow.* Point was convinced that God blessed this act of American generosity by sending a favorable tide the next day, which brought them all to the safety of New York's harbor. They arrived on December 14, 1835, a day within the Octave of the Immaculate Conception, a coincidence Point regarded as being most significant.[15]

Because there was no house of the society in New York, the four Jesuits remained there but two days, long enough, however, to record a number of impressions. "What is most striking for the European," he noted, "is the scant number of houses of prayer, always closed; the large number of houses of insurance, always opened; the extraordinary frequency of fires, always flagrant; I slept only two nights in New York and I don't know how many times I was awakened by cries: 'To fire, to fire'."[16] On the morning of the seventeenth the four men boarded a steamboat bound for Philadelphia with the intention of eventually making their way to Georgetown, the largest Jesuit house in the United States, but two-thirds of the way there they boarded a train which took them "and about two hundred other travelers at a rate of ten miles an hour all the way to Philadelphia." Here they immediately went to St. Joseph's Church on Willing's Alley with the idea of spending the day there before traveling on to Baltimore, but the journey was impossible by sea, because of the ice, and impractical by land because of the price of tickets: for the four of them it would have cost about $75.00.[17]

Fortunately, because of William Murphy's Irish connections, all the doors in Philadelphia were opened to them.[18] Bishop Henry Conwell (1745–1842) whose family occupied the greater part of the parish residence, was nearly ninety and blind, and "was occupied with no other thoughts than his own eternity." He had turned all affairs of the diocese over to his coadjutor, Bishop Francis Patrick Kenrick (1796–1863), another Irishman with connections to the Murphy family. Kenrick made sure that there were two comfortable rooms put at the disposal of Point and Murphy and the brothers were lodged with an Irish family in town. Here they settled in to spend Christmas. It was then that another Jesuit visitor made his appearance at Willing's Alley and was lodged with the overburdened Irish family.[19] This was Charles Van Quickenborne (b. Peteghem, Oost-Vlanderen, Belgium, January 21, 1788; d. Portage des Sioux, Missouri, August 17, 1837), the famous founder of the Missouri Mission who came from St. Louis in search of generous benefactors on the East Coast for his latest project: a plan for creating reductions among the North American Indians in general and in particular for the Osage and the Kickapoo.[20] Despite the fact that his venture had received support from both Father General Roothaan and President Andrew Jackson, his fund-raising efforts were not successful.[21] But he and his plan made an unforgettable impression on Nicolas Point. Van Quickenborne was a severe, parsimonious man who had the reputation for being laconic and brusque, hard on himself and on others, but he was also a man of great humility, vision, and total dedication to the Indians. The fact that he spent long hours speaking with Point indicates he found a kindred soul in the newly arrived Frenchman. Point considered his meeting with this Old Testament-like prophet as providential and "all that he heard from the mouth of this Father, about the needs, the desires, and the attitudes of the American Indians electrified his imagination and filled his heart with joy."[22]

At the very moment when Van Quickenborne was causing such transports of joy in the heart of his impressionable auditor, an event was taking place in St. Louis which would also profoundly influence Point's future and challenge Van Quickenborne's plans for the Kickapoo reduction. An Iroquois Indian named Ignace Partui, also known as Old Ignace, arrived in St. Louis with two of his sons, Charles and Francis, boys between twelve and fourteen. He was sent as a delegate from the Flathead tribe beyond the Rockies, soliciting Jesuits, the Black Robes, to work among his adopted people. This same Ignace had left his own tribe with a band of twenty-four other Iroquois between 1812 and 1820 in search of better land beyond the Mississippi Valley. These Indians, whose ancestors had been Christianized by St. Isaac Jogues in the seventeenth century, were kindly received by the Flatheads with whom they intermarried and to whom they introduced the prayers and teachings of the Catholic Church. Learning that Jesuits were in St. Louis, Ignace changed his original plans of seeking them out in Canada, the place of his birth. The delegation arrived in St. Louis late in the fall and Ignace asked the fathers to supply the solemn rites of baptism to his two sons. These were performed on the vigil of St. Francis Xavier, the same day Point baptized Marie-Philomène aboard the *John Arrow*.[23] By the end of December, Ignace had finally convinced the Superior of the Missouri mission of the importance of sending Black Robes to the Flatheads.[24] The Superior then wrote Van Quickenborne a letter suggesting the Kickapoo plan be so modified as to include the Flatheads. The unyielding stalwart would not be convinced by the arguments advanced in this letter which he received after he and Point had separated. Old Ignace and the Flatheads would have six more years to wait for the coming of their solicited Black Robes.[25] As for Point, he sat down and wrote three letters after his colloquy with Van Quickenborne. One he gave to the old missionary, the other two he addressed to the General and to his Provincial in Paris, but these he deliberately did not mail until the euphoria of his conversation with Van Quickenborne had passed.[26] He reminded his superiors that his desire to be sent to the North American Indians had been long, consistent, and confirmed by his tertianship experience. It became more pressing and apparent than ever on the night when the rudder aboard the *John Arrow* broke and the ship was spinning in circles. At this hour, when it seemed that death was imminent, he became conscious of an internal conviction that he would indeed spend his life with the Indians. Lately, his conversations with Van Quickenborne, who told him about the possibilities recently placed at the disposal of the Jesuits for a successful breakthrough with the Indians, and who invited him to be his associate in this enterprise, convinced him he should again offer his life for this apostolate: "According to the permission that you have already given to me regarding it," he pleaded with the General, "and assuming that my expressed desires are yet the same . . . I again ask Your Paternity to be sent among the poor Indians."[27] Eventually he received a favorable response, but not before six adventure-filled years had passed. Meanwhile, Point existed for the missions; the missions did not exist for Point.

The foursome left Philadelphia on the morning of the twenty-ninth, bound by rail for Columbia on the Susquehanna. With a certain amount of anticipation they disembarked at the halfway point with their fellow travelers to enjoy a sumptuous luncheon to which their railroad ticket entitled them. Both Murphy and Point commented on the event. If the latter confessed amazement on the manner in which the Americans attacked their food, the former seemed more taken by the Americans' fixation for schedules.[28] The four Jesuits joined an English preacher at one table and were enjoying their meal as civilized Europeans when all of a sudden the whistle blew to warn all the passengers to get back on the train. Flabbergasted, the five men of the cloth heard a second whistle and the train began to move. "We had a terrible time trying to make it stop, yelling at the top of our voices and running after it at full speed. Everyone was laughing at our predicament and we made up our minds to laugh along with them and to henceforth eat on the go." Even though he saw the humor in the situation, Murphy also observed that almost all the Americans suffered from digestion problems, "or from 'dyspepsia' as they call it."[29]

At Columbia they were in for another disappointment. The cold weather that had kept them so long in Philadelphia had frozen the canals and therefore they had to make the next part of the journey to Pittsburgh in four different stage coaches.[30] As he did on all of his expeditions, Point noted carefully and fondly the various types of birds and flowers he saw on the way. He had a remarkable appreciation for nature and was, as his letters published in this book show, visibly moved when man needlessly destroyed it. He was particularly impressed by the beauty of the Juniata River as it flowed down from the Alleghenies; at this point they were moving "into rattlesnake country but the rigor of the winter made dormant their striking power."[31] But not all was pleasant: "We had for a travelling companion in the distinctly unpleasant stagecoach a Presbyterian minister with a stentorian voice who had gone out to Kentucky to halt the progress of papism and to substitute Protestant women for the local [Catholic] teachers."[32] In a most insensitive way the minister kept criticizing the Church's policy on clerical celibacy, preventing, it may be supposed, Point's contemplation of the local fauna and flora. But if his comments on the minister were ironic they were also surprisingly tolerant, given his own background and the attitude of so many of his French confreres, and given the fact that the nine-passenger stage, which was without springs, jolted painfully over the rough road, which must have rendered the occupants less agreeable to discussing theological differences than might have been the case in a more commodious and comfortable setting.[33]

The stage rolled into Pittsburgh, a bustling town, "as noisy as Cyclops' cave," on the first of January "early enough to hear mass if you subscribe to the opinion of those who maintain that getting there before the offertory is sufficient."[34] The pastor at St. Stephens was another Irishman, well acquainted with the Murphy family, who did everything possible to show the Jesuits hospitality, but his pleading was in vain. Point had earlier observed that from New York to Louisville Murphy met Irishmen who tried to entertain him and show him marks of hospitality, "but he consistantly refused their invitations," and in every instance "showing himself worthy of the esteem superiors had placed in him," gave them all a wide berth.[35] On this instance he led the three Frenchmen down to the river where they selected a steamer for the next part of their journey, but later on Murphy confessed there was something about the boat he did not like, and so they changed their plans, disembarked, and still shunning the hospitality of "externs," that is non-Jesuits, they stayed the night in Pittsburgh. The next morning they congratulated themselves on their decision to tarry when they saw that their chosen steamer had sunk during the night.[36] The fare from Philadelphia to Pittsburgh was $12.50 a piece and now each one was charged about $15.00 to ride the steamer, which they caught the next day, to Louisville. This price included a bed and three big meals each day for the five days it took to reach their destination. They passed through Wheeling and Cincinnati, spending a half day at each town, "because of the fog." Thanks to the various temperance societies the only wine that was available was terribly expensive and fortified with alcohol. Murphy left it up to his superior to determine which of the two evils was to be the more lamented: the absence of good wine or the presence of bad wine. Then he woefully concluded the Jesuits had to be satisfied with tea or coffee with their meals.[37] They finally arrived at Louisville on January 6, the feast of the Epiphany, with a tremendous appetite for the traditional *gâteau des Rois,* but as Point recorded, they were forced by the place and circumstances to exercise self-restraint because, although Louisville may have had much to offer, it was not in the line of such festive *gâteaux.* Murphy, who confessed that he felt more French than anything else and that he had difficulty understanding American English, made an observation about the citizens of Louisville: he thought they spoke a peculiar mélange of English and French, a dialect that would one day become known as "American."[38] Point reported that the first priest in Louisville that the foursome met was Father Stephen Badin (1768–1853), the first priest ordained in the United States. That ceremony took place in 1793 and was officiated by Bishop John Carroll (1735–1815). Badin and another priest, an old friend of Murphy's while the two were together at Billom, advised the Jesuits not to hire a stage to take them to St. Mary's because the price, $62.00, was exorbitant, but to wait for "a kind of diligence" that would come within the week and could take them as far as Bardstown, and perhaps, for a price, even beyond.[39] At last "this stage brought us and our baggage, through wood, swamps, ice-clogged streams for $4.00. Never in my life have I seen such a horrible road, but "we arrived at St. Mary's on January 12, 1836, *more honestorum sacerdotum,* with coats, frock-coats, hats—all of which caused amazement."[40]

The same events that caused Nicolas Point to spend St. Ignatius Day, 1830, in an Amiens wheat field are responsible for the establishment of the Jesuit Mission in Kentucky. Matters had settled down pretty much in Paris by the following August 22, as Point was fleeing incognito toward the Swiss border, when Julien Druilhet wrote a letter from his place of hiding to Father Jean-Pierre Gury (Father Jean-Baptiste's nephew) in Rome advising him that "I have no news at all from Bordeaux and Le Passage. I sent good Father Petit there [on the nineteenth] to see how things are going and to keep me informed."[41] This was not the first time Nicolas Petit (b. Saint-Michel-du-Fond-des-Nègres, Haiti, July 8, 1789; d. Troy, New York, February 1, 1855) was sent on a delicate mission during troubled times. When Charles X issued the Ordinances of 1828, he and Pierre Ladavière (b. La Chapelle-de-Condrieu, Rhône, September 23, 1777; d. Spring Hill, Alabama, February 1, 1858) were dispatched on a special mission to the Channel Island of Jersey to determine if it was feasible to set up a *collège-en-exile* in British territory. They reported that Jersey was indeed an excellent location, but Roothaan vetoed the plan because its execution would prove embarrassing at the time to the British government. So, the Jersey residence and house of formation recommended by Petit and Ladavière, which was destined to be established and to flourish, would have to wait until a more fortuitous date for its beginning. In 1828 these two Jesuits were chosen for this mission because each was fluent in English. Petit had been reared in Baltimore and Ladavière had been a professor of Greek at Georgetown College before he entered the society in France in 1814.[42]

What Petit found in Bordeaux in late August 1830 was not encouraging, at least it did not appear so at the time. Point's former co-novice, Pierre Chazelle, who until the July Days was the superior of the flourishing Jesuit apostolate in that city, was still hiding in the general area, although most of the other Jesuits had fled across the Spanish border, usually to Le Passage, where some of them eventually made their way back to France, to Toulouse, where they finally established a residence that was to develop into a most important Jesuit center.[43] Meanwhile, Petit reported that Chazelle was expendable, a fact which allowed Druilhet to consider the request, made in 1829, to his predecessor Nicolas Godinot by Benedict Joseph Flaget, S.S. (1763–1850), Bishop of Bardstown, Kentucky.[44] The Bishop was alumnus of the College of Billom, the first Jesuit *collège* founded in France before the Suppression, which had been taken away from the society the year of Flaget's birth. The singular renown of Billom and the memories its very name conjured up had inspired Nicolas Godinot to reestablish a *petit séminaire* within the ancient walls of this inconspicuous town near Claremont, and in 1825 he appointed Father Julien Druilhet its first rector and sent Thomas Legoüais and William Murphy as teachers to the new Billom.[45] The anonymous author of *Notice sur le R.P. Chazelle* reported that as early as 1827 or 1828:

> Mr. [Robert] Abel [Abell], a priest from Kentucky, came to Billom in Auvergne, and offered Reverend Father Godinot, in the name of the Bishop [Flaget] . . . the College of Bardstown. It was not accepted. Probably the refusal was not absolute, and, without commiting himself one way or the other, it was understood that negotiations could be renewed at a later date providing circumstances made the project favorable. In 1830, after the July Revolution, Reverend Father Druilhet (the former Socius to Reverend Father Godinot), having a number of available priests, recalled Bishop Flaget's offer. It is probable that he wrote to the prelate . . .

At any rate, Druilhet appointed Paul Luiset superior of the inchoate community at Bordeaux and ordered Pierre Chazelle and Nicolas Petit to accept Bishop Flaget's invitation and to set off for Kentucky.[46] They were to take with them Philippe Corne (b. François, Doubs, August 18, 1800); d. Baton Rouge, Louisiana, October 28, 1862), a coadjutor brother from Le Passage, and Father Pierre Ladavière, another casualty of the Revolution who had been hiding out in Marseille.[47] The four sailed from Pauillac, near Bordeaux, November 19, 1830, thanks in part from funds received from the Society of the Propagation of the Faith, and arrived at Guadeloupe on January 5, 1831. Chazelle immediately went to the prisons where condemned slaves were awaiting execution. He ministered to these and taught catechism to small children while Petit preached to large crowds in a number of places on the island. The Jesuits finally left Guadeloupe and arrived in New Orleans on February 7. The first thing they did here was present themselves to the new bishop, Belgian-born Leo Raymond De Neckere, C.M. (1800–1833), who received them warmly, and insisted they preach in his parishes and work in the city's hospitals until

Chazelle receive an answer to the letter he dispatched to Bishop Flaget announcing the arrival of the Jesuits he had requested to take charge of his seminary.[48] At this same date Druilhet wrote to Roothaan from Lyon, which city he had judged a safer place than Paris and closer to his subjects dispersed in Savoy, Switzerland, and Spain: "Spirits seem high everywhere. We are happy to have something to suffer for our Lord. It seems to me that the spirit of faith grows and becomes stronger each day in the few [fifty-six] workers we have kept with us in France."[49]

Spirits were also high in New Orleans but not necessarily so in Bardstown. Here, during the past two years, St. Joseph's Seminary had been reorganized, was prospering, and was even drawing boys and young men from as far away as New Orleans and Mobile. Consequently, Chazelle's letter "fell as a thunderbolt on His Lordship, as well as on the priests of his diocese."[50] To say that Flaget was now on the spot would be understating the problem. As a school administrator he knew well the penchant professors have for fluttering and sputtering over matters easily handled beyond the groves of Academe. He could not now, of course, turn over St. Joseph's to the Jesuits, but at the same time his poor diocese could certainly use three more priests and a brother. Like many prelates before and since, Flaget implemented the three step approach: compromise, dialogue, prayer. After reassuring the St. Joseph faculty that he had no intention of setting up a new Billom in Bardstown, he wrote Chazelle a letter in which he was vague about the transference of St. Joseph's to the society, mentioning in passing that there were some minor difficulties to overcome, and then inviting him to travel north after the thaw, which made river traveling hazardous, was ended. Chazelle's reaction to the bishop's letter was also cautious: he ordered Ladavière and Corne to remain in New Orleans, while he and Petit left for Bardstown on April 23. When they arrived there on May 14, Flaget gave them a most cordial reception and invited them to live at St. Joseph's. As the weeks passed, Chazelle became less and less impressed by Kentucky, whereas the two Jesuits in Louisiana had all but convinced him that the opportunities for building a *collège* in that state were unlimited. Such was the situation when, toward the end of July, the bishop invited the two Jesuits to join him in making a novena to St. Ignatius of Loyola begging that, through the intercession of the founder of the Society of Jesus, a solution would be found. Before the three had completed their nine-day prayer the Gordian Knot was cut in a manner that made even skeptics wonder if the days of miracles had passed.[51]

Alexander the Great in this instance was a priest of the Bardstown diocese named William Byrne (1780–1833), "an ascetic who seldom smiled and never laughed."[52] This laconic, raw-boned man had been scarred by the violence of the Irish Rebellion of 1789 and by its bloody aftermath, and although he had an ardent desire for an education, he brought very little formal schooling with him when he arrived in the United States from his native Ireland in 1805. Eventually he managed to enroll at Georgetown, entered the society, left, and enrolled at Mount St. Mary's College at Emmittsburg, Maryland, and then transferred to St. Mary's, Baltimore. He was ordained subdeacon in December 1818 and in the following May bolted "without consideration and against the will of his superior," and traveled to Pittsburgh where he had arranged to meet Bishop Flaget. He confided to the bishop that he wanted to work in Kentucky, and Flaget accepted him, declaring at a later date that there was no better priest in his diocese.[53] If Byrne's early life handicapped him in some respects, it also made him appreciate the value of an education, and it left him with a sense of independence and perseverence under adversities. In 1820 he was assigned to take the place of Father Charles Nerinckx (1761–1824), the so-called "Apostle of Kentucky," at St. Charles Church in Marion County, some twenty miles southeast of Bardstown.[54] Six years earlier Nerinckx had founded in this parish the Sisters of Loretto, the first American established congregation of religious women, and in 1820 he was making preparations to return to his native Belgium to solicit funds for Kentucky and to recruit priests and seminarians for North America. Shortly before he left, he purchased a nearby farm, which he named "Mount Mary." It was his intention to found a boys' school for useful trades on this property, but during his absence William Byrne, his substitute, modified these plans.[55] In the spring of 1821, Father Byrne opened his new school, now re-christened St. Mary's Seminary, and in an old stone distillery on the property, he began classes for boys and young men who wanted a liberal education. When the pastor returned he found his Mount Mary very different indeed from what he had planned and "though thwarted in what he proposed to do . . . he took the disappointment with his characteristic meekness and humility."[56] The seminary became popular throughout Kentucky because of the strict discipline and the moral and academic excellence demanded by Father Byrne. A former St. Mary's student and later Archbishop of Baltimore, Martin J. Spalding (1810–1872) emphasized that this distillery school was "founded by *one man*."[57] Byrne supervised the teaching of "all branches of knowledge, except philosophy and theology" in the same place "where students learning the alphabet sat side by side with those taking Latin, Greek, and even integral calculus."[58] Himself a man of limited education, he did manage to attract and retain some good teachers and he regularly employed some of the brighter students, like Martin J. Spalding, whom he hired as his assistants.[59]

Besides being an entrepreneur Byrne was also a realist who did not let personal prejudices get in the way of making decisions regarding the future of his school, which in July 1831, included a solidly built brick building and a number of smaller structures on a 310 acre farm. The old stillhouse had probably disappeared in one of the two fires which had destroyed the main building that the eager priest had built and rebuilt, but by 1831 at least 1,200 boys and young men had already passed through St. Mary's Seminary. However, the hard work and strain had left their toll on the founder, and Byrne came to the conclusion that he could no longer manage St. Mary's. Besides, he had convinced himself there were other challenges within the scope of his competence. Consequently, he ceded St. Mary's Seminary to the bishop, requesting that he be allowed to retain the use of his saddle horse and that he be given permission to begin another school near present-day Paducah. The bishop in turn gave the school to the care of Chazelle, whose powers of persuasion at that date were in indirect ratio to his command of English. Given Byrne's personality it is surprising that he let Chazelle convince him that he should remain on as president for a year more; that is, until the French Jesuits could pass for bona fide citizens of the Bluegrass State. Perhaps Paducha's proximity to St. Mary's would have hurt the seminary or perhaps he simply succumbed to Chazelle, a man of singular charm whom a contemporary described as one who

> is admired and loved by all those who have the good fortune to know him. He combines great talents with the most edifying piety and the most attractive manner. I do not doubt that God has destined him for grand things.[60]

Whatever his reasons, Byrne's services to the Jesuits were incalculable, and at the end of the year Chazelle was able to persuade him to hold onto his presidency for another twelve months. Meanwhile, a modified plan based on the Fribourg curriculum superceded Byrne's model in which "Rhetoric properly so termed" was given a place of prominence. Spanish and Hebrew were also offered, as was bookkeeping, the one concession made to the new world.[61]

During the next few years, the school expanded and the number of Jesuits grew. While Chazelle was at St. Joseph's, Bardstown, during the summer of 1831, he gave the Spiritual Exercises to two French diocesan priests who subsequently applied and were accepted into the society by their former retreat director. The first of these was Simon Fouché (b. Paris, May 9, 1789; d. Fordham, New York, June 29, 1870), whose family had been involved in a cloak-and-dagger visitation with Marie Antoinette as she awaited her death in the Concièrgerie.[62] He had assumed the presidency of St. Joseph's when his colleague, Evremond Harissart (b. Paris, May 15, 1792; d. Paris, April 13, 1859), resigned from that position.[63] Harissart began his novitiate at St. Mary's on December 2, 1831, but he had journeyed to White Marsh, Maryland, to make a proper novitiate under the direction of the French-born master of novices sometime before September 11, 1832, the day Fouché was at last able to begin his novitiate.[64] In the meanwhile, on the previous July 7, Roothaan gave Chazelle authorization to accept novices at St. Mary's and to take over the direction of St. Mary's Seminary.[65] Harissart returned at an unknown date to complete his novitate.[66] The arrival of three new additions on the following December 22 demonstrated how committed the French Province was to its first educational institution in North America.[67] The first of these newcomers was Thomas Legoüais, Point's fellow novice at Montrouge in 1822 and William Murphy's companion at Billom in 1825, who was to be the spiritual father to the community and *Socius* to the master of novices for Harissart, Fouché, and two local men who showed short-lived interest in becoming coadjutor brothers.[68] The second was Guy Gilles, Point's spiritual father at Fribourg who subsequently became president of the ill-fated Jesuit *collège* in Baton Rouge in 1855.[69] Finally, there was Eugene Maguire (b. Slane, Meath, Ireland, June 22, 1800; d. Lebanon, Kentucky, June 11, 1833) who had entered Montrouge in 1825 as a priest after completing his seminary studies in Bordeaux. Afterwards he taught physics in Rome, and, even though a member of the French province, was assigned to a number of Italian-speaking houses in the Kingdom of Sardinia.[70] Their arrival brought the number of Jesuits up to nine and to celebrate this great event Chazelle dispensed momentarily with the strict house rule that Jesuits at St. Mary's were to use only one language, English, in reading at table and in conversing with one another.[71] Then everything went back to normal: "A day or two was allotted to repose after the fatigues of the journey from New Orleans and then the five co-laborers entered on the regular life of the society with all the punctuality and exactness observed in the oldest houses in Europe."[72] Translated, this meant for one thing the hour of rising went back to 4:00 A.M.![73]

In May 1833 Chazelle recalled Corne and Ladavière

from Louisiana. The latter remained in Kentucky only a few weeks and then returned to New Orleans;[74] the former joined the St. Mary's community where he did everything that was to be done, including taking care of the school choir and teaching boys from Kentucky, Ohio, Louisiana and Alabama, most of whom were Protestant, the songs and hymns sung at Saint-Acheul, Fribourg, and Le Passage.[75] In the spring Byrne made a trip to Nashville, Tennessee, where he found conditions ideal to set up a new pioneer school, and so he abandoned plans to follow through on the Paducha site and returned to St. Mary's to collect his ten dollars and his saddle horse. These provisions were enough to take him back to Nashville and begin a new St. Mary's Seminary.[76] But in June the cholera epidemic, which had ravished so much of the United States, reached Lebanon and claimed Father William Byrne. Six days later, June 11, the very talented thirty-two year old Eugene Maguire died. Like Byrne he too had been attending the sick and became infected. The students fled in panic and the school remained closed until the fall, and when it did open Pierre Chazelle was the president as well as the Superior of the Jesuit community.[77] On December 30 another fire, the bane of St. Mary's, destroyed the dormitory. Plans were immediately made to rebuild.[78] On July 26, 1834, St. Mary's celebrated its first Annual Commencement Day exercises which culminated in the performance of a play Chazelle wrote for the occasion entitled, "Redhawk," which was "designated to illustrate the ancient customs of the Indians and the labors of the early American settlers: all turning to the praise of Christianity."[79] Six months later; that is, when Point and his companions made their appearance, dressed as dignified, properly attired members of the cloth, St. Mary's was making slow but steady progress.

One wonders how it was done. In January 1836 there were not yet one hundred boarders whose tuition, board, room, and laundry was $32 per annum, most of which was paid in produce rather than in hard cash.[80] Each student, no matter what his age or background, was obliged, except in case of ill-health, to work one day a week on the *collège*'s farm, where all of the grain and corn for both human and animal consumption was grown. Teams of boys were organized to gather, chop, and saw wood; to plant and harvest crops; and to feed, slaughter, and dress animals.[81] Chazelle had almost doubled the farm's original acreage and had a treadmill built for grinding meal and flour, which the farmers in the area were able to use.[82] During Point's time Chazelle also put up another large brick building, but it was long after Father Nicolas had left that the Jesuits had a separate residence.[83] When Point and his three companions arrived on January 12, 1836, they were immediately put to work. Brother Ledoré took over the kitchen from Brother Corne, allowing him to spend more time on the farm, and Brother Jary was put in charge of the laundry and clothes room. William Murphy was responsible for teaching grammar, rhetoric, and literature, and Point's first job was to learn English and in his free time he was to act as prefect of studies or principal. Like the other six priests in the community Murphy was expected to "take calls" on week-ends, that is go about the diocese dispensing the sacraments and preaching. Apparently this was a chore from which Point was exempt until his English improved.[84]

Point remained one year at St. Mary's, and even though he has left some fine sketches of the *collège* buildings, he recorded almost nothing of what he did there. As principal, he presumably had a hand in the production of Chazelle's second patriotic play, "Benedict Arnold the Traitor," staged to the satisfaction and admiration of the sizeable audience that attended the Second Annual Commencement Exercises in July 1835. This extravaganza was enacted in an outdoor amphitheatre surrounded by gigantic oaks. One enormous branch overspreading the stage was utilized for the realistic hanging of Major John André (1751–1780), English soldier and spy, a fitting lesson to all on the fate of traitors.[85]

Even though he did not expound on his activities in the school, Point did record many impressions of Kentucky and its citizens. His notebook contains a verbal painting of the state's magnificent forests and he goes at length to describe how the leaves change colors during the fall.[86] The number of children in Kentucky families also impressed him, and he described how the work on the farms was allotted to different members of the family. He was amused by the fact that Kentuckians named their houses after important cities—"Paris, Versailles, Alexandria, Carthage," and after famous men, such as "Jacqueson." But he regretted that one of the Protestant ministers in Bardstown had tried to warn the people about the Jesuits by having sections of the *Monita Secreta* printed and distributed.[87]

On one occasion, probably not long after he arrived at St. Mary's, he paid a visit to a Kentucky family some of whose habits he found curious, others astonishing. For example, he was impressed by the fact that if one wanted to visit a family at home, he first had to be introduced to one of the members of the family by a mutual friend, and once proper introductions were made "the person gives you a handshake as a sign of friendship. The closer the friendship the tighter the hands are clasped." After this ritual one was no longer a stranger and could therefore present himself at the family home.[88] There were other customs quite different from those of France. For example when visiting, people liked to gather around the fireplace and

> while carrying on a conversation, Kentuckians smoke pipes, spit into the fire, and cross their legs, usually taking the most comfortable position they can. Some join their hands behind their heads or straddle a chair and then stretch out their legs; others plant themselves right in front of the fireplace with their backs toward the fire and their legs spread out like the Colossus of Rhodes. Still others, whenever they can, prop up their feet onto the mantlepiece and look at themselves in the glossy surface of their boots. Even at the table of the most well-bred there is no napkin, no soup, no desert; there is a two pronged fork and a knife with a huge blade that substitutes for a spoon. The same plate is used for every course; the most diverse foods are put on the same plate! While their mouths are busy eating—that is to say during the whole meal—their tongues stay silent and their eyes rove. One has to be able to grab flying platters in the wink of an

> eye in order to catch the main servings, and also he either has to have an American stomach or resign himself later on with a bout of indigestion. We Europeans thought we could eat at our host's table as we do at home, presenting platters of food to those sitting next to us, and carrying on polite talk during the course of the meal. But if we did that here, do you know what would happen? We would not even have reached the time for our dessert when the train of wagons would have departed, leaving us behind to carry on politely at table . . .[89]

The American practice of shaking hands and all of the nuances surrounding this ritual seemed to intrigue him. "When they meet by chance," he observed, "they do not talk, but whenever a person encounters or takes leave from another, he offers the handshake." And later:

> This shaking hands is done by both sexes, irrespective of age or social condition. They do not even make exception for bishops or Negroes; however a Negro never sits at table with a white. Should a Negro strike a white the punishment is death, and sometimes they do not always wait for the trial to carry out the execution.[90]

In addition to these general customs, Catholics had some idiosyncracies of their own that he considered worthwhile reporting. "I have seen Catholics," he wrote, "at least those who were the more devout, genuflect whenever they met a priest. Both men and women do this. The women, even the ladies among them, are ignorant of what we call a 'curtsy'." Women also manifested an informality that, in his mind, seemed to place these acts of exaggerated deference in a confusing perspective. For example, "sometimes after mass these women would come into the sacristy to light up their pipes." Black women took "gross turkey wings" and "spread them fan-like, and then stuck then on their hats." Both men and women came to Sunday mass mounted on the very finest horses, a practice which did not please "the poor missionaries," but he was realistic enough to realize that any exhortation on his part would not change this custom, for in the United States "luxury is all-pervasive."[91] Nicolas

Point would soon learn that a good mount in the United States was a necessity and did not symbolize wealth, as it did in France, nor was traveling by horse always a luxury. Since there were so few wagon roads around Lebanon in 1836 all of the Jesuits were obliged to learn to ride. Petit found his small size and pottle belly an encumbrance, but these impediments of nature did not prevent him from all but living in the saddle. It is amazing how much territory he covered preaching throughout the Ohio Valley in his deep, sonorous voice. Legoüais was less successful. He was so small he could not mount a horse unaided and when he fell off, which was often, he had to walk around leading his horse by the bridle until he found a farmer who could hoist him up again on the saddle.[92] Before he left the Northwest, Point would have many anecdotes that centered on his own ambiguous relationship with horses.

After pronouncing the final vows of the Spiritual Coadjutor before Chazelle on August 15, 1836, Father Nicolas was given a short vacation so that he could visit some of the places of interest in what is today Nelson, Washington, and Marion counties.[93] Although he does not say so explicitly, Pierre implies it was a well-deserved and much appreciated break. Nicolas wrote that he was much impressed by Bardstown, and particularly with Flaget's new cathedral and with the pieces of art donated by the Pope and by the kings of France and the Two Sicilies. But what more impressed him was Flaget's original cathedral, a twenty foot long and twelve foot wide cabin. He wrote his impression to Pierre:

> I cannot tell you what I experienced as I pressed my lips with veneration on the dusty walls of this structure, so small, so simple, so poor, so perfectly like the place where our Savior was born, and this was sentiment I have never felt in our own majestic basilica [cathedral of Reims].[94]

He visited a number of the religious houses in the neighborhood and gave a detailed, pious account of his visit with the Sisters of Loretto and his pilgrimage to the graves of the Trappist monks at Holy Cross. He had already met Father Stephen Badin when he first arrived in Louisville and was disappointed to have missed him on this excursion; however, he used the example of Badin's impressive apostolate to conclude that Kentucky "is a religious conquest inherently French."[95]

One year to the day of his arrival in the United States, December 14, 1836, Nicolas Point received the order to quit Kentucky and make his way to Louisiana to begin a new *collège* at Iberville.[96] Chazelle was not overjoyed by the appointment. Although he approved of the Iberville venture, he doubted Point was the man to head the project. On the previous December 8, he informed Roothaan that Point had been taking calls outside St. Mary's but his English was poor, and then he sounded the fatal Point motive: the man put an inordinate importance on small matters and his sensitivity was of such a nature that he easily became ill-humored.[97] Three days later, Chazelle wrote again to the General. This time it was not only to complain about Point's ignorance of spoken English, but of the fact that he did not see the need to learn it. "The superior at Iberville should know English, which is becoming a universal language, even in Louisiana," and he recommended the General send back Ladavière, who was then in France, to take over the responsibility of Iberville.[98] In later letters in which he complained that there was nobody in the St. Mary's community who had the qualities of a good superior, (a common complaint of men who have consistently held positions of authority,) Chazelle informed the General that Point had been the cause of an abortive riot at St. Mary's.[99] Kentucky boys liked their moonshine, and if the pristine distillery on campus was long since *hors de combat* there were many others in the neighborhood that supplied and oversupplied the student body. The simple fact was that St. Mary's presented problems that did not seem to exist in European *collèges-en-exile,* and the French-speaking principal was not used to them. His handling of this situation left much to be desired and was one more indication that he should not be superior of Iberville. In fairness to Point, however, it should be noted that the year after he left

St. Mary's one of the students threatened Chazelle with a pistol and on December 30, 1833, two students, miffed because they thought they had been unjustly punished, set the fire referred to above that reduced the dormitory to a heap of ashes.[100] But the young men had redeeming qualities as well. Point was silent on the matter, but in his sketch of St. Mary's he depicts the boys involved in what appears to be organized games.[101] Moreover, just as at Saint-Acheul, Fribourg, and Le Passage, they had the custom of making a visit to the Blessed Sacrament after breakfast; they celebrated Mary's month with enthusiastic devotion, and they took seriously the obligations imposed on them by the various sodalities. All of these activities came under the supervision of the principal. These and other essential elements of *éducation* the students took with them when St. Mary's moved from its humble beginnings, the Kentucky stillhouse, to the glorious towers of Fordham University.[102]

Chazelle's two letters to the General were months away from their destination when, on December 17, Nicolas Point and his two companions, Nicolas Petit and a Negro servant, set off for St. Charles's Church at Harden's Creek, where Point wanted to begin this important undertaking by making a pilgrimage to the grave of Father Charles Nerinckx to whom he had recently developed a special devotion.[103] After praying at this shrine, the three pilgrims rode seven miles to St. Stephen's where Nerinckx's Sisters of Loretto had been housed since 1826.[104] Then, the next morning after mass they plunged into the dark forest which separated them from Bardstown, and promptly got lost. After wandering aimlessly for a day and a night, they came tired, cold, and hungry to Beech Fork, a fast moving mountain stream of deceptive depth that flows a few miles south of Bardstown. Although a Breton hermit whom he had met in August had warned him then that this torrent could be dangerous,[105] still the water had to be crossed. They were not able to find a ford, so they risked swimming their gear-ridden horses through the ice-clogged waters. It was a mistake. Point led the way and recalled later that his horse was particularly skittish; he withheld judgment about the rider. The horse took four steps into the frigid waters and reared; the saddle strap broke and the rider was pitched into the deep torrent. As he was swept down the stream, he grasped for branches of rotting trees along the precipitous banks, but they broke and he was carried farther and faster down the icy, black waters. At last he was able to get his footing and rejoin his companions, albeit much worse for the wear. Evidently they had found a ford.

Point was forced to continue the journey draped in a green sheet and wearing a silk bonnet on his head. Just why these items were among his provisions he does not say, but a reader of Chateaubriand can perhaps appreciate the richness of symbolism in the adventures that brought the first superior of the Louisiana Jesuits out from an ominous forest and a freezing bath ever closer to his destination. Was he thinking of the past—of ice on the Meuse giving way under the weight of a young boy—or did he have a premonition of the future when he summed up these exploits in the following manner: "Whenever there is a mess I am in the middle of it"?[106]

The next day the threesome got in a broken-down stage from Bardstown to Louisville. "We were half way there," he wrote, "when one of the kingbolts snapped, and before we got to Louisville the springs had given out. We made out the best we could under the circumstances, but after the second mishap I had to lug my own gear."[107] On the twenty-first he bade farewell to his companions and booked passage on a steamboat, which took him down the Ohio to the Mississippi.[108] Of course he kept a journal of the events of each day: the boredom of the trip, the sameness of the scenery, the beauty of the sunsets and moonscapes; how the vegetation along the banks changed after they passed the Arkansas; the disappointment of not being able to offer mass on Christmas day, the dearth of churches on the American landscape and the plethora of banks and insurance offices; the people he met aboard ship—an Irishman, a Presbyterian minister, the crewmen—and the conversations he had with them. He commented on the American custom of celebrating holydays and holidays by having a double portion of whiskey on the night of the vigil and concluded that this too was a strange practice, and he also reflected, as the ship guided down the Mississippi, that this vast, mysterious, beautiful country had once belonged to France, a thought which made him cry out:

> Oh France, what have you done with the domain Providence entrusted to your keeping! What have you done with your divine mission which fell to you to catholicize all of this new world and to save millions of Indians. Your infidelity has all but annihilated them.[109]

He recalled how the magnificence of the Mississippi had enraptured the imagination of Chateaubriand, and at Natchez—the very word conjured up the author of *Le Génie du Christianisme*—he recalled the soil here was sacred, having drunk the blood of Frenchmen.[110] Given the author's provenance, there should be no surprise that he expressed such chauvinistic sentiments, although it would be inexact to describe Point simply as chauvinistic. For him, France was more than a country with a particular flag, language, latitudinal and longitudinal boundaries. He believed that Providence had given France a destiny: France was the transmitter of western civilization, and western civilization was Catholic christianity grafted onto the culture of the Graeco-Latin world. France was an idea, an ideal, a *Weltanschauung*, a mystery. Her roots were inexorably intermingled with, and sometimes indistinguishable from, the Church, from western civilization. Nicolas Point is unintelligible apart from this concept of France's *vocation*. The mystique of democracy, the anonymous forces of capitalism, the collapse of those customs which derive their origin and function from this civilization presented, if not the antithesis to France's role in history, then at least the appeal to those intent on destroying what was Catholic and Western. The dearth of churches and the plethora of banks so characteristic of the American landscape, the custom of wolfing down food without relish or savor, the contempt for a classical education, the mystique of material progress in a society which depended on machines as substitutes for man's industry—all of these were manifestations of the secularization, vulgarization, and dehumanization of a world which had once been impregnated by the Christian culture. Jesuits had brought this culture to the Indians in Paraguay, and it had been destroyed by similarly cynical protagonists, supporters of Mammon. Point always made a distinction between American people, so friendly, fraternal, simple, generous—people for whom he had the greatest admiration and affection—and American society which was intent on destroying what was best in the tradition of Catholic France. History showed that during the eighteenth century France repudiated her vocation; her subsequent humiliation was willed by Providence in order to bring her back to her destiny. It was from the pages of Chateaubriand that, while he was yet an adolescent, he discovered France's vocation. Such discoveries made during adolescence last a lifetime. Other authors, such as Joseph de Maistre (1753–1821) and the Vicomte Louis de Bonald (1754–1840), who were popular among his contemporaries at Fribourg, unquestionably sustained his original insights.

On December 28, the steamboat reached Iberville, some sixty miles upriver from New Orleans, where he planned to visit the property and buildings that the bishop had offered the society for the establishment of a new *collège*. Iberville was not a scheduled stop on the steamer's itinerary, but Point got a few strong deckhands to row him and his trunk to shore. They left him there and speeded back to catch their advancing ship. A black chanced by, "who was not ashamed to make a few cents," by giving him and his trunk a lift to the local parish church. There he settled in as a replacement for the absent local pastor. And from there he spent as much time as he could spare on visits to the prospective location of the *collège* at Iberville.[111]

LOUISIANA
1826–1837

In 1826, the year Point entered Montrouge for the second time, Bishop Louis William Valentine DuBourg (1766–1833) returned from France to his see in New Orleans. He reported to Bishop Rosati (1789–1843), in St. Louis: "I went to Bordeaux to see some Jesuits in regard for our project in Opelousas, which you have already proposed by letter to Father Provincial [Godinot] of Paris. I had written myself to the last-named. He does not see the affair as we do."[1] This "Opelousas project" consisted of a church and house on three hundred arpents of land in St. Landry Parish, Louisiana, where DuBourg wanted the society to build a *collège*. He had already brought the Religious of the Sacred Heart to join the Ursulines in Louisiana to provide for the education of young women in his diocese, but his efforts to establish and maintain schools for boys and young men proved futile, and this setback was one more reason for his resignation that same year. Jean-Pierre Varlet, Monsieur l'Abbé Charlier's good friend and former classmate, was the superior at Bordeaux when DuBourg visited the *collège*.

Exiled from his post two years later, Varlet would flee to Spain with Brother Philippe Corne and others to found the *collège* of Le Passage.[2] By that time DuBourg had been installed in his new see, Besançon, and from there he would continue to plead with the French provincial to send men to Louisiana.[3] We have seen his entreaties were finally answered, in a totally unexpected manner, when Varlet's successor at Bordeaux, Pierre Chazelle, ordered Brother Corne and Father Ladavière to remain in Louisiana, while he and Nicolas Petit set off for Bardstown, Kentucky, in May 1831.

The unexpected arrival of Chazelle and his companions in New Orleans was the event which made Bishop De Neckere all the more determined to implement DuBourg's plan to establish a *collège* in Lower Louisiana, and as long as Bishop Flaget seemed to be enigmatic about future plans for St. Joseph's in Bardstown, Chazelle's policy was to make sure Ladavière and Corne kept a window open in Louisiana in case the door was closed in Kentucky. By the time the St. Mary's windfall came about, Ladavière had made himself indispensable to De Neckere in New Orleans. How was it possible for Chazelle to refuse the pleading request of the prelate who had shown him and his companions such gracious hospitality in the United States? There was no way. Ladavière therefore held on to the assignment the bishop had given him: director of the school and convent of the Religious of the Sacred Heart and rector of the church at St. Michael, or Convent, Louisiana, a small town on the Mississippi, midway between New Orleans and Baton Rouge. From this central position he was able to serve a number of struggling chapels and churches on both sides of the river. He also made trips to Kentucky to confer with Pierre Chazelle. We have already seen that he and Brother Corne were in St. Mary's in May 1833, and that when he made the trip back to Louisiana that summer, he did so alone, for Brother Corne was now a permanent member of the St. Mary's community.[4]

On September 5, 1833, Bishop De Neckere died of yellow fever, leaving Father Anthony Blanc (1792–1860), a priest of the diocese, and Pierre Ladavière co-administrators of the see until a new bishop was appointed.[5] Pierre Ladavière suddenly found himself in a position of greater responsibility, and perhaps it is at this point we should interrupt our narrative to give some background of this remarkable man, whose future ministry was destined to be closely intertwined with the adventures of Nicolas Point. Ladavière exemplifies much of the individuality, single-mindedness and highly venturesome career that characterized so many of the Jesuits who came from France to the United States during the nineteenth century. In 1801, when he was twenty-four and most probably already ordained a priest, he became a member of the famous Paris *congrégation,* or sodality, founded by a Jesuit of the old society, Jean-Baptiste Bordier-Delpuits (1736–1811). A number of members of this *congrégation* distinguished themselves not only in the pursuit of holiness of life, which was the stated purpose of their organization, but also in working for the downfall of Napoleon. When the emperor was finally excommunicated, it was Ladavière who evaded the border troops and spies to smuggle back to France the proscribed Papal Bull of Excommunication, and it was he who delivered it into the hands of Bishop d'Astros. Copies were furtively printed on illegal presses and promulgated throughout the country, thanks chiefly to other members of the *congrégation.* Suspects were rounded up and thrown into prison for complicity, but the chief culprit, Ladavière, eluded the police and managed to escape from France on a ship that was seized by the British. Thinking he was a Bonapartist spy, his captors threw him into an English prison from which he finally managed to get his release in order to book passage on a ship bound for the United States. In 1812 he was teaching at Georgetown; in 1813 he was the pastor of old St. Peter's Church, New York City. The following year he returned to France, from which Napoleon had been momentarily exiled, and here at Lyon, on August 20, 1814, he entered the newly restored society.[6] As we have seen, he and Nicolas Petit were dispatched to the island of Jersey in 1828 to report on the advisability of setting up a house of formation there on British territory.[7]

Two years after Bishop De Neckere's death, in June 1835, Ladavière's co-administrator, Anthony Blanc, was appointed bishop of New Orleans. The new prelate was determined to follow through on DuBourg and De Neckere's plan to establish a Jesuit *collège* in Louisiana. Accordingly, shortly after his appointment, he wrote a letter to Father Provincial Renault in Paris, requesting men for his enterprise. When he received a negative response, he determined to go to France himself to plead his cause, and he brought along with him his former co-administrator, Pierre Ladavière. After receiving less than enthusiastic support for this project in Paris, Blanc determined to go to Rome where he could plead his cause before the General.[8] In the previous December, Roothaan had decided to divide the Province of France from the newly formed Province of Lyon, and as a consequence, when Blanc and Ladavière were received in Rome, details of the division were still being negotiated. The General was won over by Blanc's arguments and instructed the two new provincials, Achille Guidée in Paris and François Renault in Lyon, to supply men and materiel for the Louisiana project; however, "in lasting memory of our predecessors and in accordance with their ancient custom, let this mission, as that of Kentucky, be shown in the catalogue of the Province of France."[9] French superiors felt that a commitment to a new mission was more than they could support at the time, and it was the venerable Father Druilhet, a close friend of Father Roothaan's, a superior who had guided the society in France during her most critical period, who courageously expressed the opinions of the new provincials. After reminding the General that during his tenure of office he had often said no to setting up a *collège* in Louisiana, Druilhet informed the General that, "I see with considerable distress, my Very Reverend Father, that [now] you seem to have gone too fast in this matter of the Louisiana *collège* and that you have acceded *too easily* to the wishes of Bishop Blanc." Druilhet blamed Ladavière for keeping the issue alive when the facts showed there simply were not enough men available to supply a *collège* in Louisiana.[10] The fact that Guidée and

Renault were not as bold in expressing their opinions did not mean they were enthusiastic about becoming involved in Louisiana, but once the decision was made, they pooled their resources and determined to make necessary sacrifices for the new *collège-en-exile*. First of all, there was the question of who would be the superior of the new mission, and secondly there was the matter of how many and who should be sent to Louisiana. The General did not think that Ladavière would make a good superior.[11] "The only one I can see for this year," Renault wrote Roothaan on August 10, 1836, "is [someone] from St. Mary's in Kentucky. I sent Father Nicolas Point there last year; he is a man for men in the *collège*; [although] he prefers the missions, and missions to the Indians . . ."[12] Renault knew Point well and during tertianship he confirmed his vocation to be sent to the missions. But he also knew him as a *serveillant* at Saint-Acheul and respected his talents for educational administration. This quality in Point's personality was appreciated even more by his present provincial, Achille Guidée, because both men had been the assistants of Loriquet at Saint-Acheul in 1825–1826, when Guidée was in charge of *instruction* and Point of *éducation*. Nicolas Point, then, was the man selected to be the first superior of Louisiana, a mission that would one day be joined with Kentucky to form an independent province. At least, this was the plan.[13] The reality suggested something very different. Missouri, which was also interested in expanding into Louisiana, was a vibrant, thriving mission in 1836. A brief sketch of its origins and progress are in order to appreciate Nicolas Point's challenge in Louisiana and to understand the events that transpired there after the French Jesuits established their mission.

When Charles Nerinckx entrusted his parish church and the land he had purchased for building a school to Father William Byrne and left Kentucky for Europe in 1820, he stopped over at Georgetown College, near Washington D.C., just as he had done on his previous trip to Europe five years earlier. During his first stay, in

1815, the superior of the Maryland Mission had asked him to do some recruiting for the struggling American-based Jesuits. Once in Rome Nerinckx himself requested to be accepted into the society, but for some reason was dissuaded. When he returned to the United States in 1817, he brought eight Belgian candidates with him whom he delivered to Father Anthony Kohlmann (1777–1836), the master of novices in Maryland.

During his second stopover at Georgetown in 1820, Kohlmann had become superior of the Maryland Mission and as such requested the visiting Nerinckx to act again as the recruiting sergeant in Europe. Nerinckx's power of persuasion must have been extraordinary because seven of the young Flemings he brought back with him entered the Jesuit novitiate at White Marsh, Maryland, where they settled down to begin a rigorous formation under the direction of their fellow countryman, Charles Van Quickenborne, who later thrilled Nicolas Point by describing his plan for setting up Paraguay-type reductions among the Indians west of the Mississippi. Two of Van Quickenborne's novices of 1821 were to have a profound influence on the life and future of Nicolas Point: Peter Verhaegen (b. Haeght, Brabant, Belgium, June 21, 1800; d. St. Charles, Missouri, July 21, 1868) and Peter De Smet (b. Dendermonde, Oost-Vlaanderen, Belgium, February 28, 1801; d. St. Louis, May 23, 1873). One would think that the Maryland Mission would have been delighted with so many potential laborers for the harvest, but it soon became apparent that Nerinckx suffered from the Midas touch. He had been too successful. These rugged recruits had Netherlandish appetites to match their extraordinary ardor, zeal, and devotion. The Maryland Mission did not have the resources to feed them. It was at this critical point that Bishop DuBourg, the Jesuits' greatest benefactor in the United States, became the *deus ex machina.*[14] The bishop had persuaded the American government to subsidize Catholic missionaries willing to work among the Indians in the hinterlands of his vast diocese. Part of this enterprise consisted of setting up an Indian school in Missouri, a project which Van Quickenborne saw as the prelude to establishing reductions. The bishop asked why could not Van Quickenborne and all his Flemish novices come to Missouri, build an Indian school, and begin an apostolate for the Indians in the Great West. For the superiors in Maryland, struggling under the load of a terrible debt that had precipitated in a financial crisis, there could be no objection; the alternative was to dismiss the novices. For Van Quickenborne and the Flemish novices, DuBourg's solution presented an opportunity to work with the Indians, which after all, was why they had come to the United States in the first place.[15]

Accordingly, in April 1823, Father Charles Van Quickenborne and his associate Father Peter Timmermans (1788–1824) led three coadjutor brothers, seven novices, and six black slaves and their wives from White Marsh to Bishop DuBourg's farm at Florissant.[16] Their exodus is a classic in American Jesuit history. The party traveled on wagons from Baltimore to Wheeling, where Van Quickenborne purchased two large flatboats, "one to carry the missionaries and their baggage, the other, the Negro servants and horses." Thirteen years later Point and his three Louisville-bound companions would follow part of this same Ohio River itinerary in a steamer that supplied beds and three meals a day. But in 1823 Van Quickenborne could not even afford to hire an experienced pilot to guide his two boats which had been tied together, through the shoals, snags, and sawyers and down the circuitous, dangerous course of the Ohio, but he bought a pilot's guide, gave it to one of the brothers, pointed to the helm and told him to steer. The appointed bell ringer indicated the customary times for prayer, recreation, study, silence, reflective reading, rising and retiring. Mass was said each day and "grades" were strictly observed; that is, novices spoke only to novices during those times when speaking was allowed. At Shawneetown they left the Ohio and walked the remaining one hundred-and-fifty miles across southern Illinois to St. Louis where they arrived on May 31, 1823.[17] DuBourg's farm at Florissant was located a further fifteen miles northwest of the city. Here it was on the following feast of St.

Ignatius, July 31, that the formal breaking of the ground took place for, in De Smet's words, "the inauguration of the first novitiate after the suppression of the society in the great Mississippi Valley, which Marquette had dedicated two centuries before to the ever memorable Immaculate Conception of the ever glorious Blessed Virgin Mary, Queen of the Society of Jesus."[18] On this auspicious day for the history of the Missouri Mission, Nicolas Point, having recently been dismissed from the novitiate at Montrouge, was to make his way back to Rocroi and, confused about his future, would settle down there to brood about his past.

The growth of the Missouri Mission, still an integral part of the vice-province of Maryland and under the jurisdiction of its vice-provincial, was slow. In March 1824 Father Joseph Rosati, C.M. was ordained bishop and appointed coadjutor to Bishop DuBourg and set up residence in St. Louis. The following April DuBourg resigned; in March 1827, Rosati was appointed ordinary in St. Louis and administrator of New Orleans until a bishop could be appointed to that see. At last in May 1830, Rosati's vicar general in New Orleans, Leo De Neckere, was ordained bishop, splitting definitively all ties between St. Louis and New Orleans. Meanwhile, as early as February 1828, Van Quickenborne, realizing all his one-time novices were now priests and would be completing their tertianship in July, outlined plans to establish a *collège* in Rosati's new see. New vocations were essential if the Mission was to survive, and a *collège* could be a source of vocations. Garraghan reported: "No response to this petition was to come from Rome."[19] So many requests from the United States had a strident, emergency quality about them, and Roman officials were inclined to let American-based Jesuits solve their own problems. Van Quickenborne repeated his appeal to the vice provincial in Maryland, and the answer he received was that the superior in Missouri might assign his priests "to whatever duties he saw fit."[20] Van Quickenborne placed them in classrooms of the defunct St. Louis College, which had been established in 1818 by the priests of the diocese, but in 1827, because of a dearth of manpower, was forced to close its doors.

At last Rome responded in November 1829. The newly elected General, Jan Roothaan, approved "of the incipient *collège* in St. Louis," where the Jesuits had been teaching for more than a year. Such were the beginnings of St. Louis University, although this was not the first attempt the Jesuits had made at teaching. In 1825 Van Quickenborne had opened the doors at the Florissant seminary to white boys who gave promise of a religious vocation. Also, in May 1824 an Indian school was opened at Florissant, but when after seven years it failed to reach its promise, it was finally closed June 1831, by which date Van Quickenborne had become convinced that a new approach was essential in order to reach the Indians.[21] By that date other events had also taken place that changed the course of the Missouri Mission. In September 1830, Roothaan separated the Missouri Mission with its fifteen Jesuits—nine priests, six brothers—from Maryland, making it an independent mission with its own superior, Father Theodore De Theux (b. Liége, Belgium, January 25, 1789; d. St. Charles, Missouri, February 28, 1846), who superseded Van Quickenborne. This directive was implemented on February 24, 1831. By that date the seminary at Florissant had closed and the few students who had enrolled were registered at the burgeoning St. Louis College.[22] This was three weeks before Nicolas Point was ordained at Sion and three weeks after Pierre Chazelle and his party had arrived in New Orleans.

By 1832, while Point was enthusiastically involved in the "physical, moral, and intellectual development" of the students assigned to him at Fribourg, the number and quality of the St. Louis College students were less than encouraging and the institution which had begun with enthusiasm was floundering.[23] Verhaegen, the president and rector of the *collège*, had explained to Roothaan in January of the previous year that living in Missouri meant that "we live in the youngest place of the United States. . . . All things in the state seem to take on a character of infancy and change, and instability."[24] In the following month he took up this theme again: "If there is any place in the world where fickleness lords it over the souls of the young, it is unquestionably America."[25] And Missouri was the epitomy of America. It was not so much that Verhaegen was pessimistic—many adjectives could justifiably describe this boyant, good natured man, but a pessimist he never was. It was simply that he was realistic about the future of a European-type *collège* in an American frontier town where "year by year there is a great inpouring of settlers from all sides." "Our only hope of increase," he concluded, "is in Lower Louisiana" where European culture persisted.

Verhaegen wanted to open a *collège* in Louisiana, a desire which coincided with the fondest wishes of the newly ordained bishop of New Orleans.[26] No sooner had he taken office than De Neckere wrote to the Provincial of Maryland offering him the College of Iberville, built in 1824 by Father Eugene Michaud (1798–1832), a diocesan priest. "The house and land will be the property of your Fathers without any burden whatever except of the taxes," he wrote.[27] Then in 1832 he brought Father Anthony Blanc with him to St. Louis to visit the Flemish Jesuits there, and on this occasion the bishop again offered Iberville to his compatriots. Meanwhile, one of the Belgian Jesuits was sent to Louisiana to recruit boarding students, better qualified than the Missouri products, for the struggling St. Louis College. Under these circumstances it was not surprising that De Neckere "was received with eagerness at St. Louis." The rector Verhaegen and the superior James Van de Velde, (b. Lebbeke, Oost-Vlaanderen, Belgium, April 3, 1795; d. Natchez, November 13, 1855) were conspicuously sanguine about establishing themselves in Louisiana, and they wrote Roothaan, urging him to send more men to Missouri to insure that the Iberville property would not slip out of the hands of the society.[28]

Two crucial events changed the course of what seemed, in 1832, only to be a matter of time before the St. Louis Jesuits would found a *collège* in Louisiana, most probably at Iberville. First, Chazelle and his companions arrived in New Orleans on February 7, 1831, and then on September 5, 1833 yellow fever carried off De Neckere, leaving the Frenchmen Anthony Blanc and Pierre Ladavière co-administrators of the diocese. Neither man was so much anti-Flemish as he was pro-French, and understandably both were inclined to have French Jesuits operate a French-type *collège* in a colony that had been so quintessentially French. We have seen that very shortly after Anthony Blanc had been ordained to succeed the Flemish De Neckere, he and Pierre Ladavière, both natives of the Lyonnais, rushed off, in 1835, first to France and then to Rome where they were successful in persuading Roothaan to assign Lower Louisiana to the province of France, more popularly called Paris. Roothaan, who in 1833 had received letters from the American-born Father Peter Walsh (1824–1872) of the St. Louis College community, discouraging expansion on the part of the Belgian Jesuits into Louisiana, finally wrote on June 18 of that year to the Mission superior, Father James Van de Velde urging caution: ". . . if you must at all costs hasten, you hasten slowly, lest by undertaking too many things you be unable to carry on and, in fine, succeed in building nothing but ruins."[29] Consequently, the following September, as Nicolas Point was making his way to his new assignment at Le Passage and as Bishop De Neckere lay dying in New Orleans, Fathers Van de Velde and Verhaegen regretfully put their Louisiana project "on hold" until that day when St. Louis could afford to send men south to open the Iberville College.

On "Monday afternoon November 14," Achille Guidée informed Father Roothaan in a letter dated Paris, November 16, 1836, "our Louisiana group left here for Le Havre full of zeal and courage. If they have not already done so they will sail with Bishop Blanc."[30] They waited for a favorable wind until December 24 and then sailed out of the port city in two vessels bound for New Orleans, three days after Nicolas Point embarked from Louisville on the New Orleans riverboat.[31] In an age when every crossing was a horrendous adventure, the voyage of the first band of Jesuits assigned to Louisiana since the Suppression merits distinction. The two vessels managed to survive a hurricane that piled up shipwrecks along the French Atlantic coast only to be chased by pirates who preyed on the surviving ships. By the beginning of February 1837, rumors of the missionaries' peril had reached Iberville, causing the first appointed superior of the newly constituted Louisiana Mission to pack up his sketchbook and assemble his notes on the Iberville buildings and property and continue his journey southwards.[32]

In rumor-ridden New Orleans Point presented himself to the vicar-general who promptly sent him to serve as chaplain to the nuns and pupils of the Convent of the Sacred Heart in St. Landry Parish, 160 miles northwest of New Orleans and some 10 miles south of Opelousas.[33] This was the spot Bishop DuBourg spoke about to the Bordeaux Jesuits and to Father Provincial Nicolas Godinot in 1826, a location whose importance had long since paled when the more advantageous site of Iberville was offered to the society. Here Point settled in, awaiting the arrival of Bishop Blanc and his new Jesuit community, serving the spiritual needs of the nuns, students, and local people, and finding time to make notes on what he observed. The property consisted of two hundred acres. The parish church was centered on a few miles of fertile land that raised above the wooded flatlands, which stretched out to the horizon on all sides. Hence, the name of the village, Grand Coteau, perched on what appeared to be a large hill. The inhabitants of the district were chiefly Creoles and Arcadians but there was also a representative number of Catholic settlers from Maryland, generally of Irish stock, whose presence insured support for a prospective *collège*.[34] The recently constructed church of St. Charles was named after the patron saint of one of these settlers, Charles Smith, its founder. Smith was also the chief benefactor of the Sacred Heart Convent, a magnificent structure built in 1822, the year Point had been sent home from the Montrouge novitiate as an unsuitable candidate. Now, fifteen years later, a superior without a community, he wrote a long letter to the General giving him a full account of all of the events that had taken place during the past two months. In a remarkably objective manner, he outlined the advantages and disadvantages of the Iberville property and he concluded that a place like Grand Coteau seemed more promising. One of the many advantages he noted was the number of sugar and cotton planters in the neighborhood. Such people would surely support the Jesuits in exchange for the education of their sons. But whatever site was finally chosen, he impressed upon the General that teachers and coadjutor brothers were needed because "the price of Negroes and professors is exorbitant." This letter was dated February 17, 1837, the same day when, after more than two horrible months at sea, Blanc and the eight Jesuits sent from France docked at New Orleans. Point took his letter with him down to the port city where he dispatched it and greeted his companions.[35]

Besides Ladavière, who had served as their superior en route, "a valuable man for setting up [the *collège*] because of his background," there was Francis Abbadie (b. Gausson, Hautes-Pyrenées, November 5, 1804; d. Grand Coteau, Louisiana, December 16, 1890), who had entered the society at Montrouge in August 1826, two months before Point was admitted to the same novitiate. Of all the newcomers, this man was Point's closest friend, the Jesuit destined to have the greatest influence in shaping the Louisiana Mission. He was described as having "a great desire for the missions of America," which he manifested at the Jesuit *collège-en-exile* at Chambéry in the Kingdom of Savoy where he was prefect of the boarding students.[36] During this period of Abbadie's career, there was a young lay *surveillant* under his charge, an aspirant to the society named Hippolyte Gache (1817–1907), who would one day follow his mentor to the Louisiana Mission, where he would serve as minister to Father Rector Abbadie at Grand Coteau. During the War Abbadie was arrested as a Confederate spy while Gache served as a chaplain to the Tenth Louisiana Volunteer Regiment in Virginia.[37] The third priest that weathered the crossing was Joseph Soller, the reluctant sub-minister at Fribourg during Point's tenure at that *collège*, and who has been mentioned above. Renault advised Roothaan, "He has been a professor of the humanities for several years and can continue to be so; he has a great desire of exercising the holy ministry; but for *surveillance* and for the offices of minister and sub-minister he feels a repugnance that he does not sufficiently control."[38] Louisiana would not change this man who could be brutally frank in expressing his opinions and who maintained a sense of objectivity commensurate with his fierce independence. Two other of the weary voyagers had been novices with Point at Montrouge in 1827: Fathers Paul Mignard (b. Paris, August 5, 1808; d. New York, October 8, 1882) and Peter De Vos (b. Ghent, Belgium, September 24, 1797; d. Santa Clara, California, April 17, 1859). Point once described Mignard to Roothaan as a man "having a little judgment and a lot of stubbornness once he latched on to some prejudice."[39] However, in 1846 the General thought he had the necessary qualities to be a master of novices at Floissant, "but later acquiesced in the preference expressed by the fathers of Missouri."[40] Mignard, it appears, had some pretty definite opinions of his own on Point, Louisiana, and the fathers of Missouri. After being transferred to St. Louis, he wrote to Roothaan that he was happy to put Missouri between himself and Louisiana for two reasons: Point and yellow fever. But he would also like to get far away from Missouri too. Good Parisian that he was, he discerned that he would be happier among the French Jesuits at Fordham and eventually this is where he was sent, and it was here that he distinguished himself as a teacher and confessor.[41]

Peter De Vos had been assigned master to the one novice in the group, Henry Duranquet (b. Clermont, Puy-de-Dôme, December 18, 1809; d. Woodstock, Maryland, December 30, 1891). Even though Belgian by birth, De Vos entered the French Province at Montrouge, December 9, 1825, at the time when the Belgian Catholics were suffering under the oppressive rule of their Dutch Calvinist governors. But after nine months of daily order De Vos, already an ordained priest, collapsed and was sent to Saint-Acheul where in the Blamont residence he joined the lay *surveillant*

Nicolas Point, another casualty of the novitiate regime. Finally, in October 1828, after Point had returned to Montrouge for another try, De Vos was dispensed altogether from making a formal novitiate, and on the following Christmas day was allowed to pronounce his vows. On the feast of the Epiphany, January 6, 1829, four years after he had entered the society, De Vos was officially made a member of the Saint-Acheul faculty, although not as a classroom teacher, along with the scholastic Nicolas Point, who by that date had successfully finished his second try at the novitiate and had pronounced his vows in the previous March.[42] The two coadjutor brothers in the group were Joseph Chauvet (b. Velleron, Vaucluse, April 15, 1804; d. Grand Coteau, Louisiana, October 7, 1857) and Charles Alsberg (b. Ooteghem, West Flanders, Belgium, January 1, 1791; d. Fordham, New York, March 16, 1876). The former had been with Point at Le Passage, where he had been in charge of the farm since the opening of the *collège* in 1828, and was his companion on the memorable flight from Spain to Bayonne in 1834.[43] The latter had been with Point at Saint-Acheul from 1828 to 1830, and like Point, had disguised himself during the July Revolution to flee to Switzerland. At Brig he rejoined the man who, as his future superior, would welcome him to New Orleans. Alsberg was remembered as a "simple, pious, obedient brother, and his whole life in the society was a model of the life of a faithful lay-brother."[44] However, he did not hesitate to request, in 1846, after the French Jesuits reestablished St. Mary's at Fordham, New York, to be removed from the jurisdiction of Missouri and returned as soon as possible to "his real superiors."[45] When he met him in New Orleans in 1837, Point gave Brother Alsberg charge of the household needs of the new community, and once the *collège* was established, Brother Chauvet would take over the responsibility of the farm and the management of the garden.[46]

The last member of the group, the novice Henry Duranquet, may have been the only one of the eight not known to Point, although it is more than probable the two knew one another well. Henry had been a student at Saint-Acheul during his new superior's tenure there, and his brother Louis (b. Cheylade, Cantal, August 1, 1806; d. Strivegondam, Madras, India, November 8, 1843) had been a novice with Point in 1826, and was with him later at Le Passage. All five of the Jesuit Chardon du Ranquet brothers (the family's proper name; Henry alone Americanized it) were missionary priests: three had been sent to India where they died at an early age, and two came to North America.[47]

In 1827 Henry had attempted to enter the society at Montrouge, but was rejected because of health, and so he went first to Milan and then to Rome to pursue his studies. Finally, on September 3, 1836, the special friend of the family, Jan Roothaan, received him into the society and the following month sent him hurrying off to Le Harvre to join Bishop Blanc and the seven Jesuit pioneers bound for Louisiana. Ordained in 1840, he continued teaching Spanish and poetry at Grand Coteau, but when the French Jesuits opened up the Canada-New York Mission in 1842, he joined his brother Dominique (b. Châlus, Puy-de-Dôme, January 20, 1813; d. Wikwemikong, Ontario, Canada, December 19, 1900), working with the Indians in Manitoba's Far West. Then, after spending a number of years in Montreal and Guelf, Henry Duranquet was appointed minister at St. Francis Xavier Collège, New York City, from which post, in 1856, he began an apostolate with some of the most wretched people in North America: inmates of a vast complex which included a prison, hospital, poor house, work house and insane asylum, all situated on a number of islands near the city. There were some ten thousand people in this parish, "four-fifths of them are Catholics, the majority being Irish or Irish descent." He confessed that in the beginning he did not know which was worse: typhus, which had killed five of his predecessors within two succeeding years, or the anti-Catholic bigotry with which he had to contend.[48] During the late fifties he conducted an average of six funerals a day, but just before the outbreak of the Civil War, when he received help from some of his Jesuit brothers, he devoted all of his energies to caring for the prisoners at what was ghoulishly called "The Tombs" on Blackwell's

Island.[49] Finally, in 1880, Henry Duranquet, known now as "The Apostle of The Tombs," was assigned spiritual father to the scholastics studying philosophy and theology at Woodstock College, Maryland. "He was a sweet amiable old man in spite of his grim look," recalled one of his advisees, graciously adding that none of the young Jesuits "blamed the look, for his career and infirmities were calculated to impress grimness on the features of St. Francis de Sales." Although tolerance was a virtue which, in those days, sometimes bloomed late in the young, the studied charity of this unsung Boswell, cast like the cloak of Noe over his subject, has not hidden the personality of this old man who must have been the subject of many anecdotes shared by members of the Provinces. "His 'monks' in the Tombs," we are told, "were little accustomed to meditation and reading, but "he found a means of making them do a little reading by giving them as a penance a chapter of Kempis to be read once or oftener in the case a repetition of the dose was deemed necessary or advisable. He hoped the book might be taken down at other times to break the monotony of their cells. This practice he transplanted to Woodstock . . ." We are informed that the monks at the *collège* were a bit more receptive, leaving today's reader to wonder if the reason was due to the asceticism of the scholastics or to the monotony of their cells. One is left to imagine the scene of the first formal meeting of the grim looking, "sweet, amiable old man" with his spiritual charges. "His first exhortation," the chronicler informs us, "bore the odor of his discourses to his former charges, and naturally it was little suited to our Domestic Chapel. He was too old to change his style, and so his first discourse in Woodstock was his last also."[50] The old man from the French aristocratic family who ended his days "piously reading the lives of the saints" at Woodstock College was the young novice who greeted his first superior in the United States at New Orleans in February 1837.[51]

Eleven days after the French Jesuits arrived in New Orleans, the Superior of the Missouri Mission, Peter Verhaegen, wrote to the General requesting the Missouri Mission be detached from Maryland and joined to the Belgian Province, "Due to the benefits which the Belgians have lavished on this mission (whatever it has received it owes in large measure to them) . . ."[52] This desire to attach Missouri to Belgium was not new. In the summer of 1834, when the *collège* at Le Passage was in the throes of its last agony, Peter De Smet resurrected this Missouri conceived idea in a Belgium still delirious from its victorious struggle for national independence. Father Peter Kenney, Visitor of the Jesuit houses in the United States, was responsible for De Smet's being back in Belgium at that date. De Smet's health had been poor and the Visitor, falling back on a remedy prescribed by Ignatius himself in such situations, sent him to breathe his native air and thereby regain his vigor.

Vigor, however, was a quality which De Smet never seemed to lack, and now he ambitioned to be a kind of agent for the mission, but, because of certain jurisdictional problems with superiors in Europe, he found it difficult to function efficiently. Belgium had been the mission's chief supplier of men and money and therefore the union was a logical step, and it promised to be of even greater advantage for Missouri. At that date, however, the mission superior was not enthusiastic for the merger, and so in 1834 the question remained moot. But such indecision did not affect De Smet. He busied himself collecting money, altar furniture, and art works and shipped them back to Missouri. By chance he managed to come upon a whole library which he received free of charge. The generosity of his fellow countrymen seemed to know no bounds. Then he went down to France and, at Saint-Acheul, where Point began tertianship that year on November 2, he purchased at a token price Saint-Acheul's famous physics laboratory for St. Louis College. The apparatus equipment and mineral collection, which had miraculously escaped the rioters during the July Days of 1830, had stood idle since Nicolas Point put aside his experiments and ran for his life ahead of the avenging firebrands. Back in Belgium, De Smet also gathered four more stolid recruits for the mission, and these arrived at St. Louis along with Saint-Acheul's laboratory equipment in March 1835. In the following May, as Point prepared himself to take his last vows at St. Mary's, De Smet signed the demissorial papers from the society which he had requested earlier that year. Now a diocesan priest, he remained in Belgium as l'Abbé De Smet. Then, in November 1837, back at Florissant with more recruits for the mission, he was readmitted to the society by his former fellow novice and very good friend, Peter Verhaegen.[53]

Verhaegen, who became the Missouri Mission's superior in March 1836, had long before this date been a supporter of the union between the mission and the Belgian Province, but the catalyst which prompted him to request the General to act on this proposal early in 1837 was due to "the information having been given us that a *collège* of the society is shortly to be established in Louisiana, which undoubtedly, as I have often represented to your Paternity, will reduce the number of our boarders to a few [at St. Louis] and work harm according to the finances of our *collège*."[54] As Verhaegen wrote these words, Nicolas Point was apprising his travel weary companions in New Oreleans of the advantages and disadvantages of the sites he had inspected for the new *collège*. He rejected Iberville, Verhaegen's favored site, and his decision received the unanimous support of his companions. Up in Kentucky Chazelle heard the rumor that Point was about to turn down Bishop Blanc's offer of the Iberville property and buildings and promptly sat down and wrote the General of his concern about Point's judgment.[55] But Father Nicolas argued that even though the site was advantageously situated, the buildings were too near the crumbling bank of the Mississippi; moreover, the house, which was unsuitable for the needs of a *collège,* was heavily in debt. As if these were not reasons enough, "it was ascertained his Lordship was giving away property that was not entirely his own."[56] Blanc was disappointed, believing the Jesuits' decision would eventually cost the diocese dearly, but after giving written sanction that the final resolution where the *collège* was to be established was up to Nicolas Point and his consultors, the bishop left New Orleans to attend the Third Provincial Council of Baltimore.[57]

Blanc's second choice for a *collège* site was Manderville, a settlement near New Orleans, but the Jesuits decided the disadvantages they encountered there and at nearby Rome outweighed any supposed advantages, and so both locations were turned down. "Particularly in America," Pierre Point wrote paraphrasing his brother, "one had to look hard before accepting. Almost all the offerings made to the Jesuits were based on speculations most advantageous to the donors."[58] Lent came and went and no decisions had been made, even though each offer had been studied thoroughly and a detailed report on the final decision was forwarded to the General. These reports, painstakingly copied out in Point's clear, microscopic hand and embellished with sketches, stand today as witnesses to a discernment process that some have thought lay dormant in the society until recent times.[59] The only preconditions the Superior made were: (1) the site for the new *collège* had to offer the maximum advantages for all concerned—students, parents, donors, Jesuits; (2) it had to be within the boundaries of the state of Louisiana; (3) it had to be acceptable to the bishop.[60] Meanwhile, according to the practice of the early companions of Ignatius of Loyola, the priests kept themselves overoccupied preaching, dispensing the sacraments, visiting hospitals and prisons, and catechizing the young in various parts of the state.[61] Point had sent Abbadie and Ladavière to the Donaldsonville area; Mignard and De Vos to Grand Coteau, and Soller to New Orleans, where "according to the practice carried on by St. Francis Xavier and later by all the missionaries of the society [he] was at the hospital where he consoled the large number of sick, and the rest of the time he consecrated himself to the needs of the Germans, deprived until now of a priest who could speak their language."[62] In theory Father Nicolas was stationed with Soller; in fact, he was "everywhere."[63]

Besides the obvious pastoral exigencies, one of the reasons Ladavière had been sent to Donaldsonville, a river town some eighty miles north of New Orleans, was to inspect a piece of property that had showed great promise. Donaldsonville, besides being a thriving urban area that had easy access from all parts of Louisiana as well as from the adjacent states, appeared to have all of the qualifications the fathers desired, and the veteran missionary Ladavière had little difficulty in convincing all that the sale of the property where the new *collège* would be erected was reasonable. A document of sale was drawn up and the superior was about to attach his signature to it when an unexpected opposition, incited by anti-Catholic factions, flared up in the town. The Jesuits were not welcome. "Father Point withdrew at once," an early chronicler reported.[64] Now all that remained was Grand Coteau. On June 23, Point and Ladavière met with Abbadie, who had come over from nearby Assumption Parish, and in Ladavière's rectory, after kneeling in prayer for a considerable time, the three deliberated in the customary fashion of the society on the reasons advanced by De Vos from Grand Coteau for choosing that site for the *collège*. Agreement was reached at 4:00 P.M., and immediately Point set out on foot. Walking all night he reached Plaquemine at 4:00 A.M. the next day, June 24, just in time for him to catch the barge that brought him to the Grand Coteau landing. It was no preference on his part that prompted this mode of nocturnal traveling, but the absence of other alternatives—he had neither horse nor stage—forced him to rely on what experience had taught him to do well: walk far and fast.

Once he arrived at Grand Coteau he summoned De Vos and Mignard, advised them of the results of the Donaldsonville deliberation, received their approbation to the terms offered by the leading inhabitants of Grand Coteau, then sought Soller's confirmation. Soller abstained; the vote of the others was unanimous.[65] Eight hundred acres were deeded to the *collège* by the local townsmen who in turn promised to supply free labor in constructing the buildings and hauling the lumber and clay needed for bricks. They also pledged $10,000 to help defray expenses for the new *collège*. Moreover, Charles Smith's widow gave two thousand dollars and willed the remainder of Smith's fortune to the operation, which his distant relatives were successful in contending. Finally, the Religious of the Sacred Heart donated an additional one thousand dollars and provided the Jesuits, who had moved into the presbytery beside the church, with food and furniture. Point, in the name of the Provincial of France, signed the contract and sent it to Bishop Blanc. The day was the feast of Saints Peter and Paul, June 29, 1837. The people in the village, the nuns, the convent girls, and the Jesuits solemnly processed to the parish church where a *Te Deum* was sung. After sixty-four year's absence, the French Jesuits were back in Louisiana.[66]

ST. CHARLES COLLEGE

Part One: 1837–1838

A few days before St. Ignatius's feast, July 31, 1837, Charles Van Quickenborne was recalled from his last assignment.[1] When he arrived in the United States in 1817, he expressed the desire to preach to the abandoned Indians and, as he worked at the other assignments he was given, he never ceased to plan and dream about creating a reduction for them, setting up a Christian community among them far from the white man, a place where they could hear about and embrace the truths of Christianity.[2] At last, in 1836, his dream was realized. He was assigned to work among the Kickapoos, whose chief village was at the confluence of the Missouri and Salt Creek, a short distance beyond Fort Leavenworth. However, what he expected to occur and to be accomplished did not come about. So many obstacles thwarted his carefully laid out plans. According to Gilbert Garraghan, soon his "idiosyncrasies of temperament had set him at variance with those under his authority." Peter Verhaegen, who had been both a novice and a tertian under him and who was now his superior, was finally persuaded to recall him because of his "despotic manner of government." The old man, of course, obeyed immediately, but died two weeks later, ever conscious of his failure.[3] Roothaan assured him in a letter he never received that, even though his plans for an Indian reduction were hardly met with worldly success, "the obedient man will speak of virtues."[4]

The same week that the frail Van Quickenborne, who would die within a month, left the Kickapoos for St. Louis, Bishop Blanc left New Orleans bound for Grand Coteau. Here on St. Ignatius Day he laid the cornerstone of St. Charles Borromeo College and ceremoniously signed over to the Jesuits, in the name of Nicolas Point, the parish church with its properties and revenues including some two-hundred acres, "along with the usufruct of fields and woodlands, and with the right to rent, cultivate and build with pleasure in the *collège* and boarding school thereon and assume charge of the church and parish of St. Charles."[5] Point's hopes and plans, in contrast with those of his old mentor, had indeed been crowned with success.

The bishop returned to New Orleans, and Point and his community settled in to meet the challenges that faced them: perfecting their English, planting trees, expanding the garden, enlarging the church, and fitting a number of small houses into one wooden structure designed to serve as the makeshift classroom by day and the students' dormitory by night. Meanwhile, more anti-Catholic factions were forming in the neighboring Lafayette Parish, and, at the same time, the Opelousas newspaper fumed about having a Jesuit *collège* at nearby Grand Coteau, and giving the fathers fifteen days to clear out—or else! Able-bodied men in the village prepared themselves against the realization of these mean and villainous threats. Guns were loaded, horses saddled. The village took on the aspect of an armed camp. But the outlaws never showed face, and so in a few months, their threats had become part of the legend of St. Charles's past, not a menace to its future.[6]

All of this excitement, however, had the effect of intensifying a general sense of expectation: When would the classes begin? At last—relenting to the pressure of impatient parents and exasperated parishioners who would not wait for the finishing touches to be put on the small, wooden house—Point opened the *collège* on January 8, 1838. No one showed up! The day was a Friday and presumably the local people would never begin an enterprise on that day. The Jesuits had not learned enough about Cajun superstitions. The next day three youths were enrolled; by the end of the month, the number had risen to twenty-three boarders, and before the end of the school year there were fifty-six enrolled. These boys were crowded into narrow and uncomfortable quarters, the same room serving for dormitory and classroom. During the day the beds were removed and replaced with benches and tables. Since there was no means of heating the building, the alternatives when the mercury fell were to dismiss the students to their homes or to send them to bed. The cost for tuition, board, and lodging was $150 per annum. Point encouraged his companions by his extraordinary patience and resignation. Feeling that too heavy a burden might be borne by some, he spoke to his subordinates in this strain:

> "When Father General sent us hither, he sent us to the *collège* of Iberville. He had no suspicion of the sacrifices that confront us here nor any intention of imposing them upon us. Neither may I impose them upon you against your will. Are you ready then to put up with discomforts that meet us here?" The faculty was ready to accept the situation as they found it and Father Point was reassured.[7]

To ameliorate the situation he hired lay professors and servants.

Even though the Jesuit teaching faculty and administration consisted of four—Abbadie, Mignard, Duranquet and Point—all seven staff members were crowded into two small log cabins that had been designed to guarantee that the occupant would roast in the summer and freeze in the winter.[8] The two brothers were engaged in manual work and De Vos had been put in charge of the church and parish, "150 miles long and about 20 miles wide," in which there were "many poor whites . . . and very many slaves." Each day he was off visiting every house in the wide area, teaching, catechizing, forming sodalities, and organizing religious processions, which became a popular adjunct to religious instruction. Ladavière was racing all over Louisiana fundraising for the struggling *collège*. Joseph Soller, with Bishop Blanc's encouragement, continued his apostolate in New Orleans hospitals and among its German-speaking colony. Point was the factotum, although his main attention was given to adapting the "Fribourg plan" to meet the needs and talents of Grand Coteau's scholars.[9]

Evidently, however, not all of the fathers were satisfied with the rector's Spartan regime and letters began arriving in Rome complaining about his policies.[10] To make matters worse, Point did not write often enough to the General and, seemingly, when he did write, his letters were not as detailed as they could have and should have been. Roothaan informed the rector in a letter dated May 13, 1838, that he had not heard from him since December and he insisted on being apprised of all of the details about Grand Coteau so that "obedience from a distance" would be maintained.

> I insist on this point because you are new at your job and your age and background do not furnish me sufficient guarantees for [dealing with] extraordinary matters. In general, a superior in the society should not make a decision in any matter without hearing from the subjects; this is what makes governance in the society sweet and at the same time efficacious; it is also for the superior a continual exercise in abnegation and humility, which exercise can but attract graces and blessings from heaven . . .[11]

Specifically, he wanted to know what kind of a town Grand Coteau was, what the population and vocations prospectives were. For the time being he thought that it would be better to send any candidates for the society to the novitiate at Florissant. Is it possible that the General's action in this instance was influenced by Chazelle's letter about Point's asserted poor judgment, based on the way he handled a discipline problem at St. Mary's and, more importantly, on the fact that he turned down the Iberville property? Quite possibly. However, it should be remembered that Roothaan's management policy was very different in respect to

American affairs than that of his predecessor. Point answered this letter in July giving the General the details he requested and begging him for more coadjutor brothers and Jesuits who could teach mathematics, "because now our mathematics teachers are obliged to learn in the morning what they have to teach in the afternoon." Despite such minor inconveniences, he painted an optimistic picture of the *collège*, yet seemingly, he missed the point the General was making in regard to governance.[12]

The implementation of the *plan* was most satisfactory. At first there were only fifteen boys who qualified for Latin, but soon enrollment increased significantly, thanks to a number of competent lay teachers whom the rector-president had been able to attract. The most distinguished of these laymen was one who would later gain international notoriety. This was Pierce Connelly (1804–1873). In 1835, he had been the rector of Trinity Episcopal Church at Natchez when he decided, in the face of a brilliant career, to enter the Catholic Church. His resolve was supported, at first with reserve and then with enthusiasm, by his wife, Cornelia Peacock Connelly (1809–1879). She was received into the Catholic Church by Bishop Rosati at New Orleans in December 1835, at the same time Bishop Blanc and the eight Jesuit missionaries were leaving France for New Orleans. Characteristically, Pierce put off his official entrance into the Church until he was able to do so in a more dramatic setting, and so the couple set off with their children for Rome in the beginning of 1836. For the next two years this exciting couple enchanted and were in turn dazzled by the best society of the Old World, but when the 1838 depression hit, Connelly found himself without resources from the Memphis properties he shared with his brothers; consequently, he was forced to return to the United States with his family. Back home, he contacted his old friend Bishop Blanc who put him in touch with Point.[13] The rector-president of St. Charles was desperately looking for teachers and so he hired Connelly, who arrived at Grand Coteau with his family to take up his new job on June 24, 1838, a year to the day of Point's arrival from the discernment meeting at Donaldsonville and less than two weeks after the Superior wrote his report to the General.[14] Point mentioned to Roothaan that he had hired Connelly, describing him as being "completely committed to the *collège*."[15] During the coming year Pierce Connelly's brilliance and charm did wonders for the school and, despite personal sorrows, he poured himself with his true-to-type verve into teaching English literature and directing the dramatic productions. Cornelia, pregnant with her fourth child, was hired by the Religious of the Sacred Heart to give lessons in voice and instrumental music at the convent. The following month she gave birth to a daughter, Mary Magdaleine, but a few days later, July 22, the child died. This tragic event was the occasion which soldered a bond between the grieving mother and her newly found confessor and confidant, Nicolas Point.[16]

On Bastille Day, July 14, 1838, the third anniversary of the arrival of the Le Passage refugees at Bayonne (how ironic are the vagaries of history!), Roothaan directed a letter to Peter Verhaegen, Superior of the Missouri Mission, in which he advised him that, with the unanimous support of the Provincial of France and his consultors, the General had decided "to unite this French colony of the society to the Missouri Mission under one and the same superior." Grand Coteau was henceforth cut off from France and attached to the Flemish-speaking Jesuits at St. Louis. Roothaan instructed Verhaegen to make a formal visitation of Grand Coteau, meet his new subjects, replace the *collège* staff with suitable reinforcements, and find an apt substitute for Soller in New Orleans. However, he concluded: "I deem it superfluous to caution your reverence to make no immediate change in regard to customs there existing, even though they appear to be somewhat incongruous, unless indeed the rector of the *collège* and the graver among the fathers be absolutely convinced of the necessity of a change; for in matters of this kind, one must await a fuller measure of time and experience."[17]

Soller advised the General that when this news was announced at St. Charles, "we were all flabbergasted [*extra-*

ordinairement étonnés]."[18] Then he quickly added: "but we realized that it was evidentally arranged by Divine Providence." From the point of view of the Jesuits at St. Charles, this extreme reaction was understandable. In June of the previous year, when Roothaan gave Point permission to go ahead with his ambitious building program, he had informed him that the manpower problem was more serious than Point's concern, which was the shortage of funds, but that the dearth of qualified men need not be a source of concern, because "I do not think that the Provincial of Paris, upon whom your Mission depends, will forsake you."[19] However, the facts now indicated that the Louisiana colony had indeed been forsaken. Why? If not because of money or men, there must have been another reason. Was it Point's governance? In Rome and in Paris the decision seemed perfectly reasonable and the question of Point's managerial qualities was an issue that had no bearing on the case. After the separation of the newly constituted Lyon Province, the Province of France had a total of 262 Jesuits in five residences within the territorial limits of the country. Besides St. Charles, there were also two other *collèges*, both beyond the borders, one at Brugelette in Belgium and the other in St. Mary's, Kentucky. The Province was also already commited to several missions: Syria, Madura, Kentucky, and Louisiana.[20]

In 1831, the year Chazelle and his companions came to the United States, Father Benoît Planchet (b. Gap, Hautes-Alpes, January 24, 1802), who had been with Point at Saint-Acheul in 1822 and again in 1825 and 1826, initiated the mission to Syria.[21] Then, while Point was modifying the "Fribourg plan" to accommodate Louisiana boys in Grand Coteau, Planchet had implemented the principle of adaptation so well that he was indistinguishable from an Arab. Later, ordained bishop and appointed the Apostolic Delegate to Mesopotamia, he was murdered by a group of Kurdish tribesmen at Souarek, in eastern Turkey, September 21, 1859, but not before he had laid the foundations for two more famous French missions: Egypt and Armenia.[22] Reluctantly, as we have seen, the Province had pledged itself to support the Kentucky Mission, and on July 5, 1837, less than a month before Bishop Blanc laid the cornerstone of St. Charles College at Grand Coteau, Louis du Ranquet, Alexandre Martin, and two other priests had at last left Bordeaux to reestablish a French Jesuit presence in the venerable missions of Pondichery and Madura. They, too, carried with them the Province of France's commitment for support, but no one in France could have realized then how costly this commitment would be in men and money during the years to come.[23] Finally, in less than three years time, Roothaan would ask France to take on the Algerian Mission, where Point's good friend Ferdinand Brumauld's strong personality dominated a whole generation of Jesuits working among the Arab-speaking peoples of North Africa.[24] Manpower was indeed a serious problem for the Province of France, oppressed at home and overextended abroad. At the same time there was the Missouri Mission with its growing number of young, zealous Jesuits, its solid financial connections with Belgium, and its expressed desire to support a *collège* in Louisiana. Given these contingencies the 1838 decision hammered out in Rome and Paris seemed reasonable and just.

Roothaan's letter addressed to Peter Verhaegen announcing these changes reached St. Louis in October, at a time when Peter De Smet was restlessly rounding out the first year of his repeated novitiate in nearby Florissant. In compliance with the General's wishes, Verhaegen decided to waste no time in paying a visit to his newly acquired subjects in Louisiana and to inspect the buildings into which the controversial superior there had been investing so much money, energy, and time to construct. He left St. Louis on November 22 and arrived in New Orleans on December 4 with a scholastic named Isidore Boudreaux (b. Terre Bonne Parish, Louisiana, September 14, 1818; d. Chicago, February 8, 1885). Verhaegen's choice for a traveling companion does justice to his sense of tact and *délicatesse* because Isidore was the first Creole graduate of St. Louis College to enter the society. He had been sent north with three of his brothers after a parent's death had made the nine Boudreaux children orphans. In 1841 "his singularly handsome brother" Florentine Boudreaux (no Missouri name that!), followed Isidore into the society. Florentine (b. Terre Bonne Parish, May 22, 1821; d. Chicago, January 30, 1894) later became famous as an author of devotional books, but it was the gracious, outgoing, and always smiling Isidore who was destined to have a determining influence on forming the distinct character of the rank and file of the Midwestern Jesuits that perdured for a century.[25] His early career gave no hint of his future greatness, for after meeting with Father Rector Point he spent the next *ten* years as a scholastic at Grand Coteau "in regeancy," teaching French and English to his fellow cajuns and other inmates at the *collège*. In 1846, after the French Jesuits returned to St. Charles, Isidore Boudreaux was asked to which province he thought he should be assigned, Lyon or Missouri. He answered that he felt himself to be a Frenchman, and therefore would be happy to remain with the French, but he confessed that he also felt indebted to the fathers of Missouri for educating him, and for these reasons he was completely indifferent, leaving the resolution concerning his future status to superiors.[26] It was decided that he should remain with Missouri, a decision that had far-reaching consequences.

After ordination and a brief stint at St. Joseph's College, Bardstown, Kentucky, which the Missouri Jesuits took over in 1848, he moved to Xavier College, now University, Cincinnati, where he served as its fifth rector-president. Then, in 1857, he became the master of novices at Florissant, a position he held until 1880. His job there was to train young Jesuits in the society, which he saw as "a body of ecclesiastical auxiliaries, a sort of spiritual reserve, whose efficiency depended exclusively upon the spirit and availability of the rank and file." Indeed, during the twenty-three years of his tenure at Florissant, his efforts were mainly "directed toward the training of efficient Jesuits of the ranks," persuaded that "it was Providence who was to officer [the society], to make and unmake heroes." The author of his obituary wrote that "he was much more than a kind Christian gentleman and an adroit manipulator of character," although none who came in contact with him could deny that the manipulatory aspects of his complex personality were in evidence. Above all else, however, he was "eminently a spiritual man" who "set a very essential importance upon the most minute details of discipline, not because he saw in them efficient checks or goads to spiritual progress, but simply for their intrinsic merits as devout traits or their significance as interior affections." Like Xavier de Ravignan, Nicolas Point, and so many other Jesuits of that era, Isidore Boudreaux found his *raison d'être* and strength in the devotion to the Blessed Sacrament, the "unmistakable sign of a pious Jesuit," and like his first rector at Grand Coteau, Isidore "would kneel before the altar, motionless, his eyes fixed upon the tabernacle" for a period of "one, two, even three hours together."[27]

Boudreaux recounted that in 1855, while he was president of Xavier College, he traveled to Milwaukee to inspect a piece of property the bishop had offered to the Jesuits for the establishment of yet another *collège*. He got a buggy, he said, and drove out to the site, but because of the unevenness of the terrain and the thickness of the vegetation, the shaky buggy toppled over, unceremoniously dumping the venerable Isidore on the ground, where "like William the Conqueror 'he took formal possession of the soil'." After his tenure as master of novices, Isidore Boudreaux was appointed rector-president of Marquette College, now University, Milwaukee, Wisconsin, and when he arrived to assume command of his new post he was delighted to see that a monumental *collège* building had been erected over the very spot which had been so singularly stamped by his anatomy and so fulsomely fixed in his memory.[28]

On October 24, Pierce Connelly staged a play, significantly entitled "Joseph Sold by His Brethren," to finish off the 1838 fall term. It was dramatized in the finest St. Mary's, Kentucky, tradition, before Bishop Blanc, a former Louisiana governor, and some of the most distinguished citizens of the state. Prizes were distributed, according to Loriquet's recommendations, speeches made, and congratulations exchanged in the time-honored customs of the antebellum South. This tour de force received wide coverage in the press, where expressions of praise and congratulations were lavished on the Jesuits for what they were doing in Grand Coteau.[29] It was a fitting prelude for the opening of the second term on the first of December. The boys moved into Point's controversial new brick building, which was nearing completion, on the third, St. Francis Xavier Day. The mission superior arrived shortly afterwards and spent the following month learning about the disastrous split in the Jesuit community.[30] This split had begun squalidly, over budgetary matters, but the real cause was the normal human factor of personal ambition. "Never had I been a witness to such a clash of passions before I came to Grand Coteau," Joseph Soller informed Roothaan, "and particularly since the arrival of Father Verhaegen. Father De Vos, one of the combatants, had the greatest chance to reap the victory. Father Point, through harsh and arbitrary governance had alienated almost everyone in the community. Despite the advice Father Guidée had given him, he forged ahead, contemptuous of all the objections made to him." The De Vos faction was numerically stronger. It consisted of Ladavière, "who is always dissatisfied," and Mignard. "They armed themselves for the combat," and then Soller added that "until four months ago when circumstances forced me hurriedly to join their faction, I remained uncommitted, even though my inclination was to support Father Point. Father De Vos believes I am 100% behind him, but he is wrong: I cannot support his immoderations any more than I can support those of Father Point." Those who lined up behind the superior were "Father Abbadie and Brother Chauvet, both of whom are completely devoted to him."[31]

There had been superimposed on the quarrel over personal rivalry and the serious division of opinion regarding Point's personality the matter of how to handle funds for the *collège* and church. De Vos "wanted to be able to use the church's revenues according to his pleasure" and Ladavière opposed Point's asserted extravagant building program.

Point, meanwhile, aided and abetted his critics by his contempt for all opposition. The General's decision to join Grand Coteau to the Missouri Mission encouraged the De Vos faction, and before the year was out put the scrupulous-prone Point on the defensive, convincing him that his case had been misunderstood and he had been misrepresented in Rome.

Unaware of his role as the catalytic agent in this drama, in stepped the jolly Superior of the Missouri Mission. Soller describes the scene:

> As soon as Father Verhaegen arrived, he and Father De Vos were on the best of terms. They are fellow countrymen who have known one another for a long time. It is not necessary to say more about these bonds of the friendship; however, Father Visitor lodged in the presbytery where Father De Vos, an unconstrainedly crafty man, paid him regular visits. He knew about everything; he seemed to present all according to his views, his own personal interests. Constantly importuned by Father De Vos, Father Verhaegen began to mistrust him a bit, but it was too late: Father De Vos had already achieved what he had set out to do. In order to insure success, he used intrigue ("holy intrigue," as he put it); he went first to one and then to another giving his views and consolidating his faction. He never rested; such has been his way of acting ever since I have met him . . .[32]

Verhaegen spent seven weeks at Grand Coteau inspecting and researching all aspects of the *collège*, farm, and church; however, at Verhaegen's suggestion, Point was absent a whole month from the scene during the first part of the visitation. After the first session ended, he had been persuaded to take some of the boarders on a type of excursion similar to the one he had led over the Alps with the French interns at Fribourg in the summer of 1832 or 1833, and after school began he went off to give retreats and do supply work in nearby parishes.[33]

If the St. Charles boys had profited from this Louisiana holiday, their moderator confessed he had not. During his absence Father Verhaegen had executed a series of radical changes. Father De Vos was now free to administer the church as he wished and to have full say over how the revenues were to be spent. Moreover, he continued in his role as consultor and thereby was assured of a say in the administration of the *collège*.

Finally:

> to make sure his side would prevail, he recommended Father Mignard be made consultor, to the exclusion of Father Abbadie, who naturally should have had preference both because of his position in the *collège* and because of his seniority in the society. Father De Vos was overwhelmed with joy by the time Father Point returned from his excursion.[34]

Verhaegen drew up a *memoriale* making De Vos and Ladavière independent of the rector and confirming the appointment of Mignard to the list of consultors. He insisted that meat be served at the main meal, a modification which met with the approval of all, including Point.[35] There was no question that the Jesuits lived in dire poverty because every spare cent went into the building program. Abbadie was even forced to give up his own bed to a student who did not have one.[36] Finally, the new superior purchased a slave without consulting either Point or Brother Chauvet, "to the vexation of both."[37] Before leaving, Verhaegen made some modifications to this *memoriale* "but they were of little importance."[38] Point's letter to the General was moderate under the circumstances. He assured Roothaan that although the news of the attachment of St. Charles to Missouri was a surprise, it "was received by the whole community, as it should have been, with a complete submission," but because of the dissociation from France, "not without regret." He felt that Father Verhaegen had been duped into making some decisions that would lead more to division than to reconciliation. He complained that after he returned to Grand Coteau from his excursion with the students, Father Verhaegen asked him to submit written answers to a number of inquiries the Superior had drawn up. The old fear and anxiety that resulted from such a request triggered off once again a series of defense mechanisms to what he judged to be a threat. He informed Roothaan:

> All the same I answered them, but I don't know if my responses were satisfactory. I was told that in a short time I would be told what responses I could keep.

Then he requested:

> Very Reverend Father, concerning this matter, I ask your permission to maintain silence on those affairs which personally concern me.

Point then suggested the heart of the conflict was something altogether objective, something that prescinded personal differences. It was the integrity of Jesuit educational philosophy.

> One matter which I consider of the utmost urgency in my communication with Your Paternity," he wrote, "is the connection between the purpose of our studies and the method of our education, and I am at a loss to understand why we think it impossible to opt for something other than what is called a *business course*. It seems to me that with a bit of patience and talent we can *oblige* those young men who are endowed with a certain degree of intelligence to follow the *classical course*.[39]

According to Point, the crux of the matter was that Verhaegen was trying to accommodate the *plan* of studies he had set up at St. Charles to the course of studies in operation at St. Louis. This element became more apparent during the course of the year. Point had gone to great pains to transplant to the relatively new U.S. territory of Louisiana the *éducation-instruction plan* he had learned from Jean-Nicolas Loriquet and Jean-Népomucène Galicz at Saint-Acheul and Fribourg. He informed the General that "last year we attempted [to implement] the *classical course* and we must confess success has crowned our confidence; more than one half of the student body was enrolled." Total registration in the *collège* by this date had climbed over the eighty mark, and Point added that the cooperation he had received from so many parents was the reason for the achievement of the *plan*.

He repeated the classical Fribourg arguments for

"joining culture of the mind with that of the heart" during "the most critical time of the boys' lives," as the surest way "to form lasting attributes of virtue."

And he wondered:

> Why is it that almost all students spend so short a time doing their studies in practically every *collège*, even Catholic *collèges*, in America, seeing that this is the time of their lives when they have the greatest need to remain in *collège*. The only way they will stay in school is by convincing them to take a less superficial curriculum of studies. This is the reason why, most Reverend Father . . . I thought I should send you my thoughts on the subject of the method of instruction and training.

He then expressed his opinion that the Prefect of Studies, Father John Abbadie, should be one of the consultors to insure academic excellence and fidelity to the *Ratio Studiorum;* gave a financial account of the operations; and once more made a plea for more Jesuits.[40] Even though confirmed in his office, it became increasingly clear to Point that indeed Father Verhaegen's substantial administrative changes were making it difficult for him to function. From this date his letters begin to take on a strident tone; more and more his presentations become captious, defensive.

Abbadie wrote an eleven-page account of what had taken place at St. Charles between October 4 and January 19, which was as harsh as it was frank.[41] Moreover, in his capacity as consultor, Peter De Vos also wrote to the General. The tone and the content of this letter however were radically different from those of the rector and the prefect of studies:

> Desirous to fulfill my office as consultor at St. Charles, my conscience compels me to point out a few, albeit most distasteful matters to Your Paternity. For the most part these past years have been a time of the greatest distress because of mean and persistent arguments, disagreements, provocations, and what has resulted from them: grumblings, complaints, and other such grievances voiced both within the house among Ours and outside, among externs, and even

before our most excellent diocesean bishop and other prelates who seem favorably disposed toward us . . . The man who is our superior seems to be the main source of all of these [evils]. Even though Reverend Father Point appears to be a man of great virtue and singular piety, he is a man of imprudent and rash zeal, most irascible, [and] extraordinarily unpredictable, one who always relies on his own authority, who is stubbornly bound to his own opinions, imperious. From all of this, most Reverend Father, it can readily be seen how much shame he brings on himself and on us. Indeed the joining of our mission to Missouri, once regarded as the harbinger of hope for a brighter future, may now seem to be a cause for fear. Except for a few contrary opinions, Father Verhaegen is regarded as the Angel of Peace. He comes to us with prudence, affability, and truly paternal understanding, and during the time when we were blessed by his presence, he restored, and yet continues to restore, peace, to dissipate divisions, and to witness that a new spring has begun. . .[42]

On February 9, De Vos's former novice Henry Duranquet wrote a letter to Jean Jansens (1789–1847), a former friend of his Rome days, now Secretary of the society in the general's curia. Henry's lining up with forces favorable to the higher superior was contingent on Verhaegen's accepting Point's *plan,* a contingency remote from reality.

A few days ago when I wrote a letter which I took the liberty to send to Very Reverend Father General, it did not occur to me to give details about matters which did not concern me; however, today I believe it fitting to make known to you my opinion about our affairs, regardless of how displeasing it has been for me to come to a decision . . . I shall begin by stating quite simply that *all* involved here have been most tactless when it comes to representing my opinion. As far as the affairs themselves are concerned, there is no doubt in my mind that everyone has acted in good faith, and no one has ever doubted that. Therefore, what was my surprise when I learned that serious incriminations were at stake. I assure you that my purpose in writing to you today is to neutralize the effects of these serious offenses made first by one party and then by the other. However, if I must take a side, I most certainly line up with Reverend Father Superior . . .

The Rector's *plan* was submitted in a most dramatic way to the republican idol, that is to the approbation of the people. This *plan* has its pros and cons, both of which are worthy of scrutiny by a prudent judge. I confess I was against it, but Providence, which has not ceased to send up guarantees of fortuitous success, has been for it. To me, the Rector's views in dealing with class organization and school discipline have always seemed most solid. I think he has rendered a great service to this *collège* by setting up a policy of teaching by *classes* rather than by *subject matter.* His stay at Fribourg has contributed in giving him clear ideas on this point, a matter, in my opinion, in which his critics have censured him indiscretely, if only because they make their opinions public. I believe most of the teachers here can easily integrate the subjects that are taught, and actually this is a real advantage for the students, who are assembled together in one class, and it is even a greater boon for the moral and religious *éducation* of the younger boys. The particular problem we face in Louisiana has been the unfortunate custom of assigning young boys, who speak English well but know no French, with boys who know French, but who can not speak a word of English; yet I honestly do not think that this has been more of a drawback than combining older boys of mature intelligence with young lads (even in science classes) because both groups gain by becoming proficient in the two languages. For the most part, the boys and their parents understand very well that we are in a better position than they to map out an education *plan* and the overwhelming majority is satisfied with us. The influence we have enjoyed with boys and parents since the very beginning has not been lessened, and it has even gained appreciably. Moreover, Reverend Father Visitor's [Verhaegen] decision was to approve of the *plan,* and here I cannot help but see the finger of God because when he first arrived here he was quite openly against the prevailing system, and it was not until just before he took his leave that he approved it, leaving written instructions that he was totally in favor of it . . .

I do not want to overlook the mention of our distinguished Mr. Connolly. He has been quite upset lately; and I believe that he is judged too harshly. They even accuse him of having a totally Protestant mentality and of having retained all of his Protestant prejudices. Even though I have

> heard this opinion voiced many times, and even by Father Visitor himself, I assure you I find it cruel, to say the least, because I am strongly persuaded to believe that the one thing that led to his conversion was that for many years his thinking was thoroughly Catholic in regard to many particular religious questions.[43]

Pierce Connelly did not share young Henry Duranquet's optimism concerning the future of Point's *plan,* and his opinion of Father Verhaegen was no better than the Missouri superior's regard for him. He, too, wrote to the General bewailing the fact that at the very time when St. Charles was making preparations to scuttle what had made it unique, Jefferson Academy, a nearby non-catholic institution was intending to implement the Jesuit *Ratio.*[44] Just what reaction all of these complaints had in Rome has not been recorded, although Father General might well have taken consolation in that part of Soller's letter which advised him that in spite of his autocratic temperament, "Father Point has shown great courage," in the face of what obviously were personal disappointments, and "that he has risen above the difficulties which presented themselves; that he is peaceful with them; that he has great and advantageous plans for the *collège* and, most importantly, that he has a special talent for inspiring young people."[45]

On March 27 Father Verhaegen arrived at Grand Coteau for a second visitation, and he remained at the *collège* until April 2.[46] He was accompanied this time by Father Peter Walsh, no longer a Jesuit, who was eager to teach at St. Charles.[47] According to Abbadie's account, one day during recreation Father Point expressed the opinion that:

"If everything were up to me I'd be off to St. Louis," implying that he would be happy to put the problems of Grand Coteau's church and *collège* far behind him.

Verhaegen, who seemed to be encouraging him to ask for a transfer, responded, "A man should go to the missions if he wants to do good; he works only for the devil in the *collèges*."

"Permit me to disagree," said Reverend Father Point, "St. Ignatius did not think that way about the *collèges*."

"That would have been his opinion about American *collèges*," retorted Reverend Father Verhaegen."[48]

This vignette is terribly important in understanding the sequal of events, each leading to the next until the final catastrophe, because it does give some clue to the enigma of Nicolas Point. Jean-Nicolas Loriquet and the founding fathers of the restored society in France had reaffirmed Ignatius's concept of the *collège*, namely an integral part of the society itself. It was the meeting ground of Graeco-Latin tradition and Christian revolution, the foundry wherein, by means of *instruction* and *éducation,* fidelity to the purity of truth and piety were forged. The purpose of the *collège* was to imbue the young with those ideals, *ad majorem Dei gloriam,* that defined the essence of the Jesuit, and even though the environment of the *collège* was not always congenial to a spirit which was nonconformist and self-questioning, the product, like the product of the society itself, could be an originality sometimes disconcerting. That was an acceptable and even desirable effect. The *collège* was to produce lay replicas of Jean-Paul Martin, Jean-Baptiste Hus, Francis Sylvester Mahony, Xavier de Ravignan, Louis Lambillotte, and Nicolas Point. Essentially the *collège* student's training was to be no different from the training of a Jesuit scholastic because the product was basically the same—a humanist molded by the classics of Western culture, a follower of Christ as presented in the *Spiritual Exercises.* In short, a *chevalier sans reproche*. For this reason the *collège* became something sacred and there was no higher vocation for a Jesuit than to dedicate his life to the *collège*. To have heard it described as "devil's work" by his superior undoubtedly caused great anxiety in the all-too-serious soul of Nicolas Point. If such a statement was not blasphemy, it was something very much akin to it.

Peter Verhaegen was an excellent Jesuit, a man schooled in the finest classic tradition that Europe had to offer. His letters, confidently written in a number of languages, testify to his education and his broad culture. He was a fine administrator, a man of great sympathy and understanding, one who personally had the same respect for the classics as Nicolas Point. But this jolly Fleming who weighed more than 300 pounds was no *preux chavalier* whose destiny it was to die in desperate campaigns. Point was. By instinct, training, and experience, Verhaegen's merit was that he was under no obligation to any educational dogma, particularly one hatched in France. He supported the *Ratio Studiorum* because this was the Roman policy, but in this matter he seemed to be wholly pragmatic.[49] At St. Louis College in 1832 Van Quickenborne was spending two hours a day trying to teach Latin to only eight students, even though Father General Roothaan "made a strong plea for classical education as a practical ideal even in the uncongenial environment of the American West."[50] Two years later, during Verhaegen's tenure as rector-president, Greek was dropped from the curriculum at St. Louis College.[51]

Since the General himself continued to be concerned about this matter and instructed Jesuits laboring in the hostile American cultural enivronment not to compromise the society's educational philosophy, Point was persuaded he was following the General's policy when he protested so vigorously to the introduction of "commercial courses" into the curriculum at St. Charles. He was convinced he was being obedient to the General who had instructed Father Verhaegen six years earlier that the *instruction* and *éducation* imparted at St. Louis "be brought into closer alignment with the standards of the society and that the Latin and Greek languages be better cultivated."[52] For Point, the integrity of the St. Charles plan had become a near-theological rather than a practical issue, not something to be argued about but something to be committed to, and that compromise concerning it would destroy the purity of the Institute itself. It was for this reason, it seems, that he supported Abbadie's recommendation that a Visitor be sent to St. Charles, presumably to defend the society from a real threat to its integrity. He himself felt at a loss to do so. He had reason to feel, however, that the General would support him because Roothaan had taken no less an active interest in defining the Fribourg plan than he had in all other aspects of the society, however insignificant, during this period. While Point was fulfilling the job of prefect of studies or principal at St. Mary's, Roothaan wrote to Népomucène Galicz at Fribourg reminding him that Jesuit education should be "solid and sane," the very antithesis of a "soft and effeminate" mode of education that was characterized by a pursuit of the trendy, novel, and superficial. This was a reminder that Jesuit education emanated from, and was a reflection of, the Jesuit spirit itself. Jesuits were motivated by modesty, abstemiousness, and discretion, the austere ethos of combat soldiers. They were men of clear ideals and goals who received strong support from one another, and their educational philosophy should be distinguished by the same toughness, the same desire for excellence and clear-sightedness. On this occasion Roothaan warned the rector at Fribourg against compromising the ideal of Jesuit education: "It seems our modern students are pulled excessively away from the simplicity of former times; that our superiors have yielded too much to the womanish wishes of parents *(effeminata parentum placita)* and too much money is spent on the delectable, on certain luxuries, etc."[53]

Two weeks before Verhaegen's March visitation, Connelly, who had already written once to Father General Roothaan and who would write to him again within a week's time,[54] addressed a letter to his patron, Bishop Blanc in New Orleans. This letter is revealing for a number of reasons. Composed on the final day of the annual Novena of Grace in honor of St. Francis Xavier, in the midst of "a sort of spiritual tournament of prayers, acts, etc.," it is a glowing testimony to the academic excellence that Connelly considered already rooted in the soil of St. Charles. He asserted that the twofold aim of Point's plan of *"éducation et instruction,"* the "wisdom of the Greeks" expounded in an atmosphere of Catholic culture, had been achieved at the *collège* which owed its existence to the benevolence and support of Bishop Blanc. Verhaegen is depicted in this letter as the threat to the well-being of the *collège,* and it is for this reason that Connelly has formed a conspiracy against the mission superior. He was now bold enough to ask Blanc to join it (reason enough, perhaps, for Pierce Connelly's being branded a crypto-Protestant by the Mission Superior and a number of St. Charles Jesuits!). There is no indication that Point in any way was involved in this conspiracy, and if he was, there is every reason to believe that this fact would have been mentioned. Connelly's remarks, however, do substantiate Point's main objection to the "Missouri intrusion;" that is, that the quality of education at St. Charles would suffer if the St. Louis plan of studies were implemented. Finally, Connelly makes no reference to the fact, noted by Duranquet and minimized by Soller, that Verhaegen had already tabled the St. Louis curriculum and had reinstated Point's plan before leaving Grand Coteau in January. Connelly ended his letter by observing:

> The connection indeed with St. Louis *entre nous* [has been] a severe blow; but I think a letter from yourself to the Father General might put all back again in *status quo,* or at any rate relieve the good and merry Father Verhaegen from a post which he [was] put in, as he told me, so much against his will, to which he is so little fitted for, at least if Louisiana is to be part of his province. It is delightful to see him so zealous for his own College [St. Louis] and so attached to it, but he is like a child in his notions of the country in general and especially of the South and East. He seems to consider his dear Missouri and Kentucky as the center of civilization, and I believe he would like to have all Europe as well as America modeled after them. . . The temporal affairs of [this] College are far better than could possibly have been expected in so short a time. . . In Father Point especially: the more I know him the more I am astounded at our good fortune. Of *all* the Fathers of the Society of Jesus that I have met in Italy and France, in Germany, England, and America, I certainly do not think there are more than five or six who can be considered superior or equal to him.[55]

Two days before arriving at Grand Coteau, Verhaegen informed the General that he had recently received a letter from Soller assuring him that all was again calm at Grand

Coteau, and then added that Point simply had to learn to economize and not spend money he did not have.[56] This was also the constant complaint of Ladavière who wrote to the General that same month accusing Point of the ultimate crime, namely that his actions were "against the Institute."[57] Soller, however, had already informed the General that Ladavière "wanted to pass as a first-rate calculator and good bursar, and that he could account for his management." But as a matter of fact, "his books are in the greatest disorder," and Point embarrassed him each time there was a disagreement about funds.[58] The facts seem to confirm Soller's judgment. Discounting the validity of the other accusations made against him, Point's petit bourgeois instincts were sound when it came to credits and debits. As he had informed the General in January, the total debt on the *collège* was $6,109, a sum, he reckoned, that the next year's profits would wipe out, for with eighty boys enrolled, St. Charles could lay aside $10,000 per annum. In a few years the *collège* would be solvent.[59]

The constant complaints against the rector and all aspects of his governance persuaded Abbadie to write again to the General in March, persuading him for the good of all parties to assign an impartial visitor to Grand Coteau

> for the good of the *collège*, because disputes were beginning anew . . . for the good of academics [because] all of our missions in the United States should adopt Point's plan . . . and for the good of religious life [because] the spirit of independence in this country does not mesh well with the spirit of the society."[60]

It was at this same time that Pierce Connelly wrote his second letter to the General in support of Point's *plan,* and this time he complained that when he had told Father Verhaegen that Latin was important in the curriculum, the Mission Superior answered: "What good is Latin for those who are going to be planters!"[61] During this same month of March, Peter De Vos, who expressed the opinion that Point was "nothing but an imposter, the greatest imposter in the world," and that his projects were "great extravagances," left Grand Coteau to take up his new assignment, master of novices at Florissant.[62] His replacement was Theodore De Theux, who had been Van Quickenborne's successor and, therefore, the first superior of the independent Missouri Mission. He in turn was succeeded by Verhaegen. Theodore De Theux is accredited as being the first person since Marquette to suggest that the United States be dedicated to the Blessed Virgin under the title Immaculate Conception.[63] He is also the man who is responsible for the Missouri Mission's first serious commitment to the Indian apostolate.[64] Yet he, like so many of the men in this drama, was a most controversial personality. At the time of his historic visitation (1830–1852) to the United States Jesuits, the Irishman Peter Kenney informed Roothaan that he had never known two Jesuit superiors more severe in dealing with their subjects than Van Quickenborne and De Theux.[65] Isidore Boudreaux, while asserting that he would ever congratulate himself on having De Theux as his master of novices, confessed that his mentor "had great apprehension of the Judgments of God" and that he was a rigorist.[66] Point maintained he was "terrible in the confessional" and that his religious principles were "wrong, arch-wrong."[67]

St. Charles College

Part Two: 1839

During the course of 1839 there were a number of other changes that altered the make-up of the Jesuit community and, as a consequence, of St. Charles College. Soller, protected by Bishop Blanc, was to be officially assigned to New Orleans until a suitable replacement could be found to take his place. Of course, no such person was ever found. Ladavière joined him at the so-called "New Orleans Mission" residence that the bishop had insisted be established and maintained, a decision about which Verhaegen was powerless to prevent without alienating Blanc. No other Jesuit was assigned to this "residence" until the French returned in 1848, the year Jean-Baptiste Maisounabe (1805–1848) made New Orleans the headquarters for the newly constituted Louisiana Mission, dependent on the Province of Lyon.[1]

True to his word, Father Verhaegen sent a number of Missouri reinforcements to Grand Coteau, leaving no doubt that the Mission took seriously its commitment to support St. Charles. Among the priests, these newcomers included two Frenchmen, a Dutchman, a Fleming, and a Walloon (Theodore De Theux). There were also two new scholastics, both Flemish, and two brothers, both Irish. One of the French priests, Louis-Marie Pin, had entered the Florissant novitiate in 1832 and left the society in 1843.[2] His fellow countryman, Victor Paillasson (b. Lyon, June 20, 1799; d. Grand Coteau, November 9, 1840), was, like Pin, a priest when he entered the novitiate and, also like Pin, had recently finished his two year probation when he was assigned to St. Charles as De Theux's assistant. Paillasson, whom Verhaegen regarded as "a very active, zealous man with a most accommodating disposition," was the first one to serve at the new Potawatomi Mission at Council Bluffs in April 1838. He was replaced the following month by Peter De Smet, whose six-months novitiate was deemed sufficient by Verhaegen. Because of his medical background, Paillasson was sent to assist Father Van Quickenborne at the time he was stricken, and he and a brother were with him at the time of this death.[3] Another one of the pioneer fathers from Missouri was the Dutchman Theodore De Leeuw (b. Breda, Netherlands, June 13, 1810; d. Cincinnati, November 24, 1882), one of the several men recruited for the Missouri Mission by Peter De Smet, and the only one of the original Missouri fathers remaining at St. Charles when it was reposed by Maisounabe in July 1848.[4]

As we have seen, Isidore Boudreaux and Henry Duranquet remained at St. Charles, and during the course of 1839 two more scholastics joined them. These were William Mearns, who left the society, and Peter Arnoudt (b. Moere, West-Vlaanderen, Belgium, May 11, 1811; d. Cincinnati, July 29, 1865), another one of De Smet's recruits who came to the United States with De Leeuw in 1835.[5] The conduct of the scholastics, we are told, managed to scandalize one of the graver fathers, Theodore De Theux, and thereby these young Jesuit teachers manifested a quality of conduct that has remained one of the consistent factors in American Jesuit *collèges* and high schools until recent times.[6] The scholastics were defended by the rector. One of these newly arrived scholastics, Peter Arnoudt, later gained prominence as the author of a book that Garraghan has described as: "Probably the most significant book produced by a Western Jesuit . . . In the field of ascetical literature it is an acknowledged classic."[7] Ironic is the fact that Arnoudt's manuscript was turned down by the censors to whom the Latin version first had been presented. It was then sent to Rome where it was "misplaced" for fifteen years. After Roothaan's death it was found, reexamined, and cautiously approved for publication in English under the title *Imitation of the Sacred Heart of Jesus.* It became an instant sensation in American Catholic circles and was later translated and published in five more languages. Arnoudt, who always seemed to be nonplussed by all of the events preceding and following publication of his book, remains to this day an example for Jesuits who try, not always with success, to have their literary efforts published.[8]

Another one of these newly arrived Missouri Jesuits later gained some notoriety, although on a different level and with a different clientele than the devotees of Arnoudt. This was Edmund Barry who was born on February 24, 1803, someplace "in Ireland," but *where exactly,* the Netherlandish Jesuits never seemed to learn, much less record. Barry died at Bardstown, Kentucky, December 10, 1857. After his death he was described as "a famous workhand." He had been one of De Theux's first novices and Van Quickenborne's faithful companion to the Kickapoo Mission in 1836, where he served as farmer, cook, and handyman—qualifications which prepared him well for anything Grand Coteau could offer.[9] Like Barry, little is known of the other coadjutor brother, James Morris (b. Clones, Monaghan, Ireland, August 8, 1792; d. Bardstown, Kentucky, December 14, 1859), except for the fact that he and Brother Barry constituted a kind of "Pat and Mike" team, first at Grand Coteau and later at Bardstown, with himself unobtrusively taking care of the domestic chores and Brother Barry, in his own quiet way, attending to the outside tasks.[10] All of the new classroom Jesuits spoke better French than English and none of them spoke better English than those they replaced.

The long, bitter winter of discontent at St. Charles gave no signs of thawing in the spring. After Verhaegen's March visit, Point wrote him a letter registering his reactions to the visitation, a copy of which, together with a covering letter, he sent to Roothaan. He informed the General that De Vos, Soller, and Ladavière were no longer in the community and that De Theux (whom he observed was "very much against me") and Paillasson were his new consultors. In this letter Point took up a subject which he had discussed at length with the General in his letter of January 24; namely, the financial status of the *collège*. He complained that his arguments were fiscally sound, even though they failed to convince his superior, the consultors, and some of the graver fathers.[11] This letter contains what today appears to be insightful, well-balanced financial accounts placed beside wordy recriminations and lengthy vindications. In this sense it is no different in tone from all of Point's correspondence to the General after 1839. It is tempting to attribute this rhetorical style and the subject content of those letters to certain psychological quirks in Point's personality. Quirks there certainly were, and given the tensions of life at St. Charles, it is easy to see how they could have affected the superior's equilibrium. Many years later Abbadie would recall that these were "days of suffering and trial," which came about "from poverty and distress, and, too often, from the opposition to the Superior on the part of those who should have befriended him."[12] But during the spring and summer of 1839 there were other factors at work at Grand Coteau which enable today's reader to view Point's apparently bizarre conduct with a greater depth of vision and therefore approach him with better understanding. One of the facts that Point complained to the General about was that Father Verhaegen had virtually turned over the governance of the institution to the consultors who were expected to decide among themselves on matters about which they were ignorant. He wrote: *"we discuss, they decide, I execute."*[13] For the good of the school, could not the superior at least appoint the vice-president, Father Abbadie, who was also the prefect of studies, or principal, and therefore an invaluable source when it came to deciding matters pertaining to the curriculum and to the operation of the buildings and grounds?[14]

In Verhaegen's defense it should be remembered that the greatest complaint against Point by the Jesuits at Grand Coteau had been the rector's autocratic governance and that he and Abbadie were of one mind as far as policy was concerned. It should also be remembered that collegiality was a virtue Jesuits laboring in the United States during this era understood well and practiced faithfully. For example, when De Vos left Grand Coteau, Point gave him a letter addressed to the General and asked him to post it in New Orleans. De Vos, fearing that it contained accusations harmful to Verhaegen, and that it would give the General a false impression of Grand Coteau before he had the opportunity to digest Verhaegen's account, brought the letter with him to St. Louis and, in the absence of Verhaegen, put it in the hands of the rector-president of St. Louis College, John Anthony Elet (b. St. Armand, Antwerpen, Belgium, February 19, 1802; d. Florissant, Missouri, October 2, 1851).[15] Elet, like Verhaegen and De Smet, was one of the seven men who followed Charles Nerinckx to Maryland in 1821, and he was also a member of Van Quickenborne's party to Missouri in 1823.[16] He did not feel in 1839 he could make a unilateral decision on the Point letter; consequently, he assembled the consultors and some graver fathers of the community to hear De Vos's arguments and to determine whether the letter should be kept until Verhaegen's return or mailed to whom it had been addressed. The unanimous decision was that it should be mailed immediately; therefore, it was.[17]

In his letter of March 29, Abbadie warned the General that when policies are made in the midst of personal animosities, the effect is to chill the climate in which growth can be expected. This, he felt, is what had happened at Grand Coteau and the result was that public confidence in the school's administration was being corroded, thereby endangering the very existence of the institution. Again he defended Point, assuring him that he was an ideal choice as an administrator and that detraction was the cause for his being maligned.[18] The General assured Abbadie, and through him the other French Jesuits at Grand Coteau, that dissatisfaction with Point had nothing to do with the decision to place the *collège* under the jurisdiction of St. Louis, and that Point and the members of the community at Grand Coteau had been clearly informed why the transfer had taken place, namely because "the Paris Province, beset as it is with its onerous burdens would be relieved of the embarrassing responsibility of the New Orleans [sic] *collège*." Then he added, in a clear allusion to Point:

> The imagination once in motion makes a man very unhappy and causes him to commit many faults without being aware of it. It is, as St. Teresa says, the crazy member of the household. No, my dear Fathers, the reasons which brought us to unite in one body your own colony and that of Missouri remain always the same and there is nothing to change in this decision.[19]

Rather than being a message of reassurance, the General's words had the opposite effect because, as Abbadie reported, Father Verhaegen had informed the community that the reason why St. Louis had taken over the direction of St. Charles was because of the dissention that reigned at the *collège*.[20] Such confusion was one more factor that contributed to the exasperation of Point, Abbadie, and others involved in this sad drama, and it becomes one more component that helps explain why so many accusatory letters made their painfully slow way back and forth across the Atlantic.

As steam rose from Bayou Bourbeux during the oppressive heat of August, Point judged that the atmosphere at St. Charles had become stifling, intolerable. On the last day of February, at a time when the climate seemed cooler, and more bearable, Verhaegen, in a letter to Point, invited him to "forget the past" and to look forward to the future well-being of St. Charles. However well-intentioned this olive branch was, even it was misinterpreted after Verhaegen's less than successful March visitation to Grand Coteau. How could Point possibly forget the past when the *plan d'études* which constituted the very essence of the *collège* was in danger of being scuttled?[21] He complained to the General about the deplorable American practice of "politicking," and how foreign it was to the spirit of the society, and he repeated his recommendation that a "saintly visitor" be sent to disentangle misinformation about St. Charles, to refute the many accusations made against him, and also to inspect all Jesuit residences in the United States.[22] Moreover, he again advised the General of the situation at Grand Coteau, saying it was anything but satisfactory because of the impossible restrictions the mission superior had placed on him. He repeated all of these points in his letter of September 11, a missive into which he included some of his correspondence with Verhaegen, descriptions of the new buildings, and a long detailed report of the events which had transpired at Grand Coteau since the establishment of St. Charles.[23] Both letters are sad reports chiefly because, failing to see the General's position, Point supplied him with pages of material written in that minute, exact, script that had won him praise from Monsieur Briois and the officers of the *Grande Armée* twenty-nine years earlier, but must have been seen then, as it is today, as a tribute to a useless cause earnestly undertaken. At the same time, all of these *pièces justicatives* give a history of the beginnings of St. Charles from the perspective of a conscientious but slightly out-of-step visionary who either was too far ahead of his times or too far behind them. His commentaries show he had the salesman's gift for marketing the type of education he had learned so well in his early years as a Jesuit, and to which he was so passionately dedicated. Moreover, the neat, precise credit and debit columns with their accompanying financial projections testify to his knowledge of the mysteries of money management and to proper budgeting. Although in his Roman letters he included few sketches of the buildings he designed, there are many excellent line drawings of these in his "Journal."[24] These black and whites demonstrate he had a special talent for blending the decorative and tasteful with the functional and the practical, and they reveal his own architectural abilities as well as the discerning judgment of General Ney, who many years before had recognized the natural talent in Monsieur Briois's young clerk. In order to appreciate the tragedy of Nicolas Point, these sketches should be studied side by side with his August 28 and September 11 reports to Father General Roothaan. Together they demonstrate that this eager, intense, honorable, highly imaginative, and religiously motivated man, whose head was filled with thoughts of *instruction-éducation;* with daring projects for financial fundings and agricultural management, and with designs for heavy Doric columns, myriad crockets and wide-gabled verandahs, really, in spite of his aesthetic taste, lacked discrimination. He was, for all of his recognized charm and charisma, frightfully insensitive to the subtleties of human relations, totally lacking of any political instinct, and, even though seemly and wise, destitute of any critical judgment for opinions at variance with his own. In short, he was a prodigy; yet there was something terribly obtuse about his genius.

Besides the "internal problems" that began in 1838 and continued throughout the course of the next two years, the French Jesuit Jules Maitrugues (1836–1878), an early recorder of the history of St. Charles College, observed, "there was no end of trouble and vexation" for the *collège* that came from without.[25] We have seen that on December 3, 1838, the students moved into Point's newly designed three-storied brick building, which complimented the style and color of the nearby Convent of the Sacred Heart, constructed nine years earlier. The building was "almost finished," a quality that it retained well into the summer. There were disagreements and the contractors showed their dissatisfaction by slowing down their work.[26] There were also jealous reactions to the praise the Jesuits had received in the newspaper reports of October 1838, and exasperating stories about the quality of education southern boys would get at St. Charles. Michael Kenny (1863–1946), an Irish-born, New Orleans Province Jesuit historian, noted that during the course of 1839, "rumors were circulated among the parents by Methodist ministers and conductors of local boarding schools concerning the destructive influence and intent of those foreign Jesuits in Louisiana."[27] As if to crown all of these woes, in the early fall, yellow fever, an uncommon visitor to Grand Coteau, suddenly struck with a vengeance.

Faculty and students were stricken. In October two boys died; six were on the point of death, and most of the others had been withdrawn by terrified parents.[28] Brothers Charles Alsberg and James Morris had been removed to the infirmary, and Father Verhaegen sent word through Father De Theux to have Father Paul Mignard reassigned to St. Louis.[29] "These and similar calamaties have inflicted on the *collège* a wound that cannot be healed but by time," was the cheerless judgment of the anonymous chronicler of the "Annual Letters of the Missouri Mission."[30] In September, St. Charles must have had a *déjà vu* quality about it for Point, who had witnessed the results of the cholera epidemic at Le Passage in 1832. Then on October 8 he himself was stricken.[31]

Three physicians were called in and one after the other gave him up for dead. The Religious of the Sacred Heart assembled before the Blessed Sacrament and remained praying in an all night vigil for him. Finally, on the tenth, the feast of St. Francis Borgia, his agony began. His Jesuit brothers, Pierce and Cornelia Connelly, and others gathered about the sick bed. He recorded he heard a voice say the words: "He is gone." At this point he related he underwent a strange and poignant experience. While those in the room continued the prayers for the dead and dying his eyes became riveted on three pictures near his bed: St. Francis Borgia, the first general of the society to send missionaries to America; St. Francis Xavier, who had died, eyes fixed on China's shore with its millions of unbaptized; and our Lady of the Seven Sorrows, for whom he had lately developed a special devotion. The pictures of Mary and the two Jesuit saints "seemed to assure me that I would not die in this bed; that I would baptize Indians before I passed away." Despite this assurance, he felt himself slipping inexorably farther onward:

> and I thought I had touched the gates of eternity when an interior voice made me understand. It was a word of hope, coming, as it were, from the heart of the Blessed Virgin. At that very moment the bark upon which my spirit seemed to be floating appeared to turn back from the brink . . . and my strength returned to me in a perceptible way . . . When I began to come back to life, it was a new kind of life I experienced: it was as if I were in a garden where there are flowers, scents, harmony; I felt an extraordinary sense of well-being."[32]

Are these the remembered sentiments of a man endowed with a vivid imagination recorded long after the event had passed? Perhaps. But this brush with death had a profound, lasting effect on Point and influenced his future apostolate.

The ravages of the fever confined him to bed for three months, that is, until early December. According to Abbadie, the number of those who visited him during his illness was a fitting testimony to how much he was loved.[33] Then, between the end of the second term (December 10) and Christmas, he preached the Spiritual Exercises to the Religious of the Sacred Heart.[34] Cornelia Connelly was present at each conference and later recorded that this retreat was the occasion for her "real conversion." She testified that it was Point who had first kindled in her a desire for perfection. For his part, Point believed Cornelia "lived in the practice of the Third Degree of Humility," but even though she wanted to make a vow of obedience to him, he put her off.[35] By mutual consent, and with the concurrence of Point, she and Pierce had already decided to live as brother and sister, and soon Pierce was asking for further sacrifices. "She learned later," one of her biographers recorded, "that though [Point] was at the time ignorant of Mr. Connelly's intentions as she was herself, he had yet divined that the priestly and religious life would be the end of their vocations."[36] Point had taught her the Ignatian rules for discerning the will of God. But what did the "will of God" mean for her and for Pierce? During this period she confided the pros and cons of the alternatives she faced to her little diary, and concluded:: "Our confessor knows us and can judge us better than ourselves."[37] Like Teresa of Avila and Margaret Mary Alacoque, Cornelia Connelly, at this most critical period of her life, realized that scrupulous obedience to the advice of the confessor was always demanded of the penitent and a condition to advancement in one seeking perfection of union with God.[38]

The retreat ended at Christmas, and on the last day of January Cornelia took her three children, her maid, and a dog for a walk about the St. Charles property. The youngest child, Henry, not quite three, got away from the rest. Just as Henry reached a sugar boiler, the dog, who had been running with him, jumped up and knocked against him, causing the boy to fall into the scalding liquid. After suffering excruciating pains for two days, the child died on February 2, 1840. Point buried him in the parish cemetery.[39] What was the will of God for her, she continued to ask Point, who was at the time struggling with his own problems and who, himself, had fallen victim to

> "the spirit of darkness which told him all of his efforts had failed, that his superiors had judged him incompetent, that the society was rejecting him, that he had never achieved the purpose of his vocation, that all of these doubts were authentic and divinely inspired."[40]

What advice did he give her? We are not told. However, a few months later he confided his inmost thoughts to his sister, and what he wrote to her about the will of God might well be the answer he gave to Cornelia Connelly's question: "Oh yes, love the cross!" he began. "It is the interior crosses that will bring you happiness rather than the others. Whether you should be here or there—leave everything up to holy obedience."[41] Father Abbadie recorded that Cornelia bore Henry's death "with the deep sensibility of a loving mother, but at the same time with the strong resignation of the perfect Christian."[42] For the most part, Point's dealings with Cornelia Connelly are wrapped in the silence of history, but through occasional, blurred, glimpses we see that the attitudes of both confessor and penitent were identical with the struggle of those mystics during the history of the Church, who united their sufferings with Christ's Passion, struggled with the "natural will" which seeks immediate good and shuns immediate evil, and the will which seeks conformity with the Divine Will.[43] But it is into this region that Clio fears to tread.

At the same time Point went to the Northwest, where failure awaited him, the Connellys went to Rome, where Roothaan, after the couple had received a papal decree of permanent separation, was willing to receive Pierce into the society. Pierce, however, first had to make the solemn vow of chastity implicit in the priesthood; therefore, his entrance into the society was postponed until after his ordination.[44] But by then he had given up the idea of becoming a Jesuit.

Cornelia had retired into the Convent of the Trinità de' Monte, the Roman novitiate of the Religious of the Sacred Heart, after which, following the invitation of Nicholas Patrick Cardinal Wiseman (1802–1865), she opened schools in England, and later in France and in the United States. Thus was born the Society of the Holy Child Jesus. The subsequent history of this couple gained international attention when, after repudiating his ordination and returning to his former religion, Pierce attempted to have the British courts force Cornelia to return to him as his wife. Unsuccessful in this venture, he carried on a campaign of villification against her that lasted until his death.[45] These events and the fact that in 1959 the process for Cornelia Connelly's beatification was introduced in England form another part of history. The essential item here is that Point's influence on Cornelia Connelly was profound and long lasting. It was a force that permeated her critically formative days at Grand Coteau, when, as one of her biographers stated, she preached "death to self in season and out of season, and practiced it with such heroic fidelity in these years of the development of her vocation." Later on she would remember Nicolas Point, and "she would tell of his wonderful power as a missionary and say that he was believed to have the gift of miracles."[46]

On September 19, 1839, Father Peter Verhaegen had collected a list of complaints against Point from some of the actual and former members of the Grand Coteau community and sent the four-page document to Father Roothaan. Although not stated, the intent of the documentation was clear: it was time for a new rector. Many of the accusations made against him do not cause wonder or surprise to anyone having the slightest knowledge of Point's personality or of the early history of St. Charles College. There are, however, some surprises: he delegated too much to Brother Chauvet; he was too friendly with Pierce Connelly; he often forgot what he ordered members to do; he did not show enough hospitality to guests, even to the point of ruffling the bishop; it was rumored he got money from strangers to discharge debts; he made no distinction among people to whom he was introduced; his building plans were extravagant.[47] If the General had any intention of replacing him, it is certain that the news of his illness, which arrived in Rome shortly after Verhaegen's report, postponed the decision. However, it should be remembered, that Roothaan, who the previous year had discouraged Verhaegen from making any essential changes at St. Charles unless they were recommended by the graver fathers, had been getting mixed signals about the rector.[48]

In November Verhaegen requested that a selected number of these graver fathers write to Roothaan giving their opinion on the advisability of appointing a new rector for St. Charles. Again there was no clear-cut agreement.[49] By January 1840, Point had regained his strength but stopped going to recreation, gave up an interest in speaking English, and in general, demonstrated symptoms of a man in the grips of depression.[50] Various problems between the *collège* and the church pitted him against Theodore De Theux, the pastor who had been acting superior during his protracted illness. "I think he has good intentions," he said of De Theux, "and he has a good head on his shoulders, but no one could be more crotchety or cussed."[51]

Point was fearless in pointing out his disagreements with superiors when he thought their policy would be injurious to the greater good. But when these superiors decided against him, as they usually did, he accepted their decisions with obedience and docility.[52] Even his errors in judgment deserve the grace of interpretation. For example, in December 1839, Verhaegen wrote to Bishop Rosati advising him, with some poetic license, that harmony had returned to St. Charles and that there was noticeable improvement in the conduct of the students. His only complaint was the contractor's delay in completing the *collège* building and the exorbitant price he was charging for his labors. "Good Father Point, the Rector," he informed the bishop, "having no experience of Yankee tricks of the country, made only a verbal arrangement with the contractor of the building and now this gentleman does nothing but pile fraud on fraud."[53] The fact was that Point, who had been confined to bed since October, was just then bringing the matter to court and his threat persuaded the contractor to settle the dispute in an equitable manner.[54] Given Verhaegen's own unfortunate experience with the contractors of St. Louis College, one would have expected him to have been more understanding of Point's embarrassment.[55] But perhaps such an expectation is unrealistic. In matter of temperament and background the more than three-hundred-pound Fleming who found it so easy to laugh, and the intense, complex, brooding Frenchman were unfitted to work harmoniously together, and all of the religious principles they shared in common were not enough to overcome the differences.[56] The fact that public opinion outside the Jesuit community at Grand Coteau was so weighted on Point's side exacerbated the problem. Maitrugues's commentary here bears consideration. Undoubtedly, relying on the testimony of Abbadie, to whom he was closely attached, he commented that the

> tasteful building arose, as if by enchantment, and when it was completed, Father Point could not help exclaiming: *'Ah! le voilà enfin, le collège Saint-Charles, enfanté dans le douleur!'* And he could say so truly, for it is difficult to imagine the amount of vexation it had given rise to. It was a common saying that Father Point could not have a brick moved, but there was some one to find fault with it.[57]

Peter De Vos had complained to the General that Point was guilty of bringing Jesuit problems to "our most excellent diocesan bishop and to other prelates who seem favorable to us."[58] This was one of the most serious accusations one Jesuit could make against another. Was the charge justified? Point wrote but four letters, all of them short, to Bishop Blanc between November 1838 and August 1840. The first was written from St. Martinsville on January 23, 1859, shortly after the Mission Superior's first visit to Grand Coteau. Point was supplying in this Acadean town down the Têche in the absence of the local parish priest, and his stay there was coming to an end. He began this letter with an abrupt reference to the problems that bedeviled St. Charles: "Reverend Father Verhaegen is by now probably at the bishops' residence and has already apprised you of everything concerning us; I believe that he now sees things as I have always seen them. In other words, we are on the same road together." He then referred to the $6,000 debt on the *collège*, but was optimistic about paying it off soon. He asserted that this and "other little trials . . . far from discouraging me only double my confidence; indeed I am more sure than ever that one day our little *collège* shall be, Monseigneur, an object of great consolation. Rest assured that insofar as holy obedience permits, I shall keep in contact with Your Grace, for I shall always be at your dispositions to contribute all I can to support your pious wishes."[59] This letter certainly does not indicate that its author was disloyal to the society or to his fellow Jesuits; rather, it collaborates with the opinion of those who asserted that he was, despite his faults, an obedient man. But this letter does pose other questions. The day after he wrote it, Point fired off his denunciatory letter to the General against Verhaegen and his policy regarding St. Charles.[60] So, the question is: Was Point presenting Blanc with a report that was more optimistic than realistic while preparing to manifest his real opinions and feelings to Roothaan? If so, De Vos's accusations would seem unsubstantial, rash. Or, did Point truly think that the problems between himself and his superior had been ironed out, only to discover on his return to Grand

Coteau that same day, that such was not the case? If so, had his letter to Roothaan been written in haste? Whatever the case, this piece of correspondence does not seem to substantiate De Vos's accusation.

Point wrote a second letter to Blanc on March 21, 1839, advising him that certainly he would accede to the Bishop's request concerning the two students Blanc asked him to bend the rules to accept. In this letter he advised the bishop that the Jesuit community had moved into the new building on December 3; that the student population had gone up to 108, and that the community was anticipating Blanc's visitation to St. Charles on St. Ignatius Day.[61] The third letter, written in a less steady hand, was dated November 25. The convalescing rector mentions nothing about his own illness but informs Blanc that the Siena-born Italian Father Flavius Henri Rossi, the pastor at Opelousas died on the twenty-second. He laments the shortage of priests in the diocese but concludes: "It is impossible to think of anything else than our *collège* where sick students are recovering. All but four or five of them have returned; three new ones have been enrolled." The custom of speaking English among the students is prescribed, he informs Blanc, "and the future for our dear boys promises the best." There were fifteen of these preparing for confirmation, and could not the Bishop come up, "possibly for the Feast of St. Francis Xavier?"[62] Finally, on January 2, 1840, Point addressed his last letter to Blanc. Like previous letters this one was an answer to a no longer extant letter from Blanc. The Bishop had told Point he desperately needed money for covering expenses for the orphans in New Orleans, and apparently he asked him for alms. Point apologized for not being able to send, along with his best wishes, an offering for so worthy a cause but he was confident Blanc would understand because "fathers without children are no less worthy of compassion in your eyes than children without fathers." He again reminded Blanc of those at St. Charles who awaited confirmation and encouraged him to visit Grand Coteau soon, and finally, he described to the bishop how he was continuing to make improvements on the new building. For example, the recently completed domestic chapel, designed so that it could accommodate the Jesuit community, would in the future also serve the needs of the sodalists.[63] These letters to Bishop Blanc are informative, formal, discrete, at times witty, always respectful, and for the most part solicited. In none of his correspondence, which differs considerably in style and content from his letters to Jesuit superiors, does Point ever ask Blanc's council nor court the bishop's sympathy in his dealings with his fellow Jesuits.

In May, he again gave himself unsparingly to the annual Marian celebrations. As we have seen, at Saint-Acheul and Fribourg these structured May devotions were designed "for doing the faith," and so he took great pride in the fact that they were performed exactly as they had been in France and as they were still practiced in the *collèges-en-éxile*. We have seen that in addition to *instruction,* the wisdom of the Greeks, Point gave equal importance to *éducation,* practices that appealed to the heart, and that these two aspects of learning were complementary for creating and sustaining the atmosphere that distinguished St. Charles. Father Abbadie recalled that before the arrival of the Jesuits the moral and religious training of the Cajun boys had been sadly neglected. "Some of them did not know the 'Our Father' and 'Hail Mary', and as little about the catechism, as about Bacon's 'Novum Organum'." So they had to be taught their prayers and catechism along with Greek and Latin paradigms.[64] Since one of the most effective ways to teach the whole person the truths of the Faith in context with Catholic culture was by participating in the May devotions, the same prayers were said, the same songs sung, and the same processions were organized as at Le Passage. There were the same *floscoli* gatherings, the same acts of consecration, the same poetry readings and Marian sermons given by the students, and the same coronation ceremonies that had been so much a part of the *éducation* at Saint-Acheul and Fribourg. These devotions lived on at the *collège* long after Point had left. The proximity of the Convent of the Religious of the Sacred Heart heightened this annual public homage to Mary just as it fostered its pageantry. In order to enhance the dignity of the daily processions, he himself planted an avenue of live oaks joining St. Charles to the convent's formal garden, patterned after the Versailles garden of Bishop Bossuet. A number of these oaks are still living, fitting relics of Point at Grand Coteau, and their presence makes more poignant his reflections expressed to his sister in 1840.[65] He wrote that:

> Less than twenty-five years ago this Grand Coteau prairie offered no sign of, I shall not say religion, but even of civilization. And look at it today! Three brick buildings, a church, a *collège,* a convent—all rivaling with one another in some way to give glory to God. I might be wrong, but it seems to me that, judging from what we see today, maybe the day will come when this school will be on an equal footing with the boarding schools of our beloved France.[66]

The dynamo of this progress and energy was Point himself, this Frenchman whose personality at times became indistinguishable from 'the crazy member of the household', which all too frequently led him into haunted, shadowy regions.

In November 1839 some of the consultors were again asked to write to Rome giving their opinion on whether or not Point should be replaced. The answer was clear-cut as far as Fathers De Theux and De Leeuw were concerned.[67] Although Victor Paillasson's reply was more nuanced, he also answered affirmatively.[68] Consequently, a few days before St. Ignatius feast, July 31, 1840, Nicolas Point was relieved of the office of rector-president at St. Charles and, with feelings that were never recorded, he promptly took a barge as far as St. Louis.[69] He would never return. One week after he had left, Abbadie submitted a balanced budget which showed even a small increment. "In three years," Abbadie advised Roothaan, "bereft of human resources, in a foreign land, in spite of thousands of set-backs, such prosperity would not have come to us without the unmistakable assistance of divine Providence. And he whom God used to begin his work was the Rev. Father Point, who by his untoward performance has benefitted well the society in Louisiana." Abbadie included a citation from the July 11,

1840, edition of the Franklin *Gazette* offering supporting evidence to his judgment: "The order of the Jesuits have established, in this State, a *collège* which promises to be one of the most splendid institutions of the kind in the Union . . . Although not yet completed, there are few buildings in the State which can vie with it in the point of architectural beauty."[70] Pierce Connelly also commented on Point's departure in a letter, dated August 4, addressed to Bishop Blanc, who had just returned to New Orleans after participating in the Fourth Provincial Council of Baltimore:

> I received your kind letter of the 15 ult. as well as the one you were good enough to bring me from Baltimore . . . When will the vineyard be provided with labourers as are wanted? Father Verhaegen has given us a sad blow in the removal of Father Point, one who so well understood the necessities of the country and the means that should be taken to satisfy them. But God is our help. He certainly has nothing to regret; his work here has been crowned with such a success as was beyond hope—he has done what he had to do—and well. The new labours that he is called to will make up more merit and bring with them greater consolations than others of a higher and greater usefulness.[71]

Pierce Connelly "later apologized to Father Roothaan with much feeling for having taken sides with Father Point in the latter's differences with Father Verhaegen." Pierce Connelly had a way of changing his mind.[72]

Soller was named the new rector-president.[73] He came up from New Orleans, stayed just long enough to delegate Abbadie his vicar, and then got the next barge back.[74] He had previously reminded the General that he did not ask to come to Louisiana, but when Guidée and Renault begged him to volunteer he did not refuse, and now he had more work in the United States than he ever had in Europe, and so choices were necessary. He wanted to work with the people in the hospitals, and wanted nothing to do with the *collège*.[75] Although Bishop Blanc's desire was the same, he was not able to keep Soller on the hospital wards beyond December.[76] The bishop, who apparently did not comment to the Jesuit community on Point's removal, was not so circumspect among his own clergy. He was not pleased. So it was, then, that Abbadie took charge of St. Charles, just in time to face a crisis which casts the events described above in a somewhat ironic mold.

Nicolas Point had not been gone a month when a slave rebellion broke out in St. Landry and Lafayette Parishes.[77] A number of slaves, led by a few white men, formed a conspiracy to murder their masters, rob the bank at Opelousas, and then flee to Texas. The civil authorities were informed of the plot while the secret preparations were still being made. Fifteen of the guilty were hanged and others "severely punished." Ignace, the slave Point had so objected to purchasing, was falsely accused of being involved in the scheme. "He was subjected to seven days' torture, then acquitted as innocent." After his release the Grand Coteau Jesuits were denounced for having instigated the rebellion, a charge which prompted the La Fayette Volunteers to consider coming to the *collège* "to give each of them a hundred lashes with a cow-hide." One pistol-packing planter met Father De Theux on the St. Martinsville road and gave him the option of either clearing out of the parish in double quick time or getting shot.

> The principal charges brought against the fathers were: 1st, one of them had been seen shaking hands with a negro; 2d, another was known to have spent a whole night in hearing the confession of a negro in La Fayette parish, who was a relative of the man that headed the rebels; 3rd, they had furnished the negroes of St. Martinsville with weapons. These weapons, it was declared, were sent in a coffin in order not to arouse suspicion.

For almost three months local villagers kept watch during the night, and once, when the volunteers were expected to strike, "Fourteen men kept guard at the *collège*, and a patrol of thirty men lay encamped within a short distance from the grounds."[78] Such was the first act in the long tragedy at St. Charles that Nicolas Point would not have to witness.[79]

WESTPORT, MISSOURI
1840–1841

It would be unnecessarily melodramatic to suggest that Nicolas Point was removed from Grand Coteau merely because certain idiosyncracies of temperament had set him at variance with those under his authority. The reasons were more complex; their causes diverse, subtle, and not always completely understood by the parties involved at the time. Even before the Missouri Mission had taken over the administration of St. Charles, events inexorably were at work within the mission which would have given it a new direction independent of Louisiana and in spite of personalities. Yet, to match that inexorability, history could hardly have timed better manipulators of events than Peter Verhaegen, Nicolas Point, and Peter De Smet. Of these three it is easy to see how other men could have easily duplicated the roles of Verhaegen and Point. Peter De Smet, however, by the sheer power of his personality dominated the events, forging from them the dynamism out of which sprang missions in the Rocky Mountains and throughout the Northwest, and Jesuit *collèges* in California.

On the very day Nicolas Point left Grand Coteau forever, July 21, 1840, Peter De Smet was offering the first mass said in the present state of Montana, near the Idaho border, in the presence of fifteen hundred Indians.[1] The proximate reason for his presence there can be traced to an event that took place in September 1839, the date when a two-man delegation of Rocky Mountain Indians, Peter Gaucher (Left-Handed Peter) and Young Ignace, had descended from the Missouri bound for St. Louis where they hoped to find Black Robes to bring the Gospel to their people.[2] A more remote reason was that this was the fourth time such a delegation from these tribes had come to St. Louis since the fall of 1835.[3] At the time when the first delegation arrived, Nicolas Point, completing his tertianship at Saint-Acheul, was confiding to his notebook his persistent and overwhelming attraction to be sent to the forests of North America, and Abbé De Smet, a chaplain to the Carmelites at Dendermonde and no longer a member of the Society of Jesus, was negotiating with the minister of the Jesuit residence at Alost, Peter De Vos, about reestablishing a foundation of his nuns there, since Alost had been a center of Carmelite presence before the Revolution.[4]

In 1839 when the fourth Indian delegation passed through Council Bluffs on the Missouri, they met Peter De Smet, once again a member of the society, who had been "watering a dry stick" among the Potawatomis there, in obedience to his assignment by Verhaegen in 1838. De Smet, convinced that there was little hope for these hapless victims of the detestable liquor traffic, was immediately fired up by the arrival of these two Iroquois visitors whose adopted people beyond the mountains thirsted for the waters of salvation. So, while Point was writhing with fever on what was thought to be his deathbed in Grand Coteau, De Smet was promising his welcomed visitors help, and since he was eminently a man of action, he was not content merely to put his promises in a letter and send it on to Father Verhaegen. He himself would go to St. Louis. Ostensibly returning to home base to seek medical attention for a persistent ailment, he arrived back in St. Louis on February 28, 1840, and begged Verhaegen to allow him to be the one who would finally heed the persistent appeals of the Rocky Mountain Indians, and to personally investigate the possibilities for creating a reduction in the mountains of the west, far from the white man's whisky.[5] Meanwhile, both Bishop Rosati and Father Verhaegen had written letters to the General earnestly pleading that these Indians, who had been requesting missionaries for the past nine years, be assured of a commitment from the society. "For the love of God, my Very Reverend Father," the bishop wrote, "do not abandon these souls!"[6] And Verhaegen ended his letter with a similar request: "I am desirous, therefore, to know of your Paternity what he wishes done by us on behalf of those poor creatures."[7] Verhaegen wrote this letter the same time he was canvassing the consultors at Grand Coteau about the desirability for a new rector at St. Charles.[8] Undoubtedly he had plans for Point. Consequently, when De Smet arrived in St. Louis in February, the spadework had already been done for investigating the feasibility of setting up a mission among the Flatheads.[9] As a result of these preliminary steps, Verhaegen, De Smet's superior and close friend of many years, ordered him to leave for the Rocky Mountain country to investigate the possibilities of establishing a permanent mission among the Indians there. Accordingly, on March 27, 1840, De Smet departed St. Louis for Westport, which was then a frontier landing-place on the Missouri opposite the Kansas River, the eastern terminus of the Santa Fe Trail and today part of Kansas City, Missouri. There he joined a party of men from the American Fur Company, and with Young Ignace for a companion, he departed, bound for the Flathead country on April 30.[10] The party followed the usual route as far as the Platte and then up that river to Fort Laramie, Independence Rock, and finally across the Continental Divide at South Pass.[11] On June 30, he met Peter Gaucher, who had gone ahead to announce De Smet's impending arrival, with an advance guard of Flatheads at the fur company's rendezvous on the Green River, and, accompanied by these, Peter De Smet made his way to the Flathead country where he was received in triumph.[12]

Nicolas Point, who arrived at St. Louis at the end of

July, remained there until October 24, the day he, too, set out for Westport, the meeting place for merchants and fur traders en route to the great American wilderness. Here he arrived on the first of November to await the return of Peter De Smet and here he remained until the following May.[13] Before embarking on this, the first stage of his trek to the Northwest, Point presented himself at the novitiate of the Religious of the Sacred Heart at Florissant, where for a few brief hours on October 8, he was united once again with his sister.[14] After the death of their mother in 1837, both Marie-Jeanne and Pierre Point felt free to enter religious life and thereby accomplish their lifelong dream.[15] Pierre, a priest and honorary canon of the archdiocese of Reims, entered the novitiate at Saint-Acheul on January 1, 1839, four days after Marie-Jeanne was received into the Society of the Sacred Heart on the rue de Varennes, Paris.[16] Her request to work in one of the society's schools in the American Mission was granted, and so in 1840 she was appointed one of the companions to the formidable Princess Elizabeth Galitzin (1797–1843), whom St. Madeleine-Sophie Barat (1779–1865), foundress of the Religious of the Sacred Heart, sent as Visitor to the communities of the order in the United States. The autocratic Mère Galitzin's *"gouvernement à la Russe"* and her determination to mold the nuns into "lady Jesuits" came near to destroying the American foundations. She and Marie-Jeanne arrived at Florissant a few days before Point left Grand Coteau.

After pronouncing her first vows in 1841, Marie-Jeanne was assigned to St. Louis where she remained for the next two years, and then, in 1843, she was missioned to St. Michaels (present-day Convent, Louisiana), where Ladavière had been director in 1832. She arrived just in time to witness the heroic death of Mère Galitzin, who paid the ultimate price for nursing sick and dying victims of yellow fever. In 1851, Mère Point came to Grand Coteau to care for the orphans who had been so dear to Bishop Blanc, and then in 1855, she was placed in charge of the famous convent gardens, a section of which had been designed by her brother between 1838 and 1840. This "Avenue of the

Oaks," which Nicolas planted to provide shade for the Jesuits who walked each morning to the convent to say mass and for all the faithful who participated in the May and other processions, remains to this day one of the great tourist attractions at Grand Coteau, the sole and fitting monument to the founder of St. Charles College. What reader of Chateaubriand could forget that writer's reflections on the theme of gnarled trees, particularly those at Combourg?[17] The tree with its roots deeply buried in the changeless, life-giving soil was the living metaphor of tradition; the image of spontaneity, continuity, assimilation, discipline.

Late in the summer of 1853 yellow fever again struck Grand Coteau, carrying off more than thirty people, one of whom was Mère Marie-Jeanne Point, R.S.C.J., who died on October 2.[18] After their short visit on the afternoon of October 8, 1840 Nicolas and Marie-Jeanne Point never saw one another again.

Nicolas Point wrote that there were twenty-three families in his Westport parish, "each family group comprising of a Frenchman with his Indian wife and his *métis* children." He added:

> Immediately upon my arrival these people found a large place in my sympathies; for even though very poor, they somehow had contrived to build themselves a church, and again and again they had asked for a priest before succeeding in getting one. It was well though that I had sympathy to spare, there being no lack of ills awaiting cure at my hands. What with the ignorance of some, the drunkenness of others, the sensuality of almost all, there was misery enough to inspire zeal in the most laggard of missionaries. And so I went to work with great confidence, the more so because I had found that the sovereign remedy for ills of this sort lay in a little goodwill and in the use of common sense.[19]

His church, which was first staffed in 1834 by Father Benedict Roux of the St. Louis diocese, had been dedicated to the French Jesuit St. Francis Regis (1640–1737), but it was universally referred to as "Chouteau's Church," and was located two miles from the famous trading house of the same name.[20] Point, for reasons that should by now appear to the reader obvious, began calling it St. Francis Xavier's, but this innovation never seemed to catch on. With the same precision he drew up his *plan* for the students at St. Charles, he now sketched out a program calculated to deal with his first parishioners.[21] The objective had become firmly fixed in his mind "because of his frequent meditations on the spirit and examples of St. Francis Xavier, his patron and model," and because his training had taught him the importance of the relationship between *éducation* and *instruction*.[22] Westport offered him his first opportunity to implement "the means the Paraguay missionaries had adopted," which had inspired him from the days of his adolescence. Methodically, he adapted the *means* to suit the *end* and recorded how his design unfolded:

> One of my chief cares was to keep my ministry high in repute with all. To this end I tried to be as light a burden as possible on the community. My work kept me quite busy. I had a lot of knickknacks that had been given me in Louisiana, and so I turned my attention to these and with little trouble managed to find a number of articles that suited me well. Among other things I found: children's prizes, and vestments, statues, pictures, a tabernacle, and best of all a monstrance for the church. What real treasures they were to us, who when Christmas came around were able to enjoy all those blessings of devotion which we might have expected to find only in a large city. Moreover, I taught the children to sing certain short hymns with results, I may say, that fairly astonished me.[23]

His mode of operation was that of the eighteenth-century Jesuits who had sustained their Paraguay reductions according to the age-old plan of assembling a community of poorly instructed and culturally deprived Christians under the more or less patriarchal rule of the missionary.[24] Such methodology called for special emphasis placed on the dignity and beauty of the liturgy, by highlighting the visual appeal of statues, vestments, altar equipment, and by recognizing the catechetical value in such captivating, singable melodies as those created by the Lambillotte brothers and other traditional composers.[25] As he had done at Le Passage and Grand Coteau, he adapted many of Loriquet's recommendations and those suggested by Galicz for fostering competition, and therefore interest, among young people eager to be recognized and rewarded for their accomplishments. Moreover, besides the goodwill and common sense he placed at such a premium, he showed his pedagogical talents by the way he dealt with different groups in his parish. For example, as his classmate Louis Marquet would do in Brittany and Normandy, he stressed the importance of sodalities for training women, and of Eucharistic devotions for capturing the interest of, and instructing, the men. He enrolled unmarried women in a sodality dedicated to Mary Immaculate while the married women were gathered together in another sodality placed under the patronage of The Seven Sorrows. It might occur to a modern reader that Point's placing the married women of Westport under the special patronage of the Blessed Virgin of the Seven Sorrows could suggest a certain whimsical trait in the complex make-up of the pastor at Chouteau's Church. Point, however, was a man without the slightest trace of whimsy and his irony was not of the nature to suggest to him that his action might be interpreted in any way other than edifying. There was a painting in his small church of the Dolorous Virgin which attracted Indians from as far away as the Kansas plains, and this picture is undoubtedly the reason for the name given to the married women's sodality.[26] The men were encouraged to make up teams that insured the Blessed Sacrament would have appropriate honor guards during the day and night.[27] Finally, what is striking in reading his recollections of these pastoral activities, the dress rehearsal for the Rocky Mountain missions, is that here was an intelligent, compassionate, hard worker, admittedly dedicated to the principles of paternalism, but who, nevertheless, worked best when he worked alone.

An American historian described Westport during Point's stay there as an emporium, a meeting place "seething with rough Mountain Men and painted Indians and dusty immigrants, traders and wagons and buckboards, pungent mules and puffing oxen."[28] While routine events flowed unevenly but monotonously on the foreground of this hustling town, the attitudes of its Catholic population were being subtly conditioned by other forces in the background, and the source of these forces was the new pastor. He noted cautiously:

> But my good people's need extended to something beyond the singing of hymns which embodied such words as eternity, and heaven, or which alluded to the mysteries of the Church.

However attractive, such means were lures. "Solid instruction was painfully necessary," because without it, no matter how attractive the music or how inspirational the sermons, "these things passed with most of the people for an empty sound."

> Accordingly, I instructed them in the great truths of our religion, insisting particularly on the practical consequences that should be the result of the consideration of them; namely, the making of a good confession. Nor did I hesitate to address very pointed remarks to those who were included in St. Paul's catalogue of sinners, especially the drunkards.[29]

Courage, single-mindedness, clear-sightedness, determination, and, above all, an unquestionable and unflinching honesty of purpose were the salient characteristics of this man who was, and remained, first and foremost an educator, a "man of men for a *collège*" who loved the subject he was teaching, loved the people to whom he was teaching it, and saw the need to establish a relationship between subject taught and object to whom it was being taught. Like any good teacher Point was aware of his students, took a great interest in them, and adapted his teaching accordingly. After describing his "labors in behalf of the older people," he adds, "I did not neglect the children." For these:

> I had catechism classes regularly, in the course of which I paid special attention to children gifted with good memories and pliable minds, so that when scattered over different

parts of the little parish they might teach others whatever I had taught them. It is a common saying that in America it is impossible to fire children with emulation, as is done in the churches of France and Italy. In point of fact, this saying is not true. The business is a little harder to manage here, I grant, but provided you are not afraid of losing a little popularity, and with justice and prudence administer your praise and blame where it is deserved; provided also, you give out marks, and distribute medals, pictures, etc. before the parents' eyes—I warrant you success: self-love is everywhere more or less to be found and if rightly taken hold of can be molded into emulation. I tried this plan myself, at Westport, and succeeded beyond all expectations. During the week I would teach catechism, repeating the instructions on Sunday for the benefit of the whole congregation. What a picture we made up! There was the missionary in front; near him the youngest children; next those who had made their First Communion; then those studying the catechism of perseverance; last of all, the mothers and fathers. During the week marks were read out, and every Sunday the best scholars in each catechism class received a medal as a reward. At the end of each month prizes were also awarded to the most proficient in the shape of holy pictures. These pictures were afterwards hung up in some conspicuous place at home, and before them morning and evening prayers were said in common. Whenever I made my visits, I never failed to look in the direction of these objects, an action that went far towards exciting a laudable spirit of rivalry among both young and old.

As children's piety depends greatly on that of their mothers, I undertook to increase the store of piety of the latter by establishing a sodality of married women . . . Soon afterward I found another for young girls . . . These young girls I found to very modest, and so remarkable for natural piety and goodness that no words of praise was uttered of any one of them without reflecting credit on all of them . . . It is a fact that in all the twenty-three families living here, there was not a young girl whose moral conduct was not above reproach—and this marvel took place in an area where man's licentious nature brooked no bounds. A few of these young persons, encouraged by the example of a pious widow, took it upon themselves to make some artificial

> flowers for the church and I can say with truth that the work of their hands was not to be despised. Before Lent it happened that I made mention of the prayers of the Forty Hours' Devotion; when immediately men, women, children, all offered to make in turn their hour of adoration and during the three days several persons were constantly before the most Blessed Sacrament. The novena in honor of St. Francis Xavier [St. Francis Regis], the patron of our church, had also a large attendance of people; it consisted in having evening prayers and an instruction in the church. At the close of this novena, as was also the case at Christmas, two-thirds of the congregation received Holy Communion.
>
> Another thing occurred at this period that gave me great joy. The year before, balls had taken place among the people weekly; this year there were only two or three which I permitted, lest by too great a show of severity I might lose the ground I had gained with them. The means they took in securing my permission for their dancing amused me not a little. They sent as bearer of their first petition an old soldier who had served in the time of the Empire, who had also accompanied Father De Smet on his return from the Rocky Mountains, and who bore the reputation of being a man to whom I would refuse nothing. The good old fellow [Jean-Baptiste De Velder, a Belgian of Ghent and erstwhile grenadier under Napoleon who had spent fourteen years trapping beaver in the mountains[30]] came to me, and after telling me that he had a favor to ask, begged to be allowed beforehand to say a Hail Mary, for the success of his mission. The prayer said, he confidently broached his petition. The second ball was given on the occasion of a wedding; on this, so many and such restrictions had been put, that all fear of danger resulting from it seemed effectually precluded—young women for instance were not to go to it without my leave. . . .[31]

In theory, French Catholic priests during this part of the nineteenth century were uncompromising when it came to allowing their parishioners to dance, and the fact that their colleagues in Ireland not only permitted their people to dance, but sometimes even joined in the jigs and reels was a cause of the greatest scandal.[32] In this instance, even though Point congratulated himself on his ability to bend the rule for the greater good, De Smet later reported that some of the Westport parishioners complained that Father Nicolas was far too rigid for their taste. Research has not revealed the number of young women, if any, who failed to receive the pastor's leave to attend the second Westport ball, nor does there seem to be a record of their reactions. But looking back many years later, Point was pleased with his stay at Westport, and there is no evidence to suspect that the majority of people were not sorry to see him leave them again without a resident priest.

> On the Sunday before my departure, all the married women belonging to the sodality of the Seven Sorrows, the members of the young women's sodality, and all the children who had made their First Communion, approached the Holy Table. In the afternoon there was the blessing of beads, medals and pictures, the catechism prizes were distributed, Benediction of the Blessed Sacrament followed, and finally a large cross was erected in the cemetery . . . Only three marriages took place while I was at Westport, but they were exemplary marriages: the contracting parties had all the dispositions the Church desires her children should always possess. Thus from the first day of my new career did God still support my feeble steps by giving me new proofs of the care which he takes of those who put their trust in him."[33]

On the previous August 27, De Smet began his long trip back down the Missouri, past Forts Union, Clark, and Pierre. Then on October 17, as Point was making final plans to leave St. Louis for Westport, De Smet took a canoe at Vermillion, but the early ice prevented him from traveling beyond his old station at St. Joseph's Mission, Council Bluffs.[34] From there, on December 14, when the cold at Westport was "so intense as to freeze the chalice even when the altar had a chafing-dish full of live coals placed at either end,"[35] De Smet continued his journey by horse toward Chouteau's Church, where he arrived on the twenty-second, amidst the preparations for the pageantry of Christmas. This may have been the first meeting of Point and De Smet, although it is more than probable they had met in the late summer of 1834 when Monsieur l'Abbé De Smet came to Saint-Acheul—where Point, newly arrived from Le Passage, was beginning his tertianship—to purchase the physics laboratory equipment for St. Louis College. Now, however, at the end of 1840, De Smet, impatient because of his unscheduled delays, did not wait to hear the rendition of Lambillotte's cantiques by the Westport choirs nor watch the various sodalities process into the church for the Christmas midnight mass. He spent less than twenty-four hours with his host before boarding the stage, which delivered him in St. Louis on December 31, 1840.[36] Here he received a hero's welcome but not a hero's spoils. His report, recommending a permanent mission be set up among the Flatheads, was enthusiastically received by Father Verhaegen and Bishop Rosati, but they could not raise funds to support the venture. De Smet printed thousands of pamphlets describing his experiences among the Indians of the Rocky Mountains and begged for donations to support a permanent residence among them. His efforts were so successful that on February 8 he began an extensive begging expedition throughout the South and East.[37] "My fondest hopes have been more than realized," he wrote on April 27, "for notwithstanding the critical financial condition actually existing in the United States, I collected $1,100 in New Orleans. Women brought me their jewels; even the slaves contributed their mite."[38]

If Verhaegen could not supply money, he was now at least in a position to offer men for the projected mission. Less than two weeks after De Smet's return to St. Louis, he recommended Point be assigned as De Smet's companion to the Flatheads, and then while De Smet was begging in Louisiana, he submitted his name once again, and the recommendation was approved.[39] A third priest appointed to the new mission was Gregory Mengarini (b. Rome, July 21, 1811; d. Santa Clara, California, September 23, 1886), who was twenty-nine years old—young, compared to De Smet, who was already forty and to Point, who was forty-two. In December 1839, while De Smet was in Council Bluffs fulminating against whites who furnished the Potawatomis with whisky and while Point was giving the Spiritual Exercises to Cornelia Connelly in Grant Coteau, this charming Italian nobleman with a flare for scholarship was in his second year theology at the Roman College. One day during *pranzo* Bishop Rosati's letter to Father Roothaan, dated St. Louis, October 20, 1839, describing the three Flathead delegations to St. Louis, was read in the community refectory. After this reading there was an appeal from the General for volunteers. Mengarini was never the same after that meal.[40] He immediately wrote a letter, dated December 25, 1839, begging the General to assign him to the foreign missions.[41]

This appeal was accompanied by others from a number of volunteers, but the only two the General accepted were Mengarini's and one submitted by another man studying theology, James Cotting (b. Fribourg, Switzerland, May 23, 1812; d. Georgetown, D.C., July 23, 1892). The pair had their final courses plus tertianship truncated into several months, and then in the late summer of 1840, they boarded a ship bound for the United States. After the predictable perils they found themselves in Baltimore where they boarded their first train for Georgetown. Totally confused about why their fellow travelers poured off the train to eat and why all the lights went off in their car, they tried to adapt themselves to the American customs the best way they could. Meanwhile, they began making discrete inquiries in French how to get to Georgetown. No one could help them because no one could understand them. They tried six other languages without success. At last an official came to their rescue, pushed them onto another train just in time for them to continue on. Mengarini, who prided himself on being cosmopolitan could appreciate the fact that few people spoke Italian, but he was flabbergasted to learn that, unlike the rest of the world, Americans were really ignorant of French.[42] Before he published his famous Latin-Flathead grammar and other monograms in the fields of American Indian ethnology and anthropology, he would learn more astonishing facts about his adopted homeland.[43] The two ingenuous polyglots made their way from Georgetown to St. Louis in late September, and by early March Verhaegen calculated the budget would allow De Smet to take one but not two on the first excursion westward, Cotting was stronger; but, like the Paraguay missionaries, Mengarini could play a musical instrument, sing, and had a medical background; so he was deemed of greater value.[44] Cotting was given an assignment in Missouri and would be sent to the Rockies at a later date; however, this part of the plan was altered when he was subsequently accused, falsely it was asserted, of aiding and abetting a mob intent on destroying a Protestant church. Whatever his involvement in the affair it was decided the more prudent course of action would be to reassign this muscle-bound Swiss to Maryland, and it was there he ended his days. From his rather cryptic obituary one learns that "[t]hough of a gruff and uncouth nature, yet many a kind deed has been entered to his credit in the book of life".[45]

Besides the three priests assigned to the new mission, there were also three coadjutor brothers. These were: Charles Huet (b. Coutrai, Belgium, August 26, 1805; d. Old Mission, Idaho, May 31, 1856), who had been a Jesuit for six years; Joseph Specht (b. Alsace, France, September 1, 1808; d. St. Ignatius, Montana, June 17, 1884), who had entered the society in 1839, and the youngest of the party, a five-year veteran of the society, William Claessens (b. Berendrecht, Antwerpen, Belgium, September 8, 1811; d. Santa Clara, California, October 18, 1891). One day in 1835, the twenty-three year old William Claessens, who was working as a baker in Antwerp, encountered the Abbé De Smet, who promised him "a life of toil and privation, but a life, too, rich in the fruits of salvation for the poor red-skins of North America." The baker signed up immediately along with Theodore De Leeuw, Peter Arnoudt and four other Flemish candidates bound for St. Louis where they arrived in December 1835. In July 1837, Brother William was assigned to be the companion to the ailing Van Quickenborne, and he and Father Paillasson were the two men with the revered missionary when he died on the following August 17. Afterwards Brother Claessens returned to the Kickapoo Mission, and, as we shall see, witnessed its closure, before joining De

Smet and the other four on this "life of toil and privation." "Those were the pioneer days," his obituary reads, "and the life of a brother who had to exercise all trades by turns was not one of idleness and ease." The baker became a builder and in 1868 erected the second St. Mary's Mission church near Stevensville, Montana. He also constructed a small workshop which still stands, a sturdy, functional, dignified monument to the man who spent fifty years on the Indian missions. Two years before his death he was returned to the newly built novitiate at Los Gatos, California, and then to nearby Santa Clara College where he "worked at odd jobs around the house, as much as his feebleness would allow, but passed most of the time in reciting the rosary of our Blessed Mother. Thus in prayer and patience he happily closed a long life of generous self-sacrifice in the service of his good Master."[46] The other brothers assigned to this expedition were cut from the same cloth as Brother William. For example, the day before Point began his Long Retreat under Xavier de Ravignan, November 1, 1834, Brother Charles Huet and four other young candidates, together with the scientific equipment from Saint-Acheul, set sail for New York, where they arrived on December 23. The physics laboratory was received at St. Louis College on March 7, and Huet and his companions reported to Florissant two days later. Huet, an expert coppersmith, won admiration and gained praise for the work he did on the roof of the cathedral and courthouse in St. Louis in the late 1830s.[47] The sixth and final member of the founding fathers of the Rocky Mountain Mission was Brother Joseph Specht, destined to spend forty-three years in the missions, forty of them in the Northwest. He was an expert blacksmith and Mengarini credits him with having played a major role in constructing the first saw mill in Montana.[48]

On April 24, 1841, Father De Smet and Mengarini and Brothers Huet and Specht left St. Louis on a Missouri steamer bound for Westport, where they arrived on April 30.[49] Point, who had gone up to "Kickapootown" to join Brother Claessens, was not on hand to greet them. During his stay at Westport, Point had made a number of excursions to this ill-fated Kickapoo Mission. At the time when Charles Van Quickenborne had founded it in 1836, he was already so physically and mentally exhausted from a lifetime of self-imposed rigors and privations that when Verhaegen removed him the following year, he was—though not yet fifty—a dying man.

From the very beginnings of this mission Van Quickenborne had had to deal with a brilliant Indian religious leader, Kènakuk, better known as The Prophet, who had successfully synthesized a number of Catholic beliefs with traditional Indian beliefs and assertions of his own devising. Without ever confronting Van Quickenborne directly, The Prophet managed to outwit the Jesuit on every front. Then, toward the end of 1840, the United States government withdrew all appropriations to the Jesuit Kickapoo school forcing the personnel who were still serving it to begin their permanent withdrawal. It was at this time that Point appeared at the mission and was shocked at what he found: "Here had our missionaries been laboring for five years . . . yet at Sunday mass you could scarcely see more than one [Indian]." At the same time, Kènakuk, "a genius in his own way, succeeded in forming a congregation of three hundred souls." He spoke to the congregation of his revelations, the "proof of which was a chip of wood two inches wide and eight long, which were inscribed with outlandish characters symbolizing the doctrine he undertook to teach." This experience had a profound effect on Point.[50]

When spring came he returned to "Kickapootown," the concrete realization of his mentor's "Paraguay in the Plains," the first "reduction" among the North American Indians, the actualized dream Van Quickenborne outlined to him one memorable day in Philadelphia in December 1835. This time Point had come to consume the last consecrated hosts remaining in the tabernacle of Van Quickenborne's church. Significantly, it was the last day of April 1841. At Westport, De Smet and his companions had stepped off the steamer, anticipating a bright, new future, but in "Kickapootown" the last rays of the sun were fading as Point made his way to the chapel to do what he came to do. Suddenly someone stopped him and told him there was a man about a mile away who was gravely ill. He interrupted his stride to give this new situation his total attention. Searching about the village he at last found an interpreter whom he employed, and the two of them proceeded to the sick man's house. Here they found him in a state of despair. "Everyone has deserted me," he cried. Point, most gently, comforted him, instructed him simply in the most elementry principles of the Faith, and then, compulsively, almost against his better judgment as he later confessed, baptized him on the spot. Predictably, during the night, the man suddenly took a turn for the worse and died. Before the sun arose on the first day of May, Father Nicolas had gathered his first *floscolus.* This led him to comment:

> Was this not the sweetest bouquet, which the missionary upon his first entrance to the field of labor among the Indians, could offer to the Queen of Heaven, on the very day of the month consecrated to her honor begins? But how inscrutable are the judgments of God! *Unus ne desperas, Solus ne praesumas* (Lest you be the only one without hope, do not presume to act alone).[51]

Point returned to Westport with Brother Claessens, and on May 10, the expedition set off from Westport:

> taking with us all the supplies for one dear mission in five two-wheeled carts driven by two Canadians who were excellent wagoneers, and three of our brothers, still novices in that difficult art. The three priests rode horseback.[52]

ROCKY MOUNTAINS 1841–1847

Part One: St. Mary's Reduction

Ten days after Nicolas Point nailed shut Charles Van Quickenborne's Kickapoo Mission, the six Jesuits—founders of what was destined to be one of the most glamorous mission fields in North America—boarded on the first oxen-drawn carts to enter western Montana. They started out by crossing the wide Missouri River and heading westward.[1] Their guide was the famous Irishman Thomas "Broken-Hand" Fitzpatrick (1799–1854)[2] and their hunter was the Iroquois half-breed Ignace Hatchiorauquacha, better known as John Grey (?–c. 1844), two Mountain Men who knew the Oregon country well.[3] John's wife, Marianne Neketichou, who had been one of the pillars of the Sodality of the Seven Sorrows at Westport was also a member of the party.[4] Finally, there were seven or eight French Canadian trappers, a man named Baker, about whom nothing is known, and a young Englishman named Romaine.[5] After a wearisome five days' march along the south bank of the Kansas, they forded the river opposite Soldier's Creek, just below present-day Topeka, where they rendezvoused with a group led by

John Bidwell (1819–1900) at Sapling Grove.[6] Bidwell was leading the first overland party of American settlers to California and with the addition of the Fitzpatrick party, the expedition numbered seventy.[7] Despite the fact that the Bidwell contingent was anxious to begin the expedition, the group camped at Soldier's Creek for five long days, during which time De Smet renewed his aquaintance with the Kansa Indians nearby.[8]

As for Point, the more he distanced himself from the hustle and bustle of Westport, alone during much of the dreary, monotonous days and the long, restless nights, the more distorted were the phantoms and jumbled memories that came to keep him company. Did Father Roothaan ever *really* understand what had been at stake at St. Charles? Here at Sapling Grove he would endeavour once again to explain the situation in a letter to the General. This letter sadly testifies to the fact that Point was still smarting over his experience at Grand Coteau and now, under a scorching Kansas sun, surrounded by ox-carts and English-speaking emigrants, he became desperately aware of the utter futility of his efforts to instill the principles of Jesuit educational theory and practice at St. Charles. Consequently, he set about trying to deceive himself by assuring the General in four long pages that he would remain forever silent about Louisiana. This voluminous apologia, one more justification for his governance as rector and for the authenticity of his *plan d'études,* reveals a mind temporarily unbalanced. In view of the deep shock not only to his confidence from not being able to elicit the support of those he considered loyal Jesuits but also to all he ever believed in about the educational and formational principles of the society, this loss of balance becomes more understandable. In his new enforced solitude, he sought, as far as possible, to shift the blame for his failure on the cynicism of those who had misinterpreted him or on the ignorance of those who had not understood him; then immediately he felt guilt in harboring such thoughts. He would do something about it, he told the general. He would write a peace letter to Verhaegen, which indeed he did.[9] Meanwhile, he seemed to have become erratic. Faced with this peculiar behavior on the part of his colleague, the optimistic, affable De Smet naturally began to revise his opinion of him, and a state of concern and, perhaps, even disillusionment was evident when he reported he had appointed Father Nicolas the official diarist of the group "to distract him [from his] sombre and melancholy humor."[10]

On May 19, two days after Point had written to the General, the party broke camp. John Bidwell noted in his diary: "This morning the wagons started off in single file; first the 4 carts and one small wagon of the Missionaries, next 8 wagons drawn by mules and horses and lastly, 5 wagons drawn by 17 yoke of oxen."[11] As the party headed to the Northwest, De Smet, Romaine, and Point took a detour up the river to visit the principal village of the Kaw, or Kansa, Indians, near the mouth of Vermillion Creek, beyond present day St. Mary's in Potawatomie County, Kansas. Did De Smet choose Point for this excursion in order to shake him out of his lethargy, to distract him by introducing him to Indians who were, after all, the principal reason why he had come to America? It is, of course, impossible to state with certitude. However, it is refreshing to read that in his melancholy state Point found himself jolted out of his reveries when he realized that he had become an object of derision among his Indian hosts. "What could be wrong with me? I asked of myself. Then suddenly recollecting that my beard had gone unshorn for some days past, I hit upon the reason."[12] De Smet commented on the event as well, and although he sometimes let his own beard grow, Black Robes were expected to be clean shaven for apostolic reasons.[13] It is amusing to reflect that facial hair was a source of division among American Jesuits even before the 1960s, and that the reasons advanced for shaving have perdured longer and have remained more consistent than the traditional black robe or cassock that once defined the Jesuit. Since there are no reliable extant portraits or photographs of Nicolas Point, there is no visible evidence concerning his controversial moustache and beard. Presumably he left them on the Plains. Moreover, for the Kansa the length of hair was symbolic: "long hair being a sign of long mourning."[14]

Both Point and De Smet have left accounts of their visit to the Kansa village, which was subsequently destroyed by a raid of the tribe's traditional enemies, the Pawnees. Each told of having met with Chief White Plume, who had so impressed another Frenchman, Captain Benjamin Louis Eulalie de Bonneville (1796–1878) during his 1832 visit to the Kansa.[15] There were also specific impressions, two of which bear attention. The artist Point observed that it "would be no easy task, were I to render a detailed account of all the curious sights witnessed during the half-hour we spent among those strange beings. A Flemish painter would have found in them a treasure."[16] De Smet, superior of the first reduction to the Rocky Mountain Indians, observed that his hosts' "style of singing is monotonous, whence it may be inferred that the enchanting music heard on the rivers of Paraguay never cheers the voyager on the otherwise beautiful streams of the country of the Kansas."[17]

After the customary exchange of gifts the three explorers at last quit the Kansa and on their fast mounts they easily caught up with the lumbering first immigrant train to California. Fortunately, Point, De Smet, and Mengarini kept separate journals[18] during those days when, in the words of Mengarini, "slowly we toiled on while May, June, and July scorched our pathway."[19] It is remarkable how their accounts differ from one another, and how each diarist manifests in a dramatic manner his unique personality. Point never alludes to personal inconveniences, seeing all events *sub specie aeterniatis;* De Smet, the consummate personal relations man, is ever conscious of his reading public, but surprisingly it is the deputed, aesthetic, sensitive, Mengarini who most often gives the best insights of the day-to-day problems the Jesuits encountered. Father Nicolas proved that on his sea journey from Le Havre for New York he was a confirmed lover of nature who never seemed to tire watching for whales and describing waterspouts, sunsets, and the flight of birds. Later it was animals and flowers in the Alleghenies, the autumn colored leaves in Kentucky, and the vegetation along the Mississippi that captured his attention. Predictably, he now devoted pages of his journal to the fauna, flora, and rock formations he encountered on the American Plains, seeing in all of them proofs of the Divinity or an evidence of what he thought Scripture had revealed. More than twenty years after that historic march, he recalled that: "On the top of the knolls we found shells and a number of petrified substances such as are occasionally met with on some mountains of Europe." And he added: "I doubt not that an honest-minded geologist would find here as well as elsewhere indisputable proofs of the deluge. I may add that a piece of stone taken from the spot and still in my possession, furnishes abundant evidence in this respect."[20] The remembrance of prairie flowers and prairie fowl was still able, after all of those years, to conjure up beautiful memories in the artist. For instance, he recalled that on the eve of the feast of the Sacred Heart he was able to "gather a whole basket of flowers by plucking one of each kind" and he named, catalogued, and described many of them in detail. Here is what he says about what he called "Adam's needle":

> "Midway up its stem, which is about three feet high, it shoots out into a very compactly formed pyramid of flowers, light red in color. In form it is the image of an upturned diadem; its breadth dwindles down gradually towards the top where it finally develops itself into a point. At its base it has a sort of protection in a species of long, tough, prickly leaves. Its root is used in the manufacture of Mexican soap, as it is called, and again, when needs be, it serves as a nourishing substance to the Indians.[21]

Besides flowers this proto-ecologist also described with a painter's eye prairie dogs, domestic dogs, beavers, frogs, salamanders, snakes, ants, mosquitoes, buffalo, and all types of birds. But it is Mengarini who provides today's reader with the realistic account of the hardships of the journey. Neither flower gatherer nor propagandist, he demythologizes many elements of the missionary life:

> To lose the road and to be in want of water had become such an ordinary matter as to be daily expected. But why speak of a road when no such thing existed? Plains on all sides! Plains at morning; plains at noon; plains at night! And thus, day after day! The want of water was sometimes so great that we were forced to boil putrid yellow water, which we found collected in some hollow, and strive to quell the pangs of thirst at the price of others equally great.[22]

Sometimes, to amuse himself and to relieve boredom, Mengarini would shoot at the rattlesnakes he encountered en route.[23] Apparently he became a distinguished sharpshooter, but, because there were so many snakes, even this activity finally became a source of boredom and frustration. Along with the fifty men who were capable of bearing arms, both he and Point were assigned turns to stand guard duty at night. Because of their exalted positions, however, Fitzpatrick and De Smet were exempt, and if this policy was a source of scandal for the egalitarian Point (who had once assured his subjects at St. Charles that he would suffer with them) no mention of it was ever made.[24] De Smet had occasion to notice that Point's horsemanship was not of a quality to assure him a secure place of distinction among those who found a home in the saddle, and in his opinion Mengarini's equestrian skills were certainly not on a par with his ability to shoot off heads from rattlers.[25]

After traveling across territory in what is today southern Nebraska and central Wyoming, at last on June 24, the party came to the encampment on the Green River, in present-day southwest Wyoming. Here Point bade farewell to those returning to Westport: to the expedition's hunter John Grey and his family, and to a number of others, including Romaine, for whom Point seems to have developed a genuine friendship.[26] He writes about this young English Protestant who

> "in spite of his religious principles . . . promised that should Providence ever bring us together again, he should esteem it a favor to testify his gratitude for the kindness we had shown him. I recall this beautiful reflexion of his: "One must journey in the wilderness to see how Providence cares for the

> wants of man." What has become of him? I have learned that he has reached his home in safety—that is all."[27]

On the twenty-sixth, the party continued in a westerly direction to Soda Springs (Idaho). Here they separated into two groups: the Jesuits with thirty-two of the emigrants, intending to make Oregon their final destination, continued on to the north, to Fort Hall on the Snake River, and Bidwell with the others turned to the southwest and to California.[28]

> We had spent three months together, sharing the same fortunes, exposed to the same dangers, and we felt like countrymen towards each other. Our leavetaking was sad . . .[29]

During the next few weeks the missionaries spent eleven, twelve, thirteen hours on the march, and finally on August 15, the feast of the Assumption, twenty-eight years to the day from when Nicolas Point attributed his miraculous escape from Prussian military shells to heavenly intervention, "toward sunset, during the finest weather imaginable, and when all our party were in excellent health and spirits, we arrived at Fort Hall."[30] Mengarini, less ethereal, noted that their provisions were already exhausted and that they were "disappointed" that the commander of this Hudson Bay Company outpost, Francis Ermatinger (1798–1858), "even though kind and obliging," could sell them at an inflated price only two bags of toro—a mixture of buffalo meat, grease, and berries, "a luxury not sold in civilized markets."[31] At Fort Hall the missionaries were greeted by Father De Smet, who had ridden ahead of the main group, and the twenty or so Flathead advance guard who had been waiting at the fort for their arrival.[32] On the eighteenth, Jesuits and Flathead scouts set out to join the remainder of the tribe.[33] But disaster awaited them beyond the palisades of the fort when they attempted to ford the Snake. Earlier, when the wagons had reached the muddy, flood waters of the North Platte near present-day Casper, Wyoming, they halted, fearful to make the crossing. John Grey's words of assurance were to no avail. Finally Grey put his wife, Marianne Neketichou, on a horse and a one-year-old girl on a colt and guided them across the ford. "To hold back under such circumstances," De Smet observed, "would seem a disgrace for Indian missionaries."[34] But now, as the party faced the Snake, they did not have the experience of Grey nor the inspiration of Marianne to advise and encourage them. However, the Snake, "being much less deep and wide" than the Platte, "and having such limpid waters that the bottom can everywhere be seen, could only be dangerous to incautious persons."[35] Fording rivers was, however, always a precarious adventure for wagon trains and one might suspect that Point's experience at the Beech Fork in Kentucky must have given him a particular respect for the force of water power. At any rate, the crossing was attempted and the results predictable: "Down went mules, driver and vehicle . . ." The vehicle was recovered and salvaged, the driver, Brother Charles Huet, was miraculously saved, but three mules perished.[36] At this juncture De Smet's great friend Francis Ermatinger sold them more mules "for a sum truly inconsiderable, when compared with what must be paid on such occasions to those who wish to avail themselves of the misfortunes of others."[37]

"A few days after this," Point recorded, "some Indians were perceived at a short distance, and the cry was raised: 'Blackfeet! Blackfeet!' "[38] The strangers did not turn out to be Blackfeet at all, but Bannocks; however, this instance served to introduce Point to the Flatheads' most feared adversary, those formidable Algonkian-speaking, nomadic hunters who controlled the territory from the North Saskatchewan River to what is today Yellowstone Park, and on the west, from the headwaters of the Missouri, which defined the frontiers of Flathead territory, to the confluence of the Milk River with the Missouri.[39] The missionaries continued their northwestward journey through the Continental Divide, and the snow was already deep on September ninth when they set out on the last stage of their journey westward.[40] On the twenty-forth, which was the feast of Our Lady of Mercy in the Church's calender, the fact that explains why this inchoate outpost of Christian culture was baptized St. Mary's, they passed through Hell Gate, "and entered upon a plain, bordered upon the north by the territory of the Pend d'Oreilles, and on the west by that of the Coeur d'Alène."[41] This territory did not meet their satisfaction and so they took a pass southwards. Here they found the site they were looking for, a fertile valley through which the Bitter Root River flowed from south to north, a location "guarded by a mountain range against the incursions of the Blackfeet from the south," and "defended against the rigors of the northern winds by another chain of mountains covered at the base with forests which would furnish firewood and the timber needed for building purposes."[42] The place was some twenty-eight miles south of present-day Missoula, up the Bitter Root Valley, near to where the small town of Stevensville, Montana, now stands.[43]

As soon as the Jesuits erected the large cross that would mark the sign of the Reduction of St. Mary's, De Smet wrote to Verhaegen advising him that fathers and brothers had adopted a modus operandi based on the description of the Paraguay Mission by Lodovico Antonio Muratori (1672–1750).[44] Muratori, clearly one of the greatest Catholic scholars of the Age of the Enlightenment, wrote a monograph on the Jesuit reductions, which was subsequently translated into French, *Rélation des missions du Paraguay.* During the Age of the Spiritual Awakening, digest copies of this historical study went through a number of reprintings, one of which was published at Louvain in 1822, the year before Van Quickenborne led Peter De Smet, Peter Verhaegen, John Elet and four other novices from White Marsh to Florissant to begin their apostolate with the Indians.[45] "We had made it our *Vade Mecum,*" declared De Smet.[46] The Muratori *Relation* is important for another reason. The author's spiritual director, the Jesuit Paoli Segneri (1673–1713), whose biography he wrote, had a considerable influence on forming Muratori's particular type of spirituality which he described in the book *Della Regolata divozione de' cristiani* (1747). The primary purpose of this work was to renew Christian life among the clergy and people of the Age of Enlightenment, to rid it of excessive baroque devotions, and to prevent it from becoming destroyed by the Scylla of pietism or the Charybdis of Jansenistic rigorism. Muratori taught that true devotion should be "solid and essential" in the Thomistic sense; it should be based on Scripture, tradition and reason. To achieve this end Muratori exalted prayer, mortification, a humility that was centered on the Sacraments, particularly penance and the Eucharist. The means to this end were to be found in the prayerful study of the Bible, the Fathers of the Church, the ordinary magisterium, the Exercises of St. Ignatius, and in the writings of Thomas à Kempis, Teresa of Avila, and other classical authors of the spiritual life. It was a spirituality rooted in reason, good sense, practical conclusions, and it exuded Molinistic optimism.[47] The Jesuits in Paraguay created the ideal setting where this type of spirituality was planted, where it grew and flowered.

"After having seriously reflected on what Muratori relates of the establishments in Paraguay," De Smet wrote, "we have concluded that the following points should be laid down." He then proceeded to outline how the Jesuits would conduct themselves "with regard to God, neighbor, self." He reiterated their desire to convert the Flathead, and the means to achieve this end would be:

> Flight from all contaminating influence; not only from the corruption of the age, but from what the gospel calls the world. Caution against all immediate intercourse with the whites, even with the workmen, whom necessity compels us to employ, for though these are not wicked, still they are far from possessing the qualities necessary to serve as models to men who are humble enough to think they are more or less perfect, in proportion as their conduct corresponds with that of the whites. We shall confine them to the knowledge of their own language, erect schools among them, and teach them reading, writing, arithmetic and singing. Should any exception be made to this general rule, it will be in favor of a small number, and only when their good dispositions will induce us to hope that we may employ them as auxiliaries in religion. . . . To facilitate the attainment of the end in view, we have chosen the place of the first missionary station, formed the plan of the village, made a division of the lands,

> determined the form of the various buildings, etc. The buildings deemed most necessary and useful at present are: a church, schools, work houses, store houses, etc. Next, we have made regulations respecting public worship, religious exercises, instructions, catechisms, confraternities, the administration of the Sacraments, singing, music, etc. All of this is to be executed in conformity with the plan formerly adopted in the Missions of Paraguay.[48]

How much influence did Point exert on the philosophy contained in this statement of purpose? We have seen that the Paraguay reductions and Chateaubriand were the warp and woof out of which his dreams and ambitions were made long before he met Van Quickenborne. In that memorable 1835 Christmas season encounter at Philadelphia, the older missionary confirmed him in his determination to recreate Paraguay in the American West. De Smet's thinking was also influenced by Van Quickenborne, his former master of novices and superior, and like Point he was indebted to the descriptions of the Paraguay missions found in the *Lettres édifiantes et curieuses* and in Muratori. But unlike De Smet, who had a broad vision, Point was a meticulous planner. His paintings and sketches of plans for the St. Mary's and Sacred Heart reductions, are as detailed as his design of St. Charles College. It would be rash to suggest that De Smet's outline cited above owed its origin to Nicolas Point, but it would be equally rash to suggest that Point did not play a vital role in framing it. It seems likely that De Smet's specific plan for the reductions in the Northwest owes much to "that plan which had been the dream of F[ather] N[icolas] Point during the whole of his life as we have already stated: his idea was adopted by all of the Fathers and sanctioned by all major Superiors."[49] Is it possible to conclude, in evaluating the origin of the statement of purpose on how the Jesuits would conduct themselves "with regard to God, neighbor, self" and by what means they should achieve this end, by stating: The voice was the voice of Peter De Smet but the hands were the hands of Nicolas Point?

By October, as De Smet prepared to leave for Fort Colville to pick up supplies, provisions, and some livestock, as well as to renew contact with the Pend d'Oreilles, the burgeoning reduction was bustling with activity. For example, in one single day representatives from as many as twenty-four different tribes arrived to beg that Black Robes be sent to their people. Such auspicious signs as these, as well as other details of the early history of St. Mary's, have been recorded elsewhere.[50] Meanwhile, Point found outlets for his energy and talents. When not busy giving instructions to neophytes, he put his gifts for draftmanship and architecture to work designing the church, residence, utility buildings, and implementing the plan which De Smet had described to Verhaegen.[51]

> "Father Nicolas was happy," recorded Pierre Point. "He was at last in the midst of doing what he wanted to do, the chief goal of his vocation. He recognized the good dispositions [of the Indians] and foresaw great promise: much work to be done and for his human nature—the cross. He blessed the God of all, fully desiring to embrace everything the Lord wanted, and then, providing he could baptize Indians, to die."[52]

Again it is the down-to-earth Mengarini who paints a more realistic picture of what that endeavor to build St. Mary's actually entailed:

> We soon set to work to erect a log cabin and a church, and build around them a sort of fort protected by bastions. The earth was already frozen and the trench for the foundations had to be cut with axes. Trees had to be felled and trimmed in the neighboring forest, and hauled to the place destined for the buildings. The Indians were not inclined to lend a helping hand and we needed their assistance. Example is better than precept, thought I, and seizing an axe, I began to work. Some half-breeds would have deterred me by telling me that thus I would lose authority with the Indians. I let my advisers talk and worked away. Soon a chief, throwing down his buffalo-robe, stepped forward, asked for an axe and joined me in my labor. The young men hastened to follow him, and our house progressed beyond expectation.[53]

On December 8, De Smet returned in time to add 146

catechumens that Point and Mengarini had prepared for baptism to the 200 adults they had already baptized in De Smet's absence. On this occasion, Christmas Day, 1841, the first Blackfoot Indian, a chief, who significantly was given the name Nicolas, stepped forth from the font along with a Nez Percé chief and his extended family.[54] The following day Point began his annual eight-day retreat, and because De Smet had pulled him away from his drawing boards, construction work, and catechism classes and ordered him to accompany the tribe on their traditional winter buffalo hunt, this was a special retreat for him. On the twenty-ninth, he left St. Mary's in the company of forty lodges (between 240 and 320 people), bound for the territory beyond the eastern slopes of the Rockies, and before they reached their destination they were joined by hunting parties from five or six other friendly tribes, notably Pend d'Oreilles, Nez Percés and others, who were eager to learn the prayers of the Black Robes, and be guaranteed protection against the Blackfeet by their larger number.[55] The three months that followed, even though blessed by religious obedience and graced with much adventure, exacted a high price from Point for maintaining this new, nomadic sub-reduction, far from St. Mary's. For one thing, Montana winters were severe. Many years later, after Mengarini had retired to the salubrious climate of California's Santa Clara Valley, "where, palm and olive mingling," he recalled what his first winter at St. Mary's had been like. He confessed: "I scarcely dare attempt to describe the cold; for even now when I think of it a chill comes over me, so vivid is the impression upon me." He asserted that it was warmer to sleep beneath the stars than to take shelter in the log cabin because the dew which fell at night froze and furnished some insulation, which was not provided indoors.[56] De Smet also spoke of that winter and noted that it

> was so uninterruptedly severe that during the hunting season, which lasted three months, such a quantity of snow fell that many were attacked with a painful blindness, vulgarly called snow disease. One day when the wind was very high, and the snow falling and freezing harder than usual, Father

> Point became suddenly very pale, and would no doubt have been frozen to death, in the midst of the plain, had not some travellers, perceiving the change in his countenance, kindled a large fire. But neither the wind, ice, nor famine, prevented the zealous Flat Heads from performing on this journey all they were accustomed to do at St. Mary's. Every morning they assembled around the Missionary's lodge and more than three-forths of them without any shelter than the sky, after having recited their prayers, listened to an instruction, preceded and followed by hymns. At daybreak and sunset the bell was tolled three times for the Angelic Salutation. The Sunday was religiously kept; an observance which was so acceptable to God . . .[57]

Such were some of the circumstances under which Point carried on his ministry during the winter hunt of 1842. Of course, not a word describing such physical sufferings appear in his journal, although two years later, when once again he was physically and emotionally drained, he wrote to his old friend of Le Passage days, Paul Luiset, that 1842 "was a year of great drudgery and great privation . . . Reverend Father De Smet was almost always traveling about; Father Mengarini (an Italian) was almost always at the St. Mary's headquarters . . . and I was almost always off on an expedition."[58] Hardly an auspicious beginning for a Paraguay-type reduction. Shortly after Point's return to St. Mary's from the hunt, Mengarini wrote to Roothaan advising him that the exhausted Point "is under delusion or there is something wanting in his head."[59] One is left to surmise what effect this piece of news had on the General, particularly when one recalls the contents of Point's letter written from Sapling Grove the previous May. The fact was that the physical and mental sufferings he encountered on the frozen planes, where he was cut off from the source of spiritual, intellectual, and emotional nutriment, beckoned back self-doubt, depression, and scruples—old acquaintances who were really never far off.

The hunt was completed during the first week of March and Point returned to St. Mary's on Good Friday, after having baptized eighty, sixty of whom were adults. Then on

April 13, Peter De Smet set off on another westward journey during which time he visited and gave preliminary catechetical instructions to some Kootenai and Coeur d'Alène Indians in what is today northern Idaho.[60] He left Mengarini not Point in charge of the mission, a fact which in itself is significant, but encouraged the ailing Point to persevere in his many projects before the summer hunt began.[61] Added to designing, building, and catechizing, Father Nicolas began to direct his energies with characteristic intensity to new projects. Determined that the first day of May at St. Mary's would lack none of the pageantry and expressions of piety he had provided for those under his care at Saint-Acheul, Fribourg, Le Passage, and Grand Coteau, he began making elaborate plans for the traditional ceremonies celebrating Mary's month. When the first of the month came, the tribe marched in solemn procession behind banners of the various sodalities he had formed, and sang specially written hymns composed to fit Louis Lambillotte's melodies. With a combination of triumph and reverence he carried a statue of the Blessed Virgin he himself had sculpted and painted for the occasion into the newly constructed chapel, which measured twenty-five by thirty-three feet and had two galleries, one on each side, eight by thirty feet.[62] Mengarini provided instrumental music. "The pageantry was not yet on the scale of the religious ceremonies in the Paraguay reductions, described with such grace in the *Lettres Edifantes,*" which along with Chateaubriand were so important in the formation of young Nicolas's vocation, but, as Pierre Point was quick to add, "the Rocky Mountain reduction was only six months old and the missionaries were indeed poor." Each day during May the Indians gathered three times into the chapel of "Our Lady of Prayer, Patroness of the Flatheads" for special devotions.[63] These May festivities inaugurated by Point in 1842 continued to enjoy a central part of the piety of the tribe well into the next century.[64] Then, in June, the Indians looked forward to the elaborate rituals surrounding the feast of Corpus Christi when, for the first time the tribe participated in Benediction of the Blessed Sacrament, thanks to Point's design and

Brother Huet's execution of a monstrance. Finally, there were special services in honor of the Sacred Heart, by far the most important of all of Point's many cultic devotions. By the time these solemnities had all taken place, it was July, and the summer hunting expedition demanded his full attention.[65] Loriquet's instructions for the implementation of *éducation* had perhaps never before been executed on so grand a scale.

On July 12, 1842, six days before Point left St. Mary's for the summer buffalo hunt, Claude Gotteland and his two companions arrived in Shanghai to reestablish the mission, which had been taken from the society during the period of suppression sixty-seven years earlier.[66] At this same date the African mission, already three years old, numbered thirty-nine Jesuits, and in Algiers the name of Ferdinand Brumauld and the subject of his work with the orphans shared in popularity with the subjects of wars and plagues as a topic of conversation.[67] There were, however, forewarnings that presaged trouble for those Jesuits who had remained at home in France. In Paris on the first day of May, when festivities began at St. Mary's, Louis-Philippe's birthday party was interrupted by the pretended disclosure that the Jesuits were hatching a plot against the government. It was rumored they had stored arms in the cellars of Saint-Sulpice. Xavier de Ravignan was one of the chief conspirators. By mid-July, when Point left for the hunt, this outcry against the Jesuits had reached a crescendo. Beduped and vaguely fearful, the government appeared to encourage those who cried for a violent suppression of the society, but news of such events was unknown in Shanghai and among the Jesuits in the Rockies.[68] Peter De Smet was, at this date, making his way back to St. Mary's with supplies he had purchased at Fort Vancouver. He arrived at the mission post on July 27, and then, after remaining there only a few days, he went off to find Point and the hunting parties before continuing his journey back to St. Louis and other American cities in search of more funds and recruits.[69] He surprised Father Nicolas encamped in "what was more like a pious pilgrimage than a hunt of the ordinary kind," so fervent and observant had his neophytes become and so intent were they in learning their catechism.[70] But for Point, surprise quickly gave way to delight because at last he was able to talk to his superior about a project that had been on his mind almost continuously since he had instructed Nicolas and his family. He expressed his ardent desire to be sent among the Blackfeet, a people he had again encountered during the winter hunt of 1841–42, and he ended his conversation with De Smet with a request to be missioned to this tribe.[71]

Such a request might indeed appear surprising in the light of Point's apparent enthusiasm for the work in which he was engaged. Fickleness of purpose was not his vice. Moreover, he had maintained with an extraordinary courage and consistency, against the greatest privations and sufferings, his dedication to the Flatheads. What then was the line of logical development that led to this request? There seem to be at least two reasons why he began to suspect that he could not accomplish among the Flatheads what he had dreamed of doing ever since his Rocroi days. First was the fact that the Flatheads' economy was based on hunting, which meant their lives were therefore nomadic, and such a condition precluded setting up a permanent Paraguay-type reduction.[72] Second, the number of buffalo each year was decreasing at an alarming rate while at the same time the number of white settlers was increasing. The convergence of these two factors spelled doom for the Rocky Mountain tribes, a fact to which he alludes on a number of occasions in the letters published in this volume. The Blackfeet, therefore, became the key element that could break the vicious circle which spelled ruination of missionary efforts and Indian survival in the Northwest. Their incessant warfare had a dilatory effect on the conversion of their neighbors east and west, and at the same time this warfare prevented the evolution of an economic and political climate that would foster and sustain Paraguay-type reductions. But what would the future be if the Blackfeet became Christian and settled down as tillers of the soil and herdsmen? What better guarantee was there for safeguarding all of the tribes of the west from the destructive hand of white settlers than authentic Paraguay-type reductions among these Indians? Finally, even though the Blackfeet were the most warlike, they were also the most noble of all the tribes. Point therefore was attracted to them for the same reasons that Francis Xavier was attracted to China. It was St. Ignatius's idea of the *"magis,"* the greater good, and also Muratori's idea of using common sense to determine a solid, rational course of action, rather than any disillusionment with the Flatheads, that compelled Nicolas Point to dream about setting out to convert the Blackfeet to Christianity and to create a reduction-type economy that would be a buffer for them and their neighbors against the white man's progress that promised to destroy them.[73]

De Smet, however, had other plans for Point. That is why he came to seek him out. During his first trip to Fort Colville in 1841, De Smet had encountered the Coeur d'Alène whom he described as "mild, affable, polite in disposition, and above all very eager for the word of God."[74] Then, in the spring of 1842, while on his second expedition to the British trading posts for supplies, he came across the tribe again and remained some days with them. On this occasion he met and was particularly impressed by the head chief, a man named Stellam, or Thunder, who seemed to hang on every word De Smet uttered and made ardent pleas that the missionary dispatch Black Robes to his tribe where they would be warmly received.[75] De Smet obliged, promising to send Jesuits to them as soon as he returned to St. Mary's. What De Smet did not realize was that Stellam had the reputation of being the manipulator *par excellence* of the tribe known to their neighbors as past masters in shrewdness and the ability to make profitable deals as traders. To the personnel at the Hudson Bay Company Stellam was referred to as "Mon Doux," that is "My Sweet," because the employees detected not a trace of sweetness or dulcitude in him. One reason, among others, was that he

> would go to some trading post of the H. B. Company, and when not treated as well as he wanted would pick up a

> quarrel, make a great deal of noise, until to appease him they would make him a present of some pound of tobacco or something of the like; that was all he wanted: the quarrel had no other end.[76]

This same Stellam had apparently convinced the ever optimistic De Smet of the advantages for establishing a reduction among his people, while simulating the real reasons for his request, and so De Smet asked Point to forget the Blackfeet and to abandon the Flathead and to go and found a new reduction among the Coeur d'Alène.[77]

ROCKY MOUNTAINS
1841–1847
Part Two: Sacred Heart Reduction

In September the snow had already begun to fall, the weather being unusually cold, and ice had covered the mountain passes, but Point saw only the hills harmonious against the gray Montana sky and the beauty of the panorama of the Continental Divide that spread before him. "The obedient man will speak of virtues," and so, as he made his way back to St. Mary's, he took no notice of the twelve to fourteen hours spent each day in the saddle.[1] He stayed on less than a month at the reduction making preparations for his new assignment, and then, at the end of October, he and Brother Huet, accompanied by three Coeur d'Alène chiefs and their retainers, all of whom had been on hand to welcome him back to St. Mary's, set out for the country beyond the Bitter Roots where they would remain until the following September.[2] Ten days later, after "much stumbling of our horses, and upsetting of the baggage, and after many a grave accident had been avoided by the protection of Heaven," the party descended into the beautiful valley of the Coeur d'Alène River.[3] The day was the First

Friday of the month, a day when throughout the Catholic world special devotions were held in honor of the Sacred Heart of Jesus, and a day particularly dear to the members of the Society of Jesus. On the first Friday of each month, Jesuits throughout the world were expected to consecrate themselves and their work to the Sacred Heart. For this reason Point wrote that "our first duty on dismounting was to kneel down along with all those who had come to meet us, in order to renew this consecration." His first impressions of the people to whom he had been sent was anything but flattering: "What wretched misery existed amongst these poor people!" He declared:

> Some miserable huts thatched with straw, or constructed of bark were surrounded with piles of the bones of animals and fish, and filth of every description; inside there were bundles of roots flung in a corner, skins hanging from a pole, fish smoking above the fireplace. And the occupants! squalid faces, unkempt hair, hands doing duty for comb, handkerchief, knife, fork and spoon; in feeding, repulsive sounds were emitted from the mouth, nose and windpipe. This external misery, feebled, imaged forth the pitiable state of their souls. For at this date there still reigned amongst this benighted people idolatry so debasing . . . a moral abandonment which knew no check save caprice, a passion for gambling so absorbing that it trenched even upon their time for sleep, unmitigated sloth which nothing but pangs of hunger could make them shake off, and finally an habitual inclination to cheating, gluttony, and every mean vice. . . . Happily, beneath all these, there was felt an undefinable yearning towards some superior power, and this had always helped them to lend a willing ear to the least word that could give them any information in regard to Him.[4]

Nicolas Point and Charles Huet selected a site on a gentle slope along what today is the St. Joe River, some eight miles downstream from the present town of St. Mary's, Idaho, for the establishment of the second Jesuit foundation in the Rocky Mountains. Understandably, Point gave it the name Sacred Heart Reduction. Relying on his Muratori he drew a sketch based "upon the ancient plans in

Paraguay" for this new mission and, leaving Brother Huet to execute these plans the best way he could among the "Parisians," he went off to visit the "Bas-Bretons" in their fish camps and villages.[5] For him there were two types of Coeur d'Alène, the simple, untouched people, who were similar to the good Bretons of his native France and who lived in the highlands and along the Coeur d'Alène River, and the sly, cunning and deceitful members of the tribe who made their dwellings in the lowlands, the prairie through which the St. Joe ran, not altogether unlike the Seine, and where Stellam had more influence. Stellam was a "Parisian," and although all of the members of the tribe owed him allegiance, his authority was greater among his own people.[6] Consequently, Point's visitation to the fishing villages was really an act of independence from Chief Stellam, who resented having any future mission established outside his own territory. Point was French enough to realize that although one could never hold a France without conquering its Paris, Paris was by no means France.

Immediately after their arrival, Brother Huet began erecting a small church, fifty feet in length and twenty-four in breadth, at the mission site that Father Point had selected, and from where, after Easter, he would carry out peripatetic classes among people he considered more primitive than the Flatheads. Meanwhile, Stellam continued to be the ever-present, vexing problem for him. When he reflected on this trial did he ever think of "The Prophet" at Kickapoo Town who had caused similar vexations for his mentor and friend, the late Charles Van Quickenborne? He does not say. However, despite the conflicts with Stellam in the face of a number of other obstacles, he finally felt strong enough on the first Friday of December to erect a large cross on the Spokane River where he had built a temporary house of prayer. At this ceremony in a most dramatic way he rededicated the mission to the Sacred Heart. At Christmas midnight mass his prayer house "was hung with garlands of green and mats covered the ground, and various pictures, representing the different mysteries, were hung about." Then, in January he baptized sixteen "Bas-Breton" adults and increased this modest Catholic population by an additional forty-four baptisms in February.[7] Life was difficult for both Jesuits who suffered acutely from the lack of provisions, which meant that "moss from the trees had to come on the table, in rather large proportions."[8] During part of the winter Point accompanied the Coeur d'Alène on their annual hunting expedition.[9]

At the end of March, Point rejoined Brother Huet and was impressed by the progress the resourceful coadjutor had made implementing his Paraguay designs. Still, there was so much to do and so little time to do it in. He had been involved in the work of *instruction* in the villages; now it was time for *éducation* at the mission compound. He determined to create and execute, before the Easter triduum, a "Calvary," that is, an out-of-doors stations of the Cross. This meant that fourteen crosses had to be constructed and painted with tableaux on each, all in record time; then, each cross or station had to be implanted on the hill north of the unfinished church. It was during this period that Point relied more and more on sculpture as an effective pedagogical tool.[10] This latest project, however, proved too much for him. A combination of excessive physical labor and emotional anxiety with excessive penance and fasting demanded its toll: he collapsed on Good Friday. The good sense and steady judgment of Brother Huet convinced him that he was not dying, as he thought he was, and that the remedy for this fatigue would be a few sips from the meager supply of altar wine that remained at the mission. This remedy and a little food in the stomach put him back on his feet in time for the Easter services.[11]

By September 1843, the reduction was firmly established, or as established as it could be with two men doing everything that had to be done. There were unsolved problems but the future did look promising and in his journal Point now recorded many laudatory impressions about his flock.[12] Just as he had been high in praise of the moral goodness displayed by his parishioners at Westport, so now he could not say enough about the miraculous conversion of the Coeur d'Alène people for whom he clearly bore the greatest affection. Perhaps he did exaggerate their virtues, but those who accuse him of hyperbole would do well to read the subsequent opinions of disinterested commentators on the effects of the work of the Jesuits among the men and women of this tribe and on the effects Christianity had on their mores.[13] Father Joseph Joset, about whom more will be said later, declared that Point was "an indefatigable catechist and to supply the want of language on those beginning, (it was very difficult), he made several large problematic designs which helped both the understanding and the memory of the Catechumens."[14] These designs, undoubtedly similar to those teaching devices universally used by the missionaries which appear on the famous *Catholic Ladders,* seem however to have been somewhat different because Point's device presented the catechumens, through the use of visual aids, with the proper manner of arriving at moral decisions.[15] Loriquet's plan placed a premium on any means which would strengthen the understanding and memory of students. As the year progressed, however, and as Stellam became more hostile and less predictable, Point indicated in his journal that he was becoming more obsessed by Stellam. For pages, Point describes what a rascal this troublemaker was.[16] In fact, one gets the impression that Point's complaints against his adversary are already *de trop,* out of proportion. The telltale signs were there: Stellam was becoming an *idée fixe*.

By September the scarcity of supplies for the oncoming winter gave a certain urgency to Point's desire to report to De Smet, who by his calculations should have been back in St. Mary's by that date; therefore, the two Jesuits at Sacred Heart decided it was time to make the journey back to headquarters to give a progress report on the Coeur d'Alène Reduction. As they had done the year previously, they could make the journey back to Sacred Heart before mid-November. It was, of course, impossible for them to know that De Smet had altered his original plans and went to Europe in June in search of provisions of his own. The money he had managed to collect in various cities in the eastern and southern states between 1842 and 1843 enabled him to send out three more Jesuits from St. Louis to the Rocky Mountain Mission in April 1843. This would have been just after Point had returned from his good "Bretons" to the "Parisians."[17] De Smet had escorted the new missionaries from St. Louis as far as Westport and then returned to St. Louis to make the final preparations for his departure to Europe.[18] Later he was pleasantly surprised to learn that four more Jesuits—three priests and a brother—had been placed at his disposal. These men had been assigned to the Rocky Mountain Mission by Father General Roothaan and were a visible proof to De Smet of the effectiveness of his letters and recently published book on young European Jesuits.[19] But it was too late in the year to think of crossing the Great Plains and so De Smet dispatched his new men to Florissant, St. Louis, and St. Mary's Mission in Kansas, to work until the following spring.[20] The future of the mission was, indeed, promising as De Smet sailed for Ireland on June 7:[21] four men were waiting to be sent to St. Mary's in the spring of 1844; six men were making their way across the Oregon Trail with a group that included Peter Burnett (1807–1895), the first American governor of California, who would serve from 1849 to 1851;[22] Jesse Applegate (1811–1888), one of the founders of the state of Oregon;[23] and Marcus Whitman (1801–1847), the famous Protestant missionary to the Indians of the Northwest,[24] together with 366 others who made up the "great emigration of 1843."

When Point and Huet left the Sacred Heart Mission bound for St. Mary's, and, one may well imagine, looking something like Don Quixote and Sancho Panza, there were consequences at once momentous and unforeseen. Both were exhausted, suffering from malnutrition and carrying with them the ravages of a nightmarish ten months. We have already seen that when Point was in such a condition he tended to lose control of himself and of the situation. This is an important fact to keep in mind when we attempt to appreciate the impact of the news he received when, after completing the nine-day journey from Sacred Heart to St. Mary's, he arrived weary and exhausted at his destination.

First, he learned De Smet was not at the mission and would not return in the foreseeable future. Second, he was told that there was a new superior who had just recently arrived from Missouri. Third, they informed him that this superior was Peter De Vos, his bête noire of Grand Coteau days. Whatever occurred within the next few days has not been recorded. But within a matter of weeks De Vos, who had been described by Mengarini as "a jovial character," one who was always "disposed to laugh and joke," ordered the Italian to meet him and his companions "in the autumn," on the last part of their journey from Westport.[25] Mengarini, who had been sick most of the summer and who was at that time in no condition to go anywhere, obeyed, and in so doing discovered a new pass through the mountains.[26]

Three weeks later the new superior made his appearance at St. Mary's.[27] This arrival must have been almost simultaneous with the arrival of Point and Huet because, as Mengarini recorded: "A great traveller, though already advanced in years, and poor in health, [De Vos] was no sooner over the fatigues of his long journey than, in the company of two Indians, two Canadians, a brother and myself, he started for the Calispels [*sic*]."[28] Mengarini wrote his memoirs more than twenty years after the events took place and so it is understandable how he could have confused the Coeurs d'Alène with the Kalispels, among whom, as yet, there was no mission. The fact was that De Vos, Mengarini, and the unnamed brother visited Sacred Heart Mission in late September, less than four weeks after Point had left there.[29] In the light of decisions made as a result of this visit, it is strange that Point was not a member of the visiting team, all the more so since the two Jesuit priests did not know the trails from St. Mary's to Sacred Heart and, predictably, after becoming separated from the other members of the party, managed to get lost. During this time they headed in the opposite direction of Sacred Heart and came dangerously close to the Blackfeet camps before being rescued.[30] The unnamed brother, in whom the two priests placed their trust, claimed he knew the path. Was this Brother Huet? If so, Point's absence is even more striking.

Father de Vos spent a short time at Sacred Heart evaluating the situation and when he returned to St. Mary's he published his decisions concerning the mission's future. First, he approved of the site Point had made for the reduction. Second, he made mutually satisfactory arrangements with Stellam regarding the land where the mission compound would be developed. Recalling Point's past performances and his penchant for alienating people, De Vos doubtlessly placed the cause of the tension between the chief and his former rector at Grand Coteau on Point's shoulders, and given Stellam's personality, the chief must have given reasons to support the new superior's conclusions. At any rate, De Vos could congratulate himself for having brought peace where faction had been sewn. Third, De Vos changed the name of the mission from Sacred Heart to St. Joseph's, and finally, he appointed a new team to guarantee peace and progress at the mission.[31]

Two of De Vos's travelling companions from Westport, Father Adrien Hoecken (b. Tilburg, Noord Brabant, Holland, March 18, 1815; d. Milwaukee, March 19, 1897) and Brother Daniel Lyons, an Irish coadjutor brother, were assigned to replace Father Nicolas Point and Brother Charles Huet.[32] Just why the superior changed the name of the mission is a subject which invites speculation, but this much is sure: it was a decision that had long-lasting results. For one thing, it explains the origin of the name given to the St. Joe River on the banks of which the mission was built, but, as one of his contemporaries wrote, it "was a stroke upon poor Father Point; he had had in Louisiana some conflict of jurisdiction with Father De Vos which had affected him so much that his head seemed some deranged on that point, and which at intervals made his conversation very painful to his Brothers . . ."[33] We do not know what Huet's reaction was, although from what followed it probably was not very different from Point's. Brother Charles had succumbed to terrible fevers during the course of 1842–1843 because "Mosquitoes swarmed over the sloughs created by flood waters" at Sacred Heart, and therefore his health was doubly impaired.[34] It seems he was a man who spoke little and when he did say something it was epigrammatic.[35] Joseph Joset recalled after his death that:

> Brother Charles, devoted child of Mary, endured everything with an unconquerable patience. [He was an] excellent religious, humble, obedient, untiring. I believe he merited the martyr's crown because, besides the ordinary afflictions, God bestowed upon him other types of sufferings—all of which he endured with a constant patience.[36]

It does not seem that these "other types of sufferings" were physical; rather they were more akin to those Point had to endure. Joset had written to the general, while the good brother was still alive and at a time when the Coeur d'Alène mission was in difficult straits, that, "although he has goodwill, he is not altogether right in the head, and that he is more of a burden than a help."[37] There is something profoundly provocative in contemplating the fact that Nicolas Point, the artist who worked in paints, and Charles Huet, the artist who worked in metals, the two founders of the Coeur d'Alène Mission, and indeed of the church in Idaho, were what would be termed today neurotic, and yet this neurosis was the soil in which their genius, creativity, heroism,—and, may one say sanctity?—flourished.

Nicolas Point, now a member of the St. Mary's community, was ordered by Peter De Vos to accompany the Flatheads on their annual winter hunting expedition.[38] Meanwhile, Peter De Smet was finishing up his European recruiting program and on January 9, 1844, the same week that Point left St. Mary's for the hunt, De Smet disembarked from Antwerp with five more Jesuits and six sisters of Notre Dame de Namur bound for Oregon by way of Cape Horn and Valparaiso.[39] By that date Adrien Hoecken at St. Joseph's [Sacred Heart] Mission began to encounter the same problems that had so frustrated Point and by the summer, thanks to the machinations of Stellam, he managed to alienate the Coeur d'Alènes to such an extent that they planned to tie him up and whip him.[40] "He had not, perhaps, a great intellect," his obituary reads, but at least on this occasion Hoecken had the presence of mind to take literally the Gospel admonition about shaking the dust from one's feet in a situation when one's presence was judged by the locals to be something less than a boon.[41]

Hoecken, one of the great missionaries of the "second generation," came to the United States during Point's tenure at Grand Coteau and entered the novitiate at Florissant.[42] He had not yet been ordained a priest a year when he departed for the Oregon country with De Vos, Daniel Lyons, two other coadjutor novices, and Brother Peter McGean (b. ?, Ireland, May 31, 1813; d. Old Mission, Idaho, October 28, 1877), a farmer, carpenter, and jack-of-all-trades, who had worked on the Potawatomi Mission and who was destined to spend almost thirty more years among the Indians of the Northwest.[43] Six of Hoecken's brothers and sisters had entered the service of the Church as priests or religious, but none of them could possibly have worked as hard as this stolid Dutchman who literally "went native" in his efforts to bring the Gospel to the Indians. He and Brother Daniel Lyons lived six years with a Northwest tribe without ever once seeing a white man. One of the greatest tragedies of this era is that Hoecken, who remained to the end of his life "an admirer of the Indians, even retaining, in some degree, their manner of talking and their forms of expression," never recorded a single detail of his experiences as Point's successor among the Coeur d'Alène. There is one curious anecdote in Hoecken's life which says a great deal about him and about the attitude of Catholics of the post-Civil War period. After his return from the Rocky Mountains he was appointed pastor at a Cincinnati church for black Catholics. Having successfully inculturated himself to the Indians he determined to do the same among the blacks, a decision which prompted him to procure for his new church a painting of St. Benedict of Egypt, representing the saint as a black. The congregation was irate, declaring they did not believe in "nigger saints." Hoecken was forced to substitute it with a painting of a white St. Peter Claver ministering to the blacks.[44]

In early June Hoecken at last took refuge from the wrath of the Coeur d'Alène and went to live among the Pend d'Oreilles to the north, from which vantage point he notified the superior of his plight.[45] Point had long since returned to St. Mary's from the hunt, delighted with the progress the Flatheads had made. He noted with undisguised satisfaction and joy that on the last Sunday of the hunt, March 24, he had distributed Holy Communion to 104 Indians.[46] Point was the logical choice to be sent back to St. Joseph's at this time of tension; instead, De Vos dispatched Mengarini to smooth the feathers of the outraged tribe and to apprise him of the situation.[47] The timid Mengarini was not effective and so De Vos himself arrived on the scene on June 20, 1844, threatening to close down the mission altogether if the tribe could not contain Stellam.[48] This warning "brought them to their senses," but it did not have the desired effect of restoring peace and concord at St. Joseph's.[49] Hoecken returned to St. Mary's but was back with the Coeur d'Alène, where Mengarini had recently arrived sometime before August for a consultation with De Vos.[50]

In early July, during De Vos's absence, Point received a bundle of letters at St. Mary's, the most recent of which bore the date April 1842.[51] These were from a number of his old friends—Félix Martin, Dominique du Ranquet, and others—some of the nine Jesuits (six priests and three brothers), who had been waiting at Le Havre for a ship to take them to Madagascar, their new assignment, when suddenly their orders were changed.[52] "In Canada," Roothaan wrote to Father Achille Guidée, provincial of the Province of France, "the new field is vast—thousands of very well disposed Indians and there is no time to waste in view of the diabolic zeal of the Methodists."[53] So, forgetting Madagascar, they found a ship on April 24 that brought them to North America.[54] Roothaan was responding to the appeal from Monseigneur Ignace Bourget (1799–1885), then coadjutor bishop of Montreal, who had been so impressed by the retreat Pierre Chazelle had preached to him and his clergy in the summer of 1839 that he resolved Jesuits had to make their reappearance on Canadian soil.[55] In the following June, Chazelle turned over to William Murphy the superiorship of the Kentucky Mission and the presidency of St.

Mary's University, for that is what Father William Byrne's classroom in the abandoned distillery some twenty miles from Bardstown had become that very year. Chazelle was then summoned to Rome. Here he again met Bourget. The bishop had traveled the same path traversed by Bishop Blanc in 1835. Having recently succeeded to the see of Montreal, he immediately hurried off to Rome to persuade Roothaan to assign Jesuits to Canada.[56] Knowing well the Jesuit general's predilection for the missions, it was not an unusual practice for newly ordained bishops in missionary parts of the world to hasten to Rome and plead with Roothaan to send Jesuits to their diocese. Rarely did they return home completely empty handed. This time was no exception. Bourget's point about the dangers of Methodist missions proved convincing, and so Chazelle was ordered to lead the French Jesuits waiting at Le Havre to Canada. Madagascar could wait until the following year. This surprising piece of news inspired a number of the new missionaries to write to their old friend Nicolas Point who was also laboring among the Indians in America.

A few days after Point received this first packet he received another letter from Paul Luiset who had been with him at Le Passage.[57] Luiset advised him that the nine America-bound Jesuits arrived safely in New York, from which they departed on May 26, and as of June 1, were settled in at Montreal. Then a third delivery brought yet another letter, this one dated June 1844, and it was from "our good friend Mr. Blanchet," in Fort Vancouver. It, too, was full of exciting information about French Jesuit missionary activities in Canada and in other parts of the world.[58] François Norbert Blanchet (1795–1883) at this date had been appointed the new vicar-apostolic of Oregon, although he did not learn of this fact until the following November.[59] In the same way, Point had no way of knowing, as he and Huet prepared to leave their Sacred Heart reduction after the memorable winter of 1843, that his own name had been recommended for this same post. In May of that year the fathers of the Fifth Provincial Council of Baltimore submitted three names to the Holy See for the newly created vicarate that would embrace "all the territory between the Mexican Province of California on the south, and the Russian province of Alaska on the north, and which extended "from the Pacific Ocean to the Rocky Mountains." Roothaan lobbied against any Jesuit being appointed bishop and so the Holy See overlooked the three Jesuits whose names were submitted—De Smet, Point and Verhaegen—and selected as vicar general for the bishop of Quebec Point's friend Norbert Blanchet.[60] If Point's spirits were low because of De Vos's snub in late June, these letters must have changed their direction. At this moment in his life, when "his conversation was painful to his Brothers," greetings from old friends must have brought him elation. Moreover, the French Jesuits were at last establishing a mission among the American Indians! And what a mission it was for Frenchmen! What glory; what honor! "My good Father," Nicolas responded to Luiset, "and now you too are in America, in that part of America which has been bathed by the blood of our fathers," referring to the French Jesuit martyrs of the seventeenth century, Jean de Brebeuf, Isaac Jogues and their companions.[61]

On July 31, the feast of St. Ignatius, De Smet and his party arrived at the mouth of the Columbia and by mid-August they began building St. Francis Xavier Mission on the Willamette, which was destined to become the headquarters for all Jesuit reductions in the Northwest.[62] From here De Smet sent out word that he wanted to rendezvous with the acting superior, Peter De Vos, and with Gregory Mengarini at Fort Vancouver where he was going to purchase supplies for the Idaho and Montana missions. Mengarini met De Smet at the fort in early September and the two of them, with their large supply of baggage purchased for the inland missions, met Father De Vos and Brothers McGean and Specht as they were en route from Fort Vancouver to St. Joseph's Mission.[63] What was the cause of De Vos's delay? Mengarini's departure from St. Joseph's meant that Hoecken was the only priest at the Coeur d'Alène mission, a situation which, given the history of Hoecken's dealings with this tribe and his "cold feelings" toward them, could not have brought reassurance to the acting superior.[64] The reasonable solution was to forget his reservations about Point, at least for the moment, and order him to return to his beloved Coeur d'Alène, and bring Brother Daniel Coakely with him, a decision he executed in August, even though this meant that, with himself absent from St. Mary's, no priest would be stationed at the Flathead reduction.[65] The group that had left Westport in the spring, however, would be arriving momentarily at the mission. So much for Point. Now what to do with Hoecken? He sent word to have him meet him in the Kalispel's territory where the two of them agreed on a site close to the Pend d'Oreille River, near present Newport, Washington, where they set up yet another mission, which De Vos baptized St. Michael's.[66] The spring rains and thaw would prove their selection was, indeed, too hastily made, but De Vos was in a hurry to meet De Smet, who undoubtedly would be pleased to learn that the promise he had made to the representatives of this tribe he had met in 1841 was at last fulfilled: the Black Robes had at last established a permanent mission among the Kalispels.[67] De Smet's arrival, therefore, proved to be a catalyst at a time of decision for the Rocky Mountain Mission, and De Vos could have been pleased with himself as he hurried off to meet his superior, who, in turn ordered him to take charge of the newly founded St. Francis Xavier mission on the Willamette.[68]

De Smet and De Vos had been close friends for many years. We have already seen how De Vos played an important role in helping De Smet set up a Carmelite convent in Aalst and how he was very probably instrumental in De Smet's acquiring the physics laboratory at Saint-Acheul for St. Louis College. Shortly before he sailed for New Orleans in 1836 De Vos wrote a letter from Le Havre to l'Abbé De Smet, chaplain to the Carmelite nuns at his native town Dendermonde and no longer a Jesuit.[69] It was a warm letter, replete with friendly sentiments, a letter of one fund-raiser to another, full of news about such mutual friends and benefactors as the Baroness de Ghyseghem, from whom De

Smet would be authorized to borrow 125,000 francs for St. Louis College in the following year.[70] Years later, while his erstwhile rector, Nicolas Point, now assigned to the Rocky Mountain Mission, was busy organizing Lenten devotions at Westport, Peter De Vos, who was then master of novices at Florissant, wrote another letter to his old friend Peter De Smet, the appointed superior of the newly constituted Rocky Mountain Mission. He confessed his eagerness to join the mission, particularly when he considered his present job. "If I could have foreseen that my apostolate in America would be limited by a handfull of novices, perhaps—who knows? It is up to us to be ready, in the mountains or beyond them, to fulfill our *first* vocation." Obedience was always at a premium. Meanwhile, he assured De Smet that he continued to correspond with the Baroness, "and I tell her a great deal about you."[71] In April 1843 De Vos's dream finally had materialized: he bade farewell to his Florissant novices and, in De Smet's company, left Westport bound for the Rocky Mountains. The fact that he was appointed acting superior of the mission in the absence of De Smet by the vice provincial, another old friend, Peter Verhaegen, undoubtedly had De Smet's blessing.

Given the history of their long friendship, the meeting of these two Flemish Jesuits should have been nothing else but cordial. There was one piece of business, however, which cooled the encounter. De Vos had compiled a dossier of grievances against Point and Huet which he intended to send on to Rome. He gave this document to the superior and De Smet refused to give it back.[72] De Smet was a man who enjoyed an outstanding reputation among very different types of people. "He is a man of marvelous docility and simplicity," was the opinion of Father William Murphy.[73] General John Bidwell, his companion on the 1840 expedition, recorded that he was "a genial gentleman, of fine presence, and one of the saintliest men I have ever known . . . a man of great kindness and great affability under all circumstances; nothing seemed to disturb his temper."[74] Kit Carson (1809–1868), the famous frontier scout declared: "I can say of him that if ever there was a man who wished to do good he is one."[75] Father John Nobili (b. Rome, April 8, 1812; d. Santa Clara, California, March 1, 1865), founder of Santa Clara College, in 1851, and one of De Smet's companions in 1844 on the long sea voyage from Antwerp to Vancouver, declared, "this holy man helps us by the example of his life."[76] Many others attested to his character, including Point.[77] However universally admired he was, and whatever remarkable powers of attraction he seemed to have to inflame the most tepid spirits with enthusiasm, one gets the impression that he was not the best judge of character and that he knew little about the Jesuits who were his co-workers. For example, he described Brother Specht as a German tinner when he was in fact an Alsatian carpenter, and he spoke of Huet as a carpenter, not as the tinsmith he actually was.[78] As for his description of Point, he was a "Vendean as zealous and courageous for the salvation of souls as his compatriot La Rochejaquelein."[79] These glosses in no way minimize De Smet's powers of organization and leadership, nor do they call into question the charism of this man who used boundless energy for good and noble purposes. Were there Indians to be converted? He would see to it that the job was done. Were men and supplies needed? Superiors could depend on him to provide. But the glosses also reveal that there was a lack of human awareness, or better there was a disinterestedness in the personalities and backgrounds of his co-workers, and this weakness did not help solve the particular problem De Vos dropped in his lap, the problem of Nicolas Point. Stated simply, De Smet did not want to deal with a personnel problem when there was so much work to do. He wanted peace on the mission between all of his co-workers. If Point was a problem, he would look into it; there was no need to export it. This seems to have been the reason he pocketed De Vos's complaint, but in doing so he gave De Vos cause to complain to Rome.

Probably De Smet gave very little thought to this new Point problem. He had much reason to rejoice in the Rocky Mountain Mission which Roothaan considered "the apple of his eye."[80] On October 3, 1844, the day De Vos took over at his new post on the Willamette, Jesuits had missions in what today are the states of Washington, Oregon, Idaho, and Montana,[81] and on October 7, four of the five Jesuits De Smet had assigned to work in Missouri and Kansas (until they could join the 1844 expedition on the Oregon Trail) arrived at St. Mary's, bringing the total number of Jesuits on the Rocky Mountain Mission to twenty-one, an encouraging number for what was becoming an expanding enterprise.[82] As for Point, with characteristic enthusiasm he had already thrown himself into his new apostolate at St. Joseph's, placing particular attention to preparing his neophytes for their First Communion which he planned to celebrate with great pageantry.[83] Meanwhile, De Smet and Mengarini continued on their slow march bound for St. Michael's, St. Joseph's, and ultimately, St. Mary's.[84] At Fort Walla Walla they encountered Father Tiberio Soderini, the fifth man in the party that had left Westport that spring, who was on his way to Fort Vancouver. When the wagon trains arrived at Fort Hall in the early fall, Soderini determined he had had enough of his four companions and decided to place himself at the disposal of Father Blanchet. De Smet, who had a fondness for the volatile Soderini, talked him out of his decision and persuaded him to accompany him to St. Michael's, where they arrived before November 8.[85] On that day a Coeur d'Alène delegation appeared at the Kalispel mission begging De Smet not to punish them because of the altercation between their chiefs and the Kalispel missionary, Father Hoecken.[86] They invited him to come to St. Joseph's for the First Communion ceremonies and De Smet graciously accepted. Leaving Soderini to fend with Hoecken and Brother Lyons, and persuading Mengarini to proceed on to St. Mary's with the mule train of supplies intended for that mission,[87] De Smet arrived at St. Joseph's reduction on the twelfth.[88] The first thing he did was restore the original name to the mission and then presented the church with a large picture of its patron which he had brought with him from Belgium, the Sacred Heart.[89]

The anticipated First Communion ceremonies were spectacular. One hundred families gathered at the mission and De Smet recorded: "From morning to evening, and even into the night, nothing was heard throughout the camp but the recitation of prayers and the singing of canticles."[90] Point had outdone himself in paintings, sculptures, and decorations, in his use of visual teaching aids for his students, creating "images representing what they ought to believe," in order to stimulate their imaginations, insisting on repetition as a means for training the memory—methods dear to the heart of Jean-Nicolas Loriquet, practices he had learned at Fribourg. But on this occasion he confessed the "success of this method surpassed my expectations."[91] Here at the Sacred Heart Reduction, Point once again justified the wisdom of François Renault's judgment that he was "a man for the *collège*" because he was a naturally born teacher, a fact which he demonstrated in the barracks of Rocroi, the wards of Bicêtre, the boarding quarters of Blamont, the classrooms and study halls of Saint-Acheul, Fribourg, Le Passage, and St. Mary's, and in his administrative office at Grand Coteau. Even though he was "drawn by preference to the missions and the Indian missions at that, after the example of Father Van Quickenborne," he remained first and foremost a teacher.[92] All of his works, particularly his paintings, were didactic, focused on capturing the attention and gaining the interest and then the friendship of those whom he was trying to instruct. Such methods were essential to the *plan* of Jean-Nicolas Loriquet. Pierre Point explains well his brother's methodology:

> The early Paraguay missionaries charmed their Indians with music; on more than one occasion Father Point owed his safety and early successes, apart from prayer, to the inclination God gave him for drawing, about which the Indians were very curious. At one time he would show them a portrait of one of their chiefs, armed and in brilliant array; at another time he would present them with beautiful landscapes containing trees, mountains, cabins; still at another time he would show them a hunting scene with animals falling under the force of the hunters's arrows; here would be a splendid spectacle of a solemn baptism and of a First Communion ceremony; at another time there would be a battleground depicted where braves distinguished them-

selves and where they could proudly identify themselves. Civilized men are not themselves insensitive to such signs of favor. The missionaries were always well received among the Hudson Bay traders, even though for the most part these men were Protestants. Father [Nicolas] not having money to pay the debt of hospitality, would give them either a good likeness of themselves or a flattering picture of their store. It was an innocent beginning by which he gained their confidence, but at the same time, these visits ended up becoming a [spiritual] retreat for many employees at the trading posts.[93]

On September 24, 1844, three of Point's former companions from his Swiss or tertianship days—Pierre Cotain, Romain Dénieau and Ambroise Neyraguet—sailed from Le Havre bound for Ile Bourbon where they would begin the Madagascar Mission, one of the most glorious fields of French Jesuit missionary activity right up to the present day.[94] They were still on the high seas from November 12 to 19, during which time an elfin French-speaking Swiss with rosy cheeks and a child-like innocence appeared at the rebaptized Sacred Heart Reduction in search of De Smet. His name was Joseph Joset (b. Courfaivre, Bern, Switzerland, August 27, 1810; d. Desmet, Idaho, June 19, 1900), and, despite his unimpressive appearance, he had been appointed superior of the five Jesuits who had left Westport that spring and who had arrived at St. Mary's at the beginning of October. When they reached their destination, they were surprised to find that the headquarters of the Rocky Mountain Mission was a priestless reduction, manned only by Brothers Claessens, Huet and Burris. Joset, therefore, instructed his subjects to remain where they were while he and a companion set out to find someone in charge to whom he could give a full report of the expedition, deliver a pack of mail from St. Louis, and be relieved of his office.[95] One of the letters in Joset's mail pouch was addressed to Nicolas Point. It was written by Peter Verhaegen in studied, classical French and consigned to Joset shortly before the newly arrived Jesuits had left Westport. It was the answer to the letter, written in the same style, Point had entrusted to De Smet in August 1842, at the time De Smet met him at the summer hunt with the Flatheads and assigned him to found the Coeur d'Alène Mission. Point had probably written and rewritten his letter, at least in his own mind, many times over because he had spoken to the General about attempting such a letter during those days of black brooding at Sappling Grove in May 1841, at which time he was first plagued with outrage and doubts and then overcome by scruples, remorse, and feelings of guilt.

> "I received with much satisfaction," began Verhaegen, "the letter you sent me by Father De Smet, and I assure you that I very much appreciate the expressions of affections you extended to me. As far as I am concerned, dear Reverend Father, I have never ceased to love and esteem you, notwithstanding appearances which, perhaps, have led you to believe that my feelings were altered as far as you were concerned. No one is more convinced than I, that we have—all of us—imperfections, but I have learned long ago to forget the past, which causes me pain, in order to concentrate on the present, which fills me with the sweetest of consolations. The endeavors you have undertaken with so much zeal will prosper and you shall reclaim a great number of souls plunged in the darkness of infidelity, and you are tireless in your work—that, Reverend Father, is what fills me with consolation. I do not have to exhort you to persevere in your generous efforts for you know too well the value of those you have conquered to guarantee you new victories for future conquests."

Then, after proper pleasantries and some studied, general comments about the new missionaries in China, Verhaegen formally and correctly bade his farewell. It was answer to the letter written in the style and content of Point's letter to him but the formality could not disguise the mutual sincerity and honor contained in both pieces of correspondence, and this missive which Nicolas Point kept and treasured must have brought him consolation, joy, and peace each time he reread it.[96] Joset was certainly not a stranger to De Smet, whom he had met in St. Louis in 1843, and very probably he knew Point too, because he had been a student at Fribourg from 1826 to 1830, and a novice there from 1830 to 1832, years that coincided with Point's assignment in Switzerland. Like many other Jesuits mentioned in this book, Joset came from a family that gave many sons to the Church: only one brother remained a layman (there were no sisters), the other four became priests and religious. Providence arranged that his brother who had gone to China as a secular priest would play the key role in getting Claude Gotteland and his companions into that country. Another brother was a Capuchin friar; the fourth, a Jesuit lay brother who was sent to Canada and who spent his last days with the remnant of St. Mary's University, Kentucky, at Fordham, New York.[97] Father Joseph Joset, described as having "no sense of the practical," can be considered the founder of the California Mission, and certainly he was destined to play a cardinal role in the subsequent history of the Rocky Mountain Mission.[98] He was also the crucial man in determining Point's future. On this particular occasion in mid-November 1844, De Smet appointed the little Swiss superior at the Sacred Heart Reduction, with Point as his assistant and Brothers Lyons and Magri as his collaborators.[99] The latter, (b.?, Malta, November 10, 1810; d. Lewiston, Idaho, June 18, 1869), had been one of the four who arrived at St. Mary's with Joset the previous month, and he was probably the priest's companion on the journey from St. Mary's to Sacred Heart. Like Brother Peter McGean, who was with Father John Nobili at Vancouver, Magri was considered a *costaud,* a strapping, physically tough man, capable for the most challenging jobs on the mission. In 1849, Father Michael Accolti (b. Copertino, Lecce, Italy, January 29, 1807; d. San Francisco, November 7, 1878), another one of the five Jesuits who had made the voyage around Cape Horn with De Smet in 1844, requested that these two brothers, McGean and Magri, be sent to California to stake out a gold mine claim. The vast amount of money they could make would be a remedy for the financial embarrassment of the Rocky Mountain Mission and it would be an assurance that the Italian fathers in California would not have to go without "a good cup of coffee."[100] There was too much to be done at the Sacred Heart Mission in 1844, however, and the talents and strong back of the energetic Magri were essential in building the mission. Brother Huet in the meanwhile had returned to St. Mary's and Brother Lyons had taken his place. Point, of course, believed that plans for constructing the reduction were "formed upon the ancient plans in Paraguay, and each one, according to his strength and industry, contributed toward its construction."[101] Magri was able to get the Indians to work without any reassurance of pay or compensation; he loved the people dearly and was singularly loved by them in turn, and for the almost twenty-five years he spent with the Coeur d'Alène, he taught them how to prepare lumber for their new mill and how to construct private dwellings, churches, and communal buildings.[102]

After De Smet had become aware of the altercations between the Jesuits and the Stellam faction, he instructed the new Sacred Heart superior: "You judge the facts in connection with whether to close this mission . . . if you suppress it, all right."[103] Joset proceeded with great discretion and tact, dealing gently with his high-strung fellow priest and interfering seldom in the work of the two brothers, Lyons and Magri. He admitted that because he was "quite ignorant of the language, all ministry continued [to be] the lot of F. Point, who continued to apply it with his usual energy."[104] This 'usual energy' meant, as he himself explained while he prepared the catechumens at St. Mary's in December 1841, "being in the church from 8 in the morning until 10:30 at night, taking time off only for dinner, teaching catechism, saying mass and vespers, practicing hymns. "It was beautiful," he recalled, "hearing these good Indians answer questions they were asked. I shall never forget the religious tone in their responses."[105] The success of his *instruction,* would have pleased the most discerning critics at Fribourg. The four Jesuits shared a cramped and drafty log house with two orphan children. Hoecken had built this one room structure, and although it had been designed to give protection against the cold, it managed to become as wet inside as out whenever it rained.[106] The table fare offered little consolation to these hard-living conditions. "The main dish all that winter," Joset recalled, "was soup made of barley with chaff, with some tallow and without salt," and he added that this meager diet was supplemented by tree moss and occasionally by a little venison.[107] In part of January and February, Joset and Point accompanied the tribe on its annual deer hunt in the vacinity of Lake Pend d'Oreille.[108] Stellam, meanwhile, continued to be the vexing problem, undermining the work of the Jesuits, resorting to blackmail, and then, when it was obvious that he could not muster the support of the people, declaring again repentence, conversion, and attachment to the Black Robes' religion.[109]

Nicolas Point suffered greatly during these two years at Sacred Heart. In addition to the physical inconveniences was the fact that the hernia which had taken him away from his studies the year he was ordained had become the cause of continuous, aching discomfort. But his physical sufferings were mild in comparison to the mental and emotional storms that buffeted him. He had complained to De Smet, when he had the opportunity to speak with him in November 1844, of what he considered persecution at the hands of his fellow Jesuits who were in league against him. De Vos defended himself and others by reminding De Smet of the matter of mysterious documents Point had kept in his possession:

> Your Reverence should recall what Reverend Father Provincial [Verhaegen] told you shortly the day before our departure from Westport. "It would be good to seize and destroy the papers of Father Point which could compromise the society, if ever they fell into the hands of the public." Arriving at St. Mary's I communicated Father Verhaegen's wish to Father Mengarini and I authorized him to act in accord with these wishes. The good Father made immediate preparations to do so. He first purloined some papers, which were not the notes in question. I asked him not to destroy these (I had adequately advised him that the papers should be burned in case they were found), but to return them to their place. Later I asked him to make a second attempt. He did so and he succeeded. I told him to place them in a good envelope,

> sealed, and addressed to the mission superior; then to give it to Father Hoecken to bring it with him to the Coeur d'Alène, so that it could be later entrusted to the superior of the mission who had requested it. Father Mengarini assured me that he did just this, and since then I have heard nothing more about these papers. I have always believed, and I do so yet, that Father Hoecken kept them safe. I believe these were the same papers Father alluded to when I went down to the Kalispels. He told me: 'I should go back [to St. Joseph's Mission where Point had been sent in October 1844] and fetch those letters so that Father Point will not see them.' I have knowledge of no other letters than those taken away from Father Point, neither by myself nor by anyone else under my orders. The poor Father was suspicious of, and falsely accused, Father Mengarini [of persecuting him].[110]

In an age which places the highest premium on one's personal privacy and which regards any violation of that privacy as tantamount to an infringement on one's most basic rights and dignity, De Vos's actions in obtaining these so-called dangerous papers is unconscionable. It should be remembered, however, that the men of Point's generation did not deny that the superior had a perfect right to ask for such documents and if the subject did not hand them over, the superior, who had been ordered by a higher superior, had the right to obtain them even without the knowledge of the man concerned. The superior could read letters written by, or addressed to, the subject and no one could keep anything in his room without the knowledge of, and permission from, the superior. It was a right implicit in the vow of obedience, which had been freely taken, and implicit also in this vow was the concurrent duty of the subject to obey. It was part of the contract. A cursory reading of history indicates that those who hold the frantic, furious and almost ferocious attachment of a child to the notion of freedom or justice, and who harshly judge previous generations by their own criteria of what is free and what is just or hold the actions of the dead as objects of derision, often end up blindly, if not cynically perpetrating themselves the greatest injustices, in the name of freedom, on their adversaries. The transformation of Charles Péguy's *mystique* into *politique* is the fatal augury to which history attests. It is, as a matter of fact, possible to appreciate and sympathize with all of the actors involved in the drama described in De Vos's letter. The plain fact is that Point did not obey De Vos's order. Point, on the other hand, had the justifiable reputation of being a Jesuit of exemplary obedience. How does a historian reconcile these two seeming contradictions? One recalls that in 1839, when Father Peter Verhaegen made his first visitation to Grand Coteau, he requested certain information from Point which Point felt was beyond what obedience obliged him to divulge, and so he made an appeal to the General: "Very Reverend Father, concerning this matter, I ask your permission to maintain silence on those affairs which personally concern me."[111] Evidently, at that time he believed his immediate superior lacked the jurisdiction in this matter, and he appealed for a judgment to the general. That he was able to do so was also implicit in his vow of obedience, and apparently the general agreed. When De Vos asked him to turn over these mysterious papers, Point made the same appeal. Having had problems with the acting superior "over matters of jurisdiction in Louisiana,"[112] and recalling the personal disagreements these two men had at St. Mary's Reduction, it is logical to suppose that Point awaited the arrival of De Smet to settle the affair. At any rate, De Smet, who had previously pocketed De Vos's dosier of complaints against Point and Huet, returned to Point the contents of what Mengarini had taken and sealed in an envelope, and what Hoecken had kept hidden.[113] But the whole sordid history of this event left its remnant and it was a matter that would rise up again and accuse the actors.

Before 1844 had run its course, the cumulative effect of the many vexations—physical, mental and moral—caused Nicolas Point to evaluate, from a distorted viewpoint, his effectiveness on the mission. He had persuaded himself, as early as 1841, that, given the De Smet policy, it was impossible to set up authentic reductions, to function in accord with the goals and purposes outlined in the document drawn up by himself and De Smet at St. Mary's on October 26, 1841. In this matter he was in agreement with De Vos who complained to the General about the multiplication of missions which resulted in a swarm of understaffed outposts spread over a wide area of territory.[114] Added to this reality was the complicated misunderstanding about how Sacred Heart should be financed. This matter revolved about real or supposed promises made to Stellam by De Smet and De Vos and it resulted in recriminations reminiscent of the complaints and counter-complaints made to the general during the Grand Coteau crisis of 1839–1840.[115] Finally, there was his firm belief that he had been "on loan" to the "Belgian" mission, a conviction dating back to tertianship days and subsequently sustained by French superiors. Now that France had opened a mission among the American Indians, it was only logical that he should be associated with it. "It is unquestionable that the people of different nationalities, when they intermix," Henry Duranquet wrote in later years, "borrow the failings of one another, and lose to some extent their own characteristic virtues."[116] Point's experiences, since he left St. Mary's, bore out the truth of this observation. The newly arrived Italian Jesuits on the coastal missions were witnesses to this same tension. "With the sole exception of Mengarini," the new provincial James Van de Velde wrote to the General, "the Italians are the most difficult to deal with." He complained they were critical, suspicious, complainers, and were a rule to themselves.[117] De Smet added: "For the love of God let none be sent (to the Rocky Mountains) but true, humble Jesuits, men full of zeal and courage."[118] The end result of Point's brooding convinced him he could do more for the Indians among his own French Jesuits and this conviction persuaded him to seek out superiors and place the matter before them. This he did in April 1845.

De Smet had left St. Michael's the previous month for St. Mary's where, he, Hoecken, and Soderini spent Easter. On March 27, they returned to the territory of the Kalispels and chose another site along the river, near present-day

Cusick, Washington, as the new location for the Kalispel mission, which they renamed St. Ignatius.[119] Soderini and De Smet then made their way to Fort Colville where Point met them. After discussing what was on his mind with De Smet, he addressed the following letter to the general:

> I am entrusting this letter to Father De Smet hoping that in the protection of his cover it will fare better than many other letters addressed to your Paternity. For the good and peace in these parts, and for the greater good of souls, particularly my own (such is likewise the opinion of R[everend] F[ather] Joset), I must entreat Your Paternity, notwithstanding the attachments I bear the Indians of this land, kindly to send me to another Indian mission, and, may it please God that your choice will be to one entrusted to the Province of France. I say Indian mission because it seems to me my vocation is to live and die among these people. Many reasons could be given to Your Paternity for heeding my request, but I venture to assure you these reasons, whatever their worth, would never outweigh those which I could give you were I at liberty to do so. What I can say is that the provisions of the natural law which best foster union of mind and hearts do not seem to be known on the practical level by the Indians we have the good fortune to evangelize, and I am so persuaded that such shall be the case as long as I am not elsewhere (my presence here, if not the cause, is at least the occasion of such misery) and this [fact] must assure you a second time to have pity on my position.[120]

On the following day he addressed a copy of this letter to the general adding some of the same reasons in more detail which had led him to believe his situation was "deplorable," because of De Smet's policy, improper contracts and debts, and the like.[121] Shortly afterwards he and Soderini left Fort Colville together bound for Sacred Heart. It was an adventure-filled journey, but despite the many edifying experiences he chronicled, it could not have been a very happy journey.[122] Soderini had just received De Smet's permission to quit the mission and leave the society.[123]

In spite of De Smet's "covering," Point's request for transfer did not reach Roothaan until the following February and the general's response authorizing the change did not reach Point for another six months.[124] Meanwhile, Father Nicolas stayed on assisting Joset in operating the mission, instructing the people, and administering the sacraments. Both men concluded it was impossible to make a permanent site for the reduction where Point had initially decided to build the compound, and so another location was sought. There were a number of factors that entered into this decision. The flooding of the river each spring made a permanent settlement along the St. Joe impractical. The land claimed by the river curtailed acreage available for spring planting. There was also the question of the annual plague of disease carrying mosquitoes after the flooding that rendered the present site all but uninhabitable during a certain time of the year. Finally, there was the pestiferous presence of Stellam and his influence that persuaded the Jesuits that religious reasons dictated that they transfer the believers from the lowlands, away from Stellam, and to the area of the "Bas-Bretons," the true believers.[125] In November 1845, the four Jesuits agreed on the ideal place, the present site of the old mission church at Cataldo.[126] Point sketched the plan for the new reduction, and work on it was begun in spring. By summer a temporary chapel, a barn and three log houses were constructed, and wheat, potatoes and oats were planted. In late June or early July 1846 the move was made, thereby reversing the fourth and last directive De Vos, as acting superior, had legislated for the Coeur d'Alène reduction in 1843.[127]

The joy that should have accompanied this noteworthy event was muted by Point's having earlier been informed of the reply De Vos received to the letter he had written to Father Roothaan soon after he arrived at St. Francis Xavier on the Willamette. The answer was dated October 29, 1844:

> . . . Oh, how I regret that you turned over to F[ather] De Smet your notes and accounts. This father, even though superior, did not have the right to ask them from you. It is directly against the Institute. Moreover, since he has asked

> to be relieved of his post as superior, I have granted it. I have named Father Joset superior of the mission and you, Father, along with Fathers Accolti and Mengarini, his consultors. I hope that this will be better than that you seek *solidarity* among the Christians you are forming. Father Superior, with the advice of the consultors, has the authority to release from the mission, and even from the society, those who deserve to be expelled, for example Father Point, Brother Huet. After what you wrote to me, dear Father, about all of Father De Smet's running around, and about Willamette etc., I am telling Father Joset what I think. How can the neophytes of the Rocky Mountains be abandoned? How can one just baptize here and there—and then run off? No! No! Try, dear Fathers, to keep the religious spirit—that is the essential point: *religious* before all else, even before *missionary* and *apostle* because no true missionary or apostle ceases to be a religious.[128]

The new superior likewise received Roothaan's authorization to dismiss Point from the society and instructed him to serve him his dismissal papers if he saw fit. Point's qualities as a teacher, a missionary, and an apostle were of no value seeing that the essence of the religious was obedience, for "the obedient man will speak of virtues." The general had received more than one complaint about him, but the fact that he was disobedient was decisive.[129] Point pleaded with such feeling that Joset felt that he could not serve the papers, and reflecting on Point after he had left Sacred Heart, the Swiss superior observed:

> Now it is said of him that he was extraordinary, now that he was intolerable. He was disturbed over the Louisiana affair and always seemed afraid of being sent away from the society and had recourse to apologies and recriminations in hope of staying in. He would allow no exception to be taken to anything he did. For the rest, he would have been a man very well suited for the mission, a lover of poverty, generally obedient in executing orders, zealous, and pious."[130]

Other commentators have noted Point's fear of being dismissed from the society, but given the fact that indeed he was once dismissed and that this was always a contingency he faced, the fear does not seem to have been unreasonable. Furthermore, during the last days at Sacred Heart, this very insecure man had to live day by day with the sword of Damocles over his head and had to work, eat, and pray with a man who had it in his power to dismiss him without a convincing reason. It is to Joset's credit that he did not abuse his power, but he certainly did not hesitate to use it when he felt he had a good reason. In March 1848, he advised Roothaan that he had dismissed Brother Lyons, a Jesuit for thirteen years, because of his arrogance.[131] Harsh measure, of course, but it was precisely such discipline that insured the society with that quality that made for "light-armed soldiers ready for sudden battles, going from one side to another, now here, now there . . . unencumbered and free," the quality which Jean-Baptiste Gury attempted to instill in his novices at Montrouge, the quality Roothaan regarded as protected by "the Institute." The subsequent history of Nicolas Point and of the Rocky Mountain mission indicates that perhaps such an ideal was too lofty to put into practice in every instance, but this same history also shows that the ideal was never abandoned and that it remained normative both for individuals and for the corporate group. In the summer of 1845 De Smet visited each of the missions, and in the late spring of 1846 he set out from St. Francis Xavier in the Willamette bound for St. Louis. On July 29, 1846, six years to the day after Point had departed from Grand Coteau, De Smet arrived at Sacred Heart. One week later, "accompanied by the Reverend Father Point," he left the new Coeur d'Alène reduction for St. Mary's, the first leg on his journey to his new assignment—the Blackfeet.[132] Ever since 1842 Point himself had begged permission to establish a reduction among these aristocrats of the western tribes. In the chronicles that follow he reflects on the people to whom he had at last been sent and on the beginnings and end of the first mission among them.

Selected Letters, Excursions, and Anecdotes With Notes

AN OVERALL VIEW OF THE BLACKFEET

The most notorious of all the wild tribes extended along the banks of the Missouri and in the adjacent country is unquestionably, and sad to relate, the Blackfeet.[1] This tribe's reputation for brigandage is the cause of this fact. Even though still large, counting at least ten thousand, the nation has been reduced to a third of what it had been a quarter of a century ago. War, intoxicating liquor, smallpox and similar gifts presented to the people by the white man with whom they traded are causes for such an alarming drop in numbers.

In 1841, a missionary in Oregon [Peter De Smet, S.J.] wrote: "The tribes which at one time spread from the Missouri to the Pacific are daily drawing nearer to the Kingdom of Heaven. If God's thoughts were those of men, we could only despair for the future of the Blackfeet. But what was the result of the first encounter with the white man by the Chiquitos and the Chiriganos in South America? And, coming closer to our own land, what was the Iroquois' experience! Yet, with God's help, what have they not become?"[2]

After commenting on the Indians east of the Rockies, Father De Smet added, in 1845: "The Blackfeet, especially, have something hard and cruel about their features. You can read in their faces words written in blood. There is hardly one innocent hand in the whole nation. But, of course, the Almighty can bring forth sons of Abraham from the hardest of rocks."[3]

All travelers from the American Far West add to these sad testimonials: You can never rely on the Blackfeet's word; you have to treat them as enemies, etc. It is possible that such judgments are exaggerated, but the fact remains that for years the Blackfeet have been considered the worst of the Western Indians. In the light of this fact, is it any wonder that such a tribe was a mortal enemy to the nation that was consistently regarded by all newcomers into Oregon, and particularly by the missionaries, as the jewel of these extensive regions!

I speak of the Flatheads who have suffered more than any other people because of the barbarous Blackfeet. I knew a Flathead woman who, in the space of a few years, had lost four husbands, each one massacred by the Blackfeet. And I knew a Flathead chief who had fought sixty-five battles against this nation. Just one example will show the extent of the aversion these two peoples have for one another, and at the same time it will manifest the courage of the Flatheads even before this noble sentiment had been purified by our religion. One of the brothers of the chief I mentioned above [Titiche Loutso] was called "The Brave of the Braves," and after he had received a mortal wound from a party of Blackfeet, he said to them: "I know that I am going to die, and that in your sight I deserve death. For this reason I do not beg for my life; rather I request you heed my last words." He then proceeded to give a detailed account of all the Blackfeet he had killed. Next, acting as a man who knew he was about to accomplish a glorious deed by selling his life dearly, he seized his weapon and added another death to the list he had just recounted.[4]

But how was it possible that a handful of such men, irrespective of their bravery, could have resisted for so many years a nation twenty times as large as their own? And how could so perverse a nation be brought to say: "Henceforth the prayer of the Flatheads shall be ours"? These are questions which should appeal to the historian and the philosopher no less than they do to the apostle. I shall attempt to answer them here with a simple account of what I have seen and heard, and I trust, providing the God of truth and goodness bless my endeavor, the facts I relate will prove as edifying as they are interesting. First a general statement which one can easily see is confirmed by the facts: all that was virtuous or tended toward virtue has been blessed here in this world; all that was vicious or tended toward vice has been punished. Such a standard of punishments and rewards is in perfect harmony with the concepts of these people who are still so childlike. Moreover, sickness or health, abundance or famine, victories or defeats—in fact, almost every type of worldly blessing or evil is judged in the light of two great historic facts. After the coming of Catholic missions to the Rockies there was, on the one hand, the increase of the Flathead population, and on the other, the tragic decimation of the Blackfeet. Such has been the Column in the Desert by which God, in his mercy, has made himself known to the Flatheads as well as to the enemies of his people, the Blackfeet. The Column has strengthened and consoled the former and has led the latter toward the Promised Land outside of which there is no salvation.

May this little collection, in glorifying Divine Goodness, increase the fervor, generosity and zeal of pious souls, and may these, by prayers, alms, or by more direct cooperation in the apostolic work of the missionaries, bring all idolaters to the foot of the Cross.

O crux ave!

Translator's Notes

Father Nicolas Point introduced the letters and accounts that follow with this general introductory overall view of the Blackfeet. The "letters" are rather more a record that Point kept for the edification of Jesuits than a series of communications to an individual.

1. De Smet wrote: "The Blackfeet nation consists of about four-

teen thousand souls, divided into six tribes, to wit: the *Pegans* [Piegans], the *Sarcees,* the *Blood Indians,* the *Gros Ventres* (descendants of the Arapahos), the *Black-Feet* (proper), and the *Little Robes.* These last were almost entirely destroyed in 1845." Thwaites adds that these tribes "formed the Blackfoot confederacy, but the Sarcees and the Gros Ventres belonged to different stocks." Thwaits, *Early Western Travels,* 29: 259–60. John C. Ewers claims that the "Small Robes" *(Petites Robes)* were a band of the Piegans. See his *The Blackfeet (1958),* 5–6, 188. Point does not classify the Small, or Petites Robes as a specific tribe and notes that the "Sarcees and Gros Ventres speak a distinct language, entirely different from that of the other three Blackfoot tribes." The ancestors of the Sarcees came to the plains "after having wandered for a long time upon an immense lake, at the mercy of the winds and floods." The Gros Ventres "speak the same language as the Arapahos," who at that time lived at the south fork of the Platte and Arkansas. Chittenden and Richardson, *De Smet,* 3:949, note 5.

2. Thwaites, *Early Western Travels,* 27: 281–85. The Chiquitos, a Paraguayan tribe was introduced to the European reading public by Juan Patricio Fernández, alias Domingo Bandiera de Siena, Jesuit provincial in Paraguay, in his *Relación historical de las missiones de los indios que llaman Chiquitos que están a cargo de los padres de la Compañía de Jesús de la provincia del Paraguay,* (Córdoba de Tucumán, 1753). See Sommervogel, *Bibliothèque de la Compagnie de Jésus,* 1:871. Muratori, however, relied more on the reflections on the *Relación* by the French Jesuit Pierre François Xavier de Charlevoix in his *Histoire du Paraguay* (Paris: Didot, 1756), in commenting on the Chiquitos and the Chiriganos, another tribe that the Jesuits encountered in South America, whose behavior they were able to modify through the reduction system. See Erland Nordenskiöld, *The Changes in the Material Culture of Two Indian Tribes under the Influence of New Surroundings* (Göteborg: Elanders boktryekeri aktiebolag, 1920). Jean de Brébeuf, Isaac Jogues, and their companions were murdered by the Iroquois, who in turn became the precursors of Catholicism in the Rocky Mountains.

3. Thwaites, *Early Western Travels,* 29:240–41.

4. "Brave of the Braves" surname for Stiettiedloodsho who ranked beneath Victor, the chief of the confederated nation of the Flatheads, Pend d'Oreilles, and Kootenai. John Fahey, *Flathead Indians,* 97. His baptismal name was Moses because he was the patriarch of the tribe, and he was also the adopted brother of Father De Smet. Thwaites, *Early Western Travels* 29:174; Donnelly, *Wilderness Kingdom,* portrait, 49.

No. 1

RELATIONS BETWEEN THE FLATHEADS AND THE BLACKFEET

Reverend and dear Father—Pax Christi:

In 1839, seventy Flatheads, or Pend d'Oreilles, had to defend themselves over a five day period against four assembled Blackfoot camps. What was the result of such a perilous encounter? Fifty Blackfeet killed: every one of their adversaries survived. The only Flathead casualty was a brave who died four months after this celebrated affair from an arrowhead that had been impossible to dislodge from his head. And, interesting to note, he died the day after his baptism, which had been impossible to administer at an earlier date, despite his earnest wishes. To his credit and to that of his brothers-in-arms, it should be said that before encountering the enemy on the very first day of these battles, all of them knelt down and prayed for help from on high. Then the chief said: "My children, now that we have made our earnest prayer, let us not rise until the enemy rushes down upon us."

In 1841, a Blackfoot was caught redhanded stealing in the Flathead's camp. The head chief in the camp at that time was a man named Peter, who deemed it his duty to make an example of the thief by piercing him through with his spear. Justice having been requited, he took off his tunic, covered the body of the Blackfoot, and then raising his eyes toward heaven, said: "My God, be merciful to him! You know that I did not act from enmity nor from any sentiment of revenge, but only to deter those who might be tempted to walk in this man's path, from following this evil course."[1]

On Christmas Day of this same year (1841), that is on the day following the apparition of Our Lady to a young boy, two Blackfeet of the Little Robe tribe received the sacrament of regeneration.[2] One was baptized Nicolas and the other, his son, was given the name Gervais. Both had received instructions in the Faith at the same time as the Flatheads. Nicolas, probably because of his small stature, was commonly known as "Little Blackfoot," and Gervais had been called "Sata" from the time he was a child. Seeing that the boy had been a little imp right from his earliest days and that the name "sata" has almost the same meaning as "Satan" in French, Gervais had been appropriately named.[3] But whatever he had been in his early years, he—and his father too—were destined to become for their nation what the two Iroquois, both named Ignatius, had been for their adopted homeland.[4]

During the winter immediately after his baptism, Nicolas, still overflowing with fervor, resolved to provide the missionary with the opportunity to meet some members of his own nation. Taking a horse as his sole companion and a spear as his sole defender, he left camp with this resolution in mind. For seventeen days he traveled over hill and dale without encountering a single one of his fellow tribesmen. Finally he decided to return to the hunting camp where he could formulate a new plan of procedure. No sooner did he arrive than he learned that thieves had recently been scouted roaming about the neighborhood. Convinced that such visitors could only be Blackfeet, he contrived the following plan: for several nights he posted himself a short distance from the camp and then began to harangue the open air with as much gusto as if all the robbers of the whole tribe were his hearers, hoping all the while that if a few were out there, they would not be deaf to his entreaties. He was not disappointed. On one fine morning a peace pipe showed up at the edge of the hunting camp. This meant that a peace envoy would be arriving soon, and, indeed, he did arrive and informed the camp that a party of Blackfeet was coming to meet the Flatheads. Overjoyed at finally finding the opportunity he had so enthusiastically pursued, good Nicolas, accompanied by a dozen Flatheads, set out immediately to meet the Blackfeet.

About ten o'clock, we could hear Indian songs coming from the shadowed recesses of a mountain pass, and then soon in broad daylight appeared the mountain bandits themselves. What sad memories must have been stirred up by such a sight; so many Flatheads had been sacrificed to the wrath of these Blackfeet! But Christian generosity begets forgiveness. So, putting vengeful thoughts far from their minds, the Flatheads welcomed as friends those who until now had been regarded as their executioners.

Representatives of both nations met in the missionary's lodge where they smoked the peace pipe together. After protracted discussions centering on mutual advantages of a lasting peace, the Blackfeet were taken to the very best lodges and here they agreed in private converse that the declamations of the Flatheads were sincere. Needless to add that after such a happy event, everyone fell peacefully asleep. But no sooner had the camp bedded down than all were suddenly aroused by the firing of several shots. Treachery was suspected. What had happened? A Blackfoot thief caught in the act of running four Flathead horses from the camp had just been shot several times. Who was he? Luckily for the guests he was not one of their number. So, rather than blaming them for a crime in which they seemed to have had no part, and which moreover had been so promptly avenged, the Flatheads gave them leave to attend to the burial rites as they saw fit. But whether the Blackfeet feared reprisals, which certainly no one in camp would have pressed, or whether they judged the insolent thief had received his just deserts, they left to the wild beasts the performance of funeral rites, and they hastened to take their leave. Almost at the very time when this drama was taking place the Nez Percé meted out the death sentence to twelve more Blackfeet and the Pend d'Oreille, friends and allies of the Flatheads, killed an additional twenty-eight.[5]

This latter event was so remarkable as to warrant a detailed description. Four Pend d'Oreille hunters, one of whom was the son of Koulkoulokaemi, the most famous chief of the Rockies, had advanced a little ahead of their camp to see if they could find animal tracks.[6] But instead of finding animals, the group stumbled on a war party; indeed, they were Blackfeet and they numbered at least thirty. For any brave eager to make a name for himself it is always a thrill to come across the enemy like this and pounce on him. First, the son of Koulkoulokaemi the Great drove off two Blackfeet horses, and then in the scuffle that followed the Blackfoot chief was killed. Demoralized by this loss, the rest of the party allowed itself to be cornered in a box canyon. But this was only the beginning of their troubles because the gunfire, heard back in the Pend d'Oreille camp, invited many warriors to lend their support to the small hunting party. "We are lost, let us run," was a loud cry from the Blackfeet side. "No," a second voice called out, "We have found what we have been seeking." And then a third voice: "Let us fight to the death." The first Pend d'Oreille to dash out at the enemy was a woman named Kuilix, "The Red One," so named because she usually wore a red coat. Her bravery surprised the warriors who were humiliated and indignant because it was a woman who had led the charge, and so they threw themselves into the breach where nature's shelter had protected the enemy.[7] The Blackfeet immediately shot four shots almost at point-blank range; yet not a single Pend d'Oreille went down. Four of the enemy—some claim it was only two—managed to escape death by hiding in the thickets, but the rest were massacred on the spot. A few days later there were only six heads still attached to the twenty-eight bodies strewn across the bloody field, and these had been so ravaged that one would have thought that they had been there for centuries. This terrible whipping cast such fear in the hearts of the Blackfeet that from that date until the end of the hunting season, not so much as the shadow of a thief appeared near the camp. So by such severe blows did Divine Justice prepare the way for Divine Mercy.

The four that had escaped this bloodbath joined their tribe at just about the same time as the peace party, enticed by Nicolas's nocturnal exhortations, had come to the Flathead's camp. Reports from the escapees plus those given by the peace delegation added weight to the argument that it would be to the Blackfeet's advantage to become allies with the Flatheads; and by the same token there was a great deal to lose by remaining enemies. The Pend d'Oreille and the Flathead comprise one nation in the eyes of the Flatheads, and as a matter of fact they do speak the same language and have the same spirit.[8] It should come as no surprise, then, that good Chief Nicolas, who had accompanied his fellow Blackfeet back to their camp, received the highest honors there, where he was welcomed as an oracle. One of the first fruits of his zeal was the establishment of Sunday as a day of rest. Moreover, he gave on this occasion great praise both to the Flathead's prayer and the goodness of the Black Robe for teaching this prayer. The result was that the most enthusiastic members of the tribe determined to become acquainted with these Black Robes at the first opportunity.

This opportunity was not long in coming. During that same winter season, which had lasted three months because of the heavy ice and snow, the missionary had to leave his horse for a while back in Blackfeet country. A group from this nation called Little Robes took the animal, but when they learned the identity of its owner they agreed to return it. This decision on their part was all the more remarkable in that it was probably the first of its kind ever made. But how was the restitution to take place? Should they bring the horse back to St. Mary's or ask the Black Robe at St. Mary's to come and fetch it himself? The majority favored the second alternative for it would allow the whole tribe to see the Black Robe. But who should go to St. Mary's to extend the invitation? A dozen or so warriors volunteered, and off they went. On their way they met the horse's owner going to a Nez Percé camp to administer the last rites to an old chief he had but recently baptized. Everyone was delighted by the fortunate meeting. The delegation laid a few beaver pelts at the feet of the Black Robe, then invited him to a banquet where one of the guests, to everyone's astonishment, was the Nez Percé chief who was supposed to have been dying on the previous day. After the feast the Blackfeet addressed the Black Robe: "Come with us; we will give you back your horse." Pressed for time the Black Robe was not able to oblige their request, and because of the presence of an unfriendly Indian party in the neighborhood, the Blackfeet were prevented from proceeding to St. Mary's, as they had planned, to speak at length with the Black Robe. So, it was agreed that the best course for both parties would be to return to their separate homes, and not long afterwards the horse was returned to its proper owner. This was a big step toward making peace.

During the hunt in the summer which followed [1842], we had a visit from two young Little Robe Blackfeet warriors. Almost every day was a holiday for them during their stay, and they and the young people in our camp challenged one another regularly to determine who would perform the greatest hunting feats. On one occasion, one of the visitors tracked a bear he had watched going into the underbrush. But he got too close to it and in one bound the enraged animal sprang from nowhere and so savagely clawed the arm that held his bow that, were it not for the more prudent courage of one of the Flathead youths near him, it would have been the end of the rash young man. A few days afterwards, the second warrior found himself in the same position which provided yet another Flathead with the honor of coming to the rescue. And, indeed, Indians never forget such deeds nor those who perform them.

During the course of this summer hunt there was only one occasion when a Blackfoot tried to steal a horse from the Flatheads. At this time the thief was leading his prize away when he was surprised by a woman whose war cry so terrified him that, in order to give his legs speed, he left his knife and gun behind. By the time her alarm had aroused the camp, the thief had put some distance between himself and his pursuers. One of those who had responded to the woman's cry was the second chief, Michael.[9] After the confusion had abated he noticed that nearly all of his own horses had disappeared. Banishing all thought that he could be ambushed—in such circumstances it is rare that a Flathead will recoil before danger—he immediately set out in search of the horses, walking the whole night through without any success. Exhausted, and all but despairing of ever finding the object of his search, he finally knelt down on a small knoll to offer God the sacrifice of his loss. No sooner had he finished this religious act when he heard in the distance a horse neighing. Getting up, he walked toward the direction of the sound, and there he rounded up all of his horses.

A bit farther away from where this incident took place, in the country near Yellowstone, there was a poor widow, the mother of two, who came face to face one night with a Blackfoot. To stop her from crying out he put two fatal bullets in her throat. Ever since her baptism her conscience had been clear and after her death her poor children were adopted by a Flathead chief whose courage and piety were better safeguards for their virtue than the protection a poor widow could guarantee. And so it turned out that death, which gained eternal rest for the mother, was not the tragedy it might have been for the children. In fact, this widow's murder may have been fortuitous for the Flatheads since it gave them a certain moral superiority and the Blackfeet, who, for their part, were loud in denouncing the crime, asserting that shame was the only prize the murderer had taken from it. Rumor has it that later on the perpetrator of this dastardly act fell himself victim to the same violence.

In April 1843 a man of the Snake tribe was murdered near St. Mary's, and this crime presented the Flatheads and their allies with the opportunity to manifest their virtue.[10] As soon as the enormity was discovered, some young men set chase after the murderers, but they were unable to overtake them because the heavy snowdrifts made it impossible for their horses to enter the higher mountain country. So, the victim was given a decent burial and the whole tribe contributed provisions for his wife and children. A few nights after the burial—it was one of the darkest of winter nights—the mission dogs suddenly began barking. A shot was fired. A thief was wounded, very likely one of the murderers. But who had fired the weapon? Another Snake, a companion of the dead man. What happened to the wounded man? A trail of blood descended to the river and then disappeared. All evidence pointed to his having drowned, but three days later they found him in the undergrowth still very much alive. Some young Flatheads rushed in to finish him off; shots were already being fired when someone shouted, "Stop!" This was an older member of the tribe sent there by the missionary.[11] Then the dying man—he was a Blackfoot—was gently hoisted up on a horse and in less than an hour he was the object of care and compassion in the head chief's lodge. The missionary took advantage of the occasion to speak to the man about God's judgment, and the Blackfoot responded that he had never heard such truths but that he would take them to heart.

Meanwhile, the assembled chiefs were debating on how they should deal with him. After having given him all the attention demanded by Christian charity, should they then make him an example of justice in order to discourage other bandits? That was the question on the floor when the missionary, making himself the Blackfoot's advocate, said: "My dear friends, for two years now we have been teaching you to pray that God 'forgive us as we forgive others'. Several times each day you make this prayer to God. He has heard it by granting you his forgiveness. Today he has allowed one of your enemies to fall into your hands. He is guilty, very guilty, I admit. But his soul, like yours, is created in the image of God; like yours, his soul is redeemed by the Blood of Christ. Today this Blood that has redeemed you begs you to have mercy on this man. What then is your wish: that he live or that he die?" "Let him live! Let him live!" shouted all of the chiefs, and this judgment was echoed in the hearts of all their subjects.

However, the greatest threat to the absolved Blackfoot's safety was still to be reckoned with: the Snake who had wounded him was yet with us, and not being a Christian he considered vengeance a virtue, not a vice. Moreover, it appeared that he had sworn that the wounded murderer would die, and so it was only by moving the criminal from lodge to lodge each night that the Flatheads managed to save his life. Finally, when he was strong enough, they turned them over to the protection of the Pend d'Oreilles, who, as we mentioned above, are friends of the Flatheads, having the same language and are, in the eyes of the Blackfeet, people of the same nation. Selpisto, their head chief, personally took the man under his own protection, but no sooner had he been given hospitality in the camp than eleven horses vanished, all stolen by the Blackfeet. Infuriated by this theft, a few young Pend d'Oreilles, more impassioned than reasonable, wanted to blame the guest, but his noble protector reminded them of their duty. The chief's own son pursued the thieves, had actually recovered the horses, and was returning triumphantly to camp when he met another party of Blackfeet who killed him. The news of his murder exasperated even more the young Pend d'Oreille braves who now asked Selpisto to turn over to them the tribesman of his son's assassins. Before he was baptized, Selpisto would have regarded granting such a request as the right thing to do, but now he gave the Blackfoot a horse to enable him to escape from the camp. No sooner had he ridden off when some more Blackfeet came forward affirming friendship, but because no protection had been promised to these, the young Pend d'Oreille braves gave out loud war whoops. So, once again the good chief had to intervene on behalf of the Blackfeet, but this time simple persuasion did not succeed. The chief had to threaten the most intransigent of the young men that if they dared to violate the rights of hospitality, more sacred to him under these circumstances than ever before, he could no longer be their chief and he would even leave the tribe. Foiled again, or rather allowing Selpisto's magnanimity to triumph over their pettiness, the young men gave in and allowed the guests to return safe and sound to their tribes. Once home, the Blackfeet gave an account to their people of the extraordinary control Selpisto had over his people and of the power the Pend d'Oreilles' religion had over both their deepest sorrows and the most violent passions.

March 3, 1844.[12] On this day, after many and fervent prayers, the Flatheads completed an almost miraculous hunt in Blackfoot country, and in thanksgiving for such abundant and heavenly favor, the hunters began the St. Francis Xavier novena for the conversion of the Blackfeet. On the evening of the eleventh, that is on the eighth day of the novena, the missionary poured the waters of baptism over the head of the Blackfoot who had escaped from a bear's claws some eighteen months earlier, giving him the name Peter. The next day was the feast of the canonization of St. Francis Xavier, the day on which heaven and earth truly rejoiced over the event which I now relate.

The Flathead camp was but one day's march ahead, but Victor, the head chief, suddenly decided to turn about and retrace his steps. According to the testimony of those close to him, he made this decision without any apparent reason. The missionary then let it be known that he would stick with the head chief, and so the whole group turned about. Scarcely four miles had been covered when Victor halted, and climbing a mountain top, surveyed the vast lands stretched out below. On the edge of the horizon he detected some moving forms, judged by the men about him to be buffalo, but as the colors became clearer, it was suggested that the forms might be deer. Finally, clearer details revealed that these were men, in fact an approaching Blackfoot war party. As calmly as if he were directing an ordinary hunt, Victor broke away from the rest, riding before the assembled camp. When he began performing a few zigzags (this is the accepted signal for war), the braves immediately reacted by gathering around him. One of these suggested that all recite a prayer. The Black Robe made his way to Victor's side as the head chief pointed toward the mountain behind which the Blackfeet were last seen, and said: "Let us wait until we can see them up there." All eyes turned toward the summit where shortly two figures appeared. They seemed friendly, and by the way they were advancing toward us, Victor surmised that they were being pursued. Then more appeared. The head chief looked at the missionary with affection, and with joy lighting up his face, he raised his weapon, shouted, and rushed ahead followed by his most courageous men.[13]

When the terrified Blackfeet saw them pressing on, they dropped much of what they were carrying and fled. But in vain, for as quick as lightning their better-equipped pursuers swooped down upon them. Ambrose shouted his name which was cause enough for the enemy to blanch—and added with a terrible voice: "If you shoot you're dead!"[14] One Blackfoot threw down his rifle; the others put up their hands. Then a Little Robe Blackfoot approached the party. What can one do to an enemy who surrenders; to an enemy for whose conversion one has been storming heaven; to an enemy heaven itself has delivered only because the prayer to forgive one's enemies has been heard, and finally to an enemy who places himself under the protection of the Black Robe, thereby affirming his respect for, and confidence in, Christian prayer? Could a Flathead Chief think of conquering such an enemy with anything other than mercy? Of course not! So signs of mutual friendship were exchanged; a buffalo hide was spread out on the snow; the Black Robe was asked to take his seat upon it; a gift was placed at his feet; the peace pipe was brought out, then lighted, and as the peaceful smoke rose to heaven in thanksgiving, the new allies of the Flatheads declared with emotion which they had never experienced before, "From this day forward the prayer of the Flatheads will be the prayer of the Blackfeet."

Translator's Notes

These events are described in Point's letter "Henceforward the Prayers of the Flat-Heads Shall Be Ours," which De Smet incorporated in his work on the missions. Thwaites, *Early Western Travels*, 29:408–19.

1. The identity of Peter, "the apostle of his tribe," is somewhat confusing. In 1840, on his first excursion to the Rocky Mountains, Peter De Smet baptized Peter, or Walking Bear, the chief of the Pend d'Oreilles, and Paul, Tjolzhitsay, or Big Face, chief of the Flatheads. Point here seems to be confusing either Peter with Paul or the Pend d'Oreilles with the Flatheads. Donnelly, *Wilderness Kingdom,* 43. William L. Davis, *A History of St. Ignatius Mission*. (Spokane: C. W. Hill Printing Co. 1945), 89. Evans, *St. Mary's in the Rocky Mountains,* 28.

2. Donnelly, *Wilderness Kingdom,* 42.

3. Nicolas, most probably a member of the Small Robes band of Piegans, was "an old chief of the Blackfoot nation" who had received baptism "with his son [Sata] and his little family, five in all," after having received instruction from Father Point. Nicolas may have been married to a Flathead woman since Sata, who later proved so valuable to Point, was described as "a half-breed Blackfoot and Flathead." Chittenden and Richardson, *De Smet,* 2:596, note 7. It may have been that Charles Larpenteur, who is the source of this description, assumed that because Sata was perfectly bilingual, he must have been part Flathead.

4. There were two important Iroquois named Ignatius. "Young Ignatius," also known as Aeneas, had accompanied Peter "le Gaucher" to St. Louis in 1839. He and his companion had been received by Peter De Smet at Council Bluffs, who wrote, "with tears in their eyes they begged me to return with them" to the Northwest. It was they who provided De Smet with the impetus to take on the Rocky Mountain Mission. (Laveille, *The Life of De Smet,* 99–102), "Old Ignatius," also called Ignatius "La Mousse" and Ignatius "Petrui," had been baptized and married by the Jesuits at the Caughnawaga mission near Sault-au-Recollet, where Point would spend his declining years. (Point to De Smet, Sault-au-Recollet, March 17, 1862. ASJSL, LP-75). Old Ignatius brought the basic elements of Catholic Christianity to the Flatheads. He was killed by the Sioux on the 1837 expedition to St. Louis in search of Black Robes.

5. Thwaites, *Early Western* Travels, 27: 351–52.

6. Footnote in the text: "Koulkoulokaemi was baptized on his death bed by a young Indian of his tribe named Ignatius Peter. He was given the designation of 'Great' because of his exceptional feats of arms. These will be described often in what follows." It is difficult to identify with certainty Ignatius Peter, certainly it was not chief Peter who was an octogenarian. Both Indian and Christian names of many of the individuals in these letters seem to vary. Selpisto was the son of Koulkoulokaemi and head chief of the Pend d'Oreilles, a special friend of Point's. Thwaites, *Early Western Travels,* 29:174, 411 (Point letter).

7. De Smet identifies this woman as Mary Quille. Chittenden and Richardson, *De Smet,* 2:578.

8. This sentence is scored in the text.

9. Thwaites writes: "Ensyla (Insula), sometimes called Little Chief because of his station, also named Red Feather from his official emblem, and christened Michael because of his faithfulness, was one of the most influential of the Flathead chiefs . . ." Thwaites, *Early Western Travels,* 27:147, 29:333; Palladino, *Indian and White in the Northwest,* 22, 83. Point wrote that Michael was called "Little Chief" because as a child he imitated the ways of a chief. As a young man he was invited to be the head chief of "a neighboring tribe," but he turned down the honor because of his youth and because "being born on the land of the Flatheads, it is among the Flatheads that I should die." After the death of Peter (again Point confused Peter with Paul), the tribe invited Michael to be their leader. Again he refused: "I am too old; besides there is one among you who is better, and that is Victor." On the basis of this judgment Victor was chosen head chief. Michael, in Point's estimation, was the epitomy of the "noble savage," the one who incorporated all of the virtues that made work among the Indians more than simply rewarding because Michael was inspiring, clearly Point's favorite among the Flatheads. Point to De Smet (?), Sault-au-Recollet, January 13, 1863, BO-43-5, ASJSJ.

10. The following anecdote can be found in a more detailed form in Point's essay "Henceforward the Prayer of the Flat-Heads Shall Be Ours," where he indicated the action took place not in April, but in February. In Thwaites, *Early Western Travels,* 29:408–19.

11. The older chief is Selpisto, the head chieftain of the Pend d'Oreilles, who had been baptized at Easter, 1845. The missionary is Nicolas Point. In Thwaites, *Early Western Travels,* 29:411.

12. A whole year had passed. Point had returned from founding Sacred Heart, had met with De Vos, and was sent to accompany the Flatheads on their winter hunt of 1843–1844.

13. Mitt'to or Slem-cry-cre, (Little Bear Claw), was better known as Victor. As noted above, Victor became chief at the death of Big Face. Ronan incorrectly identifies him with Etsowish Semmegee-itshin, "The Grizzly Bear Erect," the famous Chief Loyola of the Pend d'Oreilles. He is also sometimes confused with another Victor, or Pitol, also a chief of the Pend d'Oreilles. Victor Mitt'to was made prefect of the Men's Sodality by Point. Point had set up this organization, modeled after the one he had founded in Westport, before the winter hunt of 1841. As prefect, Victor played an important role in the May devotions of 1842. Peter Ronan, *History of the Flathead* Indians, (Minneapolis: Ross & Haines 1890) 46. In Thwaites, *Early Western Travels,* 27:355–56. Fahey, *The Flathead Indians,* 366. Evans, *St. Mary's in the Rocky Mountains,* 72, 78, 262, 273. His nickname was "*Tas misten*" ("What can I do?") because of "the constant repetition of these words whenever he was called upon to

exercise his authority," a characteristic which may well explain why he was able to maintain for almost thirty years the reputation of being a peerless administrator. "Obituary: Gregory Mengarini," *Woodstock Letters,* 16 (1887) 95–97. See also Thwaites, *Early Western Travels,* 29, frontespiece, Victor's son was the famous Chief Slem-hah-kah (Little Claw of a Grizzly Bear), better known as Charlot. Fahey, *Flathead Indians,* 362–63. There are some interesting and amusing anecdotes about Victor, including his invitation to Pope Gregory XVI, "our Great Father, the Great chief of the Black-robes," that should he be in danger, he could take refuge in the Rocky Mountains, recorded in Chittenden and Richardson, *De Smet* 4:1347–53.

14. Ambrose or Sechelmeld. Father Hoecken was high in praise of this chief who "has affected most good" among the Flatheads in 1857. He seems to have been a naturally born leader and one of the missionaries's most faithful converts. In Mengarini's opinion he shared with Victor, Moses, and Adolph the reputation for never having "deviated from the path of honor and virtue during the 1850s, the period of stress which finally led to the dissolution of St. Mary's. In Thwaites, *Early Western Travels, De Smet's Letters and Sketches,* 27:286, note 151. Chittenden and Richardson, *De Smet,* 4:1240. Evans, *St. Mary's in the Rocky Mountains,* 142–43.

No. 2

MISDEEDS OF THE FLATHEADS PUNISHED

A peace designed to inspire optimism was signed with the Blackfeet. These new allies, exhausted by the long journey they had made on foot, then willingly accepted the generous offer made by Flathead warriors and climbed up behind their hosts to ride back on horses. Flatheads and Blackfeet sharing the same mounts—this was really a remarkable sight, undoubtedly one that the Rockies had never before witnessed. But in spite of this auspicious beginning, a quarrel soon broke out between a Blackfoot chief who had been on the trail of the Flatheads since the first days of the hunt and the chief of the party who had given hospitality at the camp. The missionaries and another Flathead chief squelched the disagreement almost as soon as it began, but shortly afterwards more wrangling began, causing the greatest concern among the peacelovers. In fact the Blackfoot who had provoked the dissension found time enough during the journey to sow dissension even in the heart of the Flathead whom he had adopted as his brother. No sooner had we halted and pitched camp when four men, not merely the two who were scrapping on the journey, faced one another as if they were in an arena. They were men regarded as outstanding in the eyes of all because of their courage and strength. Two of them demanded the weapons of their adversaries and each met with a refusal. One of the challengers was a devious Flathead who was called Thunder because of his heedless courage.[1] His antagonist, reputed to be the bravest of all Blackfeet warriors, was none other than the famous thief that had been pardoned at St. Mary's a few months earlier. Thunder had learned that this Blackfoot was contemptuous of the hospitality he had received from the Flatheads, that he gloried in this ingratitude to the extent that he boasted of having stolen horses from Thunder himself. Fuming at this disclosure, Thunder demanded the Blackfoot's gun as an indemnity. The Blackfoot refused, asserting that he would sooner give up his life than his weapon. Such then was the background for these two open conflicts, either of which could have rekindled the firebrand of dissension which all believed had been forever extinguished.

Because most of the spectators were unaware of the causes for these disputes, they stood tense and fully armed, awaiting the pronouncement of the head chief. Had he declared himself against the Blackfeet, unquestionably not a single one of them could have escaped a massacre. But when he spoke he said that he wished to know all of the facts in order to be able to render a decision. Then, selecting a few men known for prudence as well as bravery, he withdrew to a nearby hill for deliberation. Meanwhile Ambrose, who was quite familiar with the facts in each case, went throughout the camp encouraging all to remain calm and clear-headed. The Black Robe had come out of his tent to learn the cause of the trouble and found himself surrounded by those Blackfeet who, unarmed or poorly armed, huddled up to him. Ambrose's brother, Amadeus, a man reputed for bravery and blessed with the gift of eloquence, tried reason and then reproaches with the crowd, and at last succeeded in making himself heard. When Indians listen peace follows. So, the wrangling ceased. Once again the two groups smoked the calumet together, and together they again prayed asking God to strengthen the unraveling bonds of their professed friendship. The Blackfoot party then got up to leave, promising "in twenty-four hours time we shall return with four camps from our nation to confirm the treaty we have made with the Flatheads."

Beautiful words these, but the head chief and the Flathead council had reasons for not trusting them, and all agreed the wisest decision would be to break camp immediately. Why? I will record but one reason which by itself seemed sufficient to them. The Flatheads had made a double mistake in their dealings with the pardoned Blackfoot and with the quarrelsome chief. In their efforts to save the peace agreement, the Flatheads had punished with excessive severity the chief whose imprudent tongue had broken it; they had forced him to surrender his gun. As for the Blackfoot who twice owed his life to the Flatheads, it was true he was twice ungrateful. If he said the things his fellow tribesmen accused him of saying, he should have been rebuked. But to strip him of his weapon on the testimony of a troublemaking Blackfoot was, under the circumstances, imprudent, uncharitable and wrong. Again, if the error had been corrected as it should have been, that is to say by giving back the confiscated firearm, neither party would have suffered greatly. On the contrary, the chief, who was the brother of the head chief of the Pegans [Piegans], added to the imposed surrender of his rifle the voluntary gift of his calumet—a gesture which put him in an entirely good light.[2] This double mistake had not been amended, at least not sufficiently, and the Flatheads would pay the price. The twice-pardoned robber was, as we saw it, stripped unjustly of his weapon; before three weeks had passed he would be the ninth Blackfoot to break into the St. Mary's paddock, walking out with twenty Flathead horses. Granted these horses were later retrieved, but at the cost of the life of one of the owners. Moreover, Thunder would be all but mortally wounded by the Blackfeet before two years had passed.

A second Flathead blunder. During the night following the historic meeting, that is on March 13, 1844, four horses disappeared from the corral. Who had taken them? Footprints coming from the opposite direction from where the Blackfeet had been the day before exonerated the peace party. Moreover, these Blackfeet had warned their hosts: "Be on guard. Recently six men left our camp intent on robbing you"—a further proof to reasonable men that the Blackfeet in yesterday's camp were not the guilty parties, especially when traces in the snow testified that the robbers numbered six. But the horses' owner, convinced by the arguments of foreigners whose interest was to stir up trouble, determined to go to the Blackfeet's main camp where they knew nothing of the peace talks between the two nations. When the Black Robe came out of his lodge to inspect the corral where the robbery had taken place, he came upon this man, gun in hand and anxious to set off right away to the Blackfoot camp. He had found some friendly Blackfeet willing to avenge his loss, and at that moment they were sitting on their heels in a semi-circle receiving from a white man powder and bullets to use against their brothers. It was then that reasons why this adventure would turn into a triple wrong sprang into the Black Robe's mind, and he spoke so forcefully that the poor Flathead who was more muddleheaded than evil, gave up his plan. "And as for you," the Black Robe continued, addressing the Blackfeet, "I won't keep you from leaving this camp; rather I strongly advise that you do so, that you return to your tribesmen. But go as friends. Tell your chiefs, for me and for the Flatheads, what happened last night and what I said this morning. Talk them into giving back the horses. If they do so the Flatheads will continue to regard the Blackfeet as their brothers. If they will not listen, tell them the Great Spirit will favor us more than ever."

Did they follow this advice? Perhaps a few did; certainly not all. A proof of this fact was that when one of the Blackfeet did return to the camp of his tribesmen someone struck him on the head with a saber. He made his way back to St. Mary's, but his return was kept secret from the Black Robe. But if all of the friendly Blackfeet did not heed the Black Robe's advice, wasn't it perhaps also the fault of the

Flatheads, particularly those who had a personal interest in the affair? The event I now recount leads me to fear that indeed the Flatheads made a third mistake.

On March 19, the feast of St. Joseph, the head Blackfoot chief, Chetlesmelakax—a name which means Three Crows—came for a friendly visit.[3] The Flathead chiefs invited him and the principal warriors accompanying him to smoke in the missionary's lodge. After the mutual signs of goodwill were exchanged, Ambrose explained the Catholic Ladder to the visitors, and Victor, who was related to Chetlesmelakax by marriage, invited him to stay the night in his lodge. The next day the chief told the Black Robe that, near the end of the moon phase we were about to enter, he and his twenty-eight lodges would come to St. Mary's to prepare for baptism. Meanwhile, the Flathead whose horses were stolen on the 13th was driven by some evil spirit to the point where he believed himself authorized to compensate his losses. Accordingly, he snatched a rifle from one of the friendly Blackfeet visitors. Restitution soon followed this seizure, that is true. But would this forced restitution be sufficient? And wouldn't it weaken the bonds of trust our visitors had shown? I cannot answer these questions. But what I do know is this: neither Chetlesmelakax nor any of his people came to St. Mary's at the time they had indicated. Such a tragedy was followed by another, for hardly a year had passed when the chief and one half his tribe were massacred by their mortal enemies, the Crows. And this massacre took place before they were able to make good their resolution regarding baptism.

Blackfeet stole five horses from our camp the night following Chetlesmelakax's visit, that is on the night of March 19–20. Bullets felled one thief, but the horses were lost, driven off by the robbers. This sad event increased the suspicion of both nations, and after this date thefts increased, and even murders, which had not occurred during the past four years, became commonplace between the two peoples. Added to these crimes were betrayals of several friendly Blackfeet, more pilfering, rumors of war with the Crows and the Bannocks, a shortage of powder and bullets among the Flatheads—all of these give some faint idea of the terrible storm which threatened this nation at the end of 1844. The St. Mary's superior [Peter De Vos] considered the situation had become so grave that he seriously questioned the prudence of maintaining contact with the Blackfeet, irrespective of what their previous relationship with the Flatheads had been.[4] For their part the Flatheads admitted God was sending them these threats because of their sins, and so they sincerely humbled themselves before Him; performed the expected act of reparation before men, and courageously rising above human nature, they left the doors of St. Mary's open to all comers. They were convinced that if there was any way of avoiding war, this was the way to do so; yet during all of this time they did not cease to prepare for war. That summer the hunt took place without any unpleasant encounters. All was peaceful at St. Mary's where the only defenders were one Black Robe, a one-eyed chief, an old blind man, some women and a few invalids. Still, thunderclouds continued to form on the distant horizon, and, determined to ward off the storm which threatened our beloved neophytes, Father De Smet decided to visit the Blackfeet. He went down the Red River where they so often come to trade with the Hudson Bay fur traders, but all he found there were drunkards better supplied with liquor than with anything else. He felt he had to give up his plan, and so the time to approach this depraved nation still seemed distant.[5]

Translator's Notes

This letter is a continuation of the preceding letter and it describes events that took place in March 1844, toward the end of the winter hunt. Point narrated here many of the details he previously included in his letter "Henceforth the Prayer of the Flat-Heads Shall Be Ours."

1. Thunder, or Thunderbolt, who was also known as Phidel or Fidelis Teltella, was also singled out by Lawrence Palladino, in *Indian and White in the Northwest,* 83, and by Point, in Thwaites, *Early Westward Travels,* 29:415.

2. The last two sentences are scored in the manuscript.

3. St. Mary's superior at this date was Peter De Vos. The fact that he had questioned Point's prudence in maintaining contact with the Blackfeet might well have been regarded by Point as being contrary to De Smet's directives.

4. The Little Robes' Itchetles Melakas, or Three Crows, was the chief of what Point considered a band of the Piegans that was almost entirely destroyed in 1845 in the same event Point describes in this section. John Ewers explains in his book on the Blackfeet that the massacre, although frightful, was not complete, a fact to which Point attests in these letters. *Blackfeet* 188, n. 9; 298. See also Thwaites, *Early Western Travels,* 29:360, 416. This section begins the continuation of "Point's Letter," 416.

5. Chittenden and Richardson, *De Smet,* 2:526–30.

No. 3

MISDEED AMENDED

MISDEEDS FORGOTTEN

VICTORY, PROGRESS

From the time of the five-day battle, referred to above, to the meeting with the thirty-seven Blackfeet, the Flatheads' stated policy toward their enemies was consistent and exemplary. Seemingly, during this five-year period the Blackfeet were impressed by the good example of their old enemies, and they responded to it by respecting their persons and abusing only their property. And even here what they stole seemed, in reality, petty. A scarcity of crime, if one may use such an expression, and a kind of moderation, even discretion displayed by the Blackfeet when they did turn on the Flatheads, was not the least of the blessings granted to these new children of the faith. But wheat grows with chaff in this world, and virtue is never pure. So, however good the Flatheads were, they still had their blemishes, and if, like the Hebrews of old, their sins as well as their virtues did not cause us to stand in admiration of the workings of Divine Providence, I would be loathe to reveal the catalogue of their woeful deeds.[1] However, this newly formed Christian community came to see that good fortune followed good conduct and misfortune trod on the heels of evil actions. This was so consistently true that one might say, without the fear of exaggeration, that the providential cause and effect which they perceived was the light that guided, in later years, the Western tribes to the foot of the Cross, even as it had already showed the way there to the tribes of South America. A history of the Paraguay reductions verifies this fact. Relying on my own experiences in the Rocky Mountain reduction, I could substantiate what others have already written concerning this point, but in doing so I would wander beyond the bounds I have set up for myself. I shall therefore confine my reflections to the history of the events I now recount.

Our good Flatheads atoned in the best way they could for the mistakes they had made in dealing with the Blackfeet, and far from losing heart, as they considered the ominous future, they seemed to gain self-confidence. The hope they had for the future was not to be confronted either. When spring came in 1846, the number of Flathead warriors had been augmented by the Pend d'Oreilles, but together they faced a Blackfoot army four times greater in number. Pretending that they were organizing a wondrous hunt, both sides gathered together their forces. The real motive for the Blackfeet was, if they judged victory possible, to wage war. The Flatheads' purpose was to accept the challenge whatever their prospects. For the honor of their religion as well as for the peace and tranquility of their people they wanted to put an end to all this plundering. But let us now examine the site where the two armies faced each other. The Blackfoot camp was protected by a row of lodges between which they had piled branches. The Flatheads and their allies had set up their lodges in a copse. They also had cut down branches and they built a stockade with these for the women and children. Between the two camps was an open field, a most inviting theatre for those to show their courage and skill. Now, who would shoot the first arrow; who would fire the first bullet? Some of the warriors were standing, others were seated, and still others were lying on the sward, but all were armed. The Christians and the Pend d'Oreilles, who were still catechumens, waited patiently for the enemy to begin the battle, believing that as children of true prayer, it was better to defend oneself than attack the enemy. But things did not go as they should. One of the Flatheads, judging a group of Blackfeet directly opposite to him were more worked up than the others, suddenly and heedlessly aimed his barrel in their direction.[2] The shot was fired; a chief fell dead; the Blackfeet let out the war whoop, the signal for war. Everyone agrees that the initial reaction by the Blackfeet was terrible, born of their thirst for revenge and their impetuous courage. It was of such intensity that for all of their bulldog grit, the Flatheads were forced to yield. But then, realizing that all the warriors would perish on the heels of their chiefs, outstanding among whom were the proud Titiche Loutso and the hot-heated Teltella—or better, that they would be mowed down alongside them, the warriors soon realized that they would have to fight until victory was theirs. And so turning about, they began to fight with such aggressiveness that they defeated the enemy who, as one eye witness reported, fled the field like a herd of prairie cows. The battle was a total victory for the Flatheads, one that cost them four casualties: two of their own warriors and two from the allies. So ended that glorious day. And indeed glorious it was, comparable for them to Condé's victory at Rocroi. The Blackfeet were so routed that they left the twenty-one bodies unburied on the field of battle for wild beasts to devour.

One noteworthy event took place during the height of the battle's fury. A Pend d'Oreille and a Blackfoot plunging toward one another fell simultaneously from their horses, each pierced through by the arrow shot from the bow of the other. Another spectacle worth mentioning was the scene of women and children praying alongside of the missionary that heaven would bestow courage and strength on the Flathead warriors. Finally, there was the Little Robes' lack of involvement in the battle, a passivity which was more remarkable than all other extraordinary events of the day. Was it fidelity to their word that restrained this tribe of Blackfeet or was it their belief that fighting Christians meant choosing death? Whether fidelity or the conviction, it was destined to be rewarded, seeing that before two more years had passed the same Flatheads that fought in this battle would help the Little Robes avenge the Crows for the death of their head chief and half their camp. By this date the children of the tribe would have already received the sacrament of regeneration; the tribe's first baptized chief would have gone to heaven, and finally the Little Robes would have introduced ministers of the Gospel to the heart of the Blackfeet nation. This last fact is the chief topic of these letters.

But before giving details of this memorable occasion, let us say something about the prosperity following the battle which crowned the virtue and hard work of the inhabitants of St. Mary's. During the two years I was away evangelizing the Coeur d'Alènes, that is from the fall of 1844 to the summer of 1846, I had little personal knowledge of the progress of the Flatheads. But this is what I learned about them in the summer of 1846.

On the thirteenth of August that year I was traveling with Reverend Father De Smet and the head chief of the Pend d'Oreilles with several of his warriors. Toward noon we arrived at the St. Mary compound, and what a beautiful sight this first Christian village in the Rocky Mountains presented to us. Laid out as it was between two generously flowing streams, it was cool even at the height of the summer. To our right was the mill that provided the inhabitants with their flour and lumber; to the left stretched fields which last year had produced so rich a harvest and which now promised a superabundance. Beyond the fields could be seen the large building where they preserved the fruit they raised; further beyond grazed thirty-two head of cattle. And I don't know how many blooming families, contributors in every season to the prosperity of this Flathead reduction, were housed in the neighborhood. Even though at this date the compound was but four years established, its reputation had attracted many visitors, thereby offering the superior the singular opportunity to spread God's Kingdom while hardly ever leaving the mission.

Among some of the visitors in 1845 were a Bannock

chief, the head chief of the Snakes, many notable Blackfeet, and at the end of the summer and winter hunts, the whole Pend d'Oreille tribe from the large lake, nearly all of whom are baptized. An indication of these peoples' piety as well as a proof of the fellowship that exists between them and the Flatheads was a Mass followed by a Communion banquet in which they all partook. This magnificent table was also a fitting testimony to the abundance of the mission's stores, seeing that only 50 cents was spent, the rest of the supplies having been produced on the farm. The fruit was not yet ready for the harvest, but Father Mengarini managed to make a kind of sugar, almost as sweet as cane, from roots from the fields or from desert plants, and he concocted a drink which was both tasty and nourishing.[3]

Whenever religion penetrates a tribe, it works miracles in civilizing the people. One of the most remarkable temporal benefits for these Flatheads has been the increase in their population. What are the reasons for this consoling fact? I believe we can credit the following causes: greater respect and gentleness toward women; better care for children; more freedom in the choice of spouses; better care and more solicitude for the sick; fewer wars, but when wars are unavoidable, the undeniable fact that heaven protects the Christians. Today the Flatheads do not have a single enemy who has not observed that the Black Robes' medicine is powerful in making men brave in spirit as it is in making them good. We should note that the words *medicine* and *religion* are synonyms among the natives of these parts because for them the practice of these two analogous professions is never separated.

Translator's Notes

In this letter Father Point continues the specific introductory remarks he initiated in the first letter and developed in the second. Toward the end of this letter, however, he brings the reader from a consideration of events that had taken place in 1844 to what took place after he left Sacred Heart and St. Mary's for the last time, that is, in August 1846. In doing so he introduces the reader to the principal theme of his narrative: contact with the Blackfeet.

During his five year stint in the Northwest, Point had already taken part in five hunting expeditions, two with the Coeur d'Alène, in the winter of 1844 and 1846, and three with the Flathead, the winter hunt of 1841–1842; the summer hunt of 1842, and the winter hunt of 1843–1844. Now, as he asserted in the last part of this letter, he and Father De Smet were on their way to join the 1846 summer hunt with the Flatheads. The seventh and last hunt in which he would participate would be with the Piegans in the following October. When he and De Smet left Sacred Heart about August 1, the Coeurs d'Alène were at the threshold of "the rapid advancement and prosperity of that tribe." Point had participated in choosing the site for what was to shortly become this prosperous settlement: in planting, the two hundred acres, and in planning and constructing, the mission buildings and church. Soon Sacred Heart would boast of a flour mill run by horsepower, of twenty cows, eight yokes of oxen, one hundred pigs, horses and mules. But in early August 1846, as he and De Smet crossed and forded the some eighty rivers and streams that separated Sacred Heart from St. Mary's, they were returning to the first reduction of the Rocky Mountains at the height of its prosperity. When Point entered the mission compound he had designed, "according to the plans of the Paraguay missions," he felt, as he confessed in this letter, a certain pride of accomplishment. Hubert Howe Bancroft, the great historian of the West described St. Mary's in 1846. It

> consisted of 12 houses neatly built of logs, a church, a small mill and other buildings for farm use; 7,000 bushels of wheat, between 4,000 and 5,000 bushels of potatoes, and vegetables of different kinds were produced on the farm, which was irrigated by two small streams running through it. The stock of the establishment consisted of 40 head of cattle, some horses and other animals (*The Works of Hubert Howe Bancroft,* 26:604).

"The Flatheads had left for their summer hunt at least fifteen days before," Point recounted, "and we, Father De Smet and I, were still with the Coeur d'Alènes twenty-five days' journey from their camp" (Donnelly, *Wilderness Kingdom,* 188). The stay at the reduction they had founded therefore was brief. This year the number of Flatheads participating in the hunt had been reduced because the prosperity at the mission had staved off starvation, a regular visitor to the tribe, and had encouraged more people to increase this prosperity by tilling the land and tending the herds. The annual hunts, so inimical to reduction life were becoming unnecessary and with continued prosperity and more Jesuits they would be phased out altogether. Polygamy and divorce had been eliminated and the status of women greatly improved. What St. Mary's was, Sacred Heart would be in a short time. The constant threat, however, to the tender beginnings of Paraguay in the Rockies was the hostility of the Blackfeet, the encroachment of the whites, and, at least in the immediate future, the depletion of the buffalo, which in turn meant the hunting area was more restricted and hostile tribes were forced into closer contact.

Point was at least fulfilling a desire he had long fostered, but now there was a certain urgency in his need to contact the Blackfeet. By doing so he would hopefully guarantee the continued spiritual and material prosperity of St. Mary's and Sacred Heart, and at the same time he could initiate the benefits of reduction life to the "most notorious of all the wild tribes extended along the banks of the Missouri and in the adjacent country" (Bancroft, *Works*, 26:604).

The events contained in the letter correspond to those which appear in Donnelly, *Wilderness Kingdom*, 188–92 and in Thwaites, *Early Western Travels*, 29:328–35.

1. Point frequently compared the experiences of the Flatheads—wandering through the wilderness, being fed "manna," being guided by a "pillar of fire," and having a conscious awareness of their somehow being God's chosen people—to the wanderings of the Hebrews during their exodus in the desert. Such an experience, he believed, should have made them conscious of their singular vocation to witness and to bring the true faith to the other tribes.

2. Point has underscored the following in the text: *"and without reflecting on what he was doing, very probably to some divine inspiration."*

3. Mengarini, wrote Laveille, was "a skillful physician, a musician of no mean order and a remarkable linguist." He probably made the concoction that so impressed Point on this occasion from "a kind of white carrot which presumably is similar to the white carrot of Silesia," *Life of De Smet*, 120, 190. Being a "physician" meant among other healing skills he practiced, such as binding wounds, that he was "skilled in folk medicine and herbalism." *Mengarini's Recollections*, 73. See also Chittenden and Richardson, *De Smet*, 2:572.

No. 4

FLATHEADS AND BLACKFEET: BROTHERS-IN-ARMS FOR THE FIRST TIME

Almost all of the Flatheads were hunting [in August 1846], and yet war between them and the Crow, a large nation we hoped to conquer for the Lord, was imminent. So, after offering the Holy Sacrifice in honor of the Queen of Heaven, the patroness of St. Mary's, we left this pious reduction on the day of Mary's great feast. This day, August 15, [the Assumption, 1846], was also the anniversary of our first meeting with those destined to become her children.[1] On the following day, accompanied by four half-breeds of the Crow nation, three of whom were from the Red River, and by four Indians, two of whom were Blackfeet, we entered the famous pass called Hell's Gate.[2] It goes without saying we experienced the horrors of that terrifying gorge, horrors which I have described in previous letters. But in this letter it is not my intent to describe scenery but rather to record historical facts. But I will say that what struck me most on this trip was the abundance of fruit we came across, in much greater profusion this year than usual. And near Three Forks I noticed a huge variety of flowers, due to the moisture of the soil, I should think. Another day's distance approaching Crow territory, we were struck by the diversity of bushes growing everywhere, and by many deep ravines as well. Such a country offers ideal haunts for wild beasts and for the Blackfeet as well, and indeed it is regarded as headquarters for both. For this reason it is better for a small group like ours to pass through this country under cover of darkness. But since we had more reason than most travelers to put trust in Divine Providence, we decided to make our way during only part of the night and all of the day. Still, we resolved to be particularly discrete, and to walk without making any noise. Such a resolution, however, was difficult for our young escorts to keep, and as soon as four bears appeared on our right our defenders took off recklessly, shouting and firing. "Oh, how rash; how rash!" cried Father De Smet in vain, but this did not bring them back at all. Far from it. They seemed to be charging harder than usual even for a hunt, and the result was an accident. Our youngest Blackfoot charged the bears with such abandon that his horse stumbled, causing horse and rider to tumble over one another. We thought that surely both had broken their necks, but both escaped with only stiff necks. By forcing us to halt, this event gave us the opportunity to say Mass on the following morning. This we did in the middle of the brush as quietly as thieves, making up for the previous day's imprudence. After breakfast our poor little Blackfoot climbed back on his horse, but his neck was still stiffer than we had expected it would be, forcing us to begin our day's journey at a slow pace. But it wasn't long before we picked up the same trot that had brought us this far. With the Indians sprains and many other kinds of ailments heal rapidly. Besides, pending danger makes one exert oneself more.

At last we came on the Flatheads' trail, and the remains of a recently built camp our Blackfeet found were most encouraging, for here were the long poles used exclusively by their tribesmen; the pickets set in position according to the methods peculiar to the Nez Percés and the indisputable signs that the Flatheads, too, had camped here. All of these remnants convinced our guides and ourselves that all three nations had become allies to show strength against the Crow, who were not merely mighty in numbers but also ready to pick a quarrel. At this point it seemed to us that we had all but reached our tribe, and so to be united with them we took off across the fields in the direction where we thought they were. But what happened? After pressing ahead without a stop until noon, we found nothing before us but a wilderness without water. We decided not to tire all our horses further, but that the best mounts would continue the search while the others rested. But where could the tribe be? Which way should we go? Fortunately at this juncture, and to our great relief, a herd of buffalo came charging in our direction, and as everyone knows, when these animals stampede in one direction, it is a sign that they are being chased from the other. And who besides our own hunters could be pursuing them? Although this argument was not altogether convincing to us, it seemed to be so to our guides, and so off they took without further adieu. As for us, we followed their example a few minutes later, but hoping to find a safe spot to await their return, we headed in the opposite direction. Six hours later the two groups were still separated from each other. Were our guides dead or alive? Were they fighting the Crow or were they enjoying the fellowship of the Flatheads? The answers to these questions we did not know, but what we knew only too well was this: we were lost even though we were back almost to our point of departure. A short distance ahead of us we could see a gorge or, rather, a wide crevice in the middle of the prairie, and it was toward this point that we directed our steps. The crevice was quite deep and honeycombed with Indian defenses and fortifications. Presently we came upon a little spring around which we discerned human tracks. This discovery caused our Blackfeet to rejoice for a second time, and they immediately took off for a reunion with our scouts. Then in a few minutes, pale and trembling, the Blackfeet returned. What was the matter? The tracks were not left by friends but by enemies, and if we continued in the direction we had chosen we would be done for, killed. We were headed straight toward a Nez Percé camp, and it was true that the Nez Percés were anything but well disposed toward the Blackfeet. But we finally convinced our Blackfeet that they had nothing to fear if they came along with us. So, after more coaxing they agreed to continue, hiding themselves behind us as we proceeded. Finally, when we arrived among the Nez Percés, we learned that our trust in Providence had not been in vain, for this meeting became an occasion for rejoicing for everyone present. For me, because I recognized right off several catechumens I had instructed only a few months previously in the truths of our holy religion.[3] For Father De Smet, because he was delighted to make their acquaintance. And for the Blackfeet, who received nothing but the warmest welcome from the hands of the Nez Percés. This was so because they were with us and also because of the awkward position in which the Nez Percés found themselves. Despite their small number, their ignorance of the country, and the fact that large war parties were scouting the territory in all directions, these Nez Percés had rashly come into Blackfeet land. Just the day before we arrived, the best of their horses had disappeared from the corral, a proof the enemy was not far distant. As long as we remained with them we tried to make the teachings of our holy religion penetrate their hearts, which were already well disposed, thanks to their dealings with the Flatheads and Coeur d'Alène. Each evening our friends who had accompanied us—Flatheads, Pend d'Oreilles, Crees and Blackfeet—mingled with the camp's young people and then, converging from every corner of the camp, began singing, shouting, jumping up and down—in a word, Indian showing off, and in a manner I had never before seen or heard, since such demonstrations were out of character for the Flatheads, especially so since their conversion, and not according to the customs of the Oregon peace-loving Indians. But when the Blackfeet and Nez Percés have reason to believe enemies are stalking in the vicinity, they carry on like this. The fewer their numbers, the noisier their antics; the more they quake with fear, the more they strut and swagger. The reason is easy to understand.

The Nez Percés had designated August 27 [1846], three

days since we and our scouts had parted, as the day for their big hunt. By this date we were a good distance from the Nez Percé and Blackfoot camps as well as from the spot designated as our rendezvous with our scouts, a fact which meant that these scouts would now have a considerable distance to cover in order to find us. These matters were on our minds when, accompanied by a Flathead named Peter John, one of the scouts appeared in camp. Peter John, incidentally, was the first of his people to pray in the Flathead language, and for this reason he was named after Father De Smet.[4]

What news did he bring? We were about to go to war. Were the Crows numerous? Indeed they were; five times our size.

Leaving camp with Peter John, Father De Smet instructed me to remain behind to baptize some children on the morrow. Then, after placing nine souls on the road to heaven, I set out with all of our companions on the following day. As best we could we followed Father De Smet's tracks, for we had no other guide. We had traveled some distance when we spotted a camp on the horizon. Whether it was Flathead or Crow we could not yet determine. But there was one matter about which there was no question—we were in enemy territory. All about us series of trenches, battlements, earthworks, and buttresses told us plainly that war was the only purpose they served. Their presence was made all the more awesome by the fact that the countryside teemed with warriors. But as we progressed, the sharp eye of our Blackfeet served to lessen their anxiety. Finally, a knight of this wilderness came running toward us. His presence gave us assurance beyond doubt, for he was George, a dear friend of the Black Robes'. On one occasion he had saved a Black Robe's life, and now this same Black Robe stood before him![5] You can imagine our mutual delight. Yet, George's joy seemed flawed. He looked like a man who is uncertain whether he had conducted himself correctly. What had he done? On the day before he had fought the Crows alongside his brothers-in-arms with such valor that victory was theirs. But wouldn't this victory delay the conversion of the vanquished? This was his apprehension, the cause for his melancholic expression, an expression which was reflected on the faces of several others who had also participated so nobly in this same encounter. But we could only praise their behavior when, that evening, we heard from their own modest lips, the most modest perhaps that have ever existed, an account of those incidents which had forced them to use means other than patience in dealing with the Crow. We then reassured them and watched the doubts dissolve. However, all of us still had reason for apprehension, for we expected a more infuriated enemy to return and clear the record of their shameful performance on the field of battle. But our fears were for naught; the Crows, no more ashamed than terrified, dared not to renew the combat.

Among the Crow, as among all Indians who frequently engage in warfare, there are some truly brave warriors, but if one listens to those who are the least brave, he will hear that there is no nation under the sun comparable to the Crow. In describing their daring and strength, they like to compare themselves to a raging buffalo—it never retreats; no barrier can hold it back; it tears down everything that gets in its way. On the other hand, they regard their enemies as mere women or even as young calves who can but tremble. So they described the Flatheads. But, as we have already seen, this rhetoric had not prevented the Flatheads from hunting in Crow territory nor had it prevented them from taking under their protection the remnant of that wretched tribe (the Little Robes), which two years previously had escaped the wrath of the Crow. It would never do, said the Flatheads, that the Crow imagine that because now we live in the fear of the Lord, we fear men more than before. It is our intention to teach the Crow with harsh lessons that the opposite is true. God knows we want peace, that we will never be the first to break it, and that we wish the Crow well, but if they attack us we will defend ourselves with vigor. Such was the attitude and such were the words employed by the Flatheads when the Crow set up camps near them and began to threaten them.

How did these Crow, once so full of pride, now behave

toward their former friends? Instead of treating them as friends or even as sincere people, they insulted them beyond all limits. One Crow armed with a stick, they bragged, was all that it would take to chase off one hundred Flatheads. And despite their chiefs, who tried to moderate their folly, these brutes added insult to injury when they pretended to sack the Flathead camp by tearing down branches that formed the palisade, and even by going so far as to aim their rifles at Flathead chiefs, who remained as brave as they were patient. Matters had gone this far and Victor, the head chief, had felt the surge of exhaltation that immediately precedes the war cry building up in himself when another cry was heard: "The Black Robes are coming! And the Nez Percés and Pend d'Oreilles!" This news was repeated over and over again until it re-echoed throughout the camp. When the Crow chiefs heard the cry which confounded their people's intent, they added to their counsels for prudence the cry *"Amaraba! Amaraba!"* that is: "We must go! We must go!" The repetition of this word, accompanied by vigorous beating with poles, convinced even the most obstinate; so, they all decided whether they liked it or not to retreat without striking a blow.

The Flatheads spent the night thanking heaven for such a happy ending. But the next day in broad daylight the Crows stole thirty horses right from under their noses; and, because of a misunderstanding, one innocent Crow was forced to pay the price for the guilty. This mistake was all that it took to enrage all the other Crows. In spite of prompt atonement for this all too hasty injury, the fires of war flared. God allowed this evil but only because He wanted to see His own cause triumph.

Around ten o'clock in the morning the Crows came galloping in a cloud so thick it hid the hills from sight, and they pressed down on the allied camp under the illusion that nothing could stem their force. But the allies had expected a sudden attack, and so after safeguarding all who were not able to defend themselves behind a strong stockade, they ranged themselves in a line outside the camp to await the action. As soon as the attackers were within musket range,

Titiche Loutso—or Moses, as he was named at baptism—first prayed there with his little troops which formed the vanguard, then stood and addressed them. "My friends," he said, "if God wishes us to be victors, that we shall be. If He does not, may His will be done. Meanwhile, let us turn our thoughts to Him and be brave." Immediately one of his men fired at the enemy. The Crows ceased their attack and began making a series of turnings and caperings in a most swaggering fashion, all of which only served to tire their horses. Victor, seeing what was happening, shouted: "Now, brothers, mount! Forward!" Every warrior rushed the enemy with such force that the Crows' cavalry had to fall back two miles, retreating to their base of operations with the same speed they had used in charging. The head chief's two feathers were seen constantly on the road of honor just like the plume of Good King Henry in days of yore. The story was that on whatever flank Titiche Loutso directed his horse, whole rows of the enemy took flight. However, making up in numbers for what they lacked in courage, the Crows charged again and again, but each time they were made to see that God's children were invincible when they placed their trust in their heavenly Father. During these combats the youngest warriors displayed a fearlessness which astonished the elders who in turn attributed this mettle to their Christian faith. Even women proved to the Crows that if the weaker sex was to be found on the battlefield it was in their own ranks. At the very height of the melee a mother of seven threw herself with such frantic energy between her eldest and a Crow that the latter had to run off. Another younger woman went out onto the field of battle and picked up the arrows that rained down upon her and with these she replenished the depleting quivers of our warriors. A third woman, having advanced too far in pursuit of the enemy, wheeled her horse about with uncanny dexterity just as several enemy hands stretched out to pull her down and galloped back to our lines, leaving the enemy stupified by her retreat. Finally, the famous Huitix [Kuilix], mentioned above, accompanied by a few braves and armed with an axe, gave chase to a whole squadron of Crows.

When they got back to camp, she said to her companions, "I thought that those big talkers were men, but I was wrong. Truly, they are not worth pursuing."[6]

In all the fighting, nine Crows were killed and fourteen were wounded. One Flathead had fallen off his horse, but was none the worse for it, and never had the supporting Blackfeet shown such heroism. Nicolas and Gervais, the first baptized of the nation, had distinguished themselves in a special manner, and yet not one hair of their heads had been touched. Both they and the Flatheads attributed their good fortune to the fact that they had made the sign of the cross before engaging in combat. What confirmed them in this pious belief was the death of a young Nez Percé whose father, the tribe's chief, had not protected himself as they had with this sign of victory. So, with sentiments of faith and thanksgiving, they offered seventy-six of their children to be baptized. This was the greatest fruit of the whole day.

May this beautiful harvest of their Church be a continual proof of right over might, and even more of heaven over hell.

Translator's Notes

The events of this letter, which tell of the circumstances of Point and De Smet's itinerary to the Nez Percé and Blackfoot camps, and of the allies' defeat of a superior force of Crow Indians are found in Donnelly, *Wilderness Kingdom,* 188–92 and in Thwaites, *Early Westward Travels,* 29:328–35.

1. This day marked the thirty-second anniversary of what Point considered his miraculous deliverance from shells fired by the Prussian advance unit on Rocroi in 1814. This event, it will be remembered, had had a profound effect on him, inspiring him to accept the Assumption of the Virgin Mary as one of his special feast days.

2. This seems to have been the intinerary: Down the Bitter Root Valley and then up the St. Ignatius, or as it was later known, the Hellgate River, which they followed crossing to the Deer Lodge River, and then over the Cottonwood Pass, that leads from Dear Lodge County to Jefferson County, to the Boulder River, which empties into the Jefferson. From this juncture they continued on past Butte, and followed what is today Highway 10, along the Yellowstone River, past the present-day cities of

Bozeman, Livingston and Billings as far as the confluence of the Bighorn with the Yellowstone. Here they turned northwest and, crossing the Musselshell and with the Judith Mountains on their left, they passed through the Judith Basin near today's Fort Benton, below Great Falls on the Missouri. Here they found themselves at Fort Lewis. Thwaites, *Early Western Travels,* 29:340–41, nn. 195–97.

3. In Point's "Recollections," *Woodstock Letters* 13(1883):10–11; also in Point's "Letter," published in Thwaites, *Early Western Travels,* 29:341, and in Donnelly, *Wilderness Kingdom,* 99, Point claimed he met these Nez Percé "in the spring of that year." Pentland questions the accuracy of this date arguing that the meeting had taken place in the spring of 1846. Master's thesis, "The Ill-Fated Mission," p. 63. Point's comment here that he had instructed the Nez Percé "only a few months previously" gives credibility to Pentland's claim.

4. It is difficult to say with certainty which Peter John this is, possibly Peter the Iroquois.

5. George, better known as Peter George or Chalax, chief of the Pend d'Oreilles. Chittenden and Richardson, *De Smet,* 1:318, 321.

6. De Smet identifies this woman as the "celebrated Mary Quille." Chittenden and Richardson note, however: "No clue is found in Father De Smet's writings as to why the term 'celebrated' is used here." Ibid., 2:578, n. 4. Point gives the probable reason when he describes her courage in the first letter of this group, p. 252.

No. 5

LITTLE ROBE INDIANS ENTERTAIN THE BLACK ROBES

Having asked the missionaries' leave to celebrate the doubtful victory which they had just won, the Little Robe warriors set out for a more fitting place for their customary festivities. This was why they left the battlefield that had become for seventy-six of their children the cradle of a new life. Their departure was consistent with the description given by a great writer who depicted the simple and stately spirit of the Indian.[1] No need to mention that everyone was on horseback—fine mounts are seldom wanting to the errant knights of the Rockies. First in line and under the leadership of the young chief who had led them in combat, came the warriors. Behind them, and led by the bearer of the calumet, were the distinguished women of the tribe. The young chief was dressed in red; most of the others carried green branches. A few waved flags of varied shapes and colors attached to the top of their spears; one of these flags consisted simply of a few waving bands. As the phalanx started to march, the triumphal chant began, accompanied by the drums. The high voices of the women mingled agreeably with the deep voices of the men. Each phrase, no longer than the ordinary couplet, ended in a sharp cry of joy. Excited by this triumphal music, the steeds held their heads high, to all appearances in step with their riders' sentiments. This procession of warriors along a river, the banks of which resembled pictures of fortresses of old, had a picturesque feeling about it that is hard to convey in words. When they reached the campsite, there was talk of holding a scalp dance.[2] As the sun was beating down, all assembled in the shade of the tall trees; the branches of these green giants were so ideal for spectators and participants that the spot could not be passed by. So, those who were unable to find a spot in the branches or a good place on the ground sat on their horses behind the others. Sometimes two shared the same horse; the one in front sitting in the saddle, the other standing up behind him. Thus, with all assembled, the place took on the look of a vast amphitheatre, in the center of which stood the dancers in all of their finery. The more bizarre the costume, the more admiration it attracted. One man was wearing strings of small bells all of different tones; another had put over his ordinary clothes a raiment fit for a military parade. So as not to be outdone by the men, the women attached to their clothes some of the items that had contributed to the victory—here, an ornate bag carrying the shot or the powder; there, a medicine pouch. But the most striking was a headdress of eagle and other feathers wreathed with blue, red or green ribbons, according to the artist's taste. All of this regalia was put over the leather tunic that, designed to insure female modesty, the women always wore. There was something magical about the towering headdress as its undulating movement harmonized with the dance, which consisted of a little hop, more or less lively, depending on the beat of the drum. This instrument was played only by the men, but the singing, the very soul of the performance, was for everyone. From time to time to break the monotony of the chant, the sharper sounds of the whistles could be heard. If, in spite of this encouragement, the action appeared to be slowing down, there were broken cries produced by striking the mouth with the hand, lively harangues accompanied by pantomime, grotesque faces made by an old coryphaeus—all of which livened up festivities. There were two old women with black smeared all over their faces who attempted to achieve this same effect. They threw aside the staves with which they were supporting their trembling hops, swung their arms about with all the force they could muster, and jumped up and down until they could no longer move. One could judge from all of this that the criterion of beauty in such a dance was sprightliness of movement. The dance moved in a circle and as the dancers skipped about they tended to draw closer to the center. So eventually the circle became so tight that even little hops were no longer possible. Then the dancers all moved backwards to form a larger circle, and so it was that the dance began all over again with renewed vigor. I do not know how many times the dancing was thus resumed, but finally, as with all pleasures here below, the participants became weary. Alas! how brief are the pleasures of this life! A few days later, the dancers would attend the funeral of the one who had been the life and soul of the party.

Seeing that this dance was in thanksgiving for the victory achieved by all of the allies, the Flathead women were invited to take part, and they did not need much coaxing. Their dance was in a circle like the others, except that it did not draw the dancers toward the center; rather the circle maintained its shape throughout. After the dance came the procession of the calumet, which started from the left side and went around full circle. This procession was made up of only one man and three women, the four most distinguished members of their tribe. The man headed the procession with all of the dignity of a potentate, and the women followed. The most important official stood in the center holding some object; one of the others carried a calumet stem and the third one a fan. From time to time the leader turned toward the others and bowed deeply; then he made the same obeisance toward the assembled crowd which seemed to say, "My friends, the procession greets you." No doubt the purpose of this ritual was to demonstrate that the accompanying merrymaking had taken place to strengthen the bonds of friendship that united all of them. So, like the preceding dance, this ceremony was all very innocent. Green wreaths now took the place of the bloody scalps of yore, and sentiments of thanksgiving to the true God, who was honored in the person of the ministers present at the festivities, had replaced former emotions of hatred. To those who would blame a Catholic missionary for going along with the Indians in these circumstances, we would answer: with the Indians particularly, it is better to graft than to fell.

On the evening of September 9, an event took place which showed the craftiness of the Blackfeet. A Nez-Percé chief, accompanied by three Blackfeet, called at the missionaries' lodge. This chief was a close friend of the white man, believing himself to be almost white himself because, instead of plucking his beard as Indians do, he shaved as we do. The youngest of his companions, whose features were most interesting, had lost his parents—so said the interpreter—when he was too young to remember them. His mother, who had been carrying him in her arms when she was captured by the Blackfeet, had died during the first days of her captivity, and his father, who had escaped from the pursuing enemy, no longer existed as far as he was concerned. But as the orphan grew he displayed such fine qualities that he became, as it were, the adopted child of the nation, considering Blackfoot territory his own native land. That day, a woman who had taken special care of him in his childhood revealed for the first time that she was not his mother and that his father, whose name had never been mentioned previously, was living nearby in the camp. One can imagine the son's astonishment as well as the father's joy on hearing this news! But before surrendering completely to his happiness, the father wanted to make sure, and declared this would be easy to do for his son would still show a scar he had incurred as a baby on a certain part of his body. An examination ensued; the scar was discovered and the father's joy was boundless. To give the young man tangible proof of this joy, he said: "Son, I have many horses. The fastest one in the whole country belongs to me. Come with your father and it will be yours."

"Father," replied the young man, "The Black Robes are about to enter the land that has nurtured me. Give me leave to accompany them so that I might benefit by their good teaching and be baptized. After that, I shall gladly comply with your wishes."

Translator's Notes

The events in this letter can be found in Donnelly, *Wilderness Kingdom,* 192–95.

1. François-Auguste-René de Chateaubriand, *Les Natchez* (Paris: Ladvocat, 1826).

2. Ewers, *Blackfeet,* 139.

No. 6

THE BLACK ROBES' INTRODUCTION TO PIEGAN TERRITORY

On September 10, 1846 we bade adieu to the good Flatheads. It should not be difficult to understand that this separation, which we believed was final, was as hard for them as it was for us.[1] A large contingent took their leave from us right away; five or six came to our camp to spend one more night with us. I could not say whether it was because of the void caused by the absence of these our best converts or whether it was our recollection of what the Blackfeet had so recently been, but we were overcome with sadness. Moreover, as we skirted the chain of mountains that lay to our left, it seemed to us that the masses of desolate rocks, whose menacing forms grew as we progressed, were like openings of so many caverns ready to spew forth at us all of the brigands of the earth.[2] I was curious enough to enter one of these vast caverns, closed for centuries by some kind of wall that from a distance resembled the work of human hands. Nothing could be more frightening than this haunt where the sun's rays no longer penetrated. While there, I heard a rifle fire. The sound, fairly nearby, had something ominous about it. It was only a deer that had been slain, but I reflected on the fact that approaching harm is so often prefigured by such sad premonitions. The experience of men everywhere seems to affirm this. Was all of this now a warning to me of some future misfortune? Possibly. For, indeed that very evening a distinguished Blackfoot fell from his horse. Efforts to revive him were in vain; he was dead. Who was this horseman? The first baptized of his nation, a chief who for five years had been preparing the way in his country for the preaching of the Gospel; he was an upright man who, the very night before, had rejoiced in the hope that his most ardent wish was about to be fulfilled. He had resolved to have the Piegans render the Black Robes all of the honors which, he believed, they deserved, and he had hoped to see this whole nation converted ere he closed his own eyes. In a word, it was Nicolas who had been baptized at St. Mary's with the very Flatheads to whom he had just bid adieu. How impenetrable are the plans of God! What a loss for us! What sorrow for Sata, his son and our interpreter! Ordinarily, the Blackfeet express their grief in cries and by inflicting on themselves more or less serious wounds. But like his father, Sata had been baptized; he knew that the Master whom they served regards sacrifices of the heart more highly than any others; so he requested that his wife and children forego the cries, the tears, and the blood in order to concentrate on fervent prayer. "It is prayer," he said, "which will hasten the entrance of our dear departed to the good place." So, all the family passed the night praying together. The next day Sata himself ordered the funeral procession and he pronounced his father's eulogy at the side of his grave. Then the mortal remains were covered with earth, and just as the priest said, "May he rest in peace!" word spread that the Piegans were on their way to meet us. With feelings of sorrow mixed with joy we broke camp. Just then a large herd of buffalo was sighted inviting the Blackfeet to the hunt. The hunters knelt down, for the very first time on earth which had witnessed their birth, to invoke the help of Mary. Rising they mounted their horses and swept down on the black column which was approaching. They drove the herd to the very place where the Piegans were waiting. Soon in the midst of this fray of men and animals the Blackfeet and Piegans made their encounter.

That evening the hunters had returned to camp with an abundance of food and good news; fires were lighted for the cooking and royal feasts were spread everywhere. In the Black Robes' lodge—and may no one be scandalized—there were great festivities long after the meal. Such is the Indian! Yesterday he was in the depths of sorrow; today his joy is boundless! We should overlook this abrupt change of moods, remembering that before his conversion the Indian was a child and even now that he has become a Christian he retains a certain childishness. In the midst of these festivities, a Blackfoot, whose eccentricities were without limit, took the floor. Along with his *bons mots,* however, he said such sensible things that it was difficult to decide whether his wisdom or humor was uppermost. Here are some of his observations:

"When we arrived at the Flathead camp," he said, "we had plenty of meat, and of good quality, but the Flatheads and the Nez Percés were fasting. We invited them to our lodges and, as is the custom, we offered them something to eat. Since it was said that they eat differently from others, I watched to see what they would do. And what did I see? Before placing anything in their mouths, the Flatheads stand quietly and trace a cross on their bodies. After that, they say a prayer to the Great Spirit and when this is done, but never before, they eat with moderation; then they end the meal with another prayer to the Great Spirit. With the Nez Percés it was quite the contrary. As soon as we proffered them a morsel, they gobbled it up like dogs with no prayer at all, neither before nor afterwards. Let us see how they behave on God's day. On this day the Nez Percés work as on other days, but at what? They paint their faces, comb their hair, put on beautiful clothes and admire their reflections in mirrors. After approval, having had a good look at themselves and feeling pleased with their appearance, they go out to let others see them. But the Flatheads do not behave this way. On God's day they remain quiet, in their lodges, thinking how they might pray well and speak well. That's what they do. I have noticed many other similar practices. And on the day of the battle with the Crows, what did we see? Who were the braver of the two? Who let themselves be killed?"

After speaking so well of others, this unusual man then spoke about himself. "As far as I am concerned," he said, "there are two things I very much like to do—gamble and drink fire water. But now I know these things are not good; so see if I touch them again," etc.

On the thirteenth, Sata came to visit us. "What news, good Sata?"

"For two nights I have not been able to close my eyes."

"Why?"

"Because the image of my father is always before me."

"What do you do when you see him?"

"I pray. I wake up my children and we all pray together."

Sata's children are charming. This morning the oldest, who is only six, was with his brother and two little sisters, warming himself. Suddenly he left their company and went out to pick cherries. A few seconds later he returned with a little branch covered with hanging cherries. It presented a very tempting bouquet. He offered this pretty branch to his sister Adele, and she accepted it but only to give it to her little sister Marie. Marie ate the cherries after making the sign of the cross. There was also another little child eating cherries nearby, but in the style of the Nez Percés. Adele noticed it and asked her brother: "Antoine, do you see how that one eats his cherries?"

Then the group spoke of other things, while warming their hands, just like little adults.

God protects his children. One day an enormous buffalo chased by hunters passed a few feet from my lodge where little Antoine was. I saw the horn of this monstrous animal lower itself to within an inch of the child. The beast then raised his head with a force that would have uprooted a tree. But the time to ascend into heaven had not yet come for Antoine. May the virtues of a long life prove that this delay was a blessing. I beg you to forgive me for reciting all of these minor details. But Sata and the mother of these children have rendered me many invaluable services. Moreover, I have felt compelled to make special mention of this family which contributed so greatly to the advance of Christian faith and behavior among the Blackfeet.

Translator's Notes

The events in this letter correspond to those found in Donnelly, *Wilderness Kingdom,* 195–99 and Thwaites, *Early Western Travels,* 29: 345–50.

1. For Point this was indeed the *suprême adieu.* De Smet, however, would visit the Flatheads again in 1859.

2. The reference here is probably to the Elk Mountains between the two forks of the Musselshell River in today's Meagher County. Thwaites, *Early Western Travels,* 29: 345.

No. 7

THE MISSIONARIES' INTRODUCTION TO THE PIEGAN TRIBE

A remarkable harbinger, the first Piegan who came to the missionary's lodge was the chief of the party we met March 12, 1844.[1] Ever since that encounter he had kept his solemn promise: he had not borne arms against the Flatheads. "The prayer of the Flatheads shall be ours," he said. Since he had only one wife with whom he was happy, he hoped that the Black Robe would be willing to baptize the two of them soon. Akoia was his name.[2]

Two days later, toward ten o'clock in the morning, when the news was spread that the Piegans were three miles from our camp, there was great rejoicing in all of the lodges. Warriors dressed hastily in their most beautiful robes, seized their firearms, mounted their parade horses, began to sing joyful songs, beat the drums, fired their rifles and, in order to give the Piegans time to prepare themselves according to custom, advanced slowly behind the Black Robes and the notables of the band. Our approach was joyful, but the Piegans came toward us with a reserve that suggested either timidity or indifference.[3] Their head chief,

Great Lake, was not in the lead. In his place was Great Toque, the bearer of the great calumet, who received the first tokens of our friendship.[4] In a spirited improvisation an older Blackfoot spoke words bordering on ill humor. Then Sata began to speak. By his tone of voice and the fact that he gazed toward heaven, we understood that he was talking about prayer, and that his heart had not forgotten his father who had wanted to introduce God's ministers to his people. Next he explained why the orator before him had expressed discontent. He too believed the reception the Piegans gave the Black Robes was not as solemn as he would have liked it to be. Then hands were shaken and we were persuaded to believe that if their approach had been cool it was still fundamentally cordial. Great Lake, having recovered from the shyness which had caused him to assume the role of a lesser person, expressed gratitude for our friendliness.[5] The modesty of this chief, so often the most intrepid warrior on the field of battle, could have been one of his most attractive qualities if he did not sometimes exaggerate it. Under similar circumstances Flathead modesty would not have prevented expressions of warmth.

The Black Robes' lodge, enlarged to receive a number of visitors, was soon filled with representatives from the two tribes. Needless to say, the amenities began with the calumet ceremony. There is something special about this ceremony among the Blackfeet. To be properly lighted, the instrument of peace has to pass from left to right until it comes to a person of lesser distinction, that is, to someone who does not wear the special hair style or toque. (By toque I mean a big puff of hair brought from the back of the head forward toward the forehead then brushed to the side. This hair arrangement is a sign of great dignity and only the calumet bearers, who are like the nation's priests can wear it.) After this man lit the pipe it went back, passing from mouth to mouth, the way it came until it arrived at the extreme left, which is to say until it arrived at the man nearest to the door. Then it was handed back in the opposite direction, this time passing only to the great medicine men, that is, to those who wore the toque. Among the Blackfeet these medicine men smoke double rations and they are waited on but do no serving themselves. The solemnity of this ceremony, which usually lasts a long time, had destroyed the usual chattering. No sooner had the conversation begun than it was announced that the Flatheads, thought to have been far from the camp, were now on their way to pay us a visit. Immediately the entire camp got up as of one man and went to meet them; the expected pleasure of seeing them again unquestionably improved the atmosphere. The superior manners and the noble sentiments of these warriors from the wilderness rendered them even more honorable in our eyes.

While the body of the army, ranged in several lines, advanced with measured gait, singing their prescribed chants, one of the older chiefs circled about at the head with dignity and grace in a truly knightly fashion. Now there were Blackfeet in our camp from practically every tribe, and among the Flatheads were the Pend d'Oreilles and the Nez Percés, mentioned above. These were inferior to their companions as far as refinement is concerned, but the noble and simple, the sociable and cordial manner of the Flatheads gradually communicated itself to all. What happened would have been unthinkable before this time—nations so different in temperament, tastes, and beliefs were in the process of creating a fraternal union. Dances began, a repetition of the scene described above, but with this important difference: a Nez Percé dance, in which only men participated, followed the others. This dance, or better, this undisciplined charge, included wild shouting and the firing of rifles, and it was in marked contrast to the dignified, formal, and, I might add, reverential dance performed by the members of the fair sex.

After evening prayer a meeting of notables took place in our lodge. Those present gave their attention and their sympathy to Victor, the head chief of the Flatheads as he addressed the assembly, a fact that is not surprising, seeing that everything about him—his heart, his mind, his handsome features—even the tone of his voice, added charm to all that he said. First he discussed the peaceful sentiments his people entertained for the Blackfeet, and especially for the Piegans; then, giving the natural goodness of his soul free rein, he recounted a few of his own adventures, all ideally suited to gladden everyone's heart and to inspire confidence in him. Finally, combining a more solemn voice with more animated gestures, he spoke about the battle with the Crows, using pious terminology and attributing the victory to our holy religion. Here with great emphasis he singled out the efficacy of the sign of the cross in drawing down the favor of heaven. This homage to the cross was given on the very day the Church celebrates the Exaltation of the Holy Cross, September 14.

The next day we celebrated a solemn sung mass for the success of the new mission. That afternoon, as on the preceding day, there were all sorts of merrymaking. But on the day after—that is, on the day set for departing—the belligerent nature of the Nez Percés was aroused. Ambrose, that good, kind chief who had proved himself outstanding by the deeds he performed on March 12, 1844, joined with the young Flathead braves in deciding what had to be done to prevent this belligerency from expressing itself in deeds. They patrolled the camp, and whenever they spied a Nez Percé, they persuaded him, and, when necessary, forced him, to move on. Some headstrong Nez Percés stood pat and received their due; that is, the customary cane whippings. Their chief, considering he had been insulted in their persons, drew his pistol to support them. But proud Titiche Loutso, infuriated by this action, whiplashed him across the shoulders. Most certainly this action could have been the signal for a bloody confrontation had it not been for the calm courage demonstrated by another Flathead chief who happened to pass at that very moment.

A Gros Ventre, who had been in camp for all of these meetings, was so impressed by the conduct of the Flatheads that he promised, shortly before he had made his departure, that he would do everything in his power to persuade his people to establish friendship with the Flathead nation. So ended the amicable visit by the Flatheads to the Piegan camp. Further details will be supplied in the letters that follow.

SEVENTH LETTER

Translator's Notes

The events in this letter are covered in Chittenden and Richardson, *De Smet,* 2:590–93 and in Donnelly, *Wilderness Kingdom,* 198–99.

1. The circumstances surrounding this encounter are discussed in Letter Two. See also "Henceforward the Prayer of the Flat-Heads Shall Be Ours," Thwaites, *Early Western Travels,* 29:416.

2. De Smet refers to this Piegan as Akasia, stating that the Flatheads gave him his freedom out of their respect for Point. Chittenden and Richardson, *De Smet,* 2:590.

3. Point considered the Piegans "the most civilized" of all the Blackfeet tribes, "on account of relations of a portion of their people with the Flatheads," but they were also "the most noted thieves," Chittenden and Richardson, *De Smet,* 3:946–47.

4. The medicine pipe, or great calumet, was perhaps the most sacred cult item for the Blackfeet. It was carried in a bundle which was opened on solemn occasions. The one who cared for this revered object was what Point called the *Grosse Toque,* and what we have called the Great Toque. There were many in each tribe and they were easily recognizable by their peculiar headdress, or toque. One of their functions was to indicate when and where the camp should move. For a portrait see Donnelly, *Wilderness Kingdom,* 64. Ewers, *Blackfeet,* 172.

5. Great (or Big) Lake, whose Indian name was Amakzikinne, Chief of the Piegans. Chittenden and Richardson, *De Smet,* 3:952.

No. 8

ASSORTED GOSSIP

MOMENTARY SEPARATION FROM THE PIEGANS

EDIFYING RECONCILIATION

On September 17 of this same year, 1846, a Nez Percé struck a Flathead woman, and the judge in this disagreement, a Pend d'Oreille, decided against the offender who claimed that only men could be Flatheads. His punishment was basically the same as that ordered by Titiche-Loutso, and it had the same salutary results. On this same day we learned that the Nez Percés had met with more misfortune. Four members of this tribe roaming the vicinity and planning mischief were chased so effectively by an equal number of Piegans that in order to escape, the Nez Percés had to leave behind one of their robes. On the nineteenth, two Crows killed two Gros Ventres and seven Piegan lodges were hotly pursued by Crees. But all of this was merely local gossip. The big and most exciting piece of news was that several Blackfoot camps were assembling in the neighborhood of Fort Lewis to meet with the Black Robes. Each day the supply boat was expected at the Fort. Would the liquid that cheers the heart be on board? This was the crucial question posed by the non-Christian Indians; most of them hoped whiskey would be forthcoming, and we dreaded the boat's arrival with equal fervor.

On the twentieth, the feast of Our Lady of Sorrows, ninety-six children and two old men were baptized. On the twenty-first a party of Blackfeet Bloods arrived with twenty-one horses they had stolen from the Crows. One of these Bloods, the brother of the great chief, and his companion called on the Black Robes to pay a visit, assuring them that if they came to their camp they would be well received. On the twenty-second, an old Piegan who was quite influential among his people because of his gift of eloquence, was baptized and given the name Ignatius Xavier. Sata was especially hopeful because he translated the prayers. The twenty-fourth was the feast of Our Lady of Mercy and also the anniversary of our coming to the plains of St. Mary's. On this day we took our leave of the Piegans to go to Fort Lewis, accompanied by a chief of the Little Robe and another warrior, the porter of the bear knife, our interpreter Sata, and by a few métis who had been with us ever since our departure from St. Mary's. The most important of these métis was Gabriel Prudhomme, a man famous in Flathead history.[1] As we made our way we had occasion to observe the Little Robe chief.[2] Sometimes he seemed lost in deep thought; at other times he seemed to be excitingly mouthing a war song like a man who was resolved to perform some great feat. What was on his mind? I was wondering about these things when, a few miles from the fort, he came over to Father De Smet and me, sat down between us to smoke and said: "We are going to see a Blackfoot named Aponista. He has sworn to kill me because last year I fired at him to avenge the murder of a Catholic Nez Percé who had placed himself under my protection. This is what I have decided to do to compensate for the wound I gave him. I shall offer him a horse. If he accepts it, well and good. If he refuses it, I will kill him."

We advised him to behave with more wisdom and charity and promised to do our best to help him resolve the matter. We than made a vow to the Blessed Virgin, pleading with her to take in hand this young chief's interests which were so closely allied to our own. As soon as we spotted the fort we halted; rifles were loaded and checked to make sure that they were in working order. Each man made certain that he could defend himself the best way he could, should negotiations fail or should peace agreements be broken, and then we continued our march. We had already reached the long meadow that separates the fort from what is called the Blackfeet Plain when we saw two Indians riding toward us at full gallop. Our chief asked them what message they brought. "Aponista is more angry than ever at you," one of them answered. "He has said, 'I must kill a Piegan. If it is not a chief, it will be another.'"

Now, more resolved than ever, our young chief at the head of his platoon continued his way and entered the fort. I shall put off till a later time a description of this fort and my account of the gracious treatment we received there.

One of our first concerns on arriving at Fort Lewis was to ascertain the intentions of Aponista. They confirmed our apprehensions, stating that he was an evil man very much to be feared and yet that the best thing to do would be to make him an offer of peace. Consequently, we advised him of our desire to meet with him and left no doubt as to the reason. He replied, assuring us that the Black Robes could call on him at any time and with confidence, since he had already resolved, in deference to the Black Robes, to lay aside all grievances against the Flatheads. This ill-humored man was the bravest of the Blackfeet. A proof of this is the fact that eighteen months previously he had not been afraid to challenge the famous Flathead Thunder in man-to-man combat. This was the reason why, in spite of his undeniable wickedness and in spite of the evil things he had done, his people considered him almost the equivalent of a chief. His lodge was built on an island surrounded by the waters of the Missouri, sheltered by great trees and was larger than any other lodge; there was something very imposing about it. We entered and found everything spotlessly clean. A large fire illuminated the interior and brought into relief the warrior's weapons and those items which enhanced the master's dignity. Brand new buffalo robes were spread about the fireplace. The Black Robes were seated in the alcove opposite the door; the others took their places according to their rank or to the order in which they arrived. Aponista entered last, after leaving us to wait a few minutes. He was unarmed but an Indian with a rifle stood at the door. All remained silent. The calumet was prepared. Finally Father De Smet said he wished to speak. All listened intently. He began to speak eloquently and persuasively, and the effect of his words went beyond our greatest expectations. His words were supported by magnificent promises, the sincerity of which was well recognized. To further persuade Aponista with deeds our little chief came up to him, embraced him and covered his shoulders with a magnificent buffalo robe decorated with glass beads. Touched by this generosity and by all that he had heard, Aponista, in a tone that spoke of repentance said: "How can I refuse what is asked of me? I am completely satisfied. Let us forget the unfortunate circumstances that have kept us at odds, and let us henceforth think only of living as brothers."

Translator's notes

The events in this letter are referred to in Chittenden and Richardson, *De Smet,* 2:594–99 and Donnelly, *Wilderness Kingdom,* 201–2.

1. Gabriel Prudhomme had met De Smet on the banks of the Green River in 1840 and served as his interpreter when he first came to visit the Flatheads. On this occasion Prudhomme, translated the basic Catholic prayers into the Flathead language, winning the title "The Precursor" from De Smet. Chittenden and Richardson, *De Smet,* 264, 292. Palladino, *Indian and White in the Northwest,* 38.

2. It becomes evident in what follows that the chief was both a Little Robe and a Piegan, a fact which gives substance to the assertion that the Little Robes did not constitute a separate tribe, but were part of the Piegans. Point refers to this chief as "Little Chief," not to be confused with the Flathead of the same name, known as Michael.

No. 9

FIRST STAY AT FORT LEWIS

Father De Smet and I arrived at Fort Lewis on September 24, 1846. Father De Smet, who had to go to the city of St. Louis in Missouri, was given a wonderful opportunity: The clerk at the Fort was going there by boat—An invitation to Father Point to spend the winter at the Fort—Sale of liquor to the Indians strongly prohibited by the American government—All the employees at the Fort showed great respect for the missionary—There was a well-justified hope of making contact with all of the Blackfeet camps through them.

On the twenty-fifth, the supply boat arrived. Since there was a great need for provisions, there was great joy among the inhabitants as they made their way to and from the dock. The women that lived at the fort dressed themselves in imported luxuries in a manner that had something of both Indian and civilized tastes.

On the twenty-sixth, articles were brought up to the stores and displayed there. There was an exchange of news, true or false, good or bad, unpleasant or agreeable. There was talk about freedom of the press and great advances made in inventions.

On the twenty-seventh, thirty-three persons were baptized—Mass, sermon, and so forth for the first time at this fort.

On the twenty-eighth, Father De Smet left. They fired the canon; thunder rolled and the rain was torrential.

On the twenty-ninth, twenty-one Blackfeet children were baptized on Aponista's island, now called Reconciliation Isle—Anniversary of the day four years ago when I planted the cross on the highest point in Blackfeet territory. May St. Michael, whose feast we celebrate on this day, protect this nation![1]

On the first day of October, the employees of the fort asked the missionary to gather them together for evening prayer—the chief clerk [Charles Larpenteur] approved of this request. Within two months this same clerk, in disgrace, would write to the missionary: "I want to get away from civilized society and live the rest of my life as a good Christian. Allow me to be received among your Indians."[2]

On the second, we were advised the Gros Ventre were coming. A week later they assembled a mile from the fort, numbering about two hundred lodges. The agreement was that only the headmen be given entry to the fort. As I previously explained, the Indian custom is to designate as a "headman" any warrior who has performed several feats. A feat could be carrying off someone's scalp, or his gun, or a large herd of horses or some similar achievement. As the American flag fluttered in the wind and the cannon echoed along the banks of the river, the local authorities accompanied by the missionary, advanced to meet their visitors who were on foot and arranged in several lines. The chiefs and the calumet bearers were in the frontline, the young warriors in the second, and behind them soldiers proper; that is, the young men whose charge it was to maintain order.

First there were gestures of friendship and joy. These consisted in the handshake, to which the more expansive persons added the embrace, the gracious smile, the rubbing of noses,[3] the affectionate passing of the hand over the seam of the sleeve, and finally the short syllable *ai* repeated cordially three or four times. The headmen, fifty in number, were brought into the festive hall where they found the great calumet and large kettles of boiled corn and jars of water mixed with molasses. The food was heartily enjoyed and the guests praised it highly. But the missionary heard the saddest complaints from even the most docile guests about the drink; that it had not the same power to gladden the heart as firewater. The Gros Ventres are passionately fond of strong drink, but what proves that they are good people is that in their drunkenness they think only of giving one another great signs of friendship. Then they kiss like brothers. I should note in passing that this practice is not the custom beyond the Rocky Mountains.

The chief clerk, a Frenchman from Fontainebleau, [Larpenteur], stated his opinion publicly, and with true Catholic sentiments, about the Black Robes with the result that our visitors vied with one another to see who would be the first to have his child baptized. But during the night tares were sown among the wheat. It was reported that the Black Robes were very strict when it came to Indian marriages; so several were on the point of reconsidering their good intentions. All of this prompted me to pay a visit the very next day to the great chief's lodge where I went, accompanied by an interpreter, and where I was welcomed as a friend. Indeed, on the very day before this chief had given me a magnificent robe embroidered with porcupine quills. Although his lodge was surrounded by a considerable number of others equal in size, it was discernible from a distance, having above it that day a flag normally flown on holidays only as had been done with the flag at the fort on the day before. The majestic name the great chief bore probably came from the eagle which was depicted on this standard; for he called himself Chief Eagle.[4] While on the battlefield he customarily draped the American flag over his shoulders, believing that this flowing mantle had the power to inspire courage. This chief, like all chiefs in these warlike tribes, was by nature brave, but it was kindliness rather than bravery that was stamped on his features. He expressed a fatherly tenderness by lavishing caresses on his Benjamin, his youngest son and the first of the nation to be baptized. Like all true braves he spoke little and almost never about himself, but when he did speak there was a great deal of wisdom in his words. He was of average height and possibly fifty years old. He welcomed us most warmly into his royal dwelling.

Within a few minutes this Indian's palace had become a veritable sanctuary where the head of the empire and the high officials of the crown drew up in a circle and listened respectfully to the singing of the *Veni Creator.* When he had finished we showed them pictures of the Passion which my interpreters explained as best they could. My only interpreter for Blackfoot was a little *métis* boy and to interpret Gros Ventre, a totally different language, I had to rely on a young man whose knowledge of Blackfoot was indeed limited. However, we had reason to rejoice because of the reaction of the audience. Just as we were about to leave, the chief's first wife and mother of Benjamin, the youngest of our little neophytes, placed an elaborately decorated pair of mocassins at the Black Robe's feet.

Previously we mentioned that Indians associate the priesthood with medicine, and so before leaving, several sick persons were brought to me. The most common ailment among the Gros Ventres is eye inflammation, made worse by their horrible custom of plucking out eyelashes and painting the rims of their eyelids red. I gave the infected eye a few drops of clear water to alleviate the irritation and they considered I had accomplished miracles. How easy it is to acquire a reputation for scientific knowledge among the ignorant! Soon people were calling on my medical knowledge to cure all sorts of ailments, some going so far as to bring me the nearsighted and the hunchbacks. I had to declare that cures for them were beyond my power, but my protests were in vain for few believed me. Luckily, the kindheartedness in which the Gros Ventres excel prevented them from showing their disappointment in any way other than resignation.

On October 14, several war parties broke into the fort, asking the trades people for powder and the Black Robe for medicine. On the fifteenth a war party asked for a letter of recommendation for the Fort of the Crows. This party was headed by the son of Chief Eagle who had adopted me as his comrade. How could I turn a deaf ear? I therefore wrote to the captain of the aforementioned fort to ask him not only to receive this party but also to do all he could to promote peace between the Crows and the Blackfeet, two nations that had been trying for so long to annihilate one another.[5] Father De Smet had already written in this same vein two months previously. What reception were these entreaties given? God knows! Were they communicated to the Indians who could do the most good? Some Crows I later saw told me, no, this communication had not been made.

On the seventeenth the first visit from the great chief of the Piegans [Big Lake]. As all who deal with traders, he was accustomed not to commit himself until he saw the merchandise that was being offered. Seeing that we had only advice to offer him, advice that would be difficult for him to live by, he was in no hurry to pay his respects to the Black Robe. However, it had been agreed that the Blackfeets' religion would be introduced into his tribe, and so, as he was leaving, he promised me he would do all in his power to welcome me.

On the eighteenth, we left the fort and headed for Great Lake's hunting camp.

Translator's notes

The events of this letter can be found in Donnelly, *Wilderness Kingdom,* 209–12, and there are illustrations of some of the individuals Point refers to in this letter on pages 223, 226–27, 230. Moreover, Point's four-page holograph, "Journal du Père Point pendant son sejour dans la terre de pieds-noir" in the National Library, Rome, covers much of the material contained in this letter. Some factual differences should be noted. According to the Roman document, the Gros Ventres arrived on September 28, the same day De Smet departed. On the following day, the feast of St. Michael, Point baptized twenty-two children, "a bouquet the missionary offered to St. Michael seeing he was worthy of their protection." There are also other minor discrepancies, emendations and deletions. La Biblioteca Nazionale Centrale, Roma. Fondo Gesuitico, Mutlo, Sec. XIX, 9.

1. The gesture of raising a large cross was reminiscent of what he had done at St. Mary's at the foundation of that mission in September 24, 1841 and at the confluence of the Spokane River with Coeur d'Alène Lake on the first Friday of December 1842. In a sense, therefore, September 29, 1846 can be considered the official inauguration of the Blackfoot Mission. Point, "Recollections of the Rocky Mountains," *Woodstock Letters,* 12(1883), 137, 262.

2. This "clerk" was Charles Larpenteur (1803–1872), who in fact was more of a tolerated, unwelcomed guest at Fort Lewis. For the background to the events described here, cf. Hiram Martin Chittenden, *The American Fur Trade of the Far West,* 3 vols. (New York: The Press of the Pioneers, 1935) 1:391–92. Louis Pfalley, O.S.B., "Charles Larpenteur," Hafen, *Mountain Men and the Fur Trade* 1:295–311. Charles Larpenteur, *Forty Years a Fur Trader on the Upper Missouri: The Personal Narrative of Charles Larpenteur with Historical Introduction by Milo Milton Quaite,* (Chicago: Lakeside Press, 1933), 207–13.

3. Footnote in manuscript: "It should be noted that the custom of rubbing noses is practiced in almost all of the islands of Oceania."

4. For Point's portrait of Chief Eagle, see Donnelly, *Wilderness Kingdom,* 173, 182.

5. "Fort of the Crows" or Fort Alexander, which Larpenteur claimed he founded in 1842 and named in honor of Alexander Culbertson, was situated on the banks of the Yellowstone, near the confluence of the Rosebud River. It was considered the most dangerous post the American Fur Company had at the time of Point's stay at Fort Lewis. Larpenteur's claim as the founder of this fort has been challenged by Chittenden. Larpenteur, *Forty Years a Fur Trader,* 146–49, 239–40. Chittenden, *History of the American Fur Trade,* 3:995.

No. 10

FALL HUNT WITH THE PIEGANS

OBSTACLES TO CONVERSION

MEDICINE LODGES

MISCELLANEOUS MATTERS

On October eighteenth, accompanied by a twelve-year-old *métis,* who was to be my interpreter, and by a thirty-year-old Creole, who had volunteered to serve us as interpreter on special occasions, I set out in hope that, with such linguistic support, I would be able to work more effectively in teaching the Piegans.[1] But en route I was compelled to speak to my Creole companion about a certain individual he had brought along with him, and on the next day, alleging that there was no food in the camp, he disappeared. So now, if I was going to preach to the Piegans, I had only a child who didn't even know his ABC's. To encourage him I tried to teach him to read. With his help I succeeded in translating into the Blackfoot language those prayers we usually explain to the Indians.

As soon as I could read this translation well enough for it to be understood, I would read it publicly. After prayers came instruction, but here my interpreter proved defective. Having no more steadfastness than knowledge, the little scholar who was becoming a teacher, preferred to have his schoolroom in the great outdoors rather than anyplace else. Add to this difficulty that of reaching men who had neither the simplicity, nor the constancy, nor the docility of other Indians; of reaching women, who thought more of the sacrifices with which religion menaced them than of the advantages they might realize; or of reaching children, who were so influenced by the bad example with which they were surrounded, then you will easily understand that the poor missionary whose charge it was to convert them needed to have a gift for performing miracles. Sure enough, because of these obstacles all were not converted; but the children were baptized, the young people learned the prayers, and the most important truths of our holy faith became known to the more intelligent among them and found an echo in those hearts which were open to them.

The Blackfeet already had some idea of a supreme being and of an afterlife. But these notions were still so obscure that the sun was their greatest divinity and they offered sacrifices to it. When someone spoke of heaven to them, they would ask very seriously whether in our heaven there were buffalo, unable to believe that without them there could be anything good there. Then, conceiving heaven as the visible atmosphere, they consistently referred to it as 'the blue'. Thus, the older women, the physicians of the tribe, insisted this was not as good as the place they would go after death. What benefits then were offered by the place reserved for them? Pleasures of hunting, of eating, of smoking the calumet, and of conversation. Where was the place where these could be found? In the sandhills that rise up in their country![2] Also, among the Piegans there was a man who very solemnly related that one day, being dead, he found himself in the other life near a lodge in which the old ones were conversing. Not daring to enter without an invitation, he had waited at the door until someone would invite him in. But no one did, so he came among the living where he—without more ado—resumed his earthly existence.

Almost all Indian tribes build what they call medicine lodges—that is to say, chapel-like structures—to their manitous. But these structures, erected usually as a result of some dream, have a duration no less ephemeral. Indeed, within a few days they are usually ruins. Since anyone can dream that he is building a temple, everyone had the right to build one. But since this construction is expensive and because there is a far greater number of poor Indians than rich ones, it frequently happens that a good many years pass without a single lodge being built. It is for this reason that when someone says of an Indian that he has built a medicine lodge, he is saying a great deal.

The form of these structures is that of a cone built around a central pole by many long poles, far apart at the base and gathered together at the top. Once the decision is made to build a medicine lodge, those most devoutly interested in constructing it go to the forest to choose the tree that will be the central pole. Who will have the honor of striking the first blow? Men are chosen for their bravery and women for their good reputation. How can the latter be recognized? By their own witness, ratified by all those present. If a single person denies the truth of her claim and can support this denial with proof, then that candidate yields her place to another, all of which goes to prove that virginity and conjugal chastity are respected everywhere. Hence, even among the Blackfeet there is no husband or father who does not deem himself highly honored when one of these two virtues is found in his lodge.

Once the integrity of the persons involved has been acknowledged, the axes get busy. Soon the tree is felled, its branches removed, and its trunk brought to the spot designated for the construction. It is planted with respect, and the outside poles are arranged in order around it and covered with foliage. The interior is lined with mats, robes, or pieces of cloth, and rich sacrificial offerings are raised upon the central pole. Buffalo tongues, which are to be distributed to all present, are arranged in the form of wreaths, and finally, at the back of the sanctuary a niche is fashioned in which the high priest is to perform. Such are the material preparations in the erection of a medicine lodge. Who will perform the functions of the high priest? The one who has caused the lodge to be built. Who will be his acolytes? Two special dancers, one of whom is dressed in white like the celebrant and the other in black. What will be their function? To set the tone for the other dancers. How long will they dance? Two, three, and sometimes four days. What rules must the dancers observe during this time? Complete abstinence from food and drink. But if they do take something, the solid food must be covered with herbs and the liquid mixed with a certain kind of mud. Is the dance the only religious exercise? There is also a pantomime, and this is the principal ritual. What is its object? To recreate the most remarkable exploits of war. Who are the actors? The braves who boast of having accomplished these. These were the rewards: First, a drumbeat corresponding in sound with the merit and credibility of the deed; second, something to restore one's strength when the pantomime is finished; third, the right to change one's name. This last part of the reward carries the most honor. Each brave may take the name that pleases him. As a rule, however, the manitou designates the name and he is supposed to do so through a dream. Apparently the most modest and the least superstitious leave this matter to the decision of their friends, believing that in such a delicate matter the discretion of their friends can be trusted. Their generosity of recognizing greater or lesser virtue depends on the probability of being more or less rewarded. Usually in these circumstances the liberality of the man who is changing his name is so prodigal that some have been known to give away everything, keeping only what is absolutely necessary to be worthy of further honors, that is to say, keeping only their arms and their horse. Presents are made by means of a cord, one end being held by the person giving and the other by him who is to receive. The cord is a symbol of the friendship which will unite them. Young people who are present at the ceremony are there in the capacity of spectators only. They abase themselves profoundly when they see the worthiness of the high priest, and when the presentations to the great men are made. Afterwards with extreme reserve they approach the niche occupied by the high priest, persuaded that his holiness will obtain for them all that is necessary for themselves one day to become worthy of the honors granted now to their more deserving brothers. The ceremony finally ends with the distribution of the buffalo tongues. The first are offered to the highest notables, that is to say to the fearless braves and the blameless ladies who have cut down the medicine tree. This tree will remain the monument to their virtue until it is reduced to dust. Thus, at the present time, justice and honor are bestowed upon those who deserve it. But this display of justice and honor is politically inspired, and politics will balance the scales in other circumstances by multiplying acts of injustice. How many poor Indian women, tainted by the mere shadow of infidelity, will have their faces marked by the seal of ignominy, which by giving all who approach them the right to insult them will drive them into necessity, or something close to it, of behavior which justifies these insults![3]

It is the custom among the Blackfeet to buy wives. This means the great men can have three or four and prevent twenty young men from having any at all except those the great men no longer want.[4] This irregularity is the cause for a shocking abuse of morals. To preach unselfishness to parents who sell their daughters; peace to the young people; common good to the chiefs; reason to the great men, and to all religion—this is the only project whose execution will prevent the complete extermination of these poor people. But such a project would bring so much glory to religion and to humanity that the enemy of God and of man must attempt to thwart it in a thousand ways.

Another obstacle to the conversion of the Blackfeet is their attachment to superstitious practices. This is a deeply rooted attachment because being able to perform such practices greatly contributes to the building of one's reputation, which in turn advances worldly interests. It is difficult to envisage how much an Indian, once he gets a reputation for being an authority in medicine by performing a number of deceptive tricks, can enslave the gullible and take advantage of their credulity. He who is a specialist in medicine enjoys the attributes of the priest, the miracle worker, and the prophet. It is, therefore, not surprising that the more the missionary endeavors to save the people from their gullibility, the more resistance he meets. Perhaps the tricksters and knaves have never been more evident among the Piegans than when I began to speak to them seriously about religion and morality.

One day Big Lake, chief of this tribe, sent for the son of the grand calumet bearer in whom he had complete confidence, and asked him to perform a few of the tricks of his trade for me. What he was to do was to change into a piece of charcoal a lead bullet. At first this quack obstinately refused to undergo such a trial; however, he gave in to the earnest entreaties of his chief, mysteriously disappeared from the lodge, and in a few minutes returned equipped with all of the paraphernalia necessary for his charlatanism. Silently he began to trace an ellipse before the fire, and then in the center of this design he placed the object to be transformed. Next, like all Indian sorcerers, he stripped down to his loin cloth, and raising his long hair over his head pushed it forward, as if he did not want to be encumbered by it. This is how he captured the attention of the audience. We became more attentive when we saw him place the precious piece of charcoal in his left hand and seize a long flute with his right, apparently to invoke the power of his manitou. Then reverently putting down the instrument of invocation he placed his right hand over the charcoal in his left, changed the position of his hands so that the right and left were alternately one above the other. He brought them close to his body, then held them far away from it; sometimes he raised his hands; sometimes he lowered them—all of which was designed to impress the audience and to give himself time to make the transformation, or rather the substitution. And this substitution, thanks to all of these gesticulations, was becoming easier for him. His flute, his mouth, his hair—all were seen to be props for the act, even though he refused to admit it. But the proof that such was the case is that he would never repeat his trick, despite all of the offers that I made to him.

Another medicine man, yet more bold than the first, presented himself and promised to do even greater marvels for the promised reward. "By the sole power of my breath," he said, "I will cause a boulder to roll against you, one so large and heavy that it could crush you. I shall throw small pieces of iron into the fire. As many pieces I throw you shall hear that many children crying in the flames. If you drape a buffalo robe over a pole, I shall make a corpse appear under it. If you stand before me I shall, without touching you, make your head turn completely around and remain fixed in that position. . . ." This imposter arranged for us to meet the next day, after all of the lodges were set up so as to enable everyone to attend this seance. I assured him that I would be there, for to refuse would be to concede him victory. But at the appointed time he was the only one who did not show up. Rather than admit their fraud, both he and the first medicine man I described announced the following week that ever since the Black Robe had come they had lost their power.

An old Piegan had the reputation of possessing the secret of raising the dead to life. Apparently more convinced than anyone else of his power, he came to see me. I asked him how he could perform such wonders. He replied: "I have this power only after I drink great quantities of whiskey. This is the reason why those who ask for my services always provide me with all of the whiskey I want."

"How many people have you raised from the dead?"

"One woman. Many of those who saw it are still living. You may ask them about it."

"But are you sure that the person you resuscitated was indeed dead?"

"Everyone said so."

"But maybe she was really only sleeping."

"I wouldn't know about that."

One evening I was called to a lodge where a baptized child was on the point of death. An old woman doctor was there whistling in his ears and breathing on his eyes, so convinced that by these means she would cure the child that she was determined not to make room for me. The little one's mother requested that I be allowed to proceed. Seeing that his ailment was chiefly in the head, it occurred to me to bathe his feet in water. No sooner had the water touched him than the dying child began to breathe; soon afterward he opened his eyes and the next day he was running around outside. "What power the Black Robe has," everyone declared. Also, the poor people believed in my medical powers because they had seen a girl, considered to have been consumptive, come to me with her mother asking for a cure. "I saw in a dream you could cure me," she said. Had I dismissed her without at least trying to help, she would have had a poor idea of the Black Robe's charity; so I dissolved a pinch of cream of tartar in water (it was the only neutral medicine I had). She drank it, confident that she would be cured. Since then she has been, or thinks she has been, enjoying good health.

What can be concluded from these occurrences? That most of the miracles attributed to the power of medicine men are imaginary. But is this true of every one of these wonders? Does magic ever play a part in what they do? I leave the answer to this question to those who are more expert in such matters than I. However, here are a few incidents that were told to me:

An Indian stands ten feet from a white man named Picard. The white man holds a sheathed dagger in his hand. The Indian tells him to grip the dagger with all his might; yet all present witness the dagger come out of the scabbard and enter the mouth of the Indian. In the same way a larger object disappears into his mouth, followed by ten lead bullets. In the light of the next day, however, all of these items reappear.

The corpse of a man named Little Grey Head is questioned by a spirit-raiser of his tribe. The corpse answers every question posed using a tone of voice and a manner of speech that could only belong to Little Grey Head, and he answers in such a manner as to prove that he had perfect knowledge of events taking place at that very time, but at great distances, from where they were talking. The man who told me this story was seated in a Canadian *accoutoir,* a kind of armchair without legs. As he spoke the *accoutoir* was shaken by some invisible force. He attributed this power to the presence of the dead man. But what was even a more convincing proof of his presence was the fact that he himself was charged to hold the calumet and the invisible dead man was asked to smoke. He could clearly see the bowl light up when the supposed puff was taken, just as it does when someone actually smokes.

Another Indian speaks. At the sound of his voice a little plant is seen coming from the earth. The plant grows, spreads its branches. It produces leaves, then flowers and finally provides fruit which astonishes the group. But guess what kind of fruit it was. Plums!

These facts were related to me, along with many details which I have omitted, by trustworthy witnesses. These witnesses are still living and would be ready to swear upon the Gospel that they speak the truth.[5]

Translator's Notes.

Some of the topics Point discusses in this letter can be found in Donnelly, *Wilderness Kingdom,* 202, and in De Smet's letter on Religious Beliefs, *De Smet,* 3:1062–1077.

1. The name of De Smet's young interpreter was Jean-Baptiste Champagne, who was the son of Michel Champagne, the storekeeper at Fort Lewis, and of Marie Nitchetoaki, a Blackfoot. The marriage of Michel and Marie Champagne was regularized by Point on December 27, 1846. For a portrait of Jean-Baptiste and his father, see Donnelly, *Wilderness Kingdom,* 214–15.

2. These are the Sand Hills, in "a desolate country south of the Saskatchewan River," Ewers, *Blackfeet,* 184.

3. These various ceremonies are described by Ewers. He also gives a bibliography on Blackfoot religion, importance of dreams, and some of the practices Point discusses in this letter. *Blackfeet,* 162–84, 329–36.

4. Ewers writes: "My informants were very careful to remind me that white men who claimed the Blackfeet used to purchase their wives were misinformed. They stressed the importance of the exchange of gifts in the old-time Blackfoot marriage ceremony." Ewers, *Blackfeet,* 99. At first sight this statement seems to contradict Point's statement. However, since only the wealthy men were able to provide the necessary wherewithal to exchange the gifts, the contradiction is in fact only apparent.

5. This last paragraph is deleted in the manuscript.

No. 11

SUNDRY FACTS CONCERNING THE FALL HUNT AMONG THE PIEGANS ALREADY DESCRIBED IN THE NINTH LETTER

On the evening of October 28, a messenger appeared. At first we listened to him in silence, but then cries and sobs broke out on every side. What had happened? Ten friendly lodges had been exterminated, we were told. The day after the slaughter, sad to relate, only ten people had survived. And this was a circumstance that made the sorrow of the Christian Indians yet more intense. The leader of the victimized troop was an unbaptized Piegan, and between the first shot and the one which finished him off he had no time to prepare for death. He had left the Piegan camp the very day the Black Robe had come there to prepare him for baptism. Three years previously, when he and thirty-six of his men had been captured by the Flatheads, he had promised the missionary, who had obtained their pardon, that from that day on, the prayer of the Flatheads would be theirs.[1] Then, when he came to the Piegans to teach them, he, now the scout from the Big Lake tribe,[2] availed himself of our presence to renew his promise. A person must always grasp opportunities when they come his way, particularly so when the matter is something of vital importance, like the salvation of one's soul; such was the reflection of more than one Indian.

Another Piegan, not predisposed by so great a grace as the other, was nevertheless more faithful to it. During this same massacre he promised, should his life be spared, that he would be baptized. A few weeks later, he showed up with three mules that had been stolen from the Black Robe. He confirmed the news of the massacre, advised the Black Robe that the thief who had taken his mules had died before being able to get his booty to safety, and finally asked for baptism. Another remarkable story from this slaughter was about three women who were captured by the Assiniboines. They sang hymns so beautifully during the first night of their captivity that they lulled their guards to sleep and managed to escape before they awakened.

At dusk on October 31, word got around that one of our hunters, who had pursued a buffalo cow too far from our camp, had been ambushed by the Assiniboines. This news had a profound effect on the whole camp. Warriors seized their arms; terrified women scattered, and the hunter's wife cried out, *"Nina, kimmokit, kimmokit."* That is, "Father, have pity on me; have pity one me"—a sublime cry of religious trust which would move the heart of God! A large crowd mustered around the missionary; women, children, young people, even the chiefs urged him to pray that their brother would be wrested from the wrath of the enemy. We recited a prayer. After this, all of the braves left, but those in the vanguard who had not seen anything panicked and came running back toward camp, spreading fear among the warriors. Then the warriors thought they had spotted the enemy, so all, warriors and braves, turned about and came running back helter-skelter to camp. A little while later, however, they saw the man they had gone out to rescue coming toward the camp; then they listened to his account of all of the dangers he had encountered. An hour after so glorious an ending the whole camp was sleeping soundly.

It was around this period when the great hunting feats and adventures both edifying and curious took place. But I have already related such events in preceding letters written from the Flatheads' hunting camps; so I shall not dwell on them now. I'll only say what affected me most profoundly during this hunt was that the Blackfeet never fell on their prey without first calling on the protection of the Blessed Virgin.

Almost every day, visitors, both friendly and hostile, come to the Blackfeet's camp. Here there is just as much a question of politics as in civilized countries when it comes to discussing victories, defeats, battles, engagements, etc. And since news of such happenings affects them greatly, they spend three-fourths of their lives doing the war dance, mourning their dead or plotting revenge. Such practices are not conducive to developing in them sentiments of a philanthropic nature. This is why cruelty is almost a second nature even among the children. I have seen these little wretches taking great delight in gouging out the eyes of an old buffalo whose body was bristling with hunters' arrows. Given such an education is it any wonder that scalping an enemy gives such pleasure to warriors? These do not always wait until the enemy is dead either before they scalp him. The many Assiniboines who are forced to wear wigs before reaching old age are a witness to this fact.

The evening conversations usually revolve around the subject of war, or if not war, the topic is hunting. Their conversation is usually serious and not so coarse as that of the half-civilized Canadians who sometimes follow alongside of them. Here are a few examples of deeds told by those who performed them:

"In one run I killed six cows using only six bullets."

"I know some hunters who killed as many as fifteen cows in the same charge, although I don't know how many bullets they fired."

"Me, I know a hunter who killed two cows with one arrow. What a strike! Do you see, to kill the second he had to really polish off the first one."

"I know a hunter," someone else said, "who used to brag: 'See this arrow. Well, before I dismount from my horse it will have killed two cows and run through the body of a third.' And in fact, when he had killed the first two he called to his companion, 'Look,' and his friend saw that his arrow was stuck in the stomach of the third animal."

The buffalo's enraged state sometimes keeps him alive long after being struck. Some Canadian mountain men gave me these accounts:

"I once saw a buffalo that had been hit by eighteen bullets in the heart and the lungs remain standing bravely on its four legs."

"I had half-stripped the hide from a cow's back when she got up and ran off, leaving me stunned with my knife still in my hand."

"I once watched a beast with one rib already stripped from its side, its eyes glassy in death, and bullets in its heart, get up again on all fours."

"One time when I was dressing a large steer, I found an old shell in its heart; how long it had been there only God knew."

"I won't say I've seen anything that can top that," said another one, "But I know someone who could. He was dressing his animal when suddenly he stopped, stunned. Didn't he find a flint tool between the hide and the flesh?"

"Oh, come on man, you are talking nonsense now."

"Nonsense! Just listen to the end of the story and you'll see how it happened to get there."

"Go ahead, then."

"Well, you see another hunter had slit the fallen animal's hide and he began to roll it back. But then he was distracted by something, but before leaving the animal he placed his skinning instrument down on the flesh near the turned up hide. This caused the beast to itch; so it got up and ran off with the flint trapped beneath its hide."

They all burst out laughing and said: "After that one, old man, we give up. You win!"

On November 11, there was a rumor that a Little Robe chief's wife had died. The rumor was false, but it gave the Black Robe the opportunity to visit her home and it also gave him the consolation of baptizing her *in articulo mortis.* After her death, Sata delivered a kind of eulogy at her grave, as he had done for his father. In both circumstances his speech was based on the happiness of dying immediately after baptism. In this particular instance the Indian medicine man debated about the nature of the future life. On this day all agreed that it would be happy for the good and unhappy for the wicked. But what do good and evil, happy and unhappy mean? About such questions these poor Indians still need a good deal of instruction. How difficult it is to make souls still dominated by the senses see what is meant by purely spiritual happiness. But what is truly admirable is that not a single Indian has ever said: "We do not understand that; so, it is foolish to believe it." Just the opposite; when we say we ought to believe these and similar truths not because we understand them but because it is God who has revealed them, they understand perfectly that one must incline his reason because the Great Spirit must understand things we do not.

On November 17, we had an unexpected visit from Peter George, the great chief of the Pend d'Oreilles. Instead of being delighted by this visit which did them honor, some Blackfeet were resentful. They were aware of this great man's courage and that he had reason to complain about some of their own people. His visit coincided with that of two Mad Dogs, that is two Blackfeet members of the nation so named. Because the details of this visit are exceedingly interesting and seeing that as I have but a few more lines to add to finish off my account of the Piegans' hunt, I shall postpone a description of this visit until my next letter.

On November 20, a visit from a Gros Ventre, who two months previously had presented me with a gift "without intent" as he called it, that is to say, one given without any other reason save that of expressing friendship. Now as another proof of friendship, he made himself at home in my lodge, acting as if it were his very own, and wouldn't leave until he had received from me a gift, also "without intent."

The bourgeois of the post at the two Blackfeet forts shower the missionary with all kinds of consideration. The one at Fort Lewis visited me while I was at the Piegan camp, located several miles from the fort. The one at Fort Campbell sent an Indian to tell me that should I need anything I had but to express my desire and he would be happy to fulfill it.[3] Four years before this I had had the opportunity to get back the rifle that had been unjustly taken from this same Indian. This deference embarrasses me at times because it makes the Indians think that all I have to do is stamp my foot on the ground to make whatever they like spring forth. Still, I have praised the Lord for it because it shows these poor people that the Black Robes are equally friendly to all, to the white man as well as to the red. May I, even at the cost of shedding my blood, be of use to both peoples in their most serious concerns.

On November 23 the Piegan hunt came to an end. One thing special about it was that during the whole time it lasted the only blood that was spilt was that of the thousand victims slaughtered for commercial purposes. This fact did much to recommend the hunters to the traders' goodwill. And thanks to the spiritual blessings lavished upon the Piegan camp, one may say that in a more important sense, this hunt was the beginning of their coming out of Egypt.

Translator's notes

Point has repeated in the previous letters that the Blackfeet were quite impressed by the number and kind of victories the Flathead had won since the coming of the Black Robes. To the Blackfeet it seemed incontestable that these priests were in possession of some powerful medicine, and that the sign of the cross along with other prayers had given extraordinary powers to their traditional enemies. This fact explains why De Smet and Point were able to be received among the Piegans and other Blackfeet tribes with so much enthusiasm. At the end of letter seven, Point described the reception he and De Smet had received at the Piegan camp. On September 14, the feast of the Exaltation of the Holy Cross, Victor addressed the assembled Blackfeet chiefs assuring them of the goodwill of the Flathead and then:

> he spoke about the last battle with the Crows using pious terminology and attributing the victory to our holy religion. Here with great emphasis he singled out the efficacy of the sign of the cross in drawing down the favor of heaven.

On the following day, the Octave of the Nativity of the Blessed Virgin

Mary, De Smet said mass at the camp where more than two thousand lodges were assembled. Represented here were tribes from the west of the Rockies: Flatheads, Pend d'Oreille, Nez Percés; tribes from the Plains: Piegans, Bloods, Gros Ventre; and the Sarsis from the north. It was truly an impressive assembly, and when De Smet left Fort Lewis less than two weeks later, he had reason to be optimistic about the future. At the end of letter seven, Point wrote: "So ended the amicable visit by the Flatheads to the Piegan camp. Further details will be supplied in the letters that follow."

There is a logical connection between the joyous and triumphant meetings at the Piegan camp and the tragic event Point describes at the beginning of letter eleven. The animosity of the various tribes had made peace impossible and therefore any attempt to establish a reduction where Christianity, stripped from superstitious beliefs, could be taught was remote indeed. In this letter Point also mentions "the half-civilized Canadians." Even though he is always kindly toward these French speakers, who were usually *métis*, and even though it is obvious that he enjoyed their company, even as he had enjoyed the company of the soldiers at the Rocroi barracks, it is also obvious that they present another hostile factor to a successful apostolate among the Blackfeet. Christianity and civilization was what the Religious of the Sacred Heart and the Jesuits had brought to the bayoux of Têche country and it was what Point had tried to introduce to the Coeurs d'Alène. The two notions were as inseparable as *éducation* and *instruction*.

Events described in this letter can be found in Donnelly, *Wilderness Kingdom*, 204–5 and in Chittenden and Richardson, *De Smet* 2:590–9.

1. This event took place during the winter hunt of 1844 and became the subject of Point's letter "Henceforward the Prayer of the Flat-Heads Shall Be Ours," Thwaites, *Early Wastern Travels*, 29:408–19.

2. Point's footnote in the manuscript: "See the beginning section of Letter Seven."

3. When Charles Larpenteur (1833–1872) arrived at Fort Lewis from Fort Union in 1846, he mentioned that Malcom Clark (1817–1869) was the [acting] bourgeois, and that Clark left immediately for Fort Union to protest the appointment of Larpenteur as *commis* under Clark. Then, in October 1846, "Mr. Clark unexpectedly made his reappearance, having received orders at Fort Pierre to return to Fort Louis [*sic*], and take charge." Charles Larpenteur, *Forty Years a Fur Trader on the Upper Missouri*, 207–10. Before the spring of 1847 Alexander Culbertson (1809–1879), who was in fact the bourgeois, had returned to Fort Lewis. Point painted the portraits of both Clark and Culbertson, indicating that the former was the *commis*, that is clerk, and that the latter was the bourgeois. Donnelly, *Wilderness Kingdom*, 214–15. In the absence of the bourgeois, the clerk succeeded to his duties, and so Point could have

been referring to Clark in this instance. More probably, however, he was reflecting on his dealings with Culbertson in the following year. See Hiram Martin Chittenden, *The American Fur Trade of the Far West,* 3 vols. (New York: Francis P. Harper, 1902), 1:53. John E. Wickmans, "Malcolm Clark," in Hafen, *Mountain Men and the Fur Trade,* 8: 69–72, and Ray H. Mattison, "Alexander Culbertson," Ibid. 1:253–56. Larpenteur, *Forth Years a Fur Trader,* 207, 210–11, 225. Point singled out Malcom Clark for the highest praise, which says something for both men. For Clark, because Point designated him as being a man of integrity and strength of character, one who well deserved the respect and popularity accorded him both by the whites and the Indians. For Point, because even though Clark, a non-Catholic, was living in a common law marriage with his Indian wife, a practice Point never tired of condemning, he refused to judge Clark and dealt with him in a most civil and congenial manner, declaring that "everything about him indicated his religious convictions could lead him to the practice of our holy religion." Point's esteem for Clark should serve as a convincing refutation to those who assert that he was a narrow, unfeeling bigot. The fact is that he was a man who had great hope for the betterment and eternal salvation of all. Point to Van de Velde, Fort Lewis, January 14, 1847, ASJSL, AA: 407–409.

When it comes to identifying with precision the bourgeois at Fort Campbell at this date the problem becomes even more complex. Alexander Harvey (?–1854), who had instigated the ire of the Blackfeet and hatred and fear of such men as Malcolm Clark, who had attempted to kill him, formed a competing operation to the American Fur Company in 1846, known as the Harvey, Primeau and Company. He set up Fort Campbell or *Fort de l'opposition,* "just above Fort Benton." Harvey, a giant of a man, who was "inclined to be right when sober," had been temporarily in charge of Fort Chardon in 1846, and was possibly the bourgeois at Fort Campbell at least toward the end of Point's stay at Fort Lewis. See Ray H. Mattinson, "Alexander Harvey," Hafen, *Mountain Men and the Fur Trade,* 4: 119–23. Larpenteur, *Forty Years a Fur Trader,* 142–44, 198.

No. 12

A NOTEWORTHY VISIT OF A PEND D'OREILLE CHIEF AND OF TWO MAD DOG BRAVES

I have already reported that the visit of Peter George, the grand chief of the Pend d'Oreilles, far from pleasing the Piegans, had provoked them greatly. Indeed, several Piegans behaved shamelessly toward him, a fact I was not aware of at the time. Even though the two nations had only recently smoked the peace pipe together, the Piegans did not hesitate to attempt to steal at Peter George's camp. One of these thieves was caught red-handed, pardoned at the chief's request, only to turn around and steal from his own patron. This theft was all the more contemptible because Peter George had added a splendid mount to his gift of life to the pardoned offender, on condition that when he returned to his camp he would persuade his people to heed the words spoken by the Black Robes and live as brothers with the Pend d'Oreilles. Peter George had come to the Piegan camp, accompanied by his son Jules and his nephew Louis, to object to such an obvious violation of all rights. Even though born a Flathead, Peter George, because of his outstanding qualities, had been elected by unanimous vote great chief of the Larger Lake Pend d'Oreilles. He stayed in my lodge, where soon the most important warriors of the Piegans gathered. First, the noble visitor congratulated them for having a priest in their midst, an advantage which his children, even though baptized, did not enjoy. His speech was the essence of tact, not a word of blame or of self-interest escaped his lips. But the less he seemed to promote his own interests, the more incumbent it became upon the missionary to do so. I, therefore, emphasized the advantages of a peace based on justice, stressing the need for restitution in the present situation. The Piegans listened attentively and approvingly, but they declared that since the thief had left their camp with the booty, it was impossible that restitution be made, at least at the present. What gave credibility to this answer was the fact that other Indians in a similar situation had given the Piegans the same response. That evening there was a coming together for prayer at which time the missionary reiterated what he had said about justice and insisted on the obligation of making restitution. When the instruction was over, Peter George went out with his nephew, perhaps to see for himself what the results of this last recommendation would be. Suddenly we heard several rifle reports. I saw armed Indians running hither and thither, seemingly not knowing what they were doing. The whole camp took on the aspect of a fort surprised by the enemy. A cry: "The Pend d'Oreilles! The Pend d'Oreilles!" I could hear Sata delivering a forceful address. Big Lake stopped me: "Don't go in that direction," he said. More rifle reports made me dread what was happening to the Pend d'Oreilles. But like the end to a storm, the noise gradually diminished and a deep calm ensued. Silent Piegans filled up my lodge and with total composure Peter George returned as if there had been no bullets fired at all.

But what had happened? Confident that they were safe among the Piegans, our visitors had gone out for a chat. As they were leaning against a tree, a Blackfoot stealthily drew near and fired almost point blank at Peter George's nephew. Fortunately he was not a member of this tribe, and moreover his attempt did not succeed. All of the racket came about in the effort to protect Peter George, on the one hand, and on the other, to hold up the assassin. How was it that in the course of such a brawl not a hair was harmed on a single person's head? I attribute this to Heaven's protection. Since this drama the Piegans understand better that something besides noise, something even more awesome than an attempted assassination is needed to intimidate a Pend d'Oreille chief.

In order to protect our guests from another treacherous act, the Piegans, who were well disposed toward them, placed them incognito in another lodge. But why was it that during the course of that evening Big Lake came to my lodge and took away the quiver with arrows that Peter George had left there? Did he fear the Pend d'Oreille would take on the whole camp at night all by himself? Not likely. The more probable reason is that some Piegans feared that had Peter George's people heard the rifle fire, they would hasten to the aid of their great chief.

Be that as it may, the next morning when they had finished their breakfast, Peter George and his two companions got up and left. But scarce had they traveled a hundred paces from the lodge when Peter George's eagle eye spotted the horses that had been stolen from him. It took our brave only a matter of seconds to run to them, grab them and lead them back. The thieves were not there, but their fences [the receivers of the stolen goods] were bound to make an attempt to repossess their stolen goods, and this is, indeed, what they attempted to do. But Peter George, intent on defending his rights, drew his sword so fast and with such force that the fences retreated, not converted, certainly, but profoundly abashed by the failure of their efforts. Now victorious over both injustice and violence, the chief bade farewell to the Piegan camp and returned to his own, where he was welcomed with new attestations of esteem and affection.

We then had a very different type of visit, one from two Mad Dogs. Among the Blackfeet the name 'Mad Dog' is given to members of a kind of superstitious brotherhood whose principal feature is a ridiculous sort of bravery. A

Mad Dog never backs away from an enemy, no matter who he is, unless some brave among his confreres beats him back with a stick. As their peacetime rituals are all but interminable, almost always someone is overcome by exhaustion. Should someone take pity on the man and offer him some food to restore his strength, he has to throw it at him as one tosses a bone to a dog. Otherwise he will not touch it.

These rituals are contained in a dance resembling the minuet which builds up progressively, and includes every kind of bow imaginable and also a kind of humming. This humming is sometimes languid and slow and at other times fast and jerky.[1] From time to time it is interrupted by whistles and the beat is measured by a kind of rattle called a *chichiquoi*. This instrument, which they regard as more precious than we would consider the field-marshal of France's baton, consists of three distinct parts. First, there is a round poppy-like head containing the small bones that make muffled sounds to harmonize with the singing; then there is the body, somewhat narrow and decorated with the richest material that can be found; finally, there is the buffalo tail, adorned with features, fringes and ribbons of all colors. Because this object is a symbol of great courage as well as a talisman which gives courage and many other precious virtues, it is not unusual for its owner to refuse to exchange it for four horses. So, like the stem of the calumet, it is also a lucrative object; it can make a man rich and the whites have not been above making their future from it. I have heard that a simple hollowed out tube of finger size thickness and two or three feet long, decorated with large headed yellow nails, brass wire, ribbons and other baubles, has been traded for as many as six horses. But in spite of the value a Mad Dog attaches to his *chichiquoi*, three men of this breed who had talked to the Black Robe about true prayer turned theirs over to him. A fourth threw his in the middle of a field. This man had just returned safely from a perilous adventure, attributing its success to the sign of the cross he made each time he found himself in danger. This same man told me that once he was traveling with a Gros

Ventre. When the Blackfoot made the sign of the cross his companion scoffed at this new medicine in a disrespectful manner; but, he added, "he soon had cause to repent, for he wandered off just a few steps looking for a deer to kill when he was riddled with bullets from the rifles of an enemy party. My few companions and I remained hidden at the very spot where we had prayed and were not seen. If they had indeed seen us, which is doubtful, they didn't dare attack us."

This same Mad Dog and one of those who had entrusted me with his *chichiquoi* were the two visitors who came to the Piegan camp while Peter George was there. The first Mad Dog offered to exchange weapons with the Chief. Among Indians this exchange is a token of friendship, particularly so when the weapons of the one who offers are of greater worth than those of the one who accepts. And such was the case on this occasion.[2]

After having gone into some detail about the famous *chichiquoi* and about the stem of the calumet, it may not be out of order to say something now about the bear knife. This weapon, regarded as formidable by the Indians, is simply a dagger, the handle of which is fashioned from a bear's jaw bone. Like the man who possesses the *chichiquoi,* the one who carries this weapon never retreats in the presence of an enemy. Moreover, this is the only weapon he can use in attacking the enemy or in defending himself. I once heard a Frenchman brag more about capturing a bear knife than he would have had he captured the enemy's flag on a European battlefield. How is the right to carry the bear knife conferred? First of all, by buying it at a high price from its owner. Then the knife is thrown hard at the buyer who must catch it six inches from his chest. You can see that unless the brave's adroitness is on a par with his courage, it is all over for him. One bear knife I saw had the reputation of having reddened itself with the blood of three Piegans in this feat of agility and courage.

It is rare that there is more than one bear knife in each tribe. The present carrier of this knife among the Piegans was once the greatest coward known, but then he dreamt that another brave was killing him with the knife. The dream transformed his spirit, and when he awoke he found himself to be what he has since remained: the worthy carrier of the bear knife. This valiant knight has honored me by adopting me as his brother. This title is not preserved without risk if the adopter, just like the Piegan, does not join discretion with courage. This is the reason why traders, who understand their own interests better than anyone else, have one, but only one brother in each tribe.[3]

Translator's notes

Events described in the first part of this letter are related in Donnelly, *Wilderness Kingdon,* 206–7.

1. This dance was probably a part of the rituals surrounding the sun dance ceremonies described by Ewers, *Blackfeet,* 189–94.

2. Ewers did not mention either the *chichiquoi,* a special war medicine, or the Mad Dogs, apparently a men's society associated with the sun worshipping rituals. Point has painted each. Donnelly, *Wilderness Kingdom,* 182. One early traveler to the Blackfeet wrote: "In all cases they [the Blackfeet] have recourse to the drum and rattle and have great confidence in the intolerable noise caused by those instruments." Maximilian, Prince of Wieds, in *Early Western Travels,* 32 vols., ed. Ruben Thwaites, *Early Western Travels, Travels in the Interior of North America,* 23:102.

3. Ewers describes the transfer ceremony of the bear knife, "a sharp double-edge iron blade," with bear jaws and feathers attached to its handle. The bear held a special place among the Blackfoot tribes because for them this awesome animal had a secret power which it could impart to men, guaranteeing them success in war. "After they had purified themselves in a sweat lodge, the man who wished to acquire the bear knife and the owner [to whom this special power had been granted] entered the latter's lodge naked. A bed of thorns was in the lodge. The owner made a smudge of parsnip roots, donned a bearclaw necklace, sang his bear songs, and imitated a bear pawing the ground. Then he jumped upon the petitioner, pushed him on to the bed of thorns and painted him in the bear manner . . . He crawled four times around the lodge interior growling like a bear. Then holding the knife by the end of its sharp blade, he hurled it at the initiate. If the latter caught it, he became the new owner [and therefore the possessor of special powers] and the former owner congratulated him. 'You gave your life for that knife. It will make you powerful.'" *Blackfeet,* 167.

No. 13

CUSTOMS PECULIAR TO THE BLACKFEET AND TO OTHER INDIANS WHO PEOPLE THE BANKS OF THE UPPER MISSOURI

1. Buffaloes in General

What is unusual about the buffalo hunt of the Blackfeet is that they chase the animals off the cliffs that line the banks of the Missouri River. These banks are sometimes so steep that they put an end to the whole herds, who find below nothing but an enormous tomb; but it is in this tomb that the hunter finds a treasure-trove. One might wonder why these spirited animals don't stop at the abyss. The reason is that the revulsion of the first wave, which perceives the danger, can't sustain the impulse of the second, which is rushing hard behind. When the first line hurls itself over the precipice, the second, third, and all the way down to the next to last follow suit. Only the last line makes the jump to be like the rest. Another example of lack of intelligence in these animals is seen in their attempt to cross rivers dry-shod on thin ice. Moreover, it often happens that once they arrive on the opposite shore after so arduous a crossing they remain where they are and starve to death (especially the cows and calves) rather than retrace their steps, even when the river is free of obstacles[1] or when the ice has become thick enough to support their enormous weight.

These instances of buffaloes being marooned to die of starvation, of their sinking beneath the ice and of their hurling themselves over cliffs, added to the fact of their wholesale slaughter on the plains, all forbode that in a very few years the buffalo will be extinct in North America. For the Indians this could be either the greatest boon or the greatest woe. It will also be the greatest boon if missionaries in large numbers are sent to them, for when the sorry lure of purely material gain no longer consumes them, religion will bring civilization in its train, and civilization will do for their lands what religion has done for their souls. It will be the greatest woe if missionaries do not rush to their aid because without the buffaloes, they will have nothing. Since their soil does not naturally produce the food which could, as in other cultivated lands, take the place of buffalo meat, they would have no alternative other than exile or death.[2]

2. *The Missouri Buffalo*

Every once in a while in these latitudes one comes across buffaloes of an extraordinary size. I saw one hide that measured eleven feet from horns to tail, and I've seen a mane almost two feet long. A trader told me that he once saw a bone joint that was large enough to serve as a warrior's helmet. As far as colors are concerned, the most unusual shades are white, speckled, and a greenish hue. And for quality: the best hides are from heifers especially of those killed during the winter season; the rarest are the so-called beavers, and I once saw one that was as silky as beaver fur. One often encounters buffalo steers which owe their condition to the great voracity of the wolves. Their flesh is preferable to the meat of the buffalo cow. The meat of the buffalo bull is as tough as the meat of the European bull, and Indians will eat it only if there is nothing else available.

3. *Transport Contrivances*

Among the Blackfeet the most ordinary vehicle for transportation is one which is made of two poles, fifteen to eighteen feet long, joined at the upper end in such a way that the strap, which is located about fifteen to twenty inches lower than the point of intersection, rests on the horse's saddle. The other cross-bar is wide enough to take three times as much load as an ordinary horse can carry and is located between the horse's rump and the lower end of the pole. This contrivance is not only the most economic means of transport but it is also the most practical. I have just said it enables the horse to haul three times its ordinary load, and also, when not in use on the march, it serves as a ladder for erecting lodges, as a buttress to support them, as a scaffold to dry meat and as a frame to tan hides. If it has so many uses why is it that the Flatheads and other tribes of the Rockies have never adopted it? Because in their lands the rivers are deeper, the mountain passes are narrower and, in general, the roads are worse. Moreover these contrivances have some drawbacks. They tire out the horses, especially when they have to climb mountains; this is the probable reason why they are called *travails.*[3] On steep ascents the man or woman leading the horse has to place himself behind the *travail* to push it; otherwise, the horse stops dead or, in his attempt to climb, is unable to keep a straight path on a road that slopes sidewise or lengthwise, and therefore the whole load, horse and all topple down. Sometimes these catastrophies are simply comical but they can be extremely serious. Once I witnessed the *travail,* a child and the horse fall into a canyon, but the only casualty was the *travail,* which was shattered. I have also seen horses fall from a height of about two hundred feet and land on their feet and with their load intact. Once I witnessed a horse, which fortunately was not loaded down, stop on an almost perpendicular descent on a promentary where he could no longer go back up, and couldn't make up his mind to go forward. The owner made such a racket from the top of the mountain that he had to play double or quits. So, screwing up his courage and after a great many cautious gropings, he slid to the bottom and then proceeded on his way as if he had not fallen at all.

4. *Fanatical Superstitious Practices*[4]

Fanaticism makes the Blackfoot behave as cruelly toward his own as toward his enemy. Some have seen them cut two openings in a man's skin, just below the chest. They then pass leather thongs through these openings which they tie to a medicine pole. While some hold the victim's feet tight against the base of the pole, others press out with all of their might against his chest. In this way they spin him around and around the pole until either the flesh or the thongs break. On those occasions when their efforts are not successful they call on the strongest person in the group to assist them. Still others, with the same kind of thongs attached in the same way beneath their shoulder blades, are tethered to one and sometimes two horned buffalo skulls. They are then dragged around the medicine lodge and through wormwood like oxen drag a plow over a untilled field.[5]

5. *Diseases*

Rabies. It is the cruelest disease of all and I had never heard of it in the western part of the Rockies, but it is not unknown to the Indians of the Missouri. They are said to possess the best cure for this disease: wrap the patient in a freshly skinned buffalo hide and subject him to the greatest heat a man can bear. An instant cure for rattlesnake bite is more widely known. It is achieved by using blackroot, a native plant in this country.[6] When this root is not available, the Indians say this is the procedure which should be followed: dig a hole in the moist ground and bury the wound in the soil. As soon as there is contact between the wound and the earth the venom will leave the one to settle in the other. Here is another Rocky Mountain remedy: Do you feel occasional rheumatic pain or are you suffering localized pain from a fall? Make a kind of ointment from horse manure boiled in grease and apply it in small quantities to the afflicted part. If, after a few hours, the ache has not completely disappeared, there will at least be some relief. They also say that Indians have four or five kinds of herbs that prevent fire from harming a person, at least the fire in a glowing ember. To support this claim they tell of one Indian who was able, thanks to this marvelous preservative, to place a burning coal in his mouth without suffering any harm. But one day when he was drunk, he tried the same trick without using the anti-burn medicine. So badly did he burn himself that ever since they have called him 'scorched mouth'.

6. *Mourning and Funeral Ceremonies Among the Blackfeet*

Tears; wailing; sobs; self-inflicted wounds of some depth on the arms or chest; hair-cutting; amputation of the little finger up to the first joint—these are the customs that ordinarily accompany or precede funerals among the Blackfeet.[7] Except when they have the time, the heart or the disposition to do so, they do not bury their dead. Warriors who die on the battlefield are often left there for the wild beasts. But when they do have the time and the opportunity to proceed in the proper manner, this is what they do: they lay out the corpse in blankets which are more or less beautiful depending on the means of the family. Then it is strapped tightly to a *travail,* one of those contraptions I described above, and suspended from a tall tree or from the edge of a cliff. The notables are clothed in their best apparel or in rich fabric; then they are laid out in the lodge on a bed of state around which have been arranged various objects which they suppose will be of the greatest use in the other life. Both the lodge and objects, now having become sacred things, remain as long as it pleases the enemy to leave them there. They would soon disappear if the enemy were like the Blackfeet, that is for sure. So, the Flatheads take every precaution possible to hide their burial places from their enemies.[8]

7. *Inheritance*

Who are the dead person's heirs? Those he appoints before he dies. Among the Blackfeet even property of married couples is not held in common. When the husband dies the wife has a claim only on what he was willing to deed her;

likewise is the claim of the children when their father dies. For this reason the inheritance of widows and orphans almost always becomes vulnerable to force or deceit. However the bereaved are not abandoned, for there is always someone among the kinfolk willing to take care of them.

8. *Fate of the Old, Incapacitated, and Sick*

As long as their weakness allows them to drag along, they inch up hill and down dale following the camp. When they are no longer able to keep up and when the camp is pressed by hunger or by an enemy, they are abandoned to their sad fate. But, whenever possible, this is done only after a burial hammock is made for them and when some meat and roots are left by their side. Generally, the sorrow of those leaving is more vocal than that of those remaining. More often than not one sees the latter trying to cheer up the former. "My children," they say, "some day the end must come for each of us. I cannot go any further. Let me die here peacefully." What happens then between those left behind and Divine Mercy? It is a mystery.[9] Do they think of the Great Spirit? I do not know. But we must remember that Divine Mercy is infinite and saves the innocent man wherever he may be. Does innocence exist among the Blackfeet? I think a few instances may be found among them, as everywhere else,[10] among all nations.

Now we shall proceed to relate various excursions we have made among the Indians of the Upper Missouri.

Translator's notes

Some details in this letter are found scattered throughout Point's letters, others are not found anywhere in his published writings, and still others can be found in Donnelly, *Wilderness Kingdom*, 205–6.

1. Deleted in the manuscript: "People say how stupid these buffaloes are. And that is true, but how many other beings that are not buffaloes act in the same way!"

2. Point believed that the disappearance of the buffalo would have a baneful effect on the lives of the Indians, and that this loss would be an evil. However, because it would force the Indians to modify their econ-

omy and way of life and adopt a sedentary life, residing and growing their food in one spot, the disappearance of the buffalo could, in the last analysis, prove to be beneficial. Its disappearance might even be the factor that would save what was best in Indian culture. However, the determining element whether or not the buffalo's passing would be a godsend or a curse was the presence of the missionary. By setting up reductions which would bestow upon the Indians the advantages of civilization, missionaries would ultimately give them means to protect them against the whites, who threatened to destroy their culture and take their lands, and more importantly, missionaries would bring the Blackfeet and others the benefit of religion. This theme, religion and civilization for the Indians, was central to the thinking and consistent in the writings of Nicolas Point, and it was a theme he used often in his paintings. Donnelly, *Wilderness Kingdom,* 238, 243.

3. The device of two poles joined by an A-shape frame was called a travois, the Canadian corruption of the word Point uses, *travail,* which, true enough, meant 'work' or 'suffering'. But Point is probably wrong in the etymology of this vehicle of transportation for the Blackfeet and other Plains Indians because in sixteenth century French *travail* also meant a 'beam' or a 'plank', which was precisely what these two poles serving as shafts for a horse bearing a platform for the load were. Edmond Huguet, *Dictionnaire de la Langue française du seizième siècle,* 7 volumes (Paris: Didier, 1967) 7:319.

4. Point changed this heading from his original subtitle which was: *Religious or rather superstitious fanaticism.*

5. These types of maceration were part of the sun dance festivals. Ewers describes the first type of self-torture and presents a photographic illustration, *Blackfeet,* 174, 189. Point, who regarded such practices as diabolical, illustrated both of them in his paintings. Donnelly, *Wilderness Kingdom,* 135. See Also Clark Wissler, "Societies and Dance Associations of the Blackfoot Indians," *Anthropological Papers of the American Museum of Natural History,* 11 (1913), 359–460; John C. Ewers, "Self-Torture in the Blood Indian Sun Dance," *Journal of the Washington Academy of Sciences,* 38 (1948) 166–73.

6. De Smet also spoke of blackroot *(pterocaulon),* as a remedy for rattlesnake bite, a fact which aroused much interest in Europe. Chittenden and Richardson, *De Smet,* 2:663, n. 8. In his monumental work on the subject Virgil J. Voegel, *American Indian Medicine,* (Norman: University of Oklahoma Press, 1970), does not mention this antidote for rattlesnake bites which Chittenden and Richardson were not able to identify and which caused such curiosity and interest in mid-nineteenth century Europe.

7. Ewers, *Blackfeet,* 183–84.

8. Point's description of burial customs at this date differs considerably from those described in Ewers, ibid., 106–8.

9. Point deleted this sentence in his manuscript. According to Ewers the custom of leaving the feeble, sick, and aged on the plains to die was abandoned after the introduction of the horse and trevois (or travail). Point makes it clear that such a custom seemed to perdure among the nomadic Blackfeet in the late 1840s. Ewers, *Blackfeet,* 106–7.

10. In the manuscript the words "everywhere else" are deleted by the author.

INTRODUCTORY NOTES TO EXCURSIONS

Nicolas Point did not stay at Fort Lewis during the eight months he remained with the Blackfeet. Rather, he set out two days after De Smet left Fort Lewis with fifty lodges of Piegans for the annual autumn hunt. During this time, and later as well, he paid short visits to the four different Blackfoot tribes at their respective camps in a territory that included parts of what are today Alberta, Saskatchewan, and Montana.[1] In the short essays that follow in this section, he relates his impressions of the distinguishing characteristics of the tribes, describes some of his adventures, and repeats themes which the reader has learned by now to identify as typical of his thinking. Although these essays abound in the predictable, studied rhetoric so characteristic of the nineteenth-century Jesuit missionary, Point never allows the reader to know his personal feelings about the difficulties he encountered and it is impossible to discern,

[1]The Treaty of Washington was signed on June 15, 1846 establishing the 49th parallel as the boundary between the Oregon Country and the British possessions in North America.

on the basis of internal evidence, precisely what his frame of mind was during this period of his life. But are there subtle hints in these "excursions" that allow today's reader to conclude this sojourn among the Blackfeet was indeed a happy time for him? It would appear so. For one thing he was working alone. Like many creative personalities it seems he accomplished his most productive work unencumbered by the presence of others. One recalls what he was able to do with the Flathead and Coeur d'Alène while he was with them on their units or while he lived alone with them in their fishing villages. Moreover, there was no immediate danger that some other Jesuit was going to hand him papers that would expel him from the society, and this fact in itself was important for his morale because it freed him from that fear which had so often paralyzed him and made it difficult for others to live with him in peace. Given these circumstances, and given the fact that in so short a time he seemed to accomplish so much, working with the Blackfeet in their camps and with the whites and *métis* at the fort, it does not seem unreasonable to suggest that this was indeed a happy period in the life of Nicolas Point.

What was his status in the society at this period? During part of the time he spent with the Blackfeet it was uncertain, a situation which must have affected him, but then sometime between October 1846 and May 1847 he received an answer to the letter he had written to the general from Fort Colville on April 14, 1845, requesting permission to be reassigned to another Indian mission. The general advised him that he had granted request to be separated from the Rocky Mountain Mission and ordered him to go to the mission his compatriots had recently opened in Canada. On June 24, 1847 De Smet wrote to Roothaan from Brussels, and his letter gives us background to Point's leaving the Coeur d'Alène, his stay with the Blackfeet, and his final reassignment to the French mission in Canada:

> Because of Reverend Father Point's continuing troubles, difficulties and sufferings in dealing with superiors—which finally resulted in Father Joset drawing up demissorial letters—and because of my return in May 1846 from a mis-

> sion to the Blackfeet; along with the promises I had made to Father Point [in 1842 regarding a mission to the Blackfeet], and because I was convinced that everything he had done contrary [to the will of superiors] was rather due to a defect in his head rather than because of bad will, I made [Joset and his consultors] hold back his demissorial letters. In my visit of 1846 to the various missions I did my very best to smooth away problems, to pacify, even, as far as possible, to gratify tempers . . .

De Smet then informed Roothaan that he had asked for and received the permission from the consultors to leave the Williamette and to go again to Europe in search of recruits.

> I brought Father Point with me east of the mountains, and I can say I did so at the request of all the fathers and brothers. He served me as a companion in my visit to the Blackfeet, and I add in his favor that he never gave me any reason to complain on this final visit. I gave him the order and left him written permission to visit the Blackfeet in [Western] Canada during the spring of 1847. (I learned after I got to St. Louis of your Paternity's intention that Father Point was to go to [the Montreal mission in] Canada) . . .[2]

[2] De Smet to Roothaan, Brussels, June 27, 1847, Mont. Sax. 1: 1: 24., ASJR.

First Excursion

TO THE TRIBE OF THE BLACKFEET BLOODS

The very term Blackfeet Bloods normally conjures up images of what is most fearsome among the Indian hordes.[1] To what extent does this race deserve this reputation? I hesitate to say lest by starting to make excuses for them I may end up being their accusor. But what is certain is that many accusations made against them are false. Physically these Indians are usually well built. Their features have something virile, something noble about them: a high forehead, an aquiline nose, a prominent chin. To me they seem to be a better breed than the ordinary Indian. The description which follows in this account may be considered a typical portrayal of this tribe. Here are the circumstances that persuaded me to make my excursion to one of the Blackfeet camps, or more precisely to the camp of the Fish Eaters.[2] After my return from the hunt with the Piegans, I received such a cordial visit from the head chief of this camp that I could not help but feel that something good would come of it. I promised my visitor that I would return his call; this seemed to please him. However, it was not this chief I finally visited, but another named Panarkuinimaki.[3] If he was not more venerable than the other, he was better known throughout the whole area, particularly at the fort where I was at the time. Moreover, he himself seemed willing to introduce me to the camp. I was unable to accept his invitation to come to the camp the first time he extended it because I had no interpreter to go with me. They all claimed that it was not safe to trust people like the Fish Eaters. And it must be admitted that incidents like the recent stealing of horses and the murdering of a fort employee gave substance to such fear. However, this seemed such an obvious obstacle perpetrated by the enemy of mankind to what I believed were divine designs that I determined to set out with Sata as my companion, hoping with his help to baptize the children. But Sata let me know that he, too, feared for the safety of his little family. An Indian armed with a knife had invaded his lodge the previous night intent on killing either his wife or another woman to whom he had extended his hospitality. The reason was that both had been brought up among the Flatheads. I was forced to postpone my visit, but not for long. Panarkuinimaki returned to the fort shortly afterwards and, even though his feelings for the Black Robe had definitely cooled, for reasons I learned later but which at the time I already suspected, I was more than ever determined to follow up on my resolve. All the more so now because the fort's interpreter [Hamel], a Catholic who was proficient in the Blackfeet language, had to deliver a message from the manager of the post to the Fish Eaters and also to the Gros Ventres, whose camps numbering about 230 lodges were pitched one day's journey farther away. So, I said to Panarkuinimaki: "I'll go with you."

"Come if you like," he replied.

"Tell me what you think," I said. "If I go to your camp, it is only to please your people. If you think they will not be glad to see me, I shall not go."

"Get your horses," was his reply.

We set out and after we had trotted and galloped for

four or five hours, Panarkuinimaki himself walked us into his lodge.

Inflated by his ties to a trader of the American Company, this chief boasted that he was a friend of the white man. But what was the basis for such a friendship? His language would soon reveal it. Meanwhile, let us examine what was distinctive about his personality. His outstanding mannerism was a brusque arrogance, a trait which to be tolerated by even his own people had to be balanced by what they admired most in their great men—courage, generosity, skill in medicine—and it was because he possessed these qualities that he was justly famous. They tell that one day he found himself in a thick undergrowth with a handful of men, cut off from the main body of warriors; yet, with guns and arrows he killed about forty Crows from a large war party and forced the rest to retreat. Another time he gave all of nine horses in exchange for a medicine calumet. So eager was he to be set apart from the common people that on another occasion when he had serious reason to complain about the morals of one of his wives, he gave her and a beautiful horse besides to his rival. As far as supersitition was concerned, he had the reputation of being more credulous than the rank and file of his tribe. For example, he believed that a little black and yellow stuffed bird he wore on the top of his head was no less than the master of life and death for him. His other beliefs were just as bizarre. For instance, he believed that a hundred-pound hunk of iron that had come to the Blackfeet land, God knows how or when, had the capacity of producing the best horses in the land, on condition that it be given a wife as a gift. But young Indian girls, even the most eager to wed, are not desirous of such a husband. Thus the solemn bachelor kept to itself its reproductive powers. But this fact did not prevent it from receiving the honors of fatherhood, as if it and it alone had sired all the horses in the world! A second tenet of Panarkuinimaki's belief concerned a strip of land along the banks of the Missouri. It was called Steer's Head because it was thought all the fine cows emerged from it. However, in order to bring about this blessed effect, the divinity had to be offered human flesh from the feet or hands of all the pilgrims present. After the sacrifice was made, everyone went back home as he had come, that is to say, without cows, a fact which did not prevent the custom from being perpetuated. Such were the beliefs firmly held by the Great Man in whose lodge I was a guest.

As far as furniture and the layout of the quarters were concerned, these were the most striking features of the lodge. Between the fireplace and the master's seat was a reserved space where there was sketched a crescent moon with a hole fashioned for burning some sort of incense. Near it there was a most elegant perfume container, with all the material needed for the calumet ceremony, and a basin filled with water with a goblet floating on its surface. This was probably for common use. Above all of these things there was a large calumet, a sceptre with bells attached, a medicine bell, an eagle feathered headdress, and various types of weapons. Opposite the door a useful alcove had been created between two armrests.

Between these two rails the grand chief was lying very casually on an ornamental bed, his back propped up on one of the armrests. Hidden, on his right and on his left, there were two shelters, one housing a dog, the other a rooster. It was in the midst of this brilliant scene, in the presence of His Majesty surrounded by all of the headmen of the tribe, that the missionary was required to account for his visit. According to the custom, he therefore announced that he had something to say. After the calumet had passed from mouth to mouth, very slowly, very silently and in a very solemn manner, the missionary gave a succinct statement pointing out the various advantages which would accrue from a true peace made with the Flatheads and of the many benefits that would come from establishing a reduction, like St. Mary's, on the Blackfeet land. When the Indian approves of what has been said in such a situation, he utters with feeling a short sound. This time there was silence. Both the invitation to make the visit and the reception had been cold. This was proof that between Panarkuinimaki's two visits to the Fort [Fort Lewis], the Blackfeet had been influenced to oppose this desirable peace. When I had finished speaking, the assembly president turned, gazed with great self-importance at the interpreter and said: "But, is what the Black Robe just said really true?" Then without awaiting his response, he continued: "How could he speak the truth since nothing but lies comes from the mouths of white men!"

"What you say is true," answered the interpreter humbly. "The number of white men who lie is great. But not the smallest lie has ever come from the mouths of the Black Robes."

"If this is so," replied the Chief, "it is well and good."

Then in a serious manner and softening a bit his haughtiness, he said to the Black Robe: "What you have just told us proves you love the redskins no less than the whites. Therefore you may come on our lands whenever you like. You will never stand in need of anything. We shall ever be friends with the Flatheads, and if anyone should ever dare to harm you, there shall be someone there to defend you."

Thus it was that He who holds men's hearts in His hands caused at that moment one of the Blackfeet race to speak and it was the very one who had seemed unfavorable toward us. Now it was time for the other headmen to voice the syllable of approval, and on the following day, the council room, now the cradle for a newly born Christendom, became the chapel for true prayer. Despite the size of the enclosure, the priest had to repeat the baptismal ceremonies four times in his effort to satisfy the wishes of the mothers and fathers. The last children brought forward were baptized in the open air, as the lodges were being folded up. The cold was so intense that the water froze between the priest's fingers. All the partners showed the missionary the most tender affection, particularly those who came last who, not knowing how to express their gratitude, greased his seams, repeating the syllable, "Ay, Ay" so heartily that it was impossible not to have been moved.

Was Panarkuinimaki converted on this occasion? Partly, yes, but not entirely. He was too much attached to his medicine, and he reaped too much profit and too many hours from it to renounce it all at once. What was needed to straighten out the pride of this new Sicambre was not a victory but a humiliating defeat. Such a grace would not be wanting.

Toward February, wishing to acquire booty or to add something to his great name, he led a large war party against the Blackfeet's mortal enemy, the Assiniboines. To make certain this undertaking would be crowned with success, he performed every ritual his superstitions demanded. The most remarkable part of these preparations was a sacrifice to the sun, the remains of which we saw coming down the Missouri three months later. There were beautiful clothes, scarlet blankets, bales of fabric—nothing had been spared to render him more pleasing to the divinity. And what happened? First of all, one fine night our pious thieves rounded up 190 Assiniboine horses. But then on the following night the Assiniboines took revenge so effectively that not only did they recover what had been stolen, but they also routed the camp forcing the thieves to abandon robes, weapons, flags, calumet cases, medicine sacks—in a word, all of the objects in which they had so blindly placed their trust. Thus, they were completely and ignominiously defeated. But the defeat was worth more than all of the victories in the world for them, especially for the medicine man himself. It convinced them of this: to conquer against the designs of the Great Spirit, more aid is needed than that of the sun or moon. So, having been severely reproached on this score by the missionary, the hero of this unfortunate expedition removed the images of his favorite deities from his lodge. He even carried this spirit of sacrifice to the point of placing in the Black Robe's hands the black and yellow bird which this time had proved to be as powerless as his other manitous. May God grant that his future conduct will conform with the first actions of his new life, and that his example will encourage his hundred lodges to follow the road he has pioneered for them.

Translator's notes

Some of the material covered in this excursion is found in Donnelly, *Wilderness Kingdom,* 111–16.

1. The name "Bloods" is said to have come from the Crees who described the people of this tribe by their custom of painting their faces with red earth. Another explanation is that the red coloring on their faces and hands was Kutenai or Pend d'Oreille blood. The name these people gave themselves was Kahna or Kaenna, meaning many chiefs. Maximilian, Prince of Wieds, *Travels*, in Thwaites, 22:95. Ewers, *Blackfeet*, 5–6. Point to Van de Velde, Fort Lewis, January 14, 1847, ASJSL, AA: 407–9.

2. Even though fish and fowl were plentiful in the territory inhabitated by the Blackfeet, these Indians restricted their diet to buffalo, roots, and berries. One group of the Bloods did not consider fish as taboo, and they were consequently referred to as the Fish Eaters. Ewers, *Blackfeet*, 86–87.

3. "Panarquinima" is the rendition of this name in Donnelly, *Wilderness Kingdom*, 116.

Second Excursion

THE BLACKFEET PROPER

I do not know if it was because of my prejudice, but when I first saw the Blackfeet it seemed to me that the love of plundering was written all over their faces; that among their young people there was a licentiousness such as I had never observed elsewhere; that among the mature men there was less feeling for what is good than among others, and also that in their lodges there was evidence of greater disorder than among other tribes. It was for these reasons that those who showed me the greatest affection expressed apprehension whenever I spoke of paying a visit to the Blackfeet. Since then, however, I have visited their camps on several occasions. I have been in their lodges; I have smoked with them; I have baptized a good number of their children, and in no other tribe have I baptized more adults, among whom was one woman who thought she was dying. At no time did I ever experience the slightest discourtesy. Most of the headmen, the calumet bearer and the head chief came to pay me a visit. True, it was a Blackfoot who stole my three mules, but it was another who stole them back for me from the thief. And the Blackfoot Aponista, mentioned previously, swore that he would see that I would get my mules back, vowing that he was ready to kill the thief if necessary.[1] Finally, it was a Blackfoot who presented me with a most beautiful gift, that is, the collection of his own drawings.[2] So, even among the Blackfeet proper, there are elements of good, elements which can be developed with patience and perseverance. Finally, I have heard that these Indians are most hospitable.[3]

Translator's Notes

The Blackfeet proper were also known as the Sarsi Indians. Their language Siksekai or Seksekai signified Blackfoot, "and all the other nations have translated the name into their language . . . They have always manifested a more sanguinary and predatory character than the others of whom the Piekanns [Piegans] have always been remarked as the most moderate and humane of this nation." Thwaites, *Early Western Travels,* vols. 22–24, *Travels of the Interior of North America, by Maximilian, Prince of Wieds,* 22:95.

1. The incident relating to the theft of his mules is found in letter 11.

2. Most probably these are the paintings which appear in Donnelly, *Wilderness Kingdom,* 96–99, 101.

3. This last sentence seems contradictory to what Point has already said: he visited these Blackfeet, smoked with them, baptized many of their children. It is possible that his contacts with this tribe were not on their own terrain, in the territory of the North Saskatchewan River, but rather in their camps farther south. This fact may also account for the brevity of this excursion, which is really more of a description than an excursion, and in his final remarks in the Sixth Excursion where he summarized his visits to the other three tribes on their home turf.

Third Excursion

THE GROS VENTRES: THE CAMP OF THE BEARDED ONE

During the month of December, I set off, for the fifth or sixth time, with the intention of visiting the Gros Ventres. I had as my companion an interpreter from the fort, an old hand in this country.[1] As we raced quickly through the territory, he pointed out here a hill where so many Crows had scalped so many Gros Ventres, and there a hollow where an enemy party had forced him to turn back, and over there a canyon where a few years back he and his mount slid down in order to escape certain death. After these stories, he instructed me in the rules to follow in all such cases.

"For example," he said, "if you see you cannot avoid a battle, fight resolutely because boldness frightens the enemy. And a frightened enemy will leave you be. If you are in a group and your camp is not far away, try to have someone slip away to warn the camp. The reason for this is that brigands are afraid of being recognized for what they are and of receiving later what they deserve. They try to appear what they are not, and so this ploy saves your companions.

But this is not the worst that could happen. The worst is when you are caught, not by people, against whom you can fight or from whom you can escape, but, as I have been, by water, fire, cold, hunger, or by sickness. That is when you are on the spot! Ah, I shall always remember a night that was as dark as the inside of an oven, when I was trapped on a small ice flow in the middle of a big river, and it was washing away from the shore like greased lightning. What can one do in such a fix? I promised to have a mass said in honor of the Blessed Virgin. Yes, indeed! Then I jumped. And so well did I jump that it seemed to me the bank had drawn closer to me. I saw myself heading toward it as if by magic. Otherwise, it would have been lights out!"

We were riding along at a fast clip as we talked, but then we thought it wise to dismount when we had to descend through a rocky terrain. And then what happened? We found ourselves at the bottom of a valley, or better of a ravine where there was no trail. We didn't know where we were, and so we had to go up the way we had come down to the plain. "We're in a fix," my companion kept saying, "Oh, we're in a fix!" And in fact the sun had already set, leaving nothing on the horizon but a small crescent that would soon disappear. The cold of the night was becoming severe. Our feet were wet; our horses exhausted; our memories filled with the frightening tales about which we had been talking. We had only the prospect of the wilderness and the silence of the night to encourage our own faltering steps and those of our beasts. One can imagine our joy when at length we spied smoke, then horses, then men, and finally the Gros Ventre camp for which we had been hunting since morning. This camp, on the shore of a small river, was so well hidden that one was on top of it before noticing it. In the camp there was a lodge which was distinguished from the others only by its poverty. But in it there was a blazing fire on which was a kettle boiling. Sitting around it on spread-out buffalo skins were the very best Gros Ventres in the land with the head chief of the camp, a man named the Bearded One. We were introduced then and there. In addition to his beard, which is not customary among the Indians, he wore a cowl, which is not uncommon. But what made him appear to us a true Capuchin was neither his poverty, nor his cowl nor his beard. Rather, it was his charity, his modesty, his moritifed and peaceful mien.[2] I would even say his manner was that of a religious. After expressing his happiness at our arrival by serving us the best provisions he had, he had the most distinguished men of his people gather about us. They listened to us as if we were messengers sent from on high, and for us this was the crowning point of our good fortune. I explained our two-fold purpose in coming to them, and summarized all I had resolved to ask them in the following questions:

1. Would you be happy if the Black Robes were to come and live among you, to do what they had done among the Flatheads?
2. Would you prevent those with evil intentions from doing them harm?
3. Would you be friends with the Flatheads?

Yes was the unanimous answer to the first two questions. But the third was answered by total silence. What was the meaning behind such unqualified hostility? It didn't take them long to give us the answer. After a few minutes of silence, a spokesman for the rest related in detail all that had happened to them during a recent visit they made to the Flatheads. "With the best of faith," the speaker said, "we went to their camp to rejoice together over the alliance we had just made with the Flatheads. We had already smoked the calumet, exchanged gifts, and were just about to take our leave when they, who had already broken so many previous agreements, forcefully grabbed a rifle and a blanket from us."

The accusation was a serious one. Were the Gros Ventres fabricators? No. Then, were the Flatheads treacherous? Not at all. After a discussion which was not long because it was made in good faith, the following facts were established:

1. The accused were not Flatheads properly speaking, although they spoke their language. Rather, they were

Pend d'Oreilles who had not yet had the missionary among them.

2. These Pend d'Oreilles had been absent at the time of the great peacemaking between their allies and the Blackfeet.
3. Despite the treaty made with the Flatheads, allies of the Pend d'Oreilles, those Blackfeet called Piegans had just robbed the Pend d'Oreilles in a most beastly way. We have described this in the account about Peter George.[3]
4. The Pend d'Oreilles had confused the Gros Ventres with the Piegans and the Blackfeet race when they did what the Flatheads were blamed for. Understandably too, because the Gros Ventres, the Piegans and the Bloods are all included under the name Blackfeet, even though the Blackfeet proper are the smallest of these three tribes.

Finally, what completely changed the nature of the case was the fact that the mistreatment of which the Gros Ventres were justly complaining had not been perpetrated by the Pend d'Oreille tribe itself, much less by responsible men of this nation. Rather, it was the deed of a few young braves, unworthy representatives of the nation, and once their behavior was made known to the real representatives of the Pend d'Oreille, it would be highly condemned.

After such serious debates and our ten hour ride on horseback through the snow, it would seem that the travelers had earned a good rest. But the Gros Ventres would have considered themselves poor hosts if they had allowed this. So some experts in Indian courtesy came to the interpreter and others to the Black Robe. *"Come!"* they said. Like it or not we had to go. And what was worse, one went one way and the other another. Where the interpreter was taken, I do not know. But I was taken a good mile through the coldest and darkest of nights in the company of a great toque, the highest order of the headmen. Far from knowing French, he could not even speak Blackfoot. Why did the Black Robe have to make this journey? To add to the supper he had already eaten another supper which was as yet uncooked. Fortunately, my man's chef, a good-hearted fellow, began fanning the fire into a flame as soon as he saw his master. At the same time he began talking sign language in such a cordial and animated fashion that the Black Robe almost forgot his fatigue. All this good Indian succeeded in telling me could be summed up in this: For a long time he had been troubled with an ailment which prevented him from hunting buffaloes—a very serious matter for a poor fellow in his position. So, he begged me to cure him, saying that he already loved me dearly, but that should I cure him, he would love me even more. I gave him some medicine which I thought would relieve him, and I left his family delighted by my generosity and filled with hope that our patient's health would improve. I shared their optimism, seeing that the patient had promised me that whenever he made use of my prescription he would invoke the Master of Life with heartfelt love. I have said that this patient was a great toque, that is to say he was a bearer of the calumet or a priest of the Gros Ventres' religion. One proof of the natural proclivity the Gros Ventres have for Christianity is the large number of great toques who come begging me to baptize their children. Another is their humble and peace-loving nature.

The next day I had to go to the lodge of another great toque for a baptismal ceremony. What was particularly remarkable about this occasion was the extraordinary piety of the youngest child of the family. His father, after taking my crucifix and making a long invocation over it, put it in his son's hands. The boy's mother, standing at his right, took the crucifix and told him what to do. He began devoutly passing his hands over each of his arms, and then placed the two arms together on his breast. Then, taking the crucifix from his mother, he pressed it so tenderly to his heart that one could not help but be moved. It seemed at this moment he experienced, in a sensible way, the effect of the sacrament.

After the baptismal ceremony I had to register the names of the baptized and those of their parents. These names were so odd that in order to catch some semblance of them, I had to have them repeated several times. Moreover, it often happened that instead of repeating to the best of my ability these odd sounding names, I merely repeated stock phrases such as: "This is his father" or "This is his mother"; "I do not know"; "You understand"; "Not entirely"; "Yes, very good." All of this could not but bring smiles to some faces, in spite of the seriousness of the situation and of the people involved. But there was so much good nature in the little jokes they allowed themselves that one would have to be very stern to take any offense at all.[4]

As we made our farewells, preparatory to visiting another camp of the same tribe, some twenty miles distant, we were surrounded by a crowd. It was made up of young Indians, a bit older than those who had just been baptized. They seemed to be saying to us: "We would also very much like to be baptized." But for them a preparation, not necessary for the others, would have been required. So, they resigned themselves, hoping that some day they would, with greater knowledge, share the same happiness. A little further on we encountered more children playing on the ice, some spinning tops by standing over them and striking them with birchrods to keep them going; others, seated on little wooden sledges, came careening down the frozen mountain with astonishing speed; still others, standing straight as candles, were sliding over the ice, and more, bent over the edge of a kind of well they had just dug in the ice, were dabbing their hands in the cold water. But a larger number had left their games to join our escort. The scenes brought Europe back to me and years now far gone. It was a beautiful winter day that brightened this valley: the solemn calm of the solitude made up of warriors, little lodges grouped under great trees, the pious dispositions which had just been revealed to us, and finally the realistic hope that these children of the wilderness—big and little, young and old, men and women—all will soon add their names to the great family of true believers.[5] Each of these separate impressions together imprinted on my heart one of those special memories that will never be erased.

Translator's Notes

The events in this letter are described in Donnelly, *Wilderness Kingdom,* 102–7.

1. Most probably this was Alexander Hamel, generally the interpreter at Fort Union who was at Fort Lewis at this time. Records show that he was with Point at this date. "Registre des baptêmes et marriages administrés sur la terre des Pieds-Noirs par le P. N. Point missionnaire, S.J., depuis 29 septembre 1846 jusqu'à [1847]." Mont. Sax 1, 10, 1, ASJR. Hamel's portrait is in Donnelly, *Wilderness Kingdom,* 222.

2. Point painted a portrait of "Le Barbu" or "The Bearded One" which appears in Donnelly, *Wilderness Kingdom,* 172.

3. See Point's Letter #11.

4. This incident is a refreshing anecdote in the life of Nicolas Point, who often appears as an intensely dedicated man with no humor whatsoever. Here, and often in his dealings with humble people, he can laugh at himself and at incongruous situations. It was unfortunate for him and for others that this same humor was so limited.

5. Although it is regrettable Point does not record the name of the river or give any indication where these events took place, he depicts this scene in Donnelly, *Wilderness Kingdom*, 65. Ewers describes these childrens' games in *Blackfeet,* 152–53.

Fourth Excursion

FROM THE BEARDED ONE'S CAMP TO CHIEF EAGLE'S CAMP

We had to tear ourselves away from the Bearded One's camp. So we continued on our way, now winding along the river, now penetrating into thickets covered with frost looking for a way out, or going along the steep side of a mountain where landslides blocked our progress. By chance we finally saw a fresh footpath on one of the least steep sides. We followed it, almost crawling to—I should not say to the top of the mountain for there were no mountains—the edge of a plain so vast that except for the color, it looked like a sea. Not a single tree, not a blade of grass; nothing but snow. Here on this vast carpet of white a few black specks moving in the distance told of the presence of big game. From this point the deep valley from which we had just emerged did not seem any longer than the great crevices that furrow glaciers in Switzerland. But what a difference! The crevices in Switzerland offer nothing to the lost traveler but a horrible tomb. Those in America offer man—and even animals—who venture into them, perfect winter shelters against the most rigorous cold. We could feel the contrast from the moment the freezing wind from that immense plain hit our faces. It would seem that the Indian ought to give the buffalo that one finds wandering all over this region the same consideration that he gives the horse and domestic animals. But this is not the case. Far from it. Woe to the buffaloes who cross the path of a hunter! This explained why we could see on that very day Indians and buffalo racing over the plains. One could see, off in the distance, on the side where the sun shone, black lines going in every direction. Some were coming toward us, others disappeared in the distance. These were the large game and the intrepid hunters were the tiny creatures looking like ants that dash, then stop and then scramble frenetically. In a word, we were witnessing a great buffalo hunt as seen from afar. Poor buffalo! What a slaughter! And poor Indians! If you continue in this way, within a few years you will search in vain for your daily bread, your shelter, your clothing—for everything that the buffalo lavishes on you today.

Where there are buffalo there are always wolves. That is axiomatic. But why is it that the former run from man, while the latter come as close as they can? Is it that the Indian is more considerate of one than the other? No. Particularly not the Gros Ventre. Like other Indians they need wolf hides for caps, scarves or mittens. They also need what is special to the wolf alone, that is his fat in order to prepare, tan, or soften other hides. So these Indians should have been doubly or triply assiduous in hunting the wolf. Do the wolves like to hunt as allies of the Gros Ventre? Not exactly. What they like more than anything else is a good morsel, and because this prize is found only where the hunters are, the wolves draw near to them despite all danger. But this gluttony is their undoing because the hunters either stalk and then shoot them in the midst of their feasting, or by using a tempting bait, they catch them in a trap. When hungry wolves come in great numbers and the Gros Ventre want to catch many of them, they dig a pit, the depth of which is proportionate to their expectations, cover it with branches, then with dirt, and on the dirt they place a dead animal. Soon the wolves are attracted by the odor. They move in; their number increases; the branches give, and the whole predatory horde falls in, imprisoned at the bottom of the pit until the trapper decides to do them in.

This expedient serves also for capturing antelope and even eagles. To get the antelope they take branches or stones to cordon off a runway that leads to a pit prepared as we have described above. Then they encircle the antelope in such a way as to direct them into this path. Once they are within the enclosure it is not difficult to drive them further. Like the wolves they end up tumbling down into the pit, one on top of the other. Sometimes there are thirty of them, sometimes more, depending on the size of the pit or of the herd. Since eagles have means of escape not available to antelope and wolves, different tactics are used. The trapper crouches down in his trap, hiding himself in a hollow and taking care to leave an opening for one of his hands. He then patiently waits until it pleases the eagle to swoop down on the bait. When the bird takes hold of it, the trapper grabs its legs, pulls it toward him violently, and before the bird knows what is happening, he smashes its head against a rock.[1]

But of what possible use is an eagle to the Indians? It can be very useful. First, the eagle is a great manitou, so Indians search for it to enrich their medicine bundle with its relics. Second, a bone flute is one of the best ways to invoke the power of a manitou, and there is nothing better than the eagle's tibia to fashion such a flute. Thirdly, vanity is a manitou of a sort, and the Indian sacrifices to it as much as to anything. To satisfy this divinity, eagle feathers, especially those from the tail, rank as the very best among the most beautiful objects. Their place of honor is on the warrior's headdress or at the top of his bonnet, at the end of his spear, on the outer edge of his shield, in his own hair or in the tail of his mount. Indian vanity generally puts a premium on everything that flutters in the wind. Thus, he wears his hair long and his horse's mane is long. He loves little strips of cloth, of fringe, ribbons, and feathers certainly, but especially eagle feathers. These are the things that define the Indian's personality, and that of his lodge as well as the furniture in it.[2] It is only after they understand the mystery of the Cross that they feel, like all true Christians, the emptiness of all these vanities, and cry out with the wiseman par excellence: *Vanitas vanitatum . . . et omnia vanitas praeter amare Deum et illi soli servire!*[3]

Translator's Notes.

Some of the events described in this excursion can be found in Donnelly, *Wilderness Kingdom,* 110.

1. Point illustrated the manner of hunting wolves, antelope, and eagles. See Donnelly, *Wilderness Kingdom,* 146, 149.

2. Ewers, *Blackfeet,* 117–20, 162–63; illustration facing p. 111.

3. "Vanity of vanities . . . all is vanity except loving God and serving Him alone." The reference is to *Quoheleth (Ecclesiastes)* 1:1 and, more or less, to *Deuteronomy* 6:13.

Fifth Excursion

CHIEF EAGLE'S CAMP

Toward evening, exhausted and frozen stiff, we dismounted at the lodge of one who, after the chief, was considered the first of the great men. What brought him this honor was, in the opinion of my guide, his reputation for being the best trader in the tribe. In other words, of all the Gros Ventres he was the one who provided the tradesmen at Fort Lewis with the greatest number of robes. Besides, my guide said that he maintained a good lodge and we needed a rest. Indeed his lodge was one of the largest in the camp, and it was conspicuous because of two medicine animals painted on either side of the entrance.[1] It left nothing to be desired in the matter of comfort. I was placed in a kind of alcove padded with buffalo skins that made it very comfortable. But what struck me most when I entered was not the furnishings but the attitude of the master. He seemed extremely embarrassed. Why? I was asking myself the reason when his profile, outlined very clearly against the dark part of the room, reminded me of the Gros Ventre to whom I was unable to give some medicine he had asked for. I hadn't known at the time that in dealing with medicine and the Gros Ventres it is far better to give something even worthless than to give nothing at all. His recollection of this incident excused his lack of warmth, and far from reproaching him, I pretended that I had noticed absolutely nothing. Then I slipped a little something into his hand wherewith he could play the generous host in his lodge, something he could put into his pipe on this occasion of our visit. Here I should mention in praise of Fort Lewis that it was to the fort that I was entirely indebted for my show of generosity. And this was not the first time that, thanks to the kindness of the people at the fort, I was able to enjoy the pleasure of a smoke without having put out one cent of my own—a good thing too, since I didn't have a cent to put out for tobacco. But back to the Gros Ventre.

From that moment on he so changed his attitude toward me that I became his pal, that is, his alter-ego. I could use anything in his lodge. So after we enjoyed a good smoke, and an especially good meal, came the meeting that was as formal as the one in the Bearded One's lodge. The most distinguished person present was not Eagle Chief, who was tied up in his own lodge; rather it was the oldest chief in the tribe. Whites had bestowed on him the title "The General" because of his fighting ability and possibly even more because of the officer's coat with gold braid the bourgeois at the camp had given him. He was a very wise and peace-loving man. Everyone in the camp respected the old general, and for that reason he was delegated to answer my questions in the name of the others. These answers gave us an excellent indication of his goodwill and his favorable disposition.

"We have always been friends of the white man," he began, "Why shouldn't we also be friends of the Black Robes?" Then developing this idea he responded to the first questions which were asked, the same ones I had asked the Bearded One. And, like the Bearded One, he remained silent when it came to the Flatheads, but since he showed the same good faith and presented the same reasons as the Bearded One, it was not difficult to finally get the same agreement. But, as the Old Nestor added (and on this point I agree with him), it was better at the present time to show signs of friendship from afar than from near at hand. It is, indeed, difficult for two Indian nations that have been warring with one another for such a long time to stage a reunion without some imprudent word or action escaping from one side or the other. A single indiscretion of this nature would be enough to rekindle all the fires of discord. And far from this I drew the following practical conclusion: If we want to convert all of the tribes that make up the populous Blackfeet nation, we have to work with each on its own soil without deluding ourselves that we can effectively convert them in someone else's territory.

Toward the end of our friendly discussion, the General in turn asked a few questions, the principal one of which was this: "*Nina* (that is Father), you have asked me what we would do if the Black Robes came to us. But tell us, can you be sure the Black Robes will come?"

I then repeated what Father De Smet had already told one of them: If they persevered in their good dispositions we would make it a point to ask for missionaries from the other side of the great water. And if this request, supported by such a worthy reason were made, it would be heeded. Or perhaps if it were impossible to send missionaries immediately, the Blackfeet might have to wait for a short time.

The next day they brought me the children not yet baptized, just as they had done in the other camp, and I had the consolation of baptizing all of them before I left. After the ceremony I was invited to a feast by an old man, *an expert in medicine,* the first to present me with a beautiful robe and the one who had honored me by a visit at the Piegan camp. It was undoubtedly to show the high regard he had for our relations that he added this new courtesy to all the previous ones. The feast was first class. It consisted of a dish of little red fruit called *bullberries* boiled in scrapings of animal skin, and it wasn't half bad. I expressed my satisfaction, but as a missionary what caused me more delight was the desire he expressed to be baptized as soon as possible. It was a request I could certainly grant easily since his wife (who was his only one) had expressed the same desire. But with adults I have made this my rule: Always proceed slowly. So, as I did not have the time to instruct him properly, the only thing I could do was what I always do in such cases; that is, encourage him to be steadfast. I am convinced that if his feelings were as sincere as they appeared to be the good Lord would find a way to grant his wish.

The visit accomplished, I bade my farewell to the Gros Ventres. But this was not my last visit. At the end of winter I had the opportunity to pass through several of their camps. And between visits[2] those who were most attracted to Christianity came to see me.

As can be seen from the preceding, the Gros Ventres have many good qualities. In summary one could say that they have a goodness of soul which constitutes the core of their personalities. They are also endowed with rectitude, tractability, and courage. So, if they were not such beggars and if they were not so pestering, I would easily call them the Flatheads of the East. But as the Canadians here say they are awful *demandeurs,* constantly begging for favors. In other words, in spite of their good qualities, they are good for nothing in the eyes of the traders. Why? Because they bring in fewer hides than the other tribes.[3]

Are there any ways to distinguish a Gros Ventre from someone from one of these other tribes? Even if he were mixed in with others, the Gros Ventre would stand out because of the following characteristics: The absence of eyelashes and beard, both of which are plucked in the belief that they detract from comeliness; twenty or so circular lines painted from where the hair begins down the forehead; hair worn in a long queue and ending in a point; on the hair they wear two white or blue tufts of green, yellow or red feathers that look like horns because they stick out triangularly from the far corner of each eye; a pouch for buckshot with white and red ornamentation around the edges. Good weapons, elegant clothes, fine mount—in a word, everything that goes to make up *"un sauvage bien grée,"* as they say in these parts. So much for their plumage. As for their prattle—well, it is less attractive. There is no sound more disagreeable to the ear or more difficult to pronounce than the gutteral, halting vowels of the Gros Ventre language. For this reason these people will have to have a missionary young enough to be able to bend his tongue around all of these sounds; firm enough not to be disheartened by the extravagant request they make of him; loaded down with enough medicine remedies to satisfy all the imaginary needs of the people; patient enough to bear with their unceasing petitions, but above all else, this missionary will have to have the zeal of an apostle in order to distribute to these children the bread of the Divine Word. This is what I wish with all of my heart for the Gros Ventre nation.

Translator's Notes

The events that Point described as having taken place in Chief Eagle's Camp are found in Donnelly, *Wilderness Kingdom,* 110–11.

1. These medicine animals were usually bears, symbolically painted. Ewers, *Blackfeet,* 114–16, 165–66. In two of his paintings Point shows the reader the furniture contained in this tipi. Donnelly, *Wilderness Kingdom,* 132.

2. Deleted in the manuscript, "I had many occasions of receiving these at the Fort and . . ."

3. Deleted in the manuscript: "and one understands the reason, the reason why, despite all of the good which I am able to say about them, they are far from enjoying the respect in this country that they deserve." Point's scrupulosity prevented him from making the most innocent statement that might be interpreted as offending or of judging another harshly. In this case it was the personnel at the fort.

Sixth Excursion

SECOND STAY AT FORT LEWIS

This fort, which no longer exists, was built in just about the middle of the Blackfoot country by Mr. Colbertson [Culbertson], a citizen of the United States. A steamboat could possibly navigate to this point in the Missouri during the high-water period, that is from May to July. But above where the fort was constructed, navigation became impossible because there were five waterfalls within a space of eight miles. In the winter, it is almost impossible to navigate anywhere because the river freezes quite early to a thickness of two or three feet. During the dry season, which lasts from August until the frosts, barges can go up river, but only with the combined effort of all on board. When the wind is aft the crew rarely has a chance to rest. In some years a barge runs aground six to twelve times a day. Then they have to jump into the water and pull the tow line over their shoulders. This is why navigation in these waters is such a rugged occupation and why the fort in the Blackfeet country has more of a need for manpower than other forts and why they must pay more for this manpower. A common employee is paid from 150 to 230 dollars per year, as well as food, lodging, and heat. They eat simple, local food. Carpenters, blacksmiths, hunters and other indispensable craftsmen are better paid and better fed. In addition to their better salaries, the clerks, the principal interpreter and the traders eat with the captain, or bourgeois. The fort also graciously takes care of feeding the sick and infirm, women and children, visitors, in a word all the unproductive mouths which usually total more than sixty. This is not counting the chiefs, their followers, the headmen who pass through, and sometimes whole war parties. And these receive, gratuitously, almost all the powder they need. Add to this the gifts that have to be given to the principal traders to persuade them not to take their merchandise elswhere. All of which explains why the price of everything is so high, both for the inhabitants of the fort and for the Indians who come there to trade. In general, the administration of Fort Lewis, and of all other forts belonging to the American [Fur] Company, seems to me to be very mild. Apart from the great effort it takes to tow the supply barge, work at the fort is very moderate, and it is almost always completed between two meals. Some squander all of their salaries and have unfortunate relationships with Indian women, but they do so of their own free will. But I am sure that the moral conditions would be greatly improved if each legally married employee had his own little separate room, or at least was free to admit there only companions whose tastes were the same as his own.[1]

When one mentions "fort" in Europe he conjures up the idea of some overpowering structure surrounded by ramparts, protected by bastions, and defended by a goodly number of cannons. But what is a fort in the Indian country? It is simply a conglomerate of houses and warehouses, built more for solidity than for elegance. All of these are enclosed by a rampart fifteen to twenty feet high. The size of the fortification varies in proportion to the importance of the post. Two square towers several stories high and facing one another diagonally jut out about half the distance of their width are placed at the stockade's angles. It is from these towers, constructed with spares but ingeniously arranged battlements, that the designs of mischievous Indians were thwarted. People ignorant about matters of defensive warfare sometimes ask why there are only two such towers. Why not four, one at each of the corners of the square enclosure? The professional man cannot help but smile at such a question, and the experienced person excuses the questioner for his naiveté.

Such a fort with its two protruding square towers is designed to defend itself against the first attack of thousands of Indians, but how could it hold out for long against a force which it must turn to on a daily basis to keep from dying of hunger or being ruined materially? And having to defend by force is regarded as such a calamity by those traders who best understand the interests of their company that they will do anything to prevent a disagreement with the Indians. They have learned from experience that gratitude is a thousand times stronger than fear in maintaining good conduct with the Indians. Indeed fear, which is entirely natural in them, will prevent them from openly attacking you when you are stronger. But let the opportunity present itself, as it often does, for doing a person harm, without any risk to themselves, and they will take advantage of it. All the more so because for Indians vengeance is considered a virtue. But the policy of Mr. Colbertson [*sic*] the present bourgeois at the Blackfeet's fort, further demonstrates how the traders want to deal with the Indians. He has made it his rule to act with heroic moderation, and ever since he took charge of dealing with the Indians not a single Blackfoot has tried to do him the slightest harm. And more remarkably still is that during the seventeen years he has lived among the Indians (and he has always dwelt among those hardest to please), not a single Indian has ever killed a white man when it was known that he was in the area.

To come back to the subject of Fort Lewis: I received there the most generous hospitality from September 24, 1846 to May 19, 1847, the day of the fort's demise. During this time I made the excursions I described above among the Piegans, Bloods and Gros Ventres. Besides these sorties that took place during my visit three months here, I undertook several others between December and April, but these did not necessitate traveling on the river, since the ice formed solid bridges everywhere, nor even riding a horse, since the camps I visited were close to the fort. At times the number of these camps was so great that on one day between breakfast and supper I visited eleven of them. When traveling from one camp to another, either all alone or in a small group, I often came across Blackfeet notorious for their viciousness and yet never once did I encounter one who sought to do me the slightest harm. One evening after I had baptized someone, I was returning home with my young interpreter. As we crossed a thicket we heard a rustling in the brush behind us. It sounded like some kind of stalking. But it turned out to be an Indian woman running after us with something we had left behind in her lodge. A short time later we spied some armed men under cover of darkness. They were hunters, and they gave us every possible sign of friendship. It is true that on several occasions the Spirit of Lies and his henchmen, who in these parts are not always redskins, spread rumors that could have compromised the Black Robe's apostolate. But such rumors never led to an attack on the person of the Black Robe himself. Besides, they were so absurd and so convincingly refuted by contrary evidence seen by all that, if they caused some short term harm, ultimately they had the most favorable effect possible. For instance, what harm could come from the silly rumor that baptism made men foolish and caused them to die before their normal span of years, when whole tribes like the Flatheads and Pend d'Oreilles, whose intelligence was equal to their longevity, bore witness to the opposite for practically all to see! Then there were so many favorable observations from some of their own nation, as well as from other Indians we had evangelized in the Rocky Mountains and in Oregon, that the Blackfeet had to admit that our prayer was a good one. There are some noteworthy facts: Not only were there relatively fewer deaths among the baptized infants, but there were more deaths among evil-living adults than among the good, and some of the circumstances of these deaths were so startling that it would be impossible to attribute them to chance. For instance, there was the case of those who broke the peace treaty with the Flatheads; of the circumstances of the deaths of the three thieving relatives of Big Lake; of those who stole the Black Robe's three mules; of the Piegan chief who was unfaithful to the promise he had made to God; of the imposter who had passed himself off as one of the Nez Percés; of the Blackfoot and the Gros Ventre who had ridiculed the sign of the cross. Then there was the disease that killed many among the Piegans, causing blood to gush from their ears; and at the same time that the derisive mockery of the sign of the cross took place, an earthquake struck the Gros Ventre territory. In the Assiniboine nation there was the disastrous expedition of Panarkuinimaki, while among the whites a scandalous libertine was three times brought to the point of death by a disease. Conversely, there were multifold blessings obtained in trusting the true God, Catholic prayer and the strength of the sign of the cross. Blackfeet became invincible to their enemies; fugitives escaped from pursuing bandits; the successful escape of the Little Robe prisoners; a Piegan spared from death because of his promise to be baptized; a remarkable victory over the Crow that did not cost a single drop of the victors' blood. Strictly speaking, several of these events—perhaps even all, if considered singly—could be explained without recourse to divine intervention or to a miracle proper, but if we consider them all as a whole, with their attendant circumstances and their consequent effects, it is difficult not to see them as graces so remarkable that they have the force of the miraculous in the eyes of those to whom they were granted.

I would also place the following event in the same category. During a very cold and beautiful February night, a cross, perfectly formed was projected against the moon. Its beams were red in color just as the much larger disc that framed it. The extremities of the vertical beam were contained within this disc, but the horizontal beam stretched out along the horizon. Along this horizontal line, at points where it intersected the circumference of the disc, and farther where it intersected still another circle, made visible only at these points of intersection, were small equidistant, concentric rings of different and various colors. The local physicists call these rings buck-eyes. Indians report they have seen similar phenomena many times before, but never so dramatic as this one. They add that these manifestations are indicators of extreme cold, and perhaps they are merely indicators of frigid weather. Reputable physicists will find reasons to quibble in giving their explanation of this manifestation. It does not seem to me that it was a paraselene. But I can say that, although I did not see it with my own eyes, I learned about it from several people who did see it. Moreover, many travelers arriving the next day related that they had seen a cross on the solar disc at sunrise, an event which does not appear in ordinary parhelia. Now we should consider that the first of these extraordinary circumstances took place at the very same time when nothing mattered to the Blackfeet but the cross; the power of the cross; the salutation of men brought about by the cross; protection, healing, victories attributed to the sign of the cross. Moreover, it wasn't only the missionary and all of the Catholics at the fort who made the sign of the cross, but there were also a large number of non-baptized Indians who signed themselves in the same way.[2] Further, the celestial event had taken place but a few days after an infant had been baptized a Catholic at the request of its Protestant father, and only a few hours after a cross had been planted on this same child's grave. Finally, this cross planted on the grave which matched the cross seen in the heavens was first erected in this land by the missionary's hand. So, one must conclude that it is reasonable to see in the face of these happenings the indication of divine approbation, the sure sign of their similarity.

At this same time word spread throughout the fort, not only among the Blackfeet, but also among the whites, that this sublime sign of our redemption was therefore something most worthy of respect, seeing that God took delight in displaying its glory. I should also say to the credit of him who commanded the fort that the Catholics who ate at his table were not ashamed to sign themselves with the sign of the cross at the beginning and the end of their meals, even though he himself was a Protestant. In order to preserve the memory of all of these events so glorious to Catholicism, the missionary, aided by all of the children of the fort, built a stone pyramid over the grave of the child whose funeral had been so honored, and he crowned it with a wooden cross. May this little monument teach future generations of Blackfeet what the goodness of the Lord did for their forefathers during the year 1847.

In less than eight months' time there were more than seven hundred baptisms administered at Fort Lewis itself and in the neighboring camps. A dozen Indian women, after receiving baptism, were also properly married in the Church to men with but a remnant of the faith who, until then, had been more pagan than Christian. However, obedient to the voice of God calling them back to their obligations, they not only were delighted to receive communion, so as better to prepare themselves for marriage, but they also renewed this holy practice at Easter time.[3] On Easter Sunday everyone was so happy and our blessed religion was held in such high esteem that Mr. Colbertson [*sic*] suggested that all employees, irrespective of their religious affiliations, begin a collection for the benefit of the Catholic mission. And it was one of his clerks, a Protestant like himself, who considered it an honor to present the total amount to the missionary.[4] He was loath to turn down such a beautiful token of their generosity, but he accepted it only on condition that the work he had begun would continue. A few days after the collection, which amounted to almost $200, the donors added a certificate attesting to the motive that had made them so generous. In this document, designed to silence the voice of the propagators of lies, they attested that the blessings bestowed upon the preaching of the Gospel had convinced everyone that nothing could be more advantageous for the Blackfeet tribes than the establishment of a Catholic reduction on their lands. This document further certified that all of the honorable men at the fort were in accord with this principle and that for this reason they had responded to Mr. Colbertson's [*sic*] appeal to take up a collection for the missionary.

The generosity of the country's whites did not stop here. The marvelous example displayed at Fort Lewis provoked a noble emulation among the inhabitants at Fort Campbell, located but six miles distant. The inhabitants here got together not only in the same spirit as those at Fort Lewis, but they rivaled the generosity of their neighbors. The proof of their generosity was that they sent the missionary $99 in a more touching manner for they included a statement of their motives, signed by all the contributors. Considering the number of personnel here, the contributions were about the same in both forts, with the bourgeois' gift alone amounting to $30. With enthusiasm running so high, everyone now at Fort Lewis wanted to demonstrate his generosity in his own way. This was especially the case among the mothers who had become Christians. They offered some sample of their skill while the children endeavored to see who could learn more prayers or who could master the catechism. During Mary's month they laid crowns, in which every flower had been purchased by an *Ave Maria* or by a virtuous act, at the feet of the Blessed Virgin Mary. Some of them made a daily offering of several of these crowns.

I would like to be able to describe in detail all that these good children and their parents did to help realize the missionary's endeavors and the designs of Divine Mercy for the Blackfeet nation. Perhaps I shall one day have the opportunity of doing so. It is with this plan in mind that I have made notes and my heart cannot forget a single service rendered. But what I cannot put aside for long is my gratitude to everyone for the personal signs of esteem I received during the eight months I lived among them. So touching was the attention many gave me that I must attribute it to the profound respect and genuine love they have for our blessed faith and for my special ministry. Before I took my leave from them, it was my pleasure to address them in this manner (and I would not repeat all of this here were it not for the way they received my short address, thereby giving added proof of the delicacy of their feelings). "My friends," I said, "before leaving—and for some of you it will perhaps be the last time we shall meet—it is impossible for me not to feel the need to thank you for all you have done for me. Be assured that any place God's Providence may take me, I will most happily proclaim my indebtedness to you. I say this as a priest and as a Frenchman. For in addition to the countless ways you have demonstrated your kindness toward me personally, I consider as done to me the good you did for my fellow countrymen who have merited your esteem; the good you have shown one another because of my apostolate, and the good I was able to achieve for the Indians here, thanks to your generosity. I thank the good Lord for the zeal with which you have cooperated with his merciful plan. You could not have done better: to the abundance of your almsgiving you have added your good example. Thus, those who love both religion and mankind will react with pleasure, respect, and emotion when they hear all that the inhabitants of Fort Lewis have said and done to keep their vow. These people will read with their very own eyes the written account I have compiled, and these heartfelt words I have said here, they will repeat for themselves. Wonderful! What Father said is verified here in writing! My friends, may your conduct always correspond to your faith. Let us never forget that what we believe and the works that flow from that belief alone become meritorious before God and man. Faithful to the sentiments that unite us here today, may you always be united, as are our two great nations, in mutual esteem and affection. Finally, may the happiness that comes from peace, civilization and religion—subjects about which we so often talked—gently draw the numerous tribes with whom we deal to esteem religion, humanity, and honor. This same sentiment was often expressed by the bourgeois of this fort and by the heads of the American Fur Company and it is reflected by the policy of civilized nations—at least by those worthy of the name 'civilized'—as well as by you yourselves. This fact imposed upon you the duty to follow these last pieces of advice from a friend whose sole consolation at this moment of departure is the hope of seeing you one day in a better world. Farewell, my friends, farewell! Remember me, as I shall remember you—that is in the presence of Him who alone can properly reward what we have done for His glory."

I left Fort Lewis on May 19, 1847, which was the day of its destruction or, rather, of its relocation. All of the building material which could be crated up was transported on rafts three miles downstream, to a site preferable to the old one for scenic beauty, fertility of soil, and convenience for trading. Still, in quitting a land in which my heart had felt such holy emotions, I could not help but sigh and repeat the words a famous traveler said in the Roman catacombs: "So then here as everywhere does everything quickly change and pass away!" Yes, no doubt, everything passes in this world, but the benefits of the supernatural order are more permanent.

Those who witnessed the ceremonies of our holy religion in these lands will always remember with joy Christmas night, the feast of the Epiphany, the magnificent ceremonies of Easter week, the introduction of so many souls into the path of heaven at baptism, the reconciliation between God and their consciences of so many souls. And the humble cross which soars aloft this cradle of religion will tell future travelers that this land, however desolate it may appear, was a blessed land. It will tell them also that, even before our own departure, it held the bodies of those who died in the assurance that they will arise again to life eternal. May this assurance be the hope of all who, in the future, will rest here and in those vast regions that are already begging that apostles be sent to them. This was my most ardent prayer at the moment when we left Fort Lewis.

Translator's Notes

The details in the remaining part of Point's account contained in the San Francisco manuscript are similar to, but not exactly the same as, the account found in Point's Journal, housed in the archives of the French-speaking Canadian Province, Saint-Jérôme, Quebec, which Donnelly used for his rendition published in *Wilderness Kingdom,* and to the manuscript found in the Point Collection at the University of St. Louis, which was edited and published by Gilbert Garraghan under the title "A Journey in a Barge on the Missouri from the Port of the Blackfeet [Lewis] to that of the Assiniboines [Union]," *Mid-America,* 13 (1930–31): 236–54. The St. Louis manuscript and another holograph in the Jesuit archives, Rome, are the same. Some events and descriptions found in this the Sixth Excursion or Second Stay at Fort Lewis can be found in Donnelly's *Wilderness Kingdom* 212–13, and in Garraghan's version, 238–39.

1. This paragraph differs only in minor details from what is contained in the other three manuscripts.

2. Although much of the information contained in this and the following paragraphs can be found in various parts of Point's Journal, the author has departed from his account given in the other three manuscripts. It is at this juncture in the San Francisco holograph that Point returns to the topic followed in the other manuscripts. His habit of changing words and phrases common to the other renditions is common. In the following paragraph even though many facts are the same and even though some phrases are identical as those found in Garraghan, "Journey" *Mid-America,* 13 (1930–31), 139–40, and in Donnelly, *Wilderness Kingdom,* 213, there are major differences in factual presentation and in style.

3. Larpenteur, after speaking with a number of men at the Fort during Point's October excursion with the Piegans, requested that the missionary give some instructions to the personnel there, almost all of whom were nominal Catholics. Consequently, every morning after his six o'clock mass, at which a number of men, women and children attended, he would gather the young people together, teach them prayers in Blackfeet, and explain the basic elements of the faith. About six in the evening, "I gave the men an instruction which was more analytical yet practical." This time was not a convenient hour for the women and so they gathered together in the makeshift chapel later in the evening. Here Point explained to them "how they should act not only *as Christians,* but as *wives* and as *mothers.*" Sometimes the Indians outside the fort would attend these meetings at which they were always welcome. Again, it is Nicolas Point the teacher who stands out so clearly in this aspect of his missionary activity.

The result of these instructions went beyond his most optimistic expectations. "With few exceptions, all of the Catholics fulfilled their obligations." This meant regularizing their marriages, baptizing their children, hearing their confessions and giving them Communion. However, "No Indian woman was given the sacrament of baptism or marriage until she had already received sufficient instruction and gave proof of her good intentions. The solemnity of the sacramental ceremonies were so impressed upon the memory of each one that she would never forget" what she and her husband had commited themselves to and what obligations these promises entailed. The following names are of the women who were baptized and the couples whose marriages were regularized.

Extracts from Point's notes (ASJSJ, BO-50-4[2]):

Marie Nitchetoaki wife of Michel Champagne	Four children*
Hélène Atoxaki wife of Augustin Hamel	Seven children
Marie-Louise? wife of Jacques Berger	One child
Thérèse Sepsenike wife of Louis Matte	Two children
Angélique Apekrismaki wife of Charles Moitié	Four children
Geneviève Ekadepi wife of Joseph Howard	Two children
Catherine Aotatsis wife of Joseph Manuel	Two children
Veronique Itkitsine wife of John Oregon	One infant
Magdeleine Kaenike wife of Denys Yvard	One infant
Marie-Louise Itomisses wife of Henry Robert	One infant
Hélène Pestiaki wife of Cyprien Dénoyer (a Piegan)	Three children

**Point's "little interpreter" Jean-Baptiste, Josette, Marie, and Marie-Thérèse.*

In addition to these married couples, others were baptized in, or reconciled to, the faith: Michel Garcie, Victor Antoine, Basile Ménard, Louis Ménard, Georges Weiper, François Latulippe, H. Arnauld, C. Landry, L. Grangier, P. Carpentier, E. Chauvin, J-B. Deschamps, C. Choquette, B. Deroche, Louis Vachard, Iwahai, Marie, F. Loiselle, Auguste Daniel, J. B. Ouillers, Joseph Coinand, Paul Lonty, Neskapiss, Piksaki, Léandre Blin, Pierre Mathias, Thomas Holme and his wife, and Antoine Rodeur.

4. In addition to the names Point gives of those he baptized and whose marriages he solemnized at Fort Lewis, which was "placed under the protection of the heart of Mary," he has also left in his notes the names of those who contributed to establishing a reduction among the Blackfeet. He noted that "the Protestants were at the head" of this enterprise. Among those in Point's listing on the following page, there are some who later made additional contributions.

Extracts from Point's notes (ASJSJ, BO-50-4[2]):

Alex. Colbertson [*sic*]	$15	M. Clarke	$5
M. Champagne	$10	J. Berger	$7
Louis Vachard	$5	Jos. Howard	$10
Louis Matte	$10	H. Robert	$5
G. Weipper	$5	J. Loiselle	$5
D. Yvard	$4	Léandre Blin	$5
Ant. Primeau	$3	J. Aubichon	$3
Baptiste Guillers	$3	James Lee	$5
Auguste Daniel	$2	A. Hamel	$10
Ant. Breda	$5	Ch. Choquette	$5
Basile Ménard	$4	Ch. Rondin	$10
Souse	$5	John Oregon	$10
*Victor Antoine	$5	Ch. Landry	$5
*B. Deroche	?	T. Holmes	$5
Etienne Chauvin	$5	Pierre Carpentier	$3
Charles Carroll	$3	Latulippe	$2
N. Arnauld	$5	Louis Ménard	$4
Pompée	$2	Bereier	$5
*Pierre Mathias	$5	*Jean Latour	$5
*Edouard Herbot	?	*Paul Lonty	?
*Cyprien Dénoyer	$2		

*Indicates men who left before Easter to form Fort Campbell.

Seventh Excursion

BARGE TRIP FROM THE BLACKFOOT FORT TO THAT OF THE ASSINIBOINES

About eight o'clock on the morning of May 21, 1847, we said our adieux to Fort Clay and, thanks to the efforts of the oarsmen, in a few minutes we were already sailing past the rival fort, Campbell. The bourgeois there was away, but those taking his place saluted our passing with a few rifle shots, which we acknowledged the best way we could.[1] Then we plunged into such a deep wilderness that soon the only living things we saw were the wild animals. But these were so beautiful and so abundant that this trip offered us more enchantment than the finest parks of civilized lands. Within a few hours we had spotted wolves, antelopes, roe-deer, bighorns, stag deer, buffalo or bison, bears, eagles, cormorants, gulls, bustards, and so forth. As for the water-dwellers, we only had a glimpse of them in the evening. We saw a catfish, a kind of fish whose three fleshy bristles jutting out on either side of its mouth, give it the impression of a man with a mustache. Because of the delicacy of its meat it has earned the name "Missouri salmon." The smaller it is, the more tender. It can be huge, with eyes measuring as much as eighteen inches apart, depending on the expanse and depth of the waters it inhabits.

In the midst of this population so new to us, there was a scene which changed our wonder to compassion. What was it? An abandoned horse and dog. "Poor animals, why are you here?" "Look at us: we are old and crippled. All because of the many services we rendered our master." The plight of the horse we could understand. But what wearisome service does the Indian demand of his dog? When the Indian is poor it must take the place of a horse, and like a horse it is sometimes overburdened. Moreover, these open plains bristle with sharp nettles that come from a plant called the prickly pear. So, even if the poor animal were not as overworked as it is, very often the sores and the pain caused by these nettles force it to lag behind, barely able to drag itself on, until it collapses or finds someone to put an end to its sufferings. One day our faithful Carlo that had followed the Black Robe practically everywhere in Oregon, was lost like this dog in the wilderness. An Indian sent back after him told us he found Carlo near the lodge where we had spent the previous night crying like a child that had lost its mother.[2]

There is always something magical about a man gliding down a beautiful river in a boat in that the country traversed seems to be moving past him. But in certain parts of the Missouri the enchantment is increased by the destructive beauty displayed along the banks. By this, I mean the giant landslides created by the depth of the river's bed, or because of the swiftness of its course, or the weakness of the soil along its banks or because its high waters subside. When seen at close range those scenes of destruction present only hideous ravines, deep cavities, exposed roots and overturned trees—in a word, the very image of desolation. But if one moves a little distance away, these rude masses seem to take on gentler forms. Clashing colors are blended, disparate objects melt together, and sometimes, as in the shapes of clouds, effects are produced which one could not contemplate without pain, or pleasure, depending on the nature of the strange beings which appear, are transformed, and soon vanish, palpable images of the illusions of this life.

May 22, 1847. These scenes were not uniform by any means. But perhaps it was precisely this variety that brought the traveler the greatest delight. Yesterday their yellowish tinge fading to black along with their oppressive nearness gave an impression of sorrow that constricted one's heart. Today the banks of the river have expanded to embrace a softer green landscape—fresher groves, lovely islands, mountains of whitish hue tinged with pink, a feeling of spaciousness which lends some of its blue to the over-somber or over-bright colors of this vast tableau. All this stirs up in the soul an expanding feeling of joy.[3] The contrast is all the more striking because to the melancholy features to which I have already alluded was added the even sadder sight of civilization fallen into ruin. I refer to Fort McKenzie, the longest lived-in Blackfoot fort, and to Fort Fiegan, the first one built by the whites in Blackfoot territory. Allow me to dwell on the history of this latter fort, seeing that it is linked to the peace so long yearned for, the peace which was all the more desirable because before it, as many whites as fell into the hands of the Blackfeet became victims, sacrificed to their hatred.

This peace was not concluded until the spring of 1831. This is the way it came about. In the beginning of that year there was a Canadian at Fort Union named Jacques Berger (he is still alive and has confirmed the truth of the details below), a brave trader who had already spent twenty years in the forests of the Northwest. During this period these forests were frequented by the Blackfeet who came there to trade their furs, and so Berger often had the opportunity to meet the nation's headmen. He also knew enough of their language to understand them and to make himself understood. To his experience and knowledge he added a most conciliatory temperament, and so his bourgeois, who at this time was Mr. McKenzie, asked him if he would be so brave as to convey to the Blackfeet the good news which had been at issue for such a long time. To such an honorable proposal Berger gave the answer it deserved, and, despite the fact that it was winter, he set out, accompanied by four other

Canadians no less loyal than himself, well supplied with gifts for the Blackfeet and with one wish—either to die as an honorable man or to fulfill the noble mission entrusted to him. They had to march out through the snow in search of the very men from whom most people would want to escape. One can just imagine their exhaustion and their courage; for forty long days they tromped on without encountering any living beings other than wild animals. Finally, when they awoke on the forty-first day, a war party suddenly appeared before them. "We're done for," said Berger's companions, "but all the same we have to fight." "No!" replied this brave leader, "We did not come to fight. Let me deal with them," and alone he went forward to meet the enemy. It was a Piegan war party of seventeen. How great was his joy when he discovered that the chief of this party was a certain Assapake, for whom he had recently done a good turn. Now among the Indians a good deed is never forgotten, and here was one more proof of this fact. They smoked the calumet and exchanged gifts. But even though these gifts were offered cordially enough, either their quality or their quantity did not satisfy the anticipated expectations of the Piegans. So, a few malcontents took upon themselves to demand a good part of the personal property of the envoys, as well as confiscate all of the firearms, except Berger's. None of this settled well with his companions, but what could they do? Fortunately, God, who holds the hearts of all men in his hands, inclined the Indians to listen to reason, in spite of their natural inclinations. Then the chief, a good-hearted man, somehow managed to get them to restore some of the seized property. Once this had been achieved, all started out again and five days later, on March 6, they arrived with the flag unfurled at the Piegan camp where Onestenatoue (that is He Who Eats Veal) was the chief. It goes without saying that their arrival at the camp was quite an event for the tribe, and that their proffered gifts were accepted. The Indians listened to the whites' proposal, and accepted it under one condition, that the whole agreement be just what the agreement said and legally binding. At this period the Blackfeet mistrusted the traders so much that they found it difficult to believe in the sincerity of their word. But on this occasion so many convincing proofs were given that even the skeptics joined the others in proposing that they accompany the peacemakers back to Fort Union, both in order to defend them in case of attack and to confirm with greater solemnity the treaty just concluded.

After resting and feasting for twenty-two days, Berger and his companions began their return, followed by ninety-two Indian men and thirty-two women. When they had left the fort they had said: "We shall be back here on May 15, at the latest. If we are not here by that date, it will mean things did not turn out as we had hoped." Now May 15 had passed and they had not returned. "What has happened to them?" their friends began to ask one another. "What has become of them? Probably like so many others before them, they have been massacred." Such were the sinister thoughts their delay had generated. Then the shout was heard: "Here they are! Here are our men!" Just imagine the joy on all sides when they saw them standing outside the fort, flag unfurled, at the head of such a large contingent, all in good health and none showing fear or discomfort. The bourgeois particularly did not know how to express his delight, seeing that his honor and his interests were so much at stake in this venture. So, amidst congratulations and celebrations of all kinds, peace was confirmed to the complete satisfaction of all concerned.[4] It was agreed that at the beginning of summer sufficient men would be sent to build a fort in the Blackfeet country. This fort was constructed by the orders of Mr. McKenzie and under the supervision of Mr. Kipp, and it was given the name Fort Piegan in honor of the Indians of this tribe who were the first to make a treaty with the Americans from Fort Union. This was a mark of deference which honors the founder's wisdom as much as his modesty. Evidently unaware of Mr. McKenzie's peaceful intentions, the Bloods burnt this fort to the ground; but he built another farther up the river, and it received the name the first fort should have had. Fort McKenzie prospered until 1844, when reasons of prudence dictated that it should be moved. Apparently the proximity of the Judith River, plus the beauty of its surroundings, proved to be too great a temptation for those who were supposed to supply for the fort. Hindsight showed that these benefits and others which the location seemed to offer did not make up for the grave disadvantage of being too accessible to enemy attack. For this same reason, a third fort, called F.E.C.—Effeci,[5] had to be moved farther up the river just one year after its destruction. This was the origin of Fort Lewis, referred to above. But now this fort, after having achieved a full career in so short a time, was displaced by Fort Clay, presently under construction.[6]

Lest I omit anything that is connected with the present subject, I ought to include another fort of 1844. It belonged to the rival company of Fox and Livingston and lasted but one spring.[7] What is to be said of the thousand and one army forts scattered along the banks of the Missouri?[8] Very often what was built in the morning was, by evening, destroyed or abandoned. Thus, in this region, perhaps more than anywhere else, and in spite of foresight, skill and long experience (all of which the bourgeois of the American Fur Company had), it must be said that we have no permanent abode in this area.

Fort McKenzie, which lasted only twelve years, is cited as a rare example of longevity. Still its ashes deserve our respect, for it was for trade what Fort Lewis has been for religion.

To keep some continuity in the historical events of this journal, I have had to omit the events of the day and gloss over some of the monuments which merit attention. I am referring to the Citadel, the Pierced Rock and the Steamboat, which are to the Missouri what the House and the Chimney are to the Platte, with this difference: the Citadel is not merely constructed of sandstone, but is composed of rock fragments which appear to be the product of volcanic action. As for the Steamboat, which the missionary would rather call the Cathedral, and Pierced Rock, remarkable only for the hole which pierces it through and through, they, like the odd formations along the Platte, owe their formation to erosion by wind and rain. But there is this difference: the volcanic rock which is mixed with the sandstone adds an antiquity to their picturesque shape, and the possibility that they will endure gives them a more venerable aspect.

Events of the day: Almost under the enclosure of the fort, Mr. Culbertson killed a bear just as it was rearing to attack. An oarsman's hat fell into the water at the foot of the Pierced Rock, and its owner wailed: "My poor hat; there it goes up the river!" These are perhaps profane sketches from the missionary's pen as he scuds by the Cathedral.[9]

22 May, Vigil of Pentecost. We keep on rowing fast. In praise of our brave rowers I must say that I have never heard them say an unseemly word, even in the midst of their joking remarks or when pressed with hard work. In spite of the wonders they see at each moment there was more than one of them who would have preferred to seek rest on land. And they think what they would do on the morrow if, like at Easter, they had had the missionary with them. But on Sundays and feast days barges have to go on, and like it or not, the oarsmen must go on with them.

23 [May]. At least today they will have the satisfaction of hearing holy mass. How? In the most comfortable way possible. Indeed we came to a stop. It was raining and the altar took up half my cabin. So, while half the congregation squeezed up against the altar, the rest kept silence, and I suppose prayed around the fire, under the shelter they had built. After mass the weather cleared. All aboard! is shouted. We leave.

Translator's Notes

The events in this essay coincide with those described in Donnelly, *Wilderness Kingdom,* 213–16 and Garraghan, "Journey on a Barge," *Mid-America* 13 (1930–1) 241–46.

1. Fort Clay, better known as Fort Benton, was the new fort built to replace Fort Lewis. Fort Campbell, as has already been indicated, was founded by Harvey Primeau and Company. Presumably the absentee bourgeois at this date was the despicable Alexander Harvey. See Hafen, *Mountain Men of the Fur Trade,* 4:119–23.

2. Point had a great love of animals. His sentimental portrait of the dog Carlo is in Donnelly, *Wilderness Kingdom*, 235.

3. Donnelly has included some of Point's black and white sketches of a number of the scenes the author described in this section. These sketches contrast dramatically with his primitive, psychedelic-like paintings of the Indians and of his adventures among them, and they are reminiscent of the architectural drawings he executed of St. Mary's, Iberville, and Grand Coteau. Ibid, 228–29.

4. Jacques Berger's mission to the Blackfeet is described by Charles Larpenteur, *Forty Years a Fur Trader*, 93–95. What Point obviously did not know was that Berger was instrumental in actively encouraging settlers into the Indian country; moreover, he was accused of selling the Indians whisky—two activities which militated against setting up Paraguay-type reductions. Hafen, *Mountain Men and the Fur Trade*, 4:121–22; 8–71. Point painted Berger's portrait. Donnelly, *Wilderness Kingdom*, 222.

5. Footnote in the manuscript: "These three letters should be pronounced as they are in English to get Effeci."

6. Point's account of the history of the erection and destruction of the forts described in this section was obviously learned from prejudiced sources. Fort Piegan had been built at the instruction of Kenneth McKenzie by James Kipp at the angle of the Marias and Missouri Rivers in October 1831. It was burned down by the Blackfeet and another fort, McKenzie, was erected to take its place six miles up the river, in 1832. In 1843, Francis A. Chardon was the bourgeois at this fort when the Blackfeet accidentally killed his negro servant. Chardon, in conjunction with Alexander Harvey and, according to Larpenteur, with Jacques Berger, massacred a number of Bloods in retaliation. The result was disastrous for relations between the Blackfeet and the American Fur Company. Chardon was forced to abandon Fort McKenzie, and, in the summer of 1842, he built a new fort, which he modestly called Fort Francis A. Chardon (F.A.C.), at the mouth of the Judith River. Then, leaving Alexander Harvey in charge, he returned to Fort Clark. The Bloods now turned their wrath on the new establishment. In 1845 Culbertson forced the besieged Harvey to abandon this fort, burnt it, and built Fort Lewis. Meanwhile, the Blackfeet had burned the old fort, for which reason it became known in history as Fort Brulé at the site of Brulé Bottom. Hiram Martin Chittenden, *The American Fur Trade of the Far West*, 2 volumes. (New York: The Press of the Pioneers, 1935), 1:372, 2:685–86; Hafen, *Mountain Men of the Fur Trade*, 1:225–27, 2:201–5, 4:119–23; Larpenteur, *Forty Years a Fur Trader*, 186–90, 192–98, 207–9.

7. Fox and Livingston established a rival company to the American Fur Company in 1842. John A. N. Ebbetts, a former associate with the A.F.C., supplied the capital, which he got from selling liquor to the

Indians. This new company, known also as the Union Fur Company, began setting up competing posts while Point was with the Coeur d'Alène, but before he arrived at Fort Lewis the new company had been forced to sell out to the A.F.C. Its chief trading center was Fort Mortimore, near the mouth of the Yellowstone, and it is to this fort that Point most probably referred, and will mention again in the next Excursion. Hafen, *Mountain Men and the Fur Trade,* 1:170. Larpenteur, *Forty Years a Fur Trader,* 153–55. John E. Sunder, "The Decline of the Fur Trade on the Upper Missouri, 1840–65," in *The American West: An Appraisal,* ed. Robert G. Ferris (Santa Fe: Museum of New Mexico Press, 1963), 128–37.

8. In the manuscript the following sentence is deleted: "They are almost as plentiful as the grass in the fields, but they did not last as long."

9. In the manuscript this whole paragraph is deleted.

ASSORTED ANECDOTES

Amusement The wooded point to the right there was the scene of an incident that started a lot of jokes going around last year. Here is an example of one. The Count de Trent, a French traveler famous for his openhandedness in these parts, was going up the river to visit Fort Effeci. On the way he indulged in some hunting, which he had the reputation of being very fond of, and, true to his nature, he would leave his quarry for whoever wanted it. After his companion, who shared the same generous nature and the same taste for hunting, had downed a deer, two *engagés* began arguing over the hide. The dispute heated up and just as they were about to come to blows, the animal came to and took off at full speed without, of course, leaving its coat behind. What was the result? Everyone burst out laughing, even the two who had most to lose by this unexpected flight. "Shucks," they said, "That sure settled our argument."

How does the mariner new to these shores
Save face and keep his head up too?
With Gascon wit he laughs with boors
And gaily smiles, swallowing rue.

Sense of Humor à la Provençal Here is another example of a sally of wit that again shows the cheerful disposition of these boatmen as well as the seriousness of their bosses. One French-born mariner was always good-natured with everyone, a happy-go-lucky sort, a typical Provençal. One day some of his mates persuaded him to get them all some liquid refreshment from the bourgeois, a stern man if ever there was one. Despite the merits of the supplicant, his request did not meet with the desired success. "Fine. I know what we'll do then," the Provençal retorted with what sounded like a bit of temper. "Just what will you do, you scum?" replied the bourgeois, a bit hot under the collar. "What will we do?" was the Provençal's answer, "Why, we'll do without it." Unable to suppress a smile at such repartee, the bourgeois ended up by granting what at first he had refused.

Here is an example of grit in the same Provençal. In the Blackfoot country there is a job—that of horse keeper—which might seem more fitted for a child than for a man. But to do it properly requires both spunk and alertness because horse thieves are always on the prowl. The job is usually given to someone who has backbone and misses nothing. Well, the Provençal got the job and he fulfilled it as honorably as he had all the others that had been entrusted to him, so much so that I heard nothing but praise for him from all those who knew him. On more than one occasion he saved the herd and himself with it. Then one day he came back to the fort earlier than usual, and, like a noble knight in the days of yore, all he was able to say was: "All is lost except honor." What had happened? After seeing his companion killed, he was able to put the murderers to flight, but only after they had mounted the horses he was guarding. The proof, however, that he had done more than his duty in this situation was that, although his right arm had been fractured by a bullet, he held high in his left a bear knife. Now among the Blackfeet a captured bear knife is the same as the cavalry colors among the Western peoples. I met later the Indian who was responsible for the loss of the Provençal's arm in my lodge. The Provençal walked in at the same time. Now one would think that the sight of the assassin would have given rise to some feeling of vengeance in him, but he was the first to tell the Indian that he had nothing to fear, that a Frenchman knew how to fight on the battlefield but that in camp he could forgive.

The Provençal's Departure Now I must bring to an end a story I have dwelt on with some delight: my account of the gallant Provençal. As his advanced years, his filial piety, his love of country, the voice of religion—in a word, the most noble reasons compelled him to think of returning to his native land, his friends took up a collection to defray his traveling expenses. Their generosity is all the more remarkable in that these were the same men who, two months earlier, had taken up a collection in favor of the missionary. Twenty-five francs were collected for him. His conduct and the services he has rendered me surpass all of my expressions of appreciation and praise. Anyway, he deserves honorable mention here, and I feel I would lack gratitude did I not pay him this tribute. His name was Honoré Arnault.[1]

May 24. Feast of Our Lady Help of Christians. The ice all about us indicates that during the last two nights the thermometer has dropped forty-three degrees, a variation due to a cold air current sweeping in over the flat coastline. These flat banks, when wooded, are called points because they are often triangular, their apex jutting wedgelike into the river. They are more or less separated from one another by barren strips; however from the great island to the Musselshell River there are twenty-four of them, all clustered close together. Grazing animals like to take refuge in this area because of the coolness of its shade and because of its grasslands. Every hour of the day we can see several herds at close range.

To our right we see what is left of a house built during the winter of 1845 by A. [Augustin] Hamel, presently interpreter at the Blackfeet's fort, Fort Clay. He built the house there because the cold weather had made it impossible for him to proceed further up the river.[2] Nearby, through the cottonwood trees on the left bank we can see the bluish hue of Rock Mountain, called by the Indians Wolf Mountain because of the great number of wolves there.[3] Their presence means there is an abundance of buffalo and deer in the vicinity, for these gentlemen have a taste for big game.

All of a sudden the passengers' attention is irresistibly drawn to a nearby hill. What attracts them? A buffalo cow and her calf are being ruthlessly chased by a wolf pack. Immediately the barge stops to rescue them. The hunter jumps off onto the shore, the captain follows and so do I, in order to witness what could be a good deed. So as not to be detected, we go around the hill behind which the attack is taking place and there, unnoticed, we watch the dramatic scene of a desperate struggle, of ferocity sharpened by hunger, doing battle with bravery, sustained by maternal love. A thunder of rifles, a burst of ammunition, the murderers flee. Their victim, worthy alas of a better fate, falls a few feet from her calf. Poor little one, though showing a wound near your heart, you are still alive. But what will you do now that you no longer have a mother? Let the hunter solve that one. Just as he rescued the mother so will he deliver the son: he will bring death to both. Such is the tenderness of the hunter!

On these verdant shores I see the most beautiful flowers I have seen since our departure. There is one that is star shaped, blue with shades of pink, that delicately arrange its clusters around a pyramid-shaped stem along which sprouts, at regular intervals, twin leaves that gradually diminish in size as they ascend. Another is like lupin but simpler. It has beautiful yellow petals and pale green leaves shaped like clover. In honor of the feast, I call the first *Auxilienne* "Helper" and the second *Mariana* or *Printanière des Pied-noirs,* "Blackfeets' spring flower," because I had already seen it around Fort Lewis right after the end of winter.

A short way below this place juts out Dry Point, so-called because of the blanched tree trunks that cover the ground, some still standing, others fallen or leaning on similar ruins. This funeral tableau following the spectacle of the flowers is suggestive of Poussin's painting depicting the athletic fields. . . .

> . . . under the elms
> and near them a tomb where these words are written:
> "And I, I too was a shepherd in Arcadia."

The scene arouses in the soul a vague feeling of kinship because there is nothing that dies that is entirely foreign to us.[4] Further down the river we come across the remains of a sacrifice offered but a short time before. The rich trappings that tell us what it was are yet hanging from the cradle of branches that served as its altar. The Blackfeet Bloods had made this sacrifice to the sun before going to war against the Assiniboines, doubtless to ask this god to heat up their courage. But all they achieved from their expedition was to come back frozen with fear and almost dead from the cold.

May 26. We are now in sight of the round-shaped butte that separates the Blackfeet fort from that of the Assiniboines. It differs only from other buttes in its height and form. It is round and flattened on the summit, giving it the appearance of an upside down vat. A large tree located on one side looks like a plume to shade its head.[5]

Near the barge we observe felled trees, their branches stripped of bark; then we see wood arranged in piles, and finally we observe an animal displaying four very white teeth, a decidedly flat tail and hand-like paws. All of these are indications we are near a beaver haunt. Everyone knows of the industry, the cleanliness, and the gentle disposition of this animal, which has also such great commercial value. I would just like to advise hat-makers that, thanks to the substitution of silk for pelts in their shops, these animals, almost extinct in these parts, shall soon return to what they were in former days.

We watch a fawn on the shore that the barge children chase, then catch and hug. They would like to make it a playmate, but we reason that without its mother's milk it cannot survive, and so it will have to be dispatched. Consequently, the cook's knife does its work. Soon there is a sadder spectacle in a larger arena. No longer is it a question of one little one, but of the great and powerful lords of the wilderness. Now a huge herd of deer covering the slopes has to endure continuous firing from all of the barges. What will become of them, trapped as they are between our gunfire and the inaccessible river embankment? One animal, hit in the heart, drifts down with the current; another, trying to hide, gets entangled in a mass of branches. Some find no way out without braving the threat of death: the nimble leap up the embankment as if they were taking it by assault. Finally, all that have not been butchered or mortally wounded disappear, leaving to man the honor of his victory. Honor indeed! If only such a slaughter served some useful purpose—but no, we have more meat than we need and so they are killed for the thrill of killing with no thought as to whether in ten years those living in the wilderness would have anything more than roots to eat, or if even roots will be left. Roots are a rarity where buffalo abound; there is only grass.

May 27. Wind, fog, and rain. Nature's mourning is interrupted only by a symphony of cheerless sounds. There are always creatures that live only by preying on others. Here it is principally wolves. So, it is always a treat for the barge children when some wolf gets blasted, and that takes place often enough, thanks to our little interpreter's skill and his antipathy for these animals. In the evening Providence directs such a great number of catfish to our fishing hooks that there is a surfeit of food for all of the tables.

May 28. We greet the Milk River, so called because of the whiteness of its waters, although this color is noticeable only when the water level is low. Because it is such a sizeable tributary, the Missouri widens, while the mountains are lower and farther away. There is a majestic feeling in this wider perspective. In the evening Mr. Culbertson presents a "nun"; that is, a white-headed eagle, to the missionary for the honor of being painted. Although this one was a female, the "King of the Air" is depicted where it received its mortal wound, that is under the walls of its palace.

May 29. We are at Eagle's Nest, a place associated with a pleasant memory. Here, at the foot of the tree where they constructed it, the eldest daughter of our pilot, little Josette, was born eight years ago. Several rows of trees, so symmetrically aligned that they might have been planted by a royal gardener, adorn the vicinity of this cradle, adding even more to its nobility. But even this beauty is surpassed by the excellent qualities of the child born here. Except for those times when they were on the river during the month of May, she and her younger sister Marie went every day to place at the feet of the Blessed Virgin the most beautiful flowers they could find from the fields or little wreaths that they would make with their own hands. What gave the wreaths greater value than the flowers was that each wreath or crown cost the girls some virtuous act, and each segment of the wreath was purchased with a prayer. These two little girls were also the first to crown with flowers the cross that today rises aloft over the land of the Blackfeet.[6]

To our left, more ruins—all that remains of a fort a dozen whites, survivors of the 1844 opposition company, were forced to defend themselves against the Assiniboines. When this company withdrew, these men were not interested in leaving; they felt like having a taste of the Indians' freedom. But, either because they were not born to it and therefore could not make the necessary adaptations, or because they would not accept any other guide than their own whims and therefore could not come to an agreement among themselves, the fact is that just as they decided to come together so they decided to disperse, with the exception of a Canadian named Dupuis. The Assiniboines later killed him. Of course, it was an unfortunate mishap, but some good came from it: it brought good fortune to a child he had fathered by an Indian woman. I call it good fortune because otherwise the child would not have died the holy death it did, after having been baptized, at Fort Lewis.[7]

Still the 29th: Our flotilla almost had a serious accident. The wind, gustier than usual, tossed one of our barges against a tree, which penetrated both sides of it. But thanks to the skill and energy of our rowers the rest of the crew managed to unload 3,600 furs before the water got to them, and soon the damage was repaired. The pilot told us that not one of a hundred barges damaged like this could be saved. Our accident occurred almost at the same spot where, fifteen years before, a supply barge had sunk. The loss of that cargo was estimated at $10,000, but that was not the worst of it. Because the disaster took place at night, and on a very dark night, and because the barge struck the shore with a great force, some while jumping from the boat, which was drifting very rapidly along the banks, were injured, more or less seriously. A Canadian named Benoit was crushed between the barge's side and the riverbank. An eight-year-old child was drowned in his bed and an Indian woman saved her life by jumping into the middle of the river. Michel Champagne, then as now the barge's owner, was hurled ashore by a blow from the rudder, fortunately with no worse effect than to make him more aware of the sad plight of the others.

News of the disaster was sent to the bourgeois at Fort Union, who was at the time Mr. McKenzie. He received it with noble resignation. Of course, he deplored the fate of the victims as he should have, but then he said: "Don't come ashore, folks; I have still more supplies for you."

May 30. Dialogue between a young passenger and an old pilot: "Skipper, it seems that over there to the right, beyond the willows, I can see something white like a tiara. Do you know what it is?"

"It is an Indian pyramid."

"An Indian pyramid! But they told me that these fellows had no architecture."

Right. This monument is merely an exception to their careless lifestyle."

"Which Indians had the bright idea to put it up?"

"The Crow."

"The Crow? What an odd name!"

"Odd, but most fitting."

"Oh? Why?"

"Because these Indians are birds of ill omen to their neighbors."

"Why?"

"Because they are at war with almost all of them and their wars are almost always wars of extermination."

"Did they erect this monument by any chance to commemorate some outstanding victory?"

"No. They say it was to propitiate their gods."

"During what period of their history would you say it was constructed?"

"The only recollection the old timers have is that it has always been there."

"It's odd: the closer we come to this curious structure the more mysterious it seems to be. The side facing the sun glistens like silver. Is it made of silver, by any chance?"

"Not quite, but it is made of something almost as durable as silver."

"Marble then?"

"Not at all, it is neither metal nor even mineral."

"What is it, then?"

"Some branches grow like a plant; yet are not part of a plant. They have roots; yet these roots do not penetrate the soil. They belong to the animal kingdom; yet they have no sensation. Now, can you guess what it is?"

"There are buffalo around here. Could it be made of buffalo horns?"

"You are getting warm. It is made of horns all right, but of the kind that are born and die each year. That is why they are not called 'horns' *(cornes)*."

"I get it! They are 'antlers' *(bois)* right? And *bois* (antlers) that are not *bois* (wood)."

"Now you've got it!"

"But why would the architects of this monument choose such an odd material?"

"Because they believe that the stag is a medicine animal."

"Does this mean that this great heap of antlers is a religious monument?"

"That is what they say."

"And the Indian goes there just as we go on a pilgrimage?"

"Very likely."

"And each time he lays down his offering?"

"Yes, at least whenever he finds a stag with a set of antlers. So, thanks to the continuous offerings occasioned by the superstition, the Indian monument has become what you see. The first builders probably just laid its foundation."

"And no one has ever thought of tearing it down?"

"It was destroyed in 1834."

"By whom?"

"Some whites out on a pleasure outing."

"And the Crows didn't avenge their manitou?"

"Others did it for them."

"Who?"

"Fire and water."

"How?"

"First because of lack of water these imprudent navigators had to abandon their boat."

"How had they come here?"

"By steamboat."

"How did they return?"

"In a barge or raft."

"What happened to the poor steamboat?"

"After a year of penance, the water, satisfied with having given her this little lesson, offered to take her back."

"And so the story ends happily for her."

"Hardly. No sooner was she refloated than she was destroyed by fire."

[*Translators note:* Eight verses that are not decipherable in the original have been omitted here.]

Today—still May 30th—is the feast of the Holy Trinity. Thanks be to God and to the goodwill of the crew, I was able to say Holy Mass. What we give to God is never lost. Despite the threat of a contrary wind, the day was almost perfect and the evening delightful. At any rate, I have never seen a more glorious evening. The sun, just about to end his course and wrapped in a transparent haze, had exchanged his blazing gold for the vivid iridescence of the ruby. His fullness was vividly etched against an azure background;

above him, hanging like drapery, were clusters of clouds tinged with purples, blues and velvets, while below a row of giant trees cast tall shadows over the river, bringing out all this beauty in bold relief. What was the crew doing before such a beautiful scene? As the mariners' rapid oars gave our barges the look of so many chariots competing for a racing prize, their wives and children crowded together on the decks, praying and singing hymns in honor of the Queen of the Angels. Never had the wilderness heard sounds such as these. What missionary could remain unmoved, especially on hearing this refrain repeated over and over again:

How blessed are those under her rule!
What delights the pure of heart find there!
Love, innocence, and peace are her gift;
Love, innocence, and peace is their share.

On May 31, a strong wind that picked up force around noon compelled us to halt just a few miles from Fort Union. There, on the right bank, we waited for the good weather that was expected for the next day. I'll let you speculate the subject of our conversations. In a few more hours the fort's canon would answer our barge's canon. Flags would be unfurled; friends would be with one another again, and the bourgeois would vie with one another in showing generosity! What would be a missionary's chief reflection? What sentiment should fill his heart on this the thirty-first of May, the last day of Mary's month! How much did a Rocky Mountain missionary owe to Mary!

Oh Mary, what will he ask of you at the end of a report wherein your name has so often been interwoven with the names of so many Indians that have begun to call you holy. May they always bless you, and in spirit and in truth adore the One in whose name we proclaimed to them their salvation!

Translator's Notes

The events in this essay correspond to Point's description in Donnelly. *Wilderness Kingdom,* 217–25 and in Garraghan's translation in "Journey on a Barge," *Mid-America,* 13 (1930–1) 246–56.

1. The name Honoré Arnault appears frequently as a sponsor for baptisms and as a witness to marriages in Point's records. "Registre des baptêmes et marriages administrés sur la terre des Pieds-Noirs par le P. N. Point missionaire, S.J., depuis 29 septembre 1846 jusqu'à [1847], Mont. Sax. 1.10, ASJR.

2. Point sketched the Hamel house, a reproduction of which appears in Donnelly, *Wilderness Kingdom*, 236.

3. Reference here is most probably to the Little Rocky Mountains in Blaine and Philipps counties.

4. Deleted in the text: "More proofs of human poverty."

5. Most probably Point is describing here one of the Piney Buttes in present-day Garfield County.

6. Point painted the portraits of Marie and Josette, daughters of Michel Champagne and sisters of his "little interpreter," who played so important a role in introducing to the Blackfeet the May devotions practiced at Saint-Acheul, Fribourg, Grand Coteau, and the Rocky Mountain reductions. Donnelly, *Wilderness Kingdom*, 211.

7. Probably Point is referring to the ill-fated Fort Mortimore, mentioned in Excursion 7, n. 7.

CONCLUSION

Nicolas Point remained at Fort Union from May 31 until June 25, the day he boarded the steamship *Martha* bound for St. Louis.[1] The captain of this side-wheeler, the French speaker, Joseph La Barge (1815–1899), refused to allow the missionary to pay a cent for his fare.[2] La Barge was one of the Jesuits' greatest benefactors, and unquestionably the most famous riverboat captain on the Missouri.[3] Gilbert Garraghan asserts that in later years he "was perhaps De Smet's most intimate personal friend among the laity . . ."[4]

In the spring of 1847, two events took place on the *Martha* during its run from St. Louis to where Point picked it up at Fort Union that might well have been auguries. For one thing, some Indians, threatened and made angry by the number of whites pouring into territory west of the Missouri, had indiscriminately shot and killed one of the white deckhands. Up until now there had been periodic clashes between individual Indians and whites but with the beginning of the Cayuse War in 1848 until the end of the Nez

Percé war in 1877 the United States federal government became totally involved in pacifying the newly acquired Oregon country pouring millions of pre-Civil War dollars into this enterprise which would radically alter the relationship between the various tribes and the white man. Moreover, Captain La Barge had brought his wife with him, the first white woman to journey up the river from old Fort Lisa, modern day Omaha, to Fort Union. This was a sign of the opening up of that vast wilderness empire to a new emigrant—the white woman. During the next thirty years it was she who would tame, domesticate, pacify and forever transform that wilderness where only trappers, traders, mountain men and missionaries had penetrated, in ways more effectual and permanent than cavalry charges and federal armies. As for the Indians at Fort Union, they did not know what to make of her, such a strange creature she seemed to be—they had to touch her to make sure she was real.[5] These two events indicate that Point was leaving a land that would soon be ineluctably and forever changed and that he was returning to a St. Louis that reflected the quality and acceleration of changes that had already taken place during the seven years he was absent. These changes were of such a nature as to render his dreams of establishing Paraguay-type reductions among the Indians on both sides of the Rockies as curious as the fossil he had picked up on the Kansas plain in 1841, an object in which he saw incontrovertible proof of the account in Genesis of the flood. As the *Martha* chugged down the river, Point, who had been so impressed by celestial foretokens of an age of grace for the Blackfeet—luminous phenomena of streamers, arches, and crosses in the winter skies—was probably not aware of the events on the *Martha* as clear signs of a new age.

On June 29, at Fort Pierre, where the Cheyenne joins the Missouri, he baptized a number of children, just as he had at Fort Union earlier in the month and as he would do at Bellevue on July 5.[6] He was, after all, a missionary, and, as Francis Xavier had shown in action and words, the work of a missionary never stopped. On the previous day, he recorded having passed the Mormon winter quarters opposite

Council Bluffs, in what is today Omaha, and noted that there were three hundred followers of Brigham Young who had not as yet made the journey to the Great Salt Lake Basin.[7] At Bellevue he addressed a letter to the vice-provincial in St. Louis:

> I received, as you probably know, permission to return to my province and Reverend Father De Smet, who wrote to me about this matter, told me that he had advised my brother, who is the superior at Sandwich parish, that I will soon be with him. Without doubt I have, before leaving a province with which I have had such close bonds during the past ten years, many good reasons to bid farewell to you in person, but what seems to me to prevail over all considerations of my personal satisfaction is the fear that my presence at St. Louis will be an occasion of controversy for people opposed to the [American] Fur Company.[8]

This letter is definitely a farewell message. The author asks Van de Velde that his interpreter, Jean Baptiste Champagne, who was of invaluable aid to him among the Blackfeet, be given free board and room at St. Louis College until the next steamer left for the Yellowstone. The reasons Point gives Van de Velde for the embarrassment his presence at St. Louis could cause are understandable. His admitted admiration for Malcolm Clark, the clerk at Fort Lewis and arch-enemy of Charles Larpenteur, could reasonably be a source of embarrassment to the Jesuits anxious to maintain good relations with officials in both the American Fur Company and Harvey, Primeau and Company.

Two days after he wrote this letter the *Martha* sailed past Westport, which he designated Kansas, and there too, even though it looked the same, much had changed at his old mission.[9] For one thing, a woman who had a grudge against John Grey's family determined to take revenge against Grey himself. Even though in 1841 the old Iroquois guide could have taken on four bears at one time, he was no match for the fury of this woman who succeeded in making his wife, Marianne Hatchiorauquacha, a widow. And if this were not enough, the river had flooded, washing away Marianne's house.[10] Among the fifty-four pencil-drawings Point did on the journey from Fort Lewis to St. Louis there is one sketch depicting a house, like Marianne's, the victim of the rushing waters.[11] Like the Grey's house, Westport itself had become a part of a world that was breaking up and that could never be the same. Even so, there was some ironic relief: Marianne, the one-time pillar of the Sodality of the Seven Sorrows and the valiant woman who forded the Platte to prove to Gregory Mengarini and the others that fears about the unknown were generally imaginary, would soon become the sacristan at St. Francis Regis where she adopted the custom of carrying a big stick and challenging anyone near the church that she judged to be suspicious.[12]

In the summer of 1847 the *Martha* inexorably continued her journey, past Jefferson City, where, from her deck, Point sketched the impressive state capitol building, and past St. Charles, Missouri, where his pen and ink captured Philippine Duchesne's Convent of the Sacred Heart, the place where his sister may have been stationed, and finally to the busy, exciting port of St. Louis, where the *Martha* docked after her long journey.

At St. Louis, Point made his report to Father Vice-Provincial James Van de Velde, who, in turn, informed Roothaan in a letter dated August 5, that "Reverend Father Point arrived here from the territory of the Blackfeet, where he accomplished much good, baptizing almost six hundred persons. But he only remained at St. Louis a few days. He has already left for Sandwich, Canada."[13] Pierre Point wrote that Nicolas

> believed he should begin his new mission with a sacrifice. He had received permission to visit his sister, a religious of the Sacred Heart at St. Charles. It would have been a great consolation for him to see her, as well as his dear mission at Grand Coteau, but he preferred to make a sacrifice to the Sacred Heart. He went straight to his new post where they scarce expected him because they thought he had been drowned in Oregon crossing a river. His unattended arrival could not have been more joyous.[14]

For those who can understand Nicolas Point's spirituality, no explanation for his seemingly inhuman decision not to visit his sister and to refrain from traveling to Grand Coteau is needed, and, for those who cannot understand, no explanation is possible.

Father Ambroise Rubillon, Provincial of France, had written to the general on January 11, 1846, five months after Roothaan had authorized Joset to dismiss Point from the society, declaring, "I have confidence that Father Nicolas Point will recover bit by bit. His heart is excellent; his dedication without limits; his head has never been very steady [la tête n'a jamais été bien fort]. He shall have his good and holy brother as superior."[15] Although no correspondence with Rubillon during this period is extant, undoubtedly Point had been in contact with his provincial whom he considered, and with justifiable reason, his true superior, and just as he had requested in his letter to Roothaan that he be separated from the "Belgian" mission and attached to the newly established French mission to the Indians in Canada, so it is reasonable to conclude that he had made the same request to Rubillon. The slowness of the mail had almost resulted in a personal tragedy for Point and ultimately for the society, but fortunately for both, Providence had placed a man, Joseph Joset, in charge of the Rocky Mountain Mission. Ironically, Joset had been described by one of his subjects as a man "without a sense of the practical," and when the general referred to him he did so as "Pauvre Père Joset! Il n'a pas la tête."[16]

Ambroise Rubillon declared one reason why he had confidence in Point's future was because his new superior, his brother Pierre Point, knew Nicolas better than anyone else. Originally Pierre had been elected, along with Luiset, to be one of the founding fathers of the Madagascar Mission; however, the exigencies that gave priority to Canada, which were described above, added to the ecclesiastical red tape that kept the Jesuits out of Madagascar until late 1844, prompted Roothaan to change Pierre's assignment.[17] For these reasons, then, Nicolas Point's classmates, Pierre Cotain, Ambroise Neyraguet, and Romain Dénieau, rather than his brother and Paul Luiset, became the chartered members of the Madagascar Mission.[18] It so happens that when Pierre Chazelle led Félix Martin, Paul Luiset and the other three priests and three brothers to Canada in 1843, Pierre Point was doing a biennium, or an additional year of theological studies; therefore, he did not make his appearance in Canada until 1843.[19]

As soon as the first wave of French Jesuits arrived in Montreal on May 31, 1843, Chazelle gave evidence of his extraordinary organizing abilities. On May 8 of that same year, Michael Power (1804–1847), former pastor at Laprairie, across from Montreal, had been ordained bishop and appointed to the newly created see of Toronto. He invited Chazelle to take charge of his former parish, and so by July a church and a novitiate, both under the direction of Paul Luiset, were established.[20] Laprairie is a particularly rich area in Jesuit history because it was here that the first reduction for the Iroquois was established in 1647, and it was the place hallowed by the grave of Kateri Tekakawitha.[21] As early as September, Father Master Luiset had accepted the first candidates to the society into a novitiate which, if it did not resemble Montrouge externally, emulated the spirit which had so distinguished that house where Father Master had received his own training.[22] Meanwhile, in preparation for opening an Indian mission, Chazelle had sent two of his men to learn the language of a tribe north of Quebec.[23] Bishop Power had requested that Chazelle show his appreciation for Laprairie by assisting him in his diocese in Upper Canada, where priests were so sorely needed.[24] Chazelle complied and in September accepted responsibility for the management of the parish at Sandwich. He promised the bishop that as soon as Pierre Point arrived from France, he would be dispatched to take charge of that mission.[25]

In making this decision to accept the parish at Sandwich, Chazelle again was inspired by the rich tradition of Jesuit history. A reduction was first established on this spot in 1747 by the Jesuit Pierre Potier (1708–1781). It was to serve the Huron Indians, and was given the rather pretentious name of L'Assomption-de-la Pointe-de-Montréal-du-Détroit, or Assomption for short. After the old priest's death, which occurred during the time of the Suppression, the mission for all practical purposes went unattended.[26] Then in 1797, after the British had ceded Detroit to the Americans, loyalists crossed the Detroit River, settled on what was called South Side, and then renamed Assomption, Sandwich, arguing that if this village was to replace Detroit as the capital of the Western District it should bear the name of an English city.[27] In 1847, the year Pierre Point reactivated this Jesuit church, the population of Sandwich had reached an impressive 450 inhabitants, and the Catholics were divided between the indigent French and the Irish immigrants.[28] In 1935 Sandwich was incorporated into Windsor, the southernmost city in Ontario, the town which today is separated from Detroit, Michigan, by the Detroit River.[29]

From Sandwich, Chazelle established the first French Province Indian Mission on Walpole, a ten-by-four mile island in the Saint Clair River, the waterway that, together with Lake St. Clair and the Detroit River, joins Lakes Huron and Erie. In 1843, the Indian population of Walpole was about 1,150. It was here that the famous Tecumseh, brother of the Kickapoo Prophet, was put to rest after his defeat at Moravian Town on October 5, 1813.[30] After setting up the Walpole mission, Chazelle began surveying the Great Lakes for more possible mission sites, particularly sites on Manitoulin Island at Georgian Bay in the northern part of Lake Huron, where the Jesuits had had missions during the seventeenth century.[31] It was on Grand Manitoulin, the one hundred mile long and forty mile wide island, that he decided to found the second Indian mission. There were five villages on this island, which is the world's largest island surrounded by fresh water, the most important of which was Wikwemikong.[32] By this date it had become clear to Chazelle that there were two markedly different orientations that were taking shape in this vast area under his jurisdiction. The needs in Lower Canada, from Montreal to the Atlantic, were city parishes, retreat houses, and *collèges* similar to those in Europe and in the Europeanized parts of the United States. But in Upper Canada, that is, from Sandwich to points west, the needs of the Indians were the greatest priority. He represented this problem to Roothaan and accordingly, on July 31, 1844, the general signed a decree dividing into two districts the territorially vast Canadian Mission and designating Félix Martin the first superior of Lower Canada, that is Quebec, and Chazelle remained superior in Upper Canada.[33] As we have seen, Martin founded first the *petit collège* Saint Marie (1848–1851) in Montreal and later, (1851–1587), he expanded this instution to include the *grand collège*.

Chazelle, carrying on the traditional missionary apostolate of the society in the west, faced the perennial problem that bedeviled all of the missions—lack of quantatative and qualified manpower. In the summer of 1845 two more priests came to join his team, and that same summer Clément Boulanger, the former French provincial, was sent as a special visitor by Rubillon to visit all houses and establishments in North America under the jurisdiction of the Province of France. Jean-Baptiste Hus was appointed his companion and collaborator.[34] These two men evaluated the Sandwich enterprise, and with their encouragement Chazelle began a third mission at Sault Ste. Marie, the waterway between Lake Superior and Lake Huron.[35] This post on the St. Mary's River resonated in the minds of French Jesuits, for Isaac Jogues preached to the Indians there in 1641 and in 1688 Jacques Marquette founded on the south side of the falls the first permanent settlement in what became the state of Michigan.[36] That the Jesuits were eagerly sought by the Indians spurred on plans to reopen this mission. Eighteen years earlier, in 1826, an Indian chief contrasted the treatment of his people by the French with the way the Americans were treating them.

> When the French arrived at these falls they came and kissed us. They called us children and we found fathers. We lived like brethren in the same lodge and we always had wherewithal to clothe us. They never mocked our ceremonies, and they never molested the places of our dead. Seven generations of men have passed away and we have not forgotten it. Just, very just were they toward us.[37]

No doubt grievances of the Indians in the 1820s made the period they lived under the French more pleasant than it really was, but in 1670–71 there were as many as twenty Jesuit missions among as many tribes in the Great Lakes area, and the educational interests of many of the fathers were similar to those of Nicolas Point; moreover, the tactics they employed to convert the Indians were utilized by Point in the Rocky Mountains in the 1840s. Father Louis André (1631–1715) presents a fascinating comparison. This man came to Canada in 1669, labored as an Indian missionary until 1684 when he was assigned to be a professor at the Jesuit *collège* in Quebec. Like Point he saw no contradiction between purely academic and missionary activity: the essence was the same, the modality different. In 1690 André was back again in the forests with the Indians. Although, unlike Point, he did not paint, he could, again unlike Point, play the flute, and so using French country melodies of his native Lyonnais he composed songs in the Indian tongue, taught them to the children, and then organized bands of these young people to go from village to village attacking the jugglers and those who practiced polygamy, and seemingly, he rendered the catechism into singable melodies.[38]

Louis André had done much of his missionary work at St. Francis Xavier Mission, present-day De Pere on the Fox River, near Green Bay, Wisconsin.[39] This was the last mission Père Jacques Marquette (1637–1675) and Louis Jolliet (1648–1700) had visited in 1673 before they made their way up the Fox River, then down the Wisconsin—the exploration that led them to the discovery of the Mississippi; thereby opening up the west to the missionaries, the *voyageurs,* the *coureurs de bois,* and the French flag.[40] It was to this same site that Chazelle determined to visit in August 1845 in order to investigate the possibilities of reestablishing St. Francis Xavier. Accordingly he departed from Sandwich on the eighteenth bound for Sault Ste. Marie via Green Bay.[41] At Green Bay he caught a cold that quickly developed into pneumonia and on September 4, 1845, he died, passing the flag which had been handed to him by Issac

Jogues, John de Brebeuf, Louis André, Jacques Marquette, Pierre Potier, and many others, to Pierre Point, the newly appointed superior of the Upper Canada Mission.

In 1845, the year Fathers Clément Boulanger and Jean-Baptiste Hus arrived in New York to evaluate the Paris missions in North America, Archbishop John J. Hughes (1797–1864) offered the Paris Jesuits St. John's College, outside New York City. They accepted in the name of the Provincial of France. This decision necessitated abandoning St. Mary's College, which William Byrne had begun in a Kentucky stillhouse in 1821 and at which Nicolas Point had served as principal in 1836. Three years later, in the summer of 1848, the Missouri vice-province assumed responsibility for operating St. Joseph's College, Bardstown, Kentucky, and Peter Verhaegen was named its first Jesuit president. Verhaegen immediately made a most favorable impression on everyone at Bardstown. Besides being a man of unquestionable charm, he was also "remarkable for his kindness and liberality, both to the religious community and to the students." The first serious problem he encountered was with seventeen students "most of them from Mississippi," and all of them non-Catholics. They objected to the president's regulation that they kneel in the *collège* chapel during mass and public prayers. Like another trouble-making group that emerged the following year, "they were brought up . . . on the banks of the lower Mississippi where the worst inclined of them had acquired something of the profane dialect, and the ruffian manners of the steamboat rousterbouts." These students and the president could not come to terms and so the rebels "seceded as a body" from St. Joseph's.[42] There is something ironic in the defiance of these students and in the consequent intransigence of Verhaegen, particularly when one remembers Chazelle's complaint about Point's lack of firmness with Kentucky boys who were inclined to riot at St. Mary's, and when one remembers that although he did not always work well with other Jesuits, Nicolas Point did enjoy a reputation among friend and foe for getting along well with the students at Grand Coteau and with the steamboat rousterbouts on the

Missouri. But there is another anecdote which is even more poignant. Bishop Flaget had intended to make over the property at Bardstown to the Jesuits in fee-simple, and Verhaegen, contemptuous of the suggestion on the part of many in the Jesuit community that he employ a lawyer to draw up the deed of transfer, composed the document himself. This document hardly reflected the intention of the donor and when, after the old bishop's death, the mistake was realized, the scene was set for a long act in which charges and counter-charges were made by the Missouri vice-province and the Louisville diocese. "God does not bestow all good gifts on any one man," Walter Hill observed, "even if he is a saint; among Father Verhaegen's excellent gifts and acquisitions was not that of a great business capacity."[43] This observation might balance off with Verhaegen's opinion, expressed to Bishop Rosati, concerning Point's naivete in business matters. And then, too, there were frequent complaints made to Rome between 1838 and 1840 that Point often acted on his own.

After the Jesuits left Bardstown, St. Joseph's soon fell into disrepair; St. Mary's, however, continued to thrive.[44] It was purchased by the Resurrectionist fathers who kept it as a school. Later it became a seminary restricted to young men and boys intent on the priesthood. In 1977 the number of candidates for the priesthood had declined to such an extent that the seminary had become redundant. It was sold to a hippie group from San Francisco called the Cornucopias. It has been asserted the new proprietors did not maintain the buildings and grounds in a manner that would have won for them encomiums from William Byrne, Pierre Chazelle, and William Stack Murphy. The Cornucopias sold what was left of the *collège* to the state. St. Mary's now serves the community as a prison.

Blows dealt St. Charles College, Grand Coteau, after Point left in 1840 proved nearly fatal to the institution he had begun in 1837. The number of students had dropped to thirty-seven during the 1842–43 session, "and even they do not pay," complained Soller. In 1844–45 the number increased from twenty-three to sixty-three; in 1848–46 it went up to ninety-seven, but then in 1847–48 the student population dipped to eighty-six. In January 1847, the vice provincial informed Roothaan that the memory of Point, who at that time was making various excursions to the Blackfeet camps, continued to haunt Grand Coteau where Abbadie wanted to implement his famous plan of studies in its pristine purity. Abbadie had reintroduced Greek to the curriculum and there were other changes that he hoped to make. Van de Velde further informed the general that the Missouri fathers wanted to pull out of St. Charles, that he himself was "sick and tired of all the meddling of Clément Boulanger who continues to write to Fathers Duranquet and Mignard as if they were members of [the province of] France, as they claim they are." The presence of the Visitor Boulanger was understandably a source of annoyance to Van de Velde because a number of the French Jesuits in Missouri were attracted, as Point had been, to the new French missions in Canada and New York. "The love of charity and peace," concluded Van de Velde, "compels me to beg your Paternity to annul the decree of annexation [of Louisiana to Missouri]." This had already been effected and at that very time the first six Jesuits from the Lyon Province arrived in Mobile to reactivate Spring Hill College. Then, in February, Father Abbadie became rector and president of St. Charles.

If St. Charles did not prosper during Abbadie's rectorship, it did manage to stay afloat. In 1857 a new building was erected beside Point's structure, but the architects did not follow Point's grandiose design for what was to be the Louisiana Fribourg with its elegant *Pensionnat*. During the Reconstruction period the two *collèges* of the New Orleans Mission, Grand Coteau and Spring Hill, suffered from the economic and moral depression that devastated the South. In 1868, the year of Point's death, the decision was made to close St. Charles in order to assure the continuance of Spring Hill, but that year a fire destroyed the Spring Hill campus and Point's building was spared the indignity of remaining empty.

After 1872 the building served first as a novitiate and then as a scholasticate. Michael Kenny, who was a scholastic there in 1893, described Point's building as a four-story edifice built "in ante-bellum style with its heavy Doric columns supporting the gabled verandas; but additions were made to the original building, and these though comfortable and commodius enough are of no style in particular."[45] Another eye witness said:

> It was an imposing building on account of its height, its vast galleries and rows of gigantic pillars. It was to be the first of a series of buildings in the plan of its architect, Father Point, S.J.; but the plan was never carried to completion. It was not a comfortable building, and the large halls of which it originnally consisted, made poor living rooms when partitioned off.[46]

In 1900 a fire destroyed the three story building that had been constructed in 1857, and this necessitated moving the scholasticate once again. Point's building then became a day school for local boys and a house of retirement for elderly and infirm Jesuits.

Early in 1907 it was decided to reopen St. Charles as a boarding *collège*, but on July 8, fire again visited the campus; this time claiming the nearly seventy-year-old building put up by Point in 1838. By 1909 a new building, designed to accommodate two hundred boarders, was completed and St. Charles again became a boarding *collège*, but by 1922 the student population had fallen off dramatically and the *collège* was forced to close its doors. Since that date the building that replaced Point's edifice and the *collège* he founded have served as the novitiate for the New Orleans Province. It is significant that besides being a *collège* in 1838, St. Charles was also a Jesuit novitiate under the direction of Father Rector Nicolas Point and Father Master Peter De Vos, and that one hundred and fifty years later it is still a Jesuit novitiate. There may be other novitiates of the society somewhere in the world (certainly not in the United States) that can claim to be older but research has not revealed their identity.[47]

The year 1847, when Point detached himself from the mission, was the year that began the period of the great foreclosure, and between 1847 and 1852, the Rocky Mountain Mission underwent a crisis from which it never fully recovered. In April 1852, Father General Jan Roothaan bewailed this condition of the mission to De Smet:

> It seems that the idea of renewing the miracles of Paraguay amid those mountains was a Utopia. In the first place, we could not hope for the means which our Fathers received from the Crowns of Spain and Portugal. Then, it was impossible to keep the whites at a distance; then, too, the nature of the land is quite different and one cannot hope to wean the bulk of the savages from their nomadic life during a great part of the year when they are on the hunt and scattered and disbanded, some to the right and some to the left . . . I declare, my dear Father, I don't see how one can have any success at all. And where should we get the necessary men and resources! The Willamette farm has also been a stink hole. In fine, I don't see how these missions can be kept up. May the Lord enlighten us![48]

Pessimistic words these, but here was reason for discouragement. In November 1847, not long after Point had arrived among the Blackfeet, the Protestant missionary Marcus Whitman and his party were massacred at Waiilatpu thereby triggering the Cayuse Indian War and a wave of anti-Catholic feeling in the Oregon Territory.[49] There was also a morale problem among the missionaries for which De Smet placed the blame on the new batch of Jesuits.[50] As was shown earlier, there were certainly more nationalistic tensions that manifested themselves among the missionaries who arrived after 1843. Then, during the course of 1849 gold was discovered in California, causing an exodus from the territory to California. As far as the individual missions were concerned, St. Mary's seemed to fare the worst. Death took one Venetian Jesuit, Pietro Zerbinatti (1809–1845), sent to assist Mengarini and, although the dead man's replacement, Father Anthony Ravalli, (b. Ferrara, Italy, May 16, 1812; d. Stevensville, Montana, October 2, 1884), one of the five Jesuits who rounded Cape Horn with De Smet in 1844, and Montana's first medical doctor, was considered a saint and a healer by both Indians and settlers, he was not at that date a Peter De Smet or a Nicolas Point.[51] But even if he had been, one wonders how effective he could have been; so much had changed after 1847. Ravalli, as a matter of fact, pointed the finger of blame for St. Mary's woes at De Smet and, by association, at Point.[52] Roothaan seems to have held Joset responsible, and Father Aloysius Vercruysse (b. Coutrais, Oost-Flaanderen, Belgium, February 3, 1796; d. Coutrais, July 12, 1867), another one of the group who had accompanied De Smet around Cape Horn in 1844, a "good religious," but also "brusque, irritable, impatient, and highly imaginative," placed the blame for the demise of St. Mary's Reduction squarely on the shoulders of the timid Mengarini, whom he stops just short of calling a coward.[53]

But the reasons were infinitely more complex than they appeared to the eyes of contemporary witnesses. The Flatheads had been unduly influenced by the growing number of whites, frequently of the lowest quality, who settled in the mission area and who chided the Indians for following the counsel of the Black Robes.[54] Point had been able to recognize and dissipate the restless spirit among young braves, a fact to which the letters in this volume give adequate testimony. Such spirit was usually hatched during the annual hunts, when the tribe was away from the mission compound, but since 1847 there was no Jesuit available to accompany the Flatheads on these hunts, and therefore conduct incompatible with the Black Robes' teaching was given full reign. Mengarini was too timid and his many phobias prevented him from participating in the hunts; seemingly, Ravalli's services were judged to be of more value at St. Mary's. Faced with the vicious rumors spread about the Jesuits by the young, who more and more showed contempt for the reduction system and for religious practices, Mengarini appealed to Victor to avenge the Black Robes and to reinstate discipline within the tribe, only to be met with: *"Tas misten!"* (What can I do!).[55] Like many timid personalities under pressure, Mengarini apparently became dictatorial, an attitude which had a counter-productive effect on the elders of the tribe. Then, on September 7, 1850, during Mengarini's absence from St. Mary's, a party of fifty Blackfeet attacked the compound, killing some mission retainers, stealing horses, and terrifying Ravalli. This incidence convinced Mengarini that the lives of the Jesuits were at stake and, granting his request, Joset gave him the order, on November 5, 1850, to withdraw from St. Mary's.[56] Joset's reasoning seems to have been that just as in 1847–1848 he had given the Coeur d'Alène the option either to get rid of Stellam or face the closure of Sacred Heart, so, too, Mengarini could force the issue with the Flatheads.

But this time the gamble did not work. Mengarini closed the mission—it was intended to be temporary—and sold the buildings to an entrepreneur, John Owens, who turned the reduction that Point had designed into a trading post.[57] The church furniture, records, and presumably Point's carvings and Huet's monstrance, were lost when the raft carrying them capsized in the Clark's Fork.[58] At the Flatheads' request the mission was reopened in September 1854, but not at the same place. At that date the Kalispel mission of St. Ignatius, founded in 1844 by De Vos and Hoecken and relocated the following year by De Smet, moved from the Clark's Fork, near present-day Cusick, Washington, to what is now St. Ignatius, Montana. Transplanted, St. Ignatius became the new Flathead mission. John Owens's trading post eventually became Stevensville in Ravalli County, Montana.[59] Father Wilfred Schoenberg records in *Jesuits in Montana* that the epitaph over Ravalli's grave at the site which Point had designed and which was for a time called St. Mary's Reduction, reads: "Here was the first white settlement in Montana; here was the first permanent human habitation builded [*sic*] in this great state. And the first settlers were men of God. Few commonwealths have had such an auspicious beginning."[60] It is a fitting tribute.

Roothaan's pessimistic words did not pertain to the Coeur d'Alène mission. There have been a number of reasons suggested for such being the case. For geographical reasons Sacred Heart was not as vulnerable as St. Mary's to subversive influences from the whites and to terrifying raids from the Blackfeet. Moreover, Joset, who had resolved the problem which had gotten out of hand at St. Mary's by his ultimatum to the tribe during the final Stellam crisis, had achieved an authority which was lacking at St. Mary's. Indeed, the unobtrusive, vacillating Joseph Joset would assume a heroic leadership during the Indian Wars of 1858 which would justifiably win him the respect of Indians and whites far beyond the territory of the Sacred Heart Mission.[61] But De Smet may have given an additional reason for the success of Sacred Heart in a thirty-one page report he sent the general in 1845. This report lavishes praise on Nicolas Point and attributes to him the reason why the Coeur d'Alène were the best and most thoroughly instructed of all the tribes.[62] This was also the opinion of Hoecken and Vercruysse.[63] During his short time with the Coeur d'Alène Point had succeeded in implementing the concepts of *instruction* and *éducation* in a remarkable way. De Smet's testimony and the consequent history of the Coeur d'Alène during the period between 1847 and 1851 make the treatment Point received from his superiors between 1843 and 1847 appear even more tragically unfortunate.

One of these superiors was Peter De Vos, the man whose destiny had been linked so closely with his own since both men were together at Saint-Acheul in 1825, the year before Point entered Montrouge the second time. As we have seen, De Vos became superior of St. Francis Xavier on the Willamette at the end of 1844.[64] He was the only Jesuit priest in the Willamette country who could speak English, and perhaps this was one reason why Blanchet appointed him administrator of the vicariate when he left Oregon City to be ordained bishop. But there were other reasons too. De Vos was an exemplary priest and, despite Joseph Soller's harsh evaluation, he was very popular among the people he served.[65] For these reasons De Smet judged he could do more good among the American settlers in Oregon City, and so Michael Accolti replaced him as superior at St. Francis Xavier in 1845.[66] De Vos built the first Catholic church in

Oregon City and received a number of important members of the American community into the Roman Catholic Church, among whom were two of his fellow travelers on the "great emigration of 1843" over the Oregon Trail: the English-born John E. Long, M.D. (?–1846),[67] secretary of the Oregon provisional government, and Peter H. Burnett, whom we have previously identified, destined to be the first chief justice of Oregon and the first American governor of California.[68] By the time De Smet and Point left the Coeur d'Alène, the ever-smiling, affable, Father Peter was on his way to becoming one of the most respected and admired Jesuit missionaries in the Northwest. But in April 1848 someone was desperately needed to care for the Skoyelpi or Chaudière (Kettle) Indians near Fort Colville, and so Joset plucked him from his successful apostolate in Oregon City and planted him at St. Paul's Mission, Kettle Falls.[69] Here, relying on his Flemish gift for learning languages and on his propensity for hard work, De Vos settled down and mastered the Skoyelpi language so well that in 1851, when he left, he had no need for an interpreter in instructing the Indians. "The obedient man will speak of virtues." His fellow countryman Aloysius Vercruysse observed: "Alone as he was for three years, everything changed face. The Canadian employees of Fort Colville are no longer the same nor are the Indians of the locality and its environs . . . Of all the missions, this is the one where most is done for the instruction of the Indians."[70] During his tenure at St. Paul's, De Vos composed a Skoyelpi dictionary which, unfortunately, was subsequently lost.[71] Joset singled him out as being an ideal missionary,[72] but beneath the veneer of satisfaction and success, Peter De Vos faced problems similar to those Nicolas Point had experienced. He complained that he had personal problems with his superiors, particularly with Joset, and asked to be placed under the jurisdiction of his former superiors, presumably the Flemish Jesuits in the Missouri vice-province. He also complained about his health. Understandably, the man was worn out.[73]

Michael Accolti did not remain long at Willamette. In 1849 he requested Joset's permission to go to San Francisco to care for the countless emigrants attracted there by the gold rush, and he pleaded with De Vos, who was temporarily at Sacred Heart with Joset, to urge his case. Apparently De Vos was a good persuader because "very reluctantly" Joset finally gave the necessary permission.[74] Soon another Italian missionary, John Nobili, the founder of Santa Clara College joined him in California.[75] In the beginning of 1850, Accolti, obviously unaware of the fate of Point and Soderini, wrote to the general from San Francisco requesting that these two "problems," and Brother Charles Huet also, be sent to San Francisco, where he and Nobili needed men, and where, presumably, the city's gray fog contained metamorphic qualities that could change problems into assets.[76] Even though the vice-provincial in St. Louis had singled out the author of this request (along with his Italian compatriots) as a man with "too much imagination for this country," Accolti was appointed superior of the ever-extending Rocky Mountain Mission that same year.[77] He, therefore, set off to visit his subjects in the Northwest. The result was that Mengarini and De Vos rather than Point and Soderini came to California. Chief Victor tried in vain to persuade Mengarini to return to the Flatheads, but the Black Robe who, at one time, liked to shoot rattlesnakes and who expressed a fear of deep water was judged to have the right qualities to be the ideal treasurer at the recently established Santa Clara College. This new assignment in the lush land of the Santa Clara Valley, which the Indians referred to as the Valley of the Heart's Desire, was a far cry from the rigors of the Bitter Root. For this reason the anonymous author of Mengarini's obituary can only have been exercising high irony when he wrote: "The grand *collège* of the present was a thing of the undreamt future and the primitive life of the wigwam and log-house was twin-sister to that which he was called upon to lead in the adobe walls of his new dwelling."[78] In California, Peter De Vos went back to the type of ministry he had done with such distinction at Grand Coteau and Oregon City. Assigned pastor of St. Joseph's Church, in Pueblo San Jose, he also served such far away mission stations as Gilroy, San Martin, and San Juan Baptista.[79] San Jose was the capital of California until February 1851 and one of De Vos's parishioners, at least for a very short time, was his friend Peter Burnett, who had been inaugurated governor the previous March.[80] De Vos was also appointed master of novices, and set up his first novitiate in San Jose.[81] Thus, the man who lacked the physical and psychological strength to make a formal novitiate himself, and was therefore excused from Father Gury's regime at Montrouge, became a novice master in the Missouri Vice-province, and the first master of novices in the Louisiana Mission, the Rocky Mountain Mission and the California Mission. When he was appointed master of novices in Missouri, Henry Duranquet, his former novice at Grand Coteau, remarked that hopefully people in Missouri would get to know De Vos soon, otherwise the Province would end up with no novices, at all.[82] One of these Florissant novices, Adrien Hoecken, confessed that a house where De Vos was in charge was "a dungeon."[83]

In a letter dated September 22, 1847, and posted from Sandwich, Ontario, Pierre Point, superior of the Upper Canadian Mission, advised Father General Roothaan that "Reverend Father Nicolas Point arrived here on August 10, having been sent by Reverend Father De Smet, who had advised him of Your Paternity's will."[84] There is no indication in this letter that Nicolas wanted to leave the Blackfeet. On the contrary, he was ordered to do so because of the request he had made *before* he was assigned to the Blackfeet. While he was with these Indians he had baptized 651 persons, only 26 of whom were adults, and of this number, there were many who were baptized *in articulo mortis*. He was hesitant, as his correspondence shows, to baptize adults, even those who begged him to do so.[85] "The greatest obstacle to the conversion of the Indians of the Upper Missouri *in toto*," De Smet had declared, "was too much sexual inequality."[86] Point, as we have seen, agreed, but he had planted the seed, he had collected some money, and now it was up to his superiors to send someone to set up a reduction to reap what he had sown. His pleadings certainly did not meet opposition from his superiors. On the contrary, three months after Point had left St. Louis, Van de Velde pleaded with Roothaan: "We must not abandon the mission to the Blackfeet, a mission which is not forsaken. Since Father Point promised them, I must send someone to them in the spring."[87] But there was no one to send. Two months later the new vice-provincial, John Elet, recommended the potential Blackfeet mission be separated from the Rocky Mountain Mission, over which the superior in St. Louis had always held nebulous and ill-defined jurisdiction, and which Roothaan had regarded as his special care.[88] Jurisdictional ambiguities plagued the Rocky Mountain Mission from its very beginnings. Then in June of 1848, Elet wrote again to Roothaan saying that "the Mission to the Blackfeet will probably be put off until April 1, 1849, first, because a war has broken out between the Indians and the whites, and secondly, because Father De Smet arrived too late to go there by water."[89] The following years brought more delays until finally in 1859 Father Adrian Hoecken and Brother Vincent Magri established St. Peter's mission on the banks of the Teton River, near present day Choteau, Montana.[90] But during the dozen years that had passed between Point's departure from Fort Lewis and the beginnings of St. Peter's Mission, an old world had died and a new world was born.

Pierre Point had informed Roothaan that Nicolas had come to Sandwich "full of good health, joy, and with a desire to work in the Canada Mission everywhere or wherever he would be sent." His Rocky Mountain experiences had not dimmed his faith in the reduction system, and he was now anxious to try again to set up a reduction far from the influences of the whites.[91] During his first year in Canada, Nicolas remained pretty much with his brother at Sandwich, and then in 1849 he joined Dominique du Ranquet working with the Indians on Walpole Island, and in 1848 Pierre made him superior at Holy Cross Mission, Wikwemikong, on Grand Manitoulin Island.[92] In 1670 Father Joseph Antoine Poncet de la Rivière, S.J. (1610–1675), founder of the church in Detroit, established the first church at Wikwemikong, but the nineteenth-century mission was begun in 1836 by the diocesan priest, Jean-Baptiste Proulx (1808–1881). In 1844 the mission was entrusted to the Jesuits and Father Pierre Chorné (1808–1878) came to assist Father Proulx, who left the following year.[93] In a letter to Roothaan, Clément Boulanger registered doubts about the prudence which prompted Pierre Point to appoint his brother to this mission. Nicolas was now fifty, and the Visitor questioned that he would be able to master another Indian language; that, therefore, he felt Point would be hampered in the exercise of his ministry. But it is doubtful if Nicolas, who had trouble enough getting along in English, ever mastered an Indian language. In this same letter to the general, Boulanger wrote:

> "I add that anyone certainly allowed himself to be deceived who regarded this Father as dangerous and capable of publishing certain papers, which were never meant for anyone other than the Very Reverend Father General, and which were designed to clarify points that seemed to him important for religious life and for the good of the missions. What seems incontestable to me is that people have made Father Point suffer and, at the same time, that he himself has been the cause of suffering for others.[94]

Clément Boulanger, like Amboise Rubillon, had known Nicolas Point since the days the latter was a lay *surveillant* under Jean-Nicolas Loriquet and Achille Guidée at Saint-Acheul. It was altogether fitting that this man out of his past should have been the one who absolved him from all accusations of disloyalty and treachery toward the society he loved. Boulanger closed the case of the suspicious papers which had dragged so many good people into such sordid activities, and in doing so wrote a most accurate description of this aspect of Point's character: others were the cause of his sufferings and he was the cause of theirs. What were these mysterious and dangerous documents? They could have been any number of documents in which Point poured out endless arguments justifying his course of action at Grand Coteau from 1838 to 1840. A copy of a long letter he sent to Father Achille Guidée, provincial of France in 1841, with Guidée's reply, dated Paris, December 3, 1841, could well have been part of this dossier. On the top of Guidée's letter, Point, in the script of an old man, wrote: "Many believed that I was sent to the mountains out of disgrace, and therefore without a vocation. This letter can prove the contrary."[95] Nicolas Point had the reputation of being a man who did not seek honor or recognition, but his pride was of the sort that he was very much afraid of disgrace and humiliation. It is easy to understand why this man, who felt slighted because his talents and his work were not appreciated, was misjudged and often treated wrongly by those with whom he lived. It is also understandable why, ever insecure, he went to such pains to prove to others he was a good Jesuit, a good educator, a good missionary.

Although Point's ministry in Canada is beyond the scope of this book, a brief consideration of his activities at Holy Cross, or Sainte-Croix, is in order because it places in a clearer context his missionary philosophy by demonstrating how he dealt with Indians whose culture and mode of living were different from those he had encountered in the American Northwest. We have already seen he was ever convinced that the Indians would prosper spiritually and materially to the extent that they retained their own language, customs, and government, while maintaining a distance, geographical, psychological and cultural, from the whites.[96] For this reason his new assignment presented many advantages over those he had encountered in his efforts to Christianize and civilize in the tribes of the Rockies and the Upper Missouri. As a result of the so-called Treaty of 1836, the British government in Canada had given many concessions to the Indians on the Manitoulin islands. These people, remnants of a number of Algonkian-speaking tribes, the chief of which, the Ottawas, Ojibway, and the Chippewa, were sedentary, village dwellers; therefore, they were ideally prepared for reduction-type living. On the other hand, the tensions between French-speaking Catholics and English-speaking Protestants, which were becoming so much a part of life in Upper Canada, were not unknown on

Grand Manitoulin. A magnificent, well-endowed Protestant church dominated the largest village on the island, tidy, progressive Manitowaning. Built with English money and serviced by English-speaking ministers, it was referred to locally as "the eighth wonder of the world," and it stood in symbolic contrast to the broken down Catholic chapel in the small, filthy hamlet of Sainte-Croix. This chapel was begun at the end of 1844 by Father Proulx and the newly arrived Father Chorné, but it had never been finished. The symbolic significance of these two contrasting edifices was not lost on the Indians, nor was the challenge missed by Point, who complained that it was always the white man who "did things" for the Indians. "We are the ones who build mill, church, etc.," he reflected, and added:

> So long as we direct and encourage our Indians, as is proper, could not they themselves put up these structures? The skills they have already shown seem to answer: Yes. Let us therefore direct them with all of our might; let us encourage them with all of our forces, and this way put to rest the bias notions that tell us that no matter what we do, the Indian will never take on great projects; that only money can civilize mission Indians; that the religious conquest of the Northwest could not have been accomplished without money: if we do not outright discredit all of this, at least let us say that it was pertinent to another age. What we come back to stressing is this: we must give up our preconceived notions, we must avoid making a frightful mistake now because it may be the chances for success have never been more auspicious.[97]

Such optimistic sentiments counterbalance Roothaan's grim evaluation of the Rocky Mountain Mission enterprise and his dire projections for the future of setting up Paraguay-type reductions among the North American Indians. How realistic Point was vis-a-vis Roothaan is another question, but his faith in the Indian was unlimited. The crowns of Spain and Portugal could no longer be depended upon to provide money, so necessary for the conversion and civilization of the Indian. Such money was not *the* essential requisite and Nicolas Point was about to prove it. As soon as he arrived at Holy Cross, he determined that the Indians, with his direction and help, would put up a stone church, a house of God surely, but also a monument of Indian pride, a visible sign to those "who put their trust in princes."

The cornerstone of the church was blessed on July 3, 1849. Stone was brought from neighboring islands in flat-bottom boats, and the clerk of the works, an Indian named Bemanakinang, organized teams of men, women, and children to carry the stones up the hill. Point was the only white man involved in the enterprise. The all-but-completed church was blessed July 25, 1852, the twelfth anniversary of Point's departure from Grand Coteau as well as the twelfth anniversary of the first mass said in the present state of Montana by Peter De Smet, the event, at which fifteen hundred Indians were present, which inaugurated the Rocky Mountain Mission. The church was completed in time for Christmas ceremonies of 1853. Still in use today, this structure measures one hundred feet in length and forty feet in width, exclusive of the side-chapels. Except for the tableaux, which Point himself executed, the edifice was built entirely by Indians and in a manner not altogether different from the way the total population at Reims built their cathedral during the thirteenth century.[98]

In addition to the church, Point also constructed a school and provided for teachers. He formed the same type of sodalities he had established while he was at Fribourg, Le Passage, Grand Coteau, Westport, and St. Mary's, because the sodalities were the means to inculcate in lay people the spirit which so distinguished the Society of Jesus during the nineteenth century—devotion to the Sacred Heart, the Eucharist, the Virgin Mary and the saints, and a fierce unwavering loyalty to the pope. In addition to the sodalities, he also established a temperance society at this mission because he judged alcohol was the Indian's worst enemy. Once the mission at Wikwemikong was secure, he was given a new assignment, at Father Dominique du Ranquet's mission in Fort William on Thunder Bay, western Ontario, where he arrived in 1857.[99] He remained here but one year when the hernia from which he suffered for thirty years forced him to return to the parish at Sandwich.[100] But his assignment here, too, was short-lived.

In 1856 the diocese of Toronto was divided by the erection of Hamilton and London, which included Sandwich. In 1859 the new bishop at Sandwich, Pierre-Adolphe Pinsonneault, S.S. (1815–1883), requested the Jesuits turn over their church to the diocese.[101] Pierre was sent to St. John's College, Fordham, New York, where he became prefect of the church, but Nicolas was not given an immediate assignment.[102] This was the event which inspired him to write to Father Félix Sopranis (1799–1876), the special Visitor sent by Father General Peter Beckx (1795–1887) to visit all Jesuit houses from Canada to California, making once again a formal request to be missioned to the Rocky Mountains. After explaining that his desire to work among the Indians remained constant, he continued: " . . . if my presence is judged useful in whatever manner for the renewal of the abandoned reductions, particularly that of St. Mary's among the Flatheads, I am sincerely disposed to contribute all my means under whatever superior, even if it is Father De Smet." Realistically, however, he admitted he was aware of De Smet's reservations, for he had been in correspondence with him. "The source of our terribly regrettable differences was a gross mistake which perhaps we have never completely gotten over—G[rand] Coteau."[103] There are two facts here which seem important in evaluating Nicolas Point's motivation for making such a request. First, he was not dissatisfied with the Canadian Mission nor had he been seduced by romantic, rosy-hued dreams of a world he had "abandoned" twelve years earlier. His motivations were realistic and apostolic. Secondly, Grand Coteau, which even at this date remained a sore wound, was regarded objectively and, in comparison to earlier years, with a certain healthy distance. In his response, Sopranis wrote: "I received your letter you wrote me, perhaps from New York, although you forgot to mention the house and the date," and then after a few amenities, he advised Point that just a few days before his letter reached him at Georgetown he had received another letter. It was from Father De Smet and, ever since its arrival it had caused him to center his thoughts on the plight of the Rocky Mountain Mission. For this reason, he

> was even more affected by sentiments of devotion and love for these poor people who are presently deserted. This circumstance served to make your letter even more than otherwise acceptable, and I was on the point of writing: '*Mon très cher Père-allez*'- but reflecting on it before God, and realizing that certain questions had to be answered before proceeding. I believe it my duty to suspend the decision until these matters are resolved . . .[104]

Most probably Nicolas had accompanied Pierre to New York and, while he was at Fordham, he had the occasion to renew friendship with such men as Fathers Thomas Legoüais and Paul Mignard, and Brothers Charles Alsberg, Philippe Ledoré, and others. It was while he was at Fordham that he also wrote a letter to Peter De Smet, who had recently returned from the Northwest after his famous peacemaking mission resulting from the Steptoe Disaster of 1858, telling him of his desire to return to the Rocky Mountains and advising him that the superior of the Canadian Mission had counseled him to write to his old friend soliciting his opinion on this matter. Point ended his letter reminding his correspondent of the

> long painful trials which both of us had to put up with, seeing in the past only incentives to commit ourselves, from the very depths of our souls, to Him who sends us trials only to purify us. In a few days I shall go to Sault-Recollet [*sic*], near Montreal, to await the final decision on what I have written about to you. At any rate, I have permission to put a bit of order into my notes and sketches so that they can be of service to missionaries, whoever they may be.[105]

Ultimately, of course, Sopranis's decision was that Point, already sixty-one years old, would not be an asset to the Mission, which at that time was beginning a new spring. He went on to Sault-au-Recollet where, as assistant to the master of novices, he began a new career. It was here, as he had indicated to De Smet, that, at the insistence of his superiors, he began to edit his notebooks. The result was the five-volume opus, "Souvenirs et mémoires illustrés." From his new post he also served as the chaplain to the Religious of the Sacred Heart and carried on an extensive correspondence, some of which is extant, with various persons mentioned in this study.[106]

If Point's correspondence during these years of semi-retirement does not give us new insights into his complex personality, it does offer more evidence to what has already been seen. He wrote on more than one occasion to De Smet about the Flatheads, the Coeur d'Alène, and the Blackfeet. He showed particular concern for those children he had baptized while he was at Fort Lewis in 1847 and urged De Smet to do all in his power to have Jesuits assigned to the Blackfeet so that these nominal Christians should be instructed in the rudiments of their faith.[107] In 1857 De Smet informed him that even the United States government was interested in this project and was willing to add an additional $15,000 to the $200 he had collected to establish the mission.[108] As we have seen, this mission was finally begun anew in 1859. De Smet also informed Point about particular Indians he had known and he encouraged him to send biographical information on such individuals as Loyola, the chief of the Kalispels; Louise, the apostle of the Coeur d'Alène; the Flathead chiefs Michael and Victor; and a number of others.[109] Indeed, some of this information supplied by Point had already been incorporated into the text of De Smet's *Life and Travels.* In fact, much of De Smet's descriptions and impressions of the Blackfeet, as well as much of his information about the Flatheads and the Coeur d'Alène, are from Point, a fact which is perfectly understandable because Point was more directly the researcher and De Smet, the chronicler. In one letter De Smet advised Point that John Gilmary Shea had intended to write a history of the Northwest missions and encouraged him to correspond with Shea.[110] During this period of his life Point did manage to compose a fourteen-page pamphlet entitled "Quelques notes sur les Missions des Montagnes rocheuses," This work was never published, and rightly so, for it adds nothing new about the Indians although it does give some insight into the old man who composed it and how indebted he was to his Jesuit teachers, particularly Xavier de Ravignan.[111]

This sporatic and limited correspondence with De Smet also testifies to the loyalty he retained over the years to the friends he met in the Northwest. He begged De Smet for news about Alexander Culbertson and his family, Michel Champagne, A. Hamel, and others.[112] He likewise showed affectionate interest in the fate of a number of the Indians he had mentioned in the letters contained in this book.[113] Some of these had become key figures in treaties with the United States Government. For example, Victor, described as the head chief of the Flathead tribe and the head chief of the Flathead nation, was the principal signatory of the Treaty at Hell Gate, January 16, 1855. Other co-signers included Alexander, chief of the Upper Pend d'Oreilles, Ambrose, Adolph, Thunder, Paul and Moses. Fidelis and Big Lake were conspicuous in the Treaty between the United States Government, the Blackfeet and the Flatheads, which was signed at the Judith River on October 17, 1855. Gabriel played a crucial role in saving the Coeur d'Alène from certain disaster during the tragic Indian War of 1858, that followed the Steptoe disaster.[114] The portraits of many of his Indian friends, about whom he spoke in the above letters, were painted by Gustavus Sohon.[115]

Conspicuously missing from the Fordham community when Point visited during the Christmas season of 1859–1860 was one of his oldest and best friends, William Stack Murphy, who had paid him a visit at Sandwich that August.[116] Murphy had moved to St. John's College, Fordham, with the St. Mary's, Kentucky, community in 1846, but then he was appointed Visitor to the Missouri vice-province in June 1851, and named vice-provincial the following August. Garraghan writes: "None of [Murphy's] predecessors from Van Quickenborne to Elet had succeeded in governing to the complete satisfaction of Father General; they had all on one occasion or another been called to task for not measuring up to the Ignatian ideal of the Jesuit superior."[117] Now all the expectancy was on Murphy, the man Chazelle judged not to have the necessary qualities to be a superior.[118] Effectively, Roothaan had given his new vice-provincial the mandate to implement much of what was in Point's *plan* into the educational institutions of the vice-province and to improve the spiritual and intellectual training of the St. Louis Jesuits according to practices followed in France during the time that Point and Murphy had been trained there. Significantly, it was Isidore Boudreaux, who lived so long at Grand Coteau with Paris Province Jesuits, who was able to evaluate the sad, inbred, condition of his own vice-province, and who carried the oriflamme of spiritual reform after Murphy's departure. Boudreaux thereby provides an excellent precedent for those who support the policy that talented scholastics should, as a matter of policy, make theological studies outside their own assistancies. "It must be remembered," Boudreaux informed the general after he returned to Missouri, "that our Province was not begun by *trained Jesuits* but by untrained novices, who remained for years strangers to the customs of the Society."[119] Very sincere mediocrity had become the accepted mode of governance and the same type of premature and exaggerated expansion that had all but destroyed the Rocky Mountain Mission now threatened the Missouri vice-province. The Saint-Acheul trained Murphy was given peremptory instructions by Roothaan to put things in order. "Conservative by temper," as Garraghan describes him, Murphy, who liked to cite the line from Thomas à Kempis, "We are sometimes swayed by passion and fancy it is zeal," set out to revolutionize, "Fribourgize," the Missouri vice-province, and although he succeeded to some extent, the mandate was too extensive, and he was all but destroyed in the process of turning the vice-province around.[120] Following Roothaan's directive, he was determined to contract, not to expand; to build up internal organization, not to foster outward growth. For this reason, "he stood out in opposition to all his consultors against the acceptance of Milwaukee as a new field of work, and was brought to take it over only by the positive wish of Father

General."[121] Appointed vice-provincial at a crucial period, Murphy did not serve out his tenure of office, but rather returned to Fordham, only to be recalled in February 1861 to serve a second term as vice-provincial. This time he lasted less than two years in office before retiring to join his fellow French confreres in the war-torn New Orleans Mission, where he remained the rest of his days. It is, therefore, William Stack Murphy, "cher Guillaume," whose biography begs to be written, who more than anyone else, vindicated Nicolas Point, his fellow tertian and traveling companion from Le Havre to St. Mary's, Kentucky, because Murphy was able to begin the spiritual renewal and educational reform that Point had dreamed about but was so peremptorily prevented from doing fifteen years earlier.[122]

In 1864, as William Murphy was attempting to adjust to life in New Orleans, which had been occupied by Federal troops, Nicolas Point, whose health had begun to fail, moved with the novices to Quebec City.[123] In 1865 the American Civil War came to an end, Pierre returned from New York and became superior at the Quebec residence, which served as the province juniorate, and Nicolas joined him there shortly afterwards.[124] No longer able to leave the house, he confined his apostolate to the confessional and to giving conferences to the young Jesuit scholastics. Death came in July 1868, claiming Nicolas Point on the fourth, Clément Boulanger on the twelfth, and Peter Verhaegen on the twenty-first. In life the destinies of these three men were curiously, mysteriously, intertwined. Point was sixty-nine years of age. Significantly, July 4, 1868 was the First Friday of the month, a day dedicated to the Sacred Heart. On Monday, July 6, there was a low mass of burial, at which neither a homily nor a eulogy was preached, and where no music was played. After these traditional Jesuit services, however, the body was interred, at the request of Abbé Charles-Félix Cazeau (1807–1881), the justifiably famous, sometime administrator and vicar-general of the diocese in the basilica of the city of Quebec.[125]

Summing up

In 1853, three years after the closing of St. Mary's Mission, the Flatheads, contrite and ashamed, begged the Black Robes to return, and even solicited the American governor to make intercession for them. Unfortunately there was no available priest at that date to send them, and when Point learned of these facts, and after reflecting there were enough available men in the Canadian Mission, he wrote to Father General Peter Beckx requesting to be reassigned to his beloved Flatheads. Before making a decision Beckx canvassed a number of Jesuits in Canada asking their opinion on this matter. The General then responded "with a great deal of kindness" telling Point, whose health had already forced him to leave Fort William for Sandwich, that he was not the man for the job at that time. One man the General contacted, Father Joseph Hanipaux, who lived under Nicolas Point at the Holy Cross mission for more than four years and in 1854 succeeded him as superior there, gave the following evaluation:

> Father Point is equipped with all sorts of virtues, is inspired with a boundless zeal and has the deepest love for the society; but he is very often, especially at certain periods, submitted by Divine Providence to a very painful trial, painful for himself as for those about him who cannot comprehend why he entertains such ideas of them as those to which he gives expression. He has at times when the cross relaxes, at least sensibly [admitted how painful it is for him]; but it is not slow in making itself felt again. When he is in this state he cannot be persuaded that he is dealing not with realities, but with phantasms of the imagination, trials of Divine Providence, which makes certain souls pass through this state in order to have them arrive at great consolations. In spite of these torments he works and renders good service to the Mission. He has a great and ever increasing desire to return to the Rocky Mountains, where many of his former neophytes are in the greatest desolation. He would not do well there except with adequate support while this condition of trial is upon him.[126]

De Smet, who admired Nicolas Point greatly, confessed:

> I have known none of Ours [i.e. Jesuits] with whom he could live in peace or they with him. . . . All the troubles that seemed to surround him wherever he went were more to be attributed to something wrong in his mind, of which he was not master, than to his will. Nevertheless, the troubles existed and hindered in a great measure the progress of the mission. At the same time by his zeal and fervor, his deeds of mortification, etc., he has certainly done a great deal of good among the Indians.[127]

De Smet's judgment seems a bit too facile. Point did have some Jesuit friends and the troubles he encountered were not altogether the result of some psychological quirk in his personality. The Grand Coteau affair was central to so many of the problems he encountered both in Louisiana and in the Rocky Mountains, and, as we have seen, De Smet could not have been an impartial judge in this matter. In an attempt to place Point's character in an objective perspective, it is important to consider that most descriptions we have of him are those given by Jesuits. And the Jesuits introduced in this study were hard on one another. For example, Murphy claimed De Smet had the gift of blaming others for his own mistakes.[128] Van de Velde thought that he was far too independent.[129] Joset was quoted as saying he believed he was "a saint, but a saint according to his own way."[130] Another superior thought him *original*—that is, strange, eccentric.[131] De Vos, Joset, and Nobili faulted him for his bizzare mode of government.[132] For his part, De Smet considered Hoecken "vain, worldly, independent,"[133] and De Vos thought by no means should Hoecken be the superior at St. Ignatius.[134] Hoecken, admittedly an exemplary missionary, had no better an opinion of Soderini ("a tyrant") than he had for his former master of novices, De Vos.[135] Men, who were consistently spurred on by what was the ideal in every aspect of their lives and who, from their earliest days in the society were trained to be content with nothing short of perfection, tended to be intolerant of the defects and sloppiness they encountered in the real, everyday world. However spiritual, they did not manifest that same ease with the "incarnational" which is so characteristic of Franciscan spirituality. Perhaps this is one reason why their founder, St. Ignatius, placed the contemplation on the Incarnation immediately after the consideration of the Call of the King in his *Spiritual Exercises.* At any rate, the judgments made by Point's companions about him should be studied in the light of their own frank appraisal of one another. At the same time, all of his Jesuit confreres assert, independent of one another, that Point was zealous but neurotic, that he dealt well with many—students, lay faculty members, mountain men, traders, and especially Indians—but found it all but impossible to live with most of his brother Jesuits, and that, for whatever reason, there was something "loose in his head." However, they also agreed with De Smet that Point and the Indians formed a mutual admiration society. "I just learned Father Point . . . has been called to his reward," wrote Father Joseph Joset from Sacred Heart Mission to Father General Beckx, "What didn't he do for the Indians!"[136] And in 1851 Aloysius Vercruysse informed Roothaan that, in his short time among the Blackfeet, Point had become a legend; that the Indians missed him sorely and spoke about him often.[137]

Point himself, we are told, was aware of his deficiencies and defects, and in the evening years of his life he composed some reflections entitled "Some Thoughts on the Spirit of the (Religious) State, and Especially on the Spirit of the society; On Self-Will, etc."[138] Possibly these notes were intended as aids for the conferences he gave to the novices at Saut-au-Recollet or to the juniors at Quebec, and unquestionably they present a sort of *apologia pro vita sua.* They are written in his tiny script and organized according to the scholastic form Jean-Paul Martin taught him at Saint-Acheul, which is another way of saying they abound in definitions, distinctions, and sub-distinctions. What are essential virtues for a Jesuit, he inquired, and concluded obedience was first and foremost. "The obedient man will speak of virtues." Of its nature obedience was opposed to dissent. But obedience could never be appreciated, much less practiced, unless one realized that in exercising this virtue he was obeying God and God alone. This insight demanded the virtue of simplicity, which developed as a result of continual mortification, and which in turn led to prudence. "O eternal Wisdom, let me understand with a practical intelligence these great truths."[139] Finally, he who had fought so hard and paid such a price for the integrity of *le plan d'études de Fribourg* wrote: "adhesion to some truth is not obstinacy much less bullheadedness; it is the legitimate exercise of one's will and intelligence . . . it is virtue; it is discretion; it is courage, the very courage of the martyrs."[140]

Abbreviations

ASJR	*Archives of the Society of Jesus, Rome*
ASJSL	*Archives of the Society of Jesus, St. Louis*
ASJSJ	*Archives of the Society of Jesus, Saint-Jerome, Canada*
ASJLG	*Archives of the Society of Jesus, Los Gatos, CA.*
ASJNO	*Archives of the Society of Jesus, New Orleans*
ASJC	*Archives of the Society of Jesus, Chantilly, France*
JHAGU	*Jesuit Historical Archives, Gonzaga University*
UNDA	*University of Notre Dame Archives*

NOTES

for Biographical Section and Conclusion

BEGINNINGS 1799–1818: (1–15)

1. "Vie du Père Nicolas Point, S.J.," 5 (henceforth, "Vie"). This 150-page manuscript was written about 1870 by Father Pierre Point, S.J., brother of Nicolas. It is housed in the Archives de la Compagnie de Jésus, Province du Canada-français, Saint-Jérôme, Québec, Canada (ASJSJ), number 4073. See also Leon Pouliot, "Le Père Nicolas Point (1799–1868): collaborateur du P. De Smet dans les montagnes Rocheuses et missionnaire en Ontario," in *Rapport de la Société canadienne d'histoire de l'Eglise catholique* (1936) 20–30. Rufo Mendizabel, S.J. gives different birthdates for both Nicolas and Pierre Point in his *Catalogus Defunctorum in renata Societate Iesu ab a. 1814 ad a. 1970* (Romae: apud Curiam P. Gen, 1972) col. 3 no. 423 and col. 8, no. 821. This work, however, is not always reliable.

2. Cited by Henri Daniel-Rops in *The Church in an Age of Revolution, 1789–1870,* trans. John Warrington (New York: E.P. Dutton & Co., 1965), 45.

3. Archives of the Archdiocese of Reims have paid a heavy toll to the exigencies of two world wars. The result is that nothing seems to be known about Monsieur l'abbé Richer that has not been revealed by Pierre Point. Since his name does not appear on the lists of priests of the archdiocese in 1789, it is thought he was probably a religious before the Revolution.

4. P. Point, "Vie," 6.

5. Ibid.

6. Ibid., 7.

7. Ibid.

8. Ibid.

9. Ibid., 8.

10. Olwen Hufton, "Women in Revolution 1789–1796," in *Past and Present,* 53 (1971): 107–8.

11. D. G. Wright, *Revolution and Terror in France, 1789–1795* (London: Longman, 1974), 86.

12. John McManners, *The French Revolution and the Church* (New York: Harper and Row, 1969), 145.

13. Marcel Grosdidier de Matons, *Une Ame Loraine: Madame de Méjanès (Anne-Victoire Tailleur, 1763–1837), Fondatrice de la Congrégation des Soeurs de Sainte-Chrétienne* (Paris: Editions Spes, 1957). *L'Episcopat français depuis le Concordat jusqu'à la Séparation: 1802–1905* (Paris: Librairie Saint-Denis, 1907), 359–60.

14. Some details on the life of Sister St. Gabriel can be found in "Nécrologe des Soeurs," Archives Sainte-Chrétienne, Metz, France. These same archives give the following details on the school at Rocroi: "Founded in 1717 as a result of a gift given by a lady of Reims, Mlle Le Vergeur de Saint-Souplet, to support two religious. During the Revolution these two religious were dispersed, and the school was cared for by two former members of the Sisters of the Infant Jesus of Reims, who wore lay clothes. The bishop of Metz invited dispersed sisters to regroup in the Congregation of Sainte-Chrétienne and they were clothed in habit in 1808. On March 10, 1808, Sister St. Gabriel, who was then thirty, and Sister St. Thérèse, nineteen, arrived in Rocroi. Their mission was to give religious instruction and to teach reading, writing, and arithmetic. Their salary was fixed at 600 francs per year. In 1830 because of the increase in the number of students, Sister St. Gabriel was given two religious. These women received lodging and their salary was now 900 francs (300 each) per annum. In 1838, being more than 60 years of age and having taught at least thirty-one years at Rocroi, [the now] Mother St. Gabriel was replaced by Sister St. Hippolyte. The memory of dear Mother St. Gabriel remained very much alive in the neighborhood where she had developed a veritable cult of affection." "Histoire de la Maison de Rocroi," C. Rocr, 1–2, pp. 1–8, Archives Sainte-Chrétienne.

15. P. Point, "Vie," p. 9.

16. Ibid.

17. Louis Boullet, *Histoire de Rocroi,* number 3 in the series *Les Cahiers d'etudes ardennaises,* (Meziers: *Société d'études arden-*

naises, 1958), 74; *Almanach Ecclesiastique de France* (n.p., 1805, 1808, 1809, 1812), s.v. "Rocroi." "Liste des prêtes," Archives, Archdiocese of Reims.

18. P. Point, "Vie," 10.

19. A Jesuit "*collège*" of that period included three divisions (lower, middle, and upper), which roughly speaking would correspond to the combined levels of a primary school, a secondary school, and a junior college in the American system. A student who was able to read and write would enroll in the seventh section of the lower division and progress upward to the sixth section, and so on. After completing the requirements of the lower division, he would be eligible for the middle, or grammar, division, which was a three-year curriculum. Then, in the upper division, he would progress from the first year of humanities first to rhetoric and finally to philosophy. This is what is being referred to by the use of the term *collège* in connection with the system of Jesuit education. Charlier's school can not be categorized as a Jesuit *collège,* although it had a few of the same characteristics.

20. Ibid., 10, 58.

21. Ibid., 12, 47.

22. Ibid., 10–11.

23. Ibid., 12.

JESUITS 1819–1826: (16–36)

1. Joseph Burnichon, S.J., *La Compagnie de Jésus en France: Histoire d'un siècle, 1814–1914,* 4 vols. (Paris: Beauchesne, 1916), 1: 35–60.

2. Ibid., 61–68.

3. Ibid., 173–83.

4. Pierre Delattre, S.J., ed., *Les Etablissements des Jésuites en France depuis quatre siècles,* 5 vols. (Enchien, Belgium: De Meestre, 1949), 1: col. 1480–81.

5. Ibid., col. 1482, n. 1 for references; also: P. Simpson to the Fathers at Bordeaux, July 1818, cited in Delattre, 1: col. 1486; Burnichon, *Histoire d'un siècle,* 1: 289.

6. P. Point, "Vie," 10. (See Beginnings, n.1.)

7. Cited in Delattre, *Etablissements des Jésuites en France,* 1: col. 1483.

8. Ibid.

9. Ibid., col. 1484.

10. Jean-Nicolas Loriquet's published works take up twenty

columns in *The Catalogue Générale des livres imprimés, de la Bibliothèque nationale, Auteurs . . .* 231 vols. (Paris: Imprimérie nationale, 1879–1981) 100: 213–37. Burnichon, *Histoire d'un siècle,* 1:130–32; 247–64; Pierre Bliard, *Le P. Loriquet: La legende et l'histoire* (Paris: Perrin & Cie, 1922); Carlos Sommervogel, S.J., ed., *Bibliothèque de la Compagnie de Jésus,* 11 vol. (Brussels: Oscar Schaepens, 1890–1932), 5: col. 7–22. Le Baron Mattheu-Richard-Auguste Henrion, *Vie du Père Loriquet, S.J., écrite d'après sa correspondance et ses oeuvres inéditeés* (Paris: Poussielque-Rusand, 1845).

11. Burnichon, *Histoire d'un siècle,* 1:72, 475; Delattre, *Etablissements des Jésuites en France,* 1: col. 778–81; 2: col. 1045, 3: col. 1097.

12. Burnichon, *Histoire d'un siècle,* 1: 305–314; 2: 367–68; P. Point, "Vie," 12.

13. P. Point, "Vie," 12.

14. Delattre, *Etablissements des Jésuites en France,* 1: col. 205–8.

15. Delattre, *Etablissements des Jésuites en France,* 5: col. 8–12; Sommervogel, *Bibliothèque de la Compagnie de Jésus,* 5: col. 623.

16. P. Point, "Vie," 13–15.

17. Delattre, *Etablissements des Jésuites en France,* 3: col. 612–28. Burnichon, *Histoire d'un siècle,* 1:155–70.

18. St. Ignatius Loyola, *Spiritual Exercises.* (Westminister, Maryland: Newman 1943), 121, no. 353.

19. Cited in Burnichon, *Histoire d'un siècle,* 1:160.

20. Burnichon, *Histoire d'un siècle,* 1:155–60; Delattre, *Etablissements des Jésuites en France,* 3: col. 613–15; *Catalogus Provinciae Galliae, S.J.* (n.p. 1822–1823) 24–28, in *Catalogus Sociorum et Officiorum Provincial Galliae Societatis Jesu, 1818–1836,* rebound in 2 vols., ed. Alexander Vivier, (1892–1894) with a preface by Vivier signed September 27, 1894.

21. Delattre, *Etablissements des Jésuites en France,* 1: col. 1111, 1165; 3: col. 306; 4: col. 1361. Sommervogel, *Bibliothèque de la Compagnie de Jésus,* 3: col. 1976–1977.

22. Père V. Alet, S.J., *Le Père Louis Marquet de la Compagnie de Jésus. Choix de ses divers écrits et de sa correspondance. Précédé d'une notice biographique* (Paris: Oudin, 1888); Sommervogel, *Bibliothèque de la Compagnie de Jésus,* 5: col. 599–600. Delattre, *Etablissements des Jésuites en France,* 1 col. 170; 3: col. 797; 4: col. 562, 1203.

23. Delattre, *Etablissement des Jésuites en France,* 5: col. 39, 42.

24. Ibid., 1: col. 948; 4: col. 1193.

25. Armand de Ponlevoy, S.J., *The Life of Father de Ravignan, S.J.*, 2 vols. (New York: The Catholic Publication Society, 1869), 1:1–80, 123; Sommervogel, *Bibliothèque de la Compagnie de Jésus,* 5: col. 1499–1507; Delattre, *Etablissements de Jésuites en France,* 1: col. 197; Burnichon, *Histoire d'un siècle,* 2:222–24; *Nouvelle Biographie Générale depuis le temps les plus reculés jusqu'à nos jours,* 46 vols. (Paris: Firmin Didot Frères, 1862–1969), 41: col. 726–28.

26. Delattre, *Etablissements de Jésuites en France,* 2: col. 831–34, 955, 4: col. 1487.

27. Ibid., 4: col. 1361.

28. *Dictionnaire de Biographie française,* ed. J. Balteau, M. Barroux and M. Prevost, 16 vols. (Paris: Letouzey et Ané, 1933–), s.v. "Barthélemy-Louis Enfantin," by P. Hamon, 12: col. 1287. *Dizionario degli Instituti di Perfezione,* ed. Guerrino Pelliccia and Giancarlo Rocca, 7 vols. in print (Roma: Edizione Paolini, 1962–), s.v. "Louis-Barthélemy Enfantin," by G. Rocca, 3: col. 1130–1131.

29. Sommervogel, *Bibliothèque de la Compagnie de Jésus.* 8: col. 778; Burnichon, *Histoire d'un siècle,* 2:432. *Epistolae Ioannis Phil. Roothaan Societatis Iesu Praepositi Generalis XXI,* 5 volumes. Romae: Apud Postulatorem Generalem S.I., 5:588–90 (Hereafter, Roothaan, *Epistolae*).

30. "An Historical Sketch of the Missions of New York and Canada," in *Woodstock Letters,*" 4 (1875): 4; Sommervogel, *Bibliothèque de la Compagnie de Jésus,* 2: col. 1106.

31. Obituary, "Thomas Legouais," in *Woodstock Letters,* 19 (1890): 409.

32. Adrien Boudon, S.J., *Les Jésuites à Madagascar au XIXe siècle,* 2 vols. (Paris: Beauchesne, 1880), 1:97–105. Sommervogel, *Bibliothèque de la Compagnie de Jésus,* 2: col. 1913–1914.

33. *Lettres des nouvelles missions de la Chine,* 2 vols. (n.p., n.d.), 1:1841–1846, passim; Nicolas Broullion, S.J., *Mémoire su l'état actuel de la Mission du Kiang-Nan, 1842–1855* (Paris: Julien, Lavier et Cie., 1855), 1–50; Joseph de La Servière, S.J., *Histoire de la Mission du Kiang-Nam, 1840–1899,* 2 vols. (Zi-ka-wei: T'ou-sè-wè, 1944) 1:40–50, 320, 331–32. Auguste Colombel, S.J., *Histoire de la Mission du Kiangnan.* (Shanghai: T'ou-sè-wè, 1895–1905), Troisième Partie, chapter 1:598; Sommervogel, *Bibliothèque de la Compagnie de Jésus,* 3: col. 1621–1622.

34. Roothaan to Godinot, Rome, January 28, 1836, Roothaan, *Epistolae,* 2:298; Padre Pedro de Ribadeneyra, S.J., *Vida del Bienventurado Padre Ignacio de Loyola, Fundador de la Religión de la Compañía de Jesús,* 5 books in one volume (Barcelona: Imp. y Libreria de la Viuda e Hijos de J. Subirana, 1885), bk. 3, ch. 15, p. 277. For the

importance of the Exercises in the formation of Jesuit contemporaries of Nicolas Point, see Roothaan to Godinot, Rome, November 10, 1836, *Epistolae,* 2:305–9.

35. Father Gil González Dávila, cited in Cándido de Dalmases, *El Padre Francisco de Borja* (Madrid: Biblioteca de Autores Cristianos, 1983), 175.

36. St. Ignatius Loyola, *Spiritual Exercises,* no. 21.

37. St. Ignatius Loyola, "Letter to the religious of the Society in Portugal, Rome, March 26, 1553," *Monumenta Historica Societatis Iesu: Epistolae et Instructiones,* 134 vols. Series Prima, 4 (Madrid: Typis Gabriel López del Harno, 1894–) 29: 671.

38. Ibid.

39. Cited in Burnichon, *Histoire d'un siècle,* 1:170.

40. P. Point, "Vie," 15–16.

41. Ibid., 16.

42. Ibid.; Bishop Alexander Hohenlohe had the reputation among the clergy and laity on both sides of the Atlantic of being a faith healer of extraordinary powers. See the biographical artricle by Ignaz Weilner in *Dictionnaire de Spiritualité,* M. Viller, A. Rayez et A. Derville et collaborateurs, 12 vols. (Paris: Beauchesne, 1937–), 7: col. 586–88.

43. P. Point "Vie," 17.

44. *Catalogus Provinciae Galliae, S.J.* (1824–1825), 10.

45. The best description of this educational concept can be found in Ferdinand Brunetière "Education et instruction" *Revue des Deux-Mondes,* 127, Feb. 15, 1895, 914–34. See John W. Padberg, *Colleges in Controversy: The Jesuit Schools in France from Revival to Suppression, 1815–1880.* (Cambridge: Harvard University Press, 1969), 59–60.

46. St. Ignatius Loyola, *The Constitutions of the Society of Jesus.* Translated, with an Introduction and Commentary by George E. Ganss, S. J. (St. Louis: Institute of Jesuit Sources, 1970), part 1, ch. 2, no. 6, p. 129; 1, 3, 12, p. 134; 1, 3, 5, p. 156.

47. P. Point, "Vie," 17.

48. Ibid.

49. Ibid.

FORMATION

Part One: 1826–1833 (37–64)

1. Delattre, *Etablissements des Jésuites en France,* 3: col. 614.

2. P. Point, "Vie," 17.

3. Burnichon, *Histoire d'un siècle* 1:550.

4. In addition to Sommervogel, *Bibliothèque de la Compagnie de Jésus* 11: 342–56, in which there are many bibliographical references to the *Monita Secreta;* see also T. B. Chapman, "The *Monita Secreta* of the Society of Jesus," *Month* 29 (1873) 96–113; John Gerard, "The Jesuit Bogey and the *Monita Secreta,*" *Month* 98 (1901) 176–85. The two best studies on this subject are Carlos Sommervogel, "L'auteur des Monita," in *Précis historiques* 39 (1890) and Bernard Duhr, "Die *Monita Secreta* order die geheimen Verodungen der Gesellschaft Jesus," *Jesuitenfabeln* (Freiburg im Breisgau: Herder, 1904); and especially, Alexandre Brou, *Les Origines de l'antijésuitisme: les Jésuites de la Légende,* 2 vols. (Paris: Retraux, 1906), 1:275–91.

5. Marcet de la Roche-Armand, L'Abbé Martial, *Les Jésuites Modérne* (Paris: Ambroise Dupont, 1826). This is a curious biographical encyclopedia containing less than flattering biographical sketches of many of the Jesuits already mentioned in this work; idem., *Mémoires d'un jeune Jésuite ou Conjuration de Mont-Rouge* (Paris: Ambroise Dupont, 1828); idem., *Les Sept Bêtes de Montrouge, prophétie et apocalypse, manuscrit trouvé dans le novitiate de Jésuites de Paris* (Paris: Ambroise Dupont, 1827); Brou, *Origines de l'antijésuitisme,* 2:175, et seq.; *Catalogus Provinciae Galliae, S.J.* (1819–1820) 20, 36; (1822–1823), 16–17. There were former scholastics who wrote public letters disclaiming the accusations made by Marcet. See *L'Ami de la Religion et du Roi* 43 (November 8, 1826): 416 and 50 (December 13, 1826): 132.

6. Delattre, *Etablissements des Jésuites en France,* 3: col. 618.

7. Ibid.

8. P. Point, "Vie," 18; *Catalogus Provinciae Galliae, S.J.* (1827–1828), 10.

9. Burnichon, *Histoire d'un siècle,* 1: 404–9

10. *Catalogus Provinciae Galliae, S.J.* (1828–1829), 9–11.

11. Document 1605, ASJSJ; P. Point, "Vie," 17.

12. Ponlevoy, *Life of Father de Ravignan,* 1:92–93.

13. Guillaume de Bertier de Sauvigny, *The Bourbon Restoration,* tr. Lynn M. Case (Philadelphia: University of Pennsylvania Press, 1967), 440–56.

14. François Grandidier, S.J., *Vie du Révérend Père Achille Guidée* (Amiens: Lambert-Caron, 1866), 101–12.

15. P. Point, "Vie," 18–19; Ponlevoy, *Life of Father de Ravignan,* 1:98–100.

16. P. Point "Vie," 19.

17. A summary of a letter from Druilhet to Roothaan, n.d., ("Ex *notis* P. de Guilhermy"), cited in *Catalogus Provinciae Galliae, S.J. (1829–1830),* 7.

18. *Catalogus Provinciae Galliae, S.J.* (1830–1831), 40–41.

19. Ponlevoy, *Life of Father de Ravignan,* 1:53.

20. Ibid., 128.

21. Ibid.

22. These letters were published by an anonymous author in *Monsigneur Canoz, premier eveque de Trichinopoly,* 1805–1888 (Paris: Retaux-Bray, 1889); Sommervogel, *Bibliothèque de la Compagnie de Jésus,* 2: col. 689; Delattre, *Etablissements des Jésuites en France,* 1: col. 709; 2: col. 168; Burnichon, *Histoire d'un siècle,* 2:77; 3:277. A short biography appears in Auguste Jean, S.J., *Le Maduré: L'Ancien et la nouvelle Mission,* 2 vols. (Lille: Desclée de Brouwer, 1894), 2:371–78. There are references to Canoz in this work as well as in letters and reports edited by Joseph Bertrand, S.J., *Lettres édifiantes et curieuses de la nouvelle mission du Maduré,* 2 vols. (Paris: Pelagaud, 1865).

23. Delattre, *Etablissements des Jésuites en France,* 5: col. 49.

24. Lorenzo Cadieux, S.J., ed., *Lettres des Nouvelles Missions du Canada, 1843–1852* (Montréal: Les Editions Bellarmin, 1973), 890–91, 349–58, et passim; Paul Desjardins, S.J., *Le Collège Sainte-Marie de Montréal,* 2 vols. (Montréal: Collège Sainte-Marie, 1945), vol. 1, passim; Sommervogel, *Bibliothèque de la Compagnie de Jésus,* 6: col. 621–23; Raphael N. Hamilton, S.J., *Marquette's Explorations: The Narratives Reexamined* (Madison: The University of Wisconsin Press, 1970), 32–37; Arthur Edward Jones, "Félix Martin," in *Catholic Encyclopedia,* 16 vols., ed. Charles G. Habermann and collaborators (New York: Robert Appleton, 1907–1914), 6: col. 621–23.

25. Burnichon, *Histoire d'un siècle,* 3: 183–84; Delattre, *Etablissements des Jesuites en France,* 3: col. 311, 315–18.

26. Paul Mury, S. J., *Les Jésuites à Cayenne, Histoire d'une mission de vingt-deux ans dans les pénitencièrs de la Guyane* (Strasbourg: F. X. Le Rous, 1895); Burnichon, *Histoire d'un siècle,* 3: 304–10.

27. Francis X. Curran, S.J., *The Return of the Jesuits* (Chicago: Loyola University Press, 1966), 112–14.

28. Pierre-X. Poupard, S.J., *Le R.P. Augustin Laurent de la Compagnie de Jésus, son apostolate dans le diocèse de Nantes* (Paris; Retaux-Bray, 1888), 89–97; 258–66; Delattre, *Etablissements des Jésuites en France,* 5: col. 47–50.

29. Burnichon, *Histoire d'un siècle,* 4: 664–65; Delattre, *Etablissements des Jésuites en France,* 1: col. 535–36; Sommervogel, *Bibliothèque de la Compagnie de Jésus,* 4: col. 535–36.

30. Delattre, *Etablissements des Jésuites en France,* 1: col. 200, 217, 220, 729; 2: col. 589; 4: col. 1123; Burnichon, *Histoire d'un siècle,* 3: 3–19, 173, 373–75, 585–88; 4: 1–7, 38.

31. François-Pierre-Guillaume Guizot, *Memoirs to Illustrate the History of My Time,* 8 vols. (London: R. Bentley, 1858–1867), vol. 7, passim.

32. Sommervogel, *Bibliothèque de la Compagnie de Jésus,* 7: col. 1655; Delattre, *Etablissements des Jésuites en France,* 1: cols. 250, 795, 979; 2: col. 609; 5: col. 14; Burnichon, *Histoire d'un siècle,* 2: 382; 3: 177, 308–310, 435–45, 531–33; 4: 538.

33. Delattre, *Etablissements des Jésuites en France,* 4: col. 1200.

34. Burnichon, *Histoire d'un siècle,* 3: 313–314, 326–30; Delattre, *Etablissements des Jésuites en France,* 1: col. 943–48; 810–22; 3: col. 220–26; Sommervogel, *Bibliothèque de la Compagnie de Jésus,* 2: col. 242.

35. Sommervogel, *Bibliothèque de la Compagnie de Jésus,* 3: cols. 552–53; Delattre, *Etablissements des Jésuites en France,* 5: col. 179; *Dictionnaire de Biographie française,* 13: col. 645–46; Alban, le chevalier de Pidoud de Madueré, *Un Savant Jésuite franc-comtois: le R. P. Pierre Faton de Dompière, près d'Orgelet, 1805–1869* (Besançon: Jacques et Demontrovel, 1914).

36. Sommervogel, *Bibliothèque de la Compagnie de Jésus,* 5: col. 1161; Delattre, *Etablissements des Jésuites en France,* 3: col. 1327; *Nouvelle Biographie Générale,* s.v. "François-Napoléon Moigno"; *Catholic Encyclopedia* (1907–1914), s.v. "Francois Napoleon Moigno," by Henry M. Brock.

37. Sommervogel, *Bibliothèque de la Compagnie de Jésus,* 9: col. 1714–1715.

38. Delattre, *Etablissements des Jésuites en France,* 2: col. 409.

39. Burnichon, *Histoire d'un siècle,* 1: 250.

40. Delattre, *Etablissements des Jésuites en France,* 1: col. 955; Sommervogel, *Bibliothèque de la Compagnie de Jésus,* 9: col. 1715.

41. Hamilton, *Marquette's Explorations,* 41–42, 51.

42. Charles-Augustin Sainte-Beuve, "Mémoire du Père de Montezon sur les jansenistes et les jésuites," in *Port Royal,* 5 vols. (Paris: Hachette, 1858), 1: 520–48.

43. Sommervogel, *Bibliothèque de la Compagnie de Jésus,* 9: col. 1715.

44. Ponlevoy, *Life of Father de Ravignan,* 1: 100–102. Delattre, *Etablissements de Jésuites en France,* 1: col. 936–37; P. Point, "Vie," 20.

45. Delattre, *Etablissements des Jésuites en France,* 4: col. 1111–1112.

46. P. Point, "Vie," 20–21.

47. Burnichon, *Histoire d'un siècle,* 2: 50.

48. Delattre, *Etablissements des Jésuites en France,* 2: col. 622–30.

49. P. Point, "Vie," 20. *Catalogus Provinciae Galliae, S.J. (1831–1832).* 30–34.

50. Delattre, *Etablissements des Jésuites en France,* 2: col. 624.

51. Delattre, *Etablissements des Jésuites en France,* 1: col. 1390–1391; L. de Chazournes, *Vie du R. P. Joseph Barrelle,* 2 vols. (Paris: Plon, 1880), 2: 246–56; *"De Cognominibus polonicis,"* in the preface of *Catalogus Provinciae Galliae, S.J. 1819–1836,* 31–33.

52. Delattre, *Etablissements des Jésuites en France,* 1: col. 1488–1489; Burnichon, *Histoire d'un siècle,* 2: 52–60; *Catalogus Provinciae Galliae, S.J. (1831–1832),* 32.

53. Jean, *Maduré,* 2: 399–401; Sommervogel, *Bibliothèque de la Compagnie de Jésus,* 8: col. 1144.

54. Boudon, *Les Jésuites à Madagascar,* 1: 85–118. Sommervogel, *Bibliothèque de la Compagnie de Jésus,* 2: col. 1536.

55. *Catalogus Provinciae Galliae, S.J. (1822–1823),* 25; *(1831–1832),* 32.

56. *The Catholic Encyclopedia* (1907–1914), s.v. "Louis Lambillotte" (by J. B. Young); *The New Catholic Encyclopedia* (1967), s.v. "Louis Lambillotte" (by F. J. Guenther); Burnichon, *Histoire d'un siècle,* 2: 77–82. *Catalogus Provinciae Galliae, S.J. (1831–1832),* 32; *(1826–1827),* 35.

57. Sommervogel, *Bibliothèque de la Compagnie de Jésus,* 4: col. 1414–1416.

58. *Nouvelle Biographie Générale,* s.v. "Louis Lambillotte."

59. Delattre, *Etablissements des Jésuites en France,* 1: col. 964–67.

60. Burnichon, *Histoire d'un siècle,* 3: 305.

61. Roothaan to Delveaux, Rome, July 3, 1838, cited in Delattre, *Etablissements des Jésuites en France,* 1: col. 966.

62. Burnichon, *Histoire d'un siècle,* 4: 484–85.

63. "Brief report (Latin) on Kenny's visitation of the Missouri Mission, 1831–1832," cited in Gilbert J. Garraghan, S.J., *The Jesuits of the Middle United States,* 3 vols. (New York: America Press, 1938), 1: 319.

64. In addition to the references given above, see also E. Mathieu de Monter, *Louis Lambillotte et ses frères* (Paris: R. Duffer, 1871); Jules Dufour d'Astafort, *Mémoire sur les chantes liturgique réstauré par R. P. Lambillotte . . . et publiés par le P. Dufour . . . Examen des principales difficultés proposée par diverses auteurs et en particulier*

par M. l'abbé Cloet. (Paris: Ledere, 1857); Sommervogel, *Bibliothèque de la Compagnie de Jésus,* 3: col. 260–63.

65. Sommervogel, *Bibliothèque de la Compagnie de Jésus,* 3: col. 1907.

66. *Catholic Encyclopedia* (1907–1914), s.v. "Apostleship of Prayer," (by John W. Wynn); Sommervogel, *Bibliothèque de la Compagnie de Jésus,* 3: col. 1280–1286; Marius Julien, *La Nouvelle Mission de la Compagnie de Jésus en Syria (1831–1895),* 2 vols. (A. Mame et Fils, 1892), 2: 21–31; *Dictionnaire de Spiritualité,* s.v. "Xavier Gautrelet" (by Pierre Vallin).

67. P. Point, "Vie," 22.

FORMATION

Part Two: 1833–1835 (65–83)

1. Delattre, *Etablissements des Jésuites en France,* 2: col. 604, 1106.

2. P. Point, "Vie," 22.

3. Burnichon, *Histoire d'un siècle,* 2: 48–49.

4. Delattre, *Etablissements des Jésuites en France,* 2: col. 1103–1112; P. Point, "Vie," 22; *Memoriale Epistolarum Provinciae (Renault), ASJC,* 26 June 1834.

5. Auguste Séjourné, S.J., *Le Père Jeantier, ou l'apotre des petits enfants. Souvenirs de Saint-Acheul, de Fribourg, du Passage, de Turin, de Bruxelles et de Vannes* (Poitiers: Oudin, 1880); Delattre, *Etablissements des Jésuites en France,* 1: col. 230; 5: col. 65.

6. Servière, *Histoire de la Mission du Kiangnan,* 1: 159, 165, 331; Broullion, *Mémoire sur l'état actuel de la Mission du Kiang-Nan,* 304–6 et passim.

7. Roothaan to Melanie Luiset, Rome, June 6, 1846, Roothaan, *Epistolae,* 5:784. Armand Chossegros, S.J., *Histoire du Noviciat de la Compagnie de Jésus au Canada depuis ses origines, 1843, just'aux Noces d'Or de la Maison Saint-Joséph du Sault-au Recollet* (Montréal: Imprimerie du Sacré Coeur, 1903), 8–17; "An Historical Sketch of the Mission of New York and Canada (continued)," in *Woodstock Letters,* vol. 2 (1873): 194–200. Delattre, *Etablissements des Jésuites en France* 2: col. 1303; 1: col. 782; Cadieux, *Lettres des Nouvelles Missions du Canada,* 1843–1852, 344–348; Sommervogel, *Bibliothèque de la Compagnie de Jésus,* 5: col. 183.

8. Document #1605, ASJSJ.

9. Elesban de Guilhermy, S.J., *Ménologe de la Compagnie de Jésus: Assistance d'Italie,* 2 vols. (Paris: Schneider, 1893), 1:603.

10. *Dictionnaire de Spiritualité,* s.v., "Marie," (by Stephano De Fiores); Donald Attwater, comp., "Month of Mary," *Dictionary of Mary* (New York: P. J. Kennedy and Sons, 1955), 191–92.

11. Chazournes, *Vie du R. P. Joseph Barrelle,* 2:257–67.

12. Sommervogel, *Bibliothèque de la Compagnie de Jésus,* 4: col. 1414–1415.

13. Much of the narrative which follows is taken from Nicolas Point, *"Un Mois de Marie en Espagne,"* ASJSJ, where Point has the events taking place in June, rather than July; Burnichon, *Histoire d'un siècle,* 2:49–50; Delattre, *Etablissements des Jésuites en France,* 2: col. 1108–1110.

14. Burnichon, *Histoire d'un siècle,* 2:45–50. Delattre, *Etablissements des Jésuites en France* 2: col. 1110.

15. Delattre, *Etablissements des Jésuites en France,* 1: col. 948–81; Burnichon, *Histoire d'un siècle,* 2: 61–68.

16. P. Point, "Vie," 23.

17. Delattre, *Etablissements des Jésuites en France,* 1: col. 209–10.

18. Delattre, *Etablissements des Jésuites en France,* 1: col. 502–3.

19. Ponlevoy, *Life of Father de Ravignan,* 1:119.

20. Burnichon, *Histoire d'un siècle,* 2:174–77; Delattre, *Etablissements des Jésuites en France,* 1: col. 503.

21. *Memor. Epist. Prov.* Cited, as are other pieces of information pertinent to this tertianship in the footnotes to *Catalogus Provinciae Galliae, S.J. (1834–1835),* 8.

22. Ponlevoy, *Life of Father de Ravignan,* 1:121–27. See also Joseph de Guibert, S.J., *The Jesuits: Their Spiritual Doctrine and Practice,* trans. William J. Young, S. J. (Chicago: Loyola University Press, 1964), 37.

23. Leslie Stephen and Sir Sidney Lee, eds., *The Dictionary of National Biography,* 22 vols. (Oxford University Press, 1917) 13: 1236; John S. Crone *A Concise Dictionary of Irish Biography* (Liechtenstein: Nendeln Kraus Reprint, 1970), 163–64; David James O'Donoghue, *The Poets of Ireland: Dictionary of Irish Writers of English Verse* (Dublin: Hodges and Figgis, 1912), 326.

24. *Catalogus Provinciae Galliae S.J.: (1822–1823),* 25, (1823–1824), 10.

25. For the de Mac-Carthy family, see Delattre *Establissements des Jésuits en France,* 4:1360; Richard Francis Hayes, *Biographical Dictionary of Irishmen in France* (Dublin: M. H. Gill, 1949) 169–70;

Nouvelle Biographie Générale 32:481; for Nicolas de Mac-Carthy, see Richard Francis Hayes, *Ireland and Irishmen in the French Revolution* (London: Ernest Benn, 1932), 201–3; Sommervogel, *Bibliothèque de la Compagnie de Jésus*, 5: col. 238–41; Delattre, *Etablissements des Jésuites en France* 1: col. 1266; 3: col. 615; 4: col. 1363; Burnichon, *Histoire d'un siècle* 1:xix, 156, 213–14, 503–5; de Guilhermy *Ménologe de la Compagnie de Jésus: Assistance de France,* 1:575–79; *Nouvelle Biographie Générale,* s.v. "Nicolas de Mac-Carthy"; *Dictionnaire de Spiritualité,* s.v. "Nicolas de Mac-Carthy."

26. Stephen and Lee, *Dictionary of National Biography,* 13:1236–38; Crone, *Concise Dictionary of Irish Biography,* 148; Henry Boylan, *A Dictionary of Irish Biography* (Dublin: Gill and Macmillan, 1978), 216–17; O'Donoghue, *The Poets of Ireland,* 298–99.

27. O'Donoghue, *The Poets of Ireland,* 298–99.

28. Stephen and Lee, *Dictionary of National Biography* 13:1237–38; Blanchard Jerrold, collector and editor, *Final Reliques of Father Prout by Francis Sylvester Mahony* (London: Chatto & Windus, 1876).

29. Crone, *Concise Dictionary of Irish Biography,* 163–64; Desmond J. Keenan, *The Catholic Church in Ireland* (Totowa, N.J.: Barnes and Noble, 1983), 140.

30. Burnichon, *Histoire d'un siècle,* 162.

31. Renault to Roothaan, June 5, 1834, cited in n.1, *Catalogus Provinciae Galliae, S.J. (1834–1835),* 8; Ponlevoy, *Life of Father de Ravignan,* 1:119.

32. P. Point, "Vie," 24.

33. Ibid.

34. "Extraits des Chroniques" and *"Notice de la morte de Soeur Marie-Jeanne de Saint-François-Xavier par Soeur Marguerite-Marie du Sacré Coeur de Jésus. Monastère de l'Incarnation des Carmélites de Reims, le 15 Novembre 1869."* Archives, Carmelite Monastery, Reims.

35. *"Souvenirs et mémoires illustrés,"* no. 1604, ASJSJ.

36. P. Point, "Vie," 25.

37. Sommervogel, *Bibliothèque de la Compagnie de Jésus,* 2: col. 993; 4: col. 1874.

38. Jacques Terrien, S.J., *Histoire du R. P. de Clorivière de la Compagnie de Jésus* (Paris: Devalois, 1891), 40–41.

39. Delattre, *Etablissements des Jésuites en France,* 2: col. 1154–60.

40. Ponlevoy, *Life of Father de Ravignan,* 1:122–23.

41. Sommervogel, *Bibliothèque de la Compagnie de Jésus,* 7: col. 1891; Jean, *Maduré,* 1: 452–53.

42. Jean, *Maduré,* 1:452–53.

43. de Guilhermy, *Ménologe de la Compagnie de Jésus. Assistance de la France,* 1:690–92. Jean, *Maduré* 1:260, et passim.

44. Burnichon, *Historie d'un siècle,* 1:486–96; Delattre, *Etablissements des Jésuites en France,* 2: col. 1421–26.

45. Boudon, *Jésuites à Madagascar,* 1:95, 133, 183–84, 217.

AMERICA 1835–1836 (84–110)

1. Nicolas Point, "De Saint-Acheul à Sainte-Marie," essay contained in "Souvenirs et mémoires illustrés," ("Journal") p. 1, col. 1 BO-43-3, ASJSJ; Lettre du P. Point de la Compagnie de Jésus à un Père de la même Compagnie, St. Mary's, Kentucky, January 20, 1836; *Missio Kentukeiensis (1830–1846),* file 3, item 16, p. 1, ASJR.

2. N. Point, "Lettre du Père Point de la Compagnie de Jésus à un Père de la même Compagnie," St. Mary's, Kentucky, January 20, 1836, *Missio Kentukeiensis* (1830–1846), file 3, item 16, p. 1, ASJR.

3. Ibid., p. 2

4. Ibid.

5. Ibid., p. 3.

6. Ibid.

7. Ibid., p. 4; "De Saint-Acheul à Sainte-Marie," in "Journal," p. 1, col. 2.

8. "De Saint-Acheul à Sainte-Marie," in "Journal," p. 2, col. 1; Nicolas Point, letter January 20, 1836, *Missio Kentukeiensis* (1830–1846), file 3, item 16, p. 2, ASJR.

9. P. Point, "Vie," 28–29; "De Saint-Acheul à Sainte-Marie," p. 4, col. 1–2, in "Journal," BO-43-3, ASJSJ.

10. "De Saint Acheul à Sainte-Marie," p. 4, col. 2 in "Journal," BO-43-3, ASJSJ; P. Point, "Vie," 28–29.

11. "De Saint-Acheul à Sainte-Marie," p. 4, col. 2, in "Journal," BO-43-3, ASJSJ.

12. Nicolas Point, letter January 20, 1836, *Missio Kentukeiensis* (1830–1846), file 3, item 16, p. 8, ASJR.

13. P. Point, "Vie," 330–35; "De Saint-Acheul à Sainte-Marie," p. 5, col. 1–2, in "Journal," BO-43-3, ASJSJ.

14. Nicolas Point, letter 20 January 20, 1836, *Missio Kentukeiensis* (1830–1846), file 3, item 16, pp. 8–9, ASJR.

15. Ibid., 10–11; N. Point, "De Saint-Acheul à Sainte Marie," p. 4, col. 1–2; p. 5, col. 1–2, in "Journal," BO-43-3, ASJSJ.

16. N. Point, "De Saint-Acheul à Sainte-Marie," p. 5, col. 1–2, in "Journal," BO-43-3, ASJSJ. Here Point reported that the destruction of the four-block fire that he witnessed cost $100,000. "Does not Father Point fall here into one of those exaggerations that is so easy for those who arrive in a new country can make?" is the rhetorical question posed by Léon Pouliot, S.J. in his excellent essay, "Le Père Nicolas Point (1799–1868) . . .," 32, n. 12, cited in chapter 1, note 1. However, in Point's letter he states this loss was 100,000 *francs*, or approximately $22,000, a more reasonable figure. Nicolas Point, letter 20 January 1836, *Missio Kentukeiensis* (1830–1846), file 3, item 16, p. 12, ASJR.

17. *"Lettre du Père Murphy, faisant suite à la lettre du Père Point du 20 Janvier, 1836,"* St. Mary's, Kentucky, January 22, 1836, *Missio Kentukeiensis* (1830–1846), file 3, item 17, p. 1, ASJR.

18. Nicolas Point, letter January 20, 1836, *Missio Kentukeiensis* (1830–1846), file 3, item 16, p. 14, ASJR.

19. William Murphy, letter January 22, 1836, *Missio Kentukeiensis* (1830–1846), file 3, item 17, p. 1, ASJR.

20. Garraghan, *Jesuits of the Middle U.S.*, 1:22–23; 3:392–93, 411–14.

21. "Plan of a Reduction for Our North American Indians, with a letter from Father Paul M. Ponziglione, S.J." *Woodstock Letters*, 25 (1896): 353–61. Idem., "Recollections of Father Van Quickenborne and the Osage Mission," *Woodstock Letters*, 24 (1895): 37–42; see Garraghan, *Jesuits of the Middle U.S.*, 1: 170–75; 376–95.

22. P. Point, "Vie," 34.

23. Garraghan, *Jesuits of the Middle U.S.*, 1: 392. Lawrence B. Palladino, S.J., *Indian and White in the Northwest: A History of Catholicity in Montana, 1831 to 1891*. (Lancaster, Penna.: Wickersham Publishing Co., 1922), 8–12.

24. Palladino, *Indian and White in the Northwest*, 25–26.

25. Garraghan, *Jesuits of the Middle U.S.*, 1: 392.

26. P. Point, "Vie," 34. N. Point, "*De Saint-Acheul* à *Sainte-Marie*," p. 6, col. 1, in "Journal," BO-43-3, ASJSJ.

27. Point to Roothaan, December 23, 1835, Philadelphia, *Missio Kentukeiensis* (1830–1846), file 3, item 15, ASJR.

28. William Murphy, letter January 22, 1836, *Missio Kentukeiensis (1830–1846)*, file 3, item 17, pp. 1–2, *ASJR;* N. Point, "*De Saint-Acheul* à *Sainte-Marie*," p. 6, col. 2, in "Journal" BO-43-3, ASJSJ.

29. William Murphy, letter January 22, 1836, *Missio Kentukeiensis* (1830–1846), file 3, item 17, pp. 1–2, ASJR.

30. Ibid., 2.

31. Nicolas Point, *"De Saint-Acheul à Sainte-Marie,"* in "Journal," p. 6, col. 2, BO-43-3, ASJSJ.

32. Ibid.

33. Ibid.; William Murphy, letter January 22, 1836, *Missio Kentukeiensis* (1830–1846) file 3, item 17, p. 2, ASJR.

34. P. Point, "Vie," 34; William Murphy, letter January 22, 1836, *Missio Kentukeiensis* (1830–1846), file 3, item 17, p. 2, ASJR.

35. William Murphy, letter January 22, 1836, *Missio Kentukeiensis* (1830–1846), file 3, item 17, p. 2; Nicolas Point, letter January 20, 1835, *Missio Kentukeiensis,* file 3, item 16, p. 13, ASJR.

36. P. Point, "Vie," 34–35.

37. William Murphy, letter January 22, 1836, *Missio Kentukeiensis* (1830–1846), file 3, item 17, p. 2, ASJR.

38. Ibid., 3; P. Point, "Vie," 35.

39. William Murphy, letter January 22, 1836, Missio Kentukeiensis (1830–1846), file 3, item 17, p. 3, ASJR.

40. Ibid.

41. *Catalogus Provinciae Galliae, S.J., (1829–1830),* 13, n. 1.

42. Delattre, *Etablissements des Jésuites en France,* 1: col. 782–83. "Ex notis P. de Guilhermy," *Catalogus Provinciae Galliae, S.J.* (1829–1830), 7. "Father Nicolas Petit, S.J. and the Coadjutorship of Vencennes," *Woodstock Letters,* 31(1902):39.

43. J.-B. Gury, "Notice sur les resultats des 27, 28, 29 Juillet [1830] pour Compagnie de Jésus en France," ASJC, 28 (henceforth, Gury, "Notice 1830"); *Catalogus Provinciae Galliae, S.J. (1829–1830),* 30, n.1.

44. "An Historical Sketch of the Mission of New York and Canada," *Woodstock Letters,* 2(1873):111; Curran, *Return of the Jesuits,* 57–59.

45. Delattre, *Etablissements des Jésuites en France,* 1: col. 703–9. *Catalogus Provinciae Galliae, S.J. (1827–1828),* 30.

46. *Notice sur le R. P. Chazelle,* p. 1, ASJC, cited in "Praefatio" of the *Catalogus Provinciae Galliae, S.J. (1819–1836)* p. 53; Gury, "Notice 1830," 34, ASJC; *Catalogus Provinciae Galliae, S.J. (1829–1830),* 30, n.1.

47. *Catalogus Provinciae Galliae, S.J. (1829–1830),* 24, n. 1.

48. Burnichon, *Histoire d'un siècle,* 4:297. Walter H. Hill, "Some Reminiscences of St. Mary's College, Kentucky," *Woodstock Letters,* 20 (1891): 25–27 (hereafter, Hill, "Reminiscences").

49. *"Ex Notis P. de Guilhermy,"* cited in *Catalogus Provinciae Galliae, S.J. (1830–1831)*, 6.

50. "An Historical Sketch of the Mission of New York and Canada," *Woodstock Letters*, 2(1873):111.

51. The best account of St. Mary's College during this period is "The French Blackrobes Return to America," chapter 3 in Rev. Francis X. Curran's excellent book *The Return of the Jesuits: Chapters in the History of the Society of Jesus in Nineteenth-century America*, 57–80. See chapter 3, n.27.

52. Joseph Schauinger, *Cathedrals in the Wilderness* (New York: Bruce, 1952), 181–82.

53. Hill, "Reminiscences," *Woodstock Letters*, 20(1891):26.

54. *Dictionary of American Biography*, s.v. "Charles Nerinckx" (by R. J. Purcell).

55. Hill, "Reminiscences," *Woodstock Letters*, 20(1981):6.

55. Ibid.

56. "An Historical Sketch of the Mission of New York and Canada," *Woodstock Letters*, 2(1891):111.

57. Martin J. Spalding, *Sketches of the Early Catholic Missions of Kentucky from their Commencement in 1787, to the Jubilee of 1826–27* (Louisville: B. J. Webb & Brother, 1844), 273.

58. *"Notice sur le R. P. Chazelle,"* 2, ASJC, cited in *Catalogus Provinciae Galliae, S.J. (1835–1836)*, 36, n. 1.

59. Schauinger, *Cathedrals in the Wilderness*, 183.

60. Bishop Flaget to Bishop Bruté, October 4, 1831, cited in Joseph Schauinger, *Cathedrals in the Wilderness*, 265.

61. Curran, *Return of the Jesuits*, 63.

62. "Simon Fouche," *Woodstock Letters*, 19(1980):124.

63. This man sometimes signs his name François-Xavier Evremond-Harissart. On December 28, 1843, he addressed a letter to Father General Roothaan explaining that Father William Murphy had encouraged him to write a "Relation of the Kentucky Mission," in imitation of the Relations sixteenth-century French Jesuits who had written descriptions of their fields of activity. Complying with Murphy's orders, he informed the General he was including this forty-six page document in his letter. Again in imitation of the earlier French missionaries, he sent an identical copy of this work, "somewhat poetic in form," to the Paris Provincial, Father Boulanger, on March 20, 1844, thinking it might be published in the Annals. (*ASJR, Prov. Franc.* III). The "Relation" Harissart sent Boulanger is presently on permanent loan at the Gleeson Library, University of San Francisco. It has never been published and

probably never will be because neither its poetic form nor its historic value account gives a realistic picture of Kentucky in the 1840s.

64. *"Notice sur le R. P. Chazelle,"* 15, ASJC, cited in *Catalogus Provinciae Galliae* S.J. (1832–1833), 33, n. 1.

65. Curran, *Return of the Jesuits,* 60; *Catalogus Provinciae Galliae, S.J.* (1832–1833), 32.

66. *Catalogus Provinciae Galliae, S.J. (1833–1834),* 34, n. 2.

67. *Catalogus Provinciae Galliae, S.J. (1832–1833),* 32, n. 1.

68. Ibid. In a letter, dated June 21, 1833 to Chazelle, Renault appointed Legoüais master of novices. *Catalogus Provinciae Galliae, S.J. (*1833–1834),* 35, n. 1.

69. Hill, "Reminiscences," *Woodstock Letters,* 20(1891):33–34. "Some Facts and Incidents Relating to St. Joseph's College, Bardstown, Kentucky," *Woodstock Letters,* 26(1897):101. Michael Kenny, *Catholic Culture in Alabama.* (New York: The American Press, 1931), 131–132, 155–157; Cornelius M. Buckley, S.J., trans. and ed., *A Frenchman, a Chaplain, a Rebel: The War Letters of Père Louis-Hippolyte Gache, S.J.* (Chicago: Loyola University Press, 1981), 176, 185.

70. P. Gury, *"Mémoires . . . Montrouge,"* ASJC, 288. Cited in *Catalogus Provinciae Galliae, S.J. (1825–1826),* 31, n. 1.

71. "An Historical Sketch of the Mission of New York and Canada," *Woodstock Letters,* 2(1873):114.

72. Ibid.

73. Thomas J. Campbell, "Fordham University," *Woodstock Letters,* 45(1916):353.

74. *"Notice sur le R. P. Chazelle,"* ASJC, 9, cited in *Catalogus Provinciae Galliae, S.J. (1833–1834),* 34, n. 4.

75. Hill, "Reminiscences," *Woodstock Letters,* 20(1891):29.

76. Schauinger, *Cathedrals in the Wilderness,* 273.

77. Hill, "Reminiscences," *Woodstock Letters,* 20(1891):20.

78. Thomas J. Campbell, "Fordham University," *Woodstock Letters,* 45(1916):354.

79. "An Historical Sketch of the Mission of New York and Canada," *Woodstock Letters,* 2(1873):123.

80. Curran, *Return of the Jesuits,* 63.

81. Hill, "Reminiscences," *Woodstock Letters,* 20(1891):30.

82. Ibid.

83. Ibid.

84. *Catalogus Provinciae Galliae, S.J. (1835–1836),* 36–37; P. Point, "Vie," 38.

85. Hill, "Reminiscences," *Woodstock Letters,* 22(1891):28–29.

86. Nicolas Point, "Saint-Marie du Kentuky," [sic], an essay contained in *"Souvenirs* et *mémoires illustrés,"* 3, col. 2; 4, col. 1, BO-43-3, ASJSJ.

87. Ibid., 2, col. 1.

88. Ibid., 2, col. 2; 3, col. 1.

89. Ibid., 2, col. 2.

90. Ibid., 3, col. 1.

91. Ibid., 2, col. 1.

92. *Litterae annuae Societatis Jèsus in Gallia (1814–1836),* 2 vols., 2:440, ASJC; *Diarium Provinciae Galliae (1833–1844),* "27 dec. 1835," ASJC; *Catalogus Provinciae Galliae, S.J. (1835–1836),* 37, n. 1; Hill, "Reminiscences," *Woodstock Letters,* 20(1891):32.

93. *"Notice nécrologique,"* p. 3, BO-39-183, ASJSJ.

94. N. Point, "Sainte-Marie," 4, col. 2.

95. Ibid., 5, col. 2. Point and Badin did meet, however, at a later date, probably in or near the year 1853, the year of the eighty-five-year-old Badin's death; P. Point, "Vie," 38, n. 1.

96. N. Point, "Sainte-Marie," 8, col. 1.

97. Chazelle to Roothaan, St. Mary's, December 8, 1836, *Missio Kentukeiensis (1830–1846),* file 3, item 21, ASJR.

98. Chazelle to Roothaan, St. Mary's, December 11, 1836, *Missio Kentukeiensis (1830–1846),* file 3, item 22, ASJR.

99. Chazelle to Roothaan, St. Mary's, March 8, 1837 and March 10, 1837, *Missio Kentukeiensis (1830–1836),* file 3, item 4, p. 4; file 4, item 3, ASJR.

100. Edward I. Devitt, "History of the Maryland and New York Provinces," *Woodstock Letters,* 65(1936):12–14; Curran, *Return of the Jesuits,* 87.

101. N. Point, "Sainte-Marie," title page.

102. Thomas J. Campbell, "Fordham University," *Woodstock Letters,* 45(1916):67.

103. N. Point, "Sainte-Marie," 5, col. 2.

104. Ibid., 8, col. 1.

105. P. Point, "Vie," 39; N. Point, "Sainte-Marie," 8, col. 2.

106. N. Point, "Saint-Marie," 5, col. 2.

107. Ibid., 8, col. 2.

108. Ibid.

109. Ibid., 9, col. 2; 10, col. 1.

110. Ibid., 8–11; P. Point, "Vie," 40.

111. P. Point, "Vie," 39–40; N. Point, "Sainte-Marie," 11, col. 2; 12, col. 1.

LOUISIANA 1826–1837 (111–132)

1. Cited in Garraghan. *Jesuits of the Middle U.S.* 3:129.

2. *Catalogus Provinciae Galliae, S.J. (1826–1827),* 23 *(1828–1829),* 31–34.

3. Garraghan, *Jesuits of the Middle U.S.,* 3: 129–30.

4. *"Notice sur le Père Chazelle,"* 9, ASJC.

5. Garraghan, *Jesuits of the Middle U.S.,* 3:129–30; Ladavière had replaced the ubiquitous Belgian priest Charles de la Croix (1792–1869) at Convent. It was he who built the church there as well as other small chapels and mission stations in the district. He was the first Catholic missionary to the Osage Indians, a close friend of Mère Philippine Duchesne (1769–1852); as pastor of St. Ferdinand's, Florissant, Missouri, he had welcomed her and her Religious of the Sacred Heart when they arrived there in 1819. Later, in 1823, he was on hand to greet Van Quickenborne and the Jesuits. *Annales de la Propagation de la foi,* 1, 450, 484.

6. Kenny, *Catholic Culture in Alabama,* 128–29.

7. Delattre, *Etablissements des Jésuites en France,* 2:840.

8. Renault to Roothaan, Avignon, April 26, 1836, France, 3, 8:1, ASJR.

9. Roothaan to Renault, Rome, July 26, 1836, Litterae Prov. Gall. a die l Aprilis 1830–5 Septemberis, 1836, 284–86, ASJR; Garraghan, *Jesuits of the Middle U.S.,* 3:134; Delattre, *Etablissements des Jésuites en France,* 2:605.

10. Druilhet to Roothaan, Lyon, August 9, 1836, "France," file 3, item 7, p. 9, ASJR.

11. Roothaan to Renault, Rome, July 26, 1836, Litterae Prov. Gall. a die 1 Aprilis 1830–5 Septemberis, 1836, 284–86, ASJR.

12. "Praefacio" in *Catalogus Provinciae Galliae, 1819–1836,* 56.

13. Roothaan to Renault, Rome, July 26, 1836, Litterae Prov. Gall. a die 1 Aprilis 1830–5 Septemberis 1830, 284–86, ASJR.

14. Garraghan, *Jesuits of the Middle U.S.,* 1:15–72.

15. Ibid., 59–60. Garraghan cites these significant words from Bishop Fenwick's letter to Bishop DuBourg, March 13, 1823: "It was found that the former Superior [Kohlmann] had received into the Society more members than it could consequently support . . . It is somewhat

singular that the Secretary of War should make the demand of missionaries, just at the time when we could best spare them and offer a support for the same, precisely when every other means has failed us."

16. Ibid., 97–99.

17. Ibid., 88–90.

18. Ibid., 100.

19. Ibid., 283.

20. Ibid., 283–84.

21. Ibid., 147–48.

22. Ibid., 282–94.

23. Ibid., 294–308; *Catalogus Provinciae Galliae, S.J. (1832–1833),* 39.

24. Verhaegen to Roothaan, St. Louis, January 15, 1831, cited in Garraghan, *Jesuits of the Middle U.S.,* 1:300.

25. Verhaegen to Roothaan, St. Louis, February 14, 1831, cited in Garrahgan. *Jesuits of the Middle U.S.,* 1:298–99.

26. Verhaegen to Roothaan, St. Louis, January 15, 1831, cited in Garraghan, *Jesuits of the Middle U.S.,* 1:300.

27. De Neckere to Dzierzynski, St. Michel, Louisiana, July 20, 1831, cited in Garraghan, *Jesuits of the Middle U.S.,* 3:130.

28. Ibid., 132–34.

29. Walsh to Roothaan, St. Louis, February 15, 1833 and Roothaan to Van de Velde, Rome, June 18, 1833, cited in Garraghan, *Jesuits of the Middle U.S.,* 1:301.

30. Guidée to Roothaan, Paris, November 16, 1836, cited in *Praefatio in Catalogos Provinciae Galliae, 1819–1836,* 56.

31. Ibid.

32. Michael Kenny, S.J., "Jesuits in the Southland," a manuscript of unpublished notes in ASJNO (henceforth, cited as "Notes").

33. P. Point, "Vie," 4.

34. Kenny, "Notes," 32–36.

35. Point to Roothaan, Grand Coteau, February 17, 1837, N. Aur. I:1:13, ASJR.

36. Renault to Roothaan, Lyon, August 10, 1836, cited in Garraghan, *Jesuits of the Middle U.S.,* 3:135.

37. "Father John Abbadie: A Sketch," *Woodstock Letters,* 24 (1895):16–36; C.M. Widman, "Grand Coteau College in Wartimes, 1860–1866," *Woodstock Letters,* 30(1901):41; J. Maitrugues, "St. Charles College, Grand Coteau, 1835–1858," *Woodstock Letters,* 5 (1870):22; Buckley, ed., *A Frenchman, a Chaplain, a Rebel.*

38. Renault to Roothaan, Lyon, August 10, 1836, cited in Garraghan, *Jesuits of the Middle U.S.,* 3:135.

39. Point to Roothaan, Grand Coteau, August 28, 1839, N. Aur. I:2:4, ASJR.

40. Garraghan, *Jesuits of the Middle U.S.,* 1:486.

41. Mignard to Roothaan, St. Louis, December 9, 1840, N. Aur., I:2:35, ASJR.

42. *Catalogus Provinciae Galliae, S.J. (1828–1829),* 28, n. 2.

43. Ibid., 34; *(1833–1834),* 30.

44. Ibid., *(1828–1829),* 16; *(1830–1831),* 41; Alsberg obituary, *Woodstock Letters,* 21(1892):427.

45. Duranquet to Roothaan, Grand Coteau, April 1, 1846, N. Aur. 1, III, 23, ASJR.

46. Point to Roothaan, Grand Coteau, February 18, 1839, N. Aur. 1:II:11. ASJR.

47. Jean, *Maduré,* 1:277–78; J. Specht, "Father Dominic du Ranquet: A Sketch of His Life and Labors (1813–1900)," *Woodstock Letters,* 30(1901):177–95.

48. Henry Duranquet obituary, *Woodstock Letters,* 22(1893):132.

49. Ibid.

50. Patrick J. Dooley, "Woodstock and Its Makers: Spiritual Giants," *Woodstock Letters,* 56(1927):133–34.

51. Henry Duranquet obituary, *Woodstock Letters,* 22(1893):133; See also, *Woodstock Letters,* 73(1944):22–24; Sommervogel, *Bibliothèque de la Compagnie de Jésus,* 6:1440.

52. Verhaegen to Roothaan, St. Louis, February 28, 1837, cited in Garraghan, *Jesuits of the Middle U.S.,* 1:354.

53. Ibid., 350–61.

54. Ibid., 354, citing Verhaegen to Roothaan, St. Louis, February 28, 1837.

55. Chazelle to Roothaan, St. Mary's, Kentucky, March 10, 1837, Missio Kentukeiensis, file 4, item 3.

56. "Father John Abbadie: A Sketch," *Woodstock Letters,* 24(1895):20.

57. Kenny, "Notes," 34.

58. P. Point, "Vie," 41.

59. See Point to Roothaan, Grand Coteau February 17, 1837 and September 11, 1839, N. Aur. 1:I:13 and 1:II:22, ASJR for good examples of this discernment process.

60. Point to Roothaan, April 28, 1839, N. Aur. 1:II:21, ASJR.

61. P. Point, "Vie," 41.

62. Ibid.

63. Garraghan, *Jesuits of the Middle U.S.,* 3:137.

64. J. Maitrugues, "St. Charles College, Grand Coteau, 1835–1838," *Woodstock Letters* 5(1870):19.

65. Point to Roothaan, Grand Coteau, February 18, 1839, N. Aul. 1:II:11, ASJR.

66. P. Point, "Vie," 41–42; Kenny, "Notes," 34–36; Garraghan, *Jesuits of the Middle U.S.,* 3:137–38.

ST. CHARLES COLLEGE
Part One: 1837–1838 (133–156)

1. Garraghan, *Jesuits of the Middle U.S.,* 1:408.

2. Ibid., 1:22–28.

3. Ibid., 1:408–9.

4. Ibid., 1:411, citing Roothaan to Quickenborne, Rome, September 30, 1837.

5. Kenny, "Notes," 35.

6. Fr. John Francis Abbadie: A Sketch," *Woodstock Letters* 24(1895):21; J. Maitrugues, "St. Charles College, Grand Coteau," *Woodstock Letters* 5(1876):20–21.

7. Cited in Garraghan, *Jesuits of the Middle U.S.,* 3:139.

8. Burnichon, *Histoire d'un siècle,* 3:302.

9. Kenny, "Notes," 36; Garraghan, *Jesuits of the Middle U.S.,* 3:139, 149.

10. The Grand Coteau consultors' letters to the General during this period are not extant.

11. Roothaan to Point, Rome, May 13, 1838, "France" 2: 71–72, ASJR.

12. Point to Roothaan, Grand Coteau, July 5, 1838, N. Aur. 1, II:23, ASJR.

13. Kenny, "Notes," 37. Point to Roothaan, Grand Coteau, July 11, 1839, N. Aur. 1, 2:22, ASJR.

14. Mary Therese Bisgood, S.H.C.J., *Cornelia Connelly* (London Burns Otis, 1961), 23.

15. Point to Roothaan, Grand Coteau, N. Aur. 1, 2:23, ASJR.

16. Bisgood, *Cornelia Connelly,* 23.

17. Roothaan to Verhaegen, July 14, 1839, cited in Garraghan, *Jesuits of the Middle U.S.*, 3:141.

18. Soller to Roothaan, Grand Coteau, January 24, 1839, N. Aur. 1:2:44, ASJR.

19. Roothaan to Point, Rome, June 13, 1837, *France* 2:39–41, ASJR.

20. Delattre, *Etablissements des Jésuites en France,* 2:605.

21. *Catalogus Provinciae Galliae (1831–32)* 29.

22. Sommervogel, *Bibliothèque de la Compagnie de Jésus,* 6:873; Julien, *Compagnie de Jésus en Syrie,* 1:215–37. Burnichon, *Histoire d'un siècle* 1:206, 3:310–23.

23. Burnichon, *Histoire d'un siècle,* 3:272–74; Jean, *Maduré,* 1:246–47.

24. Delattre, *Etablissements des Jésuites en France,* 1:144; Burnichon, *Histoire d'un siècle,* 3:320–33.

25. Garraghan, *Jesuits of the Middle U.S.,* 2:107–9; "Obituary of Ferdinand A. Moeller, 1852–1946," *Woodstock Letters,* 76(1947):343–46.

26. Boudreaux to Roothaan, Grand Coteau, August 16, 1847, N. Aur., 2:10:4, ASJR.

27. "Obituary of Isidore J. Boudreaux," *Woodstock Letters,* 14(1855):343–46. For Point's tertian instructor's attitude toward the Blessed Sacrament, see Ponlevoy *Life of Father de Ravignan,* 1:101.

28. "Marquette College," *Woodstock Letters,* 21(1892):56.

29. Kenny, "Notes," 38–40.

30. "Fr. John Francis Abbadie: A Sketch," *Woodstock Letters,* 24(1895):22, 29; Abbadie, *"Rélation de qui est passé au collège Saint-Charles, Grand Coteau, pendant la visite du R. P. Verhaegen, depuis 4 decembre jusqu'au 19 janvier,"* Grand Coteau, February 18, 1839, N. Aur. 1:2:11, ASJR.

31. Soller to Roothaan, Grand Coteau, January 28, 1839, N. Aur.: 1:2:8, ASJR.

32. Ibid.

33. Point to Roothaan, Grand Coteau, January 24, 1839, N. Aur. 1:2:7, ASJR.

34. Soller to Roothaan, Grand Coteau, January 24, 1839, N. Aur. 1:2:8, ASJR.

35. Abbadie to Roothaan, Grand Coteau, February 18, 1839, N. Aur. 1:2:1, ASJR.

36. Soller to Roothaan, Grand Coteau, January 24, 1839, N. Aur. 1:2:8, ASJR.

37. Abbadie to Roothaan, Grand Coteau, February 18, 1839, N. Aur. 1:2:11, ASJR. Verhaegen obviously did not have philosophical problems with slavery. What Point's opinion is on the subject is not known. Both black slavery and the desire to set up reductions for the Indians could fit within the perimeters of paternalism motivated by Christian justice and charity. Van Quickenborne led Verhaegen to Missouri *"cum turba Negrorum"* in order to serve the Indians. See "Jesuit Farms in Maryland: The Negro Slaves," *Woodstock Letters,* 41(1912):22–23. The slave that Verhaegen purchased in December 1838 over the objections of Brother Chavet and Father Point was "Ignace by name," also known as "Nace," who was bought for $1,000. "John Francis Abbadie: A Sketch," *Woodstock Letters* 24(1895):22, 38. Soller to Roothaan, Grand Coteau, January 24, 1839, N. Aur. 1:2:8, ASJR.

39. Point to Roothaan, Grand Coteau, January 24, 1839, N. Aur. 1:2:7, ASJR.

40. Ibid.

41. Abbadie to Roothaan, Grand Coteau. February 18, 1839, N. Aur. 1:2:11, ASJR.

42. De Vos to Roothaan, Grand Coteau, January 24, 1839, N. Aur. 1:2:6, ASJR.

43. Duranquet to Jansens, Grand Coteau, February 9, 1839, N. Aur. 1:2:10, ASJR.

44. Connelly to Roothaan, Grand Coteau, February 28, 1839, N. Aur. 1:2:13, ASJR.

45. Soller to Roothaan, Grand Coteau, January 24, 1839, N. Aur. 1:2:8, ASJR.

46. Abbadie to Roothaan, Grand Coteau, April 19, 1839. N. Aur. 1:2:37, ASJR.

47. Ibid.; "Consultors meetings minutes," 1834, 4, ASJSL.

48. Abbadie to Roothaan, Grand Coteau, April 19, 1839, N. Aur. 1:2:37, ASJR.

49. Garraghan, *Jesuits of the Middle U.S.,* 3:116–21.

50. Ibid., 1:323–24.

51. Ibid.

52. Ibid. See also, 3:116–121.

53. Point to Verhaegen, Grand Coteau, January 24, 1839, N. Aur. 1:2:7, ASJR; Roothaan to Galicet, Rome, July 5, 1836; Roothaan, *Epistolae,* 2:201.

54. Connelly to Roothaan, Grand Coteau, February 28, 1839, N. Aur. 1:2:14, ASJR.

55. Connelly to Blanc. Grand Coteau, March 14, 1839, V-4-K, UNDA.

56. Verhaegen to Roothaan, St. Louis, March 24, 1839, N. Aur. 1:2:16, ASJR.

57. Ladavière to Roothaan, New Orleans, March 19, 1839, N. Aur. 1:2:15, ASJR.

58. Soller to Roothaan, Grand Coteau, January 24, 1839, N. Aur. 1:2:8, ASJR.

59. Point to Roothaan, Grand Coteau, January 24, 1839, N. Aur. 1:2:7, ASJR.

60. Abbadie to Roothaan, Grand Coteau, March 23, 1839, N. Aur. 1:2:17, ASJR.

61. Connelly to Roothaan, Grand Coteau, March 3, 1839, N. Aur. 1:2:13, ASJR.

62. Abbadie to Roothaan, Grand Coteau, March 23, 1839, N. Aur. 1:2:17, ASJR.

63. His full name was Theodore De Theux de Maylandt, a member of the Belgian aristocracy who renounced his title when he entered the society as a priest in 1816. W. T. Doran, "St. Stanislaus Seminary," *Woodstock Letters* 8(1910):355.

64. Garraghan, *Jesuits of the Middle U.S.*, 1:378–79

65. Ibid., 384.

66. Ibid., 486–87.

67. Abbadie to Roothaan, Grand Coteau, November 7, 1839, N. Aur. 1:2:30, ASJR.

ST. CHARLES COLLEGE
Part Two: 1839 (157–176)

1. Garraghan, *Jesuits of the Middle U.S.*, 3:150; Kenny, "Notes," 41.

2. Garraghan, *Jesuits of the Middle U.S.*, 1:345, 3:141.

3. Ibid., 1:202, 410, 432; 3:141–42.

4. Ibid., 1:358, 3:156.

5. Ibid., 1:358, 3:148.

6. Abbadie to Roothaan, Grand Coteau, November 7, 1839, N. Aur. 1, 2:30, ASJR.

7. Garraghan, *Jesuits of the Middle U.S.*, 2:105.

8. Ibid., 105–7.

9. Ibid., 1:393, 396, 403.

10. Ibid., 3:301.

11. Point to Roothaan, Grand Coteau, April 28, 1839, Aur. 1, 2: 21, ASJR.

12. "Fr. John Francis Abbadie: A Sketch," *Woodstock Letters,* 24(1895):21.

13. Point to Verhaegen, Grand Coteau, April 28, 1839 (copy sent to Reverend Father Roothaan), N. Aur. 1:2:21, ASJR.

14. Ibid.

15. Pin to Roothaan, Grand Coteau, November 7, 1839. N. Aur. 1, 2:31, ASJR.

16. Garraghan, *Jesuits of the Middle U.S.* 1:20–22, 29; W.T. Doran, "St. Stanislaus Seminary," *Woodstock Letters,* 39(1910):351.

17. Pin to Roothaan, Grand Coteau, November 7, 1839, N. Aur. 1, 2:31, ASJR.

18. Abbadie to Roothaan, Grand Coteau, March 29, 1839, N. Aur. 1, 2:17, ASJR.

19. Roothaan to Abbadie, Rome, June 25, 1839, cited in Garraghan, *Jesuits of the Middle U.S.,* 3:143.

20. Abbadie to Roothaan, Rome, November 7, 1839, N. Aur. 1, 2:30, ASJR.

21. Point to Roothaan, Grand Coteau, August 28, 1839, N. Aur. 1, 2:4, ASJR.

22. Ibid.

23. Point to Roothaan, Grand Coteau, September 11, 1839, N. Aur. 1, 2:22, ASJR.

24. "Souvenirs et mémoires illustrés: Collège Saint-Charles," ASJSJ, 1605.

25. J. Maitrugues, "St. Charles College, Grand Coteau," Woodstock Letters, 5 (1876):21.

26. "Fr. John Francis Abbadie," *Woodstock Letters,* 24 (1895):22.

27. Michael Kenny, "Notes," 38–39.

28. Abbadie to Roothaan, Grand Coteau, October 16, 1859, N. Aur. 1, II: 28, ASJR; Garraghan, *Jesuits of the Middle U.S.,* 3:142.

29. Abbadie to Roothaan, Grand Coteau, October 16, 1859, N. Aur. 1, 2:28, ASJR.

30. Cited in Garraghan, *Jesuits of the Middle U.S.,* 3:142.

31. Abbadie to Roothaan, Grand Coteau, October 12, 1859, N. Aur. 1, 2:27, ASJR.

32. P. Point, "Vie," 42.

33. Abbadie to Roothaan, Grand Coteau, November 7, 1839, N. Aur. 1, 2:30, ASJR.

34. P. Point, "Vie," 42; Bisgood, *Cornelia Connelly,* 26.

35. Marie Osmonde de Maille, S.J.C.J., *Du Marriage au cloître* (Paris: Editions France, 1962), 37.

36. *Life of Cornelia Connelly, 1809–1879, Foundress of the Society of the Holy Child Jesus by a member of the Society.* (London: Longmans, Green and Co., 1922) 33, cited in Garraghan, *Jesuits of the Middle U.S.* 3:144.

37. Bisgood, *Cornelia Connelly,* 32.

38. James Walsh, "The Vocation of Cornelia Connelly, #1," *Month* 20, New Series (1958), 266.

39. Juliana Wadham, *The Case of Cornelia Connelly* (New York: Pantheon, 1957).

40. P. Point, "Vie," 45.

41. Point to Jeanne-Marie Point, R.S.C.J., Grand Coteau, May 17, 1840, ASJSJ.

42. Cited in James Walsh, "The Vocation of Cornelia Connelly, #1," *Month* 20, New Series (1958), 267.

43. Ibid., 272.

44. Cited in James Walsh, "The Vocation of Cornelia Connelly, #2," *Month* 21, New Series (1959), 19.

45. Wadham, *Case of Cornelia Connelly,* 113–49.

46. Anon., *Life of Cornelia Connelly,* cited in Garraghan, *Jesuits in the Middle U.S.* 3:144.

47. Verhaegen to Roothaan, St. Louis, September 18, 1839, 1, 2:24, ASJR.

48. Roothaan to Verhaegen, Rome, July 14, 1838, cited in Garraghan, *Jesuits of the Middle U.S.,* 3:140.

49. Various fathers at Grand Coteau to Roothann, November 10–11, 1839, N. Aur. 1, 2:32–3, ASJR.

50. De Leeuw to Roothaan, Grand Coteau, January 14, 1840, N. Aur. 1, 2:36, ASJR.

51. Abbadie to Roothaan, Grand Coteau November 7, 1839, N. Aur. 1, 2:30, ASJR.

52. Kenny, "Notes," 40.

53. Verhaegen to Rosati, December 1839, cited in Garraghan, *Jesuits of the Middle U.S.,* 3:147.

54. Kenny, "Notes," 39; P. Point, "Vie," 43.

55. Verhaegen to McSherry, St. Louis, October 16, 1833, cited in Garraghan, *Jesuits of the Middle U.S.,* I:302.

56. Walter H. Hill, "Father Peter J. Verhaegen, S.J.: An Historical Sketch," *Woodstock Letters* 27 (1898):191–93.

57. J. Maitrugues, "St. Charles College, Grand Coteau," *Woodstock Letters* 5(1876):21.

58. De Vos to Roothaan, Grand Coteau, January 24, 1839, N. Aur. 1, 2:10, ASJR.

59. Point to Blanc, St. Martinsville, January 23, 1839, UNDA, New Orleans, V-4-h.

60. Point to Roothaan, Grand Coteau, January 24, 1839, N. Aur. 1, 2:7, ASJR.

61. Point to Blanc, Grand Coteau, March 21, 1839, New Orleans, V-4-h, UNDA.

62. Point to Blanc, Grand Coteau, November 25, 1839, New Orleans, V-4-h, UNDA.

63. Point to Blanc, Grand Coteau, January 2, 1840, New Orleans, V-4-h, UNDA.

64. "Fr. John Abbadie: A Sketch," *Woodstock Letters,* 24 (1895): 22.

65. "Academy of the Sacred Heart, Grand Coteau, Louisiana." A flyer published by the Academy, n.d. n.p.

66. Point to Mme Marie-Jeanne Point, R.S.C.J., Grand Coteau, May 17, 1840, ASJSJ.

67. De Leeuw and De Theux to Roothaan, Grand Coteau, November 11, 1839, N. Aur. 1, 2:33, ASJR.

68. Paillasson to Roothaan, Grand Coteau, November 10, 1839, N. Aur. 1, 2:34, ASJR.

69. Garraghan, *Jesuits of the Middle U.S.,* 3:145.

70. Abbadie to Roothaan, Grand Coteau, July 26–27, 1840; N. Aur. 1, 2:40, ASJR.

71. Connelly to Blanc, Grand Coteau, August 4, 1840, New Orleans, V-4-k, UNDA.

72. Garraghan, *Jesuits of the Middle U.S.,* 3:145.

73. Ibid.

74. Kenny, "Notes," 41.

75. Soller to Roothaan, Grand Coteau, January 24, 1839, N. Aur. 1, 2:42, ASJR.

76. Garraghan, *Jesuits of the Middle U.S.,* 3:146.

77. Ibid., 145–46.

78. "Fr. John Francis Abbadie," *Woodstock Letters,* 24 (1895):22–24.

79. A Jesuit shaking hands with a Black slave? A custom allowed in Kentucky. The scene invites speculation: Might this recent clasping of hands have been a farewell gesture on the part of the departing rector of St. Charles?

WESTPORT 1840–1841 (177–193)

1. Wilfred P. Schoenberg, S.J., *A Chronicle of the Catholic History of the Pacific Northwest, 1743–1960* (Spokane, Washington: Gonzaga Preparatory School, 1962), 9–10.

2. Palladino, *Indian and White in the Northwest,* 27.

3. Garraghan, *Jesuits of the Middle U.S.* 2:236–48; John Fahey, *The Flathead Indians,* (Norman: University of Oklahoma Press, 1974), 64–71; William Lyle Davis, S.J., "Peter John De Smet: The Journey of 1840," *Pacific Northwest Quarterly,* 35 (1944): 29–32.

4. P. Point, "Vie," 24; Eugene Laveille, S.J., *The Life of Father De Smet, S.J. (1801–1873),* trans. Marian Lindsay (New York: P. J. Kennedy & Sons, 1915), 72.

5. Garraghan, *Jesuits of the Middle U.S.,* 2:252.

6. Rosati to Roothaan, St. Louis, October 20, 1839, cited in Palladino, *Indian and White in the Northwest,* 29.

7. Verhaegen to Roothaan, St. Louis, November 8, 1839, cited in Garraghan, *Jesuits of the Middle U.S.,* 2:250.

8. Paillasson to Roothaan, Grand Coteau, November 10, 1839, N. Aur. 1, 2:32, ASJR.

9. Garraghan, *Jesuits of the Middle U.S.,* 2:251–52.

10. Ibid., 253; Hiram Martin Chittenden and Alfred Talbot Richardson, *Life, Letters and Travels of Father Pierre-Jean De Smet, S.J.,* 4 vols. (New York: Francis P. Harper, 1905), 1:31–32.

11. Garraghan, *Jesuits of the Middle U.S.,* 2:253.

12. Ibid., 254, Laveille, *Life of Father De Smet,* 103–6.

13. P. Point, "Vie," 46; Garraghan, *Jesuits of the Middle U.S.,* 1:261.

14. P. Point "Vie," 44.

15. Ibid.

16. *Lettres des nouvelles missions du Canada, 1843–1852, édités avec commentaries et annotations par Lorenzo Cadieux* (Montréal: Les Editions Bellarmin, 1973), 892.

17. See *François-Auguste-René Chateaubriand, Mémoires d'outre-tombe,* 4 vols., Maurice Levaillant, ed. (Paris: Flammarion, 1947), 1:80–84.

18. "Records of Religious," Society of the Sacred Heart, National Archives, U.S.A., St. Louis, Missouri; "Marie-Jeanne Point," Archives, Convent of the Sacred Heart, Grand Coteau, La.; Janet Stuart, R.S.C.J., "Elizabeth Galitzin" in *Catholic Encyclopedia* (1909) 6:346; Louise Callan, R.S.C.J., *Philippine Duchesne: Frontier Missionary of the Sacred Heart, 1769–1852* (Westminster, Md: Newman, 1957), passim.

19. N. Point, "Journal," Cahier 3, BO-43-3, ASJSJ; "Recollections of the Rocky Mountains," chapter two of "Westport, Missouri—The Kickapoo Indians," *Woodstock Letters,* 2(1882):312–21. This same section can be found in digested form in *Wilderness Kingdom: Indian Life in the Rocky Mountains: 1840–1847. The Journals and Paintings of Nicolas Point, S.J.,* translated and introduced by Joseph P. Donnelly, S.J. (New York: Holt, Rinehart and Wilson, 1967), 20–24.

20. Garraghan, *Jesuits of the Middle U.S.,* 1:254–63; P. J. De Smet, *Letters and Sketches with a Narrative of a Year's Residence among the Indian Tribes of the Rocky Mountains* (Philadelphia: Fithian, 1843), also found in Reuben Gold Thwaites, *Early Western Travels, 1748–1846,* 32 vols. (Cleveland: Arthur H. Clark, 1904–1907), 27:136, n. 2.

21. P. Point, "Vie," 46.

22. Ibid.

23. N. Point, "Recollections of the Rocky Mountains," *Woodstock Letters,* 11(1887):313–14.

24. Joseph Schmidlin, *Catholic Mission History,* trans. Matthias Braum, S.V.D. (Techny, Illinois: Mission Press, 1933), 389.

25. Fernando Pérez Acosta, S.J., *Los Missiones del Paraguay: Recuerdos Históricos de una vida feliz entre los indios Guaranies* (Barcelona: Llorens Castello, 1920).

26. N. Point, "Recollections of the Rocky Mountains," *Woodstock Letters,* 12(1888):11.

27. N. Point, "Recollections of the Rocky Mountains," *Woodstock Letters,* 11(1888):314–15.

28. Nicolas P. Hardeman, "Albert Gallatin Boon," in *The Mountain Men and the Fur Trade of the Far West,* ed. LeRoy R. Hafen, 10 vols. (Glendale, California: Arthur H. Clark Co., 1965–1972) 8:44.

29. N. Point, "Recollections of the Rocky Mountains," *Woodstock Letters,* 12(1888):314–15.

30. Thwaites, *Early Western Travels,* 27:169–70; see also Garraghan, *Jesuits of the Middle U.S.,* 1:261–63.

31. N. Point, "Recollections of the Rocky Mountains," *Woodstock Letters,* 11(1887):314–18.

32. For bibliographical material on this subject, see Cornelius M. Buckley, S.J., "French Views of Ireland on the Eve of the Famine," in *Journal of Religious History,* 8 (1975):240–54.

33. N. Point, "Recollections of the Rocky Mountains," *Woodstock Letters,* 11(1882):318.

34. Chittenden and Richardson, *De Smet,* 1:193–94.

35. N. Point, "Recollections of the Rocky Mountains," *Woodstock Letters,* 11(1887):313.

36. Garraghan, *Jesuits of the Middle U.S.,* 2:255.

37. Ibid.

38. De Smet to Francis De Smet, St. Louis, April 27, 1841, cited in Lavelle, *Life of Father De Smet,* 120–21.

39. Garraghan, *Jesuits of the Middle U.S.,* 2:256.

40. Gregory Mengarini, S.J., *Recollections of the Flathead Mission,* trans. and ed. Gloria Ricci Lothrop (Glendale, Cal.: Arthur H. Clark Co., 1977), 64. There seems to be some disagreement among authors about which letter from Rosati to Roothaan was the cause of Mengarini's determination to volunteer for the missions. See Palladino, *Indian and White in the Northwest,* 28–29. Obituary, Gregory Mengarini, *Woodstock Letters,* 16(1887):93.

41. Mengarini, *Recollections,* 64.

42. Ibid.; also Obituary: Gregory Mengarini, *Woodstock Letters,* 16(1887):93–94.

43. Some of the later publications of Mengarini include *Grammatica linguae Selicae (A* Salish or Flat-Head Grammar); Neo-Ebrorici: Cramosy Press, 1861) and "Vocabulary of the Santa Clara," in *California Notes: Indianology of California,* ed. Alexander Smith Taylor, San Francisco: 1860. Although of limited interest, both of these items are of importance to students of American Indian culture. See also "Memoires of Gregory Mengarini," *Woodstock Letters,* 17(1888):290–301; 18(1889):142–52; and Sommervogel, *Bibliothèque de la Compagnie de Jésus,* 5:246.

44. Obituary: Gregory Mengarini, *Woodstock Letters,* 16(1887):94.

45. Obituary: James Cotting, *Woodstock Letters* 22(1893):143.

46. Garraghan, *Jesuits of the Middle U.S.,* 1:358, 409, 450; Obituary: Brother William Claessens, *Woodstock Letters,* 21(1892):427; Wilfred P. Schoenberg, S.J., *Paths to the Northwest: A Jesuit History of the Oregon Province* (Chicago: Loyola University Press, 1982), 85–86.

47. Garraghan, *Jesuits of the Middle U.S.,* 1:354–56, 493.

48. Cited in Schoenberg, *Paths to the Northwest,* 37; Palladino, *Indian and White in the Northwest,* 60.

49. Garraghan, *Jesuits of the Middle U.S.,* 2:258.

50. Ibid., 1:387, 406. Point, "Recollections of the Rocky Mountains," *Woodstock Letters,* 11(1887):319–20. Kènakuk, who is also known as Pakala, the leader of the Northern Kickapoos, should not be confused with the better known Tenskwátawa (c.1786–1837), also known as "The Prophet," who was instrumental in bringing the Kickapoos and other Shawnee tribes from Illinois into Missouri and finally, in 1828, into Kansas. Tenskwátawa, also known as Elkswatawa or Lauliwaskikau, was the twin brother of Tecumseh (1768-1813), of Tippecanoe fame. Although he died in disgrace, his influence among the Indian tribes had been extraordinary. He endeavoured to unite all of the tribes south of the Great Lakes and north of Mexico into a confederation to prevent further incursions on the part of the whites. Many of his religious rites and practices were adopted by Kènakuk. For Kènakuk, see Frederick J. Dockstader, *Great American Indians: Profiles in Leadership* (New York: Van Norstad Reinhold, 1977), 133–34; for Tenskwátawa, ibid., 297–98; *Dictionary of National Biography,* 18: 375–76 and 358–60; R. David Edmunds, *The Shawnee Prophet* (Lincoln: University of Nebraska Press, c.1983). The famous American painter George Catlin (1796–1872), who painted each, wrote that Kènakuk "usually called *Shawnee Prophet* is a very shrewd and talented man," and that Tenskwátawa also "called the *Shawnee Prophet* is perhaps one of the most remarkable men." Catlin's description baffles today's researcher who stands in awe of the 'medicine' of this "Shawnee Prophet" whose identity is something of a mystery. George Catlin, *Letters, Customs, and Conditions of the North American Indians,* 2 vols. (New York: Wiley and Putnam, 1841), 2:97–8, 117–18; Frederick Webb Hodge, ed., *Handbook of American Indians North of Mexico,* 2 vols. Washington: Government Printing Office, 1912, 2:650.

51. Point, "Recollections of the Rocky Missions," *Woodstock Letters,* 11(1887).

52. Ibid., 12(1888):3.

ROCKY MOUNTAINS 1841–1847

Part One: St. Mary's Reduction (194–212)

1. Chittenden and Richardson, *De Smet* 1:279. Wilfred Schoenberg, S.J., *Jesuits in Montana, 1840–1860* (Portland: The Oregon-Jesuit, 1960), 13.

2. LeRoy and Ann W. Hafen, "Thomas Fitzpatrick," in LeRoy Hafen, *Mountain Men and the Fur Trade of the Far West: Biographical Sketches of the Participants by Scholars of the Subject,* 10 vols. (Glendale California: Arthur H, Clark Co, 1965–72), 7:87–105.

3. Merle Wells, "Ignace Hatchiorauquacha (John Grey)," in Hafen, *Mountain Men,* 7:161–75.

4. Ibid. See also Point's *Plan de Westport . . . avec indication de les 26 familles catholiques"* in Donnelley, *Wilderness Kingdom,* 29.

5. John Bidwell, *Echoes of the Past about California* (Chicago: Lakeside Press, 1928), 23–26. Bidwell noted that there were "ten or eleven French Canadians," but he made no mention of the French-speaking Jesuit brothers. Thwaites, *Early Western Travels,* 27:198, n.75.

6. *Wyeth's Oregon, or a Short History of a Long Journey,* in Thwaites, *Early Western Travels,* 21:49, note 30. LeRoy and Ann W. Hafen, "Thomas Fitzpatrick," Hafen, *Mountain Men,* 97.

7. N. Point, "Recollections of the Rocky Mountains," *Woodstock Letters,* 12(1883):6.

8. Thwaites, *Early Western Travels,* 27:197; Bidwell, *Echoes of the Past about California,* 23.

9. Point to Roothaan, 5th encampment, en route, May 17, 1840, N. Aur. 1, 2:38, ASJR. As a result of this letter, Roothaan's suspicions of Point's mental and emotional stability seemed to have been confirmed. Prov. France à die 27 Julii 1836 ad 26 novembris 1842," September 10, 1844, 265. ASJR.

10. Garraghan, *Jesuits of the Middle U.S.,* 2:455.

11. *A Journey to California in 1841: The first emigrant party to California by wagon train: The Journal of John Bidwell* (Berkeley: Friends of Bancroft Library, 1964), 10 (henceforth, *Bidwell's Journal*).

12. N. Point, "Recollections of the Rocky Mountains," *Woodstock Letters,* 12(1883):8–9.

13. Portrait of Pierre-Jean De Smet, JHAGU, Thwaites, *Early Western Travels,* 27:200.

14. Thwaites, *Early Western Travels,* 27:205.

15. Ibid., 201; N. Point, "Recollections of the Rocky Mountains," *Woodstock Letters,* 12(1883):10; Washington Irving, *The Adventures of Captain Bonneville, U.S.A. in the Rocky Mountains and the Far West digested from his journal . . .* (New York: Putnam's Sons, 1868), 49–54.

16. N. Point, "Recollections of the Rocky Mountains," *Woodstock Letters* 12 (1883):7.

17. Thwaites, *Early Western Travels,* 27:201.

18. Ibid., 27:189–254; "Memoirs of Father Gregory Mengarini," *Woodstock Letters* 17(1888):302–7; Lothrop *Mengarini's Recollection of the Flathood Mission,* 51–61; N. Point, "Recollections of the Rocky Mission," *Woodstock Letters* 12(1883):3–23; Donnelly, *Wilderness Kingdom,* 24–35.

19. Mengarini, "The Rocky Mountains: The Memoirs of Father Gregory Mengarini;" *Woodstock Letters,* 17(1888):305.

20. N. Point, "Recollections of the Rocky Mountains," *Woodstock Letters,* 12(1883):11.

21. Ibid., 13–14.

22. Mengarini, "The Rocky Mountains: The Memoirs of Father Gregory Mengarini," *Woodstock Letters,* 17(1888):304.

23. Ibid.

24. Ibid.

25. Chittenden and Richardson, *De Smet's Life, Letters and Travels,* 1:301.

26. Ibid., 295; *Bidwell's Journal,* 19.

27. N. Point, "Recollections of the Rocky Mountains," *Woodstock Letters,* 12(1883):21.

28. Thwaites, *Early Western Travels,* 27:236.

29. N. Point, "Recollections of the Rocky Mountains," *Woodstock Letters,* 12(1883):22.

30. Ibid., 133.

31. Mengarini, "The Rocky Mountains: The Memoirs of Father Gregory Mengarini," *Woodstock Letters,* 17(1888):303; Harriet D. Munnick, "The Ermatinger Brothers, Edward and Francis," in Hafen, *Mountain Men,* 8:157–73.

32. *Bidwell's Journal,* 22; N. Point, "Recollections of the Rocky Mountains," *Woodstock Letters,* 12(1883):133.

33. N. Point, "Recollections of the Rocky Mountains," *Woodstock Letters,* 12(1883):134.

34. Thwaites, *Early Western Travels,* 27:170–73; Merle Wells, "Ignace Hatchiorauquacha (John Grey)," in Hafen, *Mountain Men and the Fur Trade of the Far West,* 7:173.

35. Thwaites, *Early Western Travels,* 27:273–74.

36. Ibid.

37. Ibid, 277.

38. N. Point, "Recollections of the Rocky Mountains," *Woodstock Letters,* 12(1883):135.

39. John C. Ewers, *The Blackfeet: Raiders on the Northwestern Plains* (Norman, Oklahoma: University of Oklahoma Press, 1958), 42–43.

40. Mengarini, "The Rocky Mountains: The Memoirs of Father Gregory Mengarini," *Woodstock Letters,* 17(1888):305.

41. Point's account of the dates differs from De Smet's; although De Smet is generally more reliable, Point's account has been retained. N. Point, "Recollections of the Rocky Mountains," *Woodstock Letters,* 12(1883):137. Thwaites, *Early Western Travels,* 27:269, 281–82.

42. N. Point, "Recollections of the Rocky Mountains," *Woodstock Letters,* 12(1883):137.

43. Lucylle H. Evans, *St. Mary's in the Rocky Mountains: A History of the Cradle of Montana's Culture* (Stevensville: Montana, Montana Creative Consultants, 1976), 41–45.

44. Thwaites, *Early Western Travelers,* 27:293–97.

45. Eric Cochrane, "Muratori: The Vocation of a Historian," *Catholic Historical Review* 51 (1967): 153–72; Louis Muratori, *Relation des missions du Paraguay,* Pierre Lombert, tr. (Paris: Chez Bordelet, 1754). Louis Muratori, *Relation des missions du Paraguay* (Louvain: Chez Vanlinthout et Vandenzande, 1822).

46. Thwaites, *Early Western Travels,* 27:252.

47. *Dictionnaire de Spiritualité,* 10:1843–1847. Paolo Segneri, called "the Younger," differed from Muratori on some parts of this enlightened spirituality, particularly concerning the place of Mary and the saints; Guilhermy, *Ménologe de la Compagnie de Jésus,* 1:678–81; Sommervogel, *Bibliothèque de la Compagnie de Jésus,* 8: col. 1089–1093.

48. Thwaites, *Early Western Travels,* 27:297.

49. P. Point, "Vie," 67; Pouliot, "Le Père Nicolas Point," 24–25.

50. Schoenberg, *Paths to the Northwest,* 22–25; idem., *Jesuits in Montana,* 12–19; Garraghan, *Jesuits of the Middle U.S.,* 2:264–71.

51. P. Point, "Vie," 65.

52. Ibid.

53. Mengarini, "The Rocky Mountains: The Memoirs of Father Gregory Mengarini," *Woodstock Letters,* 17(1888): 306–7.

54. "Chronology of the Rocky Mountain Mission, 1838–1861," Joset Papers, JHAGU.

55. N. Point, "Recollections of the Rocky Mountains," *Woodstock Letters,* 12(1883):145–46. Thwaites, *Early Western Travels,* 27:348. De Smet seems to give December 23 as the date when the winter excursion left St. Mary's. A closer reading of this text indicates that Point was appointed head of the expedition, which left on December 29. P. Point, "Vie," 58.

56. Mengarini, "The Rocky Mountains: The Memoirs of Father Gregory Mengarini," *Woodstock Letters,* 17(1888):307.

57. Thwaites, *Early Western Travels,* 27:348.

58. Point to Luiset, St. Mary's, July 8, 1844, BO-43-1, ASJSJ.

59. Mengarini to Roothaan, St. Mary's, March 10, 1842, cited in Garraghan, *Jesuits of the Middle U.S.,* 2:455.

60. Chittenden and Richardson, *De Smet,* 1: 370.

61. P. Point, "Vie," 64; Laveille, *Life of De Smet,* 148–49.

62. P. Point, "Vie," 68; Evans, *St. Mary's in the Rocky Mountains,* 49.

63. P. Point, "Vie," 68.

64. Lawrence A. Palladino, S.J. (1837–1927), the famous Black Robe at St. Ignatius Mission from 1867 to 1873, and author of *Indian and White in the Northwest,* cited in this volume, published a book in 1900 entitled *May Blossoms or Spiritual Flowerets in Honor of the Blessed Virgin,* (Philadelphia: H. L. Kliner & Co.). "It owed its origin to a custom prevalent in many novitiates and provinces of the Society, of drawing each day of Our Lady's month slips containing a practical suggestion or devotional thought in honor of the Mother of God." *Woodstock Letters,* 29(1900):347. This book enjoyed immediate success and by the time the ninth edition was printed in 1909, the author had added fifty more pages of May thoughts. The devotional prayers, hymns, etc., Palladino used at St. Ignatius Mission followed the same format as those Point introduced at St. Mary's in 1842.

65. P. Point, "Vie," 68–70.

66. Burnichon, *Histoire d'un siècle,* 3:291.

67. Ibid, 312–14; Delattre, *Etablissements des Jésuites en France,* 1:143, 145–46.

68. Ponlevoy, *Life of Father de Ravignan,* 1:189–90.

69. Chittenden and Richardson, *De Smet,* 1:390–402.

70. Ibid.; P. Point, "Vie," 69.

71. Chittenden and Richardson, *De Smet,* 1:391.

72. P. Point, "Vie," 67.

73. Ibid., 69–70.

74. Chittenden and Richardson, *De Smet,* 1:374–76; 3:1144.

75. Ibid., 1:374–76.

76. "The Coeur d'Alène," 4; "History of the Coeur d'Alène Mission to 1850," 10, Joset Papers, JHAGU; also cited in Pat Allan Pentland, "The Ill-fated Mission: The Sacred Heart Mission on the St. Joe River, 1842–1846," p. 25. Masters thesis presented to the Department of History, Gonzaga University, May 1973.

77. P. Point, "Vie," 73; N. Point, "Extract from the Missionary's Journal;" Reuben G. Thwaites, *Early Western Travels,* 1748–1846, 32 vols. (Cleveland: Arthur H. Clark, 1906), *De Smet's Oregon Missions and Travels over the Rockies, 1845–1846,* vol. 29. This reference is to 29:398–407.

78. "Vie," 74–75.

NOTES TO BIOGRAPHY

ROCKY MOUNTAINS 1841–1847
Part Two: Sacred Heart Reduction (213–242)

1. P. Point, "Vie," 74–75.

2. Chapter 5 of Point's "Recollections of the Rocky Mountains," is entitled "Mission to the Coeurs d'Alène," and it appeared in *Woodstock Letters,* 12(1883):147–53; ch. 6, "Winter among the Coeurs d'Alène," is found on pages 261–68; chapters 8 and 9, "The Building of a Church in the Domain of Gabriel," and "Visit of the Ten Chiefs of the Nez Percés to the Coeurs d'Alène," appeared in *Woodstock Letters,* 13(1884):3–10 and 10–14. Parts of these chapters were reprinted with very little change in Joseph P. Donnelly, *Wilderness Kingdom*. When possible, reference to this phase of Point's life will be made from both sources.

3. N. Point, "Recollections of the Rocky Mountains," *Woodstock Letters* 12(1883):148; Donnelly, *Wilderness Kingdom,* 47.

4. N. Point, "Recollections of the Rocky Mountains." *Woodstock Letters,* 12(1883):148–49; Donnelly, *Wilderness Kingdom,* 47–50.

5. N. Point, "Recollections of the Rocky Mountains," *Woodstock Letters,* 12(1883):261–63; Donnelly, *Wilderness Kingdom,* 62–70.

6. Pentland thesis, "The Ill-Fated Mission," 38; "Comparative Ethnology of Rocky Mountain Mission Tribes," 2, Joset Papers, JHAGU.

7. Thwaites, *Early Western Travels,* 29:318–19.

8. "History of the Coeur d'Alène Mission to 1850," 3, Joset Papers, JHAGU.

9. N. Point, "Recollections of the Rocky Mountains," *Woodstock Letters,* 12(1883):266; Donnelly, *Wilderness Kingdom,* 74.

10. "History of the Coeur d'Alène Mission to 1850," 4, Joset Papers, JHAGU.

11. "Biographical Sketches," 45–55, Joset Papers, JHAGU; N. Point, "Recollections of the Rocky Mountains," *Woodstock Letters,* 13(1884):3–4. The date here is wrongly noted 1845 and corrected in Donnelly, *Wilderness Kingdom,* 78–84.

12. Most notably Governor Isaac Stevens, Governor of the Washington Territory, in his 1853 report to Washington, which is cited in part by Gilbert J. Garraghan, S.J., *Chapters in Frontier History* (Milwaukee: Bruce, 1934) 141–42.

13. See particularly, Donnelly, *Wilderness Kingdom,* 82. Also Thwaites, *Early Western Travels,* 29:317–21.

14. "History of the Coeur d'Alène Mission to 1850," 5, Joset Papers, JHAGU.

15. For the "Catholic Ladder" or the "Sah-kah-lee Stick," see

Lothrop, *Mengarini's Recollections of the Flathead Mission,* 99 and Thwaites *Early Western Travels,* "Indian Symbolical Catechism" folding plate, 27:403. Fahey states that when De Smet visited Fort Vancouver in 1842 Father Francis Blanchet showed him his " 'Catholic ladder,' a large colored drawing depicting the major events of Catholic doctrine to the present day. Aware of Point's success in instructing Indians by sketching and encouraged by Blanchet's work among the Indians, Father De Smet carried the ladder back to the Bitterroot. Later he commissioned a Paris publisher to print quantities of ladders for Indian missions, and the Flatheads learned to whittle their own: a long stick on which forty short parallel lines marked forty centuries of world history, thirty-three notches for the years of Christ's life, three crosses to show the manner of His death, carved churches, twelve notches for apostles, and eighteen more marks for the centuries since Christ's crucifixion." Fahey, *The Flathead Indians,* 77.

16. N. Point, "Recollections of the Rocky Mountains," *Woodstock Letters,* 13(1884):4–5.

17. "History of the Coeur d'Alène Mission to 1850," 3, Joset Papers, JHAGU.

18. "Biographical Sketches," 6. There were "four Irish novice lay brothers" that accompanied the two fathers. Two of them apparently left the Society without having pronounced vows. "History of the Coeur d'Alène Mission," Joset Papers, JHAGU.

19. The first of De Smet's books, *Letters and Sketches with a Narrative of a Year's Residence Among the Indian Tribes of the Rocky Mountains,* was published by Fithian in Philadelphia at this same time.

20. Garraghan, *Jesuits of the Middle U.S.,* 2:292.

21. Laveille, *Life of Father De Smet,* 154.

22. *Dictionary of American Biography,* 3:300–301; *The National Cyclopedia of American Biography,* 76 vols. (New York: J. T. White & Co., 1893–to date), 4:105–67.

23. *Dictionary of American Biography,* 1:325–26; *National Cyclopedia of American Biography,* 4:105–6.

24. *Dictionary of American Biography,* 20:141–43; *National Cyclopedia of American Biography,* 11:112.

25. Mengarini, "The Rocky Mountains: The Memoirs of Father Gregory Mengarini," *Woodstock letters,* 18(1889):38.

26. Ibid. Hubert Howe Bancroft, *The Works of Hubert H. Bancroft,* 29 vols. (San Francisco, 1886), *History of Oregon,* 1:398; cited in Schoenberg, *Paths to the Northwest,* 28.

27. Mengarini, "The Rocky Mountains: The Memoirs of Father Gregory Mengarini, *Woodstock Letters,* 18(1889):38.

28. Ibid. One of the Canadians Mengarini referred to was Louis Brown, Point's interpreter at Sacred Heart, who returned to St. Mary's with Point and Huet earlier in the month.

29. Ibid.

30. Ibid.

31. Biographical Sketches," 5, Joset Papers, JHAGU.

32. Ibid, 2.

33. Ibid.

34. Schoenberg, *Paths to the Northwest,* 26.

35. Michael Accolti to Roothaan, San Francisco, February 29, 1850, Mont. Sax. 1: 40: 8, ASJR. This description of Huet sounds very much like the description of the unnamed brother referred to above who led Mengarini and De Vos on the wrong path to Sacred Heart in September 1843. Mengarini, "Rocky Mountains: The Memoirs of Father Gregory Mengarini," *Woodstock Letters,* 18(1889): 38–39.

36. Joseph Joset to Pieter Beckx, Sacred Heart Mission, December 27, 1868, Mont. Sax. 2:12:13, ASJR.

37. Joset to Roothaan, St. Ignatius Mission, February 5, 1849, Mont. Sax, 1, 35, ASJR.

38. Donnelly, *Wilderness Kingdom,* 181–88.

39. Chittenden and Richardson, *Life, Letters and Travels of De Smet,* 2:408.

40. "Mission of the Sacred Heart," 2, "Biographical Sketches," 6, "History of the Coeur d'Alène Indians," 3, "History of the Coeur d'Alène Mission to 1850," 5–6, Joset Papers, JHAUG; cited in Pentland thesis "The Ill-Fated Mission," 50–53.

41. Walter H. Hill, S.J., "Father Adrien Hoecken: A Sketch," *Woodstock Letters,* 26(1897):368.

42. Ibid.

43. Schoenberg, *Paths to the Northwest,* 37, 45, 54. Garraghan, *Jesuits of the Middle U.S.,* 2:291.

44. Garraghan, *Jesuits of the Middle U.S.,* 2:305–13 et passim. Hill, "Father Adrien Hoecken: A Sketch," *Woodstock Letters,* 26 (1897):367. It is difficult to calculate which were the six years Father Hoecken and Brother Lyons lived together without seeing a white man. It could have been after Daniel Lyons left the society, or more probably it is an exaggeration. Mengarini, "Rocky Mountains: Memoirs of Gregory Mengarini," *Woodstock Letters,* 18(1889):38–39.

45. Pentland thesis, "Ill-Fated Mission," 52.

46. P. Point, "Vie," 20.

47. Mengarini, "Rocky Mountains: Memoirs of Gregory Mengarini," *Woodstock Letters* 18(1889):40.

48. Pentland thesis, "Ill-Fated Mission," 52.

49. Garraghan, *Jesuits of the Middle U.S.*, 2:316.

50. Mengarini, "Rocky Mountains: Memoirs of Gregory Mengarini," *Woodstock Letters*, 18(1889):40.

51. Point to Luiset, St. Mary's, July 8, 1844, BO-43-1, ASJSJ.

52. Joseph Specht, S.J., "Father Dominic du Ranquet: A Sketch of His Life and Labors (1813–1900)," *Woodstock Letters*, 30(1901):178.

53. Cited in Boudou, *Les Jésuites à Madagascar au XIXe siècle,"* 1:72.

54. Edouard Lecompte, S.J., *Les Jésuites du Canada au dixneuvième siècle,* (Montréal: Messenger Press, 1920), 36–38. Chossegros, *Histoire du Novitiate de la Compagnie au Canada,* 5–6.

55. "An Historical Sketch of the Mission of New York and Canada," *Woodstock Letters,* 2(1873):189–204.

56. Curran, *Return of the Jesuits,* 89–91.

57. Point to Luiset, St. Mary's, July 8, 1844, BO-43-1, ASJSJ.

58. Ibid.

59. Garraghan, *Jesuits of the Middle U.S.*, 2:284.

60. Ibid., 2:278–90.

61. Point to Luiset, St. Mary's July 8, 1844, BO-43-1, ASJSJ.

62. Chittenden and Richardson, *De Smet,* 2:438–46; Schoenberg, *Paths to the Northwest,* 34–35; "Short Chronology of the Beginning of the Rocky Mountain Missions," 5, Joset Papers, JHAGU.

63. Pentland thesis, "Ill-Fated Mission," 55–56. Mengarini. "The Rocky Mountains: Memoirs of Gregory Mengarini," *Woodstock Letters,* 18(1889):40; Schoenberg, *Paths to the Northwest,* 34–35.

64. Pentland thesis, "Ill-Fated Mission," 56.

65. Ibid., 55–56. "A Short Chronology of the Beginning of the Rocky Mountain Mission," 5, Joset Papers, JHAGU, Mengarini, *Rocky Mountains: Memoirs of Gregory Mengarini, Woodstock Letters* 18(1889):40. Schoenberg, *Paths to the Northwest;* 34–35.

66. Schoenberg, *Paths to the Northwest,* 35–36. "Chronological Sketch of the Rocky Mountain Missions, 1839–1855," 5, Joset Papers, JHAGU.

67. Schoenberg, *Jesuits in Montana,* 24.

68. Garraghan, *Jesuits of the Middle U.S.*, 2:298.

69. De Vos to De Smet, Le Havre, December 19, 1836, St. Louis University Library, Microfilm Roll 2829 DD, 417.

70. Garraghan, *Jesuits of the Middle U.S.*, 1:358.

71. De Vos to De Smet, St. Stanislaus Seminary, March 22, 1840. St. Louis University Library, Microfilm Roll 2829 DD, 421. There were other pieces of correspondence as well. See William Lyle Davis, S.J., "Peter John De Smet: Missionary to the Potawatomi, 1837–1840," *Pacific Northwest Quarterly*, 33 (1942):135, n. 36.

72. Roothaan to De Vos, Rome, August 8, 1845, copy in Davies Papers, no. 193, JHAGU.

73. Murphy to Beckx, April 21, 1855, cited in Garraghan, *Jesuits of the Middle U.S.*, 3:99.

74. Quaife, *Echoes of the Past about California by General John Bidwell*, 25–26.

75. Cited in Garraghan, *Jesuits of the Middle U.S.*, 3:101.

76. Nobili to Roothaan, St. Francis Xavier, November 10, 1843, ASJR, Mont. Sax. 1:4:21; also, 1:4:23.

77. Garraghan, *Jesuits of the Middle U.S.*, 3:66–107. Chittenden and Richardson, *De Smet*, 1:104–14.

78. Chittenden and Richardson, *De Smet*, 1:278.

79. Ibid.; see also Thwaites, *Early Western Travels*, 27:193, n. 68. This description of Point persisted; for example, see Palladino, *Indian and White in the Northwest*, 37.

80. De Smet to Van de Velde, April 20, 1844, Mont. Sax. 1.1.3, ASJR.

81. Pentland thesis, "Ill-Fated Mission," 55.

82. Schoenberg gives this number as seventeen. He did not count, however, the following who were members of the society: Daniel, or Michael, Lyons; Thomas Burris; Daniel Coakley and Tiberio Soderini all working at that date on the mission. *Paths to the Northwest*, 30.

83. Donnelly, *Wilderness Kingdom*, 82–94.

84. Chittenden and Richardson, *De Smet*, 2:454–55.

85. Francis A. Barnum, "The Last of the Old Indian Missionaries—Father Joseph Joset," *Woodstock Letters*, 30(1901):207. "Short Chronology of the Rocky Mountain Missions, 1836–1861," 5, Joset Papers, JHAGU. Mengarini, "The Rocky Mountains: Memoirs of Gregory Mengarini," *Woodstock Letters*, 18(1889):40; Pentland thesis, "The Ill-Fated Mission," 57.

86. Chittenden and Richardson, *De Smet*, 2:461.

87. "Short Chronology of the Beginnings of the Rocky Mountain Mission," 5, Joset Papers, JHAGU.

88. Chittenden and Richardson, *De Smet,* 2:463–64.

89. Ibid., "Biographical Sketches," 3. Joset Papers, JHAGU. In his thesis, Pentland remarks that this painting later moved to the Cataldo Mission in 1846, and then to the De Smet Mission, where it was destroyed in a church fire in 1939. "Ill-Fated Mission," 58.

90. Chittenden and Richardson, *De Smet,* 2:464.

91. Thwaites, "Point Letter, 1845," in *Early Western Travels,* 29:281.

92. Renault to Roothaan, Paris, August 10, 1836, cited in Garraghan, *Jesuits in the Middle U.S.,* 3:134–35.

93. N. Point, "Vie," 82.

94. Boudon, *Les Jésuites à Medagascar au XIXe siècle,* 1:95.

95. "History of the Coeur d'Alène Mission to 1850," 9, Joset Papers, JHAGU.

96. Verhaegen to Point, St. Louis, April 17, 1843, BO-43-5, ASJSJ.

97. Barnum, "The Last of the Old Indian Missionaries," *Woodstock Letters,* 30(1901):202–3.

98. Joset was the superior of the Rocky Mountain Mission when the California venture began. Garraghan, *Jesuits of the Middle U.S.,* 2:392–95.

99. "Short Chronology of the Beginning of the Rocky Mountain Mission," 5. Joset Papers JHAGU.

100. Garraghan, *Jesuits of the Middle U.S.,* 2:394.

101. Thwaites, "Point Letter, 1845," in *Early Western Travels,* 29:313.

102. Garraghan, *Jesuits of the Middle U.S.,* 2:429–30.

103. "History of the Coeur d'Alène Mission to 1850," 9. "Mission of the Sacred Heart," 2. Joset Papers, 71a, JHAGU.

104. "Biographical Sketches," 3 Joset Papers, JHAGU. Cited in "Ill-Fated Mission," 60, where Pentland remarks that the Baptismal Records of the Mission (JHAGU) indicate that Point had five to every one of Joset's baptisms. Records show that a third coadjutor brother was also assigned to the mission. This was Daniel Coakley, whom De Smet accepted as a novice, probably at Westport, before De Vos's group left for the Oregon country in 1843. Since he had been a Dominican novice at one time in his career, De Smet accepted him conditionally and requested a dispensation be given him from the strict rule that forbade anyone entering the society who had received a habit in another order. De Smet's request was denied and Coakley was dismissed before the winter of 1844–1845. "Short Chronology of the Beginning of the Rocky Mountain Mis-

sion," 5, Joset Papers, JHAGU. Garraghan, *Jesuits of the Middle U.S.*, 2:429.

105. P. Point, "Vie," 56.

106. "History of the Coeur d'Alène Indians." 3, Joset Papers 70a, JHAGU.

107. Ibid, 6–7, Joset Papers 43, JHAGU.

108. Pentland thesis, "Ill-Fated Mission," 62–63.

109. N. Point, "Recollections of the Rocky Mountains," *Woodstock Letters,* 13(1889):4–5.

110. Research has not uncovered the original letter; however, Mengarini sent a copy to Rome. Mengarini to Roothaan, Vancouver, November 9, 1845, Mont. Sax 1:5:6, ASJR.

111. See chapter 6, note 39. Point to Verhaegen, Grand Coteau, January 24, 1839, N. Aur. 1:2:7, ASJR.

112. See chapter 8, note 110. "Biographical Sketches," 5, Joset Papers, JHAGU.

113. Clément Boulanger to Roothaan, Sault Sainte-Marie, June 29, 1849. Canada, 1, 3, 8, ASJR.

114. Roothaan to De Vos, Rome, August 8, 1845. Roothaan, *Epistolae,* 3:500-1.

115. "Biographical Sketches," 5, Joset Papers, 45, JHAGU; Garraghan, *Jesuits of the Middle U.S.*, 2: 316–17.

116. Henry Duranquet, "The Prison Hospitals of New York," *Woodstock Letters,* 12(1883):184.

117. James Van de Veld to Roothaan, St. Louis, October 12, 1843, Miss. 4:1:45, ASJR. See also Mengarini's report on the growing nationalistic spirit on the mission. Mengarini to Roothaan, St. Mary's, September 30, 1847, Mont. Sax. 1:1:33, ASJR, and Father Aloysius Vercruysse's reflections on the animosity of the newly arrived Italians toward the Belgians. Vercruysse to Roothaan, St. Ignatius, April 29, 1851, and De Smet to Roothaan, St. Paul on the Willamette, August 29, 1844, Ibid, These comments make the Italian fathers' praise of De Smet even more significant.

118. De Smet to Van De Veld, December ? 1844, Mont. Sax. 1:3:6, ASJR.

119. Pentland thesis, "Ill-Fated Mission," 66–67.

120. Point to Roothaan, Fort Colville, April 14, 1845, Mont. Sax., 1:9:1, ASJR.

121. Ibid., 1:9:1 bis, ASJR. Mengarini made similar complaints about the defects of the society's economic policy in maintaining the missions. Lathrop, *Mengarini's Recollections,* 81–82.

122. N. Point, "Recollections of the Rocky Mountains," *Woodstock Letters,* 13(1884), 11–12; Donnelly, *Wilderness Kingdom,* 99–100, where Donnelly wrongly identifies "Father S." in this episode, and 92–3, where Point paints his adventures with Soderini. Pentland thesis, "Ill-Fated Mission," 67.

123. De Smet to Roothaan, Brussels, June 24, 1847, Mont. Sax, 1:1:24, ASJR.

124. Garraghan, *Jesuits of the Middle U.S.,* 2:450–51.

125. Pentland thesis, "Ill-Fated Mission," 68–69.

126. Schoenberg, *Chronicle of the Catholic History of the Pacific Northwest,* 20.

127. Donnelly, *Wilderness Kingdom,* 129. Pentland thesis, "The Ill-Fated Mission," 69.

128. Roothaan to De Vos, Rome, August 8, 1845; Roothaan, *Epistolae, 3:500–1.*

129. Mengarini to Roothaan, St. Mary's, March 10, 1842, Mont. Sax, 1:3:1, ASJR.

130. Joset to Roothaan, March 18 to Roothaan, Sacred Heart, March 16, 1848, Mont. Sax 1:1:34, ASJR.

131. Ibid. After the dismissal of Daniel, or Michael, Lyons, Brother Charles Huet came to Sacred Heart from St. Ignatius. Thomas Burris had entered Florissant in July 1842 and in the following year accompanied his novice master, Peter De Vos, to St. Mary's; he left the society from St. Ignatius about this same time, March 1848. Personnel Records, ASJSL.

132. Chittenden and Richardson, *Life, Letters and Travels of De Smet,* 2:564–65.

CONCLUSION (405–439)

1. Donnelly, *Wilderness Kingdom,* map of voyage, 208.

2. Point to Van de Velde, Aboard the Steamboat *Martha,* July 5, 1847. AA:415, ASJSL.

3. Hiram Martin Chittenden, *Early Steamboat Navigation on the Missouri: Life and Adventures of Joseph La Barge.* 2 vols. (New York: Francis Harper, 1903), 2:240.

4. Garraghan, *Jesuits of the Middle U.S.,* 3:88.

5. Chittenden, *Early Steamboat Navigation on the Missouri,* 1: 177–84.

6. Donnelly, *Wilderness Kingdom,* Point's map, 208; Gilbert J.

Garraghan, *Chapters in Frontier History: Research Studies in the Making of the West,* (Milwaukee: Bruce, 1934) 154.

7. On his way from Fort Lewis to St. Louis the previous fall, De Smet had visited 10,000 Mormons at their winter quarters here, "not far from the old Council Bluffs." De Smet explained to his nephew Charles that newly formed American sect, "a species of socialism and communism," had impressed him. They had just been driven out of the Union and, under Brigham Young, were resolved to move on to the Great Western Territory. De Smet had just described to his nephew the Great Salt Lake Basin, and he added: "They asked me a thousand questions about the regions I had explored," he wrote, "and the spot I have just described to you pleased them greatly from the account I gave them of it." Chittenden and Richardson, *De Smet,* 4:1402–5. The group that Point had seen were causing concern among the Omaha Indians because they consumed too much game and timber. Most of these emigrants did not join their co-religionists in the west. Rather they settled in Nebraska forming communities of Mormons separate from Salt Lake City. Federal Writers Project, *Nebraska: A Guide to the Cornhusker State,* (New York: Hastings House, 1939) 119.

8. Point to Van de Velde, aboard the *Martha,* July 5, 1847. AA:415, ASJSL.

9. Donnelly, *Wilderness Kingdom,* Point's map, 208.

10. Wells, "Ignace Hatchiorauquacha," in Hafen, *Mountain Men and the Fur Trade,* 7:173–74.

11. Donnelly, *Wilderness Kingdom,* 258.

12. Wells, "Ignace Hatchiorauquacha," in Hafen, *Mountain Men and the Fur Trade,* 7:174.

13. Van de Velde, to Roothaan, St. Louis, August 5, 1847, Missouri, 4:1:86, ASJR.

14. P. Point, "Vie," 109–10. Point specifically states "his sister, a religious of the Sacred Heart at St. Charles," a town a few miles from St. Louis. Could he have substituted St. Charles for Grand Coteau? Marie-Jeanne Point at this date was assigned neither to the convent at St. Charles nor to the convent at Grand Coteau. Rather she was at St. Michael's, Convent, Louisiana. "Personal Record: Marie-Jeanne Point," Archives, Society of the Sacred Heart, St. Louis, Missouri.

15. Rubillon to Roothaan, Paris, January 11, 1846. France, 5:3:1, ASJR.

16. Cited by Robert Ignatius Burns, S.J., "A Jesuit in the War Against the Northern Indians," *Records of the American Catholic Historical Society of Philadelphia,* 61 (March 1950):17.

17. Boudon, *Les Jésuites à Madagascar au XIXe siècle,* 1:70–72.

18. Ibid., 97–98.

19. Ibid., 72; Lecompte, *Les Jésuites du Canada au XIXe siécle,* 36–38.

20. Chossegros, *Histoire du Noviciat de la Compagnie de Jésus au Canada,* 9–10.

21. Curran, *Return of the Jesuits,* 92.

22. Chossegros, *Histoire du Noviciat de la Compagnie de Jésus au Canada,* 11–18.

23. Curran, *Return of the Jesuits,* 93.

24. Cadieux, *Lettres des Nouvelles Missions du Canada,* 892–93

25. Ibid., 892.

26. Ibid., 904; *The Jesuit Relations and allied documents; travels and explorations of the Jesuit missionaries in New France, 1610–1791; the original French, Latin, and Italian texts, with English translations and notes; illustrated by portraits, maps and fascimilies,* ed. Ruben Gold Thwaites, 73 vols. (Cleveland: The Burrows Brothers Company, 1896–1901), 69:289. Potier was sent to assist Father Armand de La Richardie (1687–1758), who had been sent to the Hurons at Detroit "who had no missionary in sixteen years." 68:333.

27. *Encyclopedia Canadiana: The Encyclopedia of Canada,* 10 vols. (Toronto: Grolier of Canada [1959]), 10:336–37.

28. Cadieux, *Lettres de Nouvelles Missions du Canada,* 904.

29. *Encyclopedia Canadiana,* 10:336–37.

30. Cadieux, *Lettres de Nouvelles Missions du Canada,* 905.

31. Ibid., 899; Curran, *Return of the Jesuits,* 95.

32. Cadieux, *Lettres de Nouvelles Missions du Canada,* 905.

33. Ibid., 885, 890–91; Curran, *Return of the Jesuits,* 94.

34. Curran, *Return of the Jesuits,* 95–96; Cadieux, *Lettres de Nouvelles Missions du Canada,* 891.

35. Curran, *Return of the Jesuits,* 96.

36. Federal Writers Project of the Works Progress Administration, *Michigan: A Guide to the Wolverine State,* (New York: Hastings House, 1964), 35.

37. Ibid., 34.

38. Thwaites, *Jesuit Relations,* 57:265–305, 318; Rt. Rev. Francis Xavier Krautburger, "Short Sketch of the History of the Menominee Indians of Wisconsin and the Catholic Missions among Them," *American Catholic Historical Records,* 4 (1887) 135; Federal Writers Project of the Works Progress Administration (WPA), *Wisconsin: A Guide to the Badger State* (New York: Hastings House, 1945) 124–25.

39. Thwaites, *Jesuit Relations,* 57:818.

40. Ibid., 39:107.

41. Curran, *Return of the Jesuits,* 96.

42. Walter H. Hill, "Some Facts and Incidents Relating to St. Joseph's College, Bardstown, Kentucky," *Woodstock Letters,* 26(1897):97.

43. Ibid., 93–94.

44. Michael Nash, "Our Fathers in Kentucky," *Woodstock Letters,* 22(1893):25–27.

45. Michael Kenny, "The Scholasticate of Grand Coteau," *Woodstock Letters,* 22(1893):207.

46. "Letter of Emile Mattern," *Woodstock Letters,* 36(1907):408.

47. Kenny, "The Scholasticate of Grand Coteau," *Woodstock Letters,* 22 (1893), 204–11. Michael McCarthy, "The Burning of the Scholasticate at Grand Coteau," *Woodstock Letters,* 29 (1900): 83–88. "Grand Coteau," *Woodstock Letters,* 43(1914): 139–40.

48. Roothaan to De Smet, April 15, 1852. Cited in Garraghan, *Jesuits of the Middle U.S.,* 2:438.

49. Robert Ignatius Burns, *The Jesuits and the Indian Wars of the Northwest* (New Haven: Yale University Press), 62–67.

50. Excerpts from Van De Velde's letter to De Smet found in De Smet's reply, April 20, 1844. Mont. Sax. 1: 1: 3, ASJR.

51. Ravalli became the best known of the Montana Black Robes, spending more than thirty-five years with the Indians. Lawrence B. Palladino, "The Catholic Church in Montana," *Woodstock Letters,* 9(1880): 97–98; idem., *Indian and White in the Northwest,* 71–76.

52. Garraghan, *Jesuits of the Middle U.S.,* 2:337–38.

53. Schoenberg, *Paths to the Northwest,* 48.

54. Fahey, *Flathead Indians,* 86–88

55. "Obituary: Gregory Mangerini," *Woodstock Letters,* 16(1887):96.

56. Garraghan, *Jesuits of the Middle U.S.,* 2:381.

57. Ibid., 2:379–80.

58. Schoenberg, *Paths to the Northwest,* 47.

59. Garraghan, *Jesuits of the Middle U.S.,* 2:386–92.

60. Schoenberg, *Jesuits in Montana,* 21.

61. Robert Ignatius Burns, "A Jesuit in the War Against the Northern Indians," *Records of the American Catholic Historical Society of Philadelphia,* 61 (1950), 9–56. Barnum, "The Last of the Indian Mis-

sionaries: Father Joseph Joset," *Woodstock Letters,* 30 (1901), 209–14. Alexander Diomini, "Studies of Modern Indian Life: The Coeur d'Alène." *Woodstock Letters* 23(1894):23–49.

62. De Smet to Roothaan, Willamette, October 1845. "Quelques remarques sur les sauvages et en particulier sur les Coeurs d'Alène," Mont. Sax. 1: 1: 6, page 18 et seq., ASJR.

63. Mont. Sax. 5: 7: 10, ASJR.

64. De Smet to Roothaan, Willamette, August 29, 1844, Mont. Sax. 1: 4: 31, ASJR.

65. Nobili to Roothaan, Vancouver, 1845, Mont. Sax., 1: 4: 9, ASJR.

66. Schoenberg, *Chronicle of the Catholic History of the Northwest,* 20–21; idem., *Paths to the Northwest,* 36–37.

67. Schoenberg, *Paths to the Northwest,* 36–37; Bancroft, *Works of Bancroft,* 29:429.

68. Peter Burnett wrote an account of his conversion: *The Path which Led a Protestant Lawyer to the Catholic Church,* (New York: Benziger, 1851).

69. Garrighan, *Jesuits of the Middle U.S.,* 2:335–37.

70. Vercruysse to Roothaan, April 25, 1851, cited in Garraghan, *Jesuits of the Middle U.S.,* 2:336–37.

71. Schoenberg, *Paths to the Northwest,* 44.

72. Joset to Roothaan, St. Paul's, Colville, October 29, 1849. Mont. Sax, 1: 4: 39, ASJR.

73. De Vos to Roothaan, St. Ignatius, Montana, April 19, 1848. Mont. Sax, 1: 8: 3, ASJR.

74. Accolti and De Vos had quarreled when the former succeeded the latter as superior at St. Francis Xavier's in 1845, but unlike Point, Accolti, who was a real 'operator', never let personal grudges get in the way of his plans. De Smet's 1845 report to Roothaan, Mont. Sax, 1: 1: 13, page 8, ASJR. Garraghan, *Jesuits of the Middle U.S.,* 2: 395. Joset's "very reluctantly" should be weighed against his admission that Accolti was "my consolation." Joset to Roothaan, Sacred Heart Mission, March 16, 1845. Mont. Sax. 1: 1: 34, ASJR.

75. Garraghan, *Jesuits of the Middle U.S.,* 2:403.

76. Accolti to Roothaan, San Francisco, February 29, 1850, Mont. Sax, 1: 1: 40, ASJR. In making such a request Accolti established one of the most perduring policies of the California Province. Then, shortly after writing this letter, which he evidently mailed at a later date, Accolti learned: "Point had returned to his own province," His reaction—"and may God be blessed!"—gives a good insight into Accolti's

mercurial character. Accolti to Roothaan, San Francisco, February 26, 1850, Mont. Sax, 1: 1: 20, ASJR; Soderini was dismissed from the society at Fort Vancouver June 27, 1846, De Smet to Roothaan, Brussels, June 24, 1847, Mont. Sax, 1: 1: 24 ASJR; and then, oddly enough, took "private vows in the society" at St. Louis on April 12, 1846, Miss. 4: 1: 67 bis. ASJR.

77. Elet to Roothaan, St. Louis August 17, 1849. Miss. 5: 1: 11, ASJR.

78. "Obituary: Gregory Mengarini," *Woodstock Letters,* 16(1887): 96.

79. "The Jesuit Mission of California," *Woodstock Letters,* 20(1891):354.

80. Burnett, a member of the Democratic Party, ran on a simple platform, one item of which was to exclude all free Negroes from the state. He had introduced this same legislation in Oregon's fundamental laws and it was later introduced into that state's constitution. He further believed that the "war of extermination will continue to be waged between the races until the Indian race becomes extinct." *National Cyclopedia of American Biography,* 76 vols. (N.Y.: J. T. White & Co., 1893–1919), 4:105; *California Biographical Dictionary,* (Wilmington, Del.: American Historical Publications, c. 1984), 37. One certainly would not expect a mid-nineteenth century politician to think or speak like a candidate running for office in the 1980s, but one might wonder how much influence De Vos, who sincerely loved the Indians and all races, actually exercised on his famous convert. There is a plaque commemorating both men in the Santa Clara Mission Church on the campus of Santa Clara University, Santa Clara, California.

81. "Catalogus Novitiorum, Societatis Jesu, Missionis Californiae, Jan. 1853–Sept. 8, 1909," ASJLG. The intitial pages of this document, written in De Vos's hand, indicate that the first novice was accepted on May 15, 1850, and that he took his first vows in Pueblo San Jose on March 30, 1855. Shortly after this date the novitiate and the master of novices had moved to Santa Clara College. Point's companion Peter De Vos should not be confused with another Peter De Vos, also a native of Ghent, who joined the Maryland mission after the novitiate was opened at Georgetown in 1806. In 1819 this Peter De Vos left the Society because it was found "that his settled habits of solitary independence rendered him unfit for community life." He labored as a diocesan priest in southern Maryland until his death in 1844. Edwin Warfield Beitzell, *The Jesuit Missions of St. Mary's County, Maryland* (Abel Md.: Edwin Warfield Beitzell, 1976) 193.

82. Abbadie to Roothaan, Grand Coteau, March 23, 1839, N. Aur. 1:2:17, ASJR.

83. De Smet to Van de Velde, Sacred Heart Mission, December 1844. Mont. Sax. 1: 1: 3, ASJR.

84. Pierre Point to Roothaan, Sandwich, September 22, 1847, Canada, 1:1:9, ASJR.

85. "Registre des baptêmes et mariages administrés sur la terre des Pieds-Noirs par le P. N. Point, missionnaire, S.J., depuis 29 septembre 1846 jusqu'au [1847]." Mont. Sax. 1: 10: 1, ASJR; Van de Velde to Roothaan, St. Louis, August 5, 1847, Miss. 4: 1: 87, ASJR. Just how accurate the number of baptisms Point administered is difficult to say. He advised James Van De Velde that he had baptized 667 persons. Point to Van de Velde, Fort Lewis, January 14, 1847, AA:411, ASJSJ.

86. De Smet's notes. Miss. 4. Document 11: 2: 9, ASJR.

87. Van de Velde to Roothaan, St. Louis, November 3, 1847, Miss. 4: 1: 94, ASJR.

88. Elet to Roothaan, St. Louis, January 31, 1848. Miss. 4: 1: 97, ASJR.

89. Elet to Roothaan, St. Louis, June 7, 1848, Miss. 4: 5:1, ASJR.

90. William N. Bischoff, S.J., *The Jesuits in Old Oregon,* (Caldwell, Idaho: Caxton, 1943), 86–93. Schoenberg, *Jesuits in Montana,* 35–36.

91. Pierre Point to Roothaan, Sandwich, September 22, 1847, Canada 1: 9: 9.

92. Cadieux, *Lettres des Nouvelles Missions du Canada,* 892, Nicolas Point, Curriculum Vitae, BO-43-1 A, ASJSJ; *Catalogus Provinciae Franciae* (1848), 49–50; P. Point, "Vie," 109–10.

93. "A Synopsis of the History of Wikwémikong, Ontario," Typewritten manuscript, Diocesan Archives, Diocese of Sault Ste. Marie, Ontario, Canada, 1; Thwaites, *Jesuit Relations,* 71:144.

94. Boulanger to Roothaan, Sault Ste.-Marie, June 29, 1849.

95. Guidée to Point, Paris, December 3, 1841 and a synopsis of various letters of Point to Guidée, BO-43-5, ASJSJ.

96. Point to Roothaan, Penetatanguishene, June 29, 1849, accompanied by "Essai d'amélioration économique dans les réductions naissantes de la Grande Manitouline, avec l'exposé de ses motifs et de ses résultats," and "Carte de la Grande Manitouline avec les noms des localités habituées et le nombre des Catholiques—Protestants—Infideles." Fonds Baraga, 8–9, ASJSJ. Characteristically, Point developed an elaborate *plan* for the education of the Manitouline Indians, one which differed both from that he had outlined for the *éducation* and *instruction* of the Rocky Mountain Indians and that which he had tried to implement,

with moderate success, at Grand Coteau. The inspiration for the Manitoulin *plan* owed much to the instruction method developed by the Reims-born educator, St. John Baptist de La Salle (1651–1719), founder of the Brothers of the Christian Schools. P. Point, "Vie," 121.

97. N. Point, "Mission Ste-Croix (Wikwémikong) Grande Ile Manitouline, Ontario: Plans, peintures, portraits," 4–5, in "Souvenirs et mémoires illustrés," 1604, ASJSJ. Cited in Pouliot, "Le Père Nicolas Point," *Rapport de la Societé canadienne d'histoire de l'Eglise catholique,* 1936–1937, 28.

98. P. Point, "Vie," 118–19.

99. "A Synopsis of the History of Wikwémikong, Ontario," 3–4, DASSM; Cadieux, *Lettres des Nouvelles Missions du Canada,* 842–43. *Catalogus Provinciae Franciae* (1856), 80. Point managed to clash with a number of people during his tenure as superior at Holy Cross, most notably with the superintendent of Indian affairs. Father Nicolas wanted two candidates of his choice elected chiefs as opposed to the candidates supported by the superintendent. Understandably Point lost (as he always did in such circumstances) and the result of this affair was instrumental in forming his desire to leave Holy Cross. "Nature, cause, occasion, prétexte et dénouement de l'intrigue ourdi contre le P. Nicolas Point dans le courant de septembre 1853." B-2-1, number 12, ASJSJ; P. Point, "Vie," 118–23.

100. *Catalogus Provinciae Franciae,* (1857), 77; Nicolas Point to Peter De Smet, Fordham, New York, January 3, 1860, AA 399–401, ASJSL.

101. Pouliot, "Le Père Nicolas Point," *La Société canadienne de histoire de l'Eglise catholique,* 1936–1937, 30.

102. *Catalogus Provinciae Franciae,* (1860), 84.

103. Point to Sopranis, n.p. [Fordham, New York] n.d. [February 1860], Mont. Sax. 2: 3: 6, ASJR.

104. Sopranis to Point, Georgetown, D.C., February 27, 1860, BO-43-5, ASJSJ.

105. Point to De Smet, Fordham, New York, January 3, 1860, AA 399-401, ASJSL.

106. Pouliot, "Le Pére Nicolas Point," *La Société canadienne de histoire de l'Eglise catholique* (Rapport, 1936–1937), 30.

107. Point to De Smet, Fordham, New York, January 3, 1860. AA 399–401, ASJSL.

108. De Smet to Point, St. Louis, September 16, 1857, BO 43–45, ASJSJ.

109. De Smet to Point, St. Louis, January 16, 1860, BO-43-5, ASJSJ.

110. De Smet to Point, St. Louis, April 28, 1862, BO-43-5, ASJSJ; P. Point, "Vie," 105.

111. "Quelques Notes sur les Missions des Montagnes rocheuses," Mont. Sax. 2: 3: 6, ASJR.

112. Point to De Smet, Sault-au-Récollet, March 17, 1862, A-LP 75, ASJSL.

113. See particularly Point to De Smet, Sault-au-Récollet, January 13, 1863, BO-43-5, ASJSJ.

114. Charles J. Kappler, comp., *Indian Affairs,* 4 vols. (Washington, D.C.: Government Printing Office, 1904), 2.

115. John C. Ewers, *Gustavus Sohon's Portraits of Flathead and Pend d'Oreille Indians,* Smithsonian Miscellaneous Collections, 100, No. 7, 1948; Burns, *Jesuits and the Indian Wars of the Northwest,* illustrations 19–28.

116. Nicolas Point to Pierre Point, Sandwich, August 9, 1859, B-1-5, no. 50, ASJSJ.

117. Garraghan, *Jesuits of the Middle U.S.,* 2:558.

118. Chazelle to Roothaan, St. Mary's, Kentucky, May 6, 1838, Missio Kentukeiensis, 4, 5, ASJR.

119. Garraghan, *Jesuits of the Middle U.S.,* 2: 579.

120. Ibid., 2:559–62.

121. Ibid., 562.

122. Ibid., 557–64.

123. *Catalogus Provinciae Campaniae* (1865), 39.

124. Leon Pouliot, "Le Père Nicolas Point," *Rapport de la Société canadienne d'histoire de l'Eglise catholique* (1936), 30.

125. "Notice necrologique," BO-39-183, ASJSJ.

126. Schoenberg, *Jesuits in Montana,* 18–19; Point to De Smet, Sandwich, September 6, 1857, AA: 403, ASJSL; Hanipaux to Beckx, May 1, 1854. Cited in Garraghan, *Jesuits of the Middle U.S.,* 2:456.

127. De Smet to Sopranis, February 1, 1860. Cited in Garraghan, *Jesuits of the Middle U.S.,* 2:456, n. 34.

128. Murphy to Roothaan, St. Louis, November 10, 1851, Miss. 5: 2: 4, ASJR.

129. Van de Velde to Roothaan, St. Louis, March 2, 1844, Miss. 4: 1: 47, ASJR.

130. De Vos to Roothaan, ?, February 22, 1849, Miss. 5: 14: 5, ASJR.

131. Cited by Burns, *Jesuits and the Indian Wars of the Northwest,* 45.

132. De Vos to Roothaan, Oregon City, April 13, 1848, Mont. Sax. 1: 8: 3; Joset to Roothaan, Sacred Heart Mission, March 26, 1849, Mont. Sax. 1: 1: 25; Nobili to Roothaan, July 25, 1845, Mont. Sax. 1: 1: 26, ASJR; Father General Beckx informed Father Sopranis that Point was not to be sent back to the Rocky Mountains. Sopranis file, June 9, 1860, 1: 5: 15, ASJR.

133. De Smet to Roothaan, Sacred Heart Mission, December 1844, Mont. Sax. 1: d: 3, ASJR.

134. De Vos to Roothaan, St. Ignatius Mission, April 19, 1848, Mont. Sax. 1: 8: 3, ASJR.

135. De Smet to Roothaan, Sacred Heart Mission, December 1844, Mont. Sax. 1: d: 3, ASJR.

136. Joset to Beckx, Sacred Heart Mission, December 27, 1868, Mont Sax. 2: 12: 13, ASJR.

137. Vercruysse to Roothaan, St. Ignatius Mission, April 29, 1851, Mont. Sax. 1: 4: 34, ASJR.

138. "Quelques pensées sur l'esprit de l'état, et spécialement sur l'esprit de la compagnie—De l'opiniâtreté etc." A nineteen page manuscript plus a title page. BO-43-1d (20), ASJSJ.

139. Ibid., 18.

140. Ibid., 19.

BIBLIOGRAPHY

ARCHIVES

Archives of the Archdiocese of Reims, France
Archives of the Carmelite Monastery, Reims, France
Archives of the Convent of the Sacred Heart, Grand Coteau, La.
Archives of Sainte-Chretienne, Metz, France
Archives of the Society of Jesus, Chantilly, France (ASJC)
Archives of the Society of Jesus, Los Gatos, Cal. (ASJLG)
Archives of the Society of Jesus, New Orleans (ASJNO)
Archives of the Society of Jesus, Rome (ASJR)
Archives of the Society of Jesus, Saint-Jerome, Quebec, Canada (ASJSJ)
Archives of the Society of the Jesus, St. Louis, Missouri (ASJSL)
Biblioteca Nationale Centrale, Fondo Gesuitico, Rome, Italy
Diocesan Archives, Sault Ste. Marie, Ontario, Canada (DASSM)
Jesuit Historical Archives, Gonzaga University (JHAGU)
National Archives of the Sacred Heart, St. Louis, Missouri
University of Notre Dame Archives (UNDA)

NICOLAS POINT'S WRITINGS (Cited)

Point, Nicolas. "Dernière semaine de Saint-Acheul." In Journal, "Souvenirs et mémoires illustrés." BO-43-3, ASJSJ.

———. "De Saint-Acheul à Sainte-Marie." In Journal, "Souvenirs et mémoires illustrés." BO-43-3, ASJSJ.

———. "Henceforth the Prayer of the Flat-Heads Shall Be Ours." In Thwaites *Early Western Travels,* 29:408–19.

———. Journal. Cahier 3-B, ASJSJ.

———. Journal du Père Point pendant son sejour dans le terre des pieds-noir. La Bibliotèca Nationale Centrale, Fondo Gesuitico, Rome, Sec. 19.

———. "A Journey in a Barge on the Missouri from the Port of the Blackfeet (Lewis) to that of the Assiniboines (Union)." In *Mid-America,* 13(1930–31):236–54, ed. Gilbert Garraghan.

———. "Mission Ste. Croix (Wikwémikong) Grande Ile Manitouline, Ontario: Plans, peintures, portraits." In Journal, "Souvenirs et mémoires illustrés," BO-43-3, ASJSJ.

———. "Un Moi de Marie en Espagne." ASJSJ.

———. "Notes de ses retraites annuelles," ASJSJ.

———. "Quelques pensées sur l'esprit de l'état, et specialement sur l'esprit de la Compagnie. De l'opineatreté etc." In Journal, BO-43-3, ASJSJ.

———. "Recollections of the Rocky Mountains." In *Woodstock Letters* 11(1882):298–321; 12(1883):13–22, 133–53, 262–77; 13(1884):2–13.

ARTICLES, LETTERS, JOURNALS, AND RECORDS

L'Ami de la Religion et du Roi. Paris. Issues: 43 (Nov. 8, 1826):416; 50 (Dec. 13, 1826):132.

Annales de l'Association de la Propagation de la foi. Lyon.

Barnum, Francis A., "The Last of the Indian Missionaries: Father Joseph Joset," *Woodstock Letters,* 30(1901):209–14.

Boudreaux, Isidore J. "Obituary: Isidore J. Bourdeaux." *Woodstock Letters* 14(1855):275–79.

Buckley, Cornelius M. "French Views of Ireland on the Eve of the Famine." In *Journal of Religious History* 8(1975):240–54

Burns, Robert Ignatius, "A Jesuit in the War Against the Northern Indians." *Records of the American Catholic Historical Society of Philadelphia,* 61 (March 1950):9–54.

Campbell, Thomas J., "Fordham University." *Woodstock Letters* 45(1916):349–70.

Chapman, T. B., "The *Monita Secreta,*" *Month* 29 (1893):96–113.

Cochrane, Eric. "Muratori: The Vocation of a Historian." *Catholic Historical Review* 51 (1965): 153–72.

Cotting, James. "Obituary: James Cotting." *Woodstock Letters* 22(1893):142–43.

Davis, William Lyle. "Peter John De Smet: The Journey of 1840." *Pacific Northwest Quarterly,* 35(1944):29–43.

———. "Peter John De Smet: Missionary to the Potawatomi, 1837–1840." *Pacific Northwest Quarterly,* 33(1942):123–52.

Davitt, Edward I. "History of the Maryland and New York Pioneers." *Woodstock Letters,* 65(1936):189–223.

Diomini, Alexander. "Studies of Modern Indian Life: The Coeur d'Alène." *Woodstock Letters* 23(1894) 23–49.

Donnelly, Joseph P. "Nicolas Point." In *Dictionnaire Biographique du Canada.* Ed. Laurentienne. Quebec: Presses de L'Université de Laval, c. 1955– . Vol. 9: 701–2.

Dooley, Patrick J. "Woodstock and Its Makers: Spiritual Giants." *Woodstock Letters* 56(1927):3–274.

Doran, W. T. "St. Stanislaus Seminary." *Woodstock Letters* 39(1910):347–62.

Duhr, Bernard. "Die *Monita Secreta* order die geheimen Verodungen der Gesellshaft Jesus." In *Jesuitenfabeln*. Freiburg im Breisgau: Herder, 1904.

Duranquet, Henry. "Obituary: Henry Duranquet." *Woodstock Letters* 22(1893):133–37.

Duranquet, Henry. "The Prison Hospitals of New York." *Woodstock Letters* 12(1883):183–85.

Epistolae Ioannis Phil. Roothaan, Societatis Iesu Praepositi Generalis XXI. Romae: Apud Postulatorum Generalem, S.I. 1940.

Ewers, John C. "Self-Torture in the Blood Indian Sun Dance." In *Journal of the Washington Academy of Sciences* 38(1948):166–73.

"Father John Francis Abbadie: A Sketch." *Woodstock Letters* 24(1895):16–36.

"Father Nicolas Petit, S.J. and the Coadjutorship of Vencennes." *Woodstock Letters* 31(1902):39–44.

Gerard, John. "The Jesuit Bogey and the *Monita Secreta*." In *Month* 98(1901):176–85.

"Grand Coteau." *Woodstock Letters* 43(1914):139–40.

Hafen, LeRoy and Ann W., "Thomas Fitzpatrick." In LeRoy Hafen, *Mountain Men and the Fur Trade of the Far West*. 7:87–105.

Hamon, P. "Barthèlemy-Louis Enfantin," in *Dictionnaire de Biographie française,* 16 vols. Ed. J. Balteau, M. Barroux, and M. Prevost. "Paris: Letouzey et Ane, 1933–.

Hill, Walter H. "Father Adrian Hoecken: A Sketch." *Woodstock Letters* 26(1897):364–68.

———. "Father Peter J. Verhaegen, S.J.: An Historical Sketch." *Woodstock Letters* 27(1898):191–202.

———. "Some Facts and Incidents Relating to St. Joseph's College, Bardstown, Kentucky." *Woodstock Letters,* 26(1897):90–108.

———. "Some Reminiscences of St. Mary's, Kentucky," *Woodstock Letters* 20(1891):25–38.

"An Historical Sketch of the Mission of New York and Canada." *Woodstock Letters* 2(1873):109–24, 189–204.

Hufton, Olwen. "Women in Revolution 1789–1796." In *Past and Present,* 53(1971):90–108.

"The Jesuit Mission of California." *Woodstock Letters,* 20(1891):347–368.

Jones, Arthur Edward. "Félix Martin." In *Catholic Encyclopedia.* 16

vols. Ed. Charles G. Habermann and collaborators. New York: Robert Appleton, 1907–1914.

Kenny, Michael. "The Scholasticate of Grand Coteau." *Woodstock Letters,* 22(1893) 207–11.

Krautburger, Rt. Rev. Francis Xavier. "Short Sketch of the History of the Menominee Indians of Wisconsin and the Catholic Missions among them." In *American Catholic Historical Records,* 4(1887) 135.

Litterae Annuae Societatis Jesus in Gallia (1814–1855) 5 vols. Pictavii: Henrici Oudin, 1865.

McCarthy, Michael. "The Burning of the Scholasticate at Grand Coteau." *Woodstock Letters,* 29(1900):83–88.

Maitrugues, J. "St. Charles College, Grand Coteau." *Woodstock Letters,* 5(1896):16–29.

"Marquette College." *Woodstock Letters,* 21(1892):55–62.

Mattern, Emile. "Letter of Emile Mattern." *Woodstock Letters,* 36(1907):406–8.

Mengarini, Gregory, "Memoires." *Woodstock Letters,* 17(1888): 298–309; 18(1889):242–52.

———. Obituary. *Woodstock Letters,* 16(1887):93–97.

———. "Vocabulary of the Santa Clara." In *California Notes: Indianology of California.* Ed. Alexander Smith Taylor. San Francisco, 1860.

Moeller, Ferdinand A. "Obituary: Ferdinand A. Moeller, 1852–1946." *Woodstock Letters,* 76(1947):343–64.

Munnick Harriet D. "The Ermatinger Brothers, Edward and Francis." In Hafen, *Mountain Men and the Fur Trade of the Far West,* 8:157–73.

Palladino, Lawrence B. "The Catholic Church in Montana." *Woodstock Letters,* 9(1880):95–106.

Pentland, Pat Allan. "The Ill-Fated Mission: The Sacred Heart Mission on the St. Joe River, 1842–46." Master's thesis. Gonzaga University, May 1973.

Pfalley, Louis. "Charles Larpenteur." In Hafen, *Mountain Men and the Fur Trade of the Far West,* 1:295–311.

"Plan of a Reduction for our North American Indians with a letter from Father Paul Ponziglione, S.J." *Woodstock Letters,* 25(1895):353–61.

Point, Pierre, "Vie du Père Nicolas Point, S.J." 150 pp. ms., 1850. #4073, ASJSJ. Archives de la Compagnie de Jésus Province du Canada-Français, Saint-Jérôme, Québec, Canada.

Ponziglione, Paul M. "Recollections of Father Van Quickenborne at the Osage Mission." *Woodstock Letters,* 24(1895):37–42.

Pouliot, Léon. "Le Père Nicolas Point (1799–1868): Collaborateur du P. De Smet dans les montagnes Rocheuses et missionaire en Ontario." In *Rapport de la Société Canadiènne d' histoire de l'Eglise Catholique,* 1936.

Rocca, Giancarlo. Giancarlo. "Louis-Barthélemy Enfantin." In *Dizionario degli Instituti di Perfezione*. 7 vols. Guerrino Pelliccia and Giancarlo Rocca, publishers. Roma: Edizioni Paolini, 1962.

Sommervogel, Carlos. "Le Véritable Auteur des *Monita Secreta*." In *Précis historiques*. 39(1890):83–88.

Specht, Joseph. "Father Dominic du Ranquet: A Sketch of His Life and Labors (1813–1900)." *Woodstock Letters,* 30(1901):177–95.

Stuart, Janet. "Elizabeth Galitzin." In *Catholic Encyclopedia* (1909 ed.)

Sunder, John E. "The Decline of the Fur Trade on the Upper Missouri, 1840–65." In *The American West: An Appraisal.* Ed. Robert G. Ferris. Santa Fe Museum of New Mexico Press, 1963.

"A Synopsis of the History of Wikwemikong, Ontario." Diocesan Archives, Diocese of Sault Ste. Marie, Ontario, Canada, 1.

(Vivier, Alexander.) *Status Assistentiae Galliae Societatis Jesus 1762–1768*. Paris: Leroy, 1899.

———. *Vita Functi in Societatis Jesu, 7 Augusti, 1819–7 Augusti, 1894.* Paris: Leroy, 1897.

———. *Catalogi Sociorum et officiorum provinciae Galliae Societatis Jesu 1819–1836*. (n.p.) 1893–1894.

Walsh, James, "The Vocation of Cornelia Connelly, 1" *Month,* New Series 20(1958):261–73.

———. "The Vocation of Cornelia Connelly, 2" *Month* 21(1959):19–33.

Weilner, Ignaz. "Alexander Hohenlohe." In *Dictionnaire de Spiritualité.* 12 vols. Ed. M. Viller, A. Rayez, A. Derville, et al. Paris: Beauchesne, 1937.

Wells, Merle. "Ignace Hatchiorauquacha (John Grey)." In *Mountain Man and Fur Trade of the Far West*. Ed. LeRoy Hafen, 7:160–175.

Widman, Conrad M. "Grand Coteau College in Wartimes, 1860–1866." *Woodstock Letters,* 30(1901):34–49.

Wissler, Clark. "Societies and Dance Associations of the Blackfoot Indians." In *Anthropological Papers of the American Museum of Natural History.* 11(1913):359–460.

Woodstock Letters: A Record of Current Events and Historical Notes connected with the Colleges and Missions of the Society of Jesus. Woodstock, Md. (1872–1969), 98 vols.

REFERENCE BOOKS

Almanach Ecclesiastique de France. N.p., 1805, 1808, 1807, 1812. Archives, Archdiocese of Reims.

Boylan, Henry. *A Dictionary of Irish Biography*. Dublin: Gill and Macmillan, 1978.

Catholic Encyclopedia. 16 vols. Ed. Charles G. Habermann, et al. New York: Robert Appleton, 1907–14.

A Concise Dictionary of Irish Biography. Ed. John S. Crone. Liechtenstein: Nendeln Kraus reprint, 1970.

Dictionary of Mary. Donald Attwater, ed. N.Y.: P. J. Kennedy & Sons, 1955.

Dictionary of National Biography. Ed. Leslie Stephen and Sir Sidney Lee. Oxford: University Press, 1917.

Dictionnaire de Biographie française. 16 vols. Ed. J. Balteau, m. Banoux, M. Prévost. Paris: Letouzey et Ane, 1933– .

Dictionnaire de la Langue française du seizième siècle. 7 vols. Ed. Edmond Huguet. Paris: Didier, 1967.

Dictionnaire de Spiritualité. 12 vols. Ed. M. Viller, A. Rayez, A. Derville, et al. Paris: Beauchesne, 1937– .

Guilhermy, Elisban de. *Ménologe de la Compagnie de Jésus: Assistance de Italie*. 2 vols. Paris: Schneider, 1892.

Mendizábel, Rufo. *Col. Catalogus Defunctorum in Renata Societatis Jesu, 1814–1970*. 2 vols. Romae: Apud Curiam P. Gen., 1972.

Monumenta Historica Societatis Iesu: Epistolae et Instructiones. Series Prima, IV. Madrid: Typis Gabriel Lopez del Harno, 1906.

National Cyclopedia of American Biography. 76 vols. New York: J. T. White & Co., 1893– .

Nouvelle Biographie Générale depuis le temps les plus réculés jusqu'à nos jours. 46 vols. Paris: Firmin Didot Frères, 1862–1969.

Sommervogel, Carlos. *Bibliothèque de la Compagnie de Jésus*. 9 vols. Brussels: Oscar Schaepens, 1894–1900.

BIOGRAPHIES AND HISTORIES

Alet, S. J., Père V. *Le Père Louis Marquet de la Compagnie de Jésus. Choix des ses divers écrits et de sa correspondance. Précédé d'une notice biographique*. Paris: Oudin, 1888.

Bancroft, Hubert Howe. *The Works of Hubert Howe Bancroft*. 39 vols. San Francisco: A. L. Bancroft Co., 1882–90.

Bertrand, Joseph. *Lettres édifiantes et curieuses de la nouvelle mission du Maduré*. 2 vols. Paris: pelagaud, 1865.

Bertier de Sauvigny, Guillaume de. *The Bourbon Restoration*. Tr. Lynn M. Case. Philadelphia: University of Penn. Press, 1967.

Bidwell, John. *Echoes of the Past about California.* Chicago: Lakeside Press, 1928.

———. *A Journey to California in 1841; the first emigrant party to California by wagon train: The Journal of John Bidwell.* Berkeley, Cal.: Friends of Bancroft Library, 1964.

Bischoff, William N. *The Jesuits in Old Oregon*. Caldwell, Idaho: Caxton, 1943.

Bisgood, Mary Therese. *Cornelia Connelly.* London: Burns Otis, 1961.

Bliard, Pierre. *Le P. Loriguet: Le légende et l'histoire*. Paris: Perris & Cie, 1922.

Boudon, Adrien. *Les Jésuites à Madagascar au XIXe siècle*. 2 vols. Paris: Beauchesne, 1880.

Boullet, Louis. *Histoire de Rocroi*. Les Cahiers d'études ardennaises #3. Méziers: Société d'études ardennaises, 1958.

Boylan, Henry. *A Dictionary of Irish Biography.* Dublin: Gill and Macmillan, 1978.

Brou, Alexandre. *Les Origines de l'antijésuitisme: les Jésuites de la Légende*. 2 vols. Paris: Retraux, 1906.

Broullion, Nicolas. *Mémoire su l'état actuel de la Mission du Kiang-Nan, 1842–1855*.

Buckley, Cornelius M., ed. *A Frenchman, a Chaplain, a Rebel: The War Letters of Père Louis-Hippolyte Gache, S. J.* Chicago: Loyola University Press, 1981.

Burnett, Peter. *The Path which Led a Protestant Lawyer to the Catholic Church.* New York: Benziger, 1851.

Burnichon, Joseph. *La Compagnie de Jésus en France: Histoire d'un siècle, 1814–1914*. 4 vols. Paris: Beauchesne, 1916.

Burns, Robert Ignatius. *The Jesuits and the Indian Wars of the Northwest*. New Haven: Yale University Press, 1966.

Cadieux, Lorenzo. *Lettres des Nouvelles Missions du Canada, 1843–1852*. Montréal: Les Editions Bellarmin, 1973.

Callan, Louise, R.S.C.J. *Philippine Duchesne: Frontier Missionary of the Sacred Heart, 1769–1852*. Westminster, Md.: Newman, 1957.

Charlevoix, Pierre François Xavier de. *Histoire du Paraquay.* Paris: Didot, 1756.

Chazournes, Léon Arcis de. *Vie du R. P. Joseph Barrlele*. 2 vols. Paris: Plon, 1880.

Chittenden, Hiram Martin. *The American Fur Trade of the Far West*. 3

vols. New York: Francis P. Harper, 1902: rep. The Press of the Pioneers, 1935.

———. *Early Steamboat Navigation on the Missouri: Life and Adventures of Joseph La Barge*. 2 vols. New York: Francis Harper, 1903.

Chittenden, Hiram Martin and Alfred Talbot Richardson. *Life, Letters and Travels of Father Pierre-Jean De Smet, S.J.* 4 vols. New York: Francis P. Harper, 1905.

Chossegros, Armand. *Histoire du Noviciat de la Compagnie de Jésus au Canada depuis ses origines, 1843, jusqu'aux Noces d'Or de la Maison Saint-Joseph du Sault-au Récollet*. Montréal: Impriméria du sacre coeur, 1903.

Colombel, Auguste. *Histoire de la Mission du Kiangnan*. Shanghai: T'ou-sè-wè, 1895–1905. Troisieme Partie.

Curran, Francis X. *The Return of the Jesuits: Chapters in the History of the Society of Jesus in Nineteenth-Century America*. Chicago: Loyola University Press, 1966.

Dalmases, Cándido de, *El Padre Francisco de Borja*. Madrid: Biblioteca de Autores Cristianos, 1983.

Daniel-Rops, Henri. *The Church in an Age of Revolution, 1789–1870*. Trans. John Warrington. New York: E. P. Dutton & Co., 1965.

Davis, William L. *A History of St. Ignatius Mission*. Spokane: C. W. Hill Printing Co., 1945.

Delattre, Pierre. *Les Etablissements des Jésuites en France dupuis quatre Siécles*. 5 vols. Enchien, Belgium: De Meestre, 1949.

Desjardins, Paul. *Le Collège Sainte-Marie de Montréal*. 2 vols. Montréal: Collège Sainte-Marie, 1945.

De Smet, P. J., *Letters and Sketches with a Narrative of a Year's Residence among the Indian Tribes of the Rocky Mountains*. Philadelphia: Fithian, 1843. Also in Thwaites.

Donnelly, Joseph P., trans. and ed. *Wilderness Kingdom: Indian Life in the Rocky Mountains: 1840–1847. The Journals and Paintings of Nicolas Point, S.J.* Intro. by J. P. Donnelly. Chicago and New York: Loyola University Press and Holt, Rinehart, and Winston, 1967.

Dufour d'Astafort, Jules. *Mémoire sur les chantes liturgiques restaurés par R. P. Lambillotte . . . et publiés par le P. Dufour . . . Examen des principales difficultés proposées par diverses auteurs et en particulier par M. L'Abbé Cloet. . . .* Paris: Ledère, 1857.

L'Episcopat français depuis le Concordat jusqu'à la Séparation: 1802–1905. Paris: Librairie Saint-Perès, 1907.

Evans, Lucylle H. *St. Mary's in the Rocky Mountains: A History of the Cradle of Montana's Culture*. Stevensville, Montana: Montana Creative Consultants, 1975.

Ewers, John C. *The Blackfeet: Raiders on the Northwestern Plains.* Norman, Oklahoma: University of Oklahoma Press, 1958.

———. *Gustavus Sohon's Portraits of Flathead and Pend d'Oreille Indians.* Washington, D.C.: Smithsonian Miscellaneous Collections 100, No. 7, 1948.

Fahey, John. *The Flathead Indians.* Norman: University of Oklahoma Press, 1974.

Federal Writers Project of the Works Progress Administration (WPA), *Michigan: A Guide to the Wolverine State*. New York: Hastings House, 1964.

Federal Writers Project of the Works Progress Administration (WPA), *Nebraska: A Guide to the Cornhusker State*. New York: Hastings House, 1939.

Federal Writers Project of the Works Progress Administration (WPA), *Wisconsin: A Guide to the Badger State*. New York: Hastings House, 1945.

Fernández, Juan Patricio. *Relacion historical de las missiones de los indios que llaman chiquitos que estàn à cargo de los padres de la Compañía de Jesus de la provincia del Paraguay.* Madrid: Manuel Fernández, 1726.

Garraghan, Gilbert J. *Chapters in Frontier History: Research Studies in the Making of the West*. Milwaukee: Bruce, 1934.

———. *The Jesuits of the Middle United States.* 3 vols. New York: America Press, 1938.

Grandidier, François. *Vie du Révérend Père Achille Guidée*. Amiens, Lambert-Caron, 1866.

Grosdidier de Matons, Marcel. *Une Ame Lorraine: Madame de Méjanès (Anne-Victoire Tailleur, 1763–1837), Fondatrice de la Congrégation des Soeurs de Sainte-Chrétienne*. Paris: Editions Spes, 1957.

Guibert, Joseph de, *The Jesuits: Their Spiritual Doctrine and Practice*. Trans. William J. Young, S. J. Chicago: Loyola University Press, 1964.

Guilhermy, Elesban de. *Ménologe de la Compagnie de Jésus. Assistance d'Italie*. 2 vols. Paris: Schneider, 1893.

Guizot, François-Pierre-Guillaume. *Memoirs to Illustrate the History of My Time*. 8 vols. London: R. Bentley, 1858–1867.

Hafen, LeRoy, R., ed. *The Mountain Men and the Fur Trade of the Far West*. 10 vols. Glendale, Cal.: Arthur H. Clark Co., 1965–1972.

Hamilton, Raphael N. *Marquette's Explorations: The Narratives Reexamined*. Madison: The University of Wisconsin Press, 1970.

Hayes, Richard Francis. *Biographical Dictionary of Irishmen in France*. Dublin: M. H. Gill, 1949.

———. *Ireland and Irishmen in the French Revolution*. London: Ernest Benn, 1932.

Henrion, Le Baron Mattheu-Richard-August. *Vie du Père Loriquet. S.J. écrit d'après sa correspondance et ses oeuvres inédités.* Paris: Poussielque-Rusand, 1845.

St. Ignatius Loyola. *The Constitutions of the Society of Jesus.* Trans. George E. Ganss, S. J. Introduction and Commentary also by George E. Ganss. St. Louis: Institute of Jesuit Sources, 1970.

———. *Spiritual Exercises.* Tr. Louis J. Puhl, S.J. Westminster, Maryland: Newman, 1943.

Irving, Washington. *The Adventures of Captain Bonneville, U. S. A. in the Rocky Mountains and the Far West digested from his journal.* New York: Putnam's Sons, 1868.

Jean, Auguste. *Le Maduré: L'Ancien et la Nouvelle Mission*. 2 vols. Lille: Desclée de Brouwer, 1894.

Jerrold, Blanchard. Collector and Editor. *Final Reliques of Father Prout by Francis Sylvester Mahoney.* London: Chatto and Windus, 1876.

Julien, Marius. *La Nouvelle Mission de la Compagnie de Jésus en Syria, 1831–1895*. 2 vols. Paris: A. Mame et Fils, 1892.

Kappler, Charles J., comp. *Indian Affairs.* 4 vols. Washington, D.C.: Government Printing Office, 1904.

Keenan, Desmond J. *The Catholic Church in Nineteenth-Century Ireland,* Barnes & Noble Import, 1984.

Kenny, Michael. *Catholic Culture in Alabama.* New York: The America Press, 1931.

Larpenteur, Charles. *Forty Years a Fur Trader on the Upper Missouri: The Personal Narrative of Charles Larpenteur with Historical Introduction by Milo Milton Quaite*. Chicago: Lakeside Press, 1933.

Laveille, Eugene. *The Life of Father De Smet, S.J.: 1801–1873*. Trans. Marian Lindsay. New York: P. J. Kennedy and Sons, 1915.

Lecompte, Edouard. *Les Jésuites du Canada au dix-neuvième siècle.* Montréal: Messenger Press, 1920.

Life of Cornelia Connelly, 1809–1879, Foundress of the Society of the Holy Child Jesus. By a member of the Society. London: Longmans, Green and Co., 1922.

McManners, John. *The French Revolution and the Church.* New York: Harper and Row, 1969.

Maillé, Marie Osmonde de. *Du Mariage au clôitre: une religieuse américaine Cornelia Connelly.* Paris: Editions France, 1962.

Marcet de la Roche-Arnaud, Martial. *Les Jésuites Moderne*. Paris: Ambroise Dupont, 1826.

———. *Mémoires d'un jeune Jésuite ou Conjuration de Montrouge.* Paris: Ambroise Dupont, 1828.

———. *Les Sept Bêtes de Montrouge, prophétie et apocalypse, manuscrit trouvé dans le novitiate de Jésuites de Paris.* Paris: Ambroise Dupont, 1827.

Mengarini, Gregory. *Grammatica linguae Selicae.* Neo-Ebrorici: Cramosy Press, 1861.

———. *Recollections of the Flathead Mission.* Trans. and ed. Gloria Ricci Lothrop. Glendale, Ca.: Arthur H. Clark Co., 1977.

Monsigneur Canoz, premier évêque de Trichinopoly 1805–1888. Paris: Retaux-Bray, 1889.

Monter, E. Mathieu de. *Louis Lambillotte et ses frères.* Paris: R. Duffer, 1871.

Munnick, Harriet D. "The Ermatinger Brothers, Edward and Francis," in Hafen, *Mountain Men.*

Muratori, Lodovico Antonio. *Relation des missions du Paraquay,* Tr. Pierre Lombert. Paris: Chez Bordelet, 1754.

———. *Relation des missions du Paraquay.* Louvain: Chez Vanlinthout et Vandenzande, 1822.

Mury, Paul. *Les Jésuites à Cayenne, Histoire d'une mission de vingt-deux ans dans les pénitencièrs de la Guyane.* Strasbourg: F. X. Le Roux, 1895.

Nordenskiöld, Erland. *The Changes in the Material Culture of Two Indian Tribes under the Influence of New Surroundings.* Göteborg: Elanders boktryekeri aktiebolag, 1920.

O'Donoghue, David James. *The Poets of Ireland: Dictionary of Irish Writers of England Verse.* Dublin: Hodges and Figgis, 1912.

Padberg, John W. *Colleges in Controversy: The Jesuit Schools in France from Revival to Suppression 1815–1880.* Cambridge: Harvard University Press, 1969.

Palladino, Lawrence. *Indian and White in the Northwest: A History of Catholicity in Montana, 1831–1891.* Lancaster, Penna.: Wickersham Publishing Co., 1922.

———. *May Blossoms or Spiritual Flowerets in Honor of the Blessed Virgin.* Philadelphia: H. L. Kliner & Co., 1900.

Pérez Acosta, Fernando. *Los Missiones del Paraguay: Recuerdos Históricos de un a vida feliz entre los indios Guaranies.* Barcelona: Llorens Castillo, 1920.

Pidoud, de Madueré, Alban, le chevalier de *Un Savant Jesuite franc-comptois: le R. P. François Faton de Dompiere, près d'Orgelet, 1805–1869.* (Besançon: Jacques et Demontrovel, 1914).

Ponlevoy, Armand de. *The Life of Father de Ravignan, S. J.* 2 vols. New York: The Catholic Publication Society, 1869.

Poupard, Pierre-X. *Le R. P. Augustin Laurent de la Compagnie de Jésus, son apostolate dans le diocèse de Nantes.* Paris: Retaux-Bray, 1888.

Ribadeneyra, Padre Pedro de. *Vida del Bienventurado Padre Ignacio de Loyola, Fundador de la Religión de la Compañía de Jésuis.* Barcelona: Imp. y Libreria de la Viuda e Hijos de J. Subirana, 1885. 5 books in 1 vol.

Ronan, Peter. *History of the Flathead Indians.* Minneapolis: Ross and Haines, 1890.

Sainte-Beuve, Charles Augustin. *Port Royal.* 5 vols. Paris: Hachette, 1858.

Schauinger, Joseph. *Cathedrals in the Wilderness.* New York: Bruce, 1952.

Schmidlin, Joseph. *Catholic Mission History.* Trans. Matthias Braum, S.V.D. Techny, Ill.: Mission Press, 1933.

Schoenberg, Wilfred P. *A Chronicle of the Catholic History of the Pacific Northwest, 1743–1960*. Portland, Oregon: Catholic Sentinel Printery, 1962.

———. *Jesuits in Montana, 1840–1860*. Portland: The Oregon-Jesuit, 1960.

———. *Paths to the Northwest: A Jesuit History of the Oregon Province*. Chicago: Loyola University Press, 1982.

Séjourné, Auguste. *Le Père Jeantier, ou l'apotre des petits enfants. Souvenirs de Saint-Acheul de Fribourg, du Passage, de Turin, de Bruxelles, et de Vannes.* Poitiers: Oudin, 1880.

Servière, Joseph de la. *Histoire de la Mission du Kiang-Nan, 1840–1899.* 2 vols. Zi-Ka-Wel: T'ou-sè-wè, 1944.

Spalding, Martin J. *Sketches of the Early Catholic Missions of Kentucky from their Commencement in 1787 to the Jubilee of 1826–27.* Louisville: B.J. Webb and Brother, 1844.

Terrien, Jacques. *Histoire du R. P. de Clorivière de la Compagnie de Jésus.* Paris: Devalois, 1891.

Thwaites, Reuben Gold, ed. *Early Western Travels, 1748–1846*. 32 vols. Cleveland: Arthur H. Clark, 1906.

———. *The Jesuit Relations and allied documents: travels and explorations of the Jesuit missionaries in New France, 1610–1791; the original French, Latin, and Italian texts, with English translations and notes; illustrated by portraits, maps amd fascimilies.*

Voegel, Virgil J. American Indian Medicine. Norman: University of Oklahoma Press, 1970.

Wadham, Juliana. *The Case of Cornelia Connelly.* New York: Pantheon, 1957.

Wright, D.G. *Revolution and Terror in France, 1789–1795*. London: Longman, 1974.

INDEX

Other books from Loyola University Press in JESUIT BIOGRAPHY:

Jacques Marquette:
1637-1675
Joseph P. Donnelly, S.J.
The only authentic biography of the Jesuit explorer and missionary who charted the Mississippi with Louis Jolliet.
Hardcover $12.95 ISBN 0-8294-0024-9

Jean de Brébeuf:
1593-1649
Joseph P. Donnelly, S.J.
The definitive biography of Jean de Brébeuf, an outstanding Jesuit missionary and martyr among the Hurons.
Paperback $8.95 ISBN 0-8294-0233-0

Jesuits of the Middle United States
Gilbert J. Garraghan, S.J., Ph.D.
A three–volume set that completely covers the Jesuits' influence on the historical development of the Midwest from 1812 to World War I.
Volume I: Hardcover $15.00 ISBN 0-8294-0444-9
Volume II: Hardcover $15.00 ISBN 0-8294-0445-7
Volume III: Hardcover $15.00 ISBN 0-8294-0446-5
$40.00 (set)

The Life of Father De Smet
E. Laveille, S.J.
Marian Lindsay, translator
A biography of the Jesuit explorer and missionary whose experiences made him a valuable confidant to both United States Presidents and Native American tribal chiefs.
Hardcover $12.95 ISBN 0-8294-0372-8

Loyola University Press
3441 North Ashland Avenue
Chicago, Illinois 60657
FOUNDED IN 1912

(800) 621-1008
in Illinois (312) 281-1818
Call us for a free catalog

Other books from Loyola University Press in JESUIT HISTORY:

Indian and Jesuit:
A Seventeenth–Century Encounter
James T. Moore
This account dramatizes the relationships between native American Indians and the French Jesuit missionaries, who strived to weave their teachings about Christ into the fabric of Indian culture and customs.
Hardcover $12.95 ISBN 0-8294-0395-7

The Chinese Rites Controversy:
From Its Beginning to Modern Times
George Minamiki, S.J.
A detailed historical account of the Chinese–rites controversy occasioned by Jesuit missionaries' attempts to adapt rituals to local customs.
Hardcover $19.95 ISBN 0-8294-0457-0

East Meets West:
The Jesuits in China, 1582-1773
Charles E. Ronan, S.J. and Bonnie B.C. Oh, editors
This collection of essays incisively evaluates the successes and failures of Jesuit missionary efforts in China.
Hardcover $19.95 ISBN 0-8294-0572-0

Lost Cities of Paraguay
C.J. McNaspy, S.J.
A textual and photographic documentation of the art, architecture, and missionary endeavors in 18th century Paraguay.
Hardcover $24.95 ISBN 0-8294-0396-5

Lineage:
A Biographical History of the Chicago Province
Edmund Fortman, S.J.
Over 200 biographical sketches of Chicago Province Jesuits; a unique approach to "family history."
Hardcover $12.95 ISBN 0-8294-0502-x

Loyola University Press
3441 North Ashland Avenue
Chicago, Illinois 60657
FOUNDED IN 1912

(800) 621-1008
in Illinois (312) 281-1818
Call us for a free catalog